The Kemetic I
The Holistic Health Guide for Body, Mind and Soul

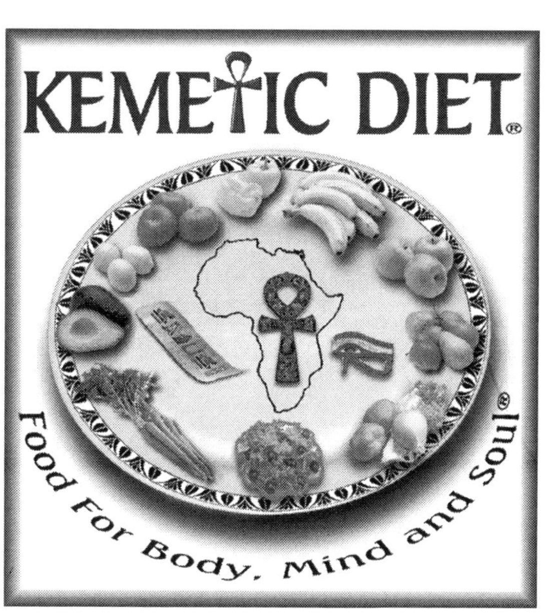

Life, Vitality and Health!

May this person's *mettu* flourish...
May this person's *mettu* be sound...
May this person's *mettu* be excellent...
May this person's *mettu* be comfortable...

-An Ancient Egyptian Doctor

SEMA UNIVERSITY

www.SemaUniversity.org

The Sema University School of Kemetic Culture and Ancient Egyptian Mysteries offers online studies leading to Associate and Bachelor degrees.

ASSOCIATE DEGREE

You may earn an Associate degree in Kemetic studies by completing 5 courses over a period of 1-1/4 years. Those who complete the Associate Degree are granted a certificate with the title of Teacher of Kemetic Culture

BACHELOR DEGREE

You may earn an Bachelor degree in Kemetic religion or philosophy within 2 years by concentrating in specific areas of study like:

	Degree Concentration area	Degree Concentration area	Degree Concentration area	Degree Concentration area	Degree Concentration area
Degree title	*Kamitan African Theology* *33 credit*	*Sema (Yoga) & Health Practitioner* *30 credit*	*Kamitan African Philosophy of Religion and Ethics* *27 credit*	*Comparative Religion and World Religion* *24 credit*	*Interdisciplinary Kamitan Studies* (Student may combine electives to create a program of their choice with approval of their mentor.) *24 credit*
FOCUS OF THE DEGREE PROGRAM Sema Institute University	Understanding the nature of Kamitan religion and its special concept of theism the nature of the Divine and its relationship to the Self as well as the main religious Kamitan paths to spiritual enlightenment.	Understanding the nature of Kamitan disciplines of SEMA or Yoga the sciences for attaining spiritual enlightenment through cultivation of body mind and soul.	Understanding the nature of Kamitan philosophy psycho-mythology and wisdom for transforming and enlightening the mind to attain higher consciousness.	Understanding the nature of world religion and its dept to Kamitan religion as well as discovering the true meaning of religion and how to get to the source and true purpose of religion: Spiritual enlightenment and human peace.	Student must complete the core courses and then choose at least 5 electives from the other degree programs

Those who complete the Bachelor degree program receive a Diploma and the title of Basu (instructor, teacher) in their chosen area of concentration.

ONLINE: The program is delivered online and via correspondence. The student receives lesson plans and interactive contact via the internet and can communicate with Sebai Dr. Muata Ashby, mentors and other students.

ACCESS TO STUDENT ONLY AREAS of the Sema University Web site containing special lectures, access to online conferences on philosophy, meditative practice, and more.

Begin your studies at any time of the year and start your path of self-discovery, learn how to promote the Kemetic path in your community and promote the upliftment of humanity through Ancient Egyptian Spirituality

www.SemaUniversity.org

☥

An Invitation to Change Your Life-Style!
Why Change? Consider the Following Statistics[1]:

- In the United States of America (USA), approximately 50% of all deaths are due to Heart Disease!
- Heart Disease is the leading cause of death worldwide, and is expected to increase in the next two decades!
- Cancer, is the second leading cause of deaths in the U.S.A.!
- Cancer is responsible for approximately 1/8th of all deaths world wide, and this figure is expected to increase in the two decades!
- The World Health Organization listed the two most significant reasons for the expected increase in Heart Disease and Cancer worldwide as (1) an increase in smoking and (2) adoption of a westernized diet!
- Cancer is the third leading cause of death in children less than 4 years of age, and the second leading cause of death in children 5 to 14 years of age!
- Children as young as four years old consuming a westernized diet are being diagnosed with fatty deposits in their blood vessels (arteriosclerosis, in other words – Heart Disease)!
- Stroke ("Brain Attack") is the number three cause of death in the USA; approximately every minute in the U.S., someone has a stroke! High Blood Pressure is a major contributing factor.
- This issue of weight is very important when one considers the following statistics: Approximately 40% of the population of the U.S.A. are overweight and approximately another 15% of the population are considered to be obese. One Health Food Store natural health magazine referred to this situation as "reaching epidemic proportions.[2]"
- **What is wrong with Milk and Dairy Products?[3]**
    - Increased milk consumption leads to HIGHER FRACTURE RISK due to osteoporosis.[4]
    - Several cancers have been linked to dairy products.[5]
    - There is a correlation between dairy products and diabetes.[6]
    - Lactose intolerance affects 95% of Asian Americans, 74% of Native Americans, 70% of African Americans, 53% of Mexican Americans, and 15% of European Americans (Caucasians)[7] Cows milk proteins, sugars, and fats leads to chronic diseases, obesity, diabetes, and atherosclerosis plaques that cause heart disease.[8]
    - Insulin-dependent diabetes (Type 1 or childhood-onset) has been linked to dairy products.[9]
    - Recombinant Bovine Growth Hormone, a genetically engineered hormone injected into cows to boost milk production stimulates the cow's liver to produce an insulin-like growth hormone (IGF-1). All of this enters into milk and even affects breastfeeding infants whose mothers drink milk.[10]

- **The Proven Benefits of Vegetarianism and the Proven Dangers of Meat Eating**
  - The prevalence of hypertension (High Blood Pressure and its associated conditions) among vegetarians is about one-third to one-half that of non-vegetarians.[11\12\13] A study of Caucasian Seventh-day Adventists found hypertension in 22 percent of omnivores (those who eat both animal and vegetable foods), but only 7 percent of vegetarians. Among African Americans, the prevalence was 44 percent of omnivores and 18 percent of vegetarians.[14] Adopting a vegetarian diet significantly lowers blood pressure in both normal and hypertensive individuals.[15]

  - Cholesterol levels are much lower in vegetarians.[16] Vegetarian diets reduce serum cholesterol levels to a much greater degree than is achieved with the National Cholesterol Education Program Step Two diet.[17] In one study published in *The Lancet*[18] total cholesterol in those following a vegetarian diet for 12 months decreased by 24.3 percent.

  - Cancer rates for vegetarians are 25 to 50 percent below population averages, even after controlling for smoking, body mass index, and socioeconomic status.[19] One study found that people who include generous amounts of fruits and vegetables in their daily diets have lower rates of cancers of the lung, breast, colon, bladder, stomach, mouth, larynx, esophagus, pancreas, and cervix compared to people who avoid such foods.[20]

  - Obesity is a major contributor to many serious illnesses, and is much less common among vegetarians, compared to the general population.[21] Vegetarians are, on average, about 10 percent leaner than omnivores.[22]

  - At least 200,000 Americans die annually at the hands of doctors![23]

  - 4,500,000 people each year are poisoned (drugged) so seriously by their physicians that they require hospitalization![24]

  - Over 40,000 die of drugs used by medical doctors each year, this number may exceed 120,000: "During 1974, Senate hearings under the chairman-ship of Senator Edward Kennedy, focused on problems of drug use and safety." Senator Kennedy said, "This is a serious public health issue, and it's one that is generally not understood among the American people ... and one that results in the death of, as we've heard estimated, anywhere from 40,000 to 120,000 deaths a year. We can't be specifically sure of the number. Some have said that it's a good deal higher ... We've had estimates before our committee from responsible researchers that say the American consumer is paying $2,000,000,000 (two billion dollars) a year more than he should because of adverse drug reactions..."[25]

On the Failure of Modern Medicine:

> "Health care has become too expensive…There are a number of reasons… Some of them are within our control and some of it is beyond our control. For example, medicine made tremendous strides in the early half of the (20th) century in dealing with *acute infectious illness* and as a result of immunization and improved public health and techniques like antibiotics we really rolled back the numbers of people affected by acute infectious illness but what that left doctors dealing with was *chronic degenerative disease* which is by nature much more difficult and not so easy to fix. **So that's a problem that I think was really beyond our control**."
>
> -Andrew Weil M.D.

Proven Benefits of The Natural Health Program

- Recovery from life threatening illnesses
- Recovery from psychological disorders like depression
- Recovery from eating disorders
- Weight loss
- Prevention and recovery from colds and flu
- Increase energy
- Will power to give up vices
- Mental clarity and spiritual awakening

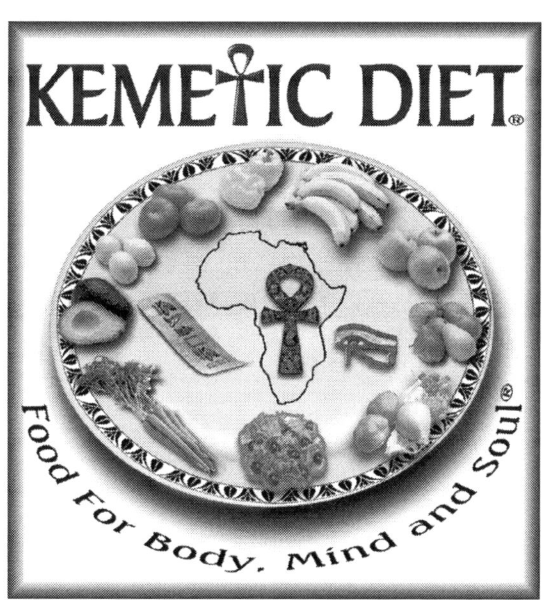

DO NOT BE CONFUSED: THERE IS AN ANSWER!

Do not be confused by the myriad of claims and the constant revelations of drugs and treatments that are being discovered to be ineffective or even dangerous to health. There is a way to find health if you are willing to take the responsibility of seeking for real answers and not being satisfied with miracle cures or medical treatments and drugs that are routinely withdrawn banned after having been touted as "breakthroughs." There is an answer for you but you must make the journey to learn about the nature of health and the real causes of disease. Then you will be empowered to promote your own health.

Cruzian Mystic Books / Sema Institute of Yoga

P. O. Box 570459
Miami, Florida, 33257
(305) 378-6253 Fax: (305) 378-6253

The author is available for group lectures and individual counseling. For further information contact the publisher.

Ashby, Muata
The Kemetic Diet, Food for Body, Mind and Spirit ISBN: 1-884564-49-6

Library of Congress Cataloging in Publication Data

1 Health 2 Vegetarianism 3 Spirituality, 4 Egyptian Philosophy, 5 Meditation, 6 Self-Help.

☥ 𓋹

Website

www.KemeticDiet.com

www.Egyptianyoga.com

About The Cover

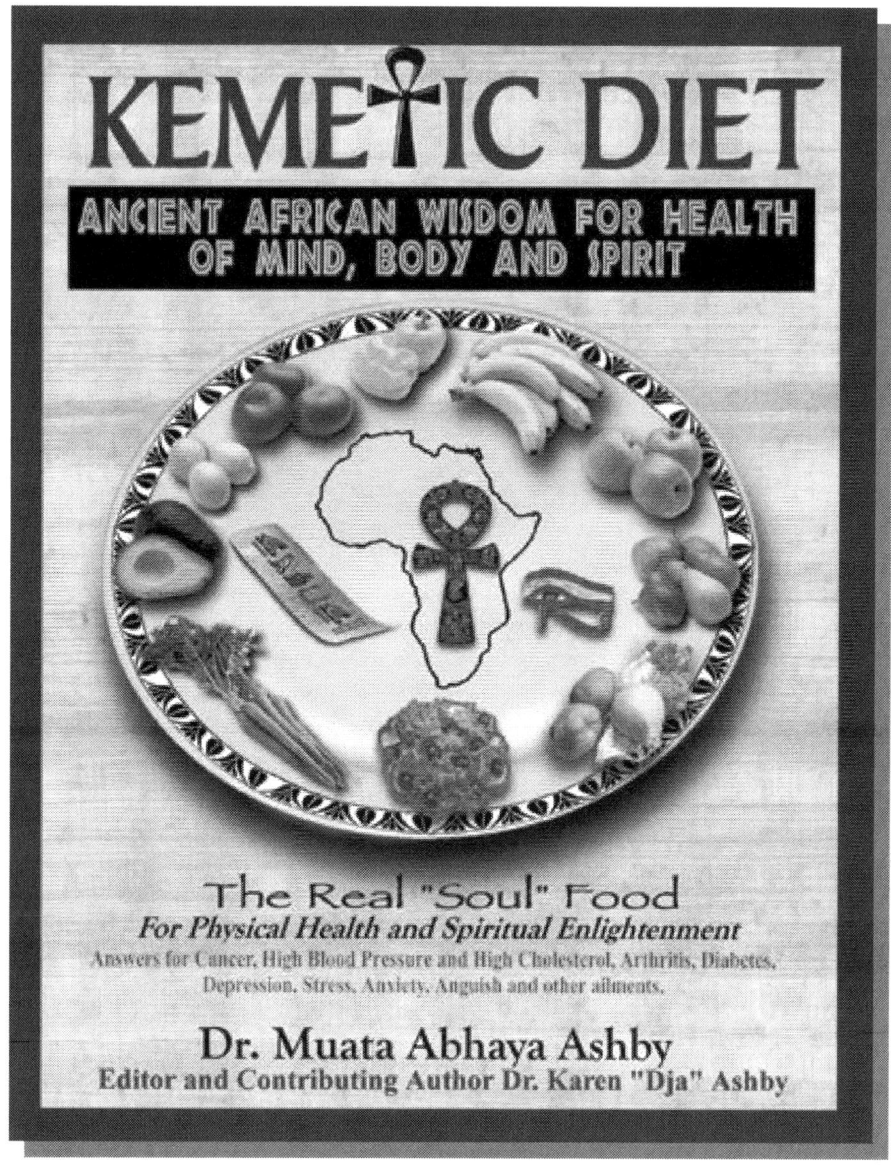

Dja Clarke-Ashby and Muata Ashby designed the cover for this book. It was developed with the idea of pictorially conveying the main concepts of the Kemetic Diet, an African (Kemetic-Ancient Egyptian) based Integral Lifestyle Enhancement Program (ABILEP), which relates to nourishment for the body, mind and soul. There are different groups of vegetarian food items that form the shape of a circle, like a plate. These items constitute the proper food for the body. Within the circle there are three Kemetic symbols. The symbol in the center, surrounded by the map of Africa, is the Ankh, meaning "Life Process." To the left of the Ankh is a small strip of Papyrus paper with an Ancient Egyptian Proverb written in hieroglyphic text. It means "feed the mind what endures," i.e. wisdom of life. To the right of the Ankh is the Eye of Heru, known as the "Divine Food Offering" or Kemetic Eucharist. This is food for the soul because it requires spiritual enlightenment. All together, these symbolize that life (Ankh) and health result when these three aspects of the constitution of a human being are fed the proper nourishment. They constitute a full meal for every human being, food for the body, food for the mind and food for the soul.

The Sema Institute of Yoga

Sema (⸸) is an Ancient Egyptian word and symbol meaning *union.* The Sema Institute is dedicated to the propagation of the universal teachings of spiritual evolution, which relate to the union of humanity and the union of all things within the universe. It is a non-denominational organization, which recognizes the unifying principles in all spiritual and religious systems of evolution throughout the world. Our primary goals are to provide the wisdom of ancient spiritual teachings in books, courses and other forms of communication. Secondly, to provide expert instruction and training in the various yogic disciplines including Ancient Egyptian Philosophy, Christian Gnosticism, Indian Philosophy and modern science. Thirdly, to promote world peace and Universal Love.

A primary focus of our tradition is to identify and acknowledge the yogic principles within all religions and to relate them to each other in order to promote their deeper understanding as well as to show the essential unity of purpose and the unity of all living beings and nature within the whole of existence.

The Institute is open to all who believe in the principles of peace, non-violence and spiritual emancipation regardless of sex, race, or creed.

SEMA INSTITUTE

About Dr. Muata Ashby

Muata Ashby D.D., P.C.

Sebai Dr. Muata Abhaya Ashby is a Priest of Shetaut Neter –African Kamitan Religion, Author, lecturer, poet, philosopher, musician, publisher, counselor and spiritual preceptor and founder of the Sema Institute-Temple of Aset, Muata Ashby was born in Brooklyn, New York City, and grew up in the Caribbean. His family is from Puerto Rico and Barbados. Displaying an interest in ancient civilizations and the Humanities, Sebai Maa began studies in the area of religion and philosophy and achieved doctorates in these areas while at the same time he began to collect his research into what would later become several books on the subject of the origins of Yoga Philosophy and practice in ancient Africa (Ancient Egypt) and also the origins of Christian Mysticism in Ancient Egypt.

Sebai Maa (Muata Abhaya Ashby) holds a Doctor of Philosophy Degree in Religion, and a Doctor of Divinity Degree in Holistic Health. He is a certified member of the American Alternative Medical Association as an Alternative Medical Practitioner. He is also a Pastoral Counselor and Teacher of Yoga Philosophy and Discipline. Dr. Ashby received his Doctor of Divinity Degree from and is an adjunct faculty member of Florida International University and the American Institute of Holistic Theology. Dr. Ashby is a certified as a PREP Relationship Counselor. Dr. Ashby has been an independent researcher and practitioner of Egyptian Yoga, Indian Yoga, Chinese Yoga, Buddhism and mystical psychology as well as Christian Mysticism. Dr. Ashby has engaged in Post Graduate research in advanced Jnana, Bhakti and Kundalini Yogas at the Yoga Research Foundation. He has extensively studied mystical religious traditions from around the world and is an accomplished lecturer, musician, artist, poet, screenwriter, playwright and author of over 25 books on Kemetic yoga and spiritual philosophy. He is an Ordained Minister and Spiritual Counselor and also the founder the Sema Institute, a non-profit organization dedicated to spreading the wisdom of Yoga and the Ancient Egyptian mystical traditions. Further, he is the spiritual leader and head priest of the Per Aset or Temple of Aset, based in Miami, Florida. Thus, as a scholar, Dr. Muata Ashby is a teacher, lecturer and researcher. However, as a spiritual leader, his title is *Sebai,* which means Spiritual Preceptor.

Plate 1: Dr. Muata Ashby

Sema Institute of Yoga/Cruzian Mystic Books P. O. Box 570459 Miami, Florida, 33257
(305) 378-6253 Fax: (305) 378-6253

EDITOR AND CONTRIBUTING AUTHOR

Dr. Karen "Dja" Ashby

ABOUT THE EDITOR AND CONTRIBUTING AUTHOR:

Karen Clarke-Ashby (Seba Dja) is a Kemetic (Kamitic) priestess, and an independent researcher, practitioner and teacher of Sema (Smai) Tawi (Kemetic) and Indian Integral Yoga Systems, a Doctor of Veterinary Medicine, a Pastoral Spiritual Counselor, a Pastoral Health and Nutrition Counselor, and a Sema (Smai) Tawi Life-style Consultant." Dr. Ashby has engaged in post-graduate research in advanced Jnana, Bhakti, Karma, Raja and Kundalini Yogas at the Sema Institute of Yoga and Yoga Research Foundation, and has also worked extensively with her husband and spiritual partner, Dr. Muata Ashby, author of the Egyptian Yoga Book Series, editing many of these books, as well as studying, writing and lecturing in the area of Kemetic Yoga and Spirituality. She is a certified Tjef Neteru Sema Paut (Kemetic Yoga Exercise system) and Indian Hatha Yoga Exercise instructor, the Coordinator and Instructor for the Level 1 Teacher Certification Tjef Neteru Sema Training programs, and a teacher of health and stress management applications of the Yoga / Sema Tawi systems for modern society, based on the Kemetic and/or Indian yogic principles. Also, she is the co-author of "The Egyptian Yoga Exercise Workout Book," a contributing author for "The Kemetic Diet, Food for Body, Mind and Soul," author of the soon to be released, "Yoga Mystic Metaphors for Enlightenment."

A WORD FROM THE AUTHOR, ABOUT THE EDITOR:

God always plans the best circumstances for all, and I feel especially blessed to have been granted the opportunity to have a partner who is dedicated to the path of enlightenment and upliftment of humanity, for there is no better human being that one can associate with than a person who is virtuous and devoted the Divine. It has been my honor to experience the good association of her company, input and suggestions, which enrich the projects I have produced. It is rare for people to discover The Divine, and also rare for people to discover The Divine in their partner, so there can be no mistaking the glorious mission we have embarked upon and which has found unqualified success, as the Egyptian Yoga Book Series has found worldwide readership. Her support, encouragement, suggestions and dedication have made this possible. This great soul is in every way the embodiment of the philosopher and Kemetic Priestess. Her skills as a scribe are unsurpassed. May God continue to bless us with her presence in life, vitality and health for many years to come.

Dr. Karen "Dja" Ashby has been an ardent supporter of the Kemetic teachings, and it was due to her devotion and strength of will that this volume was made possible in the manner in which it has come forth. As a doctor in the sciences, her knowledge of health, anatomy and physiology allowed her to make many contributions to this work. Therefore, she was an integral part of the production as well as the editing of this book.

-Dr. Muata Ashby

TABLE OF CONTENTS

TABLE OF FIGURES

TABLE OF PLATES

LIST OF TABLES

PRECAUTIONS

The programs presented in this book do not constitute as a substitute for competent advice from a qualified health professional.[1] You are advised to consult with your health professional before proceeding with any health or healing regimen.

This information is provided with the idea of presenting the options for natural health as they have been known for thousands of years. It is up to every individual to make up their own mind as to what is best for themselves with respect to diet and nutrition for health of the body and the lifestyle that will provide the best mental and spiritual health. Each individual must also decide for themselves what diet and lifestyle is appropriate at their present level of health and spiritual evolution, and if and when to make changes for the better. No one can make choices for another, only suggestions. If you find these suggestions sound, use them.

Before using this program consult your health care professional. The reader agrees not to hold
Dr. Muata Ashby personally or Cruzian Mystic Books, or The Sema Institute of Yoga responsible for any injuries or physical impairments that may result.

It is the hope of this author that this information will be used as a basis for the readers to do their own research into the nature of life and health, so as to grow, thrive and enjoy peace and happiness, as well as

☥ 𓋹

Life, Vitality and Health!

[1] The Sema Institute offers expert assistance in the form of counseling on diet and nutrition for the body, mind and soul for those wishing to adopt the Kemetic Diet Wisdom of natural health to restore and or promote better health. See the back section of this book for more information.

KEMETIC PROVERBS ON HEALTH

"The boat of the greedy is left (in) the mud,** while the bark of the silent sails with the wind. Get into the habit of praying sincerely to Aten (i.e. God, the Divine) as he rises in the sky, saying: **Grant me strength, well-being and health; He will give you your needs for this life, and you will be safe from fear."

"The blessings of thy eternal part are health, vigor, and proportion. The greatest of these is health. What health is to the body, even that is honesty to the Soul."

"The body becomes what the foods are, as the spirit becomes what the thoughts are."

"If you would preserve understanding and health to old age, avoid the allurements of Voluptuousness, and fly from its temptations.... For if thou hearken unto the words of the Adversary, thou art deceived and betrayed. The joy which it promises changes to madness, and its enjoyments lead on to diseases and death."

"The blessings of thy eternal part, are health, vigor, and proportion. The greatest of these is health. What health is to the body, even that is honesty to the Soul. Develop your spirit that it may gain strength to control the body and follow the natural Laws of nutrition and hygiene."

"Her name is Health. She is the daughter of Exercise, who begot her on Temperance. The rose blusheth on her cheeks, the sweetness of the morning breathes from her lips; joy, tempered with innocence and modesty, sparkles in her eyes and from the cheerfulness of her heart she sings as she walks."

"Yield not to emotion, for there are discarnate forces around us who desire emotional existence. In the heat of passion one surrenders to the influence of these; ill health and unwise living results. Through firm instruction one can master one's emotions and these forces, in this, make them serve one. Thus the slave becomes the master."

"If you would live, in harmony with yourself and the Earth you must follow the laws of the Earth. For your body is of the Earth; lest it lead your SOUL to the path of disease, death and reincarnation. The Neters **(angels)** ***of the divine will desert you, and those of evil will destroy your body and your spirit."***

"The source of evil is in your body. Evil entices the body through temptation of its weakest virtue. There can be no divinity in the unclean temple, not made by hands where abomination rules."

"Your spirit is of God and the Body is of Earth."

"The source of illness is the food you ingest; to purge the dreadful UKHEDU **(disease process)** ***which lurks in your bowels, for three consecutive days each month purge yourself with a cattle horn, its sharp end clipped off so as to create a small opening (for water to run through)."***

FOREWORD

"AN INVITATION TO CHANGE YOUR LIFE-STYLE"

By

"Hemit Dja Un Nefert"
(Karen Clarke-Ashby)

Editor and Contributing Author

Special thanks to Carmen Ashby (mother of Dr. Muata Ashby)
for her editorial assistance.

AN INVITATION TO CHANGE YOUR LIFE-STYLE

Introduction:

Greetings. Peace and Blessings! It is our privilege at the Sema Institute of Yoga to bring forth the knowledge and wisdom of humanity's ancient African ancestors, the Kemetic (Ancient Egyptian) Culture. Kemet, KMT, or Kamit is the ancient name for the land in Northeast Africa now called Egypt. The inhabitants of Kemet were African peoples, not to be confused with the current Arab inhabitants who were the last group to conquer Egypt, the majority of whom follow the Islamic faith. The terms Ancient Egypt(ian) or Kemet(ic) will be used interchangeably throughout this work to refer to this culture. The introduction section of this book, "Who were the Ancient Egyptians?" gives further historical insight into the timeline and people of this culture, which, according to their own historical records, reaches as far back as 25,000 to 35,000 B.C.E., and has been documented by modern scientific techniques to have existed for at least 12,000 years. What does such an ancient culture have to offer us in terms of life in the modern age? Well, think about it. We have a culture that has built monuments, which to this day, with all of our modern so-called technological advancements, still defy an explanation as to how they were made, and furthermore, duplication of the process. To give a context, consider that the United States of America is approximately 200 years old. It is obvious that Kemetic knew and did something as a culture, that mankind has not since been able to replicate. Their wisdom is embedded on the walls of the pyramids, tombs and scrolls, and it is from these sources that the wisdom on Kemetic health, for body, mind and spirit, has been taken.

It must be understood however, that though no modern society has since duplicated the phenomena that existed in Ancient Egypt at a cultural level, there have always been individuals within societies who have grasped and realized the truth of this ancient wisdom. These individuals are called sages, saints or Enlightened beings. While these individuals may or may not have specifically studied the scriptures of Ancient Egypt, they have studied the essential religious and spiritual teachings that had distilled into the various societies of the ancient world, and further developed within those societies to suit the needs of the particular culture.[2] These individuals, in turn, become the sparks that light the fire in the hearts of those who themselves seek to discover a higher truth of life, beyond the mundane and alternating cycles of joy and sorrow, pain and pleasure, gain and loss, comfort and discomfort, dis-ease and health, which have pervaded human existence since the beginning of time. Dr. Muata Ashby, or "Seba[3] Maa" as he is called by his students, the primary author of this book, is such an individual. He has worked extensively to bring forth the knowledge and wisdom of the sages of Ancient Egypt (Kemet) in the areas of mysticism, history, spirituality, and now on integral health for the body, mind and soul.

Statistics on Disease and the major Causes of Death: An Invitation to Change[4]

The issue of health, or rather, of ill-health (illness) is at the forefront of many crisis-oriented discussions in our nation right now, understandably so with statistics such as follows:

In the United States of America (USA), one out of every two deaths in is due to Heart Disease. However, this phenomena, as well as those related to the other diseases we will discuss, is not confined to the United States alone. Heart Disease is also a leading cause of death worldwide. The World Health Organization (WHO) reported that Heart Disease was the number one cause of death in all parts of the

---

[2] For more on Ancient Egyptian history, culture and philosophy, please refer to the books, *Egyptian Yoga, The Philosophy of Enlightenment* and *African Origins*, both by the author of this book.
[3] Seba or Sba means spiritual preceptor
[4] Information on WHO from the book, *Human Diseases and Conditions*, by the Nemours Foundation

world in 1998, with the exception of Africa and the western pacific, with approximately 1/3 of all deaths resulting from heart disease. In addition, the WHO predicts that the worldwide death rate from Heart Disease will climb during the next two decades, attributing this increase to the growing trend in developing nations towards increased smoking and a westernized diet!

Cancer, is the second leading cause of deaths in the U.S.A.; one out of every three Americans have cancer. The WHO reports that cancer is responsible for approximately 1/8th of all deaths world wide, and like the statistics on Heart Disease, the WHO also expects that this figure to increase in the decades to come. The WHO organization also says that lung cancer and colorectal cancer will increase worldwide in the coming decades, for the same reasons as Heart Disease, due to increased smoking and unhealthy diets, respectively.

Stroke ("Brain Attack") is the third leading cause of death in the U.S.A. According to the American Heart Association, someone has a stroke in the United States approximately every minute. The WHO reports that worldwide, stroke and related heart disease could rival infectious disease as the leading cause of death worldwide in the two decades, again citing cigarette smoking and inadequate diet, as well as lifestyle. The most contributing factor to the development of a "Brain Attack" is High Blood Pressure. Approximately sixty-five million people in the U.S.A. have High Blood Pressure (the most common form of cardiovascular disease) and High Cholesterol.

In most societies, there is a tendency to think of young children as being healthy and unaffected by the disease conditions cited above. Whereas this may have been generally true in the past, it is very unfortunate that it is no longer the case. The third leading cause of death in children less than 4 years of age (accidents are number one and congenital abnormalities are number two) and the second leading cause of death in children 5 to 14 years of age (accidents being number one) is Cancer! Approximately fourteen million people in the United States have Diabetes, and the incidence of Diabetes Type II, which results from the body being resistant to the effects of insulin that is produced, also known as adult-onset Diabetes, once rare in children, is now being diagnosed in epidemic proportions in children. School boards are only now considering that the diet they feed to children in school may be inadequate, since new findings indicate that children as young as four years of age have fatty deposits in their blood vessels (arteriosclerosis, in other words – Heart Disease).

What is disturbing about the above diseases and their statistics is that the conditions are preventable, and or even reversible. It is possible that one can be healed of these disorders, and not have to be affected by them chronically. Yes, preventable! Yes, reversible! Yes, you can be healed! You are not destined to be afflicted by them by some cruel act of nature, not even if you have a genetic predisposition. They are illnesses based primarily on lifestyle choices, and having some genetic or hereditary basis just means that you have to be disciplined and make the correct choices to prevent it and/or reverse it and heal yourself, since you have less room for error. The universe is demanding that you be more disciplined, that is, more righteous, in your lifestyle. It is giving you the impetus to develop strength of will (willpower). This is an important point to acknowledge, because it means that each person has the power to affect a state of health within his or her body. Health is a choice, and regardless of if you choose consciously or unconsciously, you are the one still choosing. Admittedly, most people have engaged in bad habits at the mental and physical levels for so long that not only do they lack the willpower to make the right choices, but also, and even more detrimental, most of their choices are being made at the unconscious level of their mind. In this capacity, one will be greatly aided by the practice of the yogic mystical disciplines, since their practice leads to increased (conscious) awareness of one's thoughts and actions, as well as increased willpower. Thus, you will be back in the driver's seat, and have the capacity to choose peace over anger and health over disease. Granted that in some cases the disease may have resulted in serious damage to organs and tissues, but under the conditions of a proper lifestyle, many of these will be alleviated to a great degree, if not completely reversed. Most organs of the body have an incredible capacity to regenerate themselves if given the proper conditions and environment.

Relative Causes of Physical Illness: The Mind –Body Connection and Diet

There are four main categories of relative causes of illness of the physical body, however, in reality there is only one. The four categories are: Smoking, Alcohol, Diet and Stress. However, smoking, alcohol and diet can all be placed under the category of stress, since most people engage in smoking, drinking alcohol, and eating a poor diet due to feeling stressed. Stress causes people to mentally feel frustrated and angry, or sad and depressed. Frustration and anger, as well as sadness and depression, affect the physical body. They cause the release of hormones and other chemicals in the body, which promote a weakening of the immune system, changes in blood pressure, redistribution of fat, ability of the blood to clot, etc., resulting in imbalances in the various systems (nervous, muscular, vascular, hormonal, skeletal, uro-genital, respiratory, lymphatic, digestive) of the physical body, leading to conditons such as cancer, heart disease, stroke, diabetes, osteoporosis, etc.

Stress:

The impact on of the emotions on health was demonstrated by an experiment on rabbits. Rabbits in this study were placed into two groups, both of which were treated exactly the same, except for one thing, that group B rabbits were not petted for the duration of the study, whereas group A rabbits were. Both groups of rabbits were fed high fat and cholesterol diets. At the end of the study, it was found that the effects of the diet on Group A rabbits which received petting and love, was negligible as compared to group B rabbits that were not handled throughout the study. The implication of this study is that health is influenced, to a great extent, by the state of one's mind (emotions). This does not mean that diet should be overlooked, because as we shall see further on in our discussion, diet does has an effect on every aspect of one's being (physical-mental-emotional-spiritual). However, it does give insight into why some people who eat a lot of "junk" food, but have a positive attitude and an "easy" way of dealing with life and its challenges, can have better physical health as compared others who eat healthier but become easily stressed when confronted by life's challenges.

Studies on the digestive system have shown that when people are feeling stressed (i.e. the participants in the study were told some terrible news while they were hooked up to monitors), the level digestive enzymes in their gastro-intestinal systems declines dramatically. This makes sense, because stress is a signal to the body of immanent danger, and the physical body reacts by triggering its survival response. When one is in danger, the last thing one is going to think about is food. So, when the mind experiences stress of any kind (anger, frustration, sadness, depression, fear, anxiety, worry, etc.), the digestive system is going to shut down, and consequently no enzymes are going to be produced. Thus, if one eats while feeling the effects of stress, the proper breakdown and absorption of nutrients will not take place. If the effect of stress is chronic, then one can actually become malnourished and ill, even though one may eating a relatively good diet, such as a vegetarian diet, and develop severe illnesses.

As mentioned above, eating a proper diet as a path to physical health cannot be overlooked. Another study demonstrated the effects of certain types of food on the mind. In a study where vegetarians were unknowingly fed meat based products, the participants were found to become increasingly restless, agitated and aggressive...more stressed! Thus, we must realize what the sages and saints of Kemet knew, and which westerners are only now starting to realize, that one's diet does have an effect on the mind. This is one of the reasons why it was strictly prohibited for the spiritual aspirants (initiates) to consume meat of any kind (including poultry, fish and seafood). Thus, if one wishes to gain control over the mind and emotions, one's diet must promote peace of mind. Vegetarian diets have been proven to have positive (calming) effect on the mind. In addition, as we will see, the vegetarian diet is also the proper biological, physiological and spiritual food for the physical human body.

In the book *Human Diseases and Conditions*, the Nemours Foundation report the results of several research studies which further document the profound mind-body connection. One study performed on animals indicated that stress in infants seemed to increase their susceptibility to stress as they grew up. Other studies found that patients with conditions such as AIDS, breast cancer, skin cancer, and HIV participating in group therapy or stress management programs had stronger immune systems and higher survival rates than those who did not.

It should be noted that although the above information from animal experimentation is being reported, the use of animals for research is not being condoned nor advocated here. As this information is already available, it is being provided to motivate those who need to see what they consider to be empirical evidence, by western standards. Such research projects are unnecessary, because the information they provide is not new. It already exists. All the information you need to know to be healthy in body, mind and spirit already exists, and has for thousands of years. Thus, the question arises, if this is true, why is the world becoming more and more disease ridden? It is because this information is generally ignored by the mainstream health organizations, the medical and scientific communities, the news media, and consequently, the public. The mind-body connection and the effects of stress on the individual, as well as the root cause of all dis-ease and stress, is the basis of mystical philosophy, and is documented in the Ancient Egyptian Mysteries System from as far back as 10,000 BCE or earlier. This knowledge has been available through all the ages, to those who have sought the path of true health, of body, mind and spirit. And still today, if one were to engage in the intensive study of mystical philosophy, such the Kemetic Wisdom, and the Kemetic Medical and Health Practices presented here and in our other books, one would not need to inflict needless pain and suffering on each other (such as in the Tuskegee Experiments[5] where African Americans were used as test specimens) or animals, only to discover what has already been known for thousands of years, but ignored. Certainly, for those who believe in paying reverence and respect to the ancient Kemetic ancestors, at least this much is owed to the Kemetic sages!

So, physical health is not a simple matter as eating some well balanced diet, and all will be well. One must also pay attention to what thoughts, and consequent emotions, are dwelling in one's mind moment by moment. Just as it is not the absorption of fat during one meal that leads to heart disease, but its accumulation over a period of time, the effects of the seemingly innocent and so called "normal" emotional experiences of stress, anger, frustration, anxiety, worry, insecurity, fear, jealousy, envy, dislike, sadness, depression, etc., also accumulate over a period of time, and promote the physical diseases people experience in their lives, in the near or distant future. For example, when one bursts out with anger, stress hormones are released. These cause physical damage to the heart tissue, in the form of microscopic scars in the heart muscle. Over a period of time of accumulating these scars in the muscle, the heart muscle becomes damaged to the point that it cannot function properly[6]. Now the person becomes diagnosed with heart disease. Thus, there is a saying in holistic (mind-body) medicine: "The body is now what the thoughts were in the past, and in the future, the body will be what the thoughts are now." We have all seen how one's thoughts affect the physical body. We have seen how a smile can be wiped off someone's face when some sad or upsetting news comes to them, and their mind becomes steeped with sadness, and likewise how a frown can become a smile when someone receives news that they find pleasing, and their

---

[5] "Beginning in the 1930s, 399 men signed up with the U.S. Public Health Service for free medical care. The service was conducting a study on the effects of syphilis on the human body. The men were never told they had syphilis. They were told they had "bad blood" and were denied access to treatment, even for years after penicillin came into use in 1947. By the time the study was exposed in 1972, 28 men had died of syphilis, 100 others were dead of related complications, at least 40 wives had been infected and 19 children had contracted the disease at birth." Quoted from CNN Interactive's Tuskegee Study Website.

[6] "Is It Worth Dying For? –How to Make Stress Work for You, Not Against You" by Dr. Robert S. Eliot (M.D.) and Dennis L Breo –copyright 1984 – Bantam Books

mind becomes joyous. The physical body is as if a shadow of the mind, following exactly in its footsteps. Thus, whatever happens in the mind, also essentially happens in the body, though the effects will register differently. Thus, whenever the mind experiences stress, the body will be bombarded by stress hormones and muscular tension, which will result in bodily distress, and over a period of time lead to those physical conditions which have been given the label "diseases" by the orthodox medical establishment. This also explains why someone can have seemingly good health in their youth, and even in their middle age years, and then become plagued by various conditions like cancer, high blood pressure, stroke, etc. It is because they have finally reached the threshold level of the assault that the body could tolerate and still be functional. So, essentially, your state of health is a refection of how you have handled your emotions, or how they have handled you during the past years in this lifetime, and also in previous lifetimes! If you are not pleased with your current health situation, you need to engage in techniques that will facilitate you to change your thoughts (emotions) and consequent behaviors (actions), so you can have the possibility of future health.

Kemetic Wisdom Teaching:

"Those who gave thee a body, furnished it with weakness; but The ALL who gave thee Soul, armed thee with resolution. Employ it, and thou art wise; be wise and thou art happy."

Kemetic Wisdom Teaching:

**"When an idea exclusively occupies the mind,
it is transformed into an actual physical state."**

The above Kemetic wisdom teachings tell us that if the mind is filled will stress-related thoughts and frustrations, these will manifest physically...and will then be referred to as "disease" (cancer, diabetes, heart attack, stroke, etc.) Thus, if one desires to have an experience of physical health, it is imperative that one develops the ability to control one's thoughts (emotions). But how is this done? It is well and good to understand that this change must occur, but as the saying goes, "old habits die hard." Yet, this task is not an impossible one. And many people, when faced with health challenges, find that they can make some changes in their lifestyle and diet that they felt they were unable to make before, but had they done so before, they very likely would have prevented the illness. However, the majority of people find that they cannot make drastic lifestyle and diet changes, even if it is a matter of life and death. I have seen both sides of the coin. A family member smoked, and of course other non-smoking family members urged him not to do so. However, he felt he was unable to stop, because of the effects of nicotine addiction. Yet, when he was told that he had lung cancer, he never again touched a cigarette. He did not wean himself off the cigarettes, but stopped immediately, just like that, something he had said he was not capable of doing. His cancer was successfully operated, and he has never smoked since. I also had the opportunity to be in a hospital waiting room area while another family member was having surgery, and while I was there, I met a gentleman who was having such severe breathing problems, that he was receiving oxygen therapy. Yet, every five to ten minutes he would to disconnect himself and leave his bed to go outside and smoke. He told me that he just could not stop smoking, even though it was killing him. What is it that affects our willpower to change our behavior, to promote positive behaviors, or to continue to engage in harmful behavior, even when it is killing us? The answer to these questions lies in the mind, so it is here we must seek further answers.

It must be noted also, that you do not have to and should not wait until you are faced with serious health conditions and drastic choices to consider altering your lifestyle. In most cases, the greatest balance, harmony and effectiveness is achieved by implementing changes over a two to five year period of time. So, you should have a firm commitment to plant the seed of change right now, not tomorrow or next week or next year, but NOW, implementing whatever small changes you can begin with, and then letting them grow and bear their sweet fruit of health, peace and vitality.

Kemetic Wisdom Teachings:

"Mind, as matter, may be transmuted, from state to state, degree to degree, condition to condition, pole to pole, vibration to vibration. Transmutation is a Mental Art."

"They who grasps the truth of the Mental Nature of the Universe are well advanced on The Path to Self Mastery."

"To destroy an undesirable rate of mental vibration, concentrate on the opposite vibration to the one to be suppressed."

Controlling the Mind- Controlling the Emotions:

In Western science, generally the mind is said to be located in the brain. However, as we shall see in our study of this book, the Kemetic view differs from this traditional western model. The ancient sages understood that mind was all, and that the physical body to be an expression of the mind, in accordance current holistic thought. They understood the nature of the mind to be fluid, and mental energy to flow though the brain and nervous system to enliven the physical body, much in the same way electricity flows though the wires of an electrical cord to run an appliance. Thus, as the mind is outside of the physical body, yet interactive with the physical body, one can only have a limited effect in affecting the mind through physical means alone. To have the most impact, one would actually have to go to the place where mind exists, a plane of consciousness existing outside of the physical body, the mental plane. This is discussed more in depth in Chapter 2 of this book, in the section entitled *The Body-Mind-Soul Relationship*. The control of mind was so important in Kemet that the initiates (spiritual aspirants) had as their first two precepts of initiatic conduct: 1- Control your thoughts, 2- Control your actions.

So, what techniques did these initiates use to control their minds (thoughts and emotions), so as to be able to control their actions (behaviors), even when they were being tempted or provoked, as they were also expected to master the following precepts: "Distinguish right from wrong," "Distinguish truth from untruth," "Be free from resentment when wronged," and "Be free from resentment when persecuted"? They used a system of disciplines, which collectively are referred to as Sema (Smai) Tawi, which today would be translated and understood as an integral process of Yoga, union of the Higher Self and lower self. The sages realized that the human personality had four basic aspects, and developed a discipline for dealing with each aspect of the personality, to control each aspect of the personality that would lead one to have negative thoughts, emotions and behaviors. Thus, for the action aspect of the personality, they developed the Sema Ari Maat, the Yoga of Righteous Action and Selfless Service. They developed the Sema Ushet, the Yoga of Devotional Love, for the emotional aspect of the personality. For the intellect aspect of the personality, they instituted the Sema Rekh, the Yoga of Wisdom, and for the will aspect of the personality, the Sema Uaa, the Yoga of Meditation. The first three practices are referred to as Informal Meditation, and the latter as Formal Meditation, and all four aspects of the disciplines were to be practiced daily in an integral fashion. Each of these disciplines will be dealt with more in depth in the book. The section on *Food for the Mind* will discuss the aspects of Informal Meditation, *while Food for the Soul* will discuss the aspects of Formal meditation, which includes the practice of Yoga Exercise postures. *Food for the Body* will discuss vegetarian-vegan-raw/live foods diet as well as the Tjef Neteru Exercise Postures. Vegetarianism falls under the categories of the Yoga of Righteous Action and the Yoga of Meditation.

These disciplines of Sema (Smai) Tawi were very scientifically and precisely worked out to be able to effect the utmost control of the mind, and eradicate negative emotions and behaviors. However, the practice of Sema Tawi disciplines was instituted by the sages not a means to attain superb physical health, but to transcend the mind and body consciousness and experience union of the lower self (ego-personality-sense of individuality) with the Higher Self (Supreme Being-sense of oneness with everything in creation)...Sema Tawi or Yoga. So, in the system of Kemetic Spirituality, called *Shetaut Neter* or *The Mystery System*, developed by the Enlightened sages of Kemet, physical health was seen as a natural by-product of the practice of the disciplines of Sema Tawi which lead one to become an Enlightened sage. Their goal therefore, was not to work for achieving good physical health, but to work to attain the goal of life and achieve the purpose of life, Sema Tawi: Union with the Higher Self (known by many other names, a few of which are: Pure Consciousness, God, Divine, Supreme Being, Allah, Goddess, Great Spirit, etc.), Enlightenment, and physical health would be a natural by-product of this sublime endeavor. *Shetaut Neter* therefore, did not allow for separation of physical and mental health and spirituality. However, when one does not know and understand the true purpose of life, and therefore lives life in an erroneous manner, mental or/and physical disbalances, commonly referred to as "diseases," will surely follow. It is a signal that something is not right, that something has strayed from how it is supposed to be. Unfortunately, most people, rather than adopting this understanding and seeking to find out why the illness is happening, feel secure in taking a pill or some treatment and continue their erroneous way of life, until the body can no longer take the assault and gives out.

The ancient Enlightened Kemetic teachers could not and did not separate physical health from spiritual health. In other words, there was only one staircase to the doorway of health. The actual doorway is attaining Sagehood or Enlightenment, and each step leading to that doorway is more steeped in peace, joy, love, compassion, understanding, patience, and health than the previous one. Everyone is somewhere on that stairway, trying to find abiding love, peace, joy and health. Those who don't care very much about their physical or spiritual health are on the lower steps. Those who care only about their body, but not about spirituality, are a little higher up. Those who care about their spiritual health, but in a limited sense which does not include proper care of the body, are a little higher up. Those who care about attaining Enlightenment are highest up on the staircase, as they take care of their physical and mental nature (diet, exercise, control thoughts and emotions) as part of their spiritual discipline. However long it takes you to get from one step to the next is up to you. By your lifestyle choices, you are choosing whether you go up to the next step, remain where you are or go down. Thus, you must reflect and determine where you are on the ladder, so as to understand what is/are the next step(s) you must take to improve your health. If you have not given much emphasis to meeting the proper needs of your physical body, now you must, and this book will guide you as to what are the proper needs of the physical body and the most effective means to meet those needs. Likewise, if you have already been practicing the proper steps of diet, nutrition and exercise, as laid out in this book, and yet find that your health is less than optimal, then you need to evaluate your spiritual (of which emotional health is a component) or lack of spiritual emphasis. Again, this book will guide you as to how to overcome the negative emotional states through the yogic practices. The Sema Tawi disciplines are gifts of the ancient teachers which are available for humanity to use to most effectively and efficiently gain control over the mind and emotions, and eventually to even go beyond mind itself, and fulfill the ultimate purpose of life, to become an extension of the Divine for establishing truth and righteous in the world... to become an Enlightened Being.

Even in the beginning stages of the practice of the disciplines, practitioners are overwhelmed by the profundity of the benefits they receive. Meditation has been documented to lower blood pressure and relieve stress, as have the yoga exercise postures. Because many patients are turning to Alternative Medicine, even the traditional orthodox medical system is researching and recommending various of the Sema Tawi disciplines to promote physical health, especially the Physical Yoga Exercise Postures (Tjef Neteru Sema Paut) and Meditation Practices, as well as dietary recommendations. Thus, by incorporating these simple but profound disciplines and techniques into your daily routine, you too can begin to enjoy peace of mind, happiness, as well as physical, mental and spiritual health.

Mind-Body and Spirit:

Kemetic Wisdom Teaching on the purpose of life:

"The purpose of all human life is to achieve a state of consciousness apart from bodily concerns."

This statement, "**state of consciousness apart from bodily concerns**" is further elucidated in the following quote from the ancient Kemetic texts:

"Know thyself as the pride of creation, the link uniting divinity and matter; behold a part of The Divine Itself within thee; remember thine own dignity nor dare descend to evil or meanness."

The "Know Thyself" phrase is referring to the spiritual process of Self-discovery, known by various names according to various religious and spiritual systems: Yoga, Union of lower and Higher Self, Kingdom of Heaven, Nirvana, Liberation, Salvation, Moksha, Self-realization, Enlightenment, etc. The Kemetic term for spiritual enlightenment is *Pert m Hru*, "Coming into the Light," also known as *Nehast*, "Resurrection," "Awakening." In this state of "Knowing Oneself," one discovers abiding happiness and love cannot be lost as a result of any condition or situation. In reality, this is what every human being is searching for in the world, without success. However, when one has not attained this lofty spiritual height, which applies to the majority of people in the world, when does not know their true essence, their Divine essence which is pure and abiding peace, pure and abiding love, pure and abiding joy, then one descends to "evil or meanness (anger, hate, doubt, worry, anxiety, envy, jealousy, hate, fear, frustration, depression, sadness, mental unrest, mental illness, physicall illness, stress, etc.)." Thus, according to Shetaut Neter System, the root cause of all physical and mental disease is NOT "Knowing Thyself." This state of lacking self-knowledge is referred to as the state of ignorance, called Kemn in the Kemetic language. Thus, Sema Tawi and other mystical philosophy teaches that kmen, ignorance of one's Self, leads to the development of mental disease which expresses as negative thoughts, emotions and behaviors, and these in turn lead to physical disease. Thus, in the strictest sense of the Sema Tawi and other mystical philosophy, anyone who is not an Enlightened personality, that is, anyone who does not "Know" themselves, is considered to be mentally ill, the degree of disease being in accordance with the extent of the lack of Self-knowledge. So what general society considers as being psychologically normal, yoga philosophy would consider as abnormal, and what general society considers as abnormal, yoga would consider as being severely affected. Thus, yoga urges the student (aspirant, initiate) to become "supernormal," and rise up against these socially accepted, but detrimental norms. It is interesting to note, that in recent statements released over the news media by the psychological association, they stated that new research indicates the condition of anger to be a temporary state of psychological imbalance, and of course we are also familiar with the term, "temporary insanity," which describes, in an almost condoning way, the psychological state where a so called rational person acts in an intensely unbalanced psychological manner. Therefore, mystical philosophy sees that the only way to achieve health of body, mind and spirit is to engage in integral practices and disciplines such as Sema Tawi (Egyptian Yoga).

First Step to Controlling the Emotions – Understanding True Happiness:

We have already established that to experience good physical health, it is imperative that one controls one's emotions. One must be able to prevent the mind from becoming angry, frustrated, worried, anxious, sad, depressed, fearful, etc. Yet, as you know, these emotions seem to as if define the nature of the mind for the majority of people. Anger and sadness are the two emotions that most predict the likelihood of heart disease and cancer, respectively[7]. Seemingly little events like someone cutting you off in traffic is enough to elicit a spark of anger, and a strike against your physical health. Think of how many strikes you make on an average day against your physical health due to your mind indulging in these negative emotional states. Why is it not possible for the ordinary person's mind to maintain a state of calmness and joy at all times?

The main reason is that most people in society have erroneously defined happiness. Most people define their experience of happiness through their relationships, work, or activities they engage themselves in. Love and happiness are almost synonymous, since people are most happy when they are in "love" with what is going on in their lives (being with a particular person or engaged in a particular activity), and when people are happy, they feel the most love flowing from their hearts. Thus, yogically, whenever one speaks of the state of true (abiding) happiness, one is also simultaneous speaking about abiding love, and abiding peace. However, depending on others or outer circumstances to experience happiness is a sure set up for eventual unhappiness, because lasting happiness is not a product of those conditions. All relationships will have their good times, and their bad times. The bad times break up the experience of elation and "love" that people experience during the good times, and therefore relationships are incapable of fulfilling one's deep longing to experience peace, ease, contentment, security, love and happiness... at every moment, that is, abidingly.

This means that if you define your happiness by your relationships, you will surely be led to the path of illness and physical disease. There have been many recent new reports of studies that have confirmed this, that one's relationships may be an important contributor to health problems. Consider for example one's cholesterol level and blood pressure. Since stress increases one's cholesterol level and blood pressure, every time you have a spat with or experience disappointment because of a spouse, child or other family member or a friend, you are contributing to blocking your arteries as well as to promoting high blood pressure, thus creating a basis to experience heart disease and/or stroke in the near or distant future.

Likewise, with respect to work, when a person enjoys their work and can apply focus and concentration when performing their tasks, this is an aspect of the concentration-meditation practice, of controlling the thoughts. Since the mind is so focused on the work at hand, it does not allow any other thoughts, negative or positive, to enter the mind, so there is an immense release of tension, and the consequent experience of peace and joy. Thus, the Kemetic scriptures advise that one should choose a line of work that is in harmony with one's personality, and based on ethical precepts, truth and righteousness, as this will promote mental and physical, and consequently spiritual health and wellbeing.

Kemetic Wisdom Teaching on Work and Happiness:

"Do not disturb a great person or distract their attention when they are occupied, trying to understand their task.
When they are thus occupied they strip their body through love of what they do.
Love for the work which they do brings people closer to their true (Divine) essence.

---

[7] Dr. Sandra A. McLanahan, M.D., founder and Executive medical Director of Integral Health Services, a holistic health care practice at Satchidananda Ashram (Yogaville), Buckingham, VA

These are the people who succeed in what they do."

However, one cannot work all day and all night. In addition, one may lose their job, or have to give it up because of injury, etc. So, depending on feeling good only because of your work will equally lead to feelings of frustration at other times, and consequently, physical illness. All situations and activities are transient experiences. They cannot be sustained in an ongoing manner to perpetuate a sense of joy and happiness. So, the experience of abiding, perpetual continuous happiness (peace, love) cannot be found in relationships or by engaging in activities of the world.

In ordinary life when people experience moments of happiness, it is because they somehow brought their mind to a more peaceful state than what it was before. The amount of happiness experienced is directly related to the release of tension in the mind. Most often this is experienced when a desire is fulfilled. What happens then is that people erroneously credit the situation, person, location or object that served to fulfill their desire and caused them to become a little more relaxed than they were before, for their experience of happiness, rather than the mental relaxation which was the actual cause of their experience of happiness. Thus, there is a yogic saying that, "True Happiness is Peace of Mind."

However, not understanding this, people are constantly running in life trying to acquire those objects and situations which in the past, their minds had linked with the experience of happiness. Of course this always will, eventually, end in frustration and failure; their efforts are in vain. Just as one cannot get apple juice from an orange, one cannot get happiness from that which does not and never has contained it. Understanding this, one can choose to embark on a spiritual journey to seek out the source of true happiness and learn how to experience it in one's own life. This is the mystical journey of "Knowing Thyself" that the Ancient Egyptian Sages espoused as the only purpose of life. This is really the journey that everyone is on, only most do not know it, and therefore, rather than facilitating the process, they are creating obstacles for themselves on the path which they will one day have to surmount, and physical disease is one such obstacle. The purpose of physical disease is to push that person to change their negative habit patterns of mind and diet, thus becoming more sagely in their behavior (control of mind and the negative emotions of the mind, developing willpower to change, learning about the nature of the body and its proper needs, learning to breath properly, etc.) For those who resist, the journey will take many lifetimes[8] and experiences of frustration before they arrive at the questions which you have probably already arrived at, "Is this all there is to life? Is there no true abiding happiness in this world?" These are the questions the universe waits for everyone to ask, and in harmony with the universal law of nature, "When the student is ready, the teacher will appear." You will be led in accordance with your spiritual inclinations and personality, to specific books, like this one, and to a spiritual teacher. Now, instead of creating obstacles for yourself on your spiritual path (journey), you now seek to remove the old obstacles, and move in such a manner that you are in harmony with the spiritual laws of the universe and therefore, are not creating new ones. In addition, the spiritual teaching as if provides a map for you to make your journey easier and more expedient.

Your vehicle for this journey is composed of your body-mind complex, and therefore these must be kept in tip-top shape, i.e., fed with proper nourishment (fuel). Thus, considering what to feed the body is not merely a matter of taking care of the body to keep it healthy so it can continue its futile, and consequently stressful, and therefore dis-ease causing, efforts in the world, of trying to find happiness through relationships or activities. As a matter of fact, no matter how much proper food is fed to the body, if one's way of understanding and dealing with practical life does not change, that is, if one does not develop a holistic spiritual perspective of life, but continues to expend energy, both physical and

[8] Reincarnation is inherent within the Ancient Egyptian Mystical (Spiritual) philosophy. It will be explained later on in the text and for more in depth information, see the book by the same author, *The Wisdom of Maati*.

mental, chasing after happiness in the world of objects, places, situations, and relationships, no diet for the body will grant the best health that is possible for that individual. There will always be an underlying basis of frustration from not being able to get what you want, absolute comfort. So there will always be a lack of ease (dis-ease) and a lack of relaxation (i.e., stress), that will result in physical and/or mental "disease." This is a crucial point to understand. One must come to see the futility behind one's efforts of seeking happiness by trying to arrange a particular situation, or moving to a different location, or acquiring a specific object or engaging in a particular relationship. When this point is grasped, only then can one become free from the clutches of the world, and being a slave to the senses. These can no longer bind you, since objects no longer dazzle your mind. Now you are free and can use your time and energy to learn about, explore and practice the specific disciplines of mystical spirituality. These will lead you to be able to get in touch with the habit patterns of your mind, and to gain control of the mind, to maintain yourself in an ever increasing state of serenity at all times, under all conditions, and eventually to transcend the mind, and discover true happiness, abiding happiness.

Understanding that the key to your experience of peace and joy in life is keeping the mind calm, you attempt to do this at all times, even in provocative conditions of ill-health. As a matter of fact, ill-health will be compounded by an upset mind, and worsen the dis-ease process. So, especially if one has any conditions of ill-health, it is of paramount importance that they submerge themselves in spiritual disciplines, which will give insight into and techniques on controlling the mind, so that it can remain calm.

Of course, maintaining a peaceful mind is quite easy when you are alone. However, while in the world interacting with other personalities, the challenge comes, especially when you are involved with people who do not have deep mystical insight into life. The challenge also comes when people erroneously perceive objects, other people and certain circumstances in the world to be the source of their happiness, they will also relate to you either as a source of their happiness, or as an obstacle on the path to their attainment of happiness. Therefore, they will either shower you with sweetness and praise when they see you as facilitating their experience of happiness, or curse you and want you out of their life when they see you as a hindrance to that process. In the world, one can go from being a friend to enemy in the wink of an eye.

For example, suppose you are a cashier, and some problem occurs with your machine as you are checking someone out. Now this person becomes upset with you. Why? Because they are perceiving you as obstructing their experience of what they believe is true happiness, which to them may mean going home in time to catch the sports section of the news on television. When one is constantly depending on certain developments in the world to be able to relax and be happy, one is setting oneself up to experience constant mental agitation and frustration, as you have no doubt discovered for yourself. There is an almost constant underlying preoccupation (mental agitation) about whether or not the situation will materialize, or will something happen to twarth it. This underlying worry (mental agitation), which may be occurring mostly at the subconscious level of mind, precludes the experience of abiding peace, and develops a psychological leaning or dependency on the world, for one's experience of happiness. If the expectations are met, as will occur at some times, then one allows themselves to feel happy for that while, until the situation ends. Then new situations must be planned to allow for the opportunity to have more happy moments in the near and distant future, and thus deepening expectations and psychological dependency on the world "to be happy" are generated, in an never ending vicious circle of constant mental preoccupation and agitation, which in itself twarths the possibility of true happiness, which is abiding. In addition, since not all situations work out the way one anticipates that they will, one's expectations will be periodically twarthed, probably more often than they will work out in the way that one had desired. When this occurs, the frustration and disappointment that ensues blocks any possibility of experiencing happiness, even a transient experience of happiness, so experiencing abiding happiness is definitely not even a possiblility under such circumstances.

"There is no happiness for the soul in the external worlds since these are perishable. True happiness lies in that which is eternal, within us."

In the example above, a customer who understands the futility in pursuing happiness in the world of objects, relationships, situations, etc., would not let the problem with the cash register dis-balance their mind. However, most customers are not in this spiritually mature category. Most would become upset and impatient. In this case, as the cashier, you need to exert your willpower so as not to allow the situation to dis-balance your mind, no matter how ridiculous it becomes, because you know the secret of being peaceful and happy. You know that your happiness is independent of the outward circumstance, and to continue to experience it all you have to do is stay calm as you continue to deal with the situation to the best of your ability, with patience. You know that happiness is your true nature, and therefore can be experienced in its fullness at every moment. This is the goal of all spiritual practices, to manifest this state of being where one is perpetually happy and joyful, no matter what is going on. Just to have this insight results in a major release of stress, because now you can stop running and chasing after the phantom of happiness, and be still and discover your true essence as the embodiment of abiding happiness. This is the state of true health, and any steps you take in this direction will lead you to become healthier. Though not easy, it must be done. In reality, you are already trying to do it; you are already constantly in pursuit of abiding happiness. What is presented here is the wisdom that is needed to do it correctly, efficiently, effectively and healthily.

Journey to Abiding Happiness—What it takes to get there:

For some, the journey will be easy, while for others, challenging. This philosophy does not lead to a morbid and austere lifestyle as some believe. It is not telling you not to love, not to interact with objects, to end all relationships, to get rid of all objects, etc. No. Rather, it is merely urging you to realize, each time you experience happiness when interacting with specific objects, situations, conditions or persons, to give credit for the experience of happiness where credit is due, to the Higher Self within you, and not the outer circumstance. If this is practiced, in addition to the other spiritual disciplines for promoting self-discovery (meditation, selfless service, righteous action, etc.), you will gradually lead yourself to the state of enlightenment. You will have attained the goal of life, that for which you have been striving, but which has eluded your grasp for countless lifetimes, the experience of abiding peace and joy (bliss).

The philosophy of Sema Rekh, the Yoga of Wisdom brings forth the understanding that true abiding happiness, that is unwavering and unaffected by any outer circumstances and conditions, can only be experienced when the mind remains calm, peaceful, and loving on a continual basis, even as one participates in the world as a seemingly “normal” person. When the most people hear and consider this teaching, especially with respect to their own personal experiences in life, they often feel a sense of disbelief, and usually conclude that this is simply not possible. They often cite circumstances where they felt the situation was so overwhelming, that even the most Enlightened saint would have become affected if they were the one who had to be involved in dealing with that situation. However, this is why the teachings also give injunctions to the neophyte (beginner) spiritual student that they must have threefold faith if they wish to progress in the process of gaining supreme control over the mind, and become Enlightened beings. They must have faith in the spiritual preceptor’s ability to lead them along the path of truth, in their own ability to accept the truth, and in their ability to act with wisdom. In other words, once you have found an authentic teacher and teaching, you must trust the process.

Stories of Buddha tell that he would not allow new students to ask questions for the first year of their stay at his spiritual center. He, like the Kemetic sages, knew that students first needed to develop a relationship with the teacher and teachings in the environment of the spiritual center, to develop trust and faith in both. He also knew that the depth of the teachings that were being given would be beyond their grasp, due to their lack of familiarity with, and insight into them. Thus, the questions they would ask would express disagreement with the teachings, rather than understanding. He knew that in the environment of the spiritual center, they would, along with the older students, practice the mystical disciplines of purification, such as vegetarian diet, selfless service, meditation, compassion, forgiveness, etc., in an integral fashion. This, he knew, would allow the seed of aspiration in their hearts, that had gotten them to this point of striving to seek something more than the so called "normal" values of worldly life, to sprout, grow, and eventually bloom into intuition. Practicing the disciplines of mystical philosophy along with listening to the teachings would allow their questions to be answered in a manner that would be effective for them, that would lead them to understanding rather than argument. In time, they would find that their questions would be answered directly by the teachings as they were being given, by more advanced students as they interacted with them, by the teacher because more a advanced student asked them, and/or by their own minds through the dawning of insight. The latter, insight or inward revelation, increasingly emerges in the mind as it becomes more purified and calm as a result of the practice of the integral Sema Tawi and other similar mystical teachings and disciplines.

In Kemet, the Temples served the same purpose. The Kemetic sages instituted *Shetaut Neter (The Mystery System),* to promote and facilitate this transformative process of spiritual growth in those students who desired it. Shetaut Neter is also referred to as The Initiatic System, and the aspiring students as Initiates. Thus, if what is being discussed here in this introduction, as well as in the entire book, seems too far-fetched, allow it the benefit of doubt for now, and continue to strive to seek, with sincerity, for inner peace, purity, truth, abiding happiness, and health of body, mind and soul. You will undoubtedly be led to circumstances, events, experiences and personalities which will bestow upon you greater understanding and insight, depending on the intensity of your sincerity, and consequently your search.

Most people don't realize that the process of Sema Tawi (Smai Tawi) or "Egyptian Yoga" is considered to be a science, as opposed to a philosophical system, although in general parlance it is often referred to as a philosophical system. Philosophy implies delving into the nature of things by logical reasoning and intellectual pursuit. Enlightenment cannot be realized through philosophy alone, as the essence of "the underlying nature of things" is transcendental, that is, beyond mind. Thus, philosophic discourses and studies of the mystical sciences form a limited part of the overall process of "Knowing Thyself." Philosophy serves primarily to promote a superficial, intellectual understanding of the teachings, practices and goal of the mystical sciences. Then the student must intently engage in the practice of the various disciplines to realize the goal. In this process, intellectual wisdom is converted to "intuitional" wisdom. Intuitional wisdom implies that the intellectual knowledge has been understood as at a deeper experiential level. Consider the example of a trainer that teacher a parrot to say the words, "I am not afraid of cats. The cat cannot hurt me because I am in a cage." Now what do you think will happen when a cat enters into the room where a parrot is? The parrot will start squawking with fear, even though it may have learned to say the above phrases perfectly well, because this learning was superficial. There was no real understanding on behalf of the parrot as to what the words really meant. Likewise, neophytes begin their level of spiritual training at this philosophical –parroting—level of understanding. However, through consistent and persistent practice, they gain insights into the teachings that lead to intuitional experiences as a result of the disciplines, and in a gradual progression, to the attainment of enlightenment.

Thus, it is important for you, the reader, to first gain the intellectual understanding of the teachings being brought forth in this book. Many insights will dawn in your mind as your are reading because of certain past experiences you have had, and more will come after you have read it as a result of experiences you will encounter. Then you should seek to gain further experiential knowledge, by attending programs, seminars and workshops which will begin to guide you to attain increasing proficiency in the practice of the disciplines. As the Kemetic wisdom teaching says, "When the student is ready, the teacher appears." So you should not worry about how or where you will find a place to receive such training, but you should strive to make yourself ready. Readiness at this level implies keeping an openness so as to be "ready" to seize the opportunities around you as they materialize or are brought into your sphere of awareness. Once you have become open to the process, you will be surprised how many opportunities which will promote your growth in these areas will seemingly "pop up" all around you, to nourish an support your early development. You may or may not find your main spiritual teacher right away. If you do not, each experience along the way will be a stepping stone in your spiritual journey, until you are able to meet his personality. In the meantime, you can certainly begin to prepare yourself for this occurrence. This is a higher level of making yourself "ready." This level of readiness implies attaining a certain degree of purification, of Body, Mind and Soul, by beginning to enter into the various practices and guidelines presented in this book. For further information on the Teacher-Student (Disciple) relationship (qualifications of an aspirant/initiate, how to evaluate a spiritual teacher in terms of authenticity, etc.), the reader is referred to the book by Dr. Muata Ashby, *Initiation in Egyptian Yoga.*

Many people, especially in western society which seemingly places much emphasis on individuality and being free spirited, recoil from the idea that they need to have a teacher or guide to enter into these practices. However, consider that when human beings are born, unlike some other animal species that can care for themselves from the time they are born, humans are totally helpless. Without care, guidance and protection from other human beings, a neonate will die. Thus there is a popular saying that the mother is the child's first teacher. And this is just the beginning. All of life is a learning process. Even an Enlightened personality can still learn new technical skills such as learning to play drums or a guitar. Also consider that for any attainment in life where one wants to achieve expertise, one must receive some training from someone else that has already mastered the experiential knowledge in that area. Sometimes this can be through an indirect process of reading books, etc., however, how would you feel about having surgery performed on you by a doctor who only read about the procedure in books, with no direct training under the direct instruction and guidance of another experienced and qualified doctor? Would you want a pilot who only read about flying from a book to fly a plane that you were on? Even basketball players undergo rigorous training under a coach's direction to become professionals. Why should the process of attaining Enlightenment be any different? If anything, it requires more guidance and coaching, as its attainment is so subtle and elusive, due to the many tricks that the egoistic mind can play and trap the initiate. Thus, in spirituality, guidance is also needed.

Consider the following example. Suppose that you are visiting our center, and during a meeting we are having on your last day of stay, I am eating something out of my bowl. You ask me what am I eating, and I reply to you that I am eating a special raw (uncooked) vegan (no animal products) ice cream that I just made. You ask me what does it taste like. I struggle to find the words to give you insight into the taste. I tell you it tastes somewhat like a combination of mangoes and peaches. You acknowledge this, knowing what mangoes and what peaches taste like, however, you still do not really know what the ice cream exactly tastes like. You have an idea, but not exact knowledge. The only way you can really know is to be able to taste it yourself. So, you ask if you may have a taste. I offer you some. You find that it is delicious, surpassing everything you have ever eaten. However, the problem is that you are leaving and would not be able to have any more of this wonderful dish that you just experienced. You also, realizing how unique and special it is, start to think of your family, and how they would easily stop eating regular ice cream if only they could have a taste of this.

So, you ask me for the recipe. I give you the recipe, and you return back home and try making the recipe. The results you got were all right, but it was not as good as the one you got from me, so you call me. In our conversation, I express some areas of nuances in the preparation of the raw ice cream. You try the technique again, a few more times, trying to apply what you were told, and your results improved, but still something is missing. You like the ice cream so much that you have decided that you want it to become the center of your livelihood. You decide to come and visit me, so that you can learn the process directly, to be sure that you are doing every thing correctly, to get the best results. When you arrive, I meet with you and you taste some of my ice cream. You are once again blown away by its wondrous taste. Yours was very good, but compared to this, you realize how much room you have for improvement in the preparation of the ice cream. To learn this, you much be able to come and spend time with me, to receive training under my supervision and instruction. You must watch me as I prepare it, giving the instructions as I go along. Next, you must try to make it yourself with my direct guidance, then you must try on your own. If it still does not come out correctly, then you must study some more, watching and observing the methodology, helping with the process, and then trying again to duplicate the technique on your own. If you wish to be successful in your business, this process of observing, listening, assisting and practicing must be continued until you have gained the understanding and mastered the technical skills to competently reproduce the ice cream, however long it takes. It must be pursued with persistence and patience, otherwise you will become upset by your seeming "failures," and stop your pursuit out of frustration and defeatism, instead of regarding each seeming "failure" as a stepping stone to success, which is what they are. Each seeming failure is in fact teaching you how to further adjust your technique or understanding so that you move closer and closer to your goal. Thus, understanding what "not to do" is part of the process of learning "what to do."

The above example gives insight into the initiatic process, which begins with aspiration. Aspiration begins as a deep inner desire or longing to experience something higher and more sublime in life, even if initially one may not know exactly what that higher, sublime pursuit is. This inner desire will lead one to pick up a book, such as this one, or attend a spiritual program where one is able to receive insight into the sublime goal of life, the attainment of Enlightenment or Self-knowledge, and the light of aspiration becomes a little brighter. This is like finding out that such a wonderful thing as raw vegan ice cream exists. You feel that there is something real there and you develop a desire to pursue it. However to properly pursue it, you must undergo a process of contact with someone who has already attained that goal, and seek their guidance and contact, at first through indirect means (books, letters, telephone, E-mail, etc.,), but even more effectively, through direct contact (being in their physical presence), so you can have the opportunity to get a taste of that Divine ice cream from being in their presence. Now having been further inspired, one begins the process of striving to attain perfection in the process of making oneself into an Enlightened being, which is related to perfecting the process of making the ice cream oneself, so one can have it all times, and not just when the teacher is around.. Thus, one must apply himself or herself in the process of following the instructions of the spiritual teacher in following the Sema Tawi recipe or scientific formula for attaining Enlightenment, that has been handed down throughout the ages by means of the initiatic process:

Enlightenment = Sema Tawi Arit Maat (Yoga of Righteousness and Selfless actions which includes a Vegetarian Diet) + Sema Tawi Ushet (Yoga of Devotion) + Sema Tawi Rekh (Yoga of Wisdom) + Sema Tawi Uaa (Yoga of Meditation which includes the physical yoga exercise postures such as Tjef Neteru and a Vegetarian Diet)

Kemetic Wisdom Teaching:

"Men and women are to become Divine-like through a life of virtue (Sema Maat), **and the cultivation of the spirit through "scientific" knowledge, practice and bodily** (Sema Ushet, Sema Rekh and Sema Uaa)."

It is important to note, as expressed in the above wisdom teaching, that the Kemetic sages regarded the system of Shetaut Neter Smai Tawi as a scienctific process. When Smai Tawi is referred to as a science, the implication is that anyone who correctly applies the formula will surely get the same result which is Enlightenment, just as chemistry scientists are each guaranteed to get the same result if they apply the same chemistry formula in the correct way. The mystical sciences affirm that the attainment of

Enlightenment can be achieved by anyone who applies themselves appropriately. Thus, everyone has the potential to become a Buddha, a Jesus Christ, an Imhotep, a Mother Teresa, etc.

Ancient Kemetic Mystical Wisdom Teachings:

"Salvation is the freeing of the soul from its bodily fetters (egoism, anger, hated, greed, etc.);
becoming a God (one who is established in virtue) through knowledge and wisdom;
controlling the forces of the cosmos instead of being a slave to them;
subduing the lower nature and through awakening the Higher Self,
ending the cycle of rebirth."

"Make your life the subject of intense inquiry,
in this way you will discover its goal, direction, and destiny."

"To free the spirit, control the senses; the reward will be a clear insight."

"O people of the earth, men and women born and made of the elements,
but with the spirit of the Divine within you, rise from your sleep of ignorance!
Be sober and thoughtful. Realize that your home is not on the earth but in the Light.
Why have you delivered yourselves unto death, having power to partake of immortality?
Repent, and change your minds. Depart from the dark light and forsake corruption forever.
Prepare to blend your souls with the Eternal Light."

"The wickedness of the soul is ignorance (of one's Higher Self and purpose of life);
the virtue of the soul is knowledge (of one's Higher Self and purpose of life)."

"Ignorance is slavery, be it to others or to one's own vices.
To become free from both so as to live in eternal happiness and
to work to establish the will of Father-Mother God[9] on earth is the sacred task."

The Ancient Egyptians were known as "the most religious people in the world,[10]" and though the details of what this means is beyond the scope of this book, suffice it to understand that every aspect of their life was dedicated to achieving the goal and purpose of life, Enlightenment. Thus spirituality was integral as to how they chose to live in every aspect of their life, and how they treated the land and nature, etc. The spiritual principles of truth and righteousness were the basis of all business developments and transactions. When life is lived in this manner, not by one or two individuals in a society, but by the majority of society, then one can easily understand how monuments such as the Sphinx and the Pyramids could be constructed, and how that culture and society could last for over 10,000 years.

[9] The Ancient Egyptian religion has been defined by Dr. Muata Ashby as "Monotheistic Polytheism." It encompasses the concept of a single absolute Supreme Divinity that expresses as the cosmic forces and elements of nature (symbolized in the form of various gods and goddesses called neteru), human beings and nature itself. This Supreme Divinity was known in what would be translated in general terms as "The God," however this term was inclusive of the female essence of creation. It was understood, as one of the scriptural quotes above gives evidence of, that this Supreme Being was a "Mother-Father" God, implying all-encompassing, unlike in modern Christianity and other religions where the implication of the term is a male Divinity. Also, their understanding of The Divine was universal in nature, thus, any of the modern denominational, religious, spiritual or scientific terminology is compatible. Thus, other names for the Divine may be represented as: Goddess, Higher Self, Supreme Being, Pure Consciousness, Brahman, Cosmic Consciousness, Great Spirit, Divine Self, etc., without contradiction. For more on the Ancient Egyptian understanding of The Divine, refer to the books by the same author entitled: **Egyptian Yoga, the Philosophy of Enlightenment, Christian Yoga, The Mystical Journey from Jesus to Christ,** and **The Egyptian Book of the Dead, (Prt M Hru).**

[10] The reader is referred to Resurrecting Osiris for further discussion on this subject.

The United States of America, reputedly the most advanced country in the world, is only a little over 200 years old, yet look at its condition in the areas of health, social justice, and spirituality. The most common remarks and jokes about the government and political leaders, the very foundation of the society, are about dishonesty, deceitfulness, corruption, pay-offs, unethical personal and political behaviors, etc. The government, in cutting itself off from religion (separation of church and state), has also cut itself off from the ethical basis that the true practice of religion demands, except for that which each individual carries within their own heart. This is, in effect, throwing the baby out with the bath water. While this may seem to offer "Religious Freedom," it is not true religious freedom, because members of society, regardless of religious affiliation, cannot practice true religion in an environment of social and political injustice, believing these to be the norm. All authentic religions have ethical precepts of conduct which are almost identical: Do not lie, Do not steal, Do not cheat, etc. So while the government can be separated from religion proper (religious dogmas, religious rituals, favoring one religion over another, etc.), it should not be separated from ethics. Thus, a system of social and political ethics should be the basis for all government and political institutions, as well as businesses in general society. Imagine if every boss and every employee decides to live by these principles, how quickly the negative aspects of society would be transformed in a positive way. Imagine what would happen if bosses knew that their employees would not steal from them, not try to cheat them, and give their very best effort in performing their work. Imagine how it would be if employees felt that their employers were honest and trustworthy, would not mis-treat or manipulate them in any way, and would pay them honestly for their work and/or share the profits with them. Some principals in the public school system have envisioned this sublime social perspective, and have instituted the teaching and practice of ethics as part of the curriculum. This is highly commendable, and is what is needed in every institution in society, government and private, including each home.

In one of the Ancient Kemetic creation myths which tells how creation came into being and is sustained, it is said that creation came into being as God, called Ra, rose out of the primeval ocean on his boat. This movement of his boat on the waters brings forth all objects in creation. Ra is depicted as standing on a pedestal. This pedestal is symbolic of the goddess known as Maat, the goddess of righteousness, order, truth, justice, and harmony. This has two very important mystical implications. First, that the very basis (foundation) of the Divine are the qualities of righteousness, order, truth, justice, and harmony, and secondly, that the very basis of creation is the same. Thus, a society which either does not have an ethical basis or does not put into practice the principles of ethics upon which it was founded, is out of harmony with the laws of the universe, and therefore will suffer dis-harmony and chaos.

Our society has some real problems that must be faced and addressed. Look at the fact that 5 % of the population controls 95 % of the wealth. Look at the homeless, and the violence in the inner cities. Look at the nursing homes filled with the discarded parents, being further mistreated and abused. Look at the divorce rate of over 50 %. Even our food supply is jeopardy due to over-farming, irradiation, and chemical and genetic manipulation. Holistic nutritionists urge consumers to purchase organic produce and products, because they have 40-70% more vitamins, minerals and other nutrients than non-organic foods. Yet, non-organic foods are the foods that fill the produce isles and shelves in the supermarkets across the country. No wonder obesity and overeating are a big problem in society. In addition to the other contributing factors of obesity, even though people consume more, their bodies are starving for the nutrients lacking in the foods, and thus, craving, bingeing and overeating develops. They are in essence malnourished. Further compounding this problem of nutrient deficient foods and soils caused by improper farming practices, is the spraying of these foods with pesticides, fungicides and herbicides, which not only poison the food supply, but also the water supply. Look at the polluted waters and uninhabitable lands. Approximately 50% of the lakes are polluted and unfit for human use. Look at animals being driven into extinction as more and more forests are cut down, and rivers, lakes and the ocean polluted. These are real problems plaguing society today. How can the wisdom of the Ancient Egyptians help?

If you were ill, and had the choice of going to a doctor that has your same condition, or another doctor that was healthy and not only knew the root cause of your condition, but also how to approach it and heal it, and what steps to take to prevent it recurrence in the future, which doctor would you choose? The best choice is of course the healthy doctor, as he/she can best give advice on how to stay healthy. The sick doctor can only commiserate with you and perhaps alleviate some of your symptoms, but obviously since he/she is sick also, he/she does not have insight into preventing the condition. Likewise, if today's society is to be changed, it must seek to learn from a system that worked extremely well and to this day withstands the test of time, instead of trying to reinvent the wheel using unnatural means.

An obvious and understandable question that usually arises when the greatness of the Ancient Egyptian culture is addressed is, "If they were so great, then why did their culture die out?" While this is true and the causes are multi-factorial, the most significant cause of the decline of any culture is the decline in justice, truth and righteousness being the basis of society. The Ancient Egyptian culture experienced this as a result of the influx of peoples from other surrounding countries who did not have the same spiritual value system. Yet, in spite of their decline, the two points still remain unchallenged, that is, they still hold the record of the longest lasting society, and their monuments still defy an explanation as to how they were created and still to this day cannot be duplicated. If you had the opportunity to learn from someone who was the most renowned person in a certain field, someone who was such a genius that no one else has even come close to surpassing him/her, but this person was now retired, or the best person in the field today who only measures up to 1/5th of the genus of the retired person, which would you choose if you wanted to gain the greatest insight into success? You would no doubt study and learn from the best person in the field today, but then go to the retired person to gain insight into his/her views and understanding, clinging to the nuances, wisdom and insights that the best person in the field today was lacking. The best person in the field would no doubt be trained in all the modernization of technology in the field. In this manner you would have the best of both, and not only be able to achieve the success of the retired genius, but perhaps be able to surpass it.

Thus, the purpose of studying and learning the wisdom of the Ancient Egyptians is not to discard the great achievements and advancements of modern society and re-create Ancient Egypt, but to use that wisdom to promote a flourishing society, where all members of society are cared for and have the opportunity to strive to attain the goal of life, spiritual enlightenment. This is possible, and becomes more possible as more and more individuals commit themselves to, as the Ancient Egyptian scripture above stated, **knowing themselves as the pride of creation, the link uniting divinity and matter, and beholding a part of The Divine Itself within themselves,** as well as **remembering their own dignity, nor daring to descend to evil or meanness.** Of course this evil or meanness includes all the vices of greed, anger, envy, jealousy, hatred, and lust. Thus, if just one person in society commits themselves and makes this change, society is improved. There is one less angry, hateful, greedy person in the world, and rather, there is one more Mother Teresa, Imhotep (Ancient Egyptian sage), Buddha or Jesus in the world. This person, just as these saints and sages mentioned, will no doubt touch many lives themselves, and ignite sparks of aspiration within many individuals that will burn until the negativity of their personality is consumed, and only the divine essence remains. Thus, the best way to promote a positive change in society is to effect a positive change in one's self. So if you are tired of the anger, hatred and greed in society, strive to free your own heart of these sentiments through the intense practice of mystical spirituality.

Diet and Mental and Spiritual Health:

So what does all this have to do with one's diet? What is the connection between diet, religion and spirituality? As implied in the title of this book, **The Kemetic Diet, Food for Body, Mind and Soul**, food must be thought of in a broader perspective. Another title of this book could perhaps be, The Kemetic Lifestyle, because it shows one how to live life for the purpose and in the manner in which it was meant to be lived, to attain spiritual fulfillment, and reap the rewards of health, physically, mentally and spiritually, as well as abundant vitality, and abiding peace and joy. The physical body and the mental body (mind, senses and emotions) together comprise the vehicle of the soul, which it uses in its journey of reconnecting with its true essence. As such, any mechanical failures in these areas (mind, body and soul) will cause a delay in reaching the final destination of experiencing abiding peace and joy (enlightenment). Thus, just as with a car or any other vehicle, the first thing one should want to know is, "What is the right fuel for my vehicle?"

Yet, very few people ask this question in relation to their bodies and mind. What should the body be fed? Is it built for eating meat, or vegetables and fruits? Is it made for consuming alcohol or water and juices? Is it made for inhaling carbon monoxide (from cigarettes)? Is it made for consuming foods that are cooked? Do the foods I eat have any influence on my mental state? Do the foods I eat have any influence on my spiritual development?

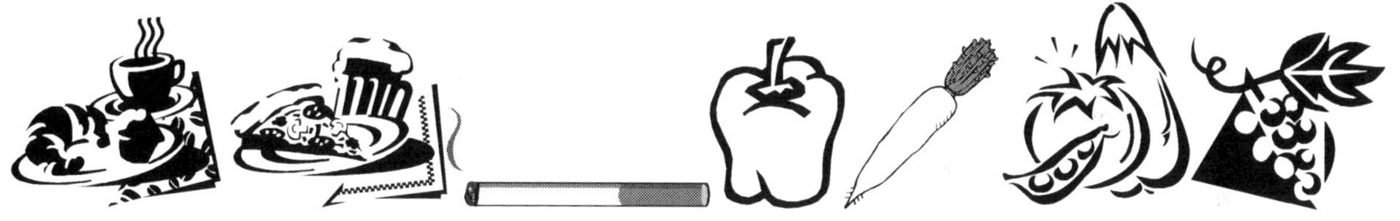

With respect to the mind, even fewer questions are asked by most people. Very few people become concerned by egoistic conversation. Gossiping is an intricate part of most relationships. How many people ask themselves, "Am I listening to or looking at something that is harmony with my spiritual development?" Obviously not too many do, otherwise how could the most popular and abundant TV shows be soap operas, sporting events, and purposeless sitcoms that incite violence, attachment, greed and sexuality? How do watching these lift one's mind to rise above "meanness" and discover one's "dignity"? In brief, they don't. Thus, just as if you were to feed your vehicle the wrong fuel there would be serious problems in its ability to function optimally, if at all, likewise putting the wrong foods in the physical and mental bodies serve to bring ill health and disease. This impedes your journey to attain that for which you have been searching all your life, every lifetime…abiding peace and abiding joy, to "Know Thyself."

The word "disease" is often said so quickly that the implication is not reflected upon, because of the emphasis placed on the specific name of the disease, such as cancer, diabetes, high cholesterol, etc. However, this important study must not be overlooked. The word disease is composed of a prefix dis- which generally implies "a lack of," as in the word disharmony, which means a lack of harmony and peace, (i.e., conflict and stress). The second part of the world is "ease." Now what does this ease refer to? It refers to the ease one attains in the state of optimum health, that is, the state of enlightenment. So the greatest ease is experienced when one overcomes their egoistic (anger, hate, envy, greed, anxiety, etc.)

tendencies, and becomes a saintly or sagely personality. One experiences abiding peace and joy that is not shaken or disturbed by any circumstance, yet one remains compassionate and unselfish. So in reality, the word disease, dis-ease, relates to a lack of spiritual awareness of one's true essence, and thus the true essence of the other people and the world around you. This lack of deep understanding (at the soul level) breeds a deep fear of the loss of one's life (death) which surfaces as the negative mental states of the subconscious mind in the form of fear of other losses. Thus one develops fear of loss (anxiety, worry, insecurity, etc.—i.e.,. stress.) with respect to one's job, status, money, friend, country, way of life, perceiving these deep within the unconscious mind as being a threat to one's very life, etc. These then surface as the negative emotional states of the conscious mind such as anger, hatred, envy, jealousy, greed, lust and fear. These negative mental states cause the release of abnormally high levels of adrenaline, cortisone and other stress hormones in the body, which reap havoc in the tissues and organs, resulting in physical dis-ease. This is compounded because mental unrest then incites stress, which leads to addictive behaviors such as smoking, overeating, emotional eating and eating the wrong foods, alcoholism and other drug use. These negative behaviors heap further assaults on the body.

So dis-ease starts at the soul level due to a disconnection from one's spiritual Self, then festers in the mind, and finally erupts in the body as the various diseases that plague a majority of society. Is it any wonder that the Western medical science, which is so adept at palliating the symptoms, has great difficulty in finding the causes of diseases plaguing Western society such as cancer, mental illness, etc.? How can they, when the cause of the cancer and other diseases is in the soul? Surgery blades cannot reach the soul, and neither can pills. So illness and dis-ease must be addressed at all three levels, the soul level through the discipline of meditation, the mental level through studying and understanding the purpose of life and how to properly achieve it, and through rigorous thinking and serenity of mind, and at the physical level with the proper diet and exercise. When these three levels are properly addressed, one's health is sure to improve. You will start to appreciate the mental and spiritual benefits immediately, however, if the damage to the physical body is too great, the physical benefits may not be fully realized in this lifetime, but certainly in the next. No effort is ever wasted; it is cumulative. Remember that in mystical spirituality, the mind is not equal to the brain, and vice versa. The mind is subtle energy which flows through the brain and nervous system to enliven the physical body, so even if someone has brain damage, they can still operate at the mental level. Thus, regardless of how severe the condition, these practices will bring about an improvement in the quality of life.

The diet of most people is just that, a die-et, a concoction for leading a person to dis-ease (absence of ease, i.e. stress) and death. Therefore, when consuming what is the correct food for the body, as dictated by the biology and physiology of the body and the laws of nature, one should not think in terms of dieting, but of embarking on a lifestyle (rather than a die-et style) of coming into harmony with the laws of nature (the Divine) as they relate to the physical body. This is the practice of truth in life as it relates to the physical body. For some this is a difficult step, as it requires that they abandon the eating habits of the culture in which they grew up or with which they now identify themselves. Thus, there is an emotional-cultural aspect that also has to be dealt with. For example, the types of food commonly known within the African American community as soul food is integral to their modern history and culture. However, this diet is probably one of the worse diets with respect to nurturing one's body, mind and soul. It is anything but "soul" food. Some call it "slave" food, as much of its development occurred during the time of American slavery. It is deadly to the physical body, and therefore does not nurture one's spiritual evolution. Since one is now free to eat as one pleases, there is really no excuse to continue to eat in this manner, certainly not with the legacy handed down from the Ancient Egyptian ancestors. Discovering and implementing the teachings they have left humanity related to diet and health is their legacy, which is yet to be claimed by this generation. As integral as "soul" food is to the African American community, the "meat and potato" diet is to the European-American community. Again, tradition, based in large part on the history of the wild west and cattle farming, is resulting in devastating numbers of people dying and suffering from ill-health. "Real beef" as it has popularly come to be known, is not the proper fuel for the human body. It is the proper food for carnivores such as dogs, cats, lion, tigers, etc., but humans are not carnivores. One only has to compare one's dentition (teeth) to a dog or cat. Every tooth, even the molars in carnivores, ends in a sharp point or a knife-like blade while the teeth of humans are for nipping (the incisors) and grinding (the molars). In addition, there are many other physiological differences, which are discussed in this book in detail. However, the point is, meat is not meant for the human body, and consequently, will result in disease.

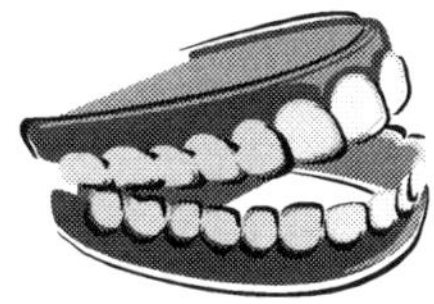

NO, IF YOU EAT FISH, YOU ARE NOT A VEGETARIAN: FACTS ABOUT FISH AND SEAFOOD – WHY YOU DO NOT WANT TO EAT THEM

Many people turn to fish when they are trying to wean themselves off of meat and poultry. The media and conventional medical establishment has led the majority of people to believe that fish is actually a healthy food, something which is good for them, and even the American Heart Association allows for the consumption of fish for people with heart disease, having less fat and cholesterol than other types of meats such as beef, pork, poultry, etc. The perpetuation of the idea that fish is good for people to eat especially gained momentum when it was revealed in the mass media that Eskimos have lower levels of heart attacks, even though their diets are rich in fat. Further research indicated that this beneficial effects the Eskimos experienced was due to the high levels of omega-3 fatty acids in fish, and thus, fish and fish oils were "established" in the minds of the public as heart healthy foods. What was not revealed or elaborated upon in the same reports about the Eskimos however, was that fish, and fish oils, being animal products, contain saturated fats and will increase one's cholesterol. High cholesterol is one of the contributing factors to heart disease. Fish oil, being derived from fish, is subject to the same problems that make eating fish undesirable. These will be discussed in this section[11].

Actual studies on the effect of eating fish and Heart Disease indicate that eating fish is of no benefit in preventing heart attacks or decreasing the incidence of heart disease. Cardiologist Dean Ornish, M.D., cites a *The Lancet* study in his book *Dr. Dean Ornish's Program for Reversing Heart Disease* on men who ate fish three times per week following their heart attack. The study found that "there was no decrease in the incidence of heart attacks." Jane Broody in her book, *The New York Times Book of Health* reports on a study by Dr. Alberto Ascherio of the Harvard School of Public Health and his colleagues which followed 44,895 men for a period of 6 years. The purpose of the study was to find out if those who ate the most fish would have the lowest incidence of heart disease. The findings of this study showed that the rate of heart disease was not affected, regardless of if the subjects ate fish once a month or six times a week.

As mentioned above, some people eat fish and yet refer to themselves as vegetarians. This is non correct, since vegetarianism refers to those who do not eat any animal flesh, and fish is animal flesh. Thus, fish, like all other animals, is not biologically, physiologically or anatomically the correct food for the human body. In addition, it spoils faster than other meats such as beef or poultry, becoming putrefied faster than the other meats and creating toxins in the body when it is eaten. Another major concern with eating fish and seafood relates to pollution of the waters worldwide with toxins such as mercury, PCB's,

[11] For more about problems with the use of fish oil, see the section: **Omega Fatty Acids: Why Flax is better than Fish Oils**

dioxin, etc., which have been linked to cancer, sterility, birth defects, etc. Dr. Cousens, M.D., in the book *Conscious Eating*, cites a Washington. Post article which attributed decreased sperm counts and increased sterility in American males primarily to PCBs. Dr. Cousens further reports that another U.S. government study found that 100% of the sperm samples from the men tested contained PCBs, and that most toxicology experts attribute human PCB contamination to the consumption of fish. He goes on to say that the Environmental Protection Agency estimates that "fish can accumulate up to nine million times the level of PCBs in the water in which they live." Because fish and shellfish are constantly being flushed by the water in which they live. As the water filters through their bodies, they concentrate toxins and microorganisms such as salmonella and hepatitis at levels far greater than found in the water they inhabit. Dr. Cousens also reports that half of the world's fish catch is fed to livestock, which further compounds the exposure to and accumulation of toxins for those who eat other types of animal meats.

Fish has also been given the reputation of being "brain" food, however, Dr. Cousens also cites studies which found correlations between mothers who ate fish while pregnant having children with lower verbal IQ scores (decreased brain development), depression, abnormal reflexes, weakness, lower birth weights and slower responses to external stimuli. He concludes, "the biggest reason of all not to eat fish is to love oneself more than being addicted to old eating patterns of culture and convenience."

Culture and Diet: From Worldly Culture to The Culture of the Higher Self

Every group (culture) has their ethnic or cultural food(s), most of which is unhealthy and unsuitable for the physical body. So what is the answer to questions about maintaining or perpetuating aspects of culture which relate to certain traditional meat dishes. Well, the answer is best summed up by the popular new age saying, "You are not a human being having a spiritual experience, but a spiritual being having a human experience." The essence of what we call a human being is the soul, and the essence of the soul is the Divine Self. This same understanding is expressed in the following teaching from the Ancient Egyptian wisdom texts: **"Men and women are mortal gods and goddesses, and the gods and goddesses are immortal men and women."** So in essence, what is required is that one claims their true culture, their higher culture, the culture of their Higher Self. Any tradition that is not in harmony with this type of culture is based on untruth and misunderstanding, and must be abandoned. The universal laws of nature will not change to suit your lack of understanding of higher truth. Rather it is you that must conform with these laws if you wish to live a life of health and spiritual prosperity, or suffer the consequences of pain and disease if you choose not to. There is really no argument, or rather all your arguments are in vain. There is patience and compassion, but there is no compromise. Look how much abuse the body takes before it rebels. Look at how many chances it gives you, each time recuperating from debilitation only to be bombarded by more attacks on its mechanism. Now it is time for you to do right by it. It is time for you to take proper care of it. Now there is no room for excuses. If you believe the recommendations in this book to be bogus, then you should do your own research and prove them incorrect, or else you will just be making an excuse so as to continue your bad habits.

Another aspect of social-societal, and sometimes cultural, conditioning that prevents people from becoming a vegetarian-vegan, and even more so from becoming a raw-live foodist, is that idea that one will lose their vitality and physical strength. In addition, with respect to consuming raw/life foods, people fear that they will become very thin. Consider that some of the strongest, most well muscled and well-built animals in the world, such as the elephant, oxen, horses, etc., are vegetarians. Some people object to the consideration of these types of animals, because their stomachs/and or intestinal tracts are specially adapted to processing and digesting vegetable matter. But then, also consider that the closest living "cousins" to human beings in the animal world, the chimpanzee and the gorilla, known for their physical prowess, are vegetarians-vegans, and not only that, but raw foodists. So, the moral is that if you want to be as strong as a cow, an ox or a gorilla, you should not eat them, but eat what they eat! Your body has the capacity to adapt with time, and in the transition phase, there are specific approaches that can be taken to compensate for problems of indigestion, malabsorption, etc.

Vegetarian-Vegan-Raw/Live Foods Diet and The Weight Problem

This issue of weight is very important when one considers the following statistics: Approximately 40% of the population of the U.S.A. are overweight and approximately another 15% of the population are considered to be obese. One Health Food Store natural health magazine referred to this situation as "reaching epidemic proportions.[12]" Being overweight and obese predisposes people to a host of physical dis-eases such as diabetes mellitus, heart disease, etc., and as shall be discussed later in the book, also has some bearing on one's spiritual evolution.

As mentioned above, being a vegetarian does not mean that one will become weak and skinny. To the contrary, one will be filled with vitality and strength, and be able to maintain a stable, balanced and healthy weight. However during the cleansing / transition periods, one may at times feel weak and lose weight, however this is not because of the new dietstyle, but because of the stress on the physical body due to the mobilization of toxins, in the body's effort to cleanse itself of them. It must be understood that the population that the Orthodox medical community generally uses to estimate what the "normal" weight of a person should be according to their height is based on data from a non vegetarinan-vegan-raw foodist population. Thus, what is skinny by that system may be quite healthy and "light" by the vegetarian-vegan-raw food standards. A general guideline to determine if one is too skinny is that if one can count one's ribs, one is too thin. One should be able to see the outline of the ribs, but not be able to count them.

Diet and Ethics:

In addition to the negative (toxic) effects of meat eating on the body, which is well addressed in the main text of this book, there are other more subtle effects. Many people want to bring an end to violence in the world, their country, their state, their community, their family, or within themselves. What they fail to realize, not understanding or believing in the cosmic laws of the universe, is that the golden rule that most people are taught as children (do unto others as you would have done unto you), is a spiritual law of nature. Just as when you break a law in society, one suffers the consequences of their action, when the universal laws of nature are broken, one suffers the repercussions, and there is no getting away from the all-seeing eye of the Divine. Thus, the abuse, violence and murder that takes place in the slaughter houses, on the fishing ships, in the poultry industry, in the dairy industry, and in the meat industry, creates a negative subtle effect on those involved and the members of society who support these industries. This manifests as wars, the violence of the inner-cities, now spilling into the violence of suburbia, etc. People may try to escape from the inner cities to suburban communities, but this subtle effect, commonly known as bad *ari*,[13] follows each individual like their shadow. There is no escape, except through changing one's understanding and behavior. Thus, currently in America, many "quiet" suburban cities are also

[12] Delicious Living, October 2001- A Penton Publication – dl.healthwell.com
[13] Kemetic word for Karma and reincarnation- the concept will be explained in more detail later.

experiencing the subtle effects of violence, in a seeming epidemic of school shootings, etc. What is the solution? Stop eating meat right away, and then further embark on discovering and acquiring the proper foods for the mind and soul.

Maat Cosmic Principle: "DO NO VIOLENCE (To any one or anything)."

•Virtue & Diet: Law of Ari (Karma) – Law of cause and effect – A Cosmic Principle!: "What you do comes back to you! In other words: "If you kill what you eat, what you eat will kill you":

- High Cholesterol (Arteriosclerosis, Heart Disease),
- Colon cancer,
- Antibiotic Residues,
- Pesticide Residues
- Environmental toxins accumulate in animals, especially in fats. Meat contains 14 times the pesticide level of an equivalent amount of commercial plant food and dairy products contain 5 ½ times the pesticide level of an equivalent amount of commercial plant food)[14],
- Hormone Residues,
- Stress Hormones released at time of death,
- Bacterial contamination of food,
- Parasites,
- Water contamination, etc.

So what is the truth with respect to the needs of the physical body? This is one-third of the purpose of this book, to elucidate the importance of vegetarianism, and especially, a mostly raw diet. I remember reading a nutritionist stating in his book that one should try to eat at least a 50% raw diet, because the positive effects of the raw diet will neutralize the toxic effects of the cooked food. So in effect, one is taking in poison and the antidote of that poison at the same time. While there is no immediate death, the body is still affected by the toxins and has to utilize energy to neutralize it and get rid of it. While in a healthy body this may not cause too many problems, in a body plagued by dis-ease, it will delay the healing process by decreasing the energy and resources available for healing. Thus, most systems that advocate vegetarian-vegan-raw/live foods usually recommend at least the ingestion of 80% raw foods, so that at least 30% more antidote is still available to nourish and cleanse the physical body after 50% of it becomes neutralized. Now consider how much benefit, in terms of nourishment and purification, a 100% "antidote" intake, that is consuming a 100% raw/live foods diet, will have?

Physical Nutrition and Enlightenment – Mysticism of the Kemetic Diet for the Physical Body:

Kemetic Wisdom Teaching:

"Spirit pervading the body, by means of veins, arteries and blood, gives the living creature motion, and as it were doth bear it in a way."

[14] According to health proponent John Robbins

From the moment of birth, we are born into our physical bodies, and they are with us until the time we die, yet, there much confusion and ignorance among the general population as to the nature and purpose of the physical body, as well as how one should care for their body. Most people know more about the anatomy of and how to maintain their cars or other vehicles and their homes, than their body, the vehicle or temple for their soul. In the wisdom teaching above, the Kemetic sages explain to us that just as the human body gives birth to a human baby, the Spirit gives birth to the physical body, and thus, as the offspring is of the same nature as the parent, the body is essentially Spirit. Just as there is no difference between the ocean and the waves it gives birth to, the body is one with the Spirit (God, Goddess, Supreme Being, etc.). Thus, one's care of one's body should not be a matter of vanity, but spirituality, and just as with any other sacred work, it should be carried out with the utmost precision, knowledge, love, and dedication (devotion of purpose). Also, as it is the Spirit pervading the mind that allows it to function, the mind must also be viewed as being inherently spiritual in nature, and thus, its purpose would have to also tie into the performance of sacred work. Thus, referring to a human being as a complex of body, mind and spirit, is a formality for being able to communicate about the different aspects of a human being, who is in reality a 100 % spiritual being. Much in the same manner, the ancient Kemetic sages used the system of gods and goddesses as tools to represent the different cosmic forces and principles (characteristics) of the one Supreme Being, for the purposes of understanding the one Divine Self.

Ignorance as to the true nature and purpose of the body, and the proper way to care for it, is pervasive in the general society, and is further complicated by the media, espousing the results of various studies, which are oftentimes contrary to the recommendations of authentic spiritual preceptors (teachers). For example, one recent study stated that the moderate daily consumption of wine and other alcoholic beverages could prolong one's life span. The unquestioning mind would readily accept this, and actually feel that they are engaging in healthy lifestyle habits by drinking alcohol. Never mind that the consumption of alcohol is responsible for many highway related deaths due to accidents and numerous health problems. And what about the fact that even one glass of wine or other alcoholic beverage kills liver cells in the physical body...which as we have said, is nothing other than Spirit itself? Would one offer an alcoholic beverage to the Divine? As will be pointed out in additional detail later in this book, alcoholic beverages (wine, beer, liquors, and other alcoholic drinks and beverages) are toxic, and should not be consumed in any quantity. People sometimes remark that wine and beer were consumed in ancient times. Yes, this may be so, but there are two important points related to this statement. First, the nature of these products in ancient times, especially brew or beer, was not as it is today. Today's system of refinement and distillation renders the end products both more potent and toxic than the ancient process. Secondly, even though there were many Enlightened spiritual leaders in Kamit, not everyone in the population was Enlightened, otherwise there would be no need for the Enlightened masters to teach about Maat, the practice of virtue and righteousness, and the other spiritual disciplines and practices which lead one to overcome the lower nature and become Enlightened. Thus, even then, the practices of the initiates and Enlightened personalities held to a higher standard than the masses. Only those who could not control themselves in a spiritually mature manner engaged in the consumption of alcohol (including wine, beer, etc.). Which category do you wish to be in? The "worldly personality" category, or the "Know Thyself – I am going to attain Enlightenment in this very lifetime" category?

Kemetic Proverb Relating to General Society:

"Drink not beer to excess! The words that come out of your mouth, you cannot recall.
You fall and break your limbs, and no one reaches out to you.
Your comrades go on drinking, they stand up and say: 'Away with this fellow who is drunk.'
If any one should seek you to ask counsel of you,
you would be found lying in the dust like a little child."

Thus, the above proverb, though it seems to be saying it is all right to drink beer (alcohol) as long as one does so in moderation, one must realize that it is being addressed to those members of society that are unable to abide by the higher code of ethical behavior, which as the quote below states, does not advocate drinking alcohol at all.

Kemetic Wisdom Teaching for Initiates:

"Oh that thou did understand that wine is an abomination."

Also, whenever the media brings forward new medical discoveries such as this one advocating the use of alcohol for health benefits, the question should arise, "What was their sample population?" Was it stressed out members of the population or did they sample a population of yogic practitioners, sages and saints? Yes, for overly stressed out people who do not know the secrets to achieving relaxation and peace through the application of authentic integral spiritual disciplines and techniques, and therefore cannot easily control their mental state, a shot of alcohol or some drug may serve in some cases to sedate them enough to insulate them from their problems (stressors) so they do not have a total meltdown in the form of a nervous breakdown, heart attack or stroke. However, to present this as a general standard for all members of society is not only misleading, but also physically, mentally and spiritually detrimental. As a Kemetic wisdom teaching tells us, one must beware of information coming to us from the Western paradigm, referred to here as the "Greek tongue":

"The Greek tongue is a noise of words, a language of argument and confusion."

This means that we must be knowledgeable about our bodies, at the very least as knowledgeable as we are about our cars and homes. We must know what is the proper fuel for our bodies. We must know about the cleansing process and how to facilitate it, as well as how to "tune-up" the body on a regular basis to maintain it in tiptop shape. We must know about the garbage disposal system of the body, where it is and how it works. Most people spend lots of energy, time and money to clean their cars and homes, both on the inside and outside, however, when it comes to their bodies, the vehicle or home of their soul, they only work to clean the outside on a regular basis. How can one begin to do serious spiritual work when they have not properly made the way for their soul to be fully present? The soul is not going to be able to exist in a temple that is defiled, filled with garbage and impurities. Imagine what would happen if you tried to have someone you really cared for and respected come and stay with you, but you do not clean out your house before you bring them into it. The house is dirty, the room you want them to stay in is cluttered and dirty, and even the bed where they are supposed to sleep is full of clutter and garbage, so they have no place to rest. They will not be able to stay. Thus, purification of the physical body through proper diet is a key component to spiritual growth, and one that is often overlooked. Thus, the Kemetic injunction: "Know Thyself," also applies to having an understanding of the body and how it works, because the physical body is an aspect of the manifestation of the Spirit in the world of time and space.

Kemetic Wisdom Teachings from "Egyptian Proverbs" by Dr. Muata Ashby

**"If you would live in harmony with yourself and the Earth,
you must follow the laws of the Earth, for your body is of the Earth;
lest it lead your SOUL to the path of disease, death and reincarnation.
The neters (gods and goddesses, cosmic forces of the universe) of the Divine will desert you,
and those of evil will destroy your body and your spirit."**

"The source of evil (egoism) is in your body. Evil entices the body through temptation of its weakest virtue. There can be no divinity in the unclean temple where abomination rules."

Most people believe that it is only the job of doctors to have an understanding of how the body functions. However, most orthodox medical doctors admit that they have received little or no training in area of nutrition and diet, much less on the spiritual dimensions of health and healing. These ideas are only now trickling into the orthodox medical establishment, not because they have pursued it themselves, but because they are loosing money because of it. As many patients continue to turn to alternative medicine now more than ever before, the orthodox medical establishment has found itself in a predicament. In an attempt to not lose any more of their patients, frustrated with the failures of modern medicine to cure their diseases or even give them relief from their symptoms, the modern medical establishment has opened its doors, albeit on a limited basis, to alternative medicine.

A new phrase has been coined by those conventionally trained medical doctors who have become pioneers in their field because of their application of alternative medical techniques. This new "branch" of medicine, as it were, is being referred to as "Integrative Medicine." It is in effect a middle ground between Alternative Medicine and Orthodox Medicine. There must still be some caution here, because since their system is still based within the traditional orthodox medical establishment, which is heavily funded by the pharmaceutical companies, the purity of the Alternative Medical care they are able to provided will be limited. Such programs will certainly be beneficial in some degree to patients who currently have no such consideration in their medical treatment and firmly believe in the orthodox medical establishment, or those who are interested in alternative medicine, but have some reservations about its use alone. However, it could be detrimental for someone seeking completely natural and holistic alternative approaches to health and healing, such as the holistic lifestyle espoused in this and other such books. Also, it must be noted that even within the Alternative Medicine field that there are various systems of healing techniques, and as in any other area, differing styles and competencies of practitioners. So, the bottom line is that you still need to be informed about your body and your health, having insight into how the various parts of the body works, and also what constitutes proper health.

Kemetic Wisdom Teachings from the book, "Egyptian Proverbs" by Dr. Muata Ashby:

"The wickedness of the soul is ignorance; the virtue of the soul is knowledge."

"Ignorance is slavery, be it to others or to ones own vices, to become free from both so as to live in eternal happiness and to work to establish the will of father-mother god on earth is the sacred task."

"The fool who does not hear, can do nothing at all; looking at ignorance and seeing knowledge; looking at harmfulness and seeing usefulness; living on the things by which one dies."

Cicero, a Roman statesman, said that in his experience, the easiest people to conquer were people without a culture. Certainly we can see this is the case today. In today's society, everyone thinks of culture more in terms of race and ethnicity. However, culture has a more universal meaning, a spiritual meaning, because a human being is more than their physical body. Rather, as the Kemetic teachings tell us, "Men and Women are mortal Gods and Goddesses, and the Gods and Goddesses are immortal human beings." Thus, men and women are divine beings, and the mortal human aspect is just one expression of Divinity. Thus, when we refer to the Kemetic High Culture, we are referring to this aspect of culture that viewed humanity in terms of spirituality. And from this perspective of Kemetic High Culture, there is only one diet for the physical body... vegetarian.

Since in the view of the Kemetic sages, the one and only purpose of life is to attain Enlightenment, then it makes sense that every aspect of one's life should be tied into this purpose, even one's diet for the physical body. This was expressed throughout the Kemetic wisdom teachings, iconography and mythology. It is expressed in the iconography depicted on the back cover of this book with the physical body of Asar, an incarnation of the Divine, laying in a coffin and wheat growing out of his body. Since the purpose of life was to become Divine, becoming one with the Divine Self in the form of Asar was seen as the goal of life in the Asarian tradition of Kamit. Asar was often depicted as green, so the spiritual meditation related to diet and eating vegetarian foods is that as one eats "green," one becomes Asar-like, a Divine being. Becoming Asar-like, that is, becoming a spiritually Enlightened personality, was seen as the state of ultimate health. This concept of a green diet and its relationship to health and attaining unity with the divine is further expressed in the following verse that was chanted in Kamit in ancient times by healers:

"Si i(e) mettu wadj" or " mettu swaj" for short

This injunction for healing calls for a "greening" of all the vital channels (vascular system, lymphatic system, circulatory system, etc.) of the physical body to restore health. It was understood that this process of bringing "green" into these conduits and channels would restore physical health, but even more importantly, mental health and spiritual health, because automatically the use of the word "swaj" meaning "greening" would render the effect of turning the mind to Asar, the Divine, the essence of all greenery in nature and the source of all healing. As a result of this, both the doctor and the patient would have an immediate experience of divine grace in the way of an experience of Divine Presence and communion with the Divine. Thus, in the process of being healed and healing with regards to the physical body, both the patient and doctor, respectively, move closer to the attainment of Enlightenment...perpetual union with the Divine, Sema (or Sma, Smai) Tawi.

There is another aspect of healing via green foods and green juices from plants. The chlorophyll molecule of the plants and the hemoglobin molecule of the animal and human red blood cells have almost the identical chemical structure. The main difference, which is primarily one of function, is that the chlorophyll molecule in plants contains the element magnesium, which allows it to trap the sun light (solar energy) for the plant in the process know as photosynthesis, while the hemoglobin molecule contains the element iron, which allows it to carry oxygen in the physical body. In the Asarian tradition, the sun is a symbol of the Divinity Ra, who is the father of Asar, and also is representative of the Divine Self. Thus, the plant stores this divine (Ra-light) energy, which is then transferred to the human body when they are consumed, leading to a union of the person eating the plant food with the Divine. Interestingly enough, when Kirlian photography, which measures the electromagnetic radiation surrounding objects (more commonly known as the "aura") is taken of plants, there is a vibrant glow. However, when this same Kirlian photography is taken of a hamburger, the only thing that glows is the lettuce. One scientist[15] found that when he measured the frequency of meat and that of cancer, they vibrated at the same (low) frequency, unlike the vibrant high energy frequency of green plant based foods, especially when in their raw unprocessed state. He literally demonstrated that you become that which you eat, so from this perspective, cancer can be described as the accumulation of "dead" meat and processed "dead" foods in the body.

Thus, the following Kemetic injunction urging humanity to seek the eternal light, Enlightenment, does not only have implications for spiritual enlightenment, but also for one's physical diet as well, because as stated previously, before one can have spiritual purity, the way must first be made though physical purity. In the end, both are still part of the same process, of attaining Sema Tawi, union with the Divine.

Kemetic Wisdom teaching from "Egyptian Proverbs" by Dr. Muata Ashby:

"O people of the earth, men and women born and made of the elements,

[15] Robert O. Young, Ph.D., D.Sc., head of the Innerlight Biological Research Center and author of "Sick and Tired?"

but with the spirit of the divine within you, rise from your sleep of ignorance! Be sober and thoughtful. Realize that your home is not on the earth but in the light. Why have you delivered yourselves unto death, having power to partake of immortality? Repent, and change your minds. Depart from the dark light and forsake corruption forever. Prepare to blend your souls with the eternal light."

How can one become "light" if one only consumes darkness (death)? To light a candle, some other source of light is needed; like begets like. Likewise, to blend with the eternal light, one must be light, physically, mentally (mental purity) and spiritually.

This aspect of consuming food with the sense of uniting with the Divine who is being represented by the food is known as the Eucharist. As can be seen from the previous discussion, this teaching was inherent in Kemetic spirituality long before its practice in Christianity. It is still evident on the reliefs on various temple walls in Egypt today where initiates, priests and priestesses, and kings and queens are seen offering a "Hetep Slab" to the Divine image. The Hetep Slab, pictured below, is symbolic of the experience of attaining oneness with the Divine. It consists of a depiction of an offering mat with a loaf of bread, as well as a goose, a thigh of an ox, and two vessels filled with an offering fluid. The word Hetep or Hotep means "Peace," not just the ordinary peace that people often refer to meaning that they are away from the hustle and bustle of the world, but abiding, perpetual peace that only comes with the attainment of Sema Tawi. The hieroglyphic symbol that means Hetep is the offering mat with a loaf of bread.

People sometimes misunderstand and believe that these symbols are to be taken to mean that the scriptures are supporting the eating of meat or making offerings of animal flesh. However, this assessment is incorrect. Rather, the bread is symbolic of Asar, in that it is made from the wheat that grows out of his body. The goose is an abbreviation for the hieroglyphic text that means female, and the thigh of the ox an abbreviation for the word male. In the ritual related to offering the Hetep Slab to the Divine, fluid in libation vessels is poured over the symbols of male (ox thigh) and female (goose). The fluid then flows over and around them, and then runs down and out a common opening. This ritual is symbolic of uniting the opposites (male and female) within one's consciousness, that is, offering every aspect of oneself to the Divine in the state of Enlightenment. Therefore, the implication of the offering of bread on a mat, in the form of the Hetep Slab is that Hetep, the Supreme Peace of Enlightenment, comes from attaining union with the Divine. Also, the libation vessels, in addition to being filled with water, were sometimes filled with wine or beer. However, again, this was not to advocate the drinking of alcohol. The pouring of the liquid from the libation vessel onto the Hetep Slab symbolizes the flowing of one's consciousness from the world of duality to the one Supreme Self, like two rivers uniting and then flowing into the ocean. Also, the use of these items on the Hetep Slab that are in fact prohibited by the scriptures for human consumption has another meaning. It symbolizes overcoming or transcending the lower animal passions such as sexuality, and the consumption of meat and alcohol.

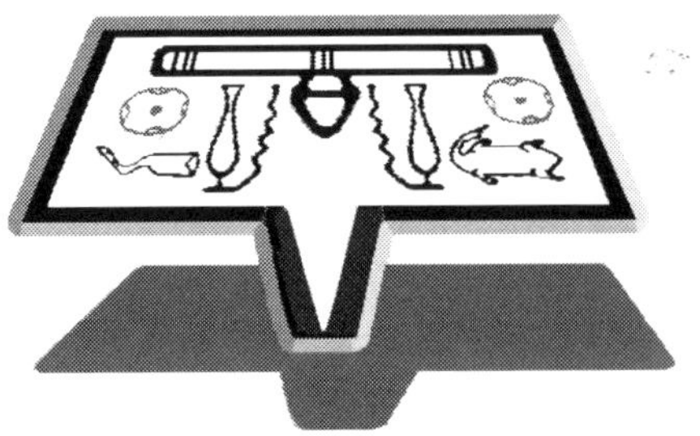

Just a little note with respect to bread, raw breads (recipes available in raw food books) can be eaten in the Kemetic Diet, but baked, processed breads, especially white breads, are not recommended. You can use natural sprouted whole grains breads in limited quantities, preferably Spelt or Kamut, available in Health Food Stores, which are baked, until you can completely wean yourself off baked breads altogether.

So, although some members of the general population in Kemet ate meat, the initiates and those who wanted to advance spiritually abstained from consuming meats of any kind. Another consideration when we say that some members of the general population ate meat is that we are not referring to the same quality, nor large quantity of meat that most people eat today. Meat, as it is generally sold in modern society, is essentially poisonous due to the fact that the "food" animals are fed rich foods (grains) and routinely medicated with various hormones and antibiotics to make them grow fatter sooner. The residues of hormones and antibiotics are now being shown to have detrimental effects on humans who consume meat. If you wish to be as strong as a friend of yours, wouldn't you just ask your friend what he or she eats and start eating that, rather than eating your friend. Likewise, if you wish to be as strong as a cow (or other vegetarian animals such an elephant or horse) why not eat what the animal eats (green foods) instead of eating the animal. With respect to fish, the lakes and oceans are so polluted that most fish contains high levels of poisons as well. The code for Initiates, Priests and Priestesses is outlined below:

Teachings from the Temple of Aset (Isis) on Vegetarianism for the Initiates (Spiritual Aspirants):

**"Plutarch, a student of the mysteries of Aset,
reported that the initiates followed a strict diet made up of vegetables and fruits
and *abstained from particular kinds of foods* (swine, sheep, fish, etc.)..."**

Teachings from the *Egyptian Book of the Dead (Pert EM Heru Text)* on Vegetarianism. Note: Chapters numbers refer to Chapters in the translated text by Dr. Muata Ashby:

In Chapter 36, of the *Pert Em Heru*, the chapter of "Entering the inner shrine, making the offering and becoming one with Asar:"

**"Henceforth, this chapter shall be recited by a person who is purified and washed;
one who has not eaten animal flesh or fish."**

Chapter 10, Verse 11:

**"...And behold, these things shall be performed by one who is clean and pure,
a person who has eaten neither meat nor fish and who has not had sexual intercourse."**

Chapter 31:69:

"This Chapter can be known by those who recite it and study it when they see no more, hear no more, have no more sexual intercourse and eat no meat or fish."

Mental and Spiritual Nutrition and Enlightenment—Mysticism of Food for the Mind and Spirit:

Kemetic prayer for health:

Hetep (Hotep) Di Si Neter Iri Ankh, Oodja and Seneb

The above prayer says: **Offerings given to cause the Neter** (the Divine) **to make happen Life (process), Vitality and Health.** Interestingly enough, one can note first and foremost, that in the Kemetic approach to praying to the Divine for health, the person propitiating the Divine first makes an offering. In other words, that person must bring something to offer to the Divine, and not come empty handed. This is in contrast to some religious systems where the ill person is simply told to pray to the Supreme Being for healing, and have faith that they will be healed. The prayer also gives insight as to what the person praying for health must bring to offer to the Divine, in the very first word of the sentence. One must bring Hetep (Hotep). We have already explored the mystical aspect of the word "Hetep" with respect to the offering mat and bread relating to a Eucharist, a union with Asar through the consumption of green foods, all well as the more comprehensive meaning related to the Hetep Slab which symbolizes the flowing of one's consciousness from the world of duality (relative reality – time and space – worldliness), to the one Supreme Self. Thus, this injunction is saying that in order to have Life, Vitality and Health, one must be able to offer a sense of Sema Tawi (Yoga), union with the Divine...enlightenment, to the Divine. The implication is that in spiritual terms, the healthiest person is an Enlightened person. This means regardless of whatever physical ailments an Enlightened sage may have, they are still healthier than an unEnlightened person who may appear to be in good physical health. This is reflected in the text from Chapter 34 of the Pert Em Heru Text, verse 10, where the initiate, having attained enlightenment says: **"There are very sick people, I go to them, I spit on the arms, I set the shoulder, and I cleanse them."**

Thus, Enlightened persons are seen as the ultimate healers, healing the very root source of all dis-eases, ignorance of one's true nature. In mystical philosophy, ignorance of one's true nature is regarded as the only true disease that exists. All other so called dis-eases, mental and physical, arise from this singular condition, which expresses as egoism in the human personality. Egoism is the experience of believing yourself to be an individual, disconnected and separate from everything around you, including the Divine. Enlightenment is the opposite. It is experiencing the underlying oneness of everything, including the Divine, and thereby acting in contradiction with Divine Order (Maat). Reflect on the metaphor of the ocean. Egoism is like believing you are one wave in the ocean, and that every other object in creation, including the Divine, are all the other waves around you, and acting from that perspective of separation and individuality. Being an Enlightened human being is understanding that even though you exist in the world as wave-like personality, as a wave, you are essentially one with the ocean and with all other waves and acting in accordance with that Divine awareness. In the latter case, as an Enlightened personality, you understand the Divine to be the ocean, and all the waves, including the wave of your individual personality, to be one with the ocean. As a matter of fact, though in the practical dealings with the world you seem to differentiate between the various wave-like objects and personalities, internally you do not differentiate between the ocean and the waves, understanding each wave to be none other than the ocean-like Divine Self.

Egoism (the sense of individuality) as discussed previously, gives rise to fear of loss of life (fear of death) deep within the unconscious mind, because one looses the perspective of one's true nature, which is universal, eternal and immortal. This fear seeps into and taints all conscious thoughts, and consequent actions, thus giving rise to anger, hated, greed, envy, jealousy, lust, insecurity, depression, anxiety, worry, nervousness, excitability, other general fear and phobias, etc.. These emotions create disturbances in the mind and with the flow of the vital Life Force energies, leading to imbalances in the nervous and hormonal (endocrine) systems of the body. Since the nervous and endocrine systems regulate all the other systems of the body, their imbalances lead to malfunctions throughout the organs and tissues of the physical body, resulting in what we have come to know as physical "dis-ease." Also, harboring the negative emotions detailed above for long periods of time, or in an intense manner, or frequently, lead to mental dis-ease, commonly referred to in our society as mental illness. Enlightened persons may still be afflicted with physical illnesses for several reasons. Some may be due to conditions in their present circumstances such as poor diet, etc., while others may be due past ari (karma – ego-based actions) from before they became Enlightened. However, regardless of which is the case, their detachment from their body and its ailments is a poignant factor, which deeply impresses the those around them, as it allows them to transcend the negative consequences of disease. Regardless, even in their state of physical illness, they are still considered to be of utmost health, because the true state of health is the state of "Knowing Thyself"... Enlightenment. The Enlightened state is associated with perfect harmony of Body, Mind and Spirit, and Transcendental (Enlightened) Consciousness, and therefore does not give rise to egoism and the downward spiraling cascade of reactions it triggers, leading to dis-ease.

Thus if one is not Enlightened, one has to seek to acquire peace (Hetep) that comes from union or oneness with the Divine. How is this Hetep attained? As we have discussed above, through the practice of the formal and informal meditation (Uaa) disciplines of Sema Tawi (Integral Kemetic or Ancient Egyptian yoga) and other authentic mystical traditions. The integral practice of these disciplines allows the practitioner to have a sense of Divine Presence all the time, by being able to be engaged in one of the disciplines at all times. Especially significant is the practice of meditation, which will grant the willpower necessary to effect the necessary positive changes in one's diet and lifestyle. The Kemetic sages understood how difficult it is to change:

Kemetic Wisdom Teaching:

**"It is very hard, to leave the things we have grown used to, which meet our gaze on every side.
Appearances delight us, whereas things that appear not make their believing hard.
Evils are the more apparent things,
whereas the good (the Divine) can never show itself unto the eyes,
for it hath neither form nor figure."**

So the ancient sages understood that the Divine will not appear as you are about to go into a fast food restaurant or take some meat from your freezer to stop you, and that worldly temptations are everywhere for the unenlightened personality. But the sages also knew that:

> "Those who gave thee a body, furnished it with weakness, but the all who gave thee soul, armed thee with resolution.
> **Employ it, and thou art wise; Be wise and thou art happy."**

-Kemetic Wisdom Teaching

Many people pray to the Divine for help, and because they do not get the response they desire, they feel that the Divine has abandoned them or that their suffering is the will of the Divine, not realizing that the Divine has already answered their prayers, first by being the very source of their inspiration to pray, secondly by bestowing upon them Hetep that comes from concentrating one's mind to the Divine (Sema, Union), and thirdly by arming them with the most powerful weapon against any physical conditions or pathogens such as viruses, cancer or bacteria, and negative personality traits: RESOLUTION. Thus, one must exercise their capacity of determination (resolution) and self-effort, which, according to the teachings, are forms of Divine grace with which every human being has been innately blessed.

The study and practice of these mystical disciplines allow the practitioner to cultivate increasing amounts of Hetep. It is this experience of Hetep, when becomes abiding, that bestows true health of body, mind and spirit... Ankh (life), Oodja (vitality) and Seneb (health)! Thus, striving to attain Enlightenment is the greatest offering you can make to the Divine, and as a result the Divine will bless you with the best health possible, of body, mind and spirit. With respect to the offering of Hetep in the prayer above, one cannot offer what one does not have, and when people become seriously ill, they usually become distraught and anxious, rather than peaceful. But as you can see, the more ill one is, it becomes that much more imperative that one practices the Sema Tawi disciplines, because to summarize the meaning of the prayer: Hetep (abiding peace that is undisturbed regardless of outer situation or circumstance) = Enlightenment = Health. Hetep does waiver with each test result and new diagnosis of the doctor! Rather, one remains the same before and after...ever unaffected, abiding in the wonderful sense of Divine Presence...which supercedes all else!!

Thus, it is not surprising that studies have found that various aspects of the mystical disciplines can have profound effects on physical as well as mental health. One study found that the practice of meditation can lower cholesterol, and another that it has the capacity to reverse arteriosclerosis. Another study by cardiologist Dr. Dean Ornish proved that heart disease could be reversed by a regimen of the integral practice of the yogic disciplines, including vegetarian diet.

What people in this world want is not meat...but the experience of Divine Presence (Divine union), not alcohol, but Divine Presence, not cigarettes, but Divine Presence, not sex, but Divine Presence, not praise, but Divine Presence. They don't want something bad to happen to someone else so they can feel good about themselves, they want Divine Presence. They don't want annoying people to leave them alone, but they want Divine Presence. They don't want what other people have; they want Divine Presence. They want Enlightenment (Divine Presence, Divine Union) because it is only the experience of Divine Presence that can grant that for which everyone searches, abiding peace, abiding joy, and abiding love. Then the activities, relationships and achievements of the world will have true meaning and be of benefit to humanity, promoting health and enlightenment.

An Invitation to Change Your Lifestyle:

One person who reviewed this book stated that though understanding the importance of everything addressed in this book, felt it would be a challenge to do everything that this book recommends. It must be understood that what is presented in this book is the ideal for which one must strive. Most changes should be implemented gradually. One change, however, which can be done abruptly, is to stop eating all meat (includes poultry, fish, eggs and dairy) products. There are enough protein packed vegetarian substitutes on the market, for just about everything. However, one should always read the labels, even of vegetarian products, even those labeled as "natural," because these too come in the category of "cheap and junkie," being filled with artificial chemicals, preservatives and other ingredients with long and unpronounceable names.

So, start small with little changes, a little Yoga exercise... even if it is one or two postures a day, a little breathing, a little fasting, a little meditation, a little reading of scriptures, a little of helping others, a little of prayer and chanting a hekau (mantra - prayer). These will gradually and holistically grow a little more each month and year, but in a way which allows the mind to remain calm and peaceful, because remember, the Divine Self is nothing but peace, bliss (happiness) and harmony. So to move towards the Divine, your steps (mind and actions) must be filled with peace, balance and harmony along the way. There is no way to reach the west if one walks to the north. So to reach the ultimate peace and harmony, one must walk in peace and harmony. Remember the children's story between the hare and the turtle: slow and steady wins the race!

With respect to fasting... or for that matter, any action you are performing in the world, for spiritual growth, there is one key question you must ask yourself, and meditate upon the answer: "Is this going to lead me towards God (truth, balance & harmony) or lead me away from that?" Many times spiritually inclined people (aspirants, initiates) engage in actions to get closer to God or the Goddess, the Higher Self, however in the struggle to perform the action, they take several steps in the opposite direction (fanaticism which leads to imbalance to dis-harmony). Instead of purifying themselves to make themselves stronger and fit to perform the work of the Divine, they weaken their physical bodies and mind, which renders it of little use in the service of the Divine, that is, moving towards that which is peaceful, joyful, good and truly divine.

Fasting does help purify the body and give will power, but a spiritual aspirant as well as worldly personality can do it for this purpose. The difference between a spiritual aspirant and a worldly personality is the purpose for doing it. As Jesus taught, "Seek ye first the kingdom of Heaven and all else will be added unto you." This means that you should do whatever you need to do to make yourself more able to serve the Divine, first and foremost... for developing greater devotion to God. If fasting is done to make the body healthy and strong to better serve the divine will (including engaging yourself in spiritual practices at a deeper level), then it is righteous action. One should strive to bring the body to a state of purity, harmony and peace. If fasting takes the body to weakness, illness and unsteadiness and renders the mind unable to study the scriptures and practice them effectively because one's concentrating ability is diminished, one's temper is more abrupt and one succumbs more easily to other aspects of the ego, then it is not promoting spiritual advancement.

Yes, there will be a period of detoxification where one may experience these negative moods, however, one should be able to exert some control over oneself through faith and self-effort to overcome them, and they should pass. If not, one may be practicing in a dis-balanced way, and should seek counseling from a qualified health care professional.[16] Remember, whatever the swing of the pendulum is to the right, it likewise will swing to the left. So in spirituality, it is best to make small movements, gradually building, so that the backlash (the body's and mind's reactions to the release of toxins) is small and controllable. If someone is very ill, they have gotten there from swinging the pendulum too far to the right or left. Now they may need to take drastic measures to live, and therefore they may have to undergo a rigorous fast, etc., i.e., swing the pendulum far to the opposite side. But even in that imbalanced condition of moving from one extreme to the next, there is a certain degree of balance and harmony being achieved. This swing will gradually decrease more and more in its intensity, leading the person more and more into a state of balance and harmony. However, for most people a high degree of intensity of implementing fasting and other cleansing techniques is not needed. For someone who is not in such a serious condition, prolonged fasting may be unnecessary and may lead to imbalance. This person may be better off spending their time purifying themselves in other ways. In addition to eating a proper diet for the body, one can choose to perform the Yoga postures, which will also detoxify the body, perform selfless service and study of scriptures which will detoxify the mind, and practice meditation, chanting and prayer which will detoxify the soul and increase one's willpower. Selfless service is especially beneficial for detoxifying the mind and ridding it of its egoistic sentiments. It gives one the opportunity to put the teachings that have been studied into practice. Eventually, you come to view every act you perform as selfless service to your Higher Self. Along with these practices, one may engage in brief fasts (12-24 hours).

When deciding to fast, pick a day that is quietest for you, when you can keep your activities and interaction with others to a minimum. Remember the purpose of the fast is to become more peaceful, loving, kind, compassionate and joyous... for this Supreme Peace is the Higher Self, God. Spend it as quietly "as is possible." This may vary from day to day. Sometimes you may be disturbed more than others, and that's alright, adjust and adapt, but still work towards minimizing outside activity ... to the extent that it is possible. You can spend time doing the Yoga exercises which are great for developing willpower, cleansing and harmonizing, and bringing peaceful vibrations to the body and mind, preparing

[16] The Sema Institute offers expert assistance in the form of counseling on diet and nutrition for the body, mind and soul for those wishing to adopt the Kemetic Diet Wisdom of natural health to restore and or promote better health. See the back section of this book for more information.

it for meditation, and reading spiritually uplifting literature or scriptures and understanding them at a deeper level. If you find that a one day fast dis-balances you, start with a half-day fast or perhaps just skip one meal one day a week. Exercise due caution and common sense, and consult with a holistic care practitioner who is experienced in this area in the event you have any questions or conditions that arise. Be sensitive to your body, but also challenge yourself to move to a state of better health.

Also, beware of making absolute recommendations to others based on your own experiences, because each individual personality (composed of body, mind and soul) is different, and what worked for you may not work for them, and vice versa, due to the nature or extent of their imbalance on any or all of the three levels (body, mind and soul). Thus, while one can share insight into the principles of natural health practices and techniques with others, it is best for each person to consult and have access to a competent and experienced health practitioner, while at the same time gaining insight into the nature of health and self-healing.

Some people will have a past basis for eating a vegetarian diet, fasting, meditating, etc., form in this or previous lifetimes, and be able to convert to this lifestyle very quickly and "effortlessly," while others are only now entering into this culture, and will find it more challenging. The most important thing is to not give up. Do not quit, regardless of if you fail a hundred times. Imagine if you held an attitude of failure when you were a baby trying to walk. If every time you fell down, and maybe even got a few bumps and bruises in the process, you decided that you were a failure and that the process of learning to walk was much too hard, where would you be today? You would still be crawling around on your hands and knees! With continued effort, no matter how long it takes you, commit to succeeding, for "as you think, so you become."

Those persons mentioned above, who can convert "seemingly" effortlessly, also had to go though the stage of striving, failures and continued effort in the past. However, this may not be evident now because they may have done it in a previous lifetime, and now their deeper memory is triggered, and all they have to do is to pick up where they left off. No one person has been more blessed with talents, special gifts or willpower than any other. Whatever talent, gifts or willpower a person has is due to their previous work in this area, in this or a past lifetime. So it is not valid to compare oneself to others, except to be inspired by those who are more advanced than you in this area. As your enthusiasm wanes and self-doubts rises, let them serve as proof to your mind that it can be achieved. Let the glow of health in their face, and the bounce of vitality in their step, inspire you and allay your fears.

Because of doubt, insecurity, fear or lack of will power or desire to change, most people resist making the corrections that are needed to practice spirituality in its highest and purest essence, yet it is only this intensity of practice that will lead them to the attain that for which they have been seeking and which cannot be attained by any other means, that is, self- knowledge and self-discovery in the state of union with the Higher Self, or to put it in simple terms, true health and true abiding happiness and peace. The fact that making these changes can be challenging is evidenced by the statement of Jesus, that "Many are called, but few are chosen." Many people take this statement to mean that there are only a few special "chosen" people who are blessed enough to become saints and sages. However, that is not what this statement means. What Jesus is remarking about here is that many people become inspired and enthusiastic, but only a few stay the course. The others give up by giving in to their weak will, insecurities, doubts, fears, laziness, etc. The coveted state (Enlightenment) is available for everyone. One only has to apply the formula. If you continue to persist, no matter how slow the pace seems, you will succeed, even in this very lifetime.

Consider the example illustrated in the following parable. A person had to walk through a dark forest to get to their destination. All they had was a little candlelight, which glowed and illumined five feet in front of them. Looking at the forest with trepidation, they wondered how they would be able to make it though that deep forest, with their little light, which only illumined five feet. When they started to walk, they noticed something amazing happened. When they got to the end of the first five feet, another five feet ahead was illumined, and likewise, when they got to the end of that five feet, yet another was illumined. Soon, little by little, five feet at a time, they made it through the entire forest. So, the moral of the story with respect to the information you will receive from this book is that though it may appear overwhelming, like the deep dark forest did to this person, start where you are with the lamp of a desire to make a righteous lifestyle change. Don't become bogged down with worry or a sense of feeling helpless or overwhelmed, or burdened with concerns as to how you can make all of these changes. Just start walking to the edge of your first five feet, which may have been your practicing the recommendations in the section "10 easy steps you can take to change your lifestyle and improve your health, right now!," or reading this book. Amazingly, you will find out about programs related to meditation, yoga, vegetarian-Vegas-raw diet, etc., on television, in your area as well as around the country. Start where you can and utilize the resources you have available to you, even if you find that at an ethnic, cultural or spiritual level a particular venue was/is not really in harmony with your personality. Still, you can learn the techniques and adapt and adjust to suit your personality, as long as the integrity of the technique is maintained. Due to past life experiences, different people are attracted to different spiritual traditions for many different reasons. So, you may find yourself involved with a particular program, but still feel that it does not resonate with your deeper personality. Continue to seek for that which is authentic and resonates with you, but in the meantime don't discard the opportunity to gain knowledge and discipline which is at hand. You must take the opportunity, walk to end of its five feet and discover the magnificence that awaits you there, as this will allow you to proceed further until you reach your destination, the state of perfect health of body, mind and soul, Enlightenment!

Peace and Blessings!

May you be blessed with Divine Communion, Life Process, Vitality, and Health – Hetep, Ankh, Oodja and Seneb!

Hemit Dja Un Nefert,
(Dr. Karen Vijaya Clarke-Ashby)

Note: Hemit Dja has also contributed research / writings on other subjects throughout this book.

10 EASY STEPS YOU CAN TAKE TO CHANGE YOUR LIFESTYLE AND IMPROVE YOUR HEALTH, RIGHT NOW!

1) Immediately after waking up, before taking any other foods or liquids, drink the coconut water of a young jelly coconut[17] if available in your area , or 1- 2 cups of purified (distilled preferred) water with Kamut Wheatgrass juice powder or other green vegetable powder you may have available, or ½-1 lime or lemon freshly squeezed into it, to alkalize and flush your system.

2) After step one, perform the following exercise. Stand tall, or sit on a chair or on the floor in a crossed-legged position. Place hands in front of you, palms together, as when one is praying. Now breathing in deeply, extend the hands and arms up while spreading them apart, then breath out and bring them back together. Repeat several times (5+), starting at a slow pace and then increasing to a faster pace. This practice will increase the oxygen and Life Force Energy intake, provide a gentle heart workout, cleanse the lymphatic or sewage system of the body for arm and chest areas, and relax the mind. You can repeat this later in the day as well, whenever possible. (For additional information on Breath and Exercise, see our book, *The Egyptian Yoga Exercise Workout Book.*)

3) Repeat the following affirmation daily:

   The Spirit is all Health
   I am One with the Spirit
   Therefore, I can be Healthy

   The Spirit is all Power
   I am One with the Spirit
   Therefore, there isn't anything I cannot do or change.

4) After performing steps 1, 2, and 3 above or anytime during the day when you can be alone and quiet for 5 minutes, lie on your back. You may also try putting one or two pillows under your knees. This will flatten out the lower back and decrease tension there, allowing you to relax more completely. Bring your attention to the movement of your abdomen (belly) as you breath in and out. Breathing in, notice the abdomen rises up, and breathing out, notice the abdomen moves in towards the spine (backbone). You can just simply focus on the rising and falling of the abdomen with the breath, or you can mentally repeat an affirmation, for example: While breathing in, mentally repeat, "The Spirit is All Peace," and while breathing out, mentally repeat, "I am One with the Spirit." It has been found that breathing quietly like this for 5 minutes twice daily can lower High Blood Pressure.

5) Go to a Health food Store that sells produce, and buy organic cucumbers. However, if you don't have access to organic cucumbers, use regular cucumbers after rinsing them with fresh lemon or lime juice or baking soda. Cucumbers are technically fruits, not vegetables, belonging to the melon family. Have cucumber in the mornings for breakfast or as a pre-breakfast snack, after your cleansing lemon or lime water drink. They are watery, which is good to continue to flush the system out in the early morning, as well as low in sugar as compared to the other melons. Thus, they are one of the most balancing (alkalinizing) foods for the body.

6) Visit one of the Health Food stores in your area and buy a bag of "Raw Organic Almonds." They come already shelled. If you cannot find organic raw almonds, still get the raw regular almonds. If you have the time, you can buy the ones in the shell and remove the shells yourself. Just be sure the

[17] Young jelly coconuts are green. The shelled brown coconuts the sell in the supermarket are "old" coconuts, and not suitable for use in the early morning.

almonds are "RAW," meaning not processed in any way. Soak one tablespoon (per person) of almonds in purified water overnight (12 hours). Drain the water the following morning, and snack on these during the day. They go great with a green leafy salad. Almonds are very high in Protein, Calcium, Magnesium, and Vitamin E. Studies have indicated that they seem to have anti-cancer properties as well. Soaking nuts makes them more easily digestible, as well as increases their protein and nutrient content.

7) While at the Health Food store, ask about a product called Stevia, a natural plant derivative that can substitute for sugar, fructose, honey or maple syrup that can be substituted for these products. It is very sweet, but it has its own taste, which the body can become used to, just as it did to sugar, natural sweeteners, or other man-made sugar substitutes, some of which are known carcinogens. If you like it great, but if you don't, be patient, but persistent and allow yourself to adapt...Remember your affirmation: "I can be Healthy. There isn't anything I cannot do or change".

8) Also, while at the Health Food store, ask about vegetarian vitamin-mineral supplements, and buy some. Use as directed. Also, ask about Flaxseed oil, and buy a bottle of that also. Take two tablespoons daily as a supplement. Also inquire about a Calcium-Magnesium supplement, and purchase that also. See appendix 1 of this book for more detailed information on these supplements. They represent the very basic foundation of nutritional supplementation.

9) If you do not have a juicer or are not currently juicing vegetables, go to a Health Food Store or a juice bar that serves "green" drinks, and order a freshly squeezed carrot and leafy green vegetable (spinach, kale, etc.) juice. Many juice bars have vegetable combinations, and sometimes will allow you to sample some of the juices they are making for other customers. Order a small juice if you are newly being introduced to it. Sip it slowly. Although such juices are best if consumed soon after they are made, most will last up to 12 hours, so if you have a lot of difficulty drinking it quickly, take your time until your body and taste buds (mind) become used to it. Also, when you are trying this for the first time, be sure wheatgrass juice is NOT added to the drink. It is a very potent blood purifier, and most people find it too strong in the beginning. If you are not used to it, you may feel faint and nauseous after drinking it due to a rapid detoxification reaction. It is best to have a green drink daily, so try to get one as often as you can, even if it is only once a week. If you do have a juicer, try to juice carrots and vegetables (kale, collards, spinach, parsley, celery, etc.) also daily, or as often as is possible (one day a week is better than none, two days are better than one, etc.) It is best to use organic vegetables, however, if you cannot get organic vegetables, juicing is even more important to maximize the your nutritional intake. Try to drink at least one cup daily, but again, a half a cup is better than none.

10) Also, while you are at a Health Food Store, speak to their personnel in the Vitamin Section and have them show you where their green drink powder mixes are. You may also ask them for recommendations. Purchase one of the green drink powders, and start to use it according to the directions and your capacity, to supplement the fresh green juices. Green drinks, as you will soon learn, are packed with enzymes, vitamins, minerals, proteins, and nutrients vital for the body. Think of it as filling up the fuel tank of your body. Try to use them instead of pasteurized juices, sodas, juice cocktails and canned juices, and caffeinated teas, and on days when you are unable to have fresh green juices.

Take a moment now, and as many moments as you can throughout the day to close your eyes, be quiet, and breathe deeply as you connect with the Peace, Love and Blessings of the Supreme Spirit, which is your own deepest essence.

Peace, Love and Blessings, for your health, in Body, Mind and Spirit! Ankh, Oodja, Seneb!

Hemit Dja

DEFINITIONS FOR THE VARIOUS LEVELS OF VEGETARIANISM

Vegetarians – generally refers to persons who does not eat meats of any kind (including poultry and fish/seafood). Some people consider themselves to be vegetarian if they do not eat red meat, but eat poultry and or fish and or seafood. This creates much confusion for those who are entering into vegetarianism. Technically vegetarianism refers to not eating meats or parts of any type of animal...of any kind. Therefore those who eat non-red meats and or fish and or seafood are really not vegetarians. This group can be further subdivided as follows:

- **Lacto-ovo-vegetarians**—Persons who do not eat meat products, but consume milk and other dairy products (lacto) and eggs (ovo).

- **Lacto-vegetarians**—Persons who do not eat meat or eggs, but consume dairy products.

- **Vegans** – Persons who do not consume any meat products or animal-by-products (i.e. no honey, no dairy, etc.). It can also imply that such persons do not wear or use items made from or containing animal products as well (i.e. no leather, etc.)

- **Raw/Live Foodists**—Persons who eat raw, fresh uncooked foods (i.e. vegetables, fruits, nuts and seeds, vegetable and fruit juices. Foods that are sun cooked (i.e. raw breads) or dehydrated at a low temperature (104-106 degrees Fahrenheit) are also permitted, as this techniques will not kill the enzymes).

- **Fruitarians** – Persons who eat only raw/live uncooked fruits. This group not only includes the fruits we are familiar with, but also some fruits that are erroneously labeled as vegetables (i.e. tomatoes, cucumbers, squash, pumpkin, olives, avocado, etc....anything with a seed inside is considered a fruit). Some fruitarians also include raw/live nuts and seeds in their diets.

Note: In this book, when references are made to "vegetarian," the understanding is of someone who does not eat meat of any kind, including poultry and fish/seafood. Egg whites and honey are permitted on a limited basis in the transition phase, as some processed vegetarian products include these items. However, one should try to transition as soon as possible to a vegan diet, either cooked and or raw, and then from a cooked vegan to a completely raw vegan.

PREFACE

"The total amount of instruction that I got in nutrition in four years of Harvard medical school and one year of internship was 30 minutes, which were grudgingly allowed to a dietitian at one hospital I worked at in Boston to tell us about the special diets that we could order for patients."
-Andrew Weil M.D.

Health issues have always been important to human beings since the beginning of time. The earliest records of history show that the art of healing was held in high esteem since the time of Ancient Egypt (5,000 B.C.E.). There are two main texts on medical science from Ancient Egypt, which have been discovered. These are the **Smith Papyrus** (2600 B.C.E) and the **Ebers Papyrus** (1500 B.C.E.).

In the early 20th century, medical doctors had almost attained the status as the most venerated members of society by the promotion of the idea that they alone were "scientists," while other healing modalities and traditional healers who did not follow the "scientific method' were nothing but superstitious, ignorant charlatans, who at best would take the money of their clients, and at worst kill them with the unscientific "snake oils" and "irrational theories." However, in the late 20th century, the failure of the modern medical establishment to lead the general public to good health has promoted many in society seek out "alternative medicine." Natural health concepts and healing techniques which were practiced in Ancient Egypt but may now be referred to as "alternative medicine" disciplines, are those healing modalities which do not adhere to the philosophy of allopathic medicine. Allopathic medicine is what mainstream medical doctors, who subscribe to the "scientific method," practice by and large. It is the theory that disease is caused primarily by agencies outside the body such as bacteria, viruses or other physical means, which affect the body. Therefore, the idea is that medicines and therapies can treat disease. This volume presents the concepts and teachings based on the Kemetic (Ancient Egyptian) philosophy of total health of the entire person, that is, health not just of the body, but also health of the mind and soul as well. For this kind of health, one must go beyond medicines and therapies to discover the source of health. Health is a lifestyle, not a medicine. It is a spiritual lifestyle that leads to health of body, mind and soul.

The natural healing method began in the absence of extensive technologies with the idea that all the answers for health may be found in nature, or putting it another way, the causes of disease can be found in discovering what the deviation from nature was, and a cure effected by correcting it. Correcting the aberration restores balance to the organism, which results in the health of the body. This is the area that will be covered in this volume. Allopathic techniques have their place in the art of healing. However, we should not forget that the body is a grand achievement of the Spirit, and built into it is the capacity to maintain itself and heal itself.

In the end, after all is said and done, one must reflect on the following. Even if there is reasonably good health, what is the purpose of having good health if there is no peace or true satisfaction in life? What is the purpose of having no major health problems, eating whatever you want and indulging in life's pleasures, if you are not truly fulfilling your deeper needs? There are many people in society who currently do not suffer from severe illness, yet, they move along and grow older, but never discover true peace or contentment. In the end they are plagued by regrets and worries, which cause them to experience fear and anguish as they leave this world. Health is more than just physical vitality. It is a manifestation of the glory of life in the whole personality, a state wherein the personality is able to truly achieve the heights of its potential. This is the exalted view of Kemetic Health. It is a program of life wherein the personality is to be made whole, and this means integrating body, mind and soul health through the disciplines of proper diet and eating habits for health of the body, spiritual studies for health of the mind and meditation practice, inner exploration, for health of the soul. In the light of the Kemetic Health teachings, this program is to be understood as "Holistic Health."

INTRODUCTION TO THE HEALTH TEACHINGS OF ANCIENT EGYPT

Firstly, Kemet or Kamit is the name for the land that is referred to as "Ancient Egypt" in modern times. Therefore, the philosophy and disciplines of health that will be discussed in this book were created by Kemetans (Kamitans).

Perhaps, second only to spirituality, health issues were the primary concern of the Ancient Egyptians. Spiritual life was the main concern because there was a recognition that the universe is an expression of the Divine. This being understood, then it follows that everything one does and all of one's actions are in and through the Divine, which manifests as cosmic forces sustaining creation and human life. Thus, there is a way to live in harmony with the universal divine intelligence. This understanding is the basis of all true spiritual traditions. The proper practice of mystical spirituality and religion necessitates one to be in optimal health. Thus, it is incumbent upon anyone who wishes to pursue further studies in Kemetic or other Mystical Traditions to also study and promote good health in order to achieve a proper understanding of the culture and spiritual teachings of Ancient Egypt or the other traditions. Health concerns were integral to the culture and spiritual life in Ancient Egypt, so much so that many of the Ancient Egyptian temples had sanatoriums (hospitals) as well as pharmacies (areas for the preparation of herbs and natural medicaments). There were special rooms for the storage and preparation of offerings to the gods and goddesses, which needed to be fresh and wholesome since they were meant for the Divine Self.

As the human being was believed to be an expression of the Divine, the consumption of food was also believed to be a divine endeavor, and thus worthy of every consideration, since this would lead to the possibility of maintaining good health and thus, attaining Divine Consciousness.

Figure 1: Remains of the Hospital at the Temple of Hetheru at Denderah Egypt complete with wards,[18] and plumbing.

[18] **3.a.** A room in a hospital usually holding six or more patients. **b.** A division in a hospital for the care of a particular group of patients. (American Heritage Dictionary)

Natural Healing Practices in Ancient Egypt

There were many natural healing practices which were part of the culture of Ancient Egypt. Some are common sense treatments, which were part of everyday life, and others, treatments instituted by professional doctors.

The ancient healing art of reflexology was first practiced by the early Ancient Egyptian, Indian, and Chinese peoples. Massage and reflexology are ancient forms of Physiotherapy, which almost anyone can learn and apply for their own health, and that of their family and community.

Physiotherapy, also known as physical therapy, involves the use of varied techniques, including heat, water, diathermy, ultrasound, massage, and exercise, to treat diseases and disorders of the musculoskeletal system in an attempt to relieve pain and to restore use of the affected parts. The work is usually performed by a physical therapist under direction of a specialist physician.[19]

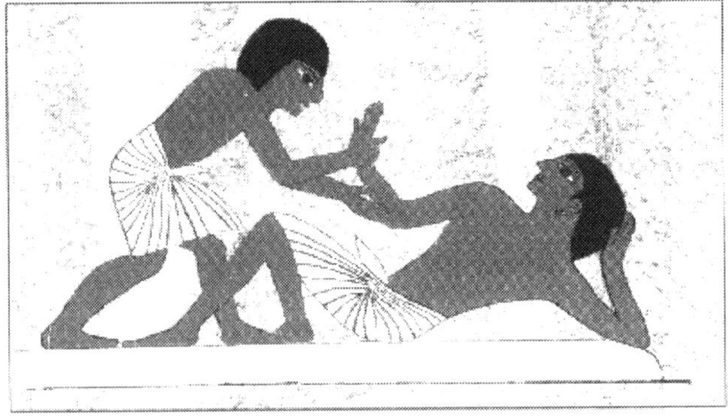

Plate 2: (left) An ancient Egyptian scene depicting doctor caring for the eyes of a patient.

Plate 3: (right) Ancient Egyptian scene depicting massage care of the hands.

[19] Random House Encyclopedia

Plate 4: Ancient Egyptian practicing foot massage, a technique known in modern times as reflexology.

Reflexology is the gentle massage on the feet which relives stress on the body and promotes the release of positive energies, and endorphins, which in turn bolster the immune system and promote physical comfort and a feeling of well being. Everyone can benefit from reflexology as well as a full body massage. The full body massage has the added benefit of helping to move the impurities of the tissues of the body so that the process of elimination can be facilitated. Studies have shown that people who receive massages daily live longer, healthier lives. Yoga exercise is a form of self-massage.

> **en·dor·phin** (ĕn-dôr′fĭn) *n.* Any of a group of peptide hormones that bind to opiate receptors and are found mainly in the brain. Endorphins reduce the sensation of pain and affect emotions.

This volume introduces and elaborates on the basic teachings and concepts of health for the body, mind and soul, which were practiced in the temples of Ancient Egypt by the spiritual initiates, as well as the customs by which the general populace lived and thrived. It will offer insights into the nature of health, and the simple but effective means by which one can restore and maintain it.

This volume explores the evidence of healing theory and practice both in the temples and by the general population, specifically focusing on the preventative health measures and natural means of restoring health. Then it elaborates on the health concepts of Ancient Egypt including the teachings about the source of disease, its cure and health maintenance. Also, it explores more deeply the spiritual dimensions of health and the impact of spirituality on the healing process as well as the health maintenance process. Next this volume elaborates on and determines the Kemetic techniques to be employed in the practice of the proper diet and fasting to restore and maintain good health. This volume also shows how modern medical science research is beginning to support the teachings of natural health, which the Ancient Egyptians knew thousands of years ago and establishes how the spiritual (Smai Tawi) practices of the Ancient Egyptians can be incorporated into one's life in order to promote a holistic movement towards the health of the body, the mind, and the soul.

Plate 5: The Imhotep Pharmacy at the Temple of Aset (Isis) in Egypt

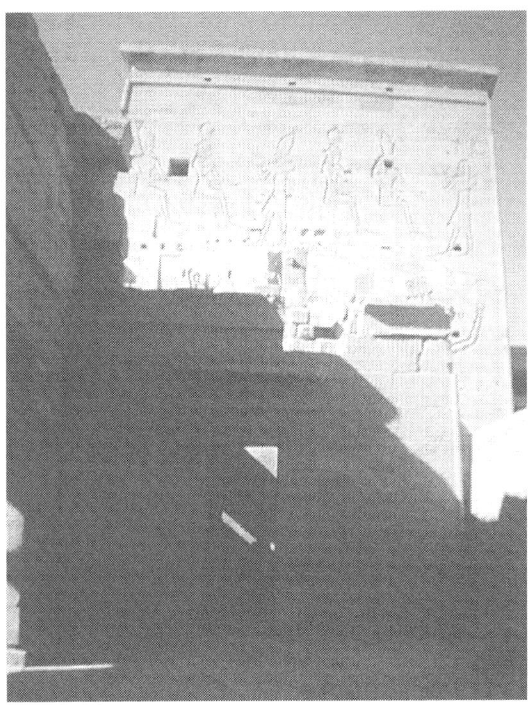

Temple of Aset with its Imhotep pharmacy/clinic (in foreground).

WHO WERE THE ANCIENT EGYPTIANS

The Ancient Egyptian religion (*Shetaut Neter*), language and symbols provide the first "historical" record of Mystical Philosophy and Religious literature. Egyptian Mysticism is what has been commonly referred to by Egyptologists as Egyptian "Religion" or "Mythology," but to think of it as just another set of stories or allegories about a long lost civilization is to completely miss the greatest secret of human existence. Mystical spirituality, in all of its forms and disciplines of spiritual development, was practiced in Ancient Egypt (Kemet) earlier than anywhere else in history. This unique perspective from the highest philosophical system which developed in Africa over seven thousand years ago provides a new way to look at life, religion, the discipline of psychology and the way to spiritual development leading to spiritual Enlightenment. Ancient Egyptian mythology, when understood as a system of *Smai Tawi*, that is, a system which promotes the union of the individual soul with the Universal Soul or Supreme Consciousness, gives every individual insight into their own divine nature, and also a deeper insight into all religions, mystical and Yoga systems.

In Chapter 4[20] and Chapter 17[21] of an Ancient Egyptian mystical text, the *Prt m Hru, The Ancient Egyptian Book of Enlightenment*, more commonly known as the *Book of the Dead,* the term "Smai Tawi" is used. It means "Union of the two lands of Egypt." The two lands refers to the two main districts of the country (North and South) and, in a mystical sense they refer to the gods Heru and Set, who are elsewhere referred to as the spiritual Higher Self and lower self of a human being, respectively. Thus, the term Smai Tawi is compatible with the Indian Sanskrit term "Yoga," which also means union of the Higher Self and lower self as well as other terms (Enlightenment, Kingdom of Heaven, Liberation, etc.) used by other systems of mystical spirituality.

Diodorus Siculus (Greek Historian) writes in the time of Augustus (first century B.C.):

> "Now the Ethiopians, as historians relate, were the first of all men and the proofs of this statement, they say, are manifest. For that they did not come into their land as immigrants from abroad, but were the natives of it and so justly bear the name of autochthones (sprung from the soil itself), is, they maintain, conceded by practically all men..."
>
> "They also say that the Egyptians are colonists sent out by the Ethiopians, Asar having been the leader of the colony. For, speaking generally, what is now Egypt, they maintain, was not land, but sea, when in the beginning the universe was being formed; afterwards, however, as the Nile during the times of its inundation carried down the mud from Ethiopia, land was gradually built up from the deposit...And the larger parts of the customs of the Egyptians are, they hold, Ethiopian, the colonists still preserving their ancient manners. For instance, the belief that their kings are Gods, the very special attention which they pay to their burials, and many other matters of a similar nature, are Ethiopian practices, while the shapes of their statues and the forms of their letters are Ethiopian; for of the two kinds of writing which the Egyptians have, that which is known as popular (demotic) is learned by everyone, while that which is called sacred (hieratic), is understood only by the priests of the Egyptians, who learnt it from their Fathers as one of the things which are not divulged, but among the Ethiopians, everyone uses these forms of letters. Furthermore, the orders of the priests, they maintain, have much the same position among both peoples; for all are clean who are engaged in the service of the gods, keeping themselves shaven, like the Ethiopian priests, and having the same dress and form of staff, which is shaped like a plough and is carried by their kings who wear high felt hats which end in a knob in the top and are circled by the serpents which they call asps; and this symbol appears to carry the thought that it will be the lot who shall dare to attack the king to encounter death-carrying stings. Many other things are told by

[20] Commonly referred to as Chapter 17
[21] Commonly referred to as Chapter 176

them concerning their own antiquity and the colony which they sent out that became the Egyptians, but about this there is no special need of our writing anything."

The Ancient Egyptian texts state:

"Our people originated at the base of the mountain of the Moon,
at the origin of the Nile river."

The ancient name for the land now called Egypt was:

"KMT" "Egypt," "Burnt," "Black people," "Black Land"

Figure 2: A map of North East Africa showing the location of the land of *Ta-Meri* or *Kamit,* also known as Ancient Egypt.

In describing the Ancient Egyptians of his time Herodotus (Greek historian c. 484-425 BC), said: *"The Egyptians and Nubians have thick lips, broad noses, wooly hair and burnt skin... ...And the Indian tribes I have mentioned, their skins are all of the same color, much like the Ethiopians... their country is a long way from Persia towards the south..."* Diodorus, the Greek historian (c. 100 B.C.) said the following, *"And upon his return to Greece, they gathered around and asked, "tell us about this great land of the Blacks called Ethiopia." And Herodotus said, "There are two great Ethiopian nations, one in Sind (India) and the other in Egypt."* Thus, the Ancient Egyptian peoples were of African origin and they had close ties in ancient times with the peoples of India.

Where is the land of Ancient Egypt?

The Ancient Egyptians lived for thousands of years in the northeastern corner of the African continent in the area known as the Nile Valley. The Nile river was a source of dependable enrichment for the land and allowed them to prosper for a very long time. Their prosperity was so great that they created art, culture, religion, philosophy and a civilization which has not been duplicated since. The Ancient Kamitans (Egyptians) based their government and business concerns on spiritual values and therefore, enjoyed an orderly society which included equality between the sexes, and a legal system based on universal spiritual laws. The *Prt m Hru* is a tribute to their history, culture and legacy. As historical insights unfold, it becomes clearer that modern culture has derived its basis from Ancient Egypt, though the credit is not often given, nor the integrity of the practices maintained. This is another important reason to study Ancient Egyptian Philosophy, to discover the principles which allowed their civilization to prosper over a period of thousands of years in order to bring our systems of government, religion and social structures to a harmony with ourselves, humanity and with nature.

Christianity was partly an outgrowth of Judaism, which was itself an outgrowth of Ancient Egyptian culture and religion. So who were the Ancient Egyptians? From the time that the early Greek philosophers set foot on African soil to study the teachings of mystical spirituality in Egypt (900-300 B.C.E.), Western society and culture was forever changed. Ancient Egypt had such a profound effect on Western civilization as well as on the native population of Ancient India (Dravidians) that it is important to understand the history and culture of Ancient Egypt, and the nature of its spiritual tradition in more detail.

The history of Egypt begins in the far reaches of history. It includes The Dynastic Period, The Hellenistic Period, Roman and Byzantine Rule (30 B.C.E.-638 A.C.E.), the Caliphate and the Mamalukes (642-1517 A.C.E.), Ottoman Domination (1082-1882 A.C.E.), British colonialism (1882-1952 A.C.E.), as well as modern, Arab-Islamic Egypt (1952- present).

Ancient Egypt or Kamit had a civilization that flourished in Northeast Africa along the Nile River from before 5,500 B.C.E. until 30 B.C.E. In 30 B.C.E., Octavian, who was later known as the Roman Emperor, Augustus, put the last Egyptian King, Ptolemy XIV, a Greek ruler, to death. After this Egypt was formally annexed to Rome. Egyptologists normally divide Ancient Egyptian history into the following approximate periods: The Early Dynastic Period (3,200-2,575 B.C.E.); The Old Kingdom or Old Empire (2,575-2,134 B.C.E.); The First Intermediate Period (2,134-2,040 B.C.E.); The Middle Kingdom or Middle Empire (2,040-1,640 B.C.E.); The Second Intermediate Period (1,640-1,532 B.C.E.); The New Kingdom or New Empire (1,532-1,070 B.C.E.); The third Intermediate Period (1,070-712 B.C.E.); The Late Period (712-332 B.C.E.).

In the Late Period the following groups controlled Egypt. The Nubian Dynasty (712-657 B.C.E.); The Persian Dynasty (525-404 B.C.E.); The Native Revolt and re-establishment of Egyptian rule by Egyptians (404-343 B.C.E.); The Second Persian Period (343-332 B.C.E.); The Ptolemaic or Greek Period (332 B.C.E.- c. 30 B.C.E.); Roman Period (c.30 B.C.E.-395 A.C.E.); The Byzantine Period (395-640 A.C.E) and The Arab Conquest Period (640 A.C.E.-present). The individual dynasties are numbered, generally in Roman numerals, from I through XXX.

The period after the New Kingdom saw greatness in culture and architecture under the rulership of Ramses II. However, after his rule, Egypt saw a decline from which it would never recover. This is the period of the downfall of Ancient Egyptian culture in which the Libyans ruled after The Tanite (XXI) Dynasty. This was followed by the Nubian conquerors who founded the XXII dynasty and tried to restore Egypt to her past glory. However, having been weakened by the social and political turmoil of wars, Ancient Egypt fell to the Persians once more. The Persians conquered the country until the Greeks, under Alexander, conquered them. The Romans followed the Greeks, and finally the Arabs conquered the land of Egypt in 640 A.C.E to the present.

However, the history which has been classified above is only the history of the "Dynastic Period." It reflects the view of traditional Egyptologists who have refused to accept the evidence of a Predynastic period in Ancient Egyptian history contained in Ancient Egyptian documents such as the *Palermo Stone, Royal Tablets at Abydos, Royal Papyrus of Turin,* the *Dynastic List* of *Manetho.* The eye-witness accounts of Greek historians Herodotus (c. 484-425 B.C.E.) and Diodorus (Greek historian died about 20 B.C.E.) corroborate the status and makeup of Kemetic culture in the late dynastic period which support the earlier accounts. These sources speak clearly of a Pre-dynastic society which stretches far into antiquity. The Dynastic Period is what most people think of whenever Ancient Egypt is mentioned. This period is when the pharaohs (kings) ruled. The latter part of the Dynastic Period is when the Biblical story of Moses, Joseph, Abraham, etc., occurs (c. 2100? -1,000? B.C.E). Therefore, those with a Christian background generally only have an idea about Ancient Egypt as it is related in the Bible. Although this biblical notion is very limited in scope, the significant impact of Ancient Egypt on Hebrew and Christian culture is evident even from the biblical scriptures. Actually, Egypt existed much earlier than most traditional Egyptologists are prepared to admit. The new archeological evidence related to the great

Sphinx monument on the Giza Plateau and the ancient writings by Manetho, one of the last High Priests of Ancient Egypt, show that Ancient Egyptian history begins earlier than 10,000 B.C.E. and may date back to as early as 30,000-50,000 B.C.E.

It is known that the Pharaonic (royal) calendar based on the Sothic system (star Sirius) was in use by 4,240 B.C.E. This certainly required extensive astronomical skills and time for observation. Therefore, the history of Kamit (Egypt) must be reckoned to be extremely ancient. Thus, in order to grasp the antiquity of Ancient Egyptian culture, religion and philosophy, we will briefly review the history presented by the Ancient Egyptian Priest Manetho and some Greek Historians.

The calendar based on the Great Year was also used by the Ancient Egyptians. The Great year is based on the movement of the earth through the constellations known as the precession of the Equinoxes and confirmed by the History given by the Ancient Egyptian Priest Manetho in the year 241 B.C.E. Each Great Year has 25,860 to 25,920 years and 12 arcs or constellations, and each passage through a constellation takes 2,155 – 2,160 years. These are the "Great Months." The current cycle or year began around the year 10,858 B.C.E. At around the year 36,766 B.C.E., according to Manetho, the Creator, Ra, ruled the earth in person from his throne in the Ancient Egyptian city of Anu. By this reckoning our current year (2,000 A.C.E.) is actually the year 38,766 based on the Great Year System of Ancient Egyptian history.

Figure 3: The land of Ancient Egypt

> Solon, Thales, Plato, Eudoxus and Pythagoras went to Egypt and consorted with the priests. Eudoxus they say, received instruction from Chonuphis of Memphis,* Solon from Sonchis of Sais,* and Pythagoras from Oeniphis of Heliopolis.*
>
> –Plutarch (Greek historian c. 46-120 A.C.E.)
>
> *(cities in Ancient Egypt-see below)

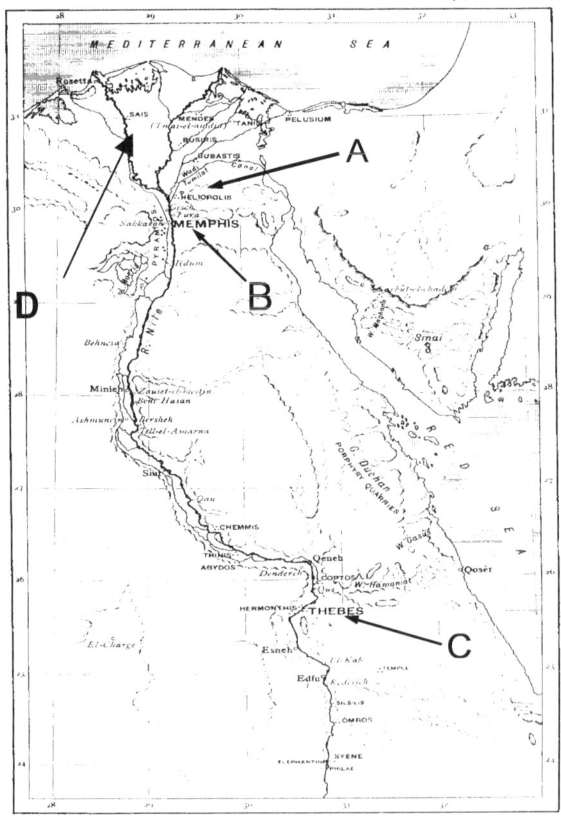

Key to the Map above: Egypt is located in the north-eastern corner of the African Continent. The cities wherein the theology of the Trinity of Amun-Ra-Ptah was developed were: A- Anu (Heliopolis), B-Hetkaptah (Memphis), C-Waset (Thebes), D- Zau (Sais).

Ancient Kemetic Terms and Ancient Greek Terms

In keeping with the spirit of the culture of Kemetic Spirituality, in this volume we will use the Kemetic names for the divinities through which we will bring forth the philosophy of the Prt M Hru. Therefore, the Greek name Osiris will be converted back to the Kemetic (Ancient Egyptian) Asar (Ausar), the Greek Isis to Aset (Auset), the Greek Nephthys to Nebthet, Anubis to Anpu or Apuat, Hathor to Hetheru, Thoth or Hermes to Djehuti, etc. Further, the term Ancient Egypt will be used interchangeably with "Kemit" ("Kamit," "Kemet"), or "Ta-Meri," as these are the terms used by the Ancient Egyptians to refer to their land and culture.

Table 1: Kemetic Names of the main Gods and Goddesses of Ancient Egypt and the Greek translation in common use.

Kemetic (Ancient Egyptian) Name	Greek Names
Asar (Ausar)	Osiris or Hades
Aset (Auset)	Isis or Demeter
Nebthet	Nephthys
Anpu or Apuat	Anubis
Hetheru	Hathor (Aphrodite)
Heru	Horus or Apollo
Djehuti	Thoth or Hermes
Maat	Astraea or Themis
Amun	Zeus
Ra	Helios
Ptah	Hephastos
Nut	Rhea
Geb	Kronos
Net	Athena
Khonsu	Heracles
Set	Ares or Typhon
Bast	Artemis
Uadjit	Leto

NOTES TO INTRODUCTION

[1] Information on WHO from the book, *Human Diseases and Conditions*, by the Nemours Foundation
[2] Delicious Living, October 2001- A Penton Publication – dl.healthwell.com
[3] Physicians Committee for Responsible Medicine (202) 686-2210 PCRM@PCRM.Org
[4] Harvard Nurses' Health Study -See Physicians Committee for Responsible Medicine (202) 686-2210 PCRM@PCRM.Org
[5] Study by Daniel Cramer M.D. -See Physicians Committee for Responsible Medicine (202) 686-2210 PCRM@PCRM.Org
[6] Study by Scott FW, and Study by Karjalainen J, Martin JM, Knip M, et al -See Physicians Committee for Responsible Medicine (202) 686-2210 PCRM@PCRM.Org
[7] Study by Bertron P, Bernard ND, Mills M, Racial bias in Federal Nutrition Polict -See Physicians Committee for Responsible Medicine (202) 686-2210 PCRM@PCRM.Org
[8] -See Physicians Committee for Responsible Medicine (202) 686-2210 PCRM@PCRM.Org
[9] See Physicians Committee for Responsible Medicine (202) 686-2210 PCRM@PCRM.Org
[10] Milk – Is it Really Good for Oour Children by Jane Sheppard – www.healthychild.com
[11]Ophir O, Peer G, Gilad J, Blum M, Aviram A. Low blood pressure in vegetarians: the possible role of potassium. Am J Clin Nutr 1983;37:755-62.
[12] 3. Melby CL, Hyner GC, Zoog B. blood pressure in vegetarians and non-vegetarians: a cross-sectional analysis. Nutr Res 1985;5:1077-82.
[13] 4. Melby CL, Goldflies DG, Hyner GC, Lyle RM. Relation between vegetarian/nonvegetarian diets and blood pressure in black and white adults. Am J Publ Health 1989;79:1283-8.
[14] Melby CL, Goldflies DG, Hyner GC, Lyle RM. Relation between vegetarian/nonvegetarian diets and blood pressure in black and white adults. Am J Publ Health 1989;79:1283-8.
[15]Rouse IL, Armstrong BK, Beilin LJ, Vandongen R. Blood-pressure-lowering effect of a vegetarian diet: controlled trial in normotensive subjects. Lancet 1983;1:5-10.
Rouse IL, Belin LJ, Mahoney DP, et al. Nutrient intake, blood pressure, serum and urinary prostaglandins and serum thromboxane B_2 in a controlled trial with a lacto-ovo-vegetarian diet. J Hypertension 1986;4:241-50.
Margetts BM, Beilin LJ, Armstrong BK, Vandongen R. A randomized controlled trial of a vegetarian diet in the treatment of mild hypertension. Clin Exp Pharmacol Physiol 1985:12:263-6.
Margetts BM, Beilin LJ, Vandongen R, Armstrong BK. Vegetarian diet in mild hypertension: a randomised controlled trial. Br Med J 1986;293:1468-71.
Lindahl O, Lindwall L, Spangberg A, Stenram A, Ockerman PA. A vegan regimen with reduced medication in the treatment of hypertension. Br J Nutr 1984;52:11-20.
[16] West RO, Hayes OB. Diet and serum cholesterol levels: a comparison between vegetarians and nonvegetarians in a Seventh-day Adventist group. Am J Clin Nutr 1968;21:853-62.
Sacks FM, Ornish D, Rosner B, McLanahan S, Castelli WP, Kass EH. Plasma lipoprotein levels in vegetarians: the effect of ingestion of fats from dairy products. JAMA 1985;254:1337-41.
Fisher M, Levine PH, Weiner B, et al. The effect of vegetarian diets on plasma lipid and platelet levels. Arch Inter Med 1986;146:1193-7.
Burslem J, Schonfeld G, Howald M, Weidman SW, Miller JP. Plasma apoprotein and lipoprotein lipid levels in vegetarians. Metabolism 1978;27:711-9.
[17] . Cooper RS, Goldberg RB, Trevisan M, et al. The selective lowering effect of vegetarianism on low density lipoproteins in a cross-over experiment. Atherosclerosis 1982;44:293-305.
Kestin M, Rouse IL, Correll RA, Nestel PJ. Cardiovascular disease risk factors in free-living men: Comparison of two prudent diets, one based on lacto-ovo-vegetarianism and the other allowing lean meat. Am J Clin Nutr 1989;50:280-7.
Ornish D, Brown SE, Scherwitz LW, et al. Can lifestyle changes reverse coronary heart disease? Lancet 1990;336:129-133.
Hunninghake DB, Stein EA, Dujovne CA, et al. The efficacy of intensive dietary therapy alone or combined with lovastatin in out patients with hypercholesterolemia. New Engl J Med 1993;328:1213-9.
[18] Ornish D, Brown SE, Scherwitz LW, et al. Can lifestyle changes reverse coronary heart disease? Lancet 1990;336:129-133.
[19] Chang-Claude J, Frentzel-Beyme R, Eilber U. Mortality pattern of German vegetarians after 11 years of follow-up. Epidemiology 1992;3:395-401.
Thorogood M, Mann J, Appleby P, McPherson K. Risk of death from cancer and ischaemic heart disease in meat and non-meat eaters. Brit Med J 1994;308:1667-70.
[20]Block G. Epidemiologic evidence regarding vitamin C and cancer. Am J Clin Nutr 1991;54:1310S-4S.
[21] . Pixley F, Wilson D, McPherson K, Mann J. Effect of vegetarianism on development of gallstones in women. Br Med J 1985;291:11-2.
Frentzel-Beyme R, Claude J, Eilber U. Mortality among German vegetarians: first results after five years of follow-up. Nutr Cancer 1988;11:117-26.
[22] Melby CL, Hyner GC, Zoog B. blood pressure in vegetarians and non-vegetarians: a cross-sectional analysis. Nutr Res 1985;5:1077-82.
Melby CL, Goldflies DG, Hyner GC, Lyle RM. Relation between vegetarian/nonvegetarian diets and blood pressure in black and white adults. Am J Publ Health 1989;79:1283-8.
Sacks FM, Ornish D, Rosner B, McLanahan S, Castelli WP, Kass EH. Plasma lipoprotein levels in vegetarians: the effect of ingestion of fats from dairy products. JAMA 1985;254:1337-41.
Pixley F, Wilson D, McPherson K, Mann J. Effect of vegetarianism on development of gallstones in women. Br Med J 1985;291:11-2.
Frentzel-Beyme R, Claude J, Eilber U. Mortality among German vegetarians: first results after five years of follow-up. Nutr Cancer 1988;11:117-26.
Burr ML, Batese J, Fehily AM, Leger AS. Plasma cholesterol and blood pressure in vegetarians. J Human Nutr 1981;35:437-41.
Rouse IL, Armstrong BK, Beilin LJ, Vandongen R. Vegetarian diet, blood pressure and cardiovascular risk. Aust NZ J Med 1984;14:439-43.
[23] *Rodale Press*
[24] *The National Enquirer*
[25] Dan Rather, in a TV broadcast "CBS Reports," on January 10, 1975

CHAPTER 1: HEALTH TEACHINGS AND PRACTICES IN KEMETIC (ANCIENT EGYPTIAN) CULTURE

"Hotep di si Neter iri Mettu wadj"

Peace Offering given (to) cause (the) Divine (to) make (the) vascular systems green (healthy)

The Divinities of Health

Healing and health maintenance is not just a matter of providing medicines. It requires the individual to restore and maintain harmony with the universe. In Ancient Africa this meant discovering and maintaining a connection with the Neteru, gods and goddesses, because they are the cosmic forces of nature from which every living being derives sustenance and vitality. In Kemet, the divinities presiding over the health of individuals were Aset (Isis), Sekhmet (lioness aspect of Hetheru), Djehuti and Heru. The doctors in ancient times invoked the power of these divinities to effect a recovery from disease, just as Aset cured and resurrected Asar, and Djehuti cured Hetheru and Heru, not just physically, but also mentally and spiritually. Therefore, some priests and priestesses of these divinities acted in the capacity of doctors. In this volume we will explore the health teachings of these divinities.

Above left: Goddess Aset (Isis) nourishes Heru (spiritual aspirant) with wisdom and love. Right: Goddess Aset prays over the body of Asar and returns it back to live. (See the book *Resurrecting Osiris* by Muata Ashby.)

Above left: God Djehuti repairs the eye of Hetheru. Right: God Djehuti repairs the eye of Heru. (See the books *The Glorious Light Meditation* and *Resurrecting Osiris* by Muata Ashby.)

Left: Goddess Sekhmet, who is the power of the sundisk of Ra, the fire spitting eye (serpent of the sundisk) presides over the vital life forces which course through the body and support the life of every individual.

The Teachings of the Temple of Aset (Isis) and The Diet of the Initiates

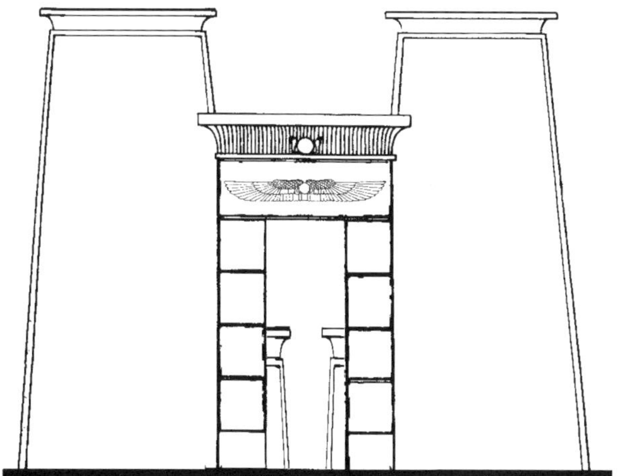

Figure 4: The Ancient Egyptian Temple

The initiates are advanced spiritual aspirants, those who are initiated into the higher mysteries of life, the secrets of mystical spirituality. They are the priests and priestesses of the temple, who while interacting with the masses, are not part of mass culture. They follow strict rules regarding health, hygiene and spiritual disciplines not followed by the common men and women. The goddess Aset was known as the goddess of healing because, in the mythology of the Asarian Resurrection,[22] she reconstituted the body of her husband Asar, after it had been mutilated by his jealous brother Set. Further, she engineered the resurrection of her son Heru, when he was bitten by a scorpion and killed, and she was known as the master of the words of power, which heal. At her temple, much more than the use of words of power were practiced within the healing arts. The following is a detailed look at those disciplines of health maintenance and restoration.

While the general population was considered to be one of the healthiest groups of the ancient world, the spiritual initiates were required to keep even more strict dietary practices. The special diets of the Ancient Egyptian initiates were a highly guarded secret as were the inner meanings of the myths, which were acted out in the mystery rituals (Shetaut Neter). For this reason, many of the special Smai Tawi (Mystical-Yogic) practices, which included a special diet and meditation, were not committed to writing in an explicit fashion. Rather, they were committed to hieroglyphic form and carried on through the initiatic process. It was not until Greek historians and initiates of the Ancient Egyptian mystery schools began to write about their experiences that the more detailed aspects of the initiatic diets were available to a wider audience. The sect of Jews called the Essenes[23] practiced an initiation period of two to three years and instituted purification diets and hygienic practices similar to those spoken about by Herodotus (484?-425 BCE) and Plutarch (46?-120 ACE). The Essenic health practices were presented in the *Essene Gospel of Peace*.[24]

---

[22] See the book *The Ausarian Resurrection: The Ancient Egyptian Bible* by Muata Ashby.

[23] The people who practiced early Judaism had originally emerged from Ancient Egypt with Moses and were ethnically Ancient Egyptians. This group included the sects known as Essenes and the Therapeuts. For more details see the book ***Christian Yoga*** by Muata Ashby.

[24] Available through the Sema Institute of Yoga – It is recommended that the reader also acquire the *Essene Science of Life,* a companion commentary by the translator.

Plutarch, a student of the mysteries of Aset, reported that the initiates followed a strict diet made up of vegetables and fruits and *abstained from particular kinds of foods* (swine, sheep, fish, etc.) *as well as indulgence of the carnal appetite.* In the following excerpts Plutarch describes the purpose and procedure of the diet observed by the initiates of Aset, and the goal to be attained through the rigorous spiritual program. This next excerpt should be studied carefully.

> *To desire, therefore, and covet after truth, those truths more especially which concern the divine nature, is to aspire to be partakers of that nature itself* (1), *and to profess that all our studies and inquiries* (2) *are devoted to the acquisition of holiness. This occupation is surely more truly religious than any external* (3) *purifications or mere service of the temple can be* (4). *But more especially must such a disposition of mind be highly acceptable to that goddess to whose service you are dedicated, for her special characteristics are wisdom and foresight, and her very name seems to express the peculiar relation which she bears to knowledge. For "Isis" is a Greek word, and means "knowledge or wisdom,"*(5) *and "Typhon," (Set) the name of her professed adversary, is also a Greek word, and means " pride and insolence."*(6) *This latter name is well adapted to one who, full of ignorance and error, tears in pieces* (7) *and conceals that holy doctrine (about Asar) which the goddess collects, compiles, and delivers to those who aspire after the most perfect participation in the divine nature. This doctrine inculcates a steady perseverance in one uniform and temperate course of life* (8), *and an abstinence from particular kinds of foods* (9), *as well as from all indulgence of the carnal appetite* (10), *and it restrains the intemperate and voluptuous part within due bounds, and at the same time habituates her votaries to undergo those austere and rigid ceremonies which their religion obliges them to observe. The end and aim of all these toils and labors is the attainment of the knowledge of the First and Chief Being* (11), *who alone is the object of the understanding of the mind; and this knowledge the goddess invites us to seek after, as being near and dwelling continually* (12) *with her. And this also is what the very name of her temple promiseth to us, that is to say, the knowledge and understanding of the eternal and self-existent Being - now it is called "Iseion," which suggests that if we approach the temple of the goddess rightly, we shall obtain the knowledge of that eternal and self existent Being.*

Figure 5: The Forms of Goddess Aset (Isis)

MYSTICAL IMPLICATIONS OF THE DISCOURSE OF PLUTARCH:[25]

1- It is to be understood that spiritual aspiration implies seeking the union (Smai Tawi, mystical union-Yoga) with or becoming one with the thing being sought, because this is the only way to truly "know" partake of something. You can have opinions about what it is like to be a whale, but you would never exactly know until you become one with it, enfolding all that exists, is the one being worthy of veneration and identification. "Knowing" Neter (God) is the goal of all spiritual practices. This is the supreme goal, which must be kept in mind by a spiritual aspirant.

2- In order to discover the hidden nature of God, emphasis is placed on study and inquiry into the nature of things. Who am I? What is the universe composed of? Who is God? How am I related to God? These are the questions which when pursued, lead to the discovery of the Self (God). Those who do not engage in this form of inquiry will generate a reality for themselves according to their beliefs. Some people believe they have the answers, that the universe is atoms and electrons or energy. Others believe that the body is the soul and that there is nothing else. Still others believe that the mind is the soul or that there is no soul and no God. The first qualification for serious aspiration is that you have a serious conviction that you are greater than just a finite individual mortal body, that you are an immortal being who is somehow mixed up with a temporal form (body). If this conviction is present, then you are stepping on the road to enlightenment. The teachings will be useful to you. Those who hold other beliefs are being led by ignorance and lack of spiritual sensitivity as a result of their beliefs. Thus, their beliefs will create a reality for them based on those beliefs. They will need to travel the road of nature, which will guide them in time toward the path of spiritual aspiration.

3-4 The plan prescribed by the teachings of Mystical spirituality (Smai Tawi – Yoga) is the only true means to effective spiritual development, because it leads to a revelation of the inner meanings of the teachings; therefore it is experiential, i.e., it is based on your own personal experience and not conjecture. Otherwise, worship and religious practices remain only at the level of ritualism and do not lead to enlightenment (Pert m Heru).

5-7 The Greek name Isis means "wisdom" which bestows the knowledge of the true Self of the initiate. In the Asarian (Osirian) Mysteries, when Set killed Asar by tearing him into pieces, he was symbolically tearing up the soul. However, Aset (Isis) restores the pieces of the soul (Asar). Set symbolizes egoism: pride, anger, hatred, fear, jealousy, etc. Therefore, pride and insolence (Set-egoism) destroy the soul and knowledge of the Self (Aset) restores it to its true nature. The Ancient Egyptian scriptures support the Greek name translation and meaning of the name Aset. One of the names of Aset is: *Rekhåt or Rekhit* (meaning "knowledge personified"). *Rekh* is also a name of the God in the "duat" or Netherworld (astral plane) who possesses knowledge which can lead the soul to the abode of the Divine. The variation, *Rekh-t* , means Sage or learned person.

8- True spirituality cannot be pursued rashly or in a fanatical way by going to extremes. Smai Tawi, Mystical Spirituality, is a science of balance. It has been developed over a period of thousands of years with well established principles, which when followed, produce the desired effect of leading the initiate from darkness to light, ignorance to knowledge, an un-enlightened state to enlightenment.

9-10 The foods referred to are flesh foods (swine, sheep, fish, etc.), pulse,[26] and salt (taken in large amounts). Indulgence in sexual activity has two relevant aspects. First, it intensifies the physical

[25] Note: The numbers at the beginning of each paragraph below correspond to the reference numbers in the text above.

experience of embodiment and distracts the mind by creating impressions in the subconscious and unconscious, which will produce future cravings and desires. This state of mind renders the individual incapable of concentration on significant worldly or high spiritual achievements. Secondly, control of the sexual urge leads to control of the sexual Life Force energy,[27] which can then be directed towards higher mental and spiritual achievement. Further, overindulgence in sexual activity tends to wear down the immunity as it wears down the mental capacity and one becomes a slave to sensual passions and susceptible to sexual and non-sex related diseases.

Chapter 30B of the Ancient Egyptian mystical text *The Book of Coming Forth By Day* states:

> *This utterance[28] shall be recited by a person purified and washed; one who has not eaten animal flesh or fish.*

Chapter 137A of the *Book of Coming Forth By Day* states:

> *And behold, these things shall be performed by one who is clean, and is ceremonially pure, a man who hath eaten neither meat nor fish, and who hath not had intercourse with women* (applies to female initiates not having intercourse with men as well).

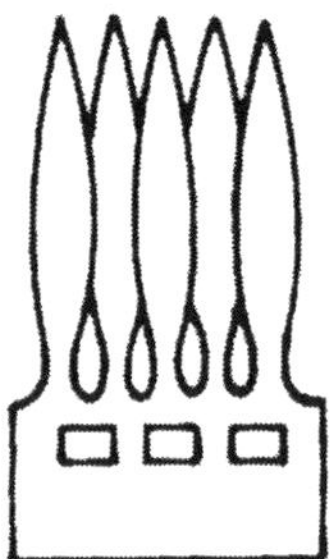

Figure 6: Kemetic Symbol for a Bed of Lettuce of Min

In the Mysteries of the Ancient Egyptian god and goddess Asar and Aset, respectively, Asar's brother Set represents the lower human nature, and Asar's son, Heru, the higher. Set kills Asar and usurps the throne, which rightfully should belong to Heru. In various renderings of the characteristics of Set, it is stated that Set is promiscuous. Most interestingly, both Heru and Set are vegetarians. Their favorite food is *lettuce.* Another form of Heru is the god Min. He symbolizes sublimated sexual energies. His favorite food is also lettuce, and in ancient times this food was seen as an aphrodisiac. Therefore, through this myth, the teaching that vegetarianism increases the potential for spiritual advancement is being given. With this understanding, it is clear that control of the sexual urge to conserve potential spiritual energy and purification of the diet are necessary practices on the spiritual path which enable the aspirant to achieve increased spiritual sensitivity.

A most important point to remember when beginning practices for the purification is that they should be implemented gradually, preferably under the supervision of an experienced person. If these changes result in an inability to perform your daily duties, then they are too extreme. The key to advancement in any area is steady, balanced practice. There must always be a balance between the practical life and the spiritual. In this way, spiritual advancement occurs in an integral fashion, intensifying every area of one's

---

[26] **pulse**[2] (pŭls) *n.* **1.** The edible seeds of certain pod-bearing plants, such as peas and beans. **2.** A plant yielding these seeds. (American Heritage Dictionary)

[27] The concept of the Life Force will be explained in detail later.

[28] Hekau, mantras, words of power, chants.

life rather than one particular area exclusively. All areas must be mastered, secular as well as non-secular, in order to attain spiritual perfection, Enlightenment.

Since the physical body and all worldly attainments are changeable, fleeting and ultimately perishable, it would be wise to pursue a way of life which directs the mind toward understanding the Self and not to pursue health as an end in itself, but as a means to your own growth and spiritual evolution, which will continue even after the death of the your physical body (i.e. carry on to your next lifetime when you reincarnate) if you have not attained enlightenment up to the time of physical death. The holistic development of an individual must be directed to achieving a state of consciousness which is not dependent on the physical body for peace and comfort. The body is an instrument, which you have created through your thoughts to allow you to pursue the goal of enlightenment and thereby experience the fullness of life.

11- See #1.

12- There are two very important points in this line. One, that good association or keeping the company of sages or other enlightened personalities is a powerful means to gain knowledge of the state of enlightenment. To this end, strive to keep good company in your family relations as well as non-family relations. Read uplifting books by the sages and the teachings of the masters. When you discover a more evolved personality, seek to maintain contact by reading their teachings and through correspondence. Do not debate with those who lack spiritual sensitivity. This form of interaction will weaken your mind. As Jesus said: *Cast not your pearls before swine, for they will trample them as they turn against you.* Trust in the omniscient Divine Self, who knows past, present and future, who manifests as Nature to lead others on the path. Spread the teachings of mystic spirituality only to those who are interested or with those whom you practice. This kind of interaction will help you both to increase your understanding and generate a positive frame of mind.

The second important point here refers to continuous reflection and meditation on the divine which is also expressed in the Ancient Egyptian prayer: *"Give thyself to God, keep thou thyself daily for God; and let tomorrow be as today."* It implies that one's mind should be constantly remembering the divine and glorifying the divine in all things. It means not allowing the mind to develop attachments to the fleeting events of human life, be they positive experiences or negative ones. It means not allowing the negative thoughts and feelings to lead you into a pursuit of illusory pleasures of the senses, which will draw you away from divine awareness and realization. It means centering the mind on self-discovery and introspection at all times, regardless of what your activities may be. However, those activities should be based solely on the principles of virtue, justice and order. This form of spiritual practice is known as "mindfulness" in Buddhism and Vedanta Philosophies.

Plutarch further reports that the Egyptian initiates:

> *...strive to prevent fatness in Apis*[29] *as well as themselves*(1)*, for they are anxious that their bodies should sit as light and easy about their souls as possible, and that their mortal part* (body) *should not oppress and weigh down their divine and immortal part...during their more solemn purifications they abstain from wine*(2) *wholly, and they give themselves up entirely to study*(4) *and meditation*(5) *and to the hearing* (3) *and teaching of these divine truths which treat of the divine nature.*

[29] Bull which was kept as a symbol of the gods Asar and Ptah.

The following dietary guidelines for spiritual and physical health are derived from the above statement.

1- Preventing "fatness"- obesity. This issue is very important, even for those without spiritual aspirations. Some people who are overweight claim that they are happy and content as they are. Some scientists claim to have discovered a gene in the human system, which causes a propensity to become overweight. All of your body's characteristics are due to your past history of experiences and desires, not only in this lifetime, but in previous ones as well. Physical weight is like a physical object which is possessed. The more you have, the more you try to hold onto, and the more stress you have trying to enjoy and hold onto "things." Desires of the body such as eating have a grounding effect on the soul, because they engender the desire to experience the physical pleasure of consuming food. Desires of the body as well as strong emotions such as hate, greed, etc., have the effect of rendering the mind insensitive to spirituality. Excess weight on the body causes innumerable health problems to arise.

Obesity is a body condition produced by the storage of excessive amounts of fat in adipose (fatty) tissue beneath the skin as well as within other organs such as the muscles, liver, etc. All mammals store some amount of body fat. In normal human females in general society, the storage of fat as a percentage of total body weight is 25 percent, and for males, 15 percent. The processing of fat can yield twice the potential energy as compared carbohydrate or protein. It is therefore another way of storing energy for times of future need. However, when there is an overabundance of fat in the body, the body works inefficiently and develops an aesthetically displeasing form which is inherently so, since it deviates from the natural form which would be dictated by the genes i.e. nature.

Obesity:

> Storage of greatly increased amounts of fat, however, is associated with impairment of health. Data from insurance company records show that persons who are 30 percent or more overweight run measurably increased risks of disease, notably diabetes, cardiovascular and gallbladder disease, and arthritis, and often encounter complications in surgery. Obesity is a result of taking in more energy in food than one uses in activity. Scientists have found that both obese and normal-weight people go on eating binges, but people of normal weight reduce their intake afterward to compensate, whereas obese people do not. Besides excess eating, obesity can also be caused by reduced activity, and this often occurs in persons who are sedentary or bedridden.[30]

There is a Kemetic Proverb which highlights the negative effects of excess bulk on the body.

> “An infant's soul is altogether a thing of beauty to see, not yet befouled by body's passions, still all but hanging from the Cosmic Soul! But when the body grows in bulk and draweth down the soul into its mass, then doth the soul cut off itself and bring upon itself forgetfulness, and no more shareth in the Beautiful and Good (God); and this forgetfulness becometh vice.”

These teachings refer to more than physical bulk. This means that fatness is more than just a factor related to the volume of excess weight. In other words, one can be physically thin and still be spiritually “fat.” The density of the matter, which comprises the cells of the body, is affected by the different kinds of foods (physical, mental, spiritual) ingested. The more earthly the physical, mental and soul foods are, the more density there is in the tissues of the body. Thus, the more resistance there is to the free flow of the vascular system and the Life Force energies. So promoting leanness implies keeping the physical weight in proper balance, but also cleansing the cells of the body as well. One can survive on a diet of

[30] "Obesity," Microsoft (R) Encarta. Copyright (c) 1994 Microsoft Corporation. Copyright (c) 1994 Funk & Wagnall's Corporation.

ham hocks, ribs, pork, lard, hamburgers, fried foods, foods high in fats, etc., and still appear lean if the food intake is at a minimum or one's metabolism is high. One can even appear lean and healthy on this diet. This is the diet and habit in many countries. However, what will the makeup of the mental, spiritual and physical constitution of a person on such a diet be? They may enjoy eating the foods, but what are the foods doing to them physically, especially in the long run, and how does this lifestyle affect their spiritual evolution now? Fatness and the carnal appetite are to be curtailed because they promote egoism and reinforce the illusoriness of life. Finally, it must be clear to the reader that the issue of diet and health go far beyond whether or not food promotes cholesterol or fat in the human body.

You can change the future condition of your body by first mentally resolving to change it, and then employing the self-effort in that direction while at the same time invoking the help of the Neters (cosmic forces - divine energies of the Higher Self, God) to assist your quest for self-improvement. This will not be easy since the temptation of food is very great. It is related to the first energy center (chakra) of the subtle spiritual body (Uraeus-Kundalini Serpent Power)[31] and it is a force which needs to be controlled in order to proceed on the spiritual path. As part of your spiritual program, begin controlling your intake of food gradually, on a daily basis, even if you cut back a tablespoonful per day until you reach a level of intake which will support the normal weight for your body structure. Be especially watchful of yourself in respect to your habits. Do you eat out of habit, for pleasure or out of necessity? If it is out of habit or for pleasure, you must break the cycle by engaging in other activities when the desire arises. Do exercise, deep breathing, study, chant, call a fellow practitioner for support. The Serpent Power will be discussed in detail in future sections.

> "Obesity is a factor in heart disease, diabetes and cancer. According to statistics cited by the senators, an estimated 61 percent of U.S. adults and 13 percent of children are overweight. An estimated 300,000 deaths per year are associated with obesity. There are twice as many overweight children and three times as many overweight adolescents as there were 30 years ago. "Obesity is our nation's fastest rising public health problem," said Bingaman, D.N.M. "As a nation, we can no longer afford to ignore the escalating costs associated with obesity and unhealthy lifestyles, such as physical inactivity and poor dietary habits." Dodd, D-Conn., said a failure to address the problem of obesity would endanger more and more children."[32]

---

[31] Note: audio tape lecture KUNDALINI - URAEUS YOGA: Workshop and Cleansing Meditation - I. Also see the book ***Serpent Power*** by Muata Ashby – both available through the Sema Institute of Yoga.

[32]

Recreational Drugs and Alcohol

2- Natural wines and other naturally brewed drinks may be acceptable in small quantities by the masses, however, you will notice that as you purify yourself, you will not be able to tolerate or desire even small amounts of intoxicants.

"Oh that thou did understand that wine is an abomination."
-Ancient Egyptian Proverb

Distilled liquor is not a natural substance. It is processed into a potent form which is injurious to the body and mind and therefore, not suitable at all for use by those advancing on the spiritual path. The same applies to narcotics and all other "recreational" drugs such as marijuana. All of these distort the spiritual perception while damaging the physical body. No drug can produce a high, which can be compared to spiritual bliss. Therefore, resolve to leave all drugs behind and become intoxicated with spiritual feelings and aspiration.

Alcohol and other drug abuse are extremely injurious factors to the personality. Drugs and alcohol kill cells in the organs, especially the brain and the liver, and impair one's thought process and sense perception, which lead to self-destruction and or injuries to others. The body is somewhat like a machine through which spiritual energy (consciousness) flows, much like electricity through electrical wires. If the wires (nervous system and brain) are damaged, the electricity (spirit) cannot operate properly. The desire for happiness and liberation of the spirit manifests as a desire of the spirit to expand beyond the confines of the body and its limitations. Not knowing that this expansion can be accomplished through meditation, or not having enough will to apply themselves, some people seek the feeling of ***"blissful freedom"*** through drug use and abuse. Drug use causes the temporary disconnection of the ego (ordinary waking consciousness), so people later recall a feeling of bliss. Along with this illusory bliss, drugs also cause critical damage to the brain and nervous system and further, the drug induced experience is unpredictable and uncontrollable, thus causing more illusions and mental agitation in the mind along with physical dependence. The feeling of bliss comes from a relief of stress. Stress is there because the person is lacking a spiritual basis in life and they are ignorantly trying to find it through the drugs. In reality, the best way (and really the only true way) to achieve true bliss and ecstasy is to train one's own mind to reach those higher levels of consciousness of the Spirit. This process may be accomplished through the practice of virtuous living and meditation. In this manner the process of discovering peace, contentment and bliss will be integrated into the psyche naturally, avoiding the mental or physical imbalances of drug abuse. Advanced spirituality entails going beyond the ego. This process occurs naturally when you sleep, in the deep-dreamless sleep state. When in deep sleep, the ego is nowhere to be found and a person experiences peace, rejuvenation and bliss. The mystic path is the art of discovering that glorious bliss, not through drugs, sleep or relationships or any worldly possessions, but through inner self-discovery. **Note:** It is important to note here that the same teaching which was practiced in Ancient Egypt of **Listening** to, **Reflecting** upon, and **Meditating** upon the teachings is the same process used in Vedanta-Jnana Yoga of India, today. This is known as the Yoga of Wisdom.

3,4,5- This outlines the main format for spiritual education:

3- Listening to the teachings.
4- Constant study and reflection on the teachings.
5- Meditation on the meaning of the teachings.

The Greek writer, *Porphyry,* gives insight into the ideal lifestyle which was upheld by the priests and priestesses of Ancient Egypt:

> The priests, having renounced all other occupation and human labor, devoted their whole life to contemplation and vision of things divine. By vision they achieve honor, safety and piety, by contemplation of knowledge, and through both a discipline of lifestyle which is secret and has the dignity of antiquity. Living always with divine knowledge and inspiration puts one beyond all greed, restrains the passions, and makes life alert for understanding. They practiced simplicity,

> restraint, self-control, perseverance and in everything justice and absence of greed.... Their walk was disciplined, and they practiced controlling their gaze, so that if they chose they did not blink. Their laughter was rare, and if did happen, did not go beyond a smile. They kept their hands always within their clothing. . . . Their lifestyle was frugal and simple. Some tasted no wine at all, others a very little: they accused it of causing damage to the nerves and a fullness in the head which impedes research, and of producing desire for sex.[33]

The General Ancient Egyptian Diet

In the West, Hippocrates (460?-377? BCE) has been called the *father of medicine.* His major teaching was that diet is the cause of disease. He was instructed in this most important link between diet and disease by the physicians of Ancient Egypt, during his documented travels to Egypt.

Herodotus witnessed an elaborate system of medical science during his travels in Egypt. The following is an excerpt from his writings where he notes the general dietary practices of the Ancient Egyptian people.

> The Egyptians who live in the cultivated parts of the country, by their practice of keeping records of the past, have made themselves much the best historians of any nation of which I have experience. I will describe some of their habits:
>
> 1. Every month for three consecutive days they purge themselves, for their health's sake, with emetics[34] and clysters,[35] in the belief that all diseases come from the food a man eats; and it is a fact - even apart from this precaution - that next to the Libyans they are the healthiest people in the world.
>
> 2. I should put this down myself to the absence of changes in the climate, for change, and especially changes of weather, is the prime cause of disease.
>
> 3. They eat loaves of Spelt - *cyllestes* is their word for them...
>
> 4....and drink a wine made from barley, as they have no vines in the country.
>
> 5. Some kinds of fish they eat raw, either dried in the sun, or salted; quails, too, they eat raw, and ducks and various small birds, after pickling them in brine; other sorts of birds and fish, apart from those which are considered sacred, they either roast or boil.
>
> 6...nevertheless they are peculiar in certain ways which they have discovered of living more cheaply: for instance, they gather the water-lilies (Lotuses) which grow in great abundance when the river is full and floods the neighboring flats, and dry them in the sun; then from the center of each blossom they pick out something which resembles a poppyhead, grind it, and make it into loaves which they bake. The root of this plant is also edible; it is round, about as big as an apple, and tastes sweet.

---

[33] Porphyry, On Abstinence from Killing Animals, trans. Gillian Clark, *De Abstentia,* Book IV, Chap. 6

[34] An *emetic* is any medicinal agent used to induce vomiting. In India, Yogis practice a similar procedure for cleansing the upper gastrointestinal tract. It is called *Jala Dhauti.* The procedure is to ingest 4-5 glasses of lukewarm water with a small amount of salt in it. Then shake up the intestines through massaging and abdominal movements and then vomit the water out using the fingers. This has the effect of removing phlegm and bile.

[35] enemas

7. There is another kind of lily to be found in the river; this resembles a rose, and its fruit is formed on a separate stalk from that which bears the blossom, and has very much the looks of a wasp's comb. The fruit contains a number of seeds, about the size of an olive-stone, which are good to eat either green or dried.

8. They pull up the annual crop of papyrus-reed which grows in the mashes, cut the stalks in two, and eat the lower part, about eighteen inches in length, first baking it in a closed pan, heated red-hot, if they want to enjoy it to perfection. The upper section of the stalk is used for some other purpose.

9. Some of these people, however, live upon nothing but fish, which they gut as soon as they catch them, and eat after drying them in the sun.

To summarize some important points from the above writings of Herodotus:

A- Another important point is that the sun was used for much of the cooking as opposed to stoves, and even worse, microwave ovens which destroy both the gross and subtle nutritional quality of foods.

B- Many foods were eaten raw and vegetables made up a major part of the diet.

C- Wheat was not a major part of the diet. Spelt was used instead. In Naturopathic medicine and Indian Ayur Veda science,[36] wheat has been found to be incompatible with some people, causing them phlegm or congestion.

D- The Ancient Egyptians lived in an area of the world where the climate was stable. This is important because their physical bodies were not subjected to drastic changes such as in those areas where seasonal temperature changes range many degrees. There are certain locations in the world where the climates change many degrees within a single day. This occurrence is jolting to the body's equilibrium and thus affects general health.

This factor of the geographical climate became a primary teaching of Jesus in the *Essene Gospel of Peace*. Also, this Gospel describes cooking with the sun, the proper methods of food combining, attitude when eating and methods of internal cleansing through fasts and enema.

[36] Ancient Medial science discipline from East India.

CHAPTER 2: THE KEMETIC CONCEPT OF HEALTH FOR BODY, MIND AND SOUL

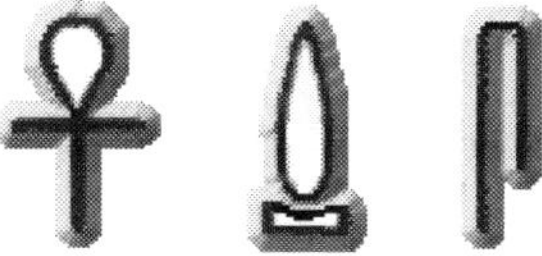

THE SOUL AND THE SPIRITUAL DIMENSIONS OF HEALTH

What is Health?

Many people do not understand the meaning of health. Health is the state in which the body and mind do not distract the vision of the Higher Self. Ill health is any condition (physical, mental or otherwise) which renders the human being ignorant of his or her true nature and thereby causes that personality to be susceptible to the miseries of life. With these definitions it must be understood that health is an issue that goes beyond the physical body, although it includes issues of the physical nature of a human being. Therefore, the physical constitution of a human being cannot be the sole criterion for the determination of whether or not a person is enjoying good health. For example, a person may be physically fit and yet be tormented with mental complexes such as worries, stress, anxieties, cravings, passions, etc. This is not good health. Conversely, another person may be very ill and yet be internally joyous, experiencing the fullness of life, peace and spiritual awareness. This person is healthier than the one mentioned earlier. Even a person who has contracted a hereditary disease and works to overcome it with a positive attitude is in better health than the one without physical disease, but living in discontent. This is because there is a mental and spiritual dimension to health, which needs to be taken into account.

Those who possess a healthy body have a better chance to achieve higher health, that is, health of the mind and soul. However, this is no guarantee. Adversities, illnesses and struggles of life come to a person as a result of their own previous actions,[37] and from the outside such a person may appear to be experiencing misery. However, if that person faces that adversity and endures or overcomes it righteously, and learns how to avoid the mistake which led them to the adversity, they are in a good position to attain higher insight, because they have overcome a karmic entanglement. Therefore, adversity, struggles in life and illness of the body cannot be automatically seen as negative developments, for there are people whose struggle to overcome illness has transformed them into better human beings, while there are perfectly physically healthy people who commit suicide and hurt others in various ways. Clearly these people who are physically healthy but who commit suicide, violence, etc., cannot be considered as being in good health. Conversely, one's social status, level of wealth, etc., are also not signs of health. There are multi-billionaires who contract fatal diseases and can do nothing about it through their money. There are those people who can easily heal themselves while there are others who need to spend excessive amounts of time and money to procure healing modalities.

Further, adversity and disease is sometimes the soul's method of promoting a change in life. Sometimes the only way that people will change their activities or explore new outlooks on life is to go through the experience of dealing with a life threatening disease. Thus, adversity is often a wakeup call from the soul. At other times, in order to atone for previous misdeeds, a person may have to spend a lot of money and suffer greatly in order to overcome a disease. The suffering and expense sometimes cannot be accounted for by the disease itself since other people go through the same disease and heal themselves without the excess of time and expense. In other words, there is a karmic dept that needs to be paid, and this heavy payment is due to the heavy karmic burden of the past actions, thoughts and feelings. This may work out in the form of ignorance about life and healing. For example, if one was previously ignorant about health maintenance and comes to believe that the only way to heal is to go to a controversial doctor and get medicines, antibiotics or surgery then, even if several naturopathic doctors were to come and administer herbs that should heal the disease easily, that person will not find relief until they go to the allopathic doctor and spend a lot of time and expense on drugs and medicines or hospital treatments. They

[37] The philosophy of Ari (Karma) will be explained in detail later. If one is unfamiliar with the concept of ari (karma), this section should be read.

themselves will not allow themselves to be healed by any other way than what they believe is necessary. Thus, they are limiting their own treatment options and leading themselves to unnecessary adversity. In addition, all of this trouble and expense is still not a permanent cure, but just a masking of the underlying problems. If, however, one expands beyond one's limited notions and concepts, then one can overstep the burden of previous ari (karma). In this case, even if the person lived in a completely negative way and ate a poor diet, their understanding will allow them to adopt a new healthy lifestyle and heal in a short time. The objective of the soul is not to cause pain and suffering, but to lead the personality to spiritual enlightenment. Ignorance is the cause of all disease, pain and suffering.

Also, many mainstream medical doctors such as Amrita McLanahan M.D., Larry Dossey M.D., Deepok Chopra M.D., Andrew Weil M.D., Christine Northrup, M.D. and others, have acknowledged the need to take into account the mental and spiritual aspects of the personality in the process of healing. Ivy League university studies have proven that there is a connection between disease and lifestyle, specifically, the spiritual aspects. Those people who are more religious suffer less disease. Those who are prayed for heal faster than those who are not. The acknowledgements by these and other mainstream doctors are signaling the end of ignorance in the general medical establishment. The placebo effect is still a medical mystery. In studies it has been shown that two groups will be chosen. One is given a medicine while the other is given a sugar pill, a placebo, which should have no effect on the medical problem. Those in the placebo group often do as well or better than those being given the medicine, and of course do not suffer from side effects. This attests to the role of the mind in health and the healing process. There are many other such proofs, however, only those who are not under the clouds of mental delusion will allow themselves to realize these truths, and then adopt the lifestyle of health, which is based on them.

The Kemetic Hieroglyphs of Health

As stated earlier, health of the physical constitution is the basis for facilitating the pursuit of mental and spiritual health. Therefore, it is the first aspect of health to be emphasized in this volume. However, we will begin by exploring the idea that physical health is sustained by the spiritual essence and is ultimately a factor of spiritual health. This concept seems at first paradoxical, but it will become clearer as we progress in our journey through the Kemetic health teachings. We will now proceed to decipher the important Kemetic hieroglyphs related to the concepts of Kemetic health philosophy.

Ankh, Oodja, Seneb = Life, Vitality, Health -The Special Kemetic Benediction

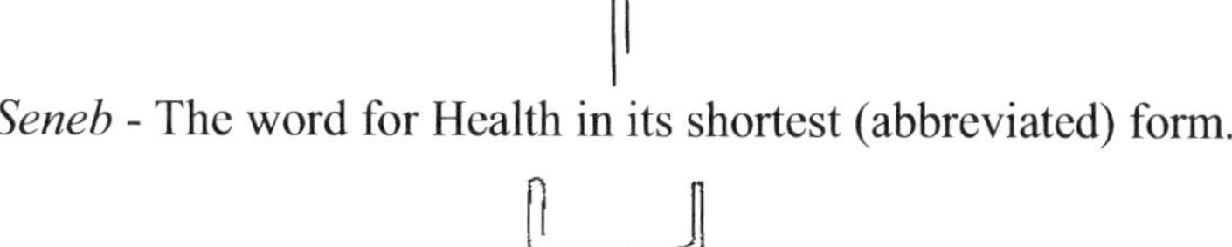

Seneb - The word for Health in its shortest (abbreviated) form.

Health - *Snb (or Seneb)* – common shortened form.

Health, Vigor- *Snbai (or Senbi)*– fully written.

A close examination of the Ancient Egyptian word for health, when fully written and spelled out, reveals the spiritual dimensions of the Kemetic concept of health. The Ancient Egyptian hieroglyphic sign, , means "ba" or soul. There are a few signs which symbolize the idea of soul, the spiritual essence of a human being, in the Kemetic language. This sign uses the image of a bird. When used in the word for health, this sign relates to the ability of the soul to fly, that is, to soar to great spiritual heights when there is good health. Thus, implied in the Kemetic understanding of health is the ability to experience elevated consciousness in the state of good health. Health therefore, is not a pursuit just for promoting long life for the indiscriminate, indefinite or unhampered pursuit of worldly pleasures, but to promote the experience of spiritual consciousness.

The Nature of the Soul and the Spiritual Constitution of a Human Being

So what is the nature of the human body and what is the purpose for the differences among human beings? How are these differences to be understood and transcended? Also, what is the underlying basis of the mind and body? What is a human being? People see themselves as different, but are they really? Don't people all over the world desire love, happiness, peace and joy? These are similarities, are they not?

"The soul belongs to heaven, the body belongs to the earth"

—Ancient Egyptian Proverb

A human being is a complex entity composed of a soul, a mind and a body. The mind and body constitute the psychophysical personality of a human being. The soul is the eternal part while the body is the transient part of a human being. The soul is the essence of the Spirit, which sustains and manifests as every human being, and indeed, all life. However, when human beings forget their eternal nature, they identify with the body and with the mind through its desires, complexes and ignorance. A person sees himself or herself as a physical body possessing a mind, and the underlying essence, the Spirit, becomes as if veiled or forgotten. Nevertheless, a human being has an innate desire to discover his or her true nature, but when this is pursued through the limited mind and body, the soul aspect of a person becomes caught in, and conditioned by, the illusions, misconceptions, prejudices and cravings of the mind and body. These ultimately lead to illnesses of the body, mind and or soul.

In addition, the individual soul of a person is in reality one with the Universal Soul, the Supreme Being, just like each wave in the ocean, though temporarily extending away from the ocean, is nevertheless essentially one with the whole ocean, always. The goal of mystical spirituality is to realize that you are not an individual, but in fact, that your true nature is universal. When you realize this goal in your own life, you will have attained enlightenment. As you move towards enlightenment, all virtuous qualities will bloom in your personality. All will be understood and loved by you as the Self, and you will have perfect health. You will become the embodiment of supreme peace (hetep) and joy (bliss). You will realize that you were always the abode of peace and bliss, even when you were identified only with your psychophysical personality.

The ego in a person develops as a result of this identification with the psychophysical personality as being who you are. Instead of realizing your true nature to be like the blue sky, expanding into infinity, you identify yourself with a small patch of blue sky created by clouds of mental delusion and ignorance.

Identified with that little patch of blue, when the mental clouds darken around you, (negative thoughts, dullness, depression, etc.) you feel gloomily. When the mental clouds are soft and fleecy (positive thoughts, elation, optimism, mind is agitated by many desires and expectation), you feel happy. When the mental clouds drift apart a little (release of tension due to agitation, contentment, harmony), you feel expansion and become peaceful. When the clouds contract again you feel worried, unsettled and miserable. The inner experience of those who are unenlightened is always conditioned by the mental clouds of ignorance and egoistic desires surrounding them, which are all of their own creation, based on wrong ways of looking at and thinking about the world. However, even then, you are really always one with the Self (blue sky), completely unaffected by the mental clouds, and always will be, deep down.

So it is the Self which sustains your psychophysical personality and is the ultimate reality behind it. This innermost Self within you is completely unaffected by any condition which affects the psychophysical personality of an individual. It feels no pain, sadness, or sorrow, but experiences these through the mind and senses of the personality. It remains always completely blissful and peaceful. It always exists in the awareness of its universal nature, but the mind and soul are as if ignorant of this deeper essence. This ignorance leads them to experience countless episodes of gain and loss, happiness and sorrow, success and failure, etc., in a never ending cycle of life, death and life again (reincarnation). However, there is a way to end the cycle, by learning the truth about one's innermost self, the Divine Self. So, the goal of true mystical spirituality is to identify more and more with your true nature, and less and less with your ego-personality. When you do this, you will be able to go beyond all the egoistic concepts, which you have tied to your existence as a psychophysical personality. This includes anger, hate, greed, envy, jealousy, fear, insecurity, and attachments. Instead you will bathe in the elixir of virtuous qualities such as compassion, universal love, understanding, peace, bliss, and these will lead to supreme fitness. You will truly "Know Thyself."

It is very important to understand that in reality, the soul within you is not affected by any happening in this world. It is only a witness. In Kemetic terms this is symbolized by the Neter (god), Amun. To understand this, think of yourself when you are dreaming. The *you,* you consider to be real is ever asleep on the bed, safe, peaceful, and calm. The dream *you* experiences all kind of situations, some very painful and some pleasurable, yet, the *you* asleep on the bed is not really experiencing any of these situations of pleasure or pain. But still, you feel that the dream character is the "real" you. Likewise, the real you, the Self, like that sleeping personality, is always resting on that bed of peace, bliss and absolute existence, remaining ever unaffected by the experiences of the psychophysical personality. If a lion is chasing you in your dream, though seemingly you have several choices of what to do such as running away, finding shelter to escape it, picking up a stick to fight with it, etc., there is in reality only one real choice which will take care of that problem for you, that is, to wake up. Likewise, the only way you will be able to deal with the problems in your life right now is to wake up from the dream of yourself being a limited psychophysical (ego) personality to realize your higher nature. Otherwise, trying to battle the forces of egoism afflicting you in life by reinforcing your existence as an ego-personality would be like deciding in your dream to turn yourself in to a lion in order to beat the lion chasing you. Even if you become a bigger lion and even kill the other one, you will still have suffered injury in the battle and in the end you have gained no real victory because another one can come out in the next moment. The only real solution is to wake up. Why go through all that pain and suffering when you could just wake up?

> "Salvation is the freeing of the soul from its bodily fetters; becoming a God through knowledge and wisdom; controlling the forces of the cosmos instead of being a slave to them; subduing the lower nature and **through awakening to the Higher Self**, ending the cycle of rebirth and dwelling with the Neters who direct and control the Great Plan."
>
> —Ancient Egyptian Proverb

So, your efforts to overcome negative sentiments within your personality or even being directed at you from another personality, which is nothing but egoism stemming from ignorance of one's true nature, should center around not attacking with more egoism, but realizing that none of the negativity of the world touches your deeper essence, the real you. When people experience hurt from others, they feel the need to see the other person suffer or to see them repent and apologize before forgiving them or to retaliate because they feel that they have personally been violated and hurt. Yet, this is not so. It is only their psychophysical personality which has been insulted or hurt. The real "them" is totally unaffected, resting on the bed of consciousness, absorbed in peace and bliss. The real you cannot be hurt. Therefore, why should you allow yourself to become more and more upset and angry over things that do not really affect the real you? This is the way in which mystical philosophy promotes health. Living by truth, you are able to remain calm even while upholding justice and standing up to those who have wronged you, not with malice or resentment, which are like poison for your own body, mind and soul, but with courage, detachment, strength and indomitable will.

"Something is added to you unlike to what thou see;
Something animates thy clay higher than all that is the object of thy senses.
Behold, what is it? Thy body remains still matter after it is fled;
therefore it is no part of it; It is immaterial."

—Ancient Egyptian Proverb

So your experience of being hurt only belongs to the unreal you, the dream you, the ego-personality, and as long as you identify with this lower aspect of who you are, you will be bound to all egoistic emotions (anger, hate, etc.). You will remain caught up in the web of strife and frustration which are the mainstay of most people's lives and not be able to experience the deeper aspect of who you are, the embodiment of peace and bliss. If you look at your own life, you will realize that all you have ever been really searching for in life through all your various actions is to be abidingly happy and peaceful. Yet, you have been searching for it in the realm of egoism where it does not exist as an abiding condition. If you really want to find true abiding peace and happiness, which remains unaffected by any condition or circumstance of life, there is only one way. You must wake up to the knowledge of your Higher Self. This process of waking up is the goal of the disciplines and practice of authentic spirituality and it requires good health in order to be successful.

The Kemetic concept of food for the mind and soul goes as far back as the Ancient Egyptian Pyramid Texts. The following ancient Egyptian selections come from the ***"Pyramid Texts of Unas"*** (you may substitute your name where *Unas* appears).

Unas pa neb sabut
Unas is the lord (mistress) of wisdom
au aart - f em apt -f
His Uraei are on his brow

Unas pa aper-a er aab khu - f
Unas is provided with power over his spirits

au Unas kha em ur pu
Unas rises (to heaven) like a mighty one

Unas pu neb hetep
Unas is the lord of the offering

Unas pa am heka - sen

Unas has eaten the words of power of the gods

Unas aam khu - sen
Unas has eaten the spirits of the gods

The text shows the initiate (Unas) "eating" the gods and goddesses, which represent *Medu Neter* (words of power), i.e. knowledge of God and Unas also eats their "Spirits." The spirits of the gods and goddesses are actually portions of the entirety of the Supreme Spirit. Therefore, eating the gods and goddesses means eating their power or cosmic force (energy), knowledge and wisdom and their essential nature. This essential nature is the nature of being. In other words, Unas, that is the initiate, has consumed the essential knowledge of Self which leads to Spiritual Enlightenment.

> "Whoever has eaten the knowledge of every God, their existence is for all eternity and everlasting in their spirit body; what they willeth they doeth."
>
> -Ancient Egyptian Proverb

The Body-Mind-Soul Relationship

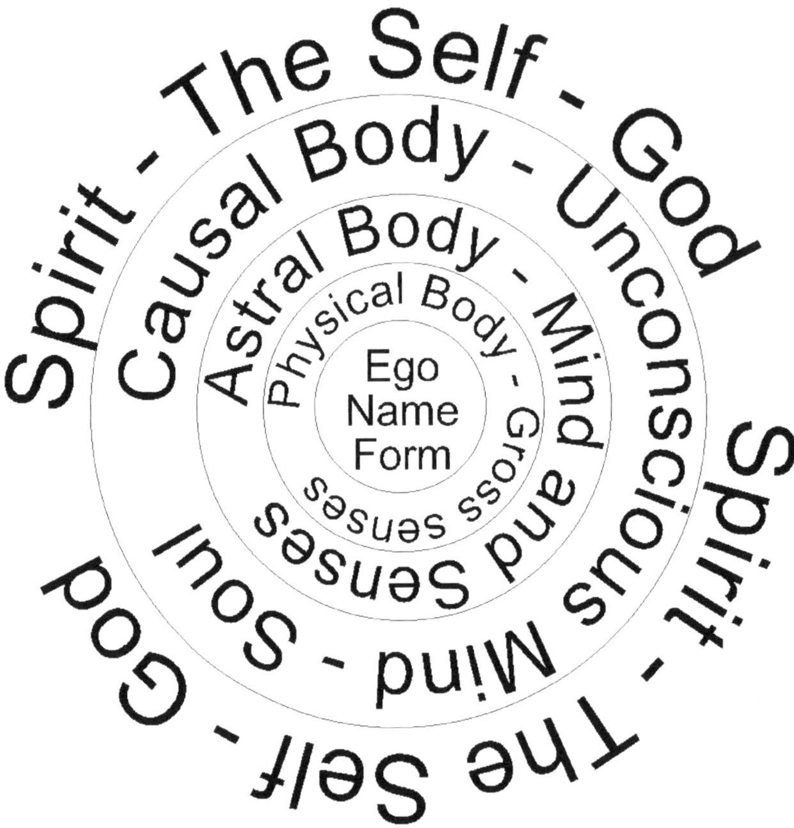

Figure 7: The Body-Mind-Soul-Spirit Connection

It is very important to understand that the soul is not a development of the body or mind and that the soul is not dependent upon the body for its existence. In fact, the body and the mind are developments of the soul, which it creates through the karmic desires of the unconscious and sustains through the Life Force. So the Spirit which is transcendental and unlimited, becomes conditioned, confined as it were, as a soul or individual focus of consciousness. This soul creates the Astral Body, and the Astral Body creates the Physical Body. A human being gains experiences through the ego (false aspect of the personality that develops as a result of the soul's identification with the mind and body as being who it is, rather than the transcendental Spirit), and its interactions with the world. When the teachings and disciplines of yogic mysticism are practiced, a human being is able to discover that there is more than the physical body and mind, that there is a larger world beyond the physical and mental planes. The more expansive a human being becomes in consciousness, the closer they are moving to the discovery of the Higher Self, the unlimited Spirit, God, and this is the glorious essential reality of every human being. In the diagram above, notice that there is no circle encompassing the Spirit. It encompasses all. Therefore, the Spirit (Universal or Cosmic Soul) is not in the body. Rather, the body is within the mind, the mind within the individual soul, and the individual soul is within the Spirit (Soul). It should be noted here that the mind (conscious, subconscious and unconscious) and the brain are not synonymous. The mind is in the Astral Body. Mental energy flows into the physical body through the nervous system (brain and spinal column) where it operates through the gross senses of the Physical Body. The Spirit is all-pervasive and transcendental, beyond time and space. The Soul, Mind and Body all exist within the realm of time and space and are therefore, limited and finite. Discovering this supreme teaching in life is referred to as Spiritual Enlightenment. It is the greatest human achievement.

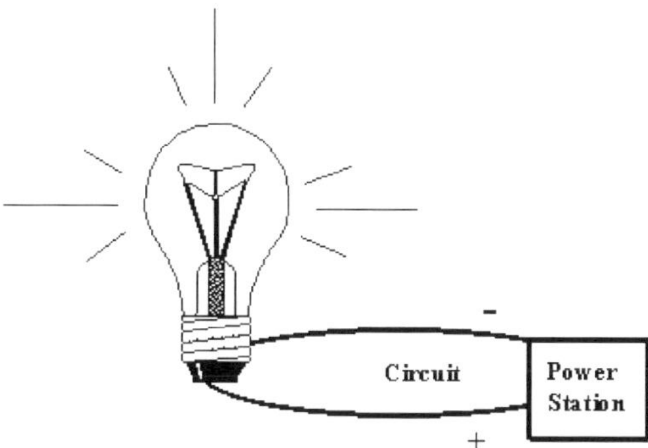

Above: The diagram of a household light bulb. It works by creating a "resistance" to the flow of electricity, which is generated by the power station. The power station sends energy in a circuit. One line is positively charged and the other is negatively charged. This flow of electricity in the lines is called the current. If the light bulb (appliance) was not there or if the lines were to cross and touch each other without passing through the appliance, there would be no resistance to the flow, thereby causing a "short circuit" in which the current would travel so fast that it would burn up the lines. If the resistance is too high (blown bulb), the flow would be restricted and the appliance would not function. Therefore, a particular balance of resistance must be maintained in order to effect the proper functioning of the appliance.

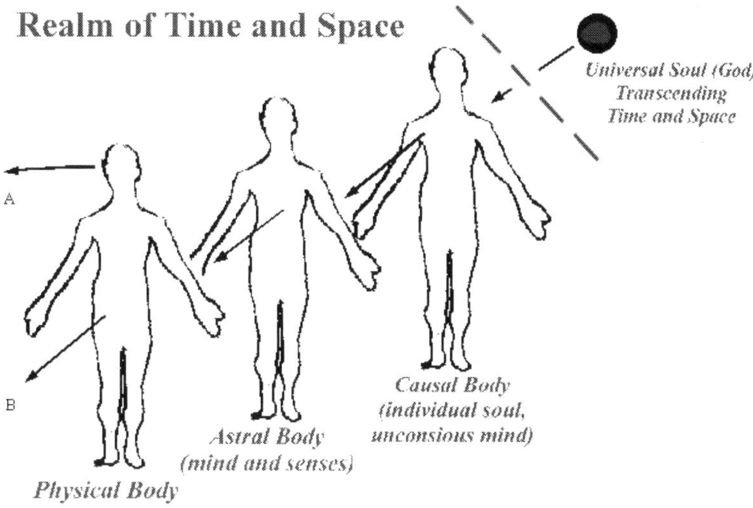

Figure 8: The Soul, Causal Body, Astral Body and Physical Body

The human body is much like an appliance in that it receives spiritual energy from the soul through the mind and transforms it into physical energy to perform physical work. Feelings of peace, contentment, harmony, equanimity, dispassion and understanding allow the proper flow of spiritual energy.

Feelings of anger, hate, fear and passionate desire cause blockages in the flow of spiritual energy through the parts of the spirit, mind and body, thereby causing illness. Also, depletion of energy occurs when the energy dissipates or flows out (open circuit) of the body due to mental attention on worldly objects (attachment), desire, worry, passion, sexual ejaculation, etc. These activities hasten the death of the individual because the energy is "used up" sooner. Therefore, one aim of concentration and meditation is to prevent the foolish loss of energy (closed circuit).

Reincarnation occurs when the soul decides to "switch off" its identification with a particular bulb (death), and then to send its light (Life Force) power to another bulb (body).

Far left: Ordinary flow of energy through the body is outward through the mental attention on the senses and mental desires (A) and sexual ejaculation (B). This mode of energy flow serves the purposes of gratification of the senses and procreation of the species, and therefore does not lead to higher spiritual attainments.

Sekhem: The Life Force Energy & The Mind-Body Connection

Figure 9: The body receives cosmic energy from the stars while the soul (hawk with the head of a person) looks on. (From an Ancient Egyptian relief.)

Plate 6: The initiate receiving Life Force (Sekhem) through the breath (touching of the noses) from the goddess Sekhmet (Sekhmit, Sekhmut, a form of the Ancient Egyptian goddess Hetheru), the divinity who presides over the Life Force. Sekhmet was also associated with Ancient Egyptian physicians. (From an Ancient Egyptian relief.)

Sekhem is the Kemetic word for the internal Life Force energy, also known as prana in East Indian Yoga and Chi or Ki in Chinese and Japanese mysticism respectively, which sustains the Physical Body. The Life Force energy comes into the body by means of the breath and the subtle energy channels in the Astral Body wherein are located seven energy centers which correspond to the central nervous system (brain and spinal cord) in the Physical Body. The Life Force energy is converted to usable energy (condensed and made less subtle) and transferred to the nerve ganglia that are associated with each energy center. From the nervous system, the energy is distributed to the endocrine system, and then to the various organs, muscles, tissues, etc.

Endocrine System, body system made up of all the endocrine, or ductless, glands that secrete chemical substances known as hormones directly into the bloodstream where they act to control body functions.

The endocrine system, together with the nervous system, controls and regulates all body functions; the endocrine system is occasionally considered the chemical control or the "liquid nervous system."[38]

Mettu of the Nerves (Nervous System) [39]

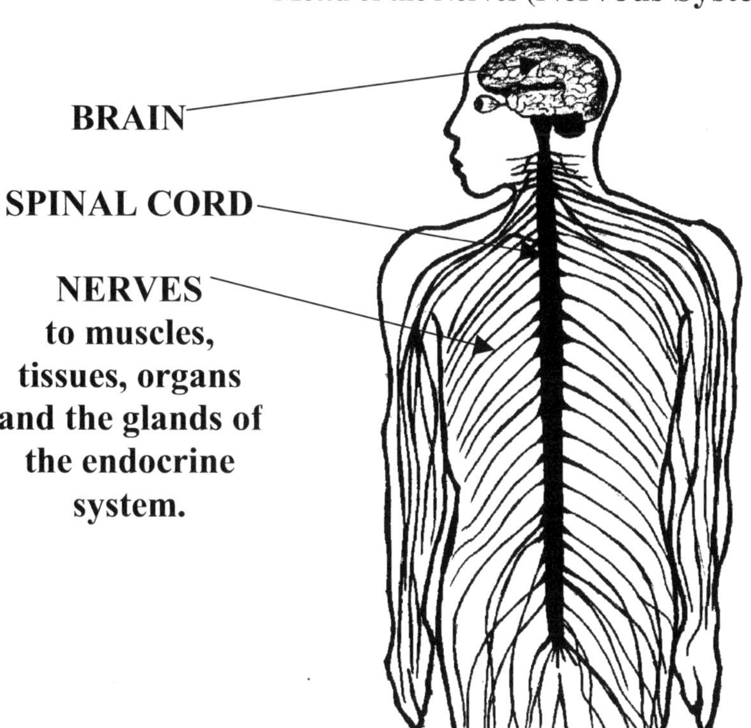

[38] Random House Encyclopedia

[39] Illustrations by Asar Oronde Reid

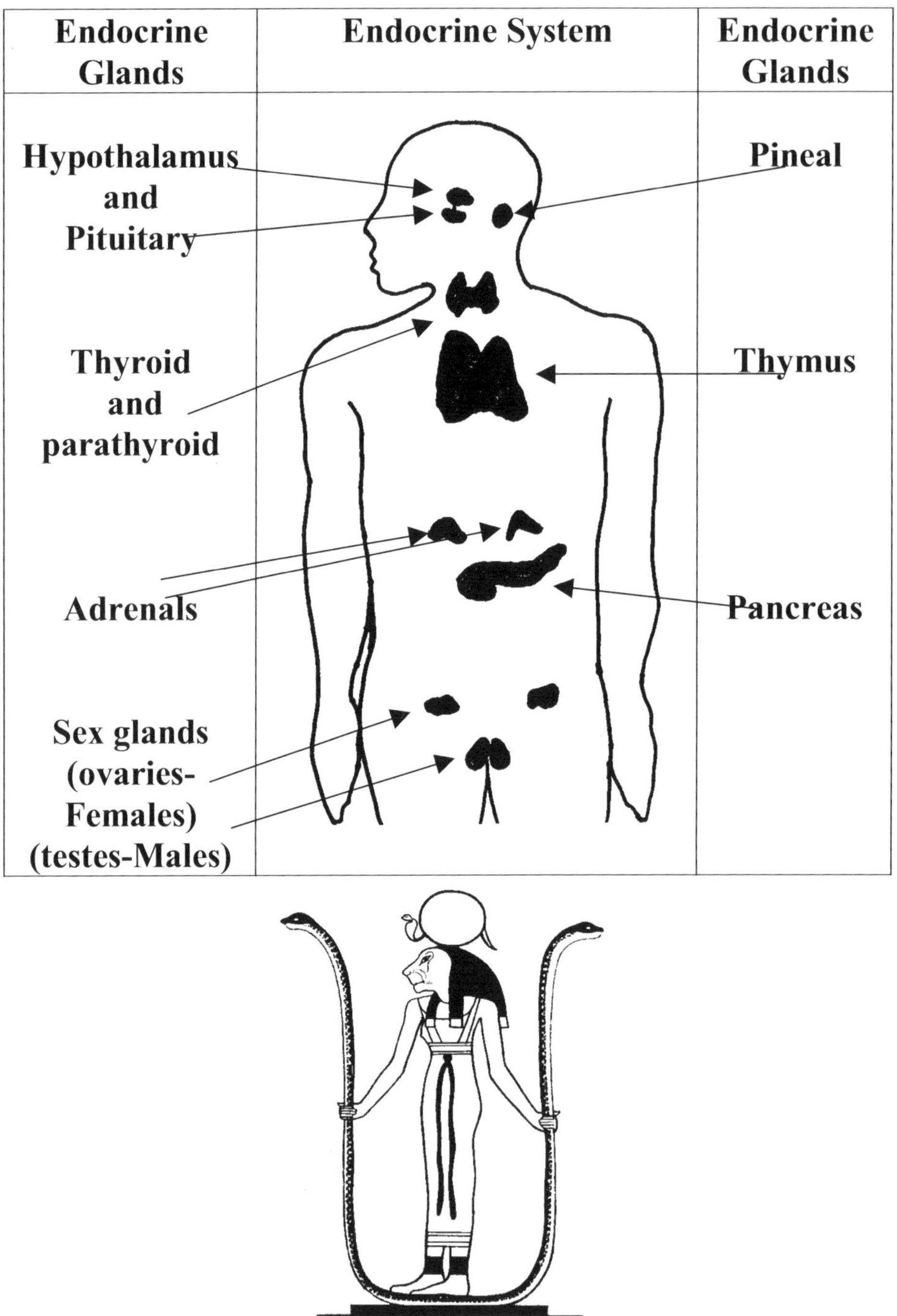

Figure 10: Ancient Egyptian Goddess Sekhmet, associated with Physicians, and Life Force, holds the serpents of the Caduceus.

Table 2: Mind-Body Connection: Energy Centers, States of Mind, the Nerve Centers and Glands

Astral Body – Mind and Subtle Senses **Physical Body and Gross Senses**

Energy Center and Location☥	Corresponding states of mind		Corresponding Nerve Ganglia	Corresponding Endocrine Gland
1. Perineum	Fear	→	Coccygeal Plexus	Adrenals
2. Genital	Sexuality Attachment	→	Sacral Plexus	Sex glands (ovaries/testes)
3. Navel/ Abdomen	Narcissism	→	Solar Plexus	Pancreas-gastrointestinal system
4. Heart/ Chest	Universal love	→	Cardiac/pulmonary plexus	Thymus
5. Neck/ Throat	Self-control	→	Cervical plexus/pharyngeal Plexus	Thyroid and parathyroid
6. Point between the eyebrows	Intuitive knowledge	→	Carotid Plexus	Pineal
7. Crown of the head	Transcendence-bliss	→	Central Nervous System	Pituitary & Hypothalamus

☥ **Although the location is described in relation to the physical spine, the energy centers are not located in the Physical Body. They are located in the Astral Body.**

When a human being is living a virtuous life and progressing on the spiritual path, the energy centers and the corresponding glands, organs and consequently the mettu, naturally remain purified, and the individual experiences above average health, vitality, peace, harmony, lucidity, inspiration and ultimately, spiritual enlightenment. For more details on the Life Force, the energy centers and the mystical wisdom of the Life Force, see the book *The Serpent Power,* by Muata Ashby.

The energy centers (chakras) in the Astral Body, wherein the Life Force energy is transformed from subtle to gross energy for use by the body are seven in number and are depicted as follows.

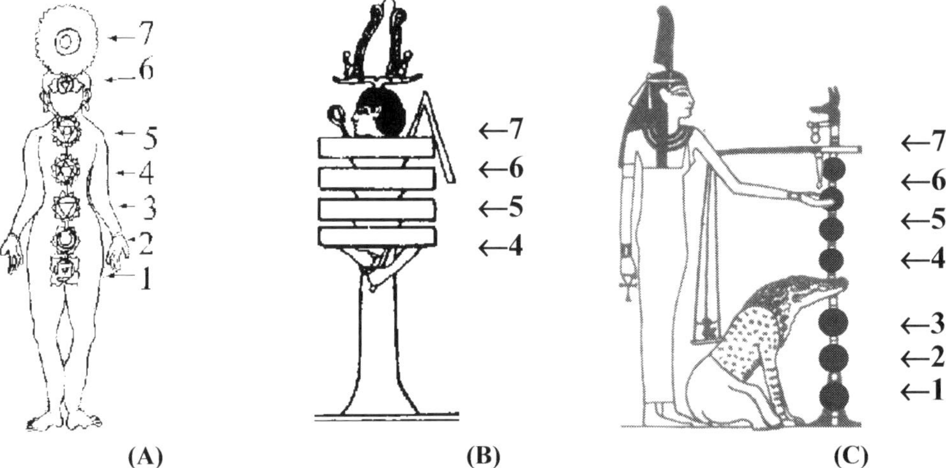

Figure 11: Left (A), the East Indian rendition of the Life Force energy centers (chakras) in the subtle spine of the individual.
Figure 12: Center (B), Ancient Egyptian rendition of the Life Force energy centers in the subtle spine of the individual. The god Asar displays the four upper centers as centers of higher consciousness.
Figure 13: The figure at right (C) shows the scales of Maat displaying the seven spheres or energy centers.

Figure (C), above, includes the Ammit demon (composite beast combining one third hippopotamus, one third lion and one third crocodile), symbolic devourer of unrighteous souls, biting between the 3rd & 4th sphere (energy center-chakra). This means that those who have not attained a consciousness level higher than the 3rd center will continue to suffer and reincarnate. The spheres represent levels of spiritual consciousness from the most ignorant (1) to the most enlightened (7). The lower three spheres are related to worldly consciousness and the upper four are related to spiritual consciousness and enlightenment, therefore, the lower must be sublimated into the higher levels. This is the project of spiritual evolution. Those who have attained higher rungs (3rd through the 7th) will move on and attain enlightenment.

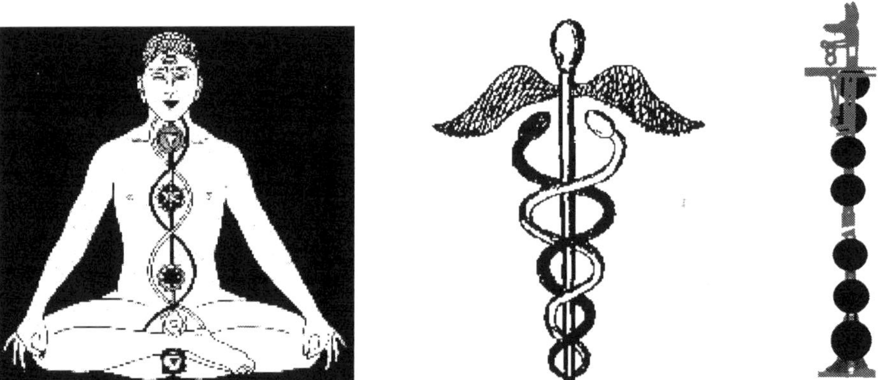

Figure 14: Left-An East Indian depiction of the Chakras with the Sushumna (central) and Ida and Pingala (intertwining conduits).
Figure 15: Center- The Kemetic Caduceus with the central Shaft (Asar), and the intertwining serpents (Uadjit and Nekhebit, also known as Aset and Nebethet)
Figure 16: Right- The Kemetic Energy Consciousness Centers (Spheres-Chakras)

The Kemetic system of the energy spheres, and of the caduceus with its central shaft symbolizing the subtle spine, and the two intertwining serpents symbolizing the dual energies into which the central shaft differentiates, concurs in every detail with the later developments in East Indian Mysticism encompassed

by the discipline known as Kundalini Yoga with its system of Chakras and the three main energy channels, Sushumna (central) and Ida and Pingala (intertwining conduits).
Thus, the flow of the Life Force energy is from most subtle and powerful at the top to the least subtle (at the bottom):

Universal Spirit
↓
Life Force Energy
↓
Individual soul
↓
The Energy Centers of the Astral Body of each human being-mind.
↓
The Nervous System
↓
The Endocrine System
↓
The organs and muscles, etc.

If there is a disturbance in the mind (Astral Body), the distribution of Life Force energy to the associated energy center will be disrupted and imbalances may occur that could lead to diseases in the areas wherein the Life Force is deficient or overabundant. This is the basis of the mind-body connection spoken about so much in current new age and alternative healing discussions. For example, anger (mental disturbance) effecting the 3rd energy center will result in the liver withholding or secreting too much bile, and the stomach secreting too much acid or not enough, resulting in physical illness. In order for the Life Force to be in harmony and function properly, the mind needs to be in harmony, peace and ease instead of dis-ease. Also evident from the above flow chart is that even higher than affecting disease at the mental level (Astral Body) is affecting it at the soul level. This is most effectively done through the practice of meditation. Thus, true freedom from stress can only come when there is a proper lifestyle, which provides for the needs of the body, mind and soul. Therefore, the practices of cleansing the mind from negative thought, meditation, and right actions are extremely important in promoting health, which is dependent to a great extent on the subtle aspects of the personality (mind and soul).

Plate 7: Left-The Ancient Egyptian God, Ra, the sun symbol of the Supreme Being, transferring energy to the initiate through lotus rays.

Figure 17: The Ancient Egyptian God, Aten (sundisk), imparts life force to the king and his family through the sunrays whose ends have hands holding the ankh (symbol of life).

DNA AND THE SPIRIT

DNA is an abbreviation for "Deoxyribonucleic acid." It is a complex giant molecule that contains the information needed for every cell of a living creature to create its physical features (hair, skin, bones, eyes, legs, etc., as well as their texture, coloration, their efficient functioning, etc.). All of this is contained in a chemically coded form. The Life Force of the soul or spirit engenders the impetus in the DNA to function. This in turn leads to the creation of the physical aspect of all living beings (human beings, animals, insects, microorganisms, etc.).

The DNA is what determines if two living beings are compatible with each other for the purpose of mating and producing offspring. If they are not compatible, then they are considered to be different species. All human beings are compatible with each other, therefore, they are members of a single species, i.e. one human race.

Therefore, DNA is an instrument of the Spirit, which it uses to create the body and thereby avail itself of physical existence and experiences. According to mystical philosophy, the soul chooses the particular world, country, family and time in history in which to incarnate in order to have the kind of experiences it needs for its spiritual evolution. This is all expressed in the physical plane through the miracle of DNA.

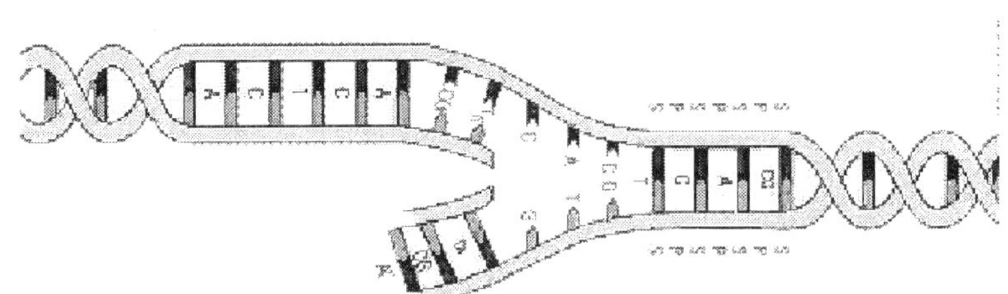

Plate 8: Example of a section of a DNA strand.

THE BASIC CONCEPT OF KEMETIC HEALTH FOR THE BODY

When Herodotus visited Ancient Egypt, he was so impressed with the medical system that he remarked: "physicians are all over the place."[40] The theory of Kemetic health is based on the understanding that the intestinal tract is the place wherein nourishment enters and waste passes through the physical body. If the process of nourishment is blocked, interrupted or corrupted, a putrefying process will take place in which the items consumed become poisons that can spread disease to any part of the body. Therefore, the Ancient Egyptian doctors placed prime importance on dietetics (the study of nutrition as it relates to health, also called sitology), and on colonic hygiene using enemas to insure the cleanliness, and therefore efficiency of the colon as a means to maintain proper health. This basic regimen of diet and colon care was thought to keep the colon free from the dreaded *Ukhedu*, a term which will be explained in detail later. Therefore, in order to heal the body it is necessary to cleanse the body from the negative foods consumed previously which have led to the present condition, and also institute the proper diet to maintain good health. This teaching of dietetics was adopted by the Greek doctor, Hippocrates, and became the hallmark of his medical practice that brought him much fame.

The Profession of Medicine in Ancient Egypt

Plate 9: (left) Imhotep- Bronze, late period sculpture now in the Louvre Museum, Paris.

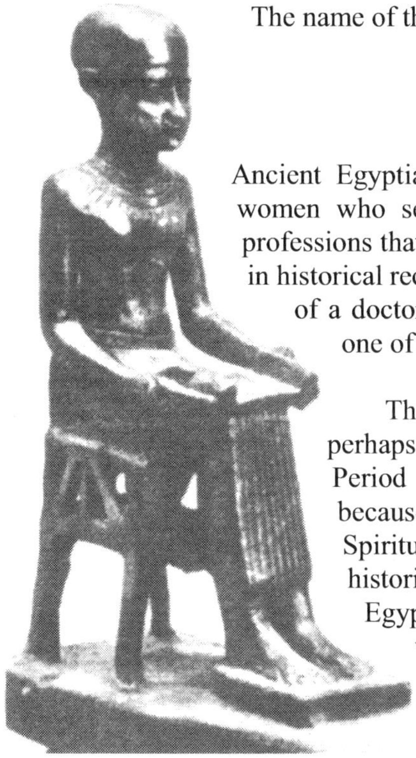

The name of the doctor in Ancient Egypt was *swn* or *swnu,* written:

Ancient Egyptian history provides us with the descriptions of the first men and women who served as medical doctors, some of whom were so good at their professions that they became legendary in their own time. The earliest female doctor in historical record was named *Mer-swnut – Peseshet.* Her position was not only that of a doctor, but she was a Chief Physician (head supervising doctor). Perhaps one of the most famous doctors in Kemetic history was Imhotep.

The name "Imhotep" means "One who comes in peace." Imhotep was perhaps the greatest Sage of Ancient Egypt, who lived in the Old Kingdom Period (5,000-2,500 B.C.E.). He was a legendary figure in his own time because he was a master healer (medical doctor), royal architect, scribe, and Spiritual Philosopher. His writings have not been discovered yet, but some historical records survive that show he was revered by both Ancient Egyptians and foreigners alike. He was deified (canonized). In the time when Hippocrates and other ancient Greeks went to study medial science in Ancient Egypt, they revered and worshiped Imhotep under the Greek name Aesculapius, as the god of medical science and healing. It must be understood that the string of movies from Hollywood called "the mummy" wherein Sage Imhotep is depicted as an evil mummy are nothing but gross misrepresentations of the truth which history records.

[40] Herodotus II/84 LB I 369

Doctor and Doctoress

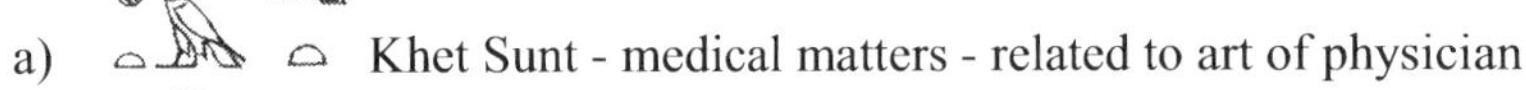

a) Khet Sunt - medical matters - related to art of physician

b) Sunt - art of physician

c) Sunu – doctor

d) Sunu ur - chief physician

e) Sunuu- doctors - physicians plural

f) Mer Peshet Sunut - overseer (Mer) female doctor Pshet

THE DIGESTIVE SYSTEM

FOOD HIEROGLYPHS

In order to have a better understanding of the Kemetic concept of food, it is necessary to enter into a brief study of the food related hieroglyphic text. Doing so will reveal the deeper meaning of the words and provide insight into the philosophy of food in Ancient Africa.

The word for meal is Asht – the day Asht and the evening Asht were very important in ancient times.

MEAL

a) Asht – meal

b) Ashtf duat - morning meal

c) Ashtf khu - evening meal

The following words provide an idea of what can be eaten at the meals. We will begin by examining the words for "sustenance," and then the varied kinds of foods that are possible.

FOOD - SUSTENANCE

a) Kau - food sustenance

b) derpu – sustenance

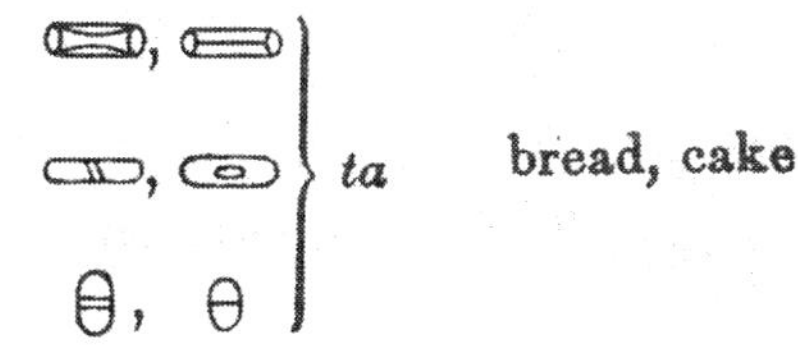

c)

d) khatnankh - staff of life - foodstuff from wood –vegetation

VEGEABLES

a) Sm - vegetables-farm fields - grasses-herbs-crops

GRAIN

a) Afau - food – bread

FLESH FOOD

a) Amait - flesh food

b) Amm - flesh food

COOKED FOOD

a) pfsit - cooked food

b) pfsu - baked cakes

Food or "that which sustains," is represented by the hieroglyph for bread which comes from grain and ultimately plants. Therefore, we are to understand that the main form of food comes from plants although flesh foods, (Amait), from animals were recognized. The ordinary Kemetic populace did consume some flesh foods, mostly poultry,[41] and some fish. However, flesh foods

[41] Note: This was domesticated poultry and wild game....plus, today, poultry is fed grain and not their natural "wild" diet, plus they are subjected to stressful conditions in which they live. Wild game is much leaner also than domestically raised animals.

were shunned by the Ancient Egyptian doctors who were also priests and priestesses and anyone coming to them for seeking health counseling was counseled to enter into rigorous purifications (detoxifications) and to then adopt a proper "living foods" (plants and fruits) diet in order to promote health. Notice that the symbol "ha", , meaning "flesh" appears in the words , "Amm" and "Amait" (flesh food) and also appears in the word , "Mtua" – poison. Thus it is notable that the detrimental effects of flesh meat are incorporated into the spelling of the word for poison. The unmistakable and obvious implication is that while flesh is a possible item that can be ingested, it is not life-promoting, and consequently not a desirable form of food.

The word for gluttony also provides some deep insights into the habit of overeating and its effects on the body. Gluttony was seen as especially unrighteous behavior. The hieroglyphic texts reveal that gluttony was likened to something not only negative or detrimental, but also in fact evil and deadly.

Gluttony

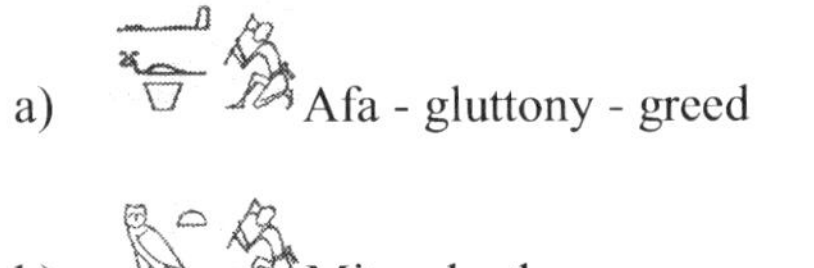

a) Afa - gluttony - greed

b) Mit – death

c) khemi - enemy-foe

d) Mitnf djsf – suicide

Death

a) Mit – death

b) khemi - enemy-foe

c) Mitnf djsf – suicide

d) Mtua – poison

Notice the glyph, (Mit – death), a man who is hitting his own head with an ax. It appears in all of the words related to the concept of gluttony as well as those related to death. The unmistakable implication is that gluttony is an unrighteous practice that leads to the ruin of an individual. Gluttony (overeating) leads to indigestion and ill health which ultimately leads to early death. Overeating is one of the main causes of obesity, and obesity leads to a myriad of health problems including arteriosclerosis, diabetes, strokes, heart disease, cancer, etc. The scriptures speak out against greed of all kinds is spoken, be it for food, wealth, power, etc. All of these forms of gluttony-greed cause indigestion in the physical body or the mental body or the soul body, and should be avoided.

Mental Anguish Food

a) amhat - eat one's own heart - remorse – repent- distraught

Eating one's own heart refers to the practice of metal torment and suffering engendered and sustained by one's own actions which cause one to look down on oneself, with anger, shame or remorse. As a form of self-punishment, one hurts oneself through recrimination (blame, reproach). There is an injunction of Maat that speaks directly to this issue.

(14) "I have not eaten my heart" (overcome with anguish and distraught). Variant: Committed perjury.

Amhat is a form of practice not enjoined in the scriptures. Remorse comes when one has acted in ways that are in contradiction with one's own higher moral code, out of ignorance or lack of will to resist temptation. It is explained that the error one has committed should be understood and corrected. There is little to be served by self-torture and recrimination once there has been true contrition and repentance. It is better to fix the error and make amends if possible, and move on with life. Further, if the higher moral code (Maat) is better understood and if life is led in a virtuous manner, the errors that lead to remorse will be reduced or eradicated. Remorse is a kind of detrimental mental food that debilitates the mind and the will of the soul. Therefore it should be avoided by adopting a virtuous way of life along with forgiveness and understanding of one's own imperfections as well as those of others.

Divine Food

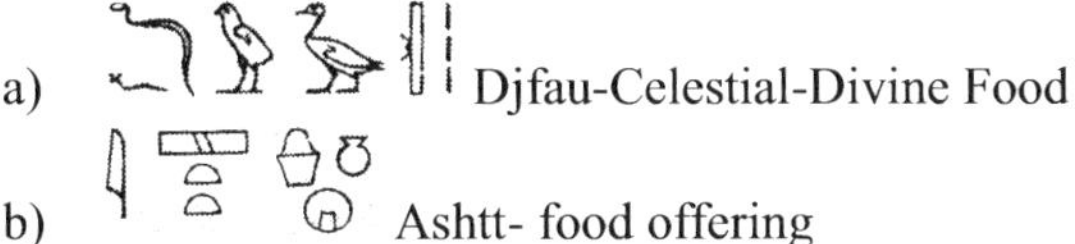

a) Djfau-Celestial-Divine Food

b) Ashtt- food offering

There are two kinds of food especially mentioned in the scriptures as being of high order. The first kind is the spiritual offering. This offering is made at the altar of the particular divinity being worshipped. In ancient times the offerings brought by people were taken (by the priests and priestesses) into the secret chambers where the Divine image was kept, and there it was placed before the divinity. The Divinity was then allowed to "take Its share," and later the priests and priestesses would come to remove the offerings and take their "share." The idea is that the Divine image lives off of the subtle essence and devotional energies with which the offerings are imbued and partakes in these, in effect taking a portion of the subtle essence of the offering, leaving the grosser aspect to nourish the physical bodies of the priests and priestesses. Celestial food is the food of the gods and goddesses in the astral plane. It is a kind of divine nectar upon which the soul (ba) and spirit (akhu) are sustained.

What is Digestion and The Digestive System?

The American Heritage Dictionary defines digestion as follows:

> **di·gest,** *v.* **di·gest·ed, di·gest·ing, di·gests.** *--tr.* **1.** *Physiology.* To convert (food) into simpler chemical compounds that can be absorbed and assimilated by the body, as by chemical and muscular action in the alimentary canal. **2.** To absorb or assimilate mentally.

The body makes use of certain organs to take in solid nourishment, break it down and extract needed nutrients in order to survive. This is the function of the gastrointestinal system, which is composed of the mouth, the esophagus, the stomach, the intestines and the rectum. If these organs are treated properly, and the correct foods ingested, they will function normally. This means that the food will be processed and the waste excreted, and the human being will enjoy pristine health and vitality. However, if the treatment of these organs is not correct, then an imbalance will develop that may affect the entire body. Thus, both in ancient and modern times, this area of the body is seen as the source of physical health, as well as disease.

Gastrointestinal body parts and other selected Anatomy Hieroglyphs

The Ancient Egyptians had described the anatomy of the body in the early period of the culture. Below are the hieroglyphic symbols which correspond to the gastrointestinal system. A close examination of them yields important ideas in reference to the concepts behind the understanding of the process of digestion.

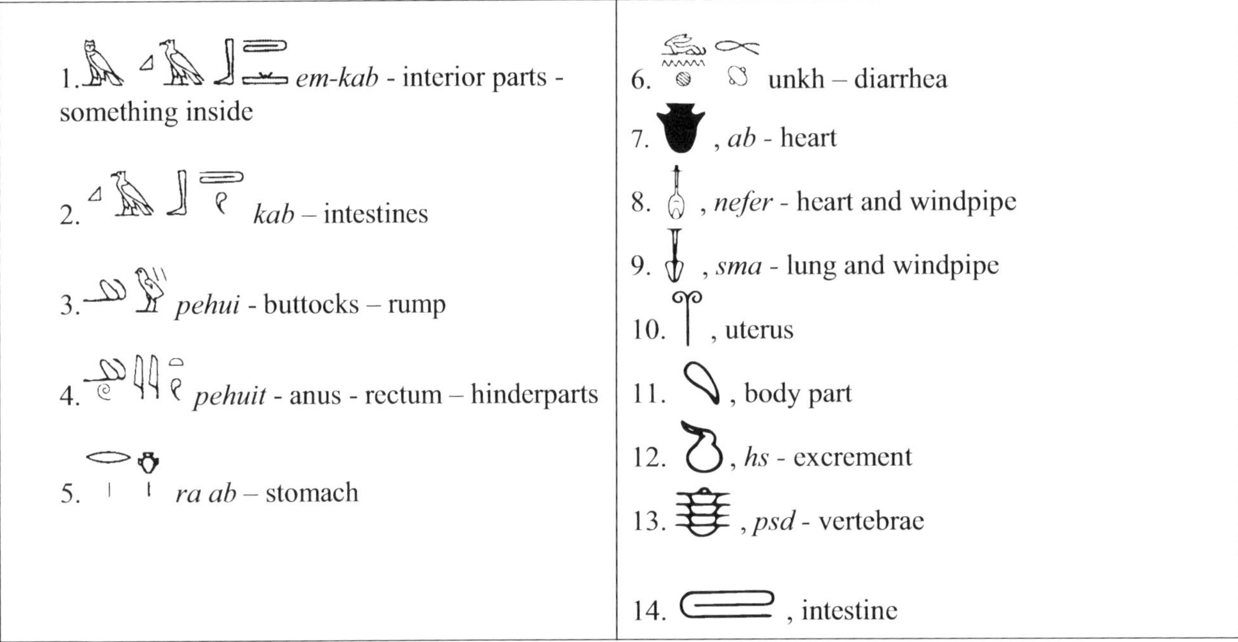

1. *em-kab* - interior parts - something inside	6. unkh – diarrhea
	7. , *ab* - heart
2. *kab* – intestines	8. , *nefer* - heart and windpipe
	9. , *sma* - lung and windpipe
3. *pehui* - buttocks – rump	10. , uterus
4. *pehuit* - anus - rectum – hinderparts	11. , body part
5. *ra ab* – stomach	12. , *hs* - excrement
	13. , *psd* - vertebrae
	14. , intestine

Notice that the word for stomach, #5, *ra-ab,* makes use of the symbol of the heart (#7, ab). This association points to the Kemetic understanding that the stomach is the heart of the digestive system, the place where the digestion of food begins in earnest. Also notice that the symbol for excrement, #12, *hs,* does not make use of the symbol for putrefaction, , in this particular case (more details on this sign will be given later in the following section). This points to the idea that there is normal excrement, and there is putrefied, pus-filled excrement due to disease, as expressed in symbol #6. It uses the pus symbol, , to denote the diseased excrement, i.e. diarrhea. The symbol, , used in #6 relates to a binding, something bound like a book that can be loosened or unbound. Thus, the Kemetic idea is given that diarrhea is a form of negative (diseased) excrement wherein there is loss of control (loss of binding) of the bowels.

What is it that causes the disease in the digestive system and what are the consequences? Also, what can be done to relieve the problem and restore health? There are two main texts on medical science from Ancient Egypt, which have been discovered. These are the **Smith Papyrus** (2600 B.C.E) and the **Ebers Papyrus** (1500 B.C.E.).

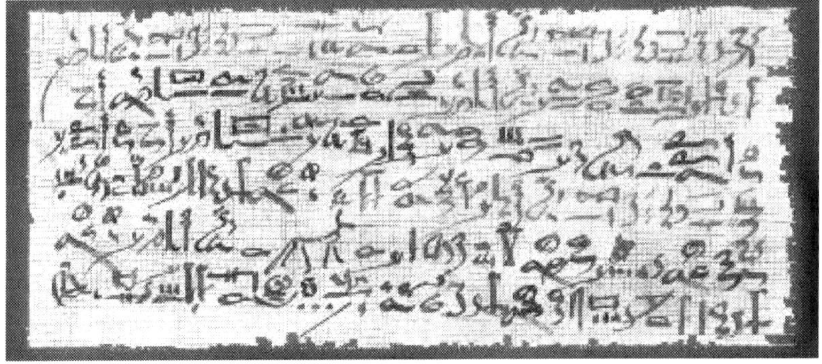

Plate 10: Section from the Smith Papyrus

Plate 11: Section from the Ebers Papyrus

Based on Ancient Egyptian teachings on health, the cause of all diseases is a disease process originating in the intestines. This disease process, Ukhedu, arises due to the following reasons:

"The source of illness is the food you ingest; to purge the dreadful UKHEDU which lurks in your bowels,
for three consecutive days each month purge yourself with a cattle horn
its sharp end clipped off so as to create a small opening (for water to run through)."
-Ancient Egyptian Teaching on Health

The Mettu of Digestion (Digestive System)[42]

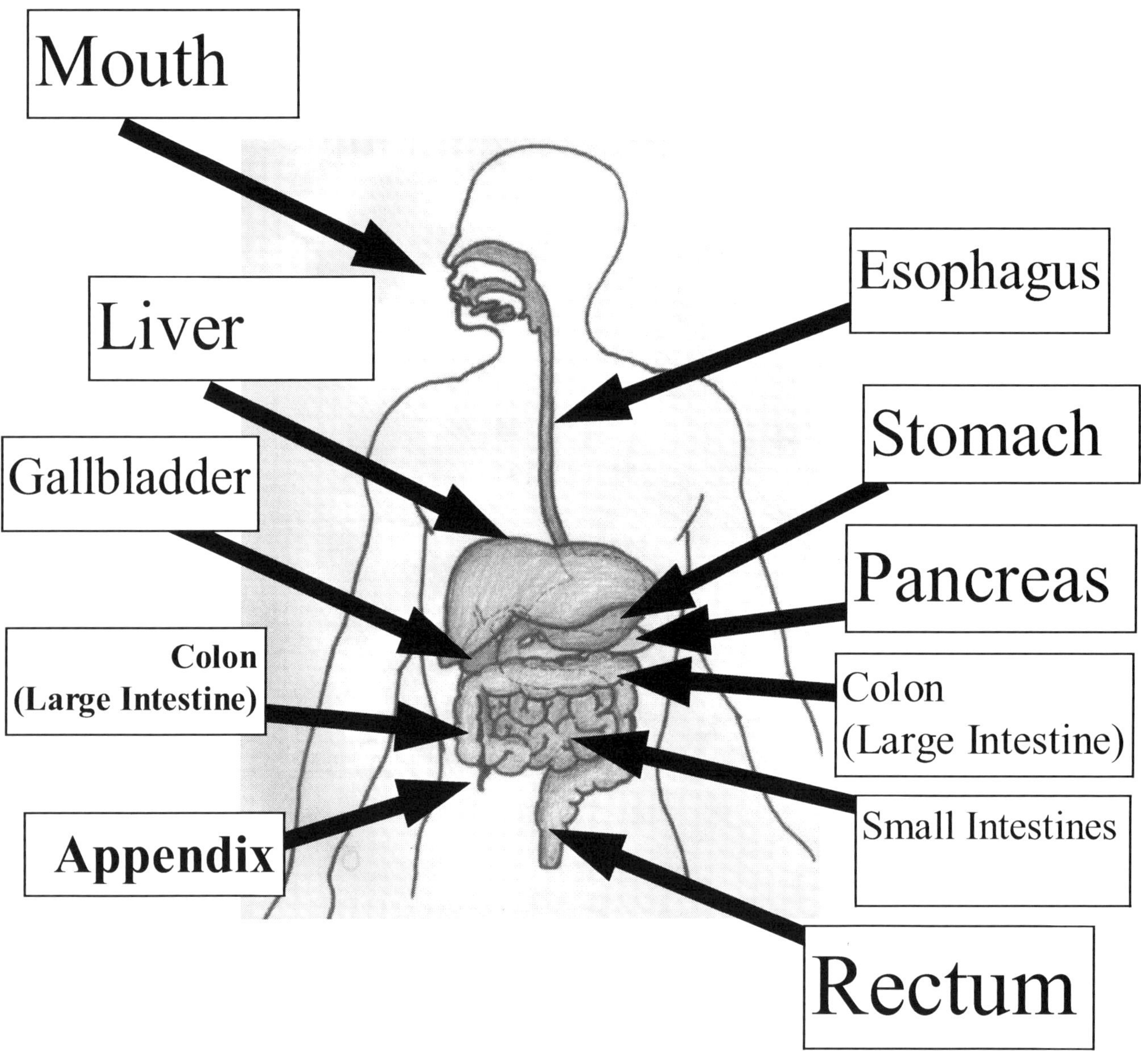

[42] Illustration by Asar Oronde Reid

Ukhedu and The channels of the Colon

Kemetic medical theory holds that there are channels which lead from the intestines, and through these, nourishment reaches all areas of the body. These same channels can also be conductors of Ukhedu and must therefore be kept free of unwholesome matter. Otherwise, if a disease process begins and is not corrected, it may expand beyond the colon and enter into the vascular systems, thereby contaminating other areas of the body, and consequently cause disease.

> **vas·cu·lar** *adj. Biology.* Of, characterized by, or containing vessels that carry or circulate fluids, such as blood, lymph, or sap through the body of an animal or a plant.[43]

The proof that the Ancient Egyptian doctors understood the existence of the circulatory system comes from the Ebers Papyrus (1500 B.C.E.).

The following statement comes from the Ebers Papyrus.

> "The beginning of the doctor's care; the knowledge of the working and nature of the heart. It contains vessels which go to all the members.
> Those points which the physician tests with his fingers whether on the head, the nape of the neck, the hands, the heart itself, the arms, the legs and any other place, all reveal something of the heart, for its vessels go to all parts of the body. This is why it speaks in the vessels of each member."

The Ancient Egyptian word "***mettu***" means "channel," "conduit" , and using the sign of the male penis, , in this case refers to "tube," "pipe" or "conduit," describing the nature of the vessels. The determinative sign, means "body part." Thus, the mettu is referring to a complex of channels, which are interconnected and extend to every part of the body.

Kemetic Healing injunction to be uttered by the healer:

May this person's *mettu* flourish...
May this person's *mettu* be sound...
May this person's *mettu* be excellent...
May this person's *mettu* be comfortable...

Thus, the concept of the *mettu*, which is affected by the presence or absence of Ukhedu, is related to the ideas of high vitality, ease as opposed to dis-ease, expansion as opposed to contraction and free-flow as opposed to stagnation and constriction.

The mettu are all over the body. They carry air, blood, tears, urine, feces, etc. They have "mouths" as it were, that is, they take in these materials (nutrients or toxins) and expel them (as excrement). They can also take in medicines. In this sense, medicines are to be understood as non-synthesized substances, which aid the body's efforts to come back to a balance of health. Medicines, according to the ancient tradition, should not be harmful man-made chemicals, which cannot be digested by the body, and thus become lodged in the tissues of the body, thereby becoming Ukhedu in the body. In modern times, that which the

[43] American Heritage Dictionary

Ancient Egyptian physicians called "Mettu," the channels that extend to every part of the body, are now referred to as the "vascular system."

Conclusion: There Is Only One Disease

Therefore, diseases, being caused by one problem, malnutrition (see definition below), are in reality all interrelated. Therefore, the particular disease process that develops is based on the particular area or organ of the body which was affected by the malnutrition.

There is no other magic bullet to combat disease except proper diet and internal cleansing. In this sense, the best "chemotherapy" is that discipline which utilizes diet and fasting, because these act on every cell of the body and produce no negative side effects which can damage other parts of the body. This is why the modern medical establishment will never succeed in finding medicines (drugs) that solve one problem, but do not create imbalances elsewhere. Further, the misguided notion that one can live a life of excesses and then seek relief through drugs, surgeries and alternative therapies must be rejected. The now recognized inability of modern medicine to cope with disease in general and the declining health of society as a whole support this point. Medicines mask symptoms and hide the disease processes which continue deeper in the body until they reach a lethal level. This disease process is then referred to by modern medical practitioners by various names, i.e. cancer, diabetes, rheumatism, impotence, high blood pressure, etc. Therefore, the natural health practitioner should strive to stay away from synthesized medicines and promote a condition wherein the body is allowed to produce its own natural chemicals, in conjunction with the chemicals contained in natural foods, to bring the body back into harmony and thereby eradicate disease.

For the purposes of the treatise, based on the Kemetic teachings, the term "malnutrition" may be defined as follows:

> *Malnutrition is the ingestion of wrong foods and or food consumption in an improper manner, which leads to indigestion, which in turn leads to the deficient nourishment of the organs and cells of the body, constituting their malnourishment and loss of strength to resist diseases (immunity) based on the type of physiological deficiencies caused by the form of the malnutrition.*

Thus, the normal processing of the fecal matter in the bowels is not Ukhedu. The putrefaction of material due to constipation, etc., caused by the ingestion of wrong foods and the subsequent disease process which develops, constitutes the Ukhedu. The Kemetic Diet Wisdom teaches that ALL disease process is understood as the deteriorated condition that the body has come to due to consuming foods that are toxic to the body. Toxins cause the body to become acidic. Therefore, Ukhedu may be thought of as a condition of "Acidosis" in the body as opposed to the natural healthy condition, "Alkaline." Acidity (toxicity) corrodes and breaks down the mettu, and the organs of the body, promoting a weakened immune system and disease. The restoration of the alkaline condition of the body, through a proper diet promotes healing and prevention of disease since the body's natural immune system is not being compromised or damaged.

THE CAUSE OF DISEASE AND ITS CURE

Table 3: The Cause of Disease

- Not experiencing the bliss of the Higher Self (no or minimal progress in spiritual evolution).
- Not living in harmony with nature
- Not thinking pure thoughts
- Not breathing clean air
- Not breathing properly
- Not enough rest and relaxation (freedom from stress)
- Eating wrong foods
- Overeating

It must be understood that bacteria and viruses are constantly in our midst. In fact you are breathing them in and out right now, and also, they are living in your skin, guts and tissues of your body, right now! This being so, why aren't you "catching" some kind of disease all the time? Why aren't people physically ill from these sources from birth to death?

The teaching is that since the cause of all diseases is the same (accumulation of Ukhedu) and since all diseases are related to the whole body, and not just the part(s) that seems to be affected, then it follows that it is not possible to create medicines to cure particular illnesses. Rather, it is necessary to get at the cause of disease and prevent it or eradicate it if a disease is already present. Further, the extensive amount of energy spent in naming diseases is in reality an exercise in segmentation of the human organism, something which is possible in theory, but not in practice and therefore, the search for specific drugs to cure certain ailments is a misguided approach to health care and health prevention because it creates the illusion that science can resolve the damage caused by wrong living. Only living by the correct rules, set by nature, will promote authentic health.

The idea that disease is caused by bacteria or viruses has been refuted by several experiments in which healthy people, who have purified themselves through the Ukhedu preventing lifestyle, have placed themselves in conditions wherein they have been exposed to supposedly contagious diseases such as malaria, cholera, the flu, etc., and have emerged unharmed. Why is it that certain people are affected by diseases and not others. In a recent airline flight, 50% of the people developed tuberculosis from being around a single sick passenger, but the other half did not. The natural health teachings and the Ukhedu concept lead to the conclusion that disease occurs when the immune system of the body is weakened. In other words, natural (non-synthesized) bacteria and viruses, which are always in the environment, take over and destroy the body because the natural processes of the body which normally keep such agents in check, coexisting with them in a natural way, loses its ability to maintain the internal balance. This means that the normal functioning of the body's ability to get rid of waste (stale air, urine and excrement) and maintain its natural level of vitality and regenerative power, as expressed in the body's destruction and creation of its own cells and the natural process of destroying foreign agents such as harmful bacteria, is impaired. Keep in mind that the practices of Kemetic health do not preclude the necessity for common sense. One should not seek to expose oneself to adverse conditions of disease to prove a point. The examples are given here to promote understanding, and not as instruction to expose oneself to disease needlessly.

Therefore, bacteria and viruses, while they may be involved in the disease process, are not the causes of disease. Thus, it is inaccurate to say that someone has "caught a cold." Stated more accurately, *the immune system of that person is so debilitated, due to toxicity, that they are experiencing a physiological imbalance which is commonly referred to as a "cold."* In other words, the body has accumulated Ukhedu and since the person is not doing anything to get rid of it (fasting, cleansing, proper diet, etc.,) the body orchestrates its own cleansing and healing process commonly known as a cold or flu. This cleansing and healing crisis aims to force the person to rest the body, to temporarily stop their food intake (a forced fast, although most people only decrease their food intake rather than completely stop it), and to facilitate the removal of Ukhedu in the form of mucus (cold).

In order to restore health, the immune system must be allowed to help the process of purification of the body. This is of course considering that the sick person will also be free from the maladies of modern culture, i.e. pollution, stress, food irradiation (from household microwave ovens or from mass produced processed food companies), radiation from powerlines, television, etc., and geographic locations with inclement weather. Natural herbs, used as antibiotics, vitamins, etc., and fasting with or without emetics or laxatives may be used to help the unburden the body and promote the flow of excrement, and with it the Ukhedu, but in reality it is the body itself which brings itself back to a state of health when it is allowed to repair the damage caused by the wrong practices which led to the original imbalance. So in reality, the healing process is an endeavor of helping the body to heal itself. Also, the need for deodorants (body odor results from excretions of toxins due to ingesting foods the putrefy and other posisons), antiseptics, germicides, disinfectants, antitoxins, sterilizing and immunizing agents is reduced when the proper hygiene is maintained and proper food for body, mind and soul is consumed. In any case, it must be understood that the myriad of surgical techniques, "cutting edge" treatments and so called "breakthroughs" that are developed by the medical establishment to cope with the thousands of diseases that have been named, are in reality unnecessary and can even be dangerous, as history has shown. It is amazing that people are eager to try any new treatment of drug from the medical establishment knowing they are taking their life in their own hands, but cringe at the thought of fasting for one to two weeks and changing their eating habits in order to heal a serious disease. In the end, they usually end up fasting anyway, before surgery to prepare the body for surgery and afterwards due to pain and discomfort.

The study of the history of science shows that one hundred years ago medical doctors thought they had or would shortly find all the answers to the questions of the body and health. No such attainment has been reached. If anything, the practices, medicines and theories developed in the last hundred years have brought into question the usefulness of medical science beyond the treatment of trauma, since the advancements most often lead to greater problems due to their side effects and loss in the quality of life. One hundred years from now the medical "breakthroughs" of today will be the equivalent of how stone-age technology is viewed by present day medical doctors. So what is the perfect knowledge, the true path? While medical science has revealed much, the knowledge of health has still eluded it, because medical scientists are pursuing an erroneous concept of health. The basis of their research has been, and for the most part still continues to be, that health issues are a separate aspect of life, not being related to spirituality, hygiene, lifestyle, diet or stress.

The laziness and vanity of people forces them to rely on factors outside of themselves to provide for their own health, and in doing so, they forsake their own power to heal. Instead of promoting preventative health, the medical establishment has chosen to support, and in some instances promote, a lifestyle of excess which allows the body to fall into imbalance and disease. Then great expense and time are devoted to seeking cures without doing the necessary work on self-healing, by restoring balance, using the body's own recuperative powers.

Health = Physiology + Psychology + Spirituality

This fragmented view of health comes from the ignorance as to the interconnectedness of life, which allows people to feel that all is separate. Therefore, the concept that the systems outside as well as inside the body can be treated at the exclusion of others is fostered. In fact, just as the organs of the body affect each other and depend on each other, nature is also composed of organs, the vegetation, the waterways, the atmosphere, etc.; are all interconnected with each other and with living organisms, so health of the body is to some degree dependent on a healthy environment, free of toxins. Holistic health means treating the entire personality, body, mind and soul. Therefore, physiology, psychology and spirituality are integral parts to the healing equation.

The spiritual Self is the source of all life, including the life of each individual human personality. It is also the spiritual Self, which sustains the mental and physical selves. At this level you should understand that the spiritual Self exists in the realm of nature (time and space) and also in another dimension, the spiritual realm, which is beyond time and space (movement and change), whereas, the mental and physical selves exist entirely in the realm of time and space. The body and mind, being instruments of the Self, operate according to the laws of nature.

Contrary to the belief system which pervades modern day society, that disease originates from factors outside of the body, it is the contention of Kemetic Smai Tawi and other mystical philosophies and the natural healing system that the root cause of ALL disease is ignorance of one's true nature as the Self. This state is referred to as the un-enlightened state. In the unenlightened state, you identify yourself with the mind, and through the mind and senses (which are merely an extension of the mind), with the body. When this occurs, the inner Self, who is in reality universal and immortal, becomes deluded by the state of ignorance into believing in the concepts of death, disease, limitation, and individuality. Because death, disease and limitation are not characteristics of the true Self, conflict and contradiction develops deep within the unconscious mind which results in a disturbance of the mental function. This distorted or inharmonious state of mind translates into a disturbance within the Life Force Energy of the astral (subtle) body and results in disease, because the flow of Life Force energy (Sekhem, Prana, and Chi) is blocked or otherwise disrupted throughout portions of the body. The presence of this energy is what constitutes "life." The absence of it is called "death."

The word disease itself gives a clue to this process by implying that disease results from lack of (dis-) ease in the body. What is this ease? It is the ease of the true Self, which is universal, free, all-encompassing, immortal, and absolute bliss and peace (Hetep). Imagine how much dis-ease would be created if you tried to confine the ocean or the sky in a jar? How much dis-ease does a wild animal, which is used to roaming in the vast forest, experience when it is captured and placed in confinement? So when body identification occurs and the soul now identifies with concepts of individuality as opposed to universality, death as opposed to immortality, dis-ease or tension arises from within the soul level of the individual which becomes manifested in the mind as fear, anger, hatred, greed, jealousy, envy and attachment. These in turn become manifested in the body as what we term illnesses and diseases, such as cancer, colds, fatigue, AIDS, and all other disease syndromes.

Thus, it is not surprising that modern medicine is finding that the most healthy activity a person can engage in is to sit quietly once or twice a day in a state of deep relaxation or meditation. Why is this? When the mind is filled with thoughts of a worldly nature, it creates ripples in the lake of consciousness, and just as when the wind blows across a lake and creates ripples, the reflection of the sky is obstructed, so too the ripples created in the lake of consciousness by tension laden thoughts obstruct the reflection of the Self (peace and joy). When these thoughts are quieted through the relaxation or meditation process, then the Self reflects in the lake of consciousness, providing one with a feeling of expansion, a sense of peace, bliss and immortality. In this state of consciousness, there is a free flow of healing Life Force Energy that heals and maintains health of the body and mind. This is what happens when you enter into deep dreamless sleep every night, however, because your consciousness is withdrawn during this process, you only know that you feel rested and relaxed when you wake up. This is why you are told to get lots of rest when you are ill or you may feel that you are becoming ill and instinctively know that if you to go to bed early, the chances are that you will not become ill. The healing comes from embracing your true nature and letting go of your body identification by relaxing the desires of the mind and temporarily giving up worldly activities. Sleep is nature's way of providing you with this experience, however, it is not the only way to have this experience. This is where the practice of mystical spirituality comes in.

Through the process and disciplines of mystical spirituality, you are able to achieve the state where you can have this experience at all times, the state of enlightenment. The formal practice of meditation provides you with this experience initially, however, when the teachings become integrated into your consciousness, your wisdom and intuitional realization of the teachings will allow you to maintain this experience, even amidst the most chaotic circumstances. So, integral and foremost to the process of maintaining or regaining optimal physical or mental health is the practice of meditation and the other disciplines of mystical spirituality, because the ultimate state of total health is in the state of enlightenment. In Indian Yoga philosophy, "true health" is termed *"Swastat"* or being established in the Self (the state of Enlightenment). Although you need to have a healthy diet, proper exercise and rest to maintain health, these factors alone can never confer total health. You must engage in spiritual practices to discover your true nature to be truly healthy. The ancient medical traditions such as the Ayurvedic system of India and The Therapeutic system of Ancient Egypt recognized this and therefore, in addition to recommending and prescribing various diets and herbs for specific illnesses, also recommended mantras and hekau repetition (spiritual chant and prayers) to calm the mind as well as the practice of meditation to promote healing.

The goal of Smai Tawi (yoga) is to promote integration of the mind-body-spirit complex in order to produce optimal health of the human being. This is accomplished through mental and physical exercises, which promote the free flow of spiritual energy by reducing mental complexes caused by ignorance. There are two roads which human beings can follow, one of wisdom and the other of ignorance. The path of the masses is generally the path of ignorance, which leads them to negative situations, thoughts and deeds. These in turn lead to ill health and sorrow in life. The other road is based on wisdom and it leads to health, true happiness and enlightenment.

"The wickedness of the soul is ignorance; the virtue of the soul is knowledge"
—Ancient Egyptian Proverb

It must be understood that being enlightened does not automatically confer a state of physical health. One's state of health is also subject to the law of ***Ari***,[44] so even someone who is enlightened may undergo serious illnesses. Yet, even amidst these physical conditions, they are able to keep their minds calm and peaceful, never losing sight of the higher nature. This is the state of optimal health. There have been many enlightened sages who have developed cancer, diabetes and other illnesses. However, this does not mean that you should not endeavor to live a healthy lifestyle. Suppose, based on ari (karma) from your previous embodiments as well as this embodiment, you develop some illness. You still have the choice to promote a healthy diet and lifestyle (good Ari, karma) or an unhealthy diet and lifestyle in this lifetime. Promoting a healthy lifestyle may add years to your life, whereas ignoring proper nutrition and exercise may result in your dying at an earlier age, not to mention the negative karmic repercussions you will still have to deal with in future lifetimes.

It is interesting that on a recent trip to Egypt, the author discovered that a great proportion of the men (over 70% or more) are chain smokers. While there, a conference of physicians on the causes and possible solutions to the increasing problem of cancer was being conducted. Notably, a listing of causes was made, but cigarette smoking was far down the list and never discussed at length. However, several presenters showed their research and displayed intricate terms and procedures for surgery, transplants and other "cutting edge" techniques for dealing with the problem. This is interesting because a natural health researcher and teacher traveled the area in the early part of the 20th century and noticed the same smoking habits, but with no large increase in cancer and disease, since the diet was pure enough and lean enough (people ate enough to survive) to compensate for the impurity of the tobacco, which by the way, did not contain the chemicals and artificially boosted nicotine content of modern cigarettes, cigars and other tobacco products.

In any case, in recent years the Egyptians, who are peoples of Arab decent and not descendants of the original inhabitants of the land, have not followed the customs of the original inhabitants of the land. In Ancient Egypt there was no smoking, and overeating was discouraged by society and nature itself, since the technology at that time did not allow the phenomena of overfarming through chemicals or machines to promote the mass production of crops or growth hormones to fatten cattle, poultry and swine. The yearly replenishing of the land, by the Nile River, insured a re-supply of nutrients that would go into the crops, thereby providing high quality

[44] Kemetic name for the concept of Karma.

vegetables and fruits and grains. In today's Egypt, meat is a staple of the diet and vegetables are not the main course. This factor also accounts for the modern problems the Egyptians are facing. Also, the new Aswan Dam prevents the yearly re-supply to the Nile Valley. Consequently the soil is becoming nutrient poor, and the problem is worsening every year.

In modern times, the causes of disease may be grouped under the following sub-headings.

Stress
Smoking
Drug abuse (includes alcohol)
Wrong diet and or wrong eating habits

In reality, stress is the root cause of the other three problems. Stress is defined in the dictionary as:

> A mentally or emotionally disruptive or upsetting condition occurring in response to adverse external influences and capable of affecting physical health, usually characterized by increased heart rate, a rise in blood pressure, muscular tension, irritability, and depression.[45]

The Kemetic concept of stress is:

> From a spiritual perspective, stress may be defined as the separation or disconnection of the soul from the Spirit. The more disconnection there is, the more stress, because the disconnected feeling leads an individual to feel alone in an ocean of life wherein human beings are in a rat race for survival, a competition for the fleeting pleasures of the world which never ends. The disconnection makes one feel that there is no purpose or plan in the world, and then one feels powerless. Ultimately, stress is the frustration of not being able to satisfy the yearning of the soul, to discover abiding peace and happiness. Since a person does not know they already have this within themselves, they search in the world of possessions, relationships and careers, but since these do not have abiding reality, they cannot satisfy the soul. The quest, which is ultimately unfulfilling, is the stress producer in life, but the cause is spiritual ignorance.

People generally feel that stress is something that is perpetuated on them by outer forces, as the dictionary definition above states. However, as the above definition based on the Kemetic concept states, stress is really the expression of a personal spiritual crisis. As discussed previously, the goal of spirituality is to stop your identification with the mind and body as being "me." This identification with the mind and body (ego-personality) as being who you are is what is called egoism. From the spiritual perspective, you are not the mind and body. These are transient projections of your true essence in the world of time and space. The real you is beyond this. The real you is the Divine Self, which is ever unaffected by the experiences of the ego-personality in the world of time and space.

The metaphor of the dream gives an understanding of this. Your Higher Self is equated with the you that is safely asleep on your bed, ever unaffected by whatever your consciousness projects in the form of a dream. In the dream you assume the form of a different subject, the dream subject. No longer are you identifying with the real you asleep on the bed, but rather with the dream character you. In the dream you, that is, you identifying yourself as the dream subject, may experience adversities and become frustrated, yet you, the real you, asleep on the bed, is totally unaffected. And though these adversities may have created a lot of stress for your dream character, perhaps even pushing the dream character to have a heart attack, when the dream is over and you reclaim your real identity as the dreamer, rather than

[45] American Heritage Dictionary

as the subject in the dream, all problems and stresses related the conditions and situations of the dream you are instantaneously dissolved along with the dream.

Just as waking up from the dream dissolved all your so-called stresses you were experiencing in your dream, similarly, waking up from the dream of the world process to your true identity resting on the bed of consciousness has the same capacity to eliminate your stress. This process of being awake to one's true Self at all times is the goal of spiritual practices, however this goal is achieved by repeated practice and in degrees. Life therefore, is designed not to give you stressful, painful and adverse situations, but rather, to give you opportunities to practice waking up to your Higher Self. If each time you are confronted with adversity, you are able to remember and identify with your true essence (I am the Divine Self, peaceful, joyful and ever unaffected), rather than the ego-personality (This is happening to *me*! *I* am being put out by this. *I* am being hurt by this. This is causing *me* pain. This is causing *me* discomfort, This is costing *me* money, This is going to make *me* suffer, *I* hate when things like this happen, etc.), you will gradually become free of ego-domination and wake up to your Higher Self. You are promoting your spiritual enlightenment. The me's and I's to which the ego-personality refers is of course related to its identification with the mind and body- the false self. Egoism is the equivalent of what western culture refers to as stress, because the ego-personality is always experiencing either gain or loss relative to the world around. And even gains have their basis in loss anyway, because all objects (including people) eventually perish. Even though at the conscious level of mind you may deny or ignore the perishable nature of objects (including people) as you acquire or interact with them, you are well aware of this fact of life at the unconscious (soul) level of mind. So, even when an object is gained, the joy experienced is not a pure joy, but a bitter sweet joy, producing numerous anxieties and worries, as you try to figure how best to secure the situation or object, so its pleasurable experience can be prolonged for as long as possible. So in the unenlightened state, no matter what life brings you, so called good situations or bad situations, there is always an underlying basis of experiencing uncontrolled mental agitation (stress).

STRESS = EGOISM

Dr. Eliot *Is it Worth Dying For?*
Early Warning Signs of Stress:

- *Feeling suspicious,*
- *Anger, Irritability, Inability to control violent impulses*
- *Defensive,*
- *Arrogant,*
- *Argumentative, Rebellious,*
- *Insecurity, Preoccupied,*
- *Sadness, the "Blahs"*
- *Grandiosity (exaggerating the importance of your activities to yourself and others),*

=

Signs of Egoism ("Fetters of Set")

- Fear (Including fear of death)
- Anger (Frustration)
- Hatred (Dislike)
- Envy
- Jealousy
- Insecurity (Anxiety)
- Greed (Craving, Desire)
- Worry
- Individualism and self-centeredness - "I" and "Me"

Sema Tawi (Yogic) Concept of Egoism, Stress and the Disease (Dis –Ease) Process:

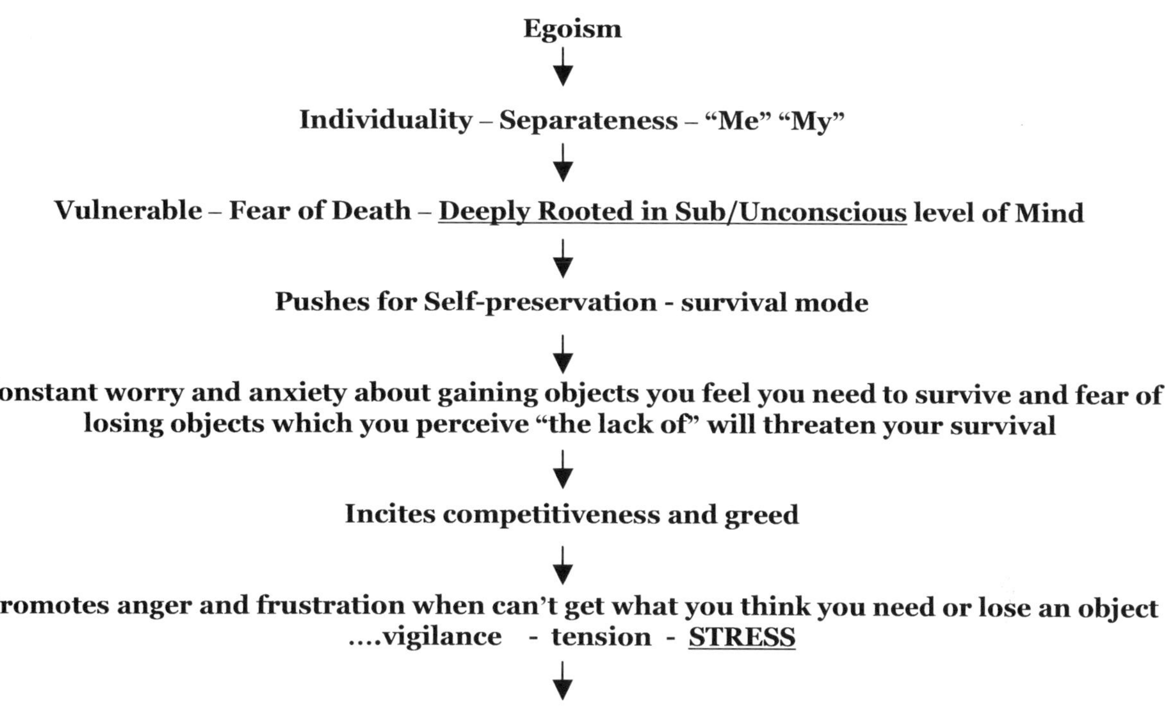

Egoism
Individuality – Separateness – "Me" "My"
Vulnerable – Fear of Death – Deeply Rooted in Sub/Unconscious level of Mind
Pushes for Self-preservation - survival mode
Constant worry and anxiety about gaining objects you feel you need to survive and fear of losing objects which you perceive "the lack of" will threaten your survival
Incites competitiveness and greed
Promotes anger and frustration when can't get what you think you need or lose an object ....vigilance - tension - STRESS
Disease (Dis-Ease) ...Mental & Physical

Your experience of stress in life will only diminish when you learn to see adverse situations, not as something orchestrated by the cosmos to cause you pain and discomfort, but as being Divinely orchestrated, the purpose being to give you opportunities to promote your spiritual advancement by identifying with your Higher Self rather than with the ego-personality crying out for validation. Just as an unwanted person knocking at your door will go away if you do not answer, so too the ego-personality will go away if you do not give it recognition, and with it the corresponding egoistic sentiments of anger, hate, greed, envy, jealousy, lust, insecurity, worries, anxieties ...stress! You will experience Supreme Peace...Hetep!

Anxiety, worry, apprehension, fear, distress, anguish, uneasiness, etc., are ways in which the vital Life Force energy is depleted since they are primary symptoms of stress. Therefore, stress is the most important health problem facing all human beings, and it should be the primary concern of the Kemetic Health Practitioner. A human being is stressed because he or she does not know how to cope with the frustrations of life. The person seeks a remedy for the stress and since no other way is known, the easier routs to stress relief, drugs, food, smoking, television, etc., are taken. While these methods relieve stress in the short run, they are actually poisoning the body further and preventing it from cleansing itself. The accumulation of toxins in the body will lead to the myriad of diseases that people suffer from later on.

The real source of stress is not understanding what life is all about. Every human being craves for contentment, love, joy, peace and understanding as well as fulfillment. The inability to discover these renders a person stressed and unhappy, discontented and disappointed with their life. This is why the Smai Tawi (yogic) lifestyle is the best promoter of health. Mystical religion and Yoga are the best way to achieve this goal because they show the personality how to achieve the satisfaction of the higher necessities of life, i.e. self-discovery, or in other words, spiritual evolution, the attainment of Divine Consciousness.

Promoting a healthy lifestyle is key to the practice of mystical spirituality, because once you realize that your body and mind are tools to take you to the destination of absolute peace and bliss, you will want to take care of them as you would a car or some other important possession you have which will be useful in helping you to achieve an important goal. In addition, unless one is very spiritually advanced, beyond identifying with the body and mind, illnesses can detract from spiritual progress because they keep the thoughts bound to the physical body and consequently also the physical world. The mind needs peace and tranquility in order to soar to the heights of philosophy and spiritual glory. To understand this, just reflect on when you have a headache or a stomachache. Where are your thoughts drawn? Usually they are more focused on the part of the body which ails you. In order to practice advance philosophy and mysticism, one must be able to essentially "forget" the body. This can only happen when there is a reasonably good measure of health. Therefore, promoting a healthy lifestyle through proper nutrition and exercise are also very important disciplines in the quest to attain union with your Higher Self.

"Spirit pervading the body, by means of veins, arteries and blood,
gives the living creature motion, and as it were does bear it in a way."

"The soul belongs to heaven, the body belongs to the earth."

—Ancient Egyptian Proverbs

The body and mind are composed of gross and subtle elements. The soul uses these in order to have experiences in the realm of time and space. When there is unhealthy living (low quality diet of food and low quality of mental experience), the soul's experiences become degraded since the impurities in the body and mind act as clouds or veils over the intellect. In this manner, all the negative aspects of the mind develop including the most severe forms of insanity such as psychotic and sociopathic behavior. Therefore, the diet of mind and body contributes heavily towards whether or not one moves closer to becoming demoniac or saintly in one's actions and thoughts.

STRESS + MEAT EATING + CAFFINE + NICOTINE + ALCOHOL = A FORMULA FOR DEATH

As the dictionary definition of stress above stated, in addition to affecting a person emotionally, it also affects physical health, causing an increase in heart rate, blood pressure and muscle tension. These physical effects are physiological manifestations of The Stress Response. The increase in heart rate can predispose a person to rapid and irregular heart beats leading to heart attack, and the increase in blood pressure can predispose to aneurysms and stroke (brain attack). Thus, over 40-50 % of those who die of heart attacks do not have predisposing factors such as vascular or heart disease. They merely die from the effects of stress. Let us take a look at how stress creates these effects which leads to death, and how this situation is further exacerbated by eating meat, smoking and taking caffeine products and alcohol.

The Stress Response is not a totally unnatural response for animals or human beings to have when faced with a challenging situation. It is an animalistic survival instinct that is supposed to kick into high gear when there is danger. It is more commonly known as the "fight or flight" response. When there is the perception of danger, the animalistic or lower part of the brain is triggered to coordinate the release of certain compounds into the bloodstream, two of the most significant being adrenaline and cortisone…to promote the survival of the animal or person. This is coordinated by the Sympathetic Nervous System (SNS).

Adrenaline and cortisone exert numerous physiological effects on the body, all of which are geared to maximizing physical strength and endurance, so that the person can escape the danger, either by running away from it or fighting their way out of it. In a true crisis (serious accidents or near accidents, etc.) where there is immanent danger, the increased heart rate allows for blood to be pumped rapidly to the muscles, so they can be mobilized to run or fight, and to the lungs so the blood can be oxygenated to supply fuel to the muscles. Other physiological changes includes dilation of the pupils, to give a larger scope of vision so one can better see their options of escape, increased blood pressure resulting from the increased heart rate coupled with a decrease in the diameter of the vessels (constriction), the mobilization of energy by releasing fats and glucose into the bloodstream, and a release of blood coagulation factors so that in the event of injury, the blood can clot quickly to minimize blood loss. In addition, blood supply is decreased to the areas of the body that are deemed not to be vital to the immediate survival, such as the digestive, urinary and integument system (skin), and sent to the parts of the body where it can be used more efficiently, namely the heart and muscles.

The First Phase of the Stress Response: The SNS Geared for Life or Death Situation:

- Hypothalamus (Brain) – Pituitary Gland (Endocrine System) – Stimulates Adrenal Glands – Produce Adrenaline & Cortisol:
- Heart Beats Faster & Harder to Pump blood ....Blood Pressure Rises abruptly
- High-energy fats dumped into the blood for energy
- Blood sugar increases
- Chemicals released to make blood clot more quickly (in case of injury)
- Other SNS responses (pupils dilate, bowels empty, sweating, etc.)

The second phase of The Stress Response is the recovery phase, where the energy plummets after the crisis has passed. This is followed by the third phase in which the physiological processes normalize; the heart rate and blood pressure return to normal.

Adrenaline has another name that it used in medical institutions. Recall any television show you watched where there was a scene where someone's heart stopped beating. What is the first drug that the doctors called for? Epinephrine. Epinephrine is another term for adrenaline. In emergency room situations where a patient's heart stops beating, epinephrine is given to stimulate the heartbeat. However, imagine what might happen if epinephrine is given to a patient with a normal heart beat. It will cause the heartbeat to become so rapid, that it may lead to arrhythmia and a heart attack. This is what people predispose themselves to each time they become "stressed out" about some situation in life.

In addition, the majority of situations that people choose to become stressed out about do not classify as a life or death emergency, yet, people have trained their minds to react as if it were so. A flat tire, a fight with a spouse, being late to work and the boss yelling at you or even firing you can all be challenging situations in the practical world and an inconvenience to the ego, however, they are not a matter of immediate life and death, and to treat them as such is truly hazardous to one's health. Even if one does not suffer an immediate heart attack, the stress hormones create lesions (tiny microscopic scars) in the heart muscle which over a period of time can predispose to heart disease. The transient increases in blood pressure eventually cause the mechanisms involved in regulating blood pressure to malfunction, leading to a permanent increase in the blood pressure, predisposing to a variety of diseases including stroke. The increased fats released into the bloodstream along with increased blood coagulation factors and constriction of the blood vessels lead to vascular obstruction and damage, again predisposing to heart disease, stroke, kidney disease, etc. The shunting of blood away from the digestive system and kidneys predispose to gastrointestinal dysfunction of all kinds and kidney disease, respectively. Thus, as a result of the mind – body connection, the mental imbalance referred to as stress, which results from a lack "Knowing Thyself," leads to a myriad of physical diseases.

People consciously choose to place or keep themselves in situations that they know are beyond their capacity to deal with (based on their level of spiritual evolution), and thus create a lot of stress for themselves. Granted, the majority of people may not understand the connection between their stressful way of living their lives and physical disease, but no one is totally clueless as to the mind-body connection. Everyone has had an experience of how a nagging headache or migraine goes away after removing oneself from a stressful situation. Many people feel they must endure these situations "to survive," but of course, except for a very few people, most do not really mean survival in the real sense of the word, which means to remain alive. Most people consider surviving to mean more than just staying alive. They must be able to have a nice house, in a nice neighborhood, and nice car, etc. So they may consider it a necessary act of survival to work two jobs or overtime, or even steal or murder, to "survive." The irony of course is, based on the effects of The Stress Response they stimulate within their bodies, they are actually shortening their life span, and whatever life span they will have, chances are they will be plagued by some form of disease. Given the above information, it is no wonder that in the U.S.A as well as other countries, the health care system is in a crisis, being overwhelmed by many middle aged and elderly patients with chronic diseases.

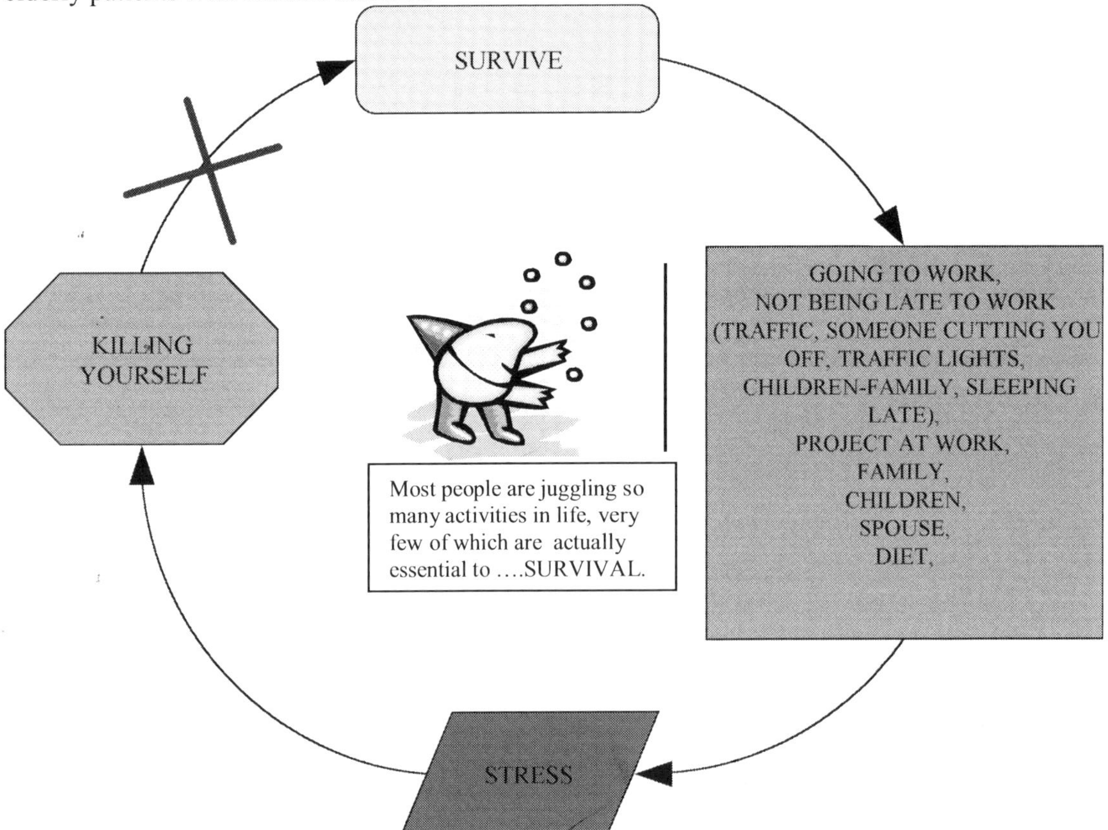

The Stress Response and The Eating of Meat and other Animal Products:

The word cholesterol normally elicits a negative connotation, however cholesterol is essential to the normal functioning of the body. Cholesterol is only produced by animals, and thus, the human body has the capacity to produce the cholesterol it needs for its functions. It does not need cholesterol from outside sources. In fact, putting additional cholesterol into the body will exacerbate the effects of The Stress Response, predisposing to high blood pressure and heart disease as cholesterol is one of the components of plaque (and also of most gallstones) which causes obstruction of the vascular system. There is some confusion about whether foods like avocado and coconut contain cholesterol. The answer is of course no. Cholesterol is found only in meat and other animal products. These foods are high in fats, but not cholesterol, and their fatty content, while for someone who eats meats are a source of additional concern, for a live (raw) foodist or vegetarian, they can be a source of fats needed for normal body function. So eating meat and animal products will only serve to exacerbate the effects of The Stress Response, increasing the likelihood of serious illness or death.

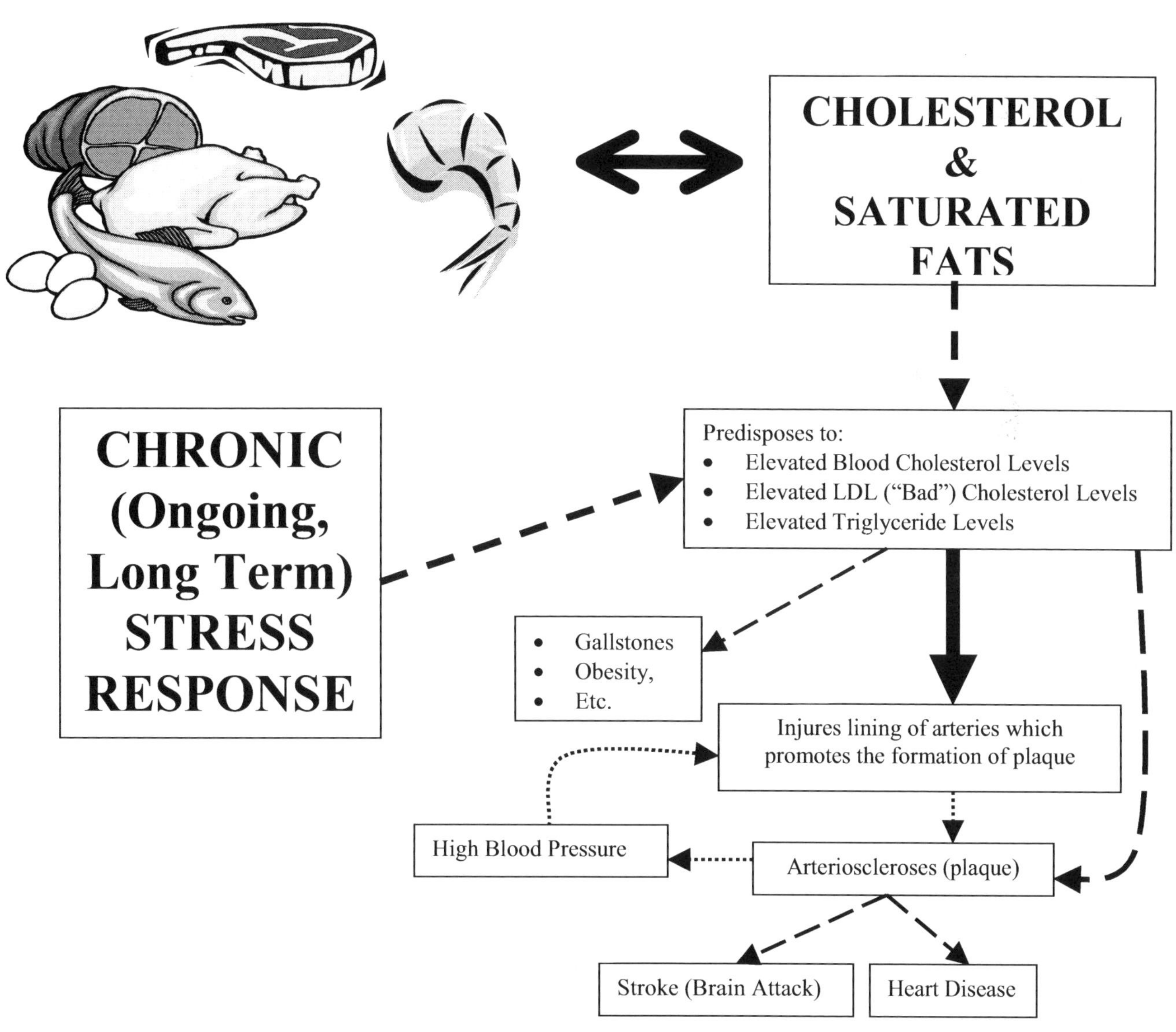

The Stress Response, Caffeine, Nicotine, and Alcohol:

Both caffeine and nicotine have the effects of increasing the production of adrenaline in the body as much as two to four times normal, and alcohol increases the production of cortisone in the body, both of which are components of The Stress Response discussed above. Thus, many of the effects that are part of The Stress Response are triggered, including, as discussed above, an increased heart rate and blood pressure. Again, prolonged exposure to these compounds (caffeine, nicotine, alcohol) in and of themselves predispose to stroke, high blood pressure, and a whole host of other system failures in the physical body. Now imagine what can happen if a smoker, coffee drinker or someone drinking alcohol becomes very upset due to some unwanted or unexpected situation and The Stress Response is triggered. Insult is added to injury, and they become a ticking time bomb waiting to go off.

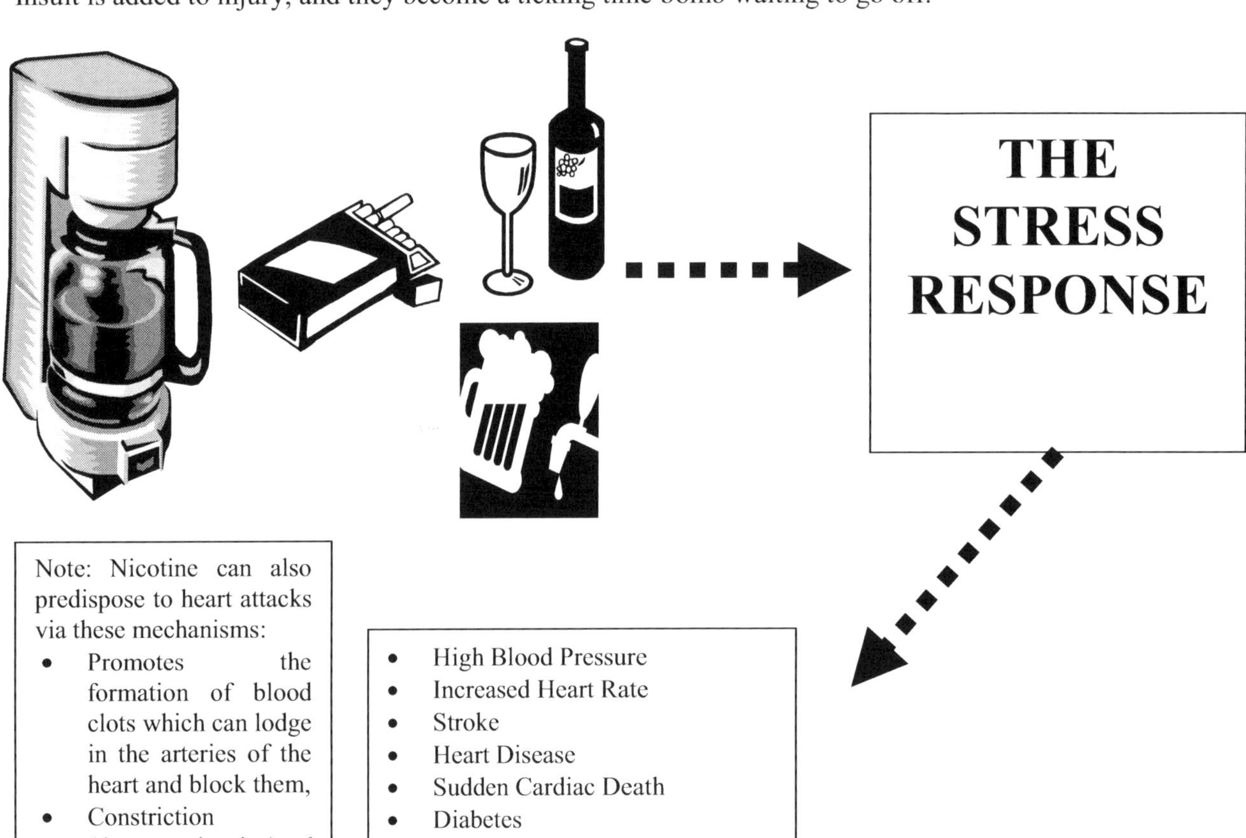

Note: Nicotine can also predispose to heart attacks via these mechanisms:

- Promotes the formation of blood clots which can lodge in the arteries of the heart and block them,
- Constriction (decrease in size) of the arteries supplying blood the heart which can obstruct the flow of blood (oxygen) to the heart
- These conditions are exacerbated if the vessels are already narrowed from plaque buildup.

- High Blood Pressure
- Increased Heart Rate
- Stroke
- Heart Disease
- Sudden Cardiac Death
- Diabetes
- Digestive Disorders
- Other Stress Related Conditions
- Injures lining of arteries which promotes the formation of plaque

Do you see (understand) how these combinations of meat eating, drinking coffee and other caffeinated beverages or taking caffeine pills, smoking and alcohol are surefire recipes for disease and death? Even taken alone they predispose disease and death. This is also why it is even more critical that one eats well and avoids alcohol, caffeine and nicotine containing products when one is experiencing stress. This is why when the orthodox medical establishment says that they do not know the cause of cancer and other forms of disease, it sounds ridiculous to the Natural Health Care Practitioner, and even more so to one who understands the connection from the level of the Spirit to the physical body. However, there are some medical doctors who are facing the truth about the inadequacies of their own profession and who are promoting the simple principles of natural health, which have been known since the time of Ancient Africa.

Sir William A. Lane, England's foremost abdominal surgeon, speaking to the staff of John Hopkins Hospital and Medical College:

> "Gentlemen, I will never die of cancer. I am taking measures to prevent it ... It is caused by poisons created in our bodies by the food we eat ... What we should do, then, if we would avoid cancer, is to eat ... raw fruits and vegetables; first, that we may be better nourished; secondly, that we may more easily eliminate waste products ... We have been studying germs when we should have been studying diet and drainage ... The world has been on the wrong track. The answer has been within ourselves all the time ... Drain the body of its poisons, feed it properly, and the miracle is done. Nobody need have cancer who will take the trouble to avoid it."

DIET FOR THE PHYSICAL BODY

The physical body is composed of the elements of creation (earth, water, air, and fire) and the four qualities of matter (hot, cold, wet, and dry). If these factors are maintained in proper balance, the physical body will be a fit conduit to operate in the physical realm and allow the mind to perceive the subtle vibrations of the spiritual realm as well. The mind is composed of subtler elements which, when purged of egoistic thoughts, is able to reflect the spiritual reality. Otherwise, the association with the grosser elements of the body renders it gross. If these factors are out of balance, the mind will be distracted with the concerns of the body (pain, illness, desire for food, etc.) and will not be able to exert self-effort toward spiritual practice in order to develop subtlety of intellect. The intellect will remain dull with the gross concerns of the physical world.

Modern physics has proven that matter is not solid but that it is in reality energy in different forms of vibration, and even energy has a subtler basis in the spiritual Self. From the perspective of mystical spirituality, what is considered to be "solid" matter (the elements) is in reality condensed subtle matter. What makes it appear solid is the level of ignorance of the seer and the intensification of the belief in it as being "real." Your body appears to be solid but in reality it is as solid as a body you might experience in a dream. Due to the soul's involvement in time and space and having been taught to believe in the world of time and space as a solid reality, ordinary people reinforce these ideas through indulgence in emotions, feelings and pleasures of the senses. One of the most powerful areas of indulgence is in the consumption of foods, which grounds and condenses spiritual energy instead of allowing it to flow freely. From a spiritual point of view, the vibratory energy in meat is very grounding to the soul. This means that the elements which compose the human body are rendered "heavier," therefore blocking perception of the subtle spiritual reality and reinforcing the gross reality as being the only reality.

Food is often used as a source of pleasure rather than necessity. Modern society advocates the consumption of good tasting, processed foods even though they may contain chemicals or excessive quantities of other substances such as processed sugars and salts which the body does not need at all or in abundance. In addition to unsanitary and inhumane living conditions in which the animals are housed and slaughtered, the chemicals and processing techniques which are used by the meat industry to raise animals for food renders the meat very toxic to the human body. Over a period of time these toxins build up in conjunction with those which are already in the environment (pollution) and lead to cancers and other diseases in later years. While for those with spiritual sensitivity and who practice the wholistic lifestyle the cause of cancer is obvious, the medical establishment still can't figure out where cancer comes from, and much less a cure, even with all the billions of dollars spent on research.

Modern Physics and Mystical Philosophy

Modern Physics appears to be "proving" Ancient Mystical Philosophy. In the past 20 years, studies that have tried to find the smallest particle or to explore the outer limits of space have come up with answers which support the ancient mystical philosophical view of the cosmos and the constitution of the human being.

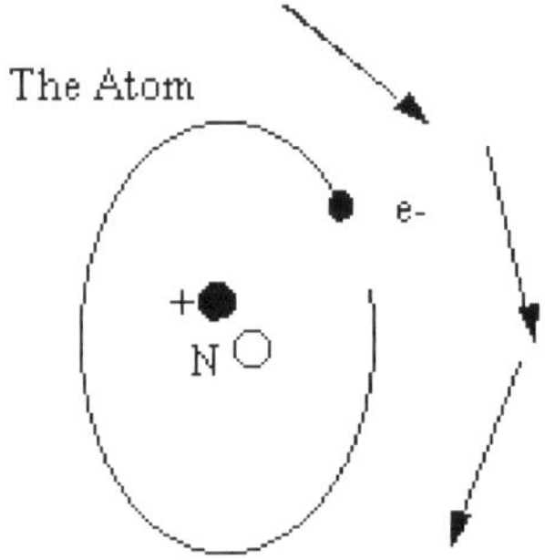

Figure 18: Structure of Atom

Science is discovering that the Universe is infinite in all directions, both at the atomic (micro) level and at the planetary (macro) level. It is also finding that what we call "matter," is not what it appears to be. In fact, studies suggest that matter is 99.9% empty space surrounded by an idea (information, thought), consciousness. Contrary to popular belief, quantum physicists have found that they cannot explain what matter is nor what holds it together. The remaining 1% of matter which appears to be visible is also theorized by quantum physics (modern physics) to be an optical illusion. The "Atom" is said to be composed of a positively (+) charged "Particle" called a "Proton" and a particle with no charge (N), called a "Neutron," in the center. These two particles are said to be surrounded by an electron which carries a negative (-) charge and revolves around the nucleus. All matter is found to be composed of the same Protons, Neutrons and Electrons. The difference in appearance comes from the different numbers of "particles" in each "Atom" and also from the combination of different atoms with varied combinations of the three particles. Further, it is known that electrons have no weight and that there is a vast "empty space" between the protons and the electrons that circulate around them; also that there is "empty space" inside of the protons, neutrons and electrons. Therefore, what we are seeing and touching by use of our senses is not at all what it appears to be.

> ***SPACE:*** Once considered as a void in which "nothing" exists, space is now known to be composed of extremely subtle matter. Modern physics has proven that space "bends" when close to an object with high gravitation such as a dense star. Therefore, the modern understanding of space, that is, the space between two people as well as the space between stars must be understood in a new way. Like ordinary "physical" matter, space itself must now be considered a "substance" which unites and binds the cosmos. Therefore, there are no "voids," "cavities" or "empty spaces" in the universe. All is ONE. Indian philosophy uses the term *"ether"* to describe space.

What we seem to perceive with our senses is in reality, only different aspects of the same substance. That is, when energy "vibrates" at a high speed (frequency), it appears as a light (less dense, less weight) material such as gas or electricity. When it "vibrates" at a lower speed, it appears as a solid (dense material) object such as rocks or metal. The higher the vibrations are, the more subtle the "material" will appear to be. The slower the vibrations are, the more solid, rigid and static it will appear to be. When matter vibrates at very high rates, it goes beyond the gaseous state; then matter appears as rays such as sun - rays or X-rays. At higher rates of vibration, it would be so subtle that it could fit in between the "empty spaces" in the slower vibrating matter. It could pass through it or "reside" in it. This is the subtle realm of the "spirit" body which "inhabits" the "physical" body. The object of all spiritual movements is to "identify" one's consciousness, one's concept of who one is, with the "subtlest reality" rather than with the gross physical reality because the physical one is perishable and transient, whereas the subtlest one is transcendental and immortal. In fact, it is the "subtle" spirit from which "gross" matter is created. For this reason, keeping a "light" lifestyle which promotes higher mental vibrations, a "light" diet and "light" thoughts are important as will be seen in further chapters.

Figure 19: Waves become particles. Left: Waves of energy are particles and particles are also waves. Both are energy in different form.

The new generation of physicists beginning with Albert Einstein has developed a "new physics." They now believe that matter, that is, everything which can be perceived with our senses, including our bodies, is an "ILLUSION." If we were to look at matter the way it truly is, we would see structures that appear as small planets and moons circling them at lightning speeds. Even the most solid looking structures are really moving; everything is in perpetual motion. Further, we would see that matter seems to come out of nowhere and then goes back into "nowhere-ness." As all "matter" is composed of the same "stuff," the different objects we see in the world are merely different combinations of the same material substance common to all things; this is what is meant by an illusion or appearance of multiplicity and variety. The "new physics" says that matter is nothing more than energy.

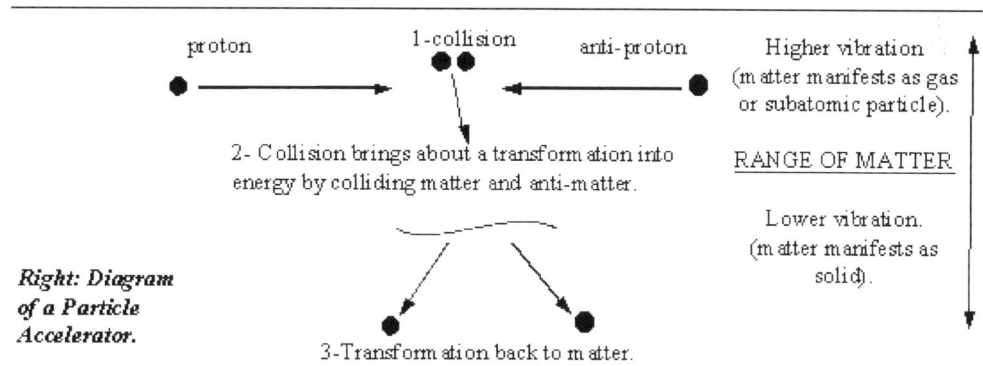

Figure 20: A particle accelerator.

Particle accelerator experiments attempted to break down atoms into smaller units by colliding them at great speeds. Scientists found that when a positively charged proton (matter) and a negatively charged proton (anti-matter) are crashed together, particles turned into energy (wave patterns) and then back to matter again. Energy and matter are therefore, interchangeable. This interchangeability of matter and energy is represented in the famous formula $E=mc^2$ by Einstein who initially developed this theory mentally (without experimentation). Therefore, even the most solid looking objects are in reality ENERGY in motion at different vibratory rates.

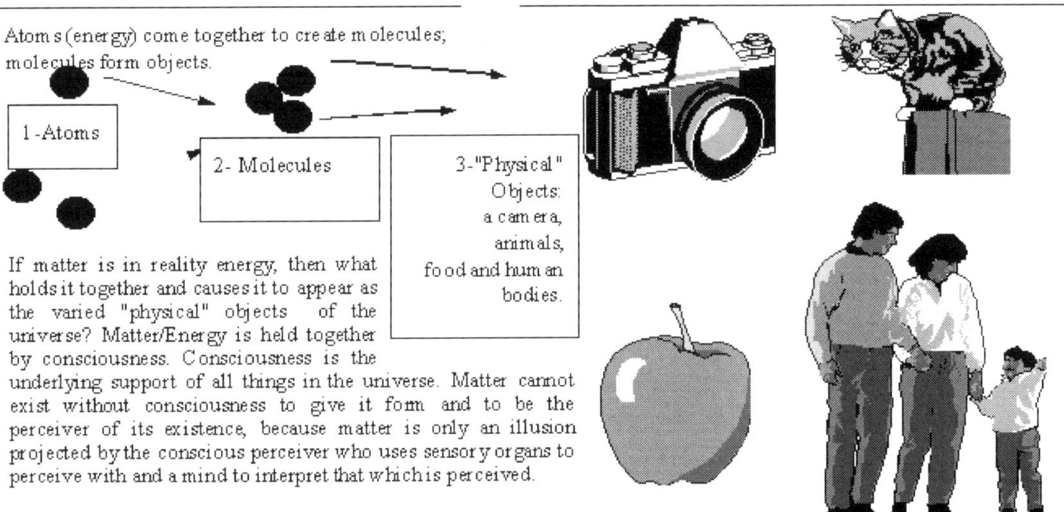

Figure 21: Atoms become molecules and molecules compose all matter.

Further, modern science has discovered that even objects of the world which appear to be separate, such as human beings, are in reality "exchanging pieces of each other" on a continuous basis. That is to say, every time we breathe out we are expelling atoms and molecules from our internal organs. Therefore, every time we breathe, we are sharing pieces of our bodies with other people and with the environment. For example, air that is breathed by someone in India may be breathed by someone in the United States two days later and vise versa. Thus, the physical world which appears to have defined boundaries is only an illusion. In reality, the world is one interrelated mass of atoms and energy which is being "caused" to move and interact by some "unknown" force.

The Ancient Mystical Philosophy of an all encompassing "force" that binds the universe together was espoused thousands of years ago in the Egyptian philosophy of SEKHEM, the Indian idea of PRANA, the Chinese idea of CHI and in the philosophies of other cultures. Philosophy further states that this "FORCE" can be controlled through mental discipline. Modern science has now, based on scientific evidence, postulated the existence of a substance called ***"DARK MATTER"*** which is described as an "unseen, unfelt substance that makes up to 99% of the Universe." This means that not only is the world one interrelated mass, but that it is a part of the greater mass called the "Universe."

This theory supports the ancient philosophical idea that the "Created" Universe really does not exist except as perceived through the mind of the individual. It is a manifestation of the Supreme Being that ebbs and flows in a time frame that encompasses an untold number (perhaps billions) of years. It is "created" and "destroyed" periodically. This supports the theory of a *"BIG BANG"* and the *"Expanding-Contracting Model of the Universe."* The last "Creation" is thought by scientists to have occurred several billions of years ago. In the future, they theorize that the universe will close in on itself (contract), and all the planets, stars, etc. will return one point, as represented by the point in the symbol of Ra ⊙. Then, a new "creation" or big bang will occur again.

This is the same information stated in age-old philosophical scriptures dating from the beginning of "historical" times. Those who are alive now will not witness the "dissolution" since it is theorized that it will not occur for millions of years in the future, however, the implications of what it means are crucial to the understanding of the nature of reality (the cosmos) with which humans are intimately related. In fact, Ancient Mystical Philosophy states that the "Created" universe is only an appearance for the generation of a stage upon which the human experience may occur. In addition, this "illusion" that has been created by our conditioned minds, is a "reality" only to the extent that we "believe" in it.

Thus, reality appears to be a relative idea. Ancient Mystical Philosophy states that the true essence of things can be seen by the liberated mind which sees what lies beyond the information given by the senses and that those whose minds are not liberated will experience the "physical" world as if it really "exists." For example: there is no blue sky. It only appears to be blue because of the limited human sense of vision.

Modern science has now accepted that so called "physical reality" cannot exist outside of the person conducting the experiments. An older theory held that the person conducting the experiment could be considered separate and apart from the phenomena being observed. Modern science now holds that nature and all phenomena occur because of an experimenters ability to conceptualize the phenomena and to interpret it. Therefore, the observer is part of the phenomena being observed. Consequently, modern science now uses a new term for the experimenter. The new term is Participant. Thus, the experimenter is really a participant in the experiment because his or her consciousness conceives, determines, perceives, interprets and understands it. No experiment or observed phenomena in nature can occur without someone to conceive that something is happening, determine that something is happening, perceive that something is happening (through instruments or the senses), and finally to interpret what has happened and to understand that interpretation. Therefore, the most recent theory in modern physics is that matter, that is to say creation, is composed of not only energy in varying degrees of density (vibration), but that it is "intelligent," or it might be better understood by saying that matter and energy are manifestations of Cosmic Intelligence (consciousness).

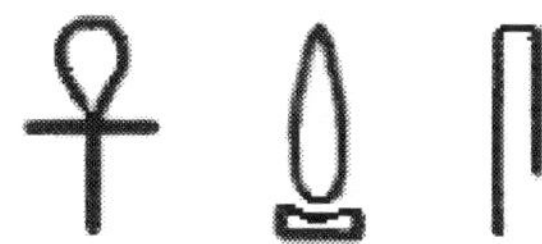

The Kemetic Concept of Ukhedu And The Modern Theory of Mucus and the Mucusless Diet

The hieroglyphs for the Ancient Egyptian term "Ukhedu" provide further insight into the nature of the concept of disease. The term may be precisely defined as "decay or disease process" and the determinative sign relates to "pustule" which releases "pus" or a "boil." Notably, the three vertical lines under the main symbol which looks like an egg, signifies that the sign is plural, meaning excess, additional, etc. In its singular form the pus symbol denotes either, , pus contained in a pocked or sac of the body tissues or , pus that is coming out of the pocket or sac, i.e. oozing material. Acne is a form of Ukhedu and this is one reason why a sensitive person can discern the emotional and physical condition of another by looking at the face. The face either shines or dims with the presence or absence of the Life Force energy, and the Life Force is affected by the presence or absence of the Ukhedu.

> **pus·tule** *n.* **1.** A small inflamed elevation of the skin that is filled with pus; a pimple. **2.** A small swelling similar to a blister or pimple. **3.** Something likened to an inflamed, pus-filled lesion.[46]

> **pus** (pŭs) *n.* A generally viscous, yellowish-white fluid formed in infected tissue, consisting of white blood cells, cellular debris, and necrotic tissue.[47]

> **boil** (boil) *n.* A painful, circumscribed pus-filled inflammation of the skin and subcutaneous tissue usually caused by a local staphylococcal infection. Also called furuncle.[48]

> **ac·ne** (ăk′nē) *n.* An inflammatory disease of the sebaceous glands and hair follicles of the skin that is marked by the eruption of pimples or pustules, especially on the face.[49]

[46] American Heritage Dictionary
[47] American Heritage Dictionary
[48] American Heritage Dictionary
[49] American Heritage Dictionary

Additional examples of words using the determinative sign will provide insight into the meaning of the

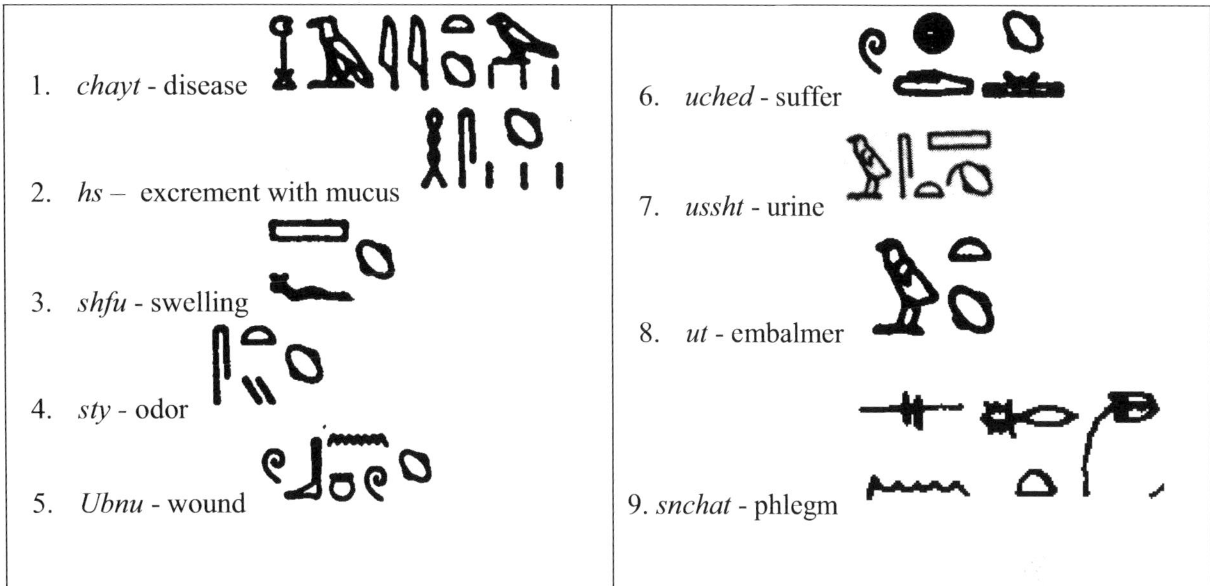

Pus or mucus is seen as the negative by-product of an abundance of Ukhedu in the body. A healthy body should not produce an abundance of purulent[50] material, but it does so when there is an imbalance in the intestinal track due to excess waste or an obstruction in the processing of waste. Thus, while there is a normal amount of mucus, white blood cells and other materials in the various parts of the body, the diseased state causes an abundance of mucus and pus to emerge out of the body. The emergence of pus and mucus in the body is a result of the body's attempts to cleanse itself of the dis-ease process, such as when one has a cold. Thus, mucus and pus are expressions of the same dis-ease process. When food or unnatural medicines are ingested, the dis-ease cleansing process is impaired, thereby exacerbating the condition or perpetuating it indefinitely, because the body's natural mechanism to repair the imbalance has been shut down in order to devote the energy towards processing the new materials that have come in. This is why there is a need to practice fasting along with the change in eating habits. Ukhedu can emerge in a wound in the form of an infection as well. One instruction reads: "Another remedy to heal the wound in which the Ukhedu has risen."

> **Mucus**, a slippery, viscous fluid containing mucin produced by mucous linings of the body. It serves for lubrication and protection: nasal mucus traps airborne particles; mucus of the stomach protects the lining from irritation by secreted hydrochloric acid during digestion.[51]

The hieroglyphic sign, refers to a "discharge" of the matter contained in the particular mettu. Sign #7 above, relates to the urinary track, which releases a form of waste called urine. However, this sign also relates to the embalming process (#8), since the dead body emanates odors and fluids related to the decay of the body after death.

In Kemet, priests and priestesses as well as others were known to bathe three times daily and to shave ***all*** hair from the body in order to maintain the highest level of external purity. They wore wigs. Long

---

[50] **pu·ru·lent** (pyo͝or′ə-lənt, pyo͝or′yə-) *adj.* Containing, discharging, or causing the production of pus. **--pu′ru·lent·ly** *adv.*

[51] American Heritage Dictionary

before the advent of modern parasitology, the Ancient Egyptians understood the problem of parasites. Parasites that affect human include rickettsias, viruses, bacteria, protozoa, fungi, flukes, and worms. These promote disease, but the underlying cause or problem which allows them to have a detrimental effect on the body is the Ukhedu, which has been allowed to develop due to unhygienic conditions externally, such as from the lack of bathing and cleaning the hair, and or internally due to the wrong diet and eating habits (in this sense the wrong diet promotes a lack of hygiene of the interior of the body). It should also be understood clearly that one's bedding should be hygienically clean. This may be accomplished by changing it on a weekly or at least bimonthly basis. There are mites and other parasites which live on the skin and on the bed sheets. Follicle mites infest human sebaceous glands and hair follicles and measure about 0.025 cm (about 0.01 in) long. In connection with the promotion of hygiene and health, the practice of bathing in hot tubs and close (intimate) contact with people who do not live in a hygienic manner needs to be avoided for the same reasons. Hot tubs themselves are breeding grounds for bacteria, and the bromide or chlorine which are used to kill these are toxic chemicals for the human constitution. Along with impeccable hygienic conditions, the priests and priestesses maintained a strict vegetarian diet, practiced fasting and enemas, and abstained from alcoholic beverages, as previously discussed.

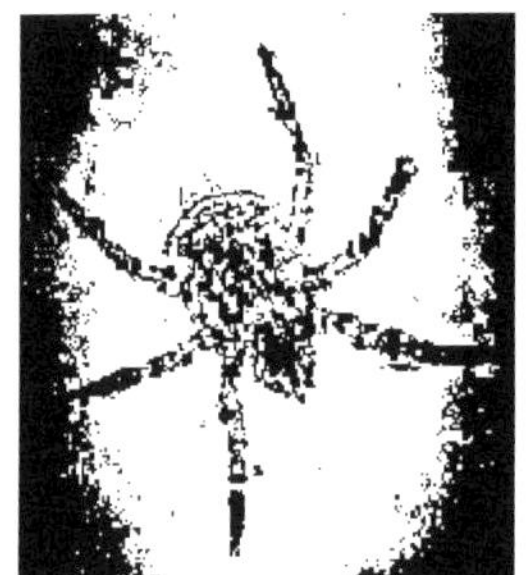

Figure 22: Chigger mite

> **Chigger**, also called harvest mite, or red bug, tiny, red larva of some kinds of mites found worldwide. Adults lay eggs on plants and hatched larvae find a host animal or human, in whom their bites cause severe rash and itching. Length: 0.01in (.25mm). Order Acarina; family Trombiculidae.[52]

According to Ancient Egyptian Medical writings, the Ukhedu is the cause of pain and disease in the physical body, however, it can be removed (cleansed) from the body. Outer physical hygiene as well as the hygiene of the intestinal track was considered a priority in the maintenance of good health. This of course implies bathing regularly and watching what is eaten, taking care that it is free from decay; in other words food should be fresh and in harmony with the body and with nature. Another contrast can be seen when comparing Ancient Egyptian and European customs of hygiene. In European medieval times, the practice of bathing was only a monthly requirement for most people, even the kings and queens. Further, the presence of parasites on the body, such as lice, was accepted as a common and even desirable feature. The lack of personal hygiene was the primary factor, which allowed Western countries to be ravaged by plagues and epidemics, while there is no record of such plagues striking Ancient Egypt throughout its long history.

> Black Death, an outbreak of plague, thought to be bubonic plague, which ravaged most of Western Europe during the 14th century and at 10-year intervals throughout the Middle Ages. Carried by the infected fleas of the black rat, the plague came west from Kaffa, a grain port in the Crimea, in 1346. It had reached England and Italy by 1348 and

[52] Random House Encyclopedia

Germany, Scandinavia, and Poland by 1349-50. The Black Death took about one third of the population of Europe in the first three years, and perhaps a total of half before the worst epidemics ceased. The results were a widespread decline in morality, a decline in the achievements of monasteries, political discontent, a labor shortage, and in Germany, the massacre of thousands of Jews, who were blamed for the plague.[53]

Bubonic Plague; disease usually transmitted to humans by fleas from rats. Symptoms include chills and fever, followed by vomiting, diarrhea, headache, and inflammation and swelling of lymph nodes, especially in the region of the groin. Sanitation is the preventive measure. See also {Plague}[54]

Epidemic; uncontained and rapid spread of a disease through a general population. The study of epidemics concerns itself with causes and patterns of contagion and methods of containing disease. Black plague, smallpox, and typhoid have been causes of historic epidemics; hepatitis, influenza, venereal disease are present concerns of epidemiologists.[55]

In Kemet, many natural treatments were used to deal with disease as opposed to using elaborate techniques requiring expensive equipment and intricate theories or methodologies. One such treatment method, which has remained part of the techniques of the natural healer today, is hyperthermia (application of heat). The following section of the Ebers Papyrus describes the treatment of a skin tumor.

"When thou meet a skin tumor on the outside part of the body above the genitals lay thy finger on it and examine his body, palpating with thy fingers. If his bowels move and he vomits at the same time, then say thou: ' It is a Skin Tumor in his body. I will treat the disease, by heat to the bladder on the front of his body, which causes the tumor to fall to the earth.' When it is so fallen, then make thou for him warm so that it may pierce his body ... (uncertain).... Heal it as the cautery[56] heals."

Many people now realize that the same processes present in disease are there also in the healthy body. For instance, abnormal cells are constantly being produced and destroyed in a normal course, but why is it that in some people this process goes haywire and is then referred to as cancer? Disease should therefore be considered as an imbalance in the normal operations of the body, a disruption in its normal functioning. A return to normalcy must then be related to bringing back the balance by correcting that action which caused the imbalance.

The Three Kinds of Foods and their Ukhedu Producing Qualities

"Twain are the forms of food-for soul and body, of which all animals consist... Some are nourished with the twofold form, while others with a single... Their soul is nourished by

[53] Random House Encyclopedia

[54] Random House Encyclopedia

[55] Random House Encyclopedia

[56] Operative procedures practiced in ancient societies included cleaning and treating wounds by cautery, poultices, and sutures, resetting dislocations and fractures, and using splints. Additional therapy included the use of purges, diuretics, laxatives, emetics, and enemas. Perhaps the greatest success was achieved by the use of plant extracts, the narcotic and stimulating properties of which were slowly discovered. So successful were these that 50 or more continue to be used today. Digitalis, a heart stimulant extracted from foxglove, is perhaps the best known. "Medicine," Microsoft (R) Encarta. Copyright (c) 1994 Microsoft Corporation. Copyright (c) 1994 Funk & Wagnall's Corporation.

the ever-restless motion of the Cosmos; their bodies have their growth from foods drawn up from the water and the earth of the inferior world."

—Ancient Egyptian Proverb

Based on the teachings of the temple of Aset, the Shetaut (religious) traditions of Kemet and the surviving medical papyri, the following disciplines of health can be derived. All living creatures need food in order to survive. There are two kinds of foods in accordance with the proverb above, food for the soul and food for the body. Food for the body complex can be further subdivided into two groups, food for body and food for mind. Thus there are three kinds of foods: food for the body, food for the mind and food for the soul. Kemetic Philosophy admonishes that the proper foods be provided for each of these aspects of the human personality, otherwise an imbalance will occur. This imbalance will lead to the emergence of the disease process called ***Ukhedu***. The food for the body is recognized to be fruits, vegetables, nuts, seeds, grains, proper breathing, rest and right actions. The food for the mind is recognized to be uplifting thoughts, positive thoughts based on truth, and proper breathing. The food for the soul is recognized to be the subtle essence of the Divine, i.e. the light of the Spirit itself, in other words, self-knowledge which is achieved through virtuous living. The following proverb directly relates to insights into the food for the soul.

"The blessings of thy eternal part are health, vigor, and proportion. The greatest of these is health. What health is to the body, even that is honesty to the Soul."

—Ancient Egyptian Proverb

FROM THE STELE OF DJEHUTI-NEFER:

"Consume pure foods and pure thoughts with pure hands, adore celestial beings, and become associated with wise ones: sages, saints and prophets; make offerings to GOD."

—Ancient Egyptian Proverb

Many people do not realize that what they consume has a strong effect on their psyche. This implies not only physical foods, but also all manner of consumption since human beings consume through the mouth, the ears, the eyes, touch, thoughts and desires, etc. These foods can have an effect on the mind, because the mind and senses are in touch with the physical body through the brain and nervous system. This effect registers, and in turn causes impressions, a sort of deep memory in the unconscious mind. These impressions in turn cause new thoughts, related to the impression, to emerge. If the impressions are for eating properly, then a cycle of virtue has been established in the diet. These thoughts are proper due to the positive impressions from which they stem and of which they will create more. If the impressions are for incorrect eating, then a cycle of vice has been established in the diet. Therefore, the issue of the nature and manner of the foods consumed can have a profound effect on the ari or karmic basis of the individual. (See the section The Role of Ari In the Health and Well-being of an Individual.)

There are three major states of consciousness on which all other states are based. These are the harmonious state, characterized by balance and equanimity, the agitated state, characterized by movement, distraction, and agitation, and the dull state, characterized by listlessness, heaviness, obtuseness, slowness and weakness. Just as there are three major states of relative consciousness, there are three basic kinds of foods. These two categories are interrelated, with agitating food promoting an agitated mind, dull foods a dull mind and lucid foods a lucid mind. The first group is composed of those foods which engender restlessness and distraction.

Ex. sugars, salty[57] foods, onions,[58] dry foods, hot spices, coffee, fish, poultry, eggs, etc.

Agitating foods promote passion, stimulate the emotions and excite the body. Foods that are too spicy, hot or sour, are considered to be agitating to the system. Also eating in a hurry promotes restlessness and distraction.

Dull Foods are the second group. This group is composed of foods which promote dullness. This group includes:

Ex. meats, tobacco, alcohol, fermented foods, processed foods, stale or overripe foods.
Overeating, even the good foods, promotes dullness.

These foods promote dullness of intellect, anger, hatred, greed, volatility, negative thoughts, disease and clouded reasoning ability. Some of these foods are filled with negativity due to the way in which they are handled in the food processing system. The addition of unnatural chemicals to food in and of itself is reason enough to classify them as tainted with poison. The killing of animals effectively poisons the food with negative hormones as well as fear vibrations from the animals. Also the human digestive tract is not designed to handle meat, so the food rots as it passes through the intestinal system, promoting an environment for diseases such as cancer to take root. Is there any wonder why medical doctors admonish those who contract cancer or experience heart trouble to stop eating meat and to stop smoking? Shouldn't they begin promoting a meat free diet for everyone (including themselves) at an early age? If smoking is known to produce cancer, shouldn't it be outlawed as are other addictive drugs and toxic agents? Poisons are sold out of greed and ignorance. Also, such poisons are consumed due to ignorance and addictive desire based on ignorance of how to satisfy the true desires of the inner self. The intellect is as if put to sleep in a fog of opaque masses of ignorance, base emotions and desires. In this condition, people can act in cruel ways to others without thinking of the consequences of their actions.

From an ordinary standpoint, the consumption of meat is not desirable due to the fact that it causes pain to other living beings in the animal level of existence. Hurting any creature should be avoided to the extent possible since it generates discordant vibrations in the universe. These vibrations disturb the balance of nature and the mental plane of existence which in turn affects human beings and their feelings, thoughts and consequently, their actions as well. Many people dislike violence in the world, however, they are sowing it everyday by supporting the violence that is performed on animals, the violence in sports, television and in ordinary human interactions.

Many people who eat meat try to rationalize their actions by saying that eating plants is a form of killing and so they may as well kill animals. Other people applaud this since animals are seen as lower forms of life. While human existence is more valuable in a certain sense than an animal's (generally speaking, one can only work to attain enlightenment in a human body, where one has access to the faculty of higher reasoning), one should not value a life form on the basis of the level of intelligence. They too are manifestations of the Self, souls at a lower level of spiritual evolution. They are feeling creatures, that have a limited ability to comprehend and love. These factors alone accord them respect as living vessels of the spirit. And actually, eating fruits and vegetables is not a form of killing because taking fruits and leaves from plants do not kill them. However, taking the legs, ribs and other body parts from any animal will certainly kill them, and or make their lives miserable and ineffective. Pruning plants and removing their fruits (seeds) is actually a help to them, promoting their health and propagation, which is their desire,

---

[57] Salt is a necessary mineral for proper health. However, amounts that make food taste salty are over the necessary nutritive amounts needed by the body and will thus cause imbalances and disease. Furthermore, common table salt is a synthesized product and some products contain unnatural chemical additives. Celtic sea salt is a good quality natural sea salt.

[58] In ancient times onions were considered to be aphrodisiacs and ancient Egyptian Priests and Priestesses avoided them for this reason.

so there is a symbiotic relationship here whereas killing animals for food is based on greed, violence and lust (for experiencing culinary pleasures). Therefore, this argument must be rejected as self-serving and ridiculous.

The argument that some people around the world, such as Eskimos, live on meat so it is ok to eat meat is also self-serving rationalizations. Just because some people eat certain things to survive does not mean that everyone should eat the same things even when they have better conditions and can do better, or can move to a more harmonious environment. There are people around the world living only on rice. Should everyone live on rice then? Other people live on bread and water only. Should everyone therefore live on bread and water? Meat eaters would be the first to squawk at that idea, but their thinking rationalizations only come up with arguments that support their point of view which will allow them to pursue their desires, the same ones which will lead them to ill health later on. Thus, the death of animals leads to the death of humans...hence the saying of the philosophy of karma, "what you do comes back to you" and the Ancient Egyptian Proverb, "He who is wrong fights against himself!" This is the way in which one's own clouded intellect acts to lead one into adversity, disease and destruction.

Violence against animals is not the same as violence against people, since human life is generally to be considered as a higher form of being, but it is a source of negative feelings and chemicals released by animals as they suffer on to death, which enters into the tissues of their bodies, and then are consumed as food by humans. These impurities enter the bodies and minds of those who eat meat. Scientific studies have proven that the blood of people who die in accidents is normal, while people who die as a result of violent situations where fear and conflict is involved, contains toxins, released into the bloodstream just prior to death.

Why is promoting life better than death? Maat is a philosophy, which from time immemorial, has promoted balance and harmony as the righteous basis of life. Nature constantly seeks a balance and repudiates extremes. The consequences of not acting in accordance with Maat is to produce negative ari or karma. Hence the Kemetic proverb, "The laws of God are the first thing the seeker will find on the way to the truth." Therefore, one's actions should seek to maintain the balance of life. The teachings of ari show that one's negative or positive actions may not show their repercussions right away. One will however, experience a result at some point, in this lifetime or after. This is why seemingly bad things sometimes abruptly happen to apparently good people and vise versa. Ari is the cause and effect principle in nature. If one acts in violence, violence will be visited upon one. Therefore, the modern problems of anger, hatred, and violence including crimes such as murder, rape, robbery, assault, etc. can be seen as repercussions for previous karmic misdeeds.

Dull foods are not good for the body or the mind, but much like the stimulating foods, they create an addictive form of dependency wherein even when the person has a full understanding of the deleterious effects of the foods, he or she continues to consume them anyway using the excuse "well I want to enjoy my life even if I shorten it." The weakened will disables a person's reasoning capacity as well as their willpower to resist the urge for the foods. The dullness of mind also prevents them from understanding that there are other methods to resolve the problems of life. However, the power of the spirit is indomitable, and if a person, no matter how dull, begins to tap into this source, they will gain the strength to overcome the negative state.

Lucid foods are those which promote harmony, inner mental peace, bright intellect, willpower, energy (vitality), etc. They foster purity of the mind as well as of the body. They are nutritious and enhance the body's ability to fight off disease. Lucid foods include:

> whole foods, cereals, fresh vegetables and fruits, legumes, seeds, nuts, sprouted seeds, herbs, teas, sunlight, clean air, etc.

All energies received by the body come from the same source, the Divine Self. However, for the sake of preciseness and understanding, the following distinctions are made in accordance with the manner in which the energy manifests. To the list above may be added the subtle energies of the environment, Cosmic Energy and Solar Energy, which are forms of the Life Force Energy, for one receives cosmic energies from the universe itself, and solar energy through whole foods indirectly and directly by being in the sunlight. On the order of density, cosmic energy is most subtle and it courses through the universe. Solar energy radiates from the sun and is less subtle. Sekhem (Life Force) energy is even less subtle. It is everywhere, available to be harnessed through the breath and other disciplines of self-control.

So one should practice being out in the direct sunlight for at least 15 to 20 minutes per day. Ideally, provisions should be made to live in areas of reduced pollution so as to be able to achieve and maintain a higher level of Life Force energy which is assimilated through the breath and the subtle energy centers of the astral body. The skin is the largest organ in the body. It takes in nutrients (producing vitamin D) from the sun as well as the air, and it should be allowed a period of time throughout the day wherein it is unencumbered by artificial coverings, i.e. clothes.

A serious spiritual aspirant must learn about the nature of food as he or she climbs the ladder of mystical spirituality. In so doing, a healthy constitution can be created which will allow for a positive and fruitful spiritual movement towards self-discovery. Since every human being is not exactly the same as another, the exact diet, which is optimal for each individual, will be slightly different. Therefore each individual should experiment with their diet within the broad guidelines given here in order to discover the right combination within the Lucid Diet – mucus-free category which is best suited for him or her.

Plate 12: Kemetic The Tree of Life[59]

In her form as the ***Tree of Life***, the goddess is the source of food and drink, mystically referred to as "breathing the air," which sustains life. The vignette above comes from the papyrus of Ani and is typical of other papyruses, which acknowledge the nourishing aspect of vegetation as the source of life for human beings. This is one aspect of the mystical teaching of the tree of life in Kemetic spirituality. Asar is the source, the Spirit, which enlivens all things. The goddess is the conduit through which that life essence is transmitted to human beings. The goddess bestows food and drink to the aspirant. Other subtle implications of this vignette are the references in the text accompanying it to the food and drink as being the "breath" which sustains life, i.e., Life Force energy. Further, the fact that the aspirant obtains these directly from the goddess who is in the tree suggests that the best food is obtained by direct contact with the goddess, that is, by picking fresh vegetables and fruits from plants directly and by listening, reflecting and meditating on the wisdom that she symbolizes.

---

[59] From the Ancient Egyptian Papyrus of Ani

NOTE ON WHAT THE WORD "VEGETARIAN" MEANS: In this sense, true vegetarianism implies eating no meat of any kind, including beef, fish, poultry, swine, eggs, etc., and no dairy products at all. Also, it must be noted that in a strict sense, processed foods are also to be avoided.

A mucus promoting diet is any food which causes the body to produce an excess of mucus due to its poisonous qualities. Any food that causes the body to produce excess mucus (Ukhedu) will force the body to use the mucus membranes to expel the excess that cannot be handled by the normal excretory systems through the skin (through the pores), lungs (waste gases), kidneys (urine) and digestive system (excrement). A distinction should be made between mucus-forming foods and mucus formation due to the natural cleansing efforts of the body when a cleansing diet is instituted.

NOTE ON THE UKHEDU (MUCUS) FORMING QUALITIES OF FOODS: If the body becomes too acid it will produce excess mucus. Therefore, foods that promote acidity should be avoided. Likewise, the more acid-binding or acid inhibiting foods should be consumed. Considering flesh foods, fish, milk, cereals, root vegetables, fruits, nuts, grains-beans, and drinks, the following listing can be made in order of their beneficial or detrimental effect on the body.

Table 4: Mucus forming and non-mucus forming foods

Acid binding or Acid inhibiting Foods (Non-Mucus Forming)	Acid Forming Foods (Mucus Forming)
Fruits Vegetables Drinks*	Flesh foods** Fish Cereals*** Milk**** Nuts***** Sodas, coffee, Artificial, processed drinks

*includes herbal teas, juices, water.

**includes chicken, rabbit, ham, venison, veal, beef, mutton, animal blood, animal flesh.

***includes refined wheat, whole wheat, farina, barley, oats, rye, rice, cornmeal, bread, cakes-pastries, pasta.

****Milk (implying other dairy products as well) is placed in the mucus forming column because it is only mildly non-mucus forming. In addition, for some people it is intensely mucus-forming. It is troublesome to most people's digestive system due to lactose intolerance, because it is designed for the offspring of that specific species of animal to consume, and not humans, and especially not adult humans. Only milk from human mothers is good for human beings (for ages up to 3 years). **Lactose intolerance** is a problem that can engender many problems in the digestive system, which include cramps, gas, and diarrhea.[60]

[60] *The Natural Pharmacy,* Healthnotes

*****includes Chestnuts, Almonds, Peanuts, Hazelnuts, Lentils, Walnuts and excludes Coconuts. Nuts and seeds are designed by nature to inhibit digestibility. Thus, while possessing the capacity of being sprouted, they can remain in a dormant state for many years. Soaking for 12 hours in water releases the digestion inhibiting agents, and therefore reduces the mucus producing effects. Thus, nuts and seeds should be eaten in their raw state after being soaked in water for 12 hours.

Some Grains and beans have both acid inhibiting and acid forming qualities. Soy beans are acid inhibiting. Other grains and beans are considered to be acid forming. This list includes dried peas, dried beans, rye flour, oat flour, oat flakes.

NOTE ON THE MUCUS FORMING PROPERTIES OF SOME VEGETARIAN FOODS: As we saw earlier, dairy products are detrimental to most people in the world, and especially troublesome for those who are lactose intolerant or who possess a weak immune system. Even some vegetables and fruits can be detrimental to the system since they have more mucus producing qualities than others. For example, some fruits with high water content such as cucumber or melon can promote mucus because they are cooling to the system. They slow down the digestive fire. This can also be said of cold drinks. Cooked vegetables are also detrimental since they are depleted in nutritional value due to the cooking process and require more energy from the digestive system in order to be processed. Starch rich foods such as root vegetables require more energy to process. So even within the vegetarian arena, one must be careful of the foods that are consumed, as well as the how and when of their consumption. Do not forget that if the digestive system is slowed or impaired, this will cause undigested foods to remain in the intestinal track, causing the problem of putrefaction to commence. This of course leads to the formation of Ukhedu.

> **Mucous Membrane**, membranes lining all body channels that communicate with the air, such as the respiratory tract, the digestive tract, and the glands secreting mucus.[61]

NOTE ON FOOD COMBINING: General guidelines- Do not mix starches and proteins. Generally, fruits and vegetables are to be eaten separately. Fruits may be eaten as a meal in themselves and are to be taken at least one half hour before vegetables. Celery and lettuce go well with most other vegetables and some fruits (tomato, avocado, bell pepper, cucumber, etc.). By definition, a fruit is considered to be any plant product that contains a seed(s) within it, such as eggplants, tomatoes, bell peppers, cucumbers, avocados, etc. Nuts (raw) should not be mixed with wet, succulent fruits but may be eaten with dried fruits. Nuts should be soaked for 12 hours, which will make them more digestible. (Note to reader: Food combining charts are available at most Natural or Health Food Stores.)

Eating Foods In Season

Along with food combining another practice of modern society should be discussed. It is the practice of cultivating foods out of season by artificial means. In order to have certain foods and vegetables all year around, special chemicals and other practices such as grafting, etc., must be used. Also, foods must often be imported from far off distances. This practice disrupts the natural rhythm of the plant and the earth as well as the physiology of the organisms that consume them, creating a situation wherein the plant is being altered and pushed out of harmony with nature and the human being is consuming the food out of season. Human beings do not need to eat the same foods all year around. Nature knows what to produce at a given time, and ideally this is what all life forms should subsist on. Therefore, an effort should be made to eat foods when in season.

---

[61] Random House Encyclopedia

NOTE: Beware of the poison. Most often we think of poisons as substances produced by nature (certain plants or animals) which are not to be consumed or chemicals produced by certain industries. It must be clearly understood by now that if the proper diet and eating habits are maintained, there should be no need for medicaments or pharmacy medicines, such as antacids to combat gas and other stomach problems. Antacids also have side effects. They have been shown to interfere with the absorption of minerals and vitamins. Therefore, the continued marketing and promotion of such drugs and the refusal of the medical establishment to point out their misuse and superfluous nature points to ignorance and greed. The only reason for the need for such drugs at present is the general ignorance of the public with respect to proper nutrition. Through the delusion of the public there is much financial gain for the food industry, which produces the poisonous foods, the advertising industry which promotes them, the drug companies which make remedies to cure the problems caused by the poisons and the doctors who treat the diseases and ailments caused by the poisons.

Starches and Carbohydrates

What is starch? Starch is a common name given to a form of carbohydrate. Carbohydrates, the most abundant organic compounds found in nature, are produced by green plants and bacteria which utilize the process known as photosynthesis. In this process, carbon dioxide is taken from the air, and with the use of solar energy, carbohydrates are produced, as well as all the other chemicals needed by the organisms to survive and grow.

Starch is almost completely insoluble in water. The human body is composed of over 80% water. Therefore, it is clear that if excess starches are ingested, they will cause a clogging of the natural systems of the body due to their quality of insolubility. The digestion process of starch begins in the mouth under the action of salivary ptyalin, but is later completed in the small intestine. This again is why it is important to chew food the proper amount of times (30-50), so that the digestive juices in saliva can adequate mix with the food and begin the process of digestion. The body converts starch into glucose for immediate use and into glycogen for later use. The glycogen is stored in the liver, and converted to glucose as it is needed by the body. Therefore, starch is a source of energy reserve storage. However, most people lead a sedentary lifestyle relative to the amount of starch they consume. Consequently, they do not burn off the starches they consume. This causes the Mettu to become "plugged up," which obstructs the cleansing process of the body and causes the Ukhedu to become "backed up." This taxing of the system is not only disease producing, but also unnecessary, since there is an easier way to get glucose and enzymes, by eating fruits. So starches should be obtained from naturally occurring sources in the raw state, and not from refined, processed sources which will produce an imbalance in the chemistry of the body, and the amount of their consumption should be gauged according to the activity level of the individual.

The Essential Ingredients of a Proper Diet: The Kemetic Diet For the 21st Century

Based on the Kemetic system of diet and natural health, the following diet is advised:

Fruits, both fresh and dried (especially figs, dates and raisins), and fruit juices
Vegetables (especially salad greens, sea vegetables and seaweed, sprouts)
Nuts and seeds (soaked/sprouted) and nut milk
Soy products (non-genetically modified or engineered)
Water (pure-not from the tap or public system, which contains chlorine, fluoride and other chemicals)

Foods from the categories listed above will provide for all of the nutritional needs of the body and will also promote colon hygiene, and therefore inhibit the Ukhedu, disease processes by allowing the body to function efficiently and maintain a strong immune system.

A spiritual aspirant should keep in mind that the body, mouth and mind also act as excretory systems, and during times of illness, the impure human being will often think unrighteous thoughts, speak unrighteous words, and exude a distasteful odor and or act in unrighteous ways. During these times the controls of the personality can be lost.

Even if a person appears to be healthy on the outside and appears to be in the best condition, yet that person can experience feelings of discontent, annoyance and dissatisfaction, as well as a general frustration with life. Periodically, famous athletes who seem to be in top shape, fall prey to debilitating diseases, and sometimes even collapse unexpectedly on the field due to some health problem. People who appear to be healthy may pick a fight and engage in belligerent behaviors and extremes of emotion. Aggression, anger, hatred, greed, lust, envy, jealousy, cravings, addictions, etc., are signs of ill health. Studies have shown that people who consume the lower quality diets including cooked foods, meats, etc., beyond developing physical illness, are quicker to experience the lower aspects of the personality (animosity, anger, hatred, greed, etc.) during the normal course of life as opposed to people who consume a higher quality diet. The production of negative excrements of this nature can lead to intensified worldly entanglements, delusions and more negative impressions lodged in the unconscious mind thereby promoting a continued cycle of psychophysical disease.

Secrets of Vitality

The term, 𓋹, oodja, the central sign in the Ancient Egyptian benediction, *Life, Vitality and Health,* gives us a very important teaching in reference to the process of human existence on earth. The sign signifies "fire drill" or an instrument used to start a fire or the commencement of the burning process. Used in this manner, the idea that is given is that the Divine Life Process, ☥(Ankh), engenders a fire (*oodja,* vitality) which courses through the body and promotes health, 𓋴, (*seneb*).

Vitality is what gives the impetus to life. It is the force, which sustains and gives a person the will to live. If there is no vitality, the entire personality is depressed and there is no enjoyment of life. Vitality sustains the immune system which keeps external as well as internal agents (bacteria, viruses, poisons, waste material, etc.) from disturbing the course of life. Vitality may also be referred to by the term Life Force or the Kemetic term Sekhem. Therefore, the following formula may be applied to the understanding of the inner processes that sustain life: Vitality = immunity = health = life. In the section, *The Body-Mind-Soul Connection,* we described the source of the Life Force and how it enters the body. Here we will look at the means for developing and maintaining the Life Force.

The primary means for assimilating the Life Force and thereby experiencing high vitality are through lucid foods, breath and calmness of mind.

1. This means that high quality (organic), fresh, uncooked foods will be best for receiving the Life Force through solid food, as this will have the highest enzyme content, and thereby facilitate the digestive process. All the metabolic processes in your body are enzyme dependent. Thus, when you eat cooked foods (dead, no live enzymes), the body has to work much harder to produce more digestive enzymes in order to properly assimilate the food, since it is not getting any help from the food itself. To meet these demands, the body has to decrease the production of other enzymes needed to run its other metabolic processes throughout the entire body, including heart function. Over a period of time, the other systems of the body become compromised and disease results. Thus, the Kemetic understanding of the digestive system as being key to one's overall health is well founded.

2. Deep breathing during the normal course of daily activities and the practice of additional breathing exercises as part of the exercise program will be best for receiving the Life Force through the breath.

3. Promoting harmony, balance, peace and relief of stress will be best for receiving the Life Force through the Astral Body (mind).

Preventing the loss of vitality

The practitioner of natural living will soon realize that even though life's challenges may not always allow one to be in complete physical or mental balance all the time, it is important to promote these principles all the time and to know how to handle the aspects of the personality, especially the mind, to bring them back to a balance quickly in order to prevent any serious or permanent damage to the immune system. It is most important to promote peace and harmony of mind. This can be accomplished by the study and practice of the teachings of mystical wisdom, developing dispassion, detachment and equanimity in all activities and in all situations. The following areas of life are to be monitored closely since they are a primary means for loss of vitality.

Table 5: Sources for loss of vitality from the human personality.

1. Agitated mind
2. Worry
3. Anxiety
4. Vain imaginations and fancies
5. Covetous nature
6. Negative thoughts
7. Talking too much
8. Talking loudly
9. Overeating
10. Oversleeping
11. Excesses of the body – too much partying
12. Too much sexual activity
13. Strenuous sports

Overfarming, The Scourge of the Land

(15) "I have not laid waste the ploughed lands."
—Ancient Egyptian precept of Maat Philosophy from the Prt M Hru or Book of Enlightenment

Overfarming is essentially the depletion of the land due to the lack of replenishment of the land that is used for farming. When a plant grows, it uses nutrients from the land. These go into the plant and the fruits of the plant. When the fruit or crop is picked, the nutrients are taken away and the land does not get it back unless it is replenished in some way. In Ancient Egypt, the annual flood of the Nile river provided this replenishment. Ordinary farming practices should include the regular replenishment of the land by rotating farmlands, allowing some fields to go un-farmed periodically as well as through composting, natural fertilizers, and other natural means for replenishing the land. Another method of overfarming is through the use of chemicals to force the increase yield of crops, introducing unnatural elements, which will in the long run cause imbalances and unforeseen chemical combinations in the nutrients of the land. In modern times the advent of genetic engineering has introduced a new method of overfarming that will in time show its negative effects. Therefore, overfarming should be stopped and the replenishment of the land should be instituted so as to bolster the nutrients that will develop in the crops. Thus, non genetically modified or engineered organic farming should be an essential endeavor of society. Further, as explained elsewhere, the body compensates for many deficiencies by manufacturing the compounds it needs. Therefore, the idea that meat must be eaten in order to survive, must be rejected by scientific evidence. If this evidence is known by the medical establishment and is available in encyclopedias, why does the American Medical Association, the United States Government and the Public Health Department allow society to continue such poisonous and destructive practices like meat eating and smoking?

Those who want good health must be able to throw off the burden of society's ignorance and greed by not being ignorant or greedy themselves. They must become wise and overcome the hypnotic influences of society which they are susceptible to only because they themselves are partaking in the culture of pleasure seeking and spiritual ignorance. Therefore, once again, the mystic path holds the keys to health of body, mind and soul, because a higher knowledge and will power is necessary in order to overcome the temptations of the world. This strength comes from the Spirit, and the mystical movement is a direct route to discovering one's spiritual powers.

Diseases of the Male and Female

Menstruation, PMS, The Uterus, Prostate Gland and the Raw (Live) Food Diet

Menstruation is defined as the process or an instance of discharging the menses, the monthly flow of blood and cellular debris from the uterus that begins at puberty in women and the females of other primates. In women, menses ceases at menopause. The natural health view on the discharge of blood during the menstrual cycle is that it is an abnormal process caused by the impurities present in the body, including chemical impurities, psychological impurities as well as spiritual impurities. The same may be said of prostate problems in men as well.

Diseases specific to the female gender include:

- Dysmenorrhea (Painful Menstruation)
- Menopause
- Menorrhagia (Heavy Menstruation)
- Menstrual Cramps
- Pap Smear (Abnormal)
- Premenstrual Syndrome (PMS)
- Infections

The medical establishment has noted an increase in PMS or premenstrual syndrome in women and prostatic irritation in men in recent years. Specific problems included in PMS are: cramping, bloating, mood changes, and breast tenderness. The presence and intensity of these problems may vary from woman to woman.

Ovulation is the process by which a mature ovum is released from the ovary, enabling it to be fertilized when it embeds itself in the uterine wall. In human females, one egg is released midway through the menstrual cycle. If it is not fertilized, it is supposed to release itself and slough off, that is, to separate from surrounding living tissue, naturally. If there are few impurities in the body, it will be discharged accompanying a mucoid substance along with normal discharges of the vagina. If there are many impurities of in the body, it will tear off, due to the body's efforts to rid itself from as much impurities as it can as soon as possible, causing bleeding and scarring. Therefore, from a natural health perspective, monthly bleeding is seen as a means which the female body uses to purify itself, and it is perhaps because of this that women generally live longer than men who do not possess the same mechanism for purification. In any case, several women have been found to revert to the bloodless cycle after adopting the raw (live foods) diet while ovulation continues normally as described above. However, naturopathic practitioners report that not all women stop bleeding after adopting the higher quality diet, perhaps due to an excess of bleeding and scarring over many years, which prevents the uterus from permanently healing itself. In any case, those women for whom bleeding does not completely stop, they experience reduced bleeding, and reduced or eliminated PMS. Thus, the idea that a woman's life needs to be encumbered with PMS, bloody discharges and discomfort as a part of normal life, must be rejected based on the teachings of natural health. What society uses as a basis to determine what is "normal" are standards of an already diseased society which has deviated from nature to a great degree. Therefore, there are few, if any, standards within that abnormal society which can be used to determine what should be normal human health. This is one of the reasons why it is important to look at ancient history and to societies which have not deviated to such an extent from the standards of hygiene and vegetarian-fruitarian diets.

Male problems include Benign Prostatic Hyperplasia and Prostate Cancer.

The prostate is a small gland that surrounds the neck of the bladder and urethra in men. It corresponds to the female uterus, and is susceptible to the same kinds of problems. One of its functions is to contribute to the seminal fluid. It is also a center of creative energy as the female uterus is a center of creative energy in the female body. If the prostate enlarges or swells, it can put pressure on the urethra, acting a bit like a clamp—this condition is known as benign prostatic hyperplasia (BPH). The urinary tract will be impaired, causing severe pain and discomfort. In extreme cases of disfunction the prostate will become cancerous. The name "benign prostatic hyperplasia" has replaced the older term "benign prostatic hypertrophy."[62] Studies have shown that a 50%-100% raw (live) food vegetarian diet (implying the elimination of toxic food intake), as well as fasting, reduce and eventually eliminate these problems.

Prostate problems can degrade into cancer. Although this form of cancer can be treated in many ways such as hormone therapy, surgery or radiation, the treatments pose serious obstructions to the normal conduct of life, not to mention their side effects. In every case of disease, the best solution is a natural remedy, and the best natural remedy is preventative, healthy living. Thus, the idea that a man's life needs to be encumbered with pain, discomfort and ultimately cancer of the prostate, as a part of normal life, must be rejected based on the teachings of natural health.

When we begin to examine the totality of life and the universality of disease, we begin to see a picture in which men and women are not as different as they may appear to be on the surface. This understanding should serve to heal the animosities, resentments and fears between the genders, which have persisted over the last several thousands of years. The following is an excerpt from the book *Egyptian Tantra Yoga* by Muata Ashby, which illustrates these issues in more detail.

Modern medical science and genetics reveal that while human beings appear to be different on the surface (sex, race, etc.), in reality all human beings are remarkably alike. They make use of the same food and their bodies are made up of the same substances, although these are arranged in slightly different ways. Skin coloration is mostly a difference based on the arrangement of pigmentation in the skin. Some people have more and some less, but all have it in varying quantities, therefore, beyond the outer appearance, all are in reality essentially the same.

Sexuality, Its Purpose and Abuse

Upon close examination, men and women are found to possess the same organs, although arranged slightly differently and exhibiting different emphasis on certain levels of development. For example, the male penis has its counterpart in the female clitoris, the male testicles in the female ovaries, and the male prostate with the female uterus. It is this understanding of the oneness of the androgynous nature which underlies male and female human bodies, that is the heart of Tantric mystical philosophy. When this understanding is reached and integrated in the human heart, it constitutes an extension (Tantra) from limited consciousness based on a sexual (dualistic) understanding, to an awareness of the non-duality, which is the ultimate reality. Thus while sexuality exists as a practical reality of life, the practitioner of Tantra discovers the a-sexuality of existence as well, thereby expanding in consciousness to encompass all (sexuality and androgyny, duality and non-duality, etc.)

Many more examples could be given.[63] The point is, from the perspective of mystical philosophy, that the true essence of a human being is not sexual, not the body, mind, senses or anything which is in the realm of time and space, because the realm of time and space is the realm of duality and illusion.

[62] Healthnotes copyright 1999

[63] For more on the philosophy of Tantra see the book *Egyptian Tantra Yoga* by Muata Ashby.

Sexuality is only an expression of the personality based on an emphasis of the Spirit, which has tended toward a pole within the range of human consciousness (male-polarity, female polarity). Human existence is based on the karmic desires of an individual soul, which is expressed within the limits allowed by the genetic basis of the organism. This means that the Spirit can express as the DNA of the particular life form allows it to be expressed. These limits are divinely ordained, and this is why they follow set rules (cosmic law-MAAT). Thus the Spirit can manifest (incarnate) as a male or female within the given species. This is the range of expression, which is allowed by the Divine Will, which created and supports all life in the universe.

Simply stated, the Spirit operates through the genes and is limited to the modes of expression which are dictated by the genes which fall within the range of either male at one extreme, or female at the other. However, human beings are in reality the same essential being. In other words, all human beings are of the self-same nature. This factor becomes most evident when the egoistic feelings and sentiments of desire are cleansed from the heart. When this occurs, the underlying unity, which supports the appearance of duality, which expresses as sexuality, becomes most evident. These are only a few examples out of hundreds, which can be presented to show that in reality human life is not separate and individual. Sexuality is a factor of nature and not of Consciousness, and Consciousness is the essential innermost essence of every human being. Therefore any notions to the contrary are based on illusion and ignorance. Further, when the mind and its dualistic notions are transcended (through mystical practices), a person can discover that they are not the body, neither male or female, but Spirit.[64]

Thus, it is the creative energy which flows from the spirit which manifests as sexual desire in human beings. Nature has implanted an innate need to unite, to procreate. All things seek their mates in nature. Therefore it is in the polarity of males and females that the attractive force can be seen most prominently. For a person who has not understood this teaching, there is no escaping the force of nature. That person is compelled by nature to enter into sexual relationships, which lead to family relations and responsibilities or other forms of entanglement (karma). For one who has transcended these impulses, the energy is redirected towards Unity, not with another ego-personality, but with the Higher Self, and creativity of a different order, that is, an expansion in consciousness which is the source of great achievements in spirituality as well as in arts and the social advancement of humanity.

> Souls, Heru (Horus), son, are of the self-same nature, since they came from the same place where the Creator modeled them; nor male nor female are they. Sex is a thing of bodies not of Souls."
>
> **-Teaching of Aset (Isis) to Heru (Horus)**

[64] For more on the findings of modern science which corroborate the ancient mystical teachings of Mystical, Yogic and Tantric Philosophy see the book, *The Hidden Properties of Matter* by Muata Ashby).

THE ROLE OF ARI IN THE HEALTH AND WELL-BEING OF AN INDIVIDUAL

An action is repaid by its like, and to every action there is a consequence.

—Sage Meri-ka-Ra[65]
From the Ancient Egyptian Wisdom Texts

The Ancient Egyptian philosophy of "Ari" and with its relationship to the Ancient Egyptian divinities Maat, Meskhenet, Shai and Rennenet, constitutes what modern Indian Yoga philosophers refer to as "Karma." From ancient times the cause and effect aspect of people's actions was well understood. Actions based on egoism and ignorance of the Divine lead a human being to frustration and the inability to discover true joy and peace. Actions based on truth and natural harmony lead to inner and outer peace and contentment. This "Hetep" or peace allows a human being to discover the higher nature or Self. Otherwise, egoistic actions lead one to bolster the lower self and ignorance. Actions based on the lower nature are characterized by egoistic desires (passion, greed, lust, envy, hatred, jealousy, anger, etc.). These actions inevitably lead to strife, violence and discontent. Actions based on Maat (righteousness-truth, selflessness, sharing, compassion, devotion to God, etc.) promote inner peace, social harmony and contentment. This is a proper environment for spiritual evolution. People who are constantly running after worldly desires will never be able to rest, while those who affirm righteousness and peace will discover the real joy of life which cannot come from wealth, conquests, fame, hurting others, etc. By turning one's mind towards righteousness and selflessness, a human being can evolve to discover the greater or deeper essence of their own being, the Higher Self, and attain "*Nehast*," (resurrection, enlightenment).

Many people believe that karma is equal to fate or destiny, however, this interpretation could not be further from the original understanding of the ancient Sages. The etymology of the word, karma, comes from the Sanskrit "karman" which means deed or action. In Yoga philosophy, karma refers to one's actions. These actions lead to certain experiences and consequences. In Ancient Egyptian philosophy, the word for karma is *Ari* or *Iri,* meaning "actions which create one's fate." It is presided over by the goddesses Maati, Rennenet and Meskhenet. Meskhenet presides over the birth circumstances and life experiences of every individual. She is the one who carries out the decree, which has been ordained by Djehuti, the god who records the results of the judgment of the soul, in the hall of Maat. The Kemetic concept of Ari (Karma) and reincarnation is that the heart of every individual is judged in accordance with the manner in which they lived in reference to the standard of order, truth and righteousness (Maat). It is Djehuti, a symbol of one's own transcendental essence, who records the deeds (actions) or karmas of every individual, and then decrees the proper Shai (destiny) and Rennenet (harvest or fortune) which are fitting for that particular individual. Then with the help of Shai and Rennenet, Meskhenet causes the individual to experience the proper birth circumstances based on their previous deeds.

Figure 23: The Heart

The Ancient Egyptian hieroglyphic symbol of the heart is a heart shaped vase, ♉. The vase is a container, which may be used for water, beer, wine, milk, etc. Likewise, the human heart is seen as a vessel, which contains thoughts, feelings, desires and unconscious memories. In mystical terms, the heart is a metaphor of the human mind including the conscious, subconscious and unconscious levels. The

[65] These are the teachings of King Kati to his son Meri-ka-Ra and are referred to by this author by the son's name since they denote his royal and spiritual enlightenment.

mind is the reservoir of all of your ideas, convictions and feelings. Therefore, just as these factors direct the path of your life, so too they are the elements, which are judged in the Hall of Maati by the two Maat goddesses.[66] The heart then is the sum total of your experiences, actions and aspirations, your conscience or ari (karma), and these are judged in the balance against the feather of Maat.

Thus, ari should be thought of as the total effect of a person's actions and conduct during the successive phases of his or her existence. But how does this effect operate? How do the past actions affect the present and the future? Your experiences from the present life or from previous lifetimes cause unconscious impressions, which stay with the soul even after death. These unconscious impressions are what constitute the emerging thoughts, desires, and aspirations of every individual. These impressions are not exactly like memories, however, they work like memories. For example, if you had a fear in a previous lifetime or the childhood of your present lifetime, you may not remember the event that caused the fear, but you may experience certain phobias when you come into contact with certain objects or people. These feelings are caused by the unconscious impressions, which are coming up to the surface of the conscious mind. It is this conglomerate of unconscious impressions which are "judged" in the Hall of Maat. They determine where the soul will go to next in the spiritual journey towards evolution or devolution, also known as the cycle of birth and death or reincarnation, as well as the experiences of heaven or hell. The following segment from the Ancient Kemetic wisdom text "Instruction to Meri-ka-Ra" explains this point.

> "You know that they are not merciful the day when they judge the miserable one..... Do not count on the passage of the years; they consider a lifetime as but an hour. After death man remains in existence and his actions accumulate beside him. Life in the other world is eternal, but he who arrives without doing wrong, before the Judge of the Dead, he will be there as a neter (divinity) and he will walk freely as do the masters of eternity."

The reference above to "his acts accumulate beside him" alludes to the unconscious impressions, which are formed as a result of one's actions while still alive. These impressions can be either positive or negative. Positive impressions are developed through positive actions by living a life of righteousness (Maat) and virtue. This implies living according to the precepts of mystical wisdom or being a follower of Heru (*Shemsu Hor*) and Aset, the goddess of mystical wisdom. These actions draw one closer to harmony and peace, thus paving the way to discover the Self within. The negative impressions are developed through sinful actions. They are related to mental agitation, disharmony and restlessness. This implies acts based on anger, fear, desire, greed, depression, gloom, etc. These actions draw one into the outer world of human desires. They distract the mind and do not allow the intellect (Saa) to function. Thus, existence at this level is closer to an animal, being based on animal instincts and desires of the body (selfishness), rather than a spiritually mature human being, based on reason, selflessness, compassion, etc.

(Purification of the heart)

How then is it possible to eradicate negative karmic impressions and to develop positive ones? The answer lies in your understanding of the wisdom teachings and your practice of them. When you study the teachings and live according to them, your mind undergoes a transformation at all levels. This transformation is the "purification of heart" so often spoken about throughout the Ancient Egyptian *Pert M Heru* or *Book of the Dead* or *Book of Coming Forth By Day*. It signifies an eradication of negative impressions, which renders the mind pure and subtle. When the mind is rendered subtle, then spiritual

[66] For more on the philosophy of Ari see the books *The Wisdom of Maati* and *The Egyptian Book of the Dead* by Muata Ashby.

realization is possible. This discipline of purifying the heart by living according to the teachings is known as the Yoga of Action or Smai Tawi Maat.

The philosophy of Maat is a profound teaching, which encompasses the fabric of creation as well as a highly effective system of spiritual discipline. In creation stories, God (Neter Neteru) is said to have established creation upon Maat. Consequently it follows that Maat is the orderly flow of energy which maintains the universe. Further, Maat is the regularity which governs the massive planetary and solar systems as well as the growth of a blade of grass and a human cell. This natural process represents the flow of creation wherein there is constant movement and a balancing of opposites (up-down, hot-cold, here-there, you-me, etc.).

Most people act out of the different forces, which are coursing through them at the time. These may be hunger, lust, fear, hatred, anger, elation, etc. They have no control over these because they have not understood that their true essence is in reality separate from their thoughts and emotions. They have *identified* with their thoughts and therefore are led to the consequences of those thoughts and the deeds they engender. As a practitioner of mystical spirituality, one must develop a higher level of spiritual sensitivity, to become aware that you have a choice in the thoughts you think and the actions you perform. You can choose whether to act in ways that are in harmony with Maat or those that are disharmonious. You have now studied the words of wisdom and must now look beyond the level of ritual worship of the Divine to the realm of practice and experience of the Divine.

In ordinary human life, those who have not achieved the state of Enlightenment (the masses in society at large) perceive nature as a conglomeration of forces which are unpredictable and in need of control. However, as spiritual sensitivity matures, the aspirant realizes that what once appeared to be chaotic is in reality the Divine Plan of the Supreme Being in the process of unfoldment. When this state of consciousness is attained, the aspirant realizes that there is an underlying order in nature, which can only be perceived with spiritual eyes.

The various injunctions of Maat are for the purpose of keeping order in society among ordinary people, people without psychological maturity and, or spiritual sensitivity, meaning that they lack an awareness of spiritual principles and moral - ethical development. Also, they provide insight into the order of creation and a pathway or spiritual discipline, which when followed, will lead the aspirant to come into harmony with the cosmic order. When the individual attunes his or her own sense of order and balance with the cosmic order, a spontaneous unity occurs between the individual and the cosmos, and the principles of Maat, rather than being a blind set of rules which one must strive to follow, become a part of one's inner character and proceeds from one in a spontaneous manner.

This means that through the deeper understanding of cosmic order and by the practice of living in harmony with that order, the individual will lead him or herself to mental and spiritual peace and harmony. It is this peace and harmony, which allows the lake of the mind to become a clear mirror in which the individual soul is able to realize its oneness with the Universal Soul.

Ari is an integral aspect of health because it is this that determines the basis with which one will begin life. Will you incarnate into a family of mystics or into that of smokers and meat eaters? Will you incarnate into the family of Yoga practitioners and the health conscious or into the family of ignorant people who abuse their bodies and do not understand the purpose of life and thereby suffer from stress, disease and frustration? However, even if one has had a negative start in life, one can improve one's conditions by engaging in righteous actions now, and gradually, life adjusts itself to the higher spiritual basis, and more favorable conditions eventually develop. One must always practice MAAT, seeking the balance in all things. If actions to be performed and or foods or other ingested substances are not in line with mental balance, this may be a signal that they are against MAAT.

The following is a complete listing of the 42 precepts of Maat. Since there are various versions of the *Pert Em Heru* which have been discovered and no two have the same exact wording, variants will also be included to elucidate on the expanded meanings accorded to the precepts by different Sages.

Affirmations of Innocence: The 42 Precepts of Maat[67]

(1) "I have not done what is wrong." Variant: I have not acted with falsehood.
(2) "I have not robbed with violence."
(3) "I have not done violence (to anyone or anything)." Variant: I have not been rapacious (taking by force; plundering.)
(4) "I have not committed theft." Variant: I have not coveted.
(5) "I have not murdered man or woman." Variant: I have not ordered someone else to commit murder.
(6) "I have not defrauded offerings." Variant: I have not destroyed food supplies or increased or decreased the measures to profit.
(7) "I have not acted deceitfully." Variant: I have not acted with crookedness.
(8) "I have not robbed the things that belong to God."
(9) "I have told no lies."
(10) "I have not snatched away food."
(11) "I have not uttered evil words." Variant: I have not allowed myself to become sullen, to sulk or become depressed.
(12) "I have attacked no one."
(13) "I have not slaughtered the cattle that are set apart for the Gods." Variant: I have not slaughtered the Sacred bull – (Apis)
(14) "I have not eaten my heart" (overcome with anguish and distraught). Variant: I have not committed perjury.
(15) "I have not laid waste the ploughed lands."
(16) "I have not been an eavesdropper or pried into matters to make mischief."
(17) "I have not spoken against anyone." Variant: I have not babbled, gossiped.
(18) "I have not allowed myself to become angry without cause."
(19) "I have not committed adultery." Variant: I have not committed homosexuality.
(20) "I have not committed any sin against my own purity."
(21) "I have not violated sacred times and seasons."
(22) "I have not done that which is abominable."
(23) "I have not uttered fiery words. I have not been a man or woman of anger."
(24) "I have not stopped my ears listening to the words of right and wrong (Maat)."
(25) "I have not stirred up strife (disturbance)." "I have not caused terror." "I have not struck fear into any man."
(26) "I have not caused any one to weep." Variant: I have not hoodwinked.
(27) "I have not lusted or committed fornication nor have I lain with others of my same sex." Variant: I have not molested children.
(28) "I have not avenged myself." Variant: I have not cultivated resentment.
(29) "I have not worked grief, I have not abused anyone." Variant: I have not cultivated a quarrelsome nature.
(30) "I have not acted insolently or with violence."
(31) "I have not judged hastily." Variant: I have not been impatient.
(32) "I have not transgressed or angered God."
(33) "I have not multiplied my speech overmuch (talk too much).
(34) "I have not done harm or evil." Variant: I have not thought evil.
(35) "I have not worked treason or curses on the King."
(36) "I have never befouled the water." Variant: I have not held back the water from flowing in its season.
(37) "I have not spoken scornfully." Variant: I have not yelled unnecessarily or raised my voice.
(38) "I have not cursed The God."
(39) "I have not behaved with arrogance." Variant: I have not been boastful.[68]
(40) "I have not been overwhelmingly proud or sought for distinctions for myself[69]."

---

[67] The following is a composite summary of "negative confessions" from several Ancient Egyptian *Books of Coming Forth by Day*. They are often referred to as "Negative Confessions" since the person uttering them is affirming what moral principles they have not transgressed. In this respect they are similar to the Yamas or ethical restraints of Indian philosophy. While all of the papyri include 42 precepts, some specific precepts vary according to the specific initiate for which they were prepared and the priests who compiled them. Therefore, I have included more than one precept per line where I felt it was appropriate to show that there were slight variations in the precepts and to more accurately reflect the broader view of the original texts. For more information, refer to the book by the same author, "The 42 Precepts of Maat: The Philosophy of Righteousness and the Ancient Egyptian Wisdom Texts," and its corresponding audio tape series, both available through the Sema Institute of Yoga (305) 378-6253.

[68] Bragging, pretentious, arrogant, egoistic.

(41) “I have never magnified my condition beyond what was fitting or increased my wealth, except with such things as are (justly) mine own possessions by means of Maat.” Variant: I have not disputed over possessions except when they concern my own rightful possessions. Variant: I have not desired more than what is rightfully mine.

(42) “I have never thought evil (blasphemed) or slighted The God in my native town.”

---

[69] Selfishness, egoistically.

CHAPTER 3: FASTING FOR HEALTH OF BODY, MIND AND SOUL

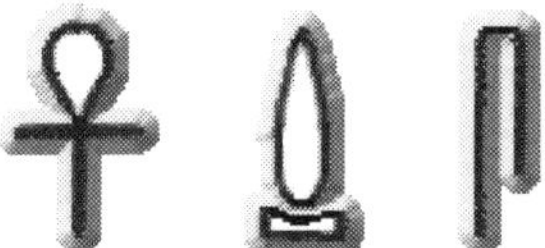

Preventative Health and Self-Healing

In the state of pristine health, the physical body of every human being exists in harmony with various bacteria, viruses and chemical processes. When the systems of the body, which keep the balance, become weakened, a situation of dis-ease develops. Due to ignorance in understanding (disharmony in the thought patterns), the mind has failed to lead the individual to internally create the proper substances (thoughts and or chemical processes that create hormones and proteins needed to have a healthy body) which will allow for the proper energy distribution throughout the mind and body.

There are several factors involved in pain, suffering and disease, however, at their most basic level, they are all related to the mind, the state of which is a reflection of the spiritual health of the individual. The body is a creation or mold of the mind, whatever the mind creates will eventually manifest in the body and the environment of the body as well. Also, if the mind is burdened by insanity (worry, anxiety, fear, delusions, stress, schizophrenia, etc.), the energy flow from the soul to the mind to the body will be disturbed or blocked. Therefore, other than ailments caused by problems in the environment or accidents, physical dis-ease is primarily due to a mental imbalance, which in turn is due to a spiritual imbalance.

Since the body is composed of inert elements, it is the Spirit, through the medium of mind (energy) and DNA, which directs and controls the elements, electrochemical composition and chemical reactions which make up the process we call life. The soul chooses the particular circumstances into which to incarnate. This means that it chooses a particular set of chromosomal factors in a family along with the life-time circumstances and situations which will allow it to gain the experiences it desires and needs for its evolution.

A problem that many people encounter in ordinary human life is that there is little concern or emphasis placed on the purity of the food, both mental and physical, that is consumed. Mental food in the form of elevated thoughts and wisdom teachings are essential in maintaining healthy reason (intellectual sharpness which comes from studying the mystical teachings) and positive mental vibrations. Nourishment in the form of solid food and exercise are prerequisites to physical health. Physical health, though not an absolute requirement for the practice of spiritual discipline, is helpful since, as stated previously, it is more difficult to focus the mind on spiritual matters when the mind is tied up in the experiences of pain and suffering.

With this in mind, there are various modes of practice which have been devised to maintain health and to deal with ailments. However, they should not be limited to just dealing with the physical signs of disease since these are only the manifestations of a deeper psycho-spiritual root cause.

The approach to health maintenance and treatment of disease should be holistic, taking the entire human being (spiritual-mental-physical) into consideration. Also, it is important to understand that doctors and other healers do not and cannot heal others. They can only help others to heal themselves by providing information and other means to assist them in bringing their constitution back into balance. It's a good idea to have conventional medical doctors examine and attempt to diagnose so that one may be pointed in a good direction toward understanding the problem, however, conventional medical treatments are usually directed to getting rid of the symptoms. This is what is often referred to as a "cure" by the medical profession. Sometimes it is critical to alleviate the symptoms, however, the deeper root cause of the disease should also be addressed. The drugs used in conventional medicine usually mask the symptom(s) of disease, creating the illusion that the problem has gone away when in fact, it is only suppressing the disease and pushing it deeper in the body. Hence, it is not surprising that so many people who have submitted themselves to this system of health care have developed cancer and other debilitating dis-eases.

Other drawbacks of many man made drugs is that drugs themselves cause side effects that damage other organs and tissues, and there is the ever-present possibility of getting the wrong prescription from the doctor or the wrong drug from the pharmacist by mistake (something that happens hundreds of times each year). They are only human after all, and should only be trusted when there is no other choice. The only entity capable of creating a correct prescription for an ailment in the form of hormones and other chemicals released into the blood stream and immune system is the body itself. What it needs in order to do that is peace of mind, proper nutrition, and internal cleansing from poisonous substances which block its operation, i.e. too much negative or too much positive emotions, unwholesome foods, overeating, negative thoughts, lack of sleep, etc.

The mysterious aspect of health is an area which is beyond the understanding of any science, and thus falls into the realm of that which is not even discussed by the conventional medical establishment. This area includes the miraculous healings, the placebo effect, as well as the unexplained deaths and ailments. This area is mysterious because it encompasses many unknown factors. These include the soul of the individual and its previous involvements, previous exposure to toxic substances, deep psychological distress which may not be apparent at the conscious level, karmic entanglements of the present and from previous lives and the mission of the soul in the present incarnation. Since no two people are alike, no treatment can be exactly alike, however, there are some guidelines to health and healing which may be performed by oneself or with the assistance of others. Except in emergency or trauma cases, surgery should be the last form of treatment considered.

FASTING FOR THE BODY

The Use of Fasting and Enemas

In order to promote internal hygiene, the Ancient Egyptians practiced regular fasting as well as cleansing with enemas. The following quote from Herodotus[70] provides further insight.

> "For three consecutive days in every month they purge themselves, pursuing after health by means of emetics and drenches; for they think it is from the food they eat that all sickness come to men and women"[71].

The ancient Naturopathic healers recognized the natural tendency of the body to lose appetite when feeling ill, and thus imparted the disciplines of fasting on a regular basis to promote physical health. This practice continues today in the Naturopathic sciences. Fasting allows the body to eliminate waste material since it can use the energy that would normally be used in trying to digest food, for processing and eliminating waste materials and poisons.

In the Digestive System, food enters the mouth (top), goes down the esophagus into the stomach, then to the small intestine, and then the large intestine; the left over material (feces) after nutrients are extracted, exits through the colon (bottom).

---

[70] *Random House Encyclopedia* Herodotus (c. 484-425 BC), Greek historian and geographer. Little is known of him. He made lengthy journeys through the ancient world (Asia Minor, Mesopotamia, Babylon, and perhaps Egypt), spent long periods in Athens, and helped colonize Thurii in South Italy. He is most known for his lengthy, vivid, frequently anecdotal history of the Persian Wars. Considered the beginning of Western history writing, his work contains diverse information and is rich in anecdotes. See also {Thucydides}

[71] Herodotus II, 77

It is a good practice to give the digestive system a break regularly, and it is even more advantageous to integrate and harmonize this into your spiritual practice. Many people believe that it is necessary to enter into rigorous water only fasts. These can certainly be practiced and there will be a benefit. However, if the lifestyle presented here is followed, such extremes should not be necessary, since this way of life promotes a constant cleansing process. However, if an imbalance occurs, special fasts may be indicated to resolve the problem. Often the body itself will signal the need for a fast by temporarily shutting off the desire for food. At these times one should follow the wisdom of the body and not eat out of habit or fear. It is very possible that by the time Herodotus visited Egypt, which was then being controlled by foreign forces, he may have observed more extreme practices, which were instituted by those foreign governments, that had not been part of the normal practices of the Egyptians previously because of the excesses of those times. In any case, colon care was paramount in importance from early on in Kemetic history.

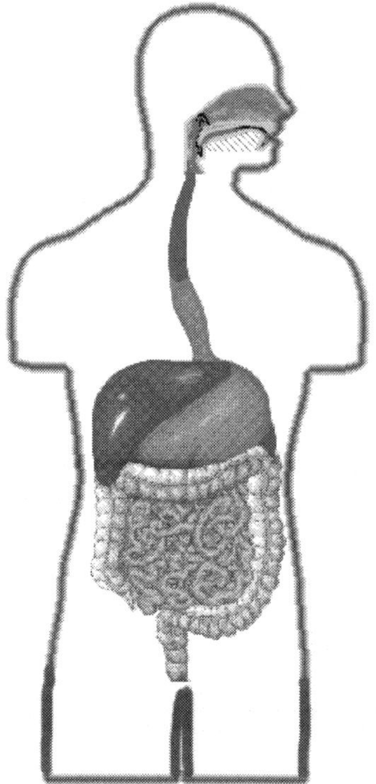

Plate 13: The Digestive System

In Ancient Egypt, there were doctors who specialized on the eyes, the teeth, the belly, and the "hidden diseases."[72] The importance given to colon health was such that specialist doctors emerged in the field of health, called *Shepherds of the Anus.*[73] It should be noted that the concerns of the Ancient Egyptian doctor of the anus went far beyond the modern medical proctologist,[74] since the shepherds were concerned with the entire functioning of the mettu system throughout the body.

It should be kept in mind that while the Ancient Egyptians may at first appear to be fanatical in their concern about the colon, their results were so impressive that even in the twentieth century, researchers are discovering the benefits of colon cleansing. The connection between colon hygiene and mental health has also been established.

---

[72] Herodotus II 84/LB I369

[73] Jonckheere 1958 p.99

[74] Random House Encyclopedia - Proctology, branch of medicine dealing with the diagnosis and treatment of diseases of the rectum and lower intestine.

F. S. Jameson. *"Colonic therapy. Its usefulness for the relief of constipation and systemic diseases and the indications for its employment."* American Medicine 36:469-474 (1930). Colonic irrigation is the most effective for chronic constipation, and benefits nervous diseases, especially neurasthenia, chronic deforming diseases of the joints, blood dyscrasias (diseased blood), and certain forms of chronic nephritis. Systematic colon treatments and dietary changes are effective in the control of high blood pressure.

N. W. Kaiser. *"Colonic therapy in mental disease."* Ohio State Medical Journal 26:510-16 (1930). In the past year some 70 patients suffering from of dementia praecox, manic depressive and psychoneurotic types and after treatment limited largely to colonic irrigations 2-3 times a week the patients showed improvement.

H.K. Marshall and C.E. Thompson. *"Colon irrigation in the treatment of mental disease." New* England Journal of Medicine 207: 454-57 (1932). Colon irrigation enables a faster return to mental stability in many cases. Sedation is obtained in active cases, strikingly shown by a reduction in the number of wet sheet envelopments required and the destruction of mattresses has fallen by approximately 50%.

In modern times, the late Dr. Denis Burkitt (of Burkitt's Lymphoma fame) exposed the cancer-prevention properties of dietary fiber. Dr. Burkitt made the "Fiber story" famous due to his work among native Africans. Dr. Burkitt, a British researcher, along with his colleagues Hugh Trowell and Alan Walker, spent many years in Africa studying the differences between the Western and African diets. They wanted to know why diseases typically found in Western countries were rare in Africa. His discoveries became world famous. The finding was that diets that are high in fiber seemed to be associated with a reduced cancer incidence in the large bowel, as well as the incidence of many other diseases common to Western countries. This means that the SWD (Standard Western Diet) is inherently detrimental to the proper functioning of the human body.

Dr. Burkitt was quoted as saying about the United States, that is, "the most constipated country in the world."

con·sti·pa·tion *n.* **1.** Difficult, incomplete, or infrequent evacuation of dry, hardened feces from the bowels.[75]

Under normal conditions there should be at least one to two bowel movements per day. The most important problems causing constipation are the consumption of wrong foods and the consumption of foods in an improper manner. Constipating consumables are processed foods in general, and especially foods such as pastries, candies, overcooked foods, fried foods, etc. However, constipation is not a phenomena which affects the intestines alone. Blocked arteries become "constipated" due to the buildup of cholesterol, plaque (arterial), or due to whatever other substance may cause an obstruction. The mental process then becomes dull and atrophied due to obstructions from stored up impurities. The accumulation of Ukhedu in certain parts of the body is a form of constipation that will cause a disease in that part of the body later on. As discussed, certain thoughts are Ukhedu forming for the mind as well. If the mind is cramped by fear, ignorance, worry, anger, hatred, desire, etc., the movement of the Life Force energies will be impaired, i.e. constipated, leading to disease later on as well.

[75] American Heritage Dictionary

Guidelines for correct eating habits

The normal eating habits that should be followed by all human beings are as follows. If these ideals are maintained, the body will cleanse itself in a natural way. Further, these habits will also promote dental health, as dental caries was relatively unknown in pre-dynastic Ancient Egypt, but gradually became prominent as Ancient Egyptian culture and diet degraded over time, and contact with less advanced cultures increased.[76] Keep in mind that the following are guidelines. Adopt any of them as your situation allows, and do not become discouraged or frustrated if you are not able to follow everything all at once. Move in accordance with your ability, and with time and patience, you will succeed.

- Start the day with no breakfast but with coconut water[77], or freshly juiced or powdered green drink, or freshly squeezed lemon or lime juice with water {bottled, from a pure source}
- No overeating – eat when hungry only.
- Food for the body: Eat only a vegetarian diet, least 50-80% raw fruits and vegetables
- Ideally, eat one item alone- the stomach will have an easier time digesting one kind of food at a time. Otherwise ideally do not eat more than three different items at one time.
- Drink sufficient fruit juices throughout the day; water consumption will decrease, as you will be getting more liquid through the fruits, fruit juices and other raw foods.
- Ideally, do not drink when eating, and up to 1 hour after.
- Chew all food thoroughly, 30-50 times per mouthful (drink your food – by proper mastication solid foods should turn to liquids before being swallowed).
- Yoga exercises daily.
- Breathing exercises daily.
- Sunbathing daily for 10-20 minutes.
- Food for the mind: Attend lectures on high philosophy and spiritual issues – allows the mind to produce positive impressions which will promote the flow of the Life Forces (Sekhem) from circulating throughout the body. Right actions – being ethical and non-violent conserves energy and promotes harmony.
- Food for the soul: Practice of meditation daily – allowing quiet time for the mind so that one can experience the glory of the eternal Self within.
- Use only starch free or reduced starch vegetables when breaking the fast and thereafter.
- Try to have no more than two major meals per day.
- Do not eat at lunchtime simply because it is lunchtime – eat when the body alerts you that there is true hunger.
- Due to the problem of overfarming, which depletes the land of its natural nutrients and thereby causes crops to be nutrient poor, try to eat organic foods, otherwise one may supplement the diet with vegetarian vitamins (formulation especially designed for people who practice vegetarianism) which may be found at your local health food store.

The following are general fasting guidelines of programs designed for maintaining a high degree of internal cleansing. However, if the above eating habits are maintained, the body will cleanse itself in a natural way and the more rigorous fasting practices will not be necessary under normal conditions. Again, the reader is advised to consult a Natural Health Care Practitioner before embarking on a fasting program beyond the 12-16 hour program outlined below.

---

[76] Ebers papyrus introduction-commentary.

[77] The clear liquid inside the young coconut.

12 - 16 hour Fast – Nature's Natural Cleansing Fast

One may consume solid food during the day, and not consume anything except liquids after the hour of 6-7 pm, until the next morning at 6-7 am or later. This is the 12 - 16 hour fast. Instead of having "breakfast" in the morning, one should rather "break" "fast," that is, break the fast you engaged in all night as you slept in a manner that will allow the toxins generated to be cleansed from the system. Break the fast with coconut water, or green vegetable juice (freshly juiced or from powdered form) or lemon/lime and water, later on with some tea (not too hot in temperature), or juice, and later on with some fruits (watery fruits such as melons first, and then the pulpier fruits). Do not start consuming other foods until noon.

If one starts the day with a solid meal, the typical idea of breakfast in most countries, the toxins are pushed back into the system. Furthermore, if this typical breakfast consists of meat products and heavy starches, not only are the toxins pushed back into the system, but additional toxins are being dumped on an already toxic system. This will exacerbate the buildup of toxins (Ukhedu) in the system which will lead to future disease. Imagine what would happen if you never took out the garbage in your home, but rather, simply kept piling garbage upon garbage, or your toilet stopped flushing. In either situation, you are going to have a serious problem in your home. Similarly, not allowing for the proper elimination of the garbage within the body-temple, your soul's home, will also lead to serious problems there. Thus, though the cause of cancer and other diseases remain a mystery to the scientific community, from the holistic physiological and biological viewpoint, it is not so inconceivable to understand why cancers and other dis-eases occur. They are merely expressions of a very toxic system.

24 hour Fast

One may consume solid foods once a day at the same time of day, eating fruits first, and then vegetables ½ hour later, considering this as one meal. In between meals one may drink fruit and green juices, teas, nut milks, and water. This program can be maintained indefinitely as a normal way of food consumption if you choose to do so, once the body is purified to a high degree and the diet consists of the high quality fruits, nuts and vegetables. This is the 24 hour fast. It can be practiced once per week or it may be used as the normal daily practice. Break the fast as above.

36 Hour Fast

After a light dinner, eat nothing solid the following day, and until "break-fast" the day after. Use the same fasting guidelines as for the three day fast (below) and the same guidelines for breaking the fast as for the 12 -16 hour fast.

Three Day Fast and Purging- Break the Fast on the Morning of the Second Day

This program is for more advanced practitioners of fasting. Beginners should use the program presented at the end of this volume in the section titled ***Your 30 day Diet and Fasting Plan for Body, Mind and Soul.***

For three consecutive days, once per month, one is to consume nothing but coconut water, lemon or lime water, or juices, in conjunction with the use of mild laxatives[78] such as castor oil, prune juice, aloe juice, senna tea or similar natural juices or herbs. These items would be eaten in servings at the exclusion

[78] Favorite laxatives in ancient times were figs, dates, and castor oil. Tannic acid, derived principally from the acacia nut, was valued in the treatment of burns. "Medicine," Microsoft (R) Encarta. Copyright (c) 1994 Microsoft Corporation. Copyright (c) 1994 Funk & Wagnall's Corporation.

of other foods. Their effect cleanses the body and naturally flushes out impurities. These may be used along with aloe juice to soothe and heal the digestive track. However, this program will accelerate the discharge of Ukhedu if there are many impurities in the body, if there is severe disease, or if one has taken in a lot of medicines in one's lifetime, as drug residues can remain in the system for many years. If these conditions are present, you should be monitored by a competent health professional.[79] Caution should be observed until the practitioner attains a high level of purity and body sensitivity to practice on his or her own.

Fruit Only Diet and or Fast

A fruit diet in itself acts as a cleanser. One may practice eating a diet completely devoid of vegetables. This will also act as a natural laxative. Certain fruits, in particular, grapes, figs and dates, have laxative qualities, and also provide nutrients to support the body. So these can be eaten alone, and one can even survive on these alone for a long time if needed. This diet may be practiced on an extended basis according to one's capacity, however, some health practitioners feel that such a stringent diet, especially considering the soil depletion factors, are more apt to result in vitamin and mineral deficiencies. Thus, fruitarian diets are often supplemented with nuts and seeds. However, as a means of cleansing the body, one may practice the fruit only diet for three to seven days or more, and then return to the regular vegetarian program.

NOTE ON FRUITS: Some conventional doctors advise their patients to cut fruits out of their diet, because, they feel, it will result in elevated blood glucose and predispose the patient to developing diabetes mellitus. So instead they recommend a diet filled with meat and starches, which is usually a continuation, if not an exacerbation (since the patient more than likely ate some fruit before) of the patient's previous diet which led them to their current state of disease in the first place. While the consumption of fruits does lead to an elevated blood glucose, when the Mettu are unclogged (free of Ukhedu), the fruit sugars can be properly absorbed and assimilated without taxing the system. However, if the system is very toxic and the Mettu clogged with many impurities, such as the accumulation of plaque from ingested animal fats and starchy foods, the consumption of fruits may predispose to hyperglycemia (increase blood glucose), since the Mettu will not be able to properly absorb or transport the glucose. The solution however, should not be simply to dump more toxins in the already overloaded system, but to engage in a process of cleansing to remove the buildup of the plaque. It has been scientifically proven that a holistic system of cleansing and healing which includes yoga exercises, meditation and vegetarianism (with cooked or raw "live" foods) can result in the removal of accumulated plaque. Thus, the process is reversible, and once the system is cleansed, the consumption of fruits should no longer pose a problem. Rather, they will promote a life of health and vitality.

Juice Fast

One may consume nothing but juices for several days. Lemon or lime and water or diluted juices can be used. This program will accelerate the discharge of Ukhedu, and beginners should be monitored by a competent health professional[80] until the practitioner attains a high level of purity and body sensitivity to be on his or her own.

Vegetable juices from raw starch-free vegetables can also be used, and should be considered for very toxic or ill persons, or long fasts, as they induce a slower and less intense cleanse than fruit juices. In addition, if the system is very toxic and the Mettu clogged with many impurities, such as the

[79] The Sema Institute offers expert assistance in the form of counseling on diet and nutrition for the body, mind and soul for those wishing to adopt the Kemetic Diet Wisdom of natural health to restore and or promote better health. See the back section of this book for more information.
[80] ibid

accumulation of plaque from ingested animal fats and starchy foods, the fruit juices may predispose to prolonged hyperglycemia (an increase blood glucose), since the Mettu will not be able to properly absorb or transport the fruit sugars. Thus, for initial cleansing in very toxic persons, vegetable juices may be preferred over fruit juices. However, once the system regains its health and balance, one should be able to fast on fruit juices as well.

Regardless of which juice is chosen for the fast, one must observe caution, since the strong action of the juice may cause a rapid discharge of impurities, wastes and poisons that may overwhelm the circulatory system and possibly lead to a crisis. So, when fasting, always take juices slowly and, in a diluted form, observing for reactions before continuing further.

Vegetable Juice Fast

If you can, consume freshly juiced vegetables at the regular meal times (Live Juice of your choice – carrot juice, celery, spinach, etc. {6-8 ounces}). If fresh juices are not available use Kamut Wheatgrass Juice prescribed for the Kemetic Diet Daily program. The cleansing effect will enhanced and the body will have the nutrient building blocks to rebuild healthy cells and maintain high energy throughout the day.

Coconut Water Fast

A coconut water only fast is beneficial because it allows the cleansing benefits of a fast without the energy loss. Coconut water is one of the purest sources of nutriment for the body.

Plain Water Fast

For an intensified fast you may consume only pure water during the time of your fast. However, this program will accelerate the discharge of Ukhedu, so you should be monitored by a competent health professional[81] until you attain a high level of purity and body sensitivity to do this on your own.

Enemas

It is beneficial to administer one or two enemas during the time of fasting in order to assist the cleansing process. However, if a high quality diet and the proper eating habits are maintained, the need for enemas as well as purgatives, is reduced.

How to Conduct the Cleansing Process: The Kemetic Healing Program

Important Points to Keep in Mind Before, During and After Fasting

- Before a fast, gradually eat lighter foods and use the mild laxatives.
- Remain in a stress free environment.
- Remain in the fresh air.
- Take air and sun baths daily.

[81] The Sema Institute offers expert assistance in the form of counseling on diet and nutrition for the body, mind and soul for those wishing to adopt the Kemetic Diet Wisdom of natural health to restore and or promote better health. See the back section of this book for more information.

- Be active only to the extent you feel comfortable. Generally, during a fast one should remain calm and inactive. Follow the rhythm of the body. Move, sleep and do activities as the body dictates, not as you desire.
- If you feel a little ill, it is most likely due to the cleansing process; wastes and impurities are being cleaned from the body. Consult with a health care professional,[82] and if all is well, simply observe the process, and do not allow negative thoughts to persuade you to end the fast or the cleansing program.
- When you get up after lying down, be extremely careful. Move very slowly, since your blood pressure is reduced and therefore will require more time to replenish the brain. Getting up too fast will cause a shortfall in oxygen to the brain, and this will cause you to faint, fall and possibly injure yourself.
- Use only starch free or reduced starch vegetables when breaking the fast (after the initial "break-fast" protocol).

Step 1

Along with the following disciplines for the body, one should take up the study of spiritual philosophy and meditation practice.

There is a mistaken notion that long-term chronic problems can be cured by a long intense fast. This is incorrect. The process of healing disease should be thought of more as the adoption of a healthy lifestyle rather than as a curing technique or one time medicament. If there is much impurity in the body from years of consuming the wrong diet or from drugs or medications, a severe fast may kill the patient, because it will cause too many impurities to be cleansed from the cells of the body at one time. This sudden infusion of impurities, into the lymph and circulatory systems which have been stored perhaps for years, may impair their functioning altogether and lead to severe illness or death. Therefore, short term fasts, along with a permanent change to the proper diet and proper eating habits, using the transition diets in conjunction with the practice of the disciplines of mystical spirituality, is the best course of action for those suffering chronic disease or who carry a lot of impurities. Further, overweight people suffer mostly from mechanical obstructions to the systems of the body. Leaner people suffer mostly from physiological obstructions such as the development of acids and pus due to meat eating. Therefore, the desired course for people encumbered with severe disease, chronic disease, physical or chemical obstructions, constipation, etc., is to make slow changes in the diet and lifestyle, moving towards gradual purification. Those who are less encumbered may move at a faster pace.

Step 2

The three-day fast may be used as a diagnostic tool. Fast for one, two or three days on water and juices alone, or simply eat fruits only. If you suffer from severe headaches, nausea, dizziness, or if heart palpitations occur, then it is a sign that there is much impurity (mucus, pus, and Ukhedu) in the systems of the body. If the reaction is severe, you should proceed slowly with the healing and fasting program and you should use the transition diets. Also, you should not practice the water only fasts during the first 1-2 years of making these dietary changes. You should not attempt the water only fast until you are purified to a greater degree, and the severe symptoms disappear. (You should also seek the advice of a qualified health practitioner).

If your symptoms are mild, you may proceed at your own pace in applying more stringent fasts, using only water or juices, and or extending the length of the fast up to one week. However, you still should be monitored by a qualified health professional.[83]

[82] ibid

Step 3

Now begin reducing your usual quantity of food intake and consume only natural, mucus inhibiting foods (starchless vegetables and fruits).

Step 4

It will require anywhere from one to three years for a person in an ordinary condition of health to be cleansed. This will be accomplished through a regular process of fasting and permanently changing to a proper diet as described in this volume. It will take this long for the mass quantities of impurities, accumulated over many years, to be completely removed from the body.

Regular Fasting Program to be used with the Special Diet

Choose a regular fasting program that suits your health needs and your personality. If you have a specific, serious ailment, you may wish to enter into longer fasts (1-2 weeks), but this should be done under the guidance of a qualified health professional. [84] In most other cases, including chronic diseases, health will be restored by:

A. Making a **PERMANENT** change to the proper diet.
B. Instituting the correct eating habits.
C. Practicing regular fasting systematically (1/2 day fast, 24 hour fast, one day per week fast, or three days per month fast).
D. Mystical spirituality practices.

Symptoms of cleansing during a fast

As the movement towards a high quality vegetarian diet and correct eating habits progresses, the body will enter into a natural process of cleansing. One may experience headaches, hunger pangs (cravings), insomnia, bursts of energy, bursts of weakness, intestinal discomforts, etc., at times due to the previous habits. These are the body's attempts to adjust to the new regimen after being encumbered with impurities for a long time. It is advisable to have a qualified health professional[85] monitor your progress so that you will not break the cleansing cycle out of ignorance of what is happening, which may lead to fears about the process. As you practice the fast, you will experience some other effects of the cleansing process. You may get headaches, nausea, coated tongue, unpleasant odor, mucus in the urine, etc. Do not be discouraged, since these are good signs. Continue drinking a lot of water and doing breathing exercises (discussed in the "Proper Breathing" section of this book).

NOTE: One may experience additional symptoms of cleansing beyond the physical aspect (body). Mental irritation, anger, annoyance, acting out, etc., may occur since the mind will also want to release pent up frustrations, prejudices, vices and other negative thoughts which have been stored up as negative impressions in the unconscious level of the mind.

[83] The Sema Institute offers expert assistance in the form of counseling on diet and nutrition for the body, mind and soul for those wishing to adopt the Kemetic Diet Wisdom of natural health to restore and or promote better health. See the back section of this book for more information.
[84] The Sema Institute offers expert assistance in the form of counseling on diet and nutrition for the body, mind and soul for those wishing to adopt the Kemetic Diet Wisdom of natural health to restore and or promote better health. See the back section of this book for more information.
[85] ibid

Breaking a fast

Generally, you should take as much time breaking a fast as you did practicing the fast. So if the fast lasted three days you should take three days to gradually break it as follows. Gradually, move from lighter to denser foods. So if you fasted with water alone, begin with juices diluted with water, then undiluted juices, then watery fruits (melons), then the pulpier fruits (papaya, apples, pears, bananas, etc.,- consult fruit combining chart), then reduced starch or starch free vegetables, then steamed vegetables, etc., The idea is to slowly work your way back to your normal diet.

NOTE 1: For Meat Eaters and the Overweight- People who had extremely acidic diets (meat based) and or are overweight, should not break the fast with fruits, since the high sugar content in these foods may cause an adverse reaction with the acids and other impurities that have been released through the fast. Also, do not practice excessively long fasts. Break the fast with (in order of succession) a mild laxative, vegetable juice, starch-free raw vegetables, lightly cooked vegetables and cabbage. No fruits should be eaten for some time. Also, such a person should be put on the transition diet for some time prior to the fast.

> **starch** *n.* **1.** A naturally abundant nutrient carbohydrate, $(C_6H_{10}O_5)_n$, found chiefly in the seeds, fruits, tubers, roots, and stem pith of plants, notably in corn, potatoes, wheat, and rice, and varying widely in appearance according to source but commonly prepared as a white, amorphous, tasteless powder. Foods having a high content of starch, as rice, breads, and potatoes.

NOTE 2: The first foods eaten after a fast should have a laxative quality as opposed to nutritional value. This is because during the fast there will be no bowel movement since the body is naturally holding on to the food until more is taken in. Therefore, what is most desirable is to get rid of the impurities that have remained in the system as soon as possible. This action will bring immediate relief to the system from disease and will promote vitality and a sense of unparalleled well being.

For people in good health, who are following a proper vegetarian and or fruit diet, the best foods with laxative qualities are fruits.

For average people the best course is to continue breaking the fast (meals after "break-fast" protocol) with raw and lightly cooked vegetables. Steamed spinach has above average cleansing properties.

NOTE 3: If there are no problems at this point, one may continue eating as much as is naturally desired, but only from the foods listed in the program. This will promote the cleansing and excretion process. As part of the natural course of life after the fast, eat only when you are truly hungry. The natural desire to eat or real hunger does not go away in a short time. If you wait a while, your feeling of hunger may go away. If it does, it was not real hunger. Real hunger will stay with you until it is satisfied. If this rule about eating is kept, all other health issues will fall into place easily. However, developing this habit may take some time, so be patient.

Notes of Caution on Fasting

NOTES:

How to Cope with Awakening of the Serpent Power During a Fast

Since there is a spiritual dimension in the practice of fasting, it is important to understand that the inner Life Force (*Serpent Power* or *Kundalini*), that sustains the body's functions and leads the soul to spiritual enlightenment, may be released in a powerful way after being obstructed. This may occur in a natural way because it is one's time as the body becomes lighter and ceases to obstruct the mind and soul. It may also occur by excess fasting or misapplication of the teachings related to meditation and the practice of the mystical disciplines. Extremes and fanaticism have no part in the scientific movement towards spiritual enlightenment. If one is not prepared to experience higher consciousness through the purification of the mind, philosophy and right action, the emergence of the Life Force can be a negative, even frightening and dangerous experience. This is referred to as a "premature release" of the Life Force. Therefore, spiritual enlightenment cannot be forced by severe fasting just as it cannot be brought about through drugs or other artificial means.

In accordance with the person's karmic background, the emergence of the energy may cause visions, out of body experiences and other psychic phenomena. If the person is ready to integrate these experiences, they can be beautiful and joyous movements towards self-discovery. If the person is not ready, that is, if they are ignorant as to what is happening or if too much is occurring too soon, they may become fearful and even come to believe they are losing their mind. In this case it is best to break the fast and seek spiritual counseling. Consuming grounding foods (cooked vegetables and transition diet type foods) will be the best course of action to bring the mind back to a normal level functioning. Your personality is to become integrated. Integration of the personality means that the experiences, if they occur, are to be blended with your preexisting knowledge. You cannot remain in an out of body state forever. You must at some point end the fast and continue your life as a human being. The difference now however is that you will be more conscious of the spiritual dimensions within yourself. This growing integration will allow you to become spiritually enlightened (achieve a perennial awareness of Divine Cosmic Consciousness), even while continuing to live in society and even when you are not fasting.

Mental Disorders

In any case, those suffering from mental disorders, not related to spiritual evolution, may be benefited by fasting since this practice will cleanse the body from chemical imbalances and other physiological irregularities which are affecting the brain and consequently distort the perceptions and functioning of the mind. However, this process should be monitored by a health professional. [86]

It must be clearly understood that fasting is not the goal of life. It is a tool to be used wisely and purposefully. Through the extended practice of fasting for even a short time or after a few times, it is possible to experience a loss of desire for eating at all. At this point the body can become very emaciated. This can affect the physiology of the brain, which in turn affect the cognitive functions of the mind. The misguided notion that becoming emaciated and losing the desire to eat is to be equated with spiritual enlightenment must be eradicated before entering into the fast. At this point the adage: "Eat to live; do not live to eat" comes in handy. One may have to force oneself to eat at this point, but not what was eaten previously.

[86] The Sema Institute offers expert assistance in the form of counseling on diet and nutrition for the body, mind and soul for those wishing to adopt the Kemetic Diet Wisdom of natural health to restore and or promote better health. See the back section of this book for more information.

It must be clearly understood that loss of appetite for eating at all is easier to achieve than a balance between eating too much and not enough. Reaching this balance is the ultimate goal of these practices, and the goal, which will help in the endeavor of promoting spiritual enlightenment. Fasting for fasting sake, fasting to prove one's ability to fast or becoming emaciated due to a misguided movement towards health is an effect of the dull intellect, and should be avoided. The discipline of health, when practiced with wisdom and insight into the nature of life, yields the true fruits of health, i.e. vitality, inspiration, detachment and freedom from the world, and ultimately self-discovery.

Injunctions from the Precepts of Maat on Food

(10) "I have not snatched away food."
(14) "I have not eaten my heart" (overcome with anguish and distraught). Variant: Committed perjury.
(36) "I have never befouled the water." Variant: held back the water from flowing in its season.

There is a proper balance to be discovered. In this balance you are trying to maintain a harmony so that you have sufficient vitality to sustain the normal activities of life, but without the extraneous weight and impurities that drag the mind down to worldliness. You want to be consuming just enough so that you may be able to remain in touch with and have enough vitality to operate in the world, but not so much that your spiritual sensitivity is hampered. You must carefully monitor what and how much you eat, and also adopt the philosophy that you are eating out of duty to sustain the body, so that your soul may carry out its divine duty on earth (attain enlightenment) and not for the mere pleasure of eating.

Fasting is not a discipline for hurting or punishing the body, but rather a practice of austerity. Austerity and asceticism are disciplines for controlling the lower nature of a human being, including the desires and other worldly aspects of the personality, to bring them under the control of the mind and its directing principle, the intellect. The encumbered intellect cannot function properly. The practices of asceticism have been devised for disciplining the mind and body by controlling the interaction between the body and the world, so that a clarity of mind may develop, and with it, spiritual enlightenment. So austerity and asceticism are not disciplines of harshness or grimness or deprivation. Rather, they are to be entered into by those who understand that you are developing a true luxury and wealth, which is control of your own mind. You are not losing or giving up anything except your troubles, and dis-ease. Rather, you are gaining the tools to be successful in life, self-control and vitality as well as health. Therefore, fasting is a tool for maintaining a clean body, and not for turning the world off. That can only be done by the mind, and the mind can only do that when there is understanding of the philosophy, which then leads to the divine experience.

Unnatural Sex Desires

Foods with growth hormones, such as those used in meat and dairy production, overcooked foods, spicy foods, etc. cause a human being to experience heightened levels of passion and desire, in general. In children, the effect of growth hormones present in the food leads to the premature onset of puberty. The mind becomes extremely agitated as the sex organs and urges develop before their normal time, as proven by the increasing reports of children experiencing sexual urges, and girls starting their menstrual cycles and becoming pregnant before the age of ten. Therefore, the disruptive elements of the growth hormones (taken in when eating meat and dairy products) on the human body must be avoided since they confuse the natural cycle of the male and the female, and lead to all kinds of sexual dysfunction, identity crisis and diseases specific to the male and female gender.[87] The factors above are exacerbated by a culture which is inordinately concerned with sexual matters. This constant over-stimulation, through the media,

[87] See the section on *Diseases of the Male and Female* for more on this topic.

entertainment and in personal life, coupled with the weak will due to the constant mental agitation from engaging in other non-virtuous behaviors, thoughts or speech, renders a person susceptible to mental as well as physical illnesses.

Cravings

Another aspect of the physiology that is strongly distorted in most people is the desire to eat. In an attempt to satiate the desire that cannot be satisfied by other means, the body craves more and more food. This craving is akin to coveting for possessions, relationships, and anything else that the mind fancies as a possible means to achieve the abiding happiness and contentment it so desperately wants. But the abiding contentment and happiness never comes in this manner, and the human being becomes more frustrated. Having no insight into the source and means to achieve this, the cycle of desiring and consuming continues until disease strikes or death terminates the soul's use of that particular body. But the soul's cravings do not end at the time of death. They continue in the astral plane wherein the soul continues to have experiences with the astral body, based on the desires lodged deep in the heart (unconscious mind) until the soul reincarnates once again into a physical body, and once more engages in the same process of desiring and craving all over again. If this cycle continues, the soul will not be able to discover higher consciousness but will remain ignorant of the higher glory that is possible.

Thus, with the program outlined here, the problems above will be alleviated and even eradicated. In reality, through the proper eating practices, one will now be able to discover one's true eating needs, and the body will go to the weight that it should have been able to achieve if the eating habits had been correct all along. So if your friends tell you that you are too skinny, you should check with a qualified medical practitioner to have an independent assessment. Use this as your guide if you are not sure. Do not expect to carry around the same weight as before, but do not also expect to be like a twig that will blow away in the wind either. Also, you want to be vital and energetic, otherwise, what is the use of your efforts? If you will go back to the way you were, why waste your time? If your friends want you to be worldly and disease prone like them, what kind of friends are they? You'd be better off making friends with other practitioners of mystical spirituality who are on the same path, who will understand you and support your efforts.

Ancient Egypt, Vegetarianism, Fasting and their impact on Christianity and Islam

The Judeo-Christian spiritual tradition emerged out of Ancient Egyptian religion.[88] As with the healing systems of Egypt and India, which encompassed Naturopathic approaches to health maintenance and natural treatment of disease, the *Therapeuts*, an Egypto-Jewish sect in Ancient Egypt, were renowned for their mastery of the healing arts. For thousands of years the temples of Egypt had been centers for healing where the public could go for help in spiritual as well as physical health matters. For this reason they were called *Per Ankh,* "House of Life." Like Hippocrates, the famous Greek physician who studied with the Egyptian doctors, the Therapeuts[89] assimilated the healing wisdom of Egypt, which included dietetics, fasting and surgery. Another important significance of the word "Therapeut" is its meaning: "servant of God" or priest of the mysteries. The Kemetic term for priest is *hem-Neter* or "servant of God." The term "therapeutic" is derived from the great healing work of these initiates.

The mind-body connection and its relation to physical and mental health, which was established in the health systems of Egypt for thousands of years before, was well understood by the Therapeutæ and the

[88] See the book *Christian Yoga: The mystical Journey From Jesus to Christ*

[89] The Essenes were a group of Jewish ascetic communities which had cultural and religious ties to Ancient Egypt and the Near East. The *Therapeuts* were another Jewish sect of Egypt that did not follow the established Jewish authorities.

Essenes. The modern day medical establishment had, until recently, rejected the idea of the mind-body connection. The ancient science of *Ayur-Veda* from India is similar in many respects to the therapeutic methods of preventative health care and holistic disease treatments described in the *Essene Gospel of Peace*[90]. In much the same way as many Mystical, Yoga and Hindu sects promote vegetarianism, the *Gospel of Peace* emphasizes vegetarianism as a way to health. While there are a few passages in the Bible which declare that humans should eat fruits and vegetables, the *Gospel of Peace* devotes a great deal of attention to the subject and, in addition, considers food as a medicine.

Genesis 1

29. And God said, Behold, I have given you every herb bearing seed, which [is] upon the face of all the earth, and every tree, in which [is] the fruit of a tree yielding seed; to you it shall be for food.

Today, there are few, if any, Christian denominations which openly and actively promote vegetarianism, since it, like celibacy and detaching from family, friends and possessions, is not seen as a pleasant, attractive or pleasurable practice. It seems to cut into a person's enjoyment of life and is considered a "hard teaching" to follow by many. There is no doubt that many people who will read this book and explore the teachings of the Bible, in the context that they have been discussed, will find the teachings distasteful or even incongruous (not consistent with what is logical, customary, or expected; inappropriate). When people begin to realize that the goal of the teachings is to lead them to liberation or resurrection from the world of human experience, many become internally shaken with fear and immediately change the subject of conversation or leave the room. Talking about God and going to live with God in some kind of future afterlife state is comfortable for many people, but the thought of actually giving up all and surrendering your very personality to God can cause a deep fear to enter the mind. This happens because the teachings are not correctly understood. Further, people are attached to their egoistic desires and to the illusory pleasures of the senses due to ignorance of the nature of the world. It should be understood that vegetarianism, prayer, rituals, etc., in and of themselves, do not make a person automatically "spiritual." However, they do aid in purifying the mind and body so that spiritual disciplines may be carried out more effectively.

The *Gospel of Peace* describes disease as the work of demons, and indicates that it is caused by sinful behavior. The sinful behavior is related to lifestyles which create negative physical and or mental conditions. These may be too much worry, poor eating habits or poor hygiene. The prescribed treatment given by Jesus is to balance the spiritual through prayer and meditation, and the physical through vegetarianism (proper diet), regular fasting and internal cleansing (enema) according to the needs of the individual and then to: *"go in peace and sin no more.*" Below Jesus emphasizes physical purification by keeping the laws of hygiene and diet (laws of the Earth Mother), and the spiritual, by keeping the practice of prayer and devotion to the Heavenly Father (the laws of the Father).

From the *Gospel of Peace*:

> "Follow, therefore, first, the laws of your Earthly Mother, of which I have told you. And when her angels shall have cleansed and renewed your bodies and strengthened your eyes, you will be able to bear the light of our Heavenly Father."

In the following passages from the *Gospel of Peace*, Jesus expands on the parable of Genesis 1:29.

> For I tell you truly, he who kills, kills himself, and whosoever eats the flesh of slain beasts, eats of the body of death. For in his body every drop of their blood turns to poison; in his bones their bones to chalk; in his bowels their bowels to decay... And their death will become his death.

[90] Healing text of the ancient Essene community.

> Behold, I have given you every herb bearing seed which is upon the face of all the earth, and every tree in which is the fruit of a tree yielding seed; to you it shall be for meat. And to every beast of the earth, and to every fowl of the air, and to everything that creepeth upon the earth, wherein there is breath of life, I give every green herb for meat...But flesh, and the blood, which quickens it, shall ye not eat.

Another important aspect of the Christian doctrines related to vegetarianism is to be found in the ritual observance of *Lent.* Lent is a period of fasting, abstaining from eating meat and practice of penitence (austerity) which is traditionally observed by Christians in preparation for Easter. In the fourth century A.C.E., a tradition was established of eating only what was necessary to survive. The length of time was established as 40 days, beginning on Ash Wednesday and then extending (omitting Sundays) to the day before Easter. The observance varies within Anglican and Protestant churches. Also, the time of the observances has been questioned. According to an apostolic constitution in February 1966, issued by Pope Paul VI, fasting and abstinence during the Lent period are mandatory only on Ash Wednesday and Good Friday. However, in many other mystical traditions, these observances were espoused as integral parts of the spiritual discipline to be followed all year around. Further, there is evidence to suggest that the Gnostic Christian sects also observed these vows perennially.

While it is true that Jesus fed the multitudes with fish, this episode should be understood for its deeper symbolism. The fish in Ancient Egyptian and Gnostic Christian mythology is the symbol of guidance and chastity. Also, Jesus realized that he needed to reach the people at their current stage of culture. Therefore, he used what they would accept. However, it is to be understood that ordinary people who do not know any better may eat whatever they like. This is a factor of their ignorance. Thus, the Bible accepts them. However, the other teachings of the Bible clearly direct serious Christians toward the path of vegetarianism as a means to promote physical and mental purity and thereby spiritual evolution as well.

Many times people use the excuse that many cultures eat meat and have done so for generations, and so this means that anyone can. This is an expression of a person's egoistic desire to continue eating meat out of ignorance. Most people do not know that the human body is not designed to eat meat. Thus, it is no wonder that chronic degenerative illnesses are highest in countries with the highest meat consumption. Just because people live in areas with harsh climate where there is no other food available, it does not excuse others from following the better path for the reasons outlined here. If you have to eat meat in order to survive, then of course you should eat meat. However, as soon as you are able to develop better conditions, you should leave meat behind.

The Islamic faith has a similar tradition to Lent, called *Ramadan.* The observance of Lent and Ramadan implies an understanding that fasting, vegetarianism and abstinence are means to bringing a person closer to their divine essence. So why don't these religions institute this policy every day of the year instead of just on Ash Wednesday, and Good Friday or Ramadan?

One factor which shaped Western Christianity is the fact that the peoples of the European and Middle Eastern culture have lived for thousands of years on a diet which includes meat. Very possibly the practice of vegetarianism was difficult to institute since eating meat is somewhat addictive, like a drug. However, all vices need to be corrected if a human being expects to attain higher spiritual realization. How can a person profess to love humanity and nature if they promote the killing and eating of animals? Animals have minds, which are developed to a lesser degree than those of human beings are, but they feel pain and anguish nevertheless, and they express this in two ways when they are killed. First, the negative mental vibrations of anger, hatred and anguish go into the environment and degrade the planet. A sensitive person can feel these vibrations just as one feels vibrations of good will or ill will when entering a room filled with other people. Secondly, at the time of death the animals secrete toxins into their tissues, which act as poisons in the human body. Is it any wonder that Western countries have a higher incidence of gastrointestinal (colon) cancers? Meat also is very grounding to the soul. This means that it helps to intensify body-consciousness and dulls spiritual sensitivity.

Further, the meat industry is constantly experiencing scandals about antibiotics and hormones fed or implanted in cattle to make them grow faster, chemicals added to preserve the meat in stores, and deaths occurring from meat contaminated with deadly bacteria. Yet meat is advocated by the industry under the guise of serving the public health needs. Is it good service to humanity to promote something which leads to death?

Greed plays an important part in deluding a person into selling poison to another. Delusion, ignorance and weak will play important roles in compelling a person to do things even when they know those things are not good for them. If you want to reach for the heights of spirituality, you must strive to purify your physical body as well as your mind. If it means going against the norm of society, then Amen (so be it). Vegetarianism and the control of the sex-urge are two important ways of channeling the energies of the mind, enabling you to direct it towards spiritual realization. There is a vegetarian saying that goes "One should make one's stomach into a garden and not a graveyard." When you eat meat, it rots (putrefies) in your guts because there is no proper digestion there to deal with it. In addition, the human gastrointestinal system is extremely long like herbivores (animals which live on plants), in contrast to the very short intestinal tract of carnivores (animals which eat other animals to survive). This further exacerbates the process of putrefaction and sets the stage for colon cancer. When you see a dead animal on the side of the road, reflect on what is happening to it and realize that when you eat meat, you are poisoning yourself as if you were eating from that same carcass! One other point as we are discussing dead carcasses, is that if you were truly carnivorous, every time you see a dead animal on the road, you should start salivating and licking your lips, as a dog would!

FASTING FOR THE MIND

Just as there is food for the mind, so too there should be fasting for the mind. Many people are constantly taking in thoughts, feelings and desires from the time they wake up in the morning until they go to bed at night. This is a very detrimental way of life. The mind swells with concepts and thoughts of a worldly nature and these cause the mind to be agitated. One of the purposes of sleep is to relieve this pressure so that the mind can regenerate. However, the amount of pressure from worldly living in conjunction with the imbalanced way of life in other areas (physical and spiritual) renders the mind weak and perpetually disturbed. This constant state of disturbance leads to chronic mental and physical problems such as insomnia, worry, uneasiness, and later develop into more severe problems.

The mind needs to have space. One needs to get enough sleep, but this is not enough. One also needs quiet time to reflect on life, to gather one's ideas. Further, one's life must be meaningful and useful. There must be a basis of righteousness and truth in life, otherwise deep down one becomes disappointed and frustrated with life.

Therefore, several disciplines should be practiced as part of normal life, to promote mental health and vitality, as well as sharpness, which lead to development of the faculties of understanding and intuition, which are necessary for spiritual realization.

- Daily –proper sleep. Depending on one's age (older people needing less sleep) and one's level of practice in meditation (the more often and intense the meditation, the less sleep is needed), one may need from 8 to 4 hours of sleep.
- Quiet time – fast the mind by practicing fasting of the speech. Do not speak for at least ½ hour per day.
- Spend some time each day reading uplifting books, or listening to uplifting speeches, etc., as opposed to negative and agitating books or shows which promote violence, conflict and passion. So as you refrain from allowing negative mental foods to come in, put in positive foods also.
- Spend some time in quiet reflection – not reading or doing anything else, just reflecting, allowing the thoughts of the unconscious mind to arise normally. When fasting the mind, many thoughts will arise from the unconscious. They are being cleansed. You should allow this process to proceed normally. Do not judge these thoughts or hold onto them; simply observe them.
- Practice a minimum of 20 minutes each day of positive affirmation or chanting the Divine Names of God (Goddess). This cleanses the mind and leads to the promotion of positive vibrations in the personality, control of the senses and positive impressions.

Watching the Emotions, Cleansing the Emotions

Watching your emotions, controlling them and not allowing them to go to extremes is a form of fasting for the feeling aspect of the mind, the heart. You will notice that when you are tense and upset, the body assumes constrictive poses and breathing becomes shallow. When this happens you need to start taking control by practicing the proper and deep breathing techniques. From now on you must try to take notice of when you experience mood swings. Spiritual energy is dissipated through indiscriminate indulgence in emotional behavior. Most people are taught to vent their emotions freely in order to be healthy. In reality, the source of emotionality needs to be dealt with in order to have true mental peace and health. Otherwise, the venting of frustrations will form mental impressions, which will cause habitual and uncontrollable outbursts of anger and other emotions. The true way to eradicate emotional and other psychic problems is to get to the root-cause of these problems: ignorance of your true Self. Try to make a conscious effort to control your emotional outbursts. When you notice you are out of control, stop yourself and go to a private place and practice your breathing exercises and hekau (mantra, chants, prayers). This is the ongoing battle of Heru and Set, of positive and negative, within you. Each time you exercise your self-effort to your capacity in each of these battles, you are building momentum to win the war of Heru over Set within yourself.

Patience and perseverance are the keys to success. Over a period of time, you will discover how your practice of Smai Tawi has changed your life for the better. Perhaps you would have argued with someone or cried for two hours in a particular situation, but now that you have been practicing Smai Tawi, you argue or cry only for one hour or not at all. Perhaps after a year of practicing Smai Tawi you discover that it takes more to get you upset now than it did a year ago. This is achieving victory over Set and success on the spiritual path. Many people judge themselves in an all or nothing manner, "I was upset a year ago and I'm still not able to control myself now, so there is no spiritual progress," and then they give up. For most people, spiritual progress occurs in degrees. At times you may notice that you are able to make giant strides in what seems to be a quantum leap. This is because you have been gathering momentum by practicing your spiritual disciplines, so it is important that you continue to do so on a regular basis.

FASTING FOR THE SOUL

Technically speaking, the soul is the entire complex making up the individual personality as a conditioned expression of the Universal Spirit due to ignorance. However, in our study, we will confine our definition of the soul as the unconscious level of mind that contains the impressions of individuality, which cause the creation of the subconscious and the conscious mind, which in turn sustains the physical body. These impressions, called Ari's in Kemetic Philosophy, are the karmic causes of the inclinations, desires and tendencies of the personality. The impressions surface as desires in the mind, and engender thoughts which impel the personality to perform actions in the world of time and space. Among this group of impressions are to be found the main causes of disease, the impressions that promote the idea of individuality and the delusion of mortal existence. If these impressions were cleansed, the mind would understand its true source and nature, and thus become enlightened. This is the ultimate goal of all spiritual practices. There would be no more burden and pressure on the personality. There would be an experience of supreme peace, joy and health, since there would no longer be any obstruction between the Spirit and its energy (Life Force) reaching every aspect of the personality.

- Practice meditation daily- the soul needs transcendental food that is not available in the world of time and space. It needs to imbibe of its own divine and eternal nature. No car, house, boat, relationship, fame or fortune will suffice. This is why people who seem to have it all still remain miserable and unfulfilled in life. Practice a minimum of 20 minutes of meditation each day.
- Train the intellect to refrain from allowing negative thoughts to remain lodged in the unconscious mind. Do not harbor feelings of anger, hatred, and greed towards anyone or anything.
- Discover the path of detachment. Since you are ultimately one with the Universal Self, in reality you are one with all things so you need not desire anything or anyone. Discover the fullness that is within you already.

The Sublime Dimensions of Fasting

Fasting promotes the development of will power and control over the mind and senses. It also promotes the ability to concentrate the mind. These are prerequisites on the path towards spiritual enlightenment. Therefore, it is no surprise that almost all spiritual traditions advocate some form of fasting as part of the spiritual disciplines.

It is a wonder that most people talk about fasting as a discipline of abstaining from food, but they really are referring to solid food. In essence, the discipline of fasting really includes fasting from everything that impedes the experience of the Divine. This means that you must think of food as more than just items on a plate at breakfast, lunch or dinnertime. Food is everything you hear, see, smell, touch and taste and much more. Food is also your thoughts that you engender and support in your mind. Desires, longings and cravings are also food for the mind. You are feeding these to your personality and your personality will consume whatever you offer it like a sponge. The following proverb indicates that purity is something that goes beyond the internal and external cleansing of the body.

I am pure. I am pure. I am Pure.
I have washed my front parts with the waters of libations, I have cleansed my hinder parts with drugs which make wholly clean, and my inward parts have been washed in the liquor of Maat.

— Ancient Egyptian Proverb

Maat is a philosophy of life, and cleansing with it means becoming righteous, honest and forthright. It means living by truth, justice, harmony and non-violence. Therefore you must also plan on fasting from the elements of the lower nature, anger, hatred, greed, lust, envy, jealousy, etc. Conveniently, you do not have to set a special time for this practice because you have ample opportunities throughout the day to practice abstaining from these expressions of the ego. When you fast and change your diet, you stop eating certain items and feed yourself new, wholesome items. In the same manner you need to stop feeding yourself selfishness and replace it with selfless service. Stop feeding yourself vanity and replace it with humility. Stop indulging in the useless search for pleasures of the world and replace this with the food of introspection and contentment. In short you must fast from egoistic behavior and discover the glory of self-knowledge. This is the greatest fast, the fast which when accomplished, all fasts are complete.

MODERN RESEARCH SUPPORTS THE PRINCIPLES OF THE KEMETIC DIET, FASTING, YOGA, MEDITATION AND HERBS FOR HEALTH

"Vegetables lower cancer risk"
-University of Wisconsin (Madison) 5/2000

Factors Which Affect the Immune System

Severe obesity and excessive thinness are associated with impaired immune responses.[91]

Obesity increases the risk of infection, at least in hospitalized patients, according to preliminary research.[92]

The higher the intake of fat and the higher the level of body fat, the greater the risk of breast and other gynecological cancer.[93] Tests have shown a similar effect in the male, whereby cancer of the prostate, the "male uterus," was promoted. The Standard Western Diet (high in fat and sugar and low in complex carbohydrates) is therefore the prime promoter of disease. Other problems it promotes include excess body fat, increased cardiovascular disease, gallstones, constipation, osteoporosis, intensified menstrual bleeding, increased tenderness of the breast and cysts, intensifies mood swings and PMS in women. Scientific testing showed the benefits of the vegetarian diet to be: lower risk of bowel cancer, promotes feeling of emotional wellness, relief of the symptoms of PMS, reduced risk of ovarian, breast and uterine cancers, reduced cardiovascular disease, reduced breast tenderness, reduced menstrual bleeding, reduced risk of gallstones, reduced constipation, promotes natural body weight.[94]

All forms of sugar (including honey) interfere with the ability of white blood cells to destroy bacteria.[95] [96] Followers of the Kemetic Diet Program should take care to use unprocessed maple syrup, dates, stevia

---

[91] Chandra RK. Nutrition and the immune system: an introduction. *Am J Clin Nutr* 1997;66:460–63S [review].)
[92] Stallone DD. The influence of obesity and its treatment on the immune system. *Nutr Rev* 1994;52:37–50.
[93] Low Fat-High Fiber Diet and Serom Estrone Sulfate in Premenopausal Women *M. Woods* American Journal of Clinical Nutrition, vol. 49 (1989), p. 1179; Effect of Low-Fat Diet on Female Sex Hormone Levels, *D. Ingram*, Journal of National Cancer Institute, Vol 79 (1987), p. 1225; and Diet and Plasma Androgens in Postmenopausal Vegetarian and Omnivorous Women and Postmenopausal Women with Breast Cancer, *H. Aldercreutz,* American Journal of Clinical Nutrition, vol. 49 (1989), p. 433..
[94] Women's Bodies, Women's Wisdom *Christine Northrup, M.D.*
[95] Sanchez A, et al. Role of sugars in human neutrophilic phagocytosis. *Am J Clin Nutr* 1973;26:1180.
[96] Ringsdorf WM, et al. Sucrose, neutrophilic phagocytosis and resistance to disease. *Dental Survey* 1976;52(12):46.

herb as sweeteners if needed- instead pf processed sugars (including brown rice syrup). Honey was used in Ancient Egypt but not in large quantities nor in a processed form.

Alcohol intake, including single episodes of moderate consumption, interferes with a wide variety of immune defenses.[97]/[98]

Chronic mental and emotional stress can reduce immune function.[99] [100]

The immune function has been increased by stress-reducing techniques such as relaxation exercises, biofeedback, and other approaches.[101] [102] Various tests conducted by Maharishi University (Iowa, U.S.A.) and other research institutions have shown the benefits of Yoga and meditation in the promotion of stress relief and general mental and physical health.

Heart Disease was successfully treated by Dr. Dean Ornish who documented the reversal of coronary artery disease through diet change (low fat vegetarian diet), exercise (which included yoga), and emotional support.[103]

Other areas of health research include the aspects of drug interactions and the increasing immunity of bacteria and viruses. The long held idea that disease can be treated solely with medicines such as antibiotics and other drugs, is slowly showing itself to be an illusory panacea. In the late 20th century, the medical establishment has had to face the problem of drug interactions which affect all patients, especially those growing older, and who experience varied ailments. The proliferation of the numbers of different drugs and their wide prescription to the same person has been found to cause unplanned complications. This is because when the drugs mix, they combine in unknown ways and affect the body in unforeseen ways, sometimes leading to death. So this problem of drug interaction is to be added to the already known problem of drug side effects. Further, antibiotics not only kill the bacteria that have overgrown due to an unhealthy lifestyle that has rendered the body toxic and created an environment suitable for their multiplication. Antibiotics also kill the friendly bacteria (probiotics) that normally live in the digestive tract that are needed for proper digestion. This therefore, further complicates the issue of healing, as the compromised digestive system will be unable to produce enough energy to bolster the immune system and bring the body back to balance.

Another problem that promises to become a health crisis in the future is the issue of bacterial and viral immunity. In the late 20th century, bacteria and viruses have been found to be transforming themselves into forms that are resistant to the antibiotics which were invented less than 100 years ago. It must be understood that the crisis may occur simply because the medical establishment and society in general, have based their health care on the theory of health through drugs. It is the dependency that is the problem. Like a child who wants to have his cake and eat it too, society has desired to pursue lifestyles that are not in harmony with the human body. When diseases have arisen, the short cut method of dealing with the problem has been to invent a new drug, but the drugs do not eradicate the problem, because the behavior which leads to the problem again and again, remains unchanged.

---

97 Ahmed FE. Toxicological effects of ethanol on human health. *Crit Rev Tox* 1995;25(4):347–67.
98 Szabo G. Monocytes, alcohol use, and altered immunity. *Alcohol Clin Exp Res* 1998;22:216–19S.
99 Herbert TB, Cohen S. Stress and immunity in humans: a meta-analytic review. *Psychosom Med* 1993;55:364–79 [review].
100 Palmblad JE. Stress-related modulation of immunity: a review of human studies. *Cancer Detect Prev Suppl* 1987;1:57–64 [review].
101 Kemeny ME, Gruenewald TL. Psychoneuroimmunology update. *Semin Gastrointest Dis* 1999;10:20–29 [review].
102 Halley FM. Self-regulation of the immune system through biobehavioral strategies. *Biofeedback Self Regul* 1991;16:55–74 [review].
103 Dr. Dean Ornish, "Can Lifestyle Changes Reverse Coronary Heart Disease?" Lifestyle Heart Trial, Lancet, vol. 336 (July 21, 1990), pp. 129-33

Modern medical science has documented the beneficial effects of comedy and laughter in the treatment of illness because it engenders a positive feeling that allows the body to relieve stress and release positive hormones as opposed to self-destructive agents into the system. It in effect, bolsters the immune system by reducing stress. The following is an excerpt from an article, which appeared in the newspaper "USA TODAY" that illustrates the point most succinctly.

Humor as a Healing Force

A chuckle a day does indeed help keep ills at bay

Mom said it, editor Norman Cousins wrote it, and now researchers are proving it: Laughter is the best medicine.

A good belly laugh boosts the body's immune system and reduces hormones that cause stress. A positive state of mind helps keep healthy people well and helps the sick recover.

"Silliness is very serious stuff," says Dr. Lee Berk, one of the USA's foremost researchers on humor and health. "This is not alternative medicine, this is real medicine," says Berk, of the Loma Linda University Medical Center, Calif. He'll review his research Nov. 3 before the American Association for Therapeutic Humor in Orlando, Fla.

Researchers, says conference presenter and mind-body expert Dr. Barry Bittman, have "taken the wisdom of the ancients and tested it with the technology of today, providing solid, scientific research showing this stuff really works."

The research "is not yet taught in traditional medical schools, but that is going to be changing," says Patty Wooten, the group's president, a nurse and author of *Compassionate Laughter: Jest for Your Health.*

Ancient wisdom speaks volumes about the need to remain stress free, to be cheerful, courteous and free of worry by trusting in the Divine. Now modern science is beginning to realize the benefits of ancient healing wisdom. In the spirit of mirth, the author discovered the following joke, which fits exactly into the general theme of this volume-for your enjoyment and good health!

History Lesson: A brief history of Medicine:

2000 B.C.E. Here, take this root.
1000 A.C.E. That root is for a heathen. Here, say this prayer.
1850 A.C.E. That prayer is superstition. Here, drink this potion.
1940 A.C.E. That potion is snake oil. Here, swallow this pill.
1985 A.C.E. That pill is ineffective. Here take this antibiotic.
2000 A.C.E. That antibiotic is artificial. Here, eat this root.

CHAPTER 4: INTRODUCTION TO KEMETIC SMAI TAWI (YOGA) FOR HEALTH OF BODY, MIND AND SOUL

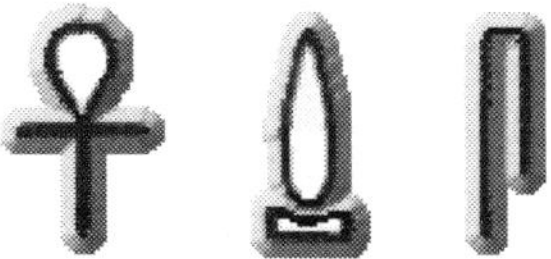

WHAT IS SEMAI TAWI (EGYPTIAN YOGA)?

Smai Tawi
(From Chapter 4 of the *Prt m Hru*)

The term Smai (Sema, Sama) Tawi, or "Sma" for short, is compatible with the Indian Sanskrit word "Yoga" which means union of the Higher Self and Lower self. In Chapter 4[104] and Chapter 17[105] of the *Prt m Hru,* or "Book of Enlightenment," a term "Smai Tawi" is used. It means "Union of the two lands of Egypt." The two lands refers to the two main districts of the country (North and South) and, in a mystical sense they refer to the gods Heru and Set, who are elsewhere referred to as the spiritual Higher Self and lower self of a human being, respectively. Ergo we arrive at the term "Egyptian Yoga."

The personality of every human being is somewhat different from every other. However the ancient Sages of Yoga identified four basic factors which are common to all human personalities and human life. These factors are: Emotion, Reason, Action and Will. Also, the human personality expresses in three basic formats. These are ***Dullness, Agitation*** and ***Lucidity (Harmony and Purity)***.[106] This means that in order for a human being to properly evolve, all aspects of the personality must develop in an integral fashion.

All forms of spiritual practice are directed toward the goal of assisting every individual to discover the true essence of the universe both externally, in physical creation, and internally, within the human heart, as the very root of human consciousness. Thus, many terms are used to describe the attainment of the goal of spiritual knowledge and the eradication of spiritual ignorance, according to the different mystical spirituality systems. Some of these terms are: *Enlightenment, Resurrection, Salvation, The Kingdom of Heaven, Moksha or Liberation, Buddha Consciousness, One With The Tao*, *Self-realization, Know Thyself,* etc. Also, many names have been used to describe that transcendental essence: *God, Allah, Asar, Aset, Krishna, Buddha, The Higher Self, Supreme Being* and many others.

Smai Tawi or Egyptian Yoga is the philosophy and disciplines based on Ancient Egyptian mysticism which promote spiritual enlightenment. Spiritual enlightenment means a movement towards transcending death. In this context death is not regarded as a miserable event, but a transition into a higher form of being if one's earthly life has been lived in accordance with the teachings of Maat. In ancient times, the Ancient Egyptians were often referred to by people in neighboring countries as "the most religious people of all the world," because they seemed to constantly affirm spiritual principles in every aspect of their lives. This was the first practice of what has come to be known as Integral Yoga in East Indian Mystical Spirituality.

The term Yoga has received wide popularity in recent years from the East Indian perspective. The disciplines of Yoga fall under five major categories. These are: Yoga *of Wisdom, Yoga of Devotional*

[104] Commonly referred to as Chapter 17
[105] Commonly referred to as Chapter 176
[106] For more on the three states of consciousness see the books *Egyptian Yoga Vol. 2* and *The Glorious Light Meditation.*

Love, Yoga of Meditation, Tantric Yoga and *Yoga of Selfless-Righteous Action.* Within these categories there are subsidiary forms which are part of the main disciplines.

Essentially, the practice of any discipline that leads to oneness with the Supreme Consciousness can be called Yoga. If you study, rationalize and reflect upon the teachings, you are practicing Yoga *of Wisdom.* If you meditate upon the teachings and your Higher Self, you are practicing Yoga *of Meditation.* If you practice rituals, which identify you with your spiritual nature, you are practicing Yoga *of Ritual Identification* (which is part of the Yoga of Wisdom and the Yoga of Devotional Love of the Divine). If you develop your physical nature and psychic energy centers, you are practicing *Serpent Power (Kundalini or Uraeus) Yoga* (which is part of Tantric Yoga). If you practice living according to the teachings of ethical behavior and selflessness, you are practicing Yoga *of Action* (Maat) in daily life. If you practice turning your attention towards the Divine by developing love for the Divine, then it is called *Devotional Yoga* or Yoga *of Divine Love.* The practitioner of Yoga is called a yogin (male practitioner) or yogini (female practitioner), and one who has attained the culmination of Yoga (union with the Divine) is called a yogi. In this manner, Yoga has been developed into many disciplines, which may be used in an integral fashion to achieve the same goal: Enlightenment. Therefore, the aspirant should learn about all of the paths of Yoga and choose those elements to concentrate on which best suithis or her personality and practice them all in an integral, balanced way.

INTEGRAL PRATICES OF MYSTICAL SPIRITUALITY

Contentment	Understanding	Peace	Fulfillment
↑	↑	↑	↑
Emotion	Reason	Action	Will.
↑	↑	↑	↑
Devotion	Wisdom	Service	Meditation

Thus, Smai Tawi is a discipline of spiritual living which transforms every aspect of personality in an integral fashion, leaving no aspect of a human being behind. This is important because an unbalanced movement will lead to frustration, more ignorance, more distraction and more illusions leading away from the Higher Self. For example, if a person develops mostly the reasoning aspect of personality, he or she may come to believe that they have discovered the Higher Self, however when it comes to dealing with some problem of life, such as the death of a loved one, they cannot control their emotions, or if they are tempted to do something unrighteous, such as smoking, they cannot control their actions; they have no will power to resist. The vision of Yoga is a lofty goal, which every human being can achieve with the proper guidance, self-effort and repeated practice. The integral practice of Yoga and mystical spirituality (practice of the four main disciplines) is to allow you to grow spiritually in every aspect of your life. During the course of the day you may find yourself doing various activities. Sometimes you will be quiet, at other times you will be busy at work, at other times you might be interacting with people, etc. The four Yoga disciplines give you the opportunity to practice Yoga at all times. When you have quiet time you can practice meditation. When at work you can practice righteous action and promote the attitude of selfless service. When you have leisure time you can study and reflect on the teachings, and when you feel the sentiment of love for a person or object you like, you can practice remembering the Divine Self who made it possible for you to experience the company of those personalities or the opportunity to acquire those objects, and who is the essence and source of the love you are experiencing. From a higher perspective, you can practice reflecting on how the people and objects in creation are expressions of the Divine, and this movement will eventually lead you to a spontaneous and perpetual state of ecstasy, peace and bliss which are the hallmarks of spiritual enlightenment. The purpose of the disciplines of Yoga therefore, is to promote integration of the whole personality of a human being, which will lead to complete spiritual enlightenment. Thus, Integral practice of Yoga should be understood as the most effective and holistic method to practice mystical spirituality.

The important point to remember is that all aspects of Yoga can and should be used in an integral fashion to generate an efficient and harmonized spiritual movement in the practitioner. Therefore, while there may be an area of special emphasis, other elements are bound to become part of the Yoga program as needed. For example, while a yogin may place emphasis on the Yoga of Wisdom, they may also practice Devotional Yoga and Meditation Yoga along with the wisdom studies. Further, it must be understood that as you practice one path of yoga, others will also develop automatically. For example, as you practice the Yoga of Wisdom, your faith will increase, or as you practice the Yoga of Devotion, your wisdom will increase as you will desire to seek more information about that which you love. If this movement does not occur, your wisdom alone will by dry intellectualism or your faith alone will be blind faith. So when we speak of wisdom here, we are referring to wisdom gained through experience or intuitional wisdom and not intellectual wisdom which is speculative. If you do not practice the teachings through the Yoga of Action, your wisdom and faith will be shallow, because you have not experienced the truth of the teachings and allowed yourself the opportunity to test your knowledge and faith. If you do not have introspection and faith, your wisdom and actions will be externalized, agitated and distracted. Your spiritual realization will be insubstantial, weak and lacking stability. You will not be able to meet the challenges of life nor will you be able to discover true spiritual realization in this lifetime or even after death. Therefore, the integral path of yoga, with proper guidance, is the most secure method to achieve genuine spiritual enlightenment.

Health of mind, body and soul is an essential ingredient to the promotion of spiritual evolution. Therefore, health may be seen as a means to the end of discovering the glory of one's divine essential nature. There are several components to health, but these are simple to understand. If their principles are correctly applied the human body and mind becomes a proper vessel to behold the grandeur of the spirit.

The Daily Schedule for Kamitan Yoga Practice

Sheti is the Kemetic word meaning "spiritual practices that lead to enlightenment." A practitioner of Smai Tawi must be able to integrate the main practices of Smai Tawi into daily life. This means that you need to begin adding small amounts of time for Prayer, Repetition of the Divine Name (Hekau-Ancient Egyptian words of power, similar to East Indian mantras-chanting), Exercise (includes proper breathing exercise), Study of the Teachings, Silence, Selfless Service, Meditation, and Daily Reflection. This also means that you will gradually reduce the practices which go against yogic movement, as you gain more time for Sheti.

Below you will find an outline of a schedule for the beginning practice of Smai Tawi. The times given here are a suggested minimum time for beginners. You may spend more time according to your capacity and personal situation, however, try to be consistent in the amount of time and location you choose to practice your discipline as well as in the time of day you choose to perform each of the different practices. This will enable your body and mind to develop a rhythm, which will develop into the driving force of your day. When this occurs you will develop stamina and fortitude when dealing with any situation of life. You will have a stable center which will anchor you to a higher purpose in life whether you are experiencing prosperous times or adverse times. In the advanced stages, spiritual practice will become continuous. Try to do the best you can according to your capacity, meaning your circumstances. If your family members are not interested or do not understand what you are trying to do, simply maintain your practices privately and try to keep the interruptions to a minimum. As you develop, you may feel drawn toward some forms of practice over others. The important thing to remember is to practice them all in an integrated fashion. Do not neglect any of the practices even though you may spend additional time on some versus others.

Practicing spirituality only during times of adversity is the mistake of those who are spiritually immature. Any form of spiritual practice, ritualistic or otherwise is a positive development, however, you will not derive the optimal spiritual benefits by simply becoming religious when you are in trouble. The masses of people only pray when they are in trouble...then they ask for assistance to get out of trouble. What they do not realize is that if they were to turn their minds to God at all times, not just in times of misfortune, adversity would not befall them nor affect them in the same manner as before. As you progress through your studies you will learn that adversities in life are meant to turn you toward the Divine. In this sense they are messages from the Divine to awaken spiritual aspiration. However, if you do not listen to the message and hearken to the Divine intent behind it, you will be in a position to experience more miseries of life and miseries of a more intense nature.

Basic Schedule of Spiritual Practice

1a- Proper breathing, using the *proper breathing technique.*

1b- Deep Breathing exercise (10 minutes in Am and in PM),

2-Prayer (10-30 minutes in Am and in PM),

3-Exercise (10-30 minutes in am and before study time),

4-Repetition of the Divine Name in the form of your chosen hekau-mantra –Chanting-Positive Affirmation (10 minutes in am and in pm),

5-Silent practice (10-20 minutes in Am, should be practiced after exercise, prayer and repetition of the Divine Name),

6-Study of the teachings (reading 15-30 minutes per day),

7-Silence time (30 minutes per day),

8-Listening to the teachings: Choose an audio recording of a yogic spiritual preceptor and listen for a minimum of 30 minutes per day without any distractions if possible. If possible, go to a spiritual center (Temple, Ashram, Wat,) where teachings are presented by a qualified teacher of mystical wisdom. If this is not possible, form a study group wherein the teachings may be discussed and explored.

9-Selfless service (as required whenever the opportunity presents itself) as well as volunteering some time in service to the community. This is a very important part of cleansing out the impurities of the heart.

10-Daily reflection: Remembering the teachings during the ordinary course of the day and applying them in daily living situations- to be practiced as much as possible.

NOTE: The preceding list is to be used as a guideline. Choose those practices that are in line with your personality and current availability of time.

THE FRUITS OF THE DISCIPLINES OF SMAI TAWI

The following are general outlines of Smai Tawi practices, which you can apply in your life to maintain mental Health. You should make every reasonable effort to make sure that these elements are present in your spiritual program. Therefore, you should reflect on them daily and evaluate your ability to follow them. They are all designed to promote peace and harmony within you, and from this space of peace and harmony, your progress in understanding the teachings and inner discovery of yourself will be promoted.

☥

CHAPTER 5: FOOD FOR THE BODY

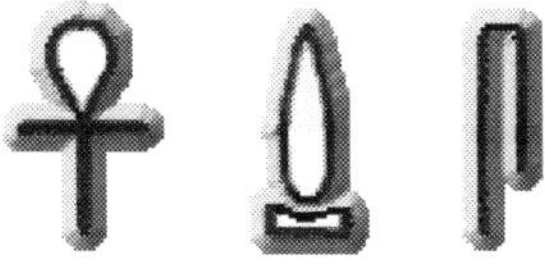

The Proper Diet for the Human Body: What Foods are OK to Eat!

When the teeth of humans is studied and compared to those of true carnivores in nature, it is discovered that the teeth of predatory animals such as dogs, cats, tigers, lions, etc. are designed for tearing flesh and quickly swallowing it. This is very different from what is found in humans. The teeth and jaws of human beings are designed for chewing, much like those of cows and elephants. This factor, coupled with the understanding that the intestinal tract of humans and other herbivores is long, designed to process vegetation, signifies in no uncertain terms that the proper diet for human beings is the vegetarian diet. However, there is much more evidence to support this conclusion.

Vegetarianism VS Eating Meat, Dairy and Starch

The Cambridge-Oxford China study is one of the best examples of the effect of food on the human body. The two universities joined in a study of food consumption and health in China and obtained remarkable results. China has three major regions, in which the inhabitants consume three different diets. The people of the north eat mostly meat and dairy products. The people of middle China eat mostly fruits and vegetables since this is the main farming area. The people of the south eat mostly rice. It was found that the farther one strays from the vegetarian-fruitarian diet, the more disease and cancer will be found.

Table 6:Cambridge-Oxford China Study

Region of China	Diet	Incidence of disease
Northern	Meat and dairy	Most disease and cancer
Southern	Rice	Moderate disease and cancer
Middle	Vegetables and Fruits	Least disease and cancer

The Proper Diet for the body is a vegetarian-fruitarian diet. The human intestinal track is not designed to handle anything else and still maintain health at the same time. But there are many levels of vegetarianism. The following is a hierarchical view of the diet showing the most effective at the top, as the ideal for all human beings.

1. Fruits, Fruit juices, Nut milk, Vegetable juices, and Vegetables Raw* (100%), Organic; Eating no more than 1 item at a time.
2. Fruits, Fruit juices, Nut milk, Vegetable juices, Nuts and Vegetables Raw (100%), Organic; Combining no more than three items
3. Fruits, Fruit juices, Nut milk, Vegetable juices, Nuts and Vegetables Raw (100%) Organic
4. Fruits, Fruit juices, Nut milk, Vegetable juices, Nuts and Vegetables Raw (100%), including slightly steamed vegetables and lightly cooked soups
5. **General Diet-Fruits, fruit juices, Nut milk, Vegetable juices, Nuts and Vegetables Raw (at least 50%-65%), lightly cooked (50%-35%), including soups
6. Fruits, Fruit juices and Cooked Vegetables including soups, soya meat substitutes.
7. Fruits, Fruit juices and Vegetables Processed, soya meat substitutes.
8. Fruits, cooked vegetables, grains, soya meat substitutes.
9. Fruits, Cooked Vegetables, Grains and Meat and Dairy products, Organic
10. Cooked Vegetables, Grains and Meat and Dairy products Processed

*<u>**Raw food diet**</u> means foods that are uncooked or sun-cooked, also termed "live" foods. This includes fruits and vegetables and some sprouted sun-cooked breads. Cooking acts to release nutrients in some

foods that would otherwise be difficult to digest (i.e. grains, beans), but also alters the chemistry of food, breaking down the nutrients and thereby rendering the food less nutritious. Therefore, an easily digestible raw food diet would me more advantageous. However, it must be understood that the raw food diet necessitates a strong digestive fire in order to be processed in the intestinal tract. The transition from a cooked to an uncooked diet must be made carefully and gradually, allowing the body to make the necessary adjustments. The changes are accelerated and facilitated when regular fasting is practiced during the transition to the raw diet.

While it is possible to make the raw food diet interesting through varied recipes, the basic raw food diet may consist of salads, sprouts, nuts and fruits. Some bonuses from this are that there is no longer a necessity for spending lengthy time in food preparation, washing pots and pans, spending additional electricity or gas to run the stove or oven, etc.

Documented evidence by raw food practitioners has shown the ability to eradicate mental and physical diseases from stress to cancer, through the raw diet.

It should be clear to the reader by now that in general, the diet of human beings should come from vegetarian sources. Also, there should be no synthesized products in the diet. In our context, the words synthesized means products that are combined, processed or otherwise manipulated by human hands (including cooking). This does not include natural food preparation such as washing, light steaming, etc. It should be kept in mind that the move towards purifying your diet should not be made with fanatical zeal. The preferred manner is slowly and with rational intent, understanding what you are doing, why you are doing what you are doing, and how it is supposed to help you. If you enter into these teachings with stress and tension, you will defeat the purpose of the program, for your stress will destroy any benefits you have achieved. It will take the average person with great determination one to three years in order to make the transition from meat eating to a complete adherence to the ideal of the practices presented here. Therefore, move with patience and faith that you will succeed, maybe not tomorrow, but soon. It is not necessary for all human beings to achieve the same level of practice. Therefore, carefully determine how far you need to go in order to satisfy the goals you have set for yourself. Remember that your goals should be reasonable, otherwise your fanatical attempt to achieve them will fail and you will abandon the righteous efforts to change, out of disgust and frustration.

All Fruit Diet – Frutarian Diet: An all fruit diet implies a diet composed only of the ripened product of a seed-bearing plant, together with their accessory parts, containing the seeds. Generally, a fruit is any product of a plant that has seeds and is used for the procreation of the plant (or tree). The World Health Organization has stated, after experimental research, that as a group of possible foods, fruits are the only group that are completely non-toxic to humans. This means that while there are (non-toxic) good food items in the vegetable class, not all vegetables are non-toxic. Even some beneficial vegetables have toxic aspects, but fruits as a whole, are all non-toxic, which means non-Ukhedu producing. Even the mango, which is related to poison oak, was found to be non-toxic in its inner, edible portion, but slightly toxic in its skin portion.

While there are no living beings on earth that subsists on an entirely fruitarian diet as a normal diet, there are some species of primates that eat a mostly fruit diet. It should also be noted here that fruits are the #1 source of vitamins. Further, studies have shown that the more fruit there is in the diet, the more seratonin is found in the system. Seratonin is a hormone related to positive well being and the absence of which is related to depression.

Purity of Mind and The Eating Habits

A small mention here should be made on reverence in relation to the eating habits. Firstly, praying over toxic foods such as meat, does not clean it of its toxic qualities any more than uttering magic words over motor oil will turn it into water. This is a measure some people use to avoid the responsibility of providing a proper diet for themselves. Also, it is an effect of the weakness of will to resist the temptation to satisfy the sense pleasures gained by satisfying the taste buds and the physiological makeup of the meat eater's body, not unlike that of a drug addict. While prayer does infuse the food with positive vibrations and cleanses it from negative vibrations, the grosser aspects of the food need to be taken care of, by seeking to eat foods from the lucid group in the first place.

It is good to eat the vegetarian-fruitarian diet, but if it is done with the wrong attitude, the benefits may not be fully realized. Firstly, one should not eat on the run, i.e. while driving, walking, working, and ideally even while talking. One should concentrate on the foods, chewing them well (30-50 times per bite) and allowing one's energies to focus on digestion. When eating, one should not curse one's food with thoughts such as "I wish I had something better to eat" or "this food is not appetizing and I don't like it." These kinds of thoughts infuse food with negative vibrations, and thus one eats negative vibrations and one's food becomes a source of negative feeling instead of health. Further, one should eat with reverence and gratitude towards nature, who produced the food, and even more so towards the Divine who ultimately IS the food itself. These positive forms of thinking spiritualize the food and even if the food you have to eat is substandard, it will not promote ill health.

Table 7: Detrimental Foods

Specifically, the detrimental foods include but are not limited to the following list:

- All products with refined sugars
- Artificial sweeteners, flavorings and colors
- Pastries
- Ice cream
- Cake
- Jell-O
- Candies
- Preserves
- Salted foods such as potato ships or salted nuts
- All meats
- Sulfur dioxide in dried fruits
- White flour
- Margarine
- Butter
- Hydrogenated oils
- Eggs
- Fried foods
- White rice
- Any foods with preservatives
- Cookies
- Coffee (regular and decaffeinated)
- Pasta
- Foods containing saturated fats and or grease
- Foods containing corn syrup or rice syrup
- Salads that are not fresh
- Cooked vegetables that are more than one day old
- Processed foods of all kinds – generally anything that does not come from the produce section of the supermarket. However, beware that these products, found at ordinary supermarkets, are usually heavily laden with pesticides. So at least they should be washed but this only takes care of the outside. What of the pesticides that the plant assimilated from the sprayed soil?

NOTE: *"Natural"* does not necessarily mean *"Good For You."*

> **nat·u·ral** *adj. Abbr.* **nat. 1.** Present in or produced by nature. **2.** Of, relating to, or concerning nature. **3.** Conforming to the usual or ordinary course of nature. **4.a.** Not acquired; inherent. **b.** Having a particular character by nature. **c.** *Biology.* Not produced or changed artificially; not conditioned. **5.** Characterized by spontaneity and freedom from artificiality, affectation, or inhibitions. **6.** Not altered, treated, or disguised. **7.** Faithfully representing nature or life.[107]

You may find the word "natural" on some food packaging, this does not necessarily mean that the food is fit for consumption. These foods may contain ingredients that may have been taken from natural sources, but which still pose a health risk. For example, sugars are often taken from natural sources, such as corn, rice or sugar cane, and concentrated in foods in the form of corn sweetener or rice syrup, and then labeled as "naturally sweetened." Juices are routinely "enriched" with vitamins and other materials such as vitamin C and Calcium. This may seem to make the product more healthy, but in reality the chemical

---

[107] American Heritage Dictionary.

balance of the original product has been disturbed and therefore, the body will not be able to treat this item as one which comes directly from nature. Also, animals are natural, however we do not want to consume animal products in the diet, do we?

Generally, food products labeled "Organic" will be safe to consume, although many organic products may be processed in various ways. However, organic foods in any form are better than the same products in a non-organic form. They contain up to 40-70% more nutrients than non-organic foods. Again, these products will be more expensive, but the reduced amount needed offsets the cost. Further, there is a running joke in natural circles, that one pays less up front for non healthy food, but ends up paying for it in later life by suffering with disease and early death!

****General Vegetarian diet-*** This is the diet that all human beings should follow as a matter of normal course. Raw (at least 50%-80% if possible), fruits, nut products (natural-organic if possible).

Transition diet (A): Currently there are several companies manufacturing meat substitutes such as veggie hot dogs, veggie burgers, veggie sausages, etc., which taste and feel like the ordinary products but contain wholesome, nutritious matter. Some are listed below. The transition from a meat eating diet to a healthy vegetarian diet should begin with these products first and a full transition to the point where even the meat substitute can be reduced to a minimal level or eliminated altogether (since they are also processed) from the diet may require months or years depending on the level of toxicity of the body of the individual. However, a word of caution is needed here. A lot of the soybeans (and therefore products made from them) that are available in the stores have been genetically engineered and manipulated so try to find organic, non-genetically engineered products if possible.

Table 8: Soy products available to the public as substitutes for meat.

- Sprout burger
- Nut burger
- Soy sausages
- Soy bacon
- Tofu bologna and salami, etc.
- Soy burgers,
- Tofu chicken
- Tofu turkey
- Soy cheese
- Soy milk
- Soy ice cream

NOTE: Soy products have been clinically proven to promote health of the female uterus and male prostate.

Transition diet (B): Once the movement away from meats has been successful, the individual may proceed to the General Vegetarian diet.

Transition to Higher Quality diets: From here, moving above the general diet, you must move at your own pace in light of your personal health and or spiritual goals. You must decide what level of purity you wish to strive for. Do not forget that attaining absolute perfection in the diet or any other aspect of physical health is not possible, nor is it to be desired as an ultimate goal of life. From a spiritual standpoint you do not want to be worrying about health issues to the exclusion of your formal spiritual disciplines or the normal duties of life which need to continue. However, the closer you move towards perfection, the easier it will be for you to understand and assimilate the teachings, and thereby attain the coveted goal of life, spiritual enlightenment. But it should also be clearly understood that perfection in the physical culture does not automatically confer spiritual enlightenment. This is why physical culture is part of the spiritual disciplines and not the other way around. Spiritual enlightenment requires an integral practice of all mystical disciplines and physical health is the basic first step on the road to self-knowledge.

The higher quality diets should not be attempted when there is mental agitation from the environment or if one must carry out worldly duties which require a lot of physical strain until one is able to make the slow transition to a body which is free from wastes and is operating at peak efficiency. So slowly change your diet and eating habits, and gradually adopt the teachings at your own pace. In the mean time, they should be looked upon as a ritual diet for those who can seclude themselves from the stresses of the world, preferably under the guidance of a spiritual preceptor. Otherwise, a healthy vegetarian diet will be adequate for normal spiritual development. Heavy foods such as overly cooked foods and meats are poisonous to the body and produce aggressive, agitated mental tendencies. Change slowly, even if it's only to one vegetarian meal per week. The secret of success in the spiritual discipline lies in slow but incremental change in a set program leading towards a permanent change in lifestyle. Also do not eat to excess (more than is required to sustain the body). If you normally overeat, change by eating one teaspoonful less per meal until you eat two thirds or three quarters of the normal serving.

Over cooked foods means any consumable that has been subjected to anything beyond light steam for a few minutes. For example, steaming carrots beyond the point where they begin to become soft would be considered overcooking, by these standards. Overcooking tends to destroy the chemical constitution of the food in such a way that the body rejects it as a foreign substance (poison); toxic conditions may arise over a short time or over long periods.

The Kemetic Diet Program recommends an organic and uncooked diet as the best food for human beings. However, as it is difficult for most people to make the transition to an uncooked diet the minimal use of cooked foods is allowed for moderately health people (people who are not suffering from disease at present.) They may adopt the Kemetic Diet Maintenance Program at the end of this book. Those in a diseased state should avoid all cooked foods and chemicals. They should adopt the Kemetic Diet Healing Program at the end of this book.

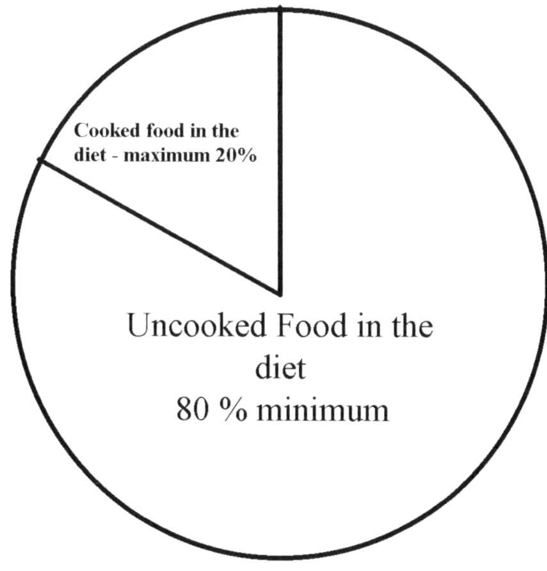

WHICH DIET IS BEST? The suggested diets above are to be used as guidelines, ideals. One can certainly live a fairly long life or even become an enlightened personality while eating a less than perfect diet. However, for the general population, that is, for most people, the quality of life on a low quality diet and or poor eating habits will be degraded, and it will be extremely difficult to attain the heights of spirituality. Chances are that even if one succeeds in living a long life on the lower quality diet and lifestyle, one's life will hardly be worth living; as with the diet, one's life will also be poor in quality. Making improvements in the diet will allow a person to deal with mental and physical disturbances and to grasp the higher essence of life in a much easier and more natural way, thereby simplifying and speeding up the process of purification of the personality. Further, the ideal diet for one personality may be different than that of another due to karmic differences, which lead to variations in the personality (body types). One person may need to purify the diet to a very high degree, while another may need only a moderate improvement. Never forget that since all beings are evolving at different levels, needs will vary according to the individual. Therefore, you must be the final judge of what is best for yourself, based on accurate knowledge of nutrition and of your own body. The ability to be in touch with the true needs of the body comes from living a lifestyle which allows one to "listen" to the body so that one may be in tune with its needs. This requires a reflective, caring and honest way of being with respect to one's own life, nature and the Spirit. It would not be worthwhile to change to a diet of health foods only to increase the stress level and agitate the mind in other areas.

NOTE ON THE NECESSITY OF PROTEIN IN THE DIET: No discussion about health and nutrition can be complete without a statement on protein. Protein is an important component of the human body, as it is estimated to compose 50% of the dry weight of the body. Human beings have over 30,000 different proteins. They are compound chemicals that function in growth and cell maintenance, and are also responsible for muscle contraction. Examples of proteins are: the antibodies of the immune system, hemoglobin, which carries vital substances throughout the body, digestive enzymes and insulin as well as most other hormones. The following is an excerpt from a modern encyclopedia containing important information in reference to our discussion. Pay special attention to the sections in italics.[108]

> All proteins in humans or in single-celled bacteria are made up of units of about 20 different amino acids, which, in turn, are composed of carbon, hydrogen, oxygen, nitrogen, and sometimes sulfur. To synthesize its life-essential proteins, each species needs given proportions of the 20 main amino acids. ***Although plants can manufacture all their amino acids from nitrogen, carbon dioxide, and other chemicals through photosynthesis, most other organisms can manufacture only some of them.*** The remaining ones, called essential amino acids, must be derived from food. *Eight essential amino acids are needed to maintain health in humans: leucine, isoleucine, lysine, methionine, phenylalanine, theonine, tryptophan, and valine.* ***All of these are available in proteins produced in the seeds of plants,*** but because plant sources are often weak in lysine and tryptophan, nutrition experts advise supplementing the diet with animal protein from meat, eggs, and milk, which contain all the essential acids. Most diets—***especially in the United States, where animal protein is eaten to excess***—contain all the essential amino acids. For adults, the Recommended Dietary Allowance (RDA) for protein is 0.79 g per kg (0.36 g per lb.) of body weight each day. For children and infants this RDA is doubled and tripled, respectively, because of their rapid growth.[109]
>
> Most plants and microorganisms are able to use inorganic compounds to make all the amino acids they require for normal growth. Animals, however, must obtain some of the standard amino acids from their diet in order to survive; these particular amino acids are called essential. ***They (Amino***

[108] Italics emphasis by this author.

[109] "Protein," Microsoft (R) Encarta. Copyright (c) 1994 Microsoft Corporation. Copyright (c) 1994 Funk & Wagnall's Corporation.

> ***Acids) are found* in adequate amounts in protein-rich foods from animal sources or *in carefully chosen combinations of plant proteins*.**[110]

The use of the quotation above from the encyclopedia has been for the purpose of showing the information that is available to the public and is considered the latest "medical knowledge." In it there is an admission that plants provide all of the necessary nutrients needed to sustain life and that animal products are not necessary for human survival. The directive to eat meat to supplement the diet and the subsequent move to scare people by telling them they need to eat meat daily, to satisfy the protein requirements of the body, is a factor of expediency in the mass healthcare system and an impetus from the cattle industry which developed early in the history of the United States as well as other Western countries. The cattle industry has become the modern day meat industry. The impetus is a quick way to get people to consume their nutrients, by the public health department, but this effort has essentially backfired because the excess intake (acknowledged in the excerpt above) of animal products has led to the myriad of diseases which we have already described elsewhere in this volume.

The meat and dairy industries have, for reason of greed, engendered a move towards greater and greater consumption of meat and dairy products much in the same way that the tobacco industry has engendered a desire to consume cigarettes and other tobacco products, through advertising, hormones and/or other chemicals placed inside the products, along with promoting the idea that consuming these products is a sign of social status and a vital source of pleasure in life. If meat eating was necessary for animal life forms how do we explain the robust, massive and powerful constitution of cattle, which are strict vegetarians or elephants, which are strict vegetarians and the largest land mammals on earth? A vegetarian joke goes, "If you want top be as strong as a cow, why not eat what the cow eats and not the cow." The protein argument is the most common reason advocates of meat eating give for the necessity to eat meat. The evidence given in this volume (which is also available in all the libraries of the world) shows that this is a bogus argument which has little to do with science and much to do with egoism, greed, and the desire for sense pleasure.

Vegetarian Sources for Protein

In short, human beings do not need meat products to survive. If there is a weakness in the elements of some plants, they should be identified and the correct plants should be used. For example, legumes are the best sources for lysine while grains are poor in lysine but sufficient in methionine. So the ordinary diet should include these in order to get these vital nutrients. The answer is not to get lysine or methionine from animal products. Therefore, the project is to choose certain foods that will provide the essential amino acids so that the body will be able to create the protein compounds that it needs, while not getting the essential amino acids from mucus forming foods. Once again, this information is readily available in reference sources (encyclopedias) and medical schools in libraries all over the world.

> The family is worldwide in distribution, but its greatest concentration is in tropical and subtropical regions. About 12,000 species exist, including such plants as peas, beans, peanuts, and soybeans; clover and alfalfa; and sweet pea, broom, and lupine. This subfamily contains about 3000 species, of which about 535 form a single genus, and includes such plants as brazilwood, carob, honey locust, Judas tree, logwood, and tamarind. Also, Barley Grass, a seedling of the barley plant; Barley Grass may be added to this list since it provides all nine essential amino acids.[111]

---

[110] "Amino Acids," Microsoft (R) Encarta. Copyright (c) 1994 Microsoft Corporation. Copyright (c) 1994 Funk & Wagnall's Corporation.

[111] "Legume," Microsoft (R) Encarta. Copyright (c) 1994 Microsoft Corporation. Copyright (c) 1994 Funk & Wagnall's Corporation.

Since there are few foods that are complete sources for all the necessary amino acids, a vegetarian needs to wisely include foods that will provide adequate sources for all the needed amino acids, such as legumes and grains. However, as previously discussed, most grains have mucus-forming qualities. For the purpose of this program, the best grain source is millet, followed by quinoa. Also soy products (soybeans, soymilk, tofu, etc.), contain most of the proteins needed and have other important additional benefits.

Due to natural differences in body types, some people may be allergic to soy products. There are other vegetarian sources for protein, which can be eaten in the raw state as well: salad greens, most other vegetables, avocado, sprouts and nuts. Herbs such as spirulina and alfalfa are also rich sources of protein as well as other important vitamins and minerals.

The human body does not need excessive amounts of protein to be in good health. It only requires fifty grams of protein per day, which amounts to about ten percent of the total calories taken in as food. Too much protein from animals predisposes one to calcium deficiencies, heart problems, colon cancer, as well as other problems. Vegetarian sources of protein are also more digestible than the animal sources. So in reality, less protein is needed if it comes from the vegetarian source to meet the same need.

NOTE: Some raw foodists say they do not worry about this issue of protein and getting the "right" amino acids. They feel that the body eventually adapts and makes what it needs, as evinced by the fact that they have never had a problem due to nutritional deficiencies. How else, they say, can you explain animals like the koala bear that exists on a diet of only eucalyptus leaves?

PROMOTING GOOD DIGESTION

in·di·ges·tion *n.* **1.** Inability to digest or difficulty in digesting something, especially food. **2.** Discomfort or illness resulting from this inability or difficulty.[112]

Since the central theory of Kemetic Health science holds that indigestion is caused by eating incorrect foods, eating foods in an incorrect manner as well as the lack of periodic fasting, this volume will not provide an extensive listing of herbs and treatments for individual diseases, since these are to be recognized as extensions from the main problem which is a lack of proper digestion. Therefore, we will concern ourselves here with those important natural herbs that are widely available, safe, and which assist the digestive process, that is, to bring itself back to a balance wherein the immune system functions optimally and maintains that balance which promotes the health of the entire organism. The use of these herbs should be in their natural form or in teas as indicated, as opposed to distillates and juices. This statement is made because many times people follow the mechanistic logic of medicine, thinking that the herb's curative power can be increased if the herb is made more powerful by concentrating it or if the curative agents could be distilled and isolated. Therefore, while tinctures[113] using alcohol or glycerin or other agents can be useful to some people, the preferred method of usage should be the natural form. Otherwise, check with your health care professional[114] for more guidance.

One must be careful not to go overboard with the idea that the body is a machine. It has some aspects that are machine-like however, it is much more than a machine since, if given the opportunity (proper rest and relief from stress) and the proper building blocks or raw materials (nutritious food and vital Life Force energy), it can manufacture all of the necessary chemicals to sustain a high quality of life. Therefore, we must never forget that we are helping the body, working with it and not manipulating it.

Once again, remember that digestion has three aspects, physical digestion of the body, mental digestion relating to the mind and spiritual digestion relating to the soul. We have already spoken about the spiritual and mental dimensions of life and what constitutes "good food" for the mind and soul, and will go in to specific details in the last two sections. In this section we will be concerned with herbs for the physical body.

col·ic *n.* **1.** Severe abdominal pain caused by spasm, obstruction, or distention of any of the hollow viscera, such as the intestines. Often a condition of early infancy, colic is marked by chronic irritability and crying.

Colic is a term used to refer to a problem from which infants suffer. However, it is only the beginning of gastrointestinal problems that will later be referred to as indigestion in older age. It is a problem that develops weeks after birth, and then appears to fade after the fourth month. The problem would be alleviated if infants were fed on demand as opposed to a set time schedule. Once again, the body knows its needs. If the lifestyle of following the body's needs is observed, the need for special herbs and remedies is reduced.

---

112 American Heritage Dictionary

113 An alcohol solution of a nonvolatile medicine.

114 The Sema Institute offers expert assistance in the form of counseling on diet and nutrition for the body, mind and soul for those wishing to adopt the Kemetic Diet Wisdom of natural health to restore and or promote better health. See the back section of this book for more information.

hem·or·rhoid (hĕm′ə-roid′) *n.* **1.** An itching or painful mass of dilated veins in swollen anal tissue. **2. hemorrhoids**. The pathological condition in which such painful masses occur. In this sense, also called piles.

Hemorrhoids are a side effect of indigestion. Medical doctors are not sure why hemorrhoids develop but there is a belief among some the medical field as well as those in the alternative medical field that they are caused by poor nutrition, constipation and the straining[115] that goes along with such problems, as well as diarrhea.[116] It has been noted that countries with high fiber intakes have a very low incidence of hemorrhoids.[117] The following herbal remedies along with a change in lifestyle, diet and practice when eliminating (not holding back the elimination process for a later time, not straining, not remaining on the toilet seat too long), will assist in alleviating and reversing the problem of hemorrhoids.

1. Psyllium
2. Fiber Horse chestnut
3. Witch hazel
4. Butcher's broom

Aids For Proper Digestion

There are several dietary and herbal remedies that can improve digestion. However, it must be understood that the best method of avoiding gastrointestinal problems is to maintain hygienic conditions and a strict control of the diet along with natural fasting, that is, not eating when the body is not hungry and eating when you are hungry. Some natural digestive and appetite enhancers are:

Ginger.
Acidophilus - also known as probiotics – friendly bacteria needed for proper digestion.
Vegetarian digestive enzymes.
Chamomile .
Aloe juice.
Apple juice.
Apple sauce.

Indigestion, Gas and Upset Stomach

The term "indigestion" refers to a varied number of gastrointestinal problems. These can include gas or wind and upset stomach. Various herbs have been used to relieve symptoms of indigestion, especially when there is excessive gas. These are referred to as carminatives[118]. The following are perhaps the most popular and well-studied herbs used as carminatives: ***peppermint, caraway, and fennel***. A combination of peppermint, fennel, caraway, and wormwood as well as combinations of peppermint and caraway oil have been shown to help people with indigestion in double blind studies.[119]/[120]

---

[115] Prescription for Nutritional Healing, James F. Balch M.D. and Phyllis A Balch, C.N.C.
[116] Johanson JF, Sonnenberg A. Constipation is not a risk factor for hemorrhoids: a case-control study of potential etiological agents. *Am J Gastroenterol* 1994;89:1981–86.
[117] The Natural Pharmacy, Healthnotes
[118] A drug or agent that induces the expulsion of gas from the stomach or intestines.
[119] May B, Kuntz HD, Kieser M, Kohler S. Efficacy of a fixed peppermint/caraway oil combination in non-ulcer dyspepsia. *Arzneim Forsch* 1996;46:1149–53.
[120] Westphal J, Hörning M, Leonhardt K. Phytotherapy in functional upper abdominal complaints. Results of a clinical study with a preparation of several plants. *Phytomedicine* 1996;2:285–91.

Unhealthy (toxic) foods, chlorinated drinking water, stress and disease create acidic conditions that destroy the friendly bacteria in the gut, which lead to indigestion, and constipation.

Heartburn is a burning feeling caused by stomach acid regurgitating into the esophagus from the stomach due to indigestion.

For relief of indigestion and excessive gas:

peppermint,
fennel,
caraway and
rosemary
sage
Lemon and water
Goldenseal
Grapefruit seed extract

Some important points:

Peppermint oil has been known to cause burning and gastrointestinal upset in some people.[121] People who suffer from chronic heartburn, inflammation of the gallbladder, severe liver damage, or obstruction of the bile ducts should also avoid it.[122]

Chamomile is useful in relieving heartburn and irritated or swollen mucus membranes along the digestive tract. Though rare, allergic reactions to chamomile have been reported.[123] It also promotes natural digestion.

Ginger and Garlic aid the digestive process and is also a help to the Circulatory System. In high doses (10 grams) ginger inhibits platelet aggregation, so it reduces the risk of atherosclerosis.[124] Ginger acts as a tonic in the digestive system and is useful for preventing ulcers and it also alleviates motion sickness and the nausea of pregnancy. Garlic, like ginger, also has anti-clotting properties. So, anyone using anti-coagulant drugs should check with their health professional[125] before using these herbs. Therefore, these two herbs assist in digestion and also in keeping the digestive system and the circulatory system free of obstructions. When used in high doses, garlic also acts as a booster to the immune system. It works against intestinal parasites and microbial infections. One raw clove may be taken per day. Higher doses, up to 10 cloves or more, may be taken for short periods when dealing with specific problems. Garlic may be used to heal and relieve the mucus membranes. For the treatment of the gastrointestinal mucus membranes, garlic may be added to food or eaten alone. For the nasal passages, a piece of garlic may be cut and soaked in water. The water may be passed through one nostril and out the other to wash the nasal passages. This can help in the treatment of sinusitis. Garlic also has antibacterial prosperities.

Goldenseal was used by the Native Americans as a treatment for irritations and inflammation of the mucous membranes of the respiratory, digestive, and urinary track. It has anti-microbial action so it is used for infectious diarrhea, upper respiratory track infections, and vaginal infections. Its use is often

---

[121] Sigmund DJ, McNally EF. The action of a carminative on the lower esophageal sphincter. *Gastroent* 1969;56:13–18.

[122] Blumenthal M, Busse WR, Goldberg A, et al, eds. *The Complete Commission E Monographs: Therapeutic Guide to Herbal Medicines.* Boston, MA: Integrative Medicine Communications, 1998, 180–82.

[123] Brown DJ. *Herbal Prescriptions for Better Health.* Rocklin, CA: Prima Publishing, 1996, 49–56.

[124] Brown DJ. *Herbal Prescriptions for Better Health.* Rocklin, CA: Prima Publishing, 1996, 97–109.

[125] The Sema Institute offers expert assistance in the form of counseling on diet and nutrition for the body, mind and soul for those wishing to adopt the Kemetic Diet Wisdom of natural health to restore and or promote better health. See the back section of this book for more information.

recommended with echinacea, which is another herb that is effective in treating colds, flu and yeast infections.

Echinasea – Echinasea is a natural herb which acts as a form of antibiotic and immune booster if used in the correct manner. The effectiveness of echinasea in treating disease has been documented in double blind scientific studies.[126/127/128]

Grapefruit seed extract is useful in dealing with gastrointestinal infections such as those caused by eating contaminated foods.

NOTE: While some herbs like goldenseal and echinacea have antibiotic-like properties, even these should not be abused. This means that one should rightly seek to live a life that avoids the need for antibiotics altogether. Herbs should be taken as a means to promote balanced nutrition primarily.

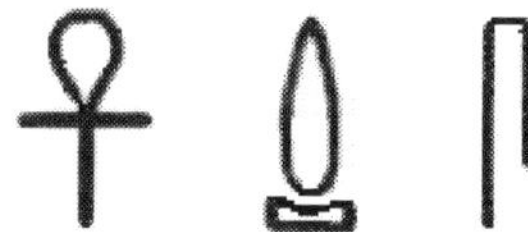

[126] Melchart D, Linde K, et al. Immunomodulation with Echinacea—a systematic review of controlled clinical trials. *Phytomed* 1994;1:245–54.
[127] Hoheizel O, Sandberg M, Bertram S, et al. Echinacea shortens the course of the common cold: a double-blind, placebo-controlled clinical trial. *Eur J Clin Res* 1997;9:261–68.
[128] Dorn M, Knick E, Lewith G. Placebo-controlled, double-blind study of Echinacea pallida redix in upper respiratory tract infections. *Comp Ther Med* 1997;5:40–42.

Overeating: The Problem of Gluttony and Greed

"Strive to prevent fatness so as that the weight on thy body will not weigh down thy Soul"

—Ancient Egyptian Proverb
from the Temple of Aset (Isis)

"An infant's Soul is altogether a thing of beauty to see, not yet befouled by body's passions, still all but hanging from the Cosmic Soul! But when the body grows in bulk and draweth down the Soul into it's mass, then doth the Soul cut off itself and bring upon itself forgetfulness, and no more shareth in the Beautiful and Good (God); and this forgetfulness becometh vice."

—Ancient Egyptian Proverb

"By keeping in subjection the belly, thou wilt be listened to. If thou hast eaten three loaves of bread, and hast drunk two vessels of beer, if you are not full contend against greediness."

—Ancient Egyptian Proverb

"Do not be greedy in the division of things. Do not covet more than your share.

—Ancient Egyptian Proverb

The problem of overeating is in reality a dysfunction caused by a deep-seeded greed that is lodged in the unconscious mind. It is a manifestation of a misguided desire to achieve something that will bring abiding happiness and satisfaction. Since that something they are looking for is lacking, the desire is projected unto an object, in this case, food. Food is also used as a pacifier, which is served to calm the body and mind temporarily from the discomfort of the functions of the excretory and cleansing systems of the body. The act of eating shuts down the process that cleanses the waste from the body temporarily. Since the waste is not being eliminated completely from the body, it accumulates in the form of deposits all over the body including the organs, and this causes their dysfunction. One example of this problem is obesity, which can lead to all manner of diseases including diabetes, and arteriosclerosis as well as malnutrition.

However, when the body is allowed to consume the normal amount of food it requires, the body comes back to its proper weight and there is more vitality on the lesser amount of food being consumed. This is because the efficiency with which the food is processed allows the body to extract more energy and nutrients from it. The following excerpt provides more information about the disease of arteriosclerosis (italics emphasis is from this author).

> **Arteriosclerosis**, several diseases of the arteries, including atherosclerosis, the most common form. It is caused by deposits of fatty materials and sometimes calcium on the arterial walls, narrowing the passage for blood, with the calcium also decreasing elasticity of the arteries. There are usually no overt symptoms until the disease is well advanced. Serious cases can lead to coronary disturbance, in which case symptoms may include excruciating chest pains radiating to the arms or neck (angina pectoris). So-called senile forgetfulness or confusion may occur if brain vessels are involved. ***There is evidence that predisposition to the disease is hereditary and that it is more likely to strike cigarette smokers, sedentary persons, or those with high fat diets. Prevention and control of***

arteriosclerosis through low fat/low cholesterol diet and exercise is currently favored. Anticoagulant drugs are sometimes effective on a short-term basis.[129]

NOTE: In the encyclopedic statement above there is an acknowledgement that the means to promote health is by a low fat, low cholesterol diet, which is of course a diet that limits meat consumption **(since cholesterol is only found in animal based products)** and processed foods. It is ironic that when people get sick with diseases such as colon cancer and arteriosclerosis, doctors will prescribe less meat and more vegetables and fruits. The question is why not prescribe this diet in the first place before people become sick? The greed of the tobacco industry, the meat industry and the drug industry perpetuates the ill health of all by influencing most physicians to also smoke, eat meat and not speak out against it. Instead of seeking real cures, the process of drug therapies is continued because it benefits doctors and drug companies. However, in recent years the movement towards alternative health approaches has gained momentum. What is being presented in this manual is actually a guide to healthy living so as to avoid the necessity for medical treatment. While modern medial science has some positive uses, especially in the treatment of trauma[130], the teachings of righteous living were and continue to be the only real means to health of mind, body and soul. Therefore, once again we are admonished to turn towards the vegetarian diet. Vegetables also have fats, but these are more digestible than those from meats.

> **Fat**, substance used by animals to store energy and shield them from the cold. Fats are esters of glycerin with carboxylic acids such as palmitic, lauric, and stearic acid, which have 16 or 18 carbon atoms. Vegetable oils are similar to fats, but are viscous liquids rather than semisolids, and have double chemical bonds in the acid molecules, that is, they are unsaturated.[131]

Along with an impairment in the elimination of impurities from the body, the excess intake of food causes a reduced ability of the body to assimilate and process nutrients. This condition leads to malnutrition, and malnutrition leads to deficiencies in the ability of the various organs of the body to process food and convert it into usable nutritious elements for the body. When the body is young, it can cope with much mistreatment, but as the body gets older, it is less forgiving and right living becomes a critical imperative for maintaining proper health.

Thus, the Kemetic teachings of health admonish that one should eat only when hungry and eating should not be out of habit, lust or greed. Further, the adage of eating to live and not living to eat should be applied in all walks of life. Food can become addictive, but perhaps no other people have sunk to the decadent state of the Ancient Romans, who created special rooms called "vomatoriums" for the express purpose of providing a place where guests could vomit up their dinner so as to go back in to the hall and experience the pleasure of eating more and more food, over and over again. This is surely the uttermost expression of excess, gluttony and greed for sensual pleasure in history. Greed for food or other worldly pleasures is like a drug, which can never satisfy the body. One needs more and more until the body collapses due to the excesses. Ironically, less is more. The more self-control is perfected in life, the more life is appreciated and the more spiritual abundance develops. In this the state of control and health, the body and its earthly nature do not hamper the experience of the heights of spiritual awareness.

Further, under this teaching, it must be understood that the idea of being overweight as an acceptable condition is erroneous. The condition in reality signifies an excess of stored up Ukhedu, which is causing an undue strain on the organs of the body and will have a deleterious effect eventually. Thus, there is no way to maintain optimal health in this condition. Further, the existence of undue weight that the person

---

[129] Random House Encyclopedia
[130] *Medicine.* A serious injury or shock to the body, as from violence or an accident.
[131] Random House Encyclopedia

must carry around, constitutes a force which causes a tendency towards worldliness, and all of its components, i.e. lack of spiritual sensitivity, intensification of worldly desires, dullness of mental processing, etc. Therefore, this condition is undesirable for the ordinary human being and extremely detrimental to the spiritual aspirant's efforts towards attaining spiritual enlightenment.

There are some important bonuses for eating less. First, the body ages more slowly, providing an extended life span. Also, while certified organic food is more expensive, when the reduced amount of food needed to survive on is considered, the savings balances off the cost of eating healthier foods. The food that would ordinarily be wasted in overeating and excess could be used for feeding others, and the environment will be spared the excess of overfarming and excrement from sewage and garbage sources, which end up in streams, lakes, oceans and landfills. Also, proper breathing extends the life span as well.

Proper Breathing[132]

Proper breathing is one effective way to store and accumulate vital Life Force energy in the body. Other means are control of emotions, thoughts, actions, etc. Proper breathing is a practice that should be used especially before and during meditation since it acts to harmonize the energies of the mind and consequently also the mind.

Most people in the modern world do not know how to breathe properly. Most people (especially males) have learned to breathe by pushing out the chest (A) in a "manly" or "macho" fashion. This mode of breathing is harmful for many reasons. The amount of air taken in is less and vital cosmic energy is reduced and becomes stagnant in the subtle vital energy channels, resulting in physical and mental diseases. The stagnation of the flow of energy through the body has the effect of grounding one's consciousness to the physical realities rather than allowing the mind and body to operate with lightness and subtlety.

"Belly breathing" or abdominal breathing massages the internal organs and develops Life Force energy (Sekhem, Chi or Prana). One breathes in an out through the nostrils, the normal breathing apparatus which filters and humidifies the air being brought into the body. The mouth is closed. It will be noticed that it is your natural breathing pattern when you lie down on your back. Instruction is as follows: B-Breathe in through the nostrils (mouth closed) and push the stomach out, swelling it out like a balloon. C-Breathe out again through the nostrils with the mouth closed, and pull the stomach in towards the spine (back). This form of breathing is to be practiced at all times, not just during meditation. It allows the natural Life Force in the air to be rhythmically supplied to the body and nervous system. This process is indispensable in the achievement of physical health and mental-spiritual power to control the mind (meditation).

Breathing exercise: With eyes closed, allow the abdomen to expand as you breathe in. Visualize that you are taking in Life Force energy along with the air. See it remaining in your body as you expel the air. Visualize that all the nutrients of the air are being used and that impurities are being carried away.

[132] Illustrations by Asar Oronde Reid

Figure 24: A- Incorrect " Chest" Breathing B& C- Proper "Belly" Breathing Technique

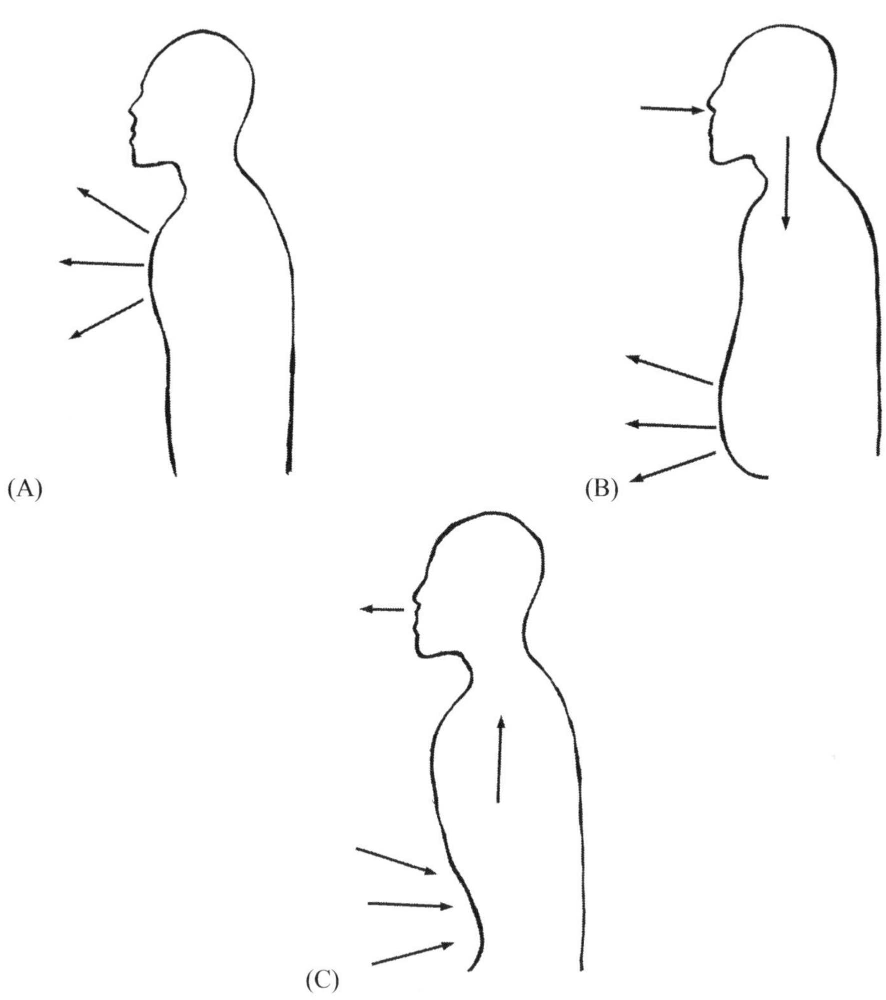

Mettu of the Respiratory System[133]

[133] Illustration by Asar Oronde Reid

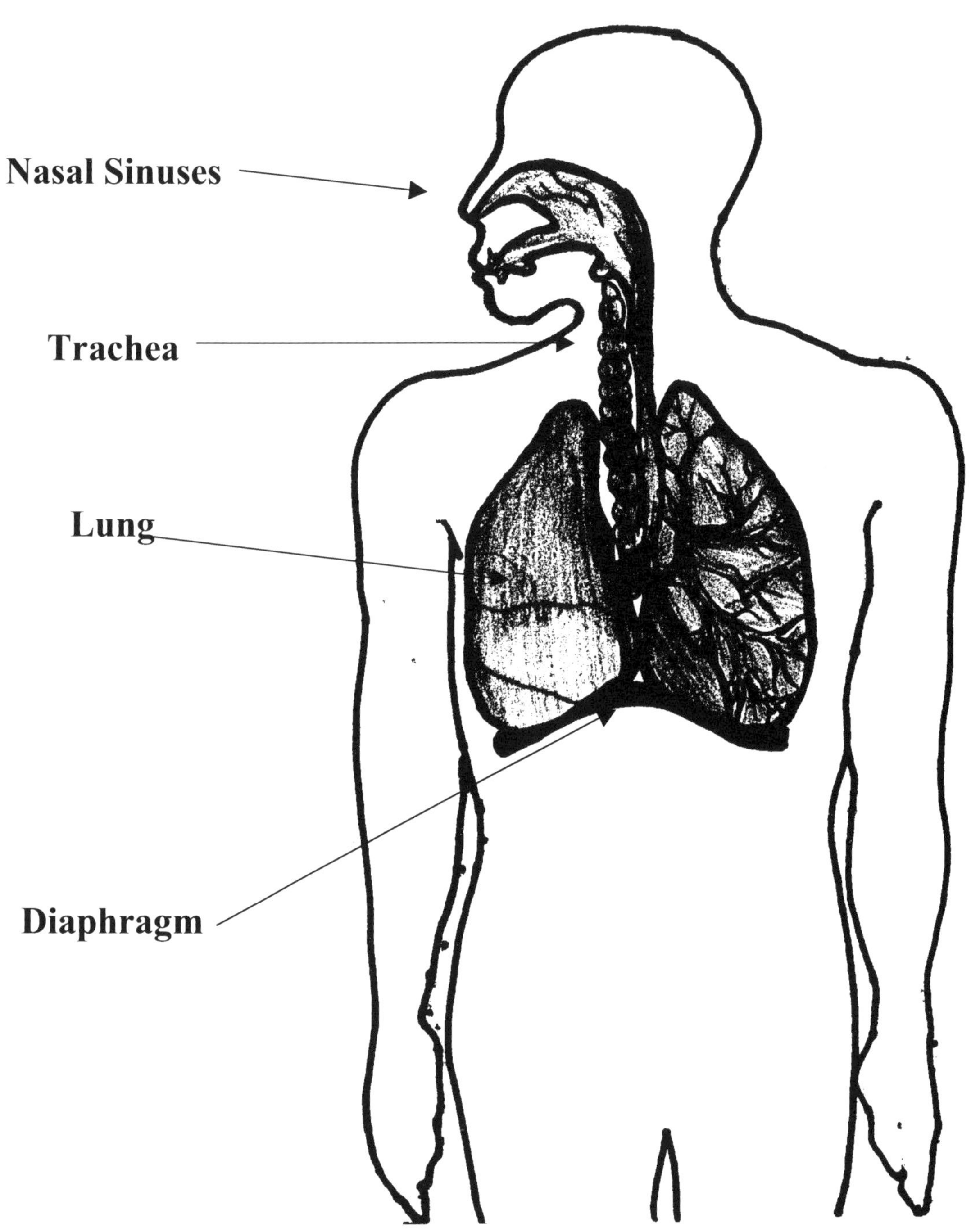
Nasal Sinuses
Trachea
Lung
Diaphragm

Physical Exercise

"Her name is Health: she is the daughter of Exercise, who begot her on Temperance. The rose blusheth on her cheeks, the sweetness of the morning breatheth from her lips; joy, tempered with innocence and modesty, sparkleth in her eyes and from the cheerfulness of her heart she singeth as she walketh."

—Ancient Egyptian Proverb

Physical and mental health are the basis of spiritual health. Therefore, Smai Tawi philosophy also includes the practice of special postures and exercises coupled with breathing techniques to promote the health of the mind and body. These exercises are psychophysical in nature, affecting both the mind and body. These postures have an effect on one's mental attitude and physical health by stimulating, cleansing and balancing the various energy centers (chakras), nerves, endocrine glands, organs and tissues of the body. Physical disturbance and preoccupation with physical illness may distract one's consciousness from higher, more sublime thoughts and aspirations. This branch of Smai Tawi is actually under the same discipline as meditation.

Physical exercise, and especially Yoga physical exercise is very effective in mobilizing the Ukhedu and assisting the circulatory and lymphatic systems in transporting impurities to the excretory organs. The headstand and shoulder-stand are extremely effective in this area. In addition, each of the Yoga exercise postures affect the energy centers (chakras) within the Serpent Power Yoga System, and thereby balances the associated psychological states of mind and physical organs in the body. It should also be understood that the best exercise for the personality as a whole is to have a sublime purpose in life that keeps one busy and active daily, working to improve oneself and the world. This acts to keep one involved in projects and endeavors which will require physical, mental and spiritual exercise of the body, mind and soul.

It must be understood that physical exercise is not the goal of life. It is a means to the end of promoting a healthy body in which the proper disciplines for discovering the higher consciousness can be maintained.

Essential Postures of Kemetic Smai Tawi (Yoga) Mystical Spirituality

Due to the extensive nature of the Kemetic Yoga Exercise Program, the reader is referred to a separate book which treats that subject exclusively. It is the *Egyptian Yoga Exercise Workout Book* by Muata Ashby and Karen Vijaya Ashby. The main purpose of physical exercise is to maintain the body in good enough condition to allow the soul to have entry into the world and to have the opportunity to experience through interaction with the world. Through interaction with the outer-world (universe), the inner-world (soul) becomes aware of itself as a living entity, and thereby has the opportunity to achieve the highest possible goal, to achieve all that is achievable, to become "Godlike," to "know itself." Even though there is much knowledge, wisdom and experience to be gained from pain, disease and suffering, in the task of achieving supreme self knowledge, a healthy body is indispensable.

To this end, exercises which will assist the proper distribution of vital energies (sexual energies) and mental peace should be practiced. Preferably, the following exercises or other systems of yoga exercise should be practiced under the supervision of a qualified instructor to insure that they are performed properly, so as to avoid injury.

The following posters show the postures of Smai Tawi Kemetic Yoga Exercise (called "Thef Neteru - The Movement of the Gods and Goddesses") that may be performed prior to the meditation practice.

Figure 25: The Egyptian (Kemetic) Thef Neteru Yoga Exercise Poster,[134] showing the exercise postures to promote the health of the physical body.

Plate 14: The author demonstrating the Kemetic Yoga postures.[135]

[134] Available from the Sema Institute of Yoga. Also, Smai Tawi Thef Neteru postures video available.
[135] Available from the Sema Institute of Yoga

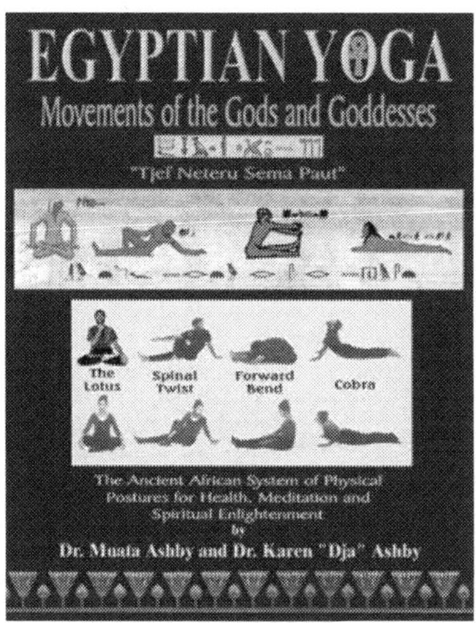

NOTE: For more information on the Kemetic Yoga Postures see (above) the book *Egyptian Yoga Exercise Workout Book* by Muata Ashby and Karen Vijaya Ashby.[136]

[136] Available from the Sema Institute of Yoga

CHAPTER 6: FOOD FOR THE MIND

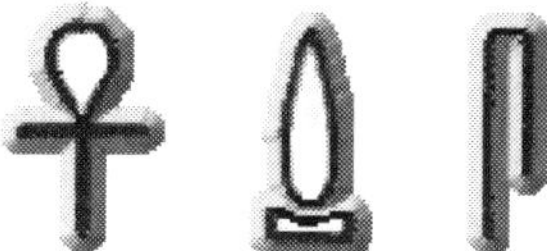

According to the *1999 United States Surgeon Generals Report on Mental Health:*

Depressive illness affects more than 19 million adults in the United States. This number does not include their family members.

According to the year *2000 World Health Organization:*

The WHO examined seven countries and found that almost half of the people who suffered some form of mental illness in their lifetime came from the United States.

Dr. Gro Harlem Bruntland (WHO's General Director):

Mental illness is the "crisis of the 21st century."

Dr. Gabriel Cousens:

"In every generation on a universally poor diet, there is a successive increasing degeneration in our mental and physical state. This has been shown in animal studies and we are now finding it in human studies. We have at least 8 million children on Ritalin. At least 10% of our children have hyperactivity, where 20 years ago that was not the case at all. We have 500 thousand children on antidepressants, particularly Prozac. One hundred thousand children are active alcoholics. It has to do with the poor nutrition of the parents, which affects the developing brain of the fetus. Then the child is raised on a very poor diet, so the brain, which may be a genetically weakened, becomes even more significantly weakened. Their neurotransmitters have lower amounts, their endorphins are not working quite right and so their brain is actually altered to the point where they need to do something to feel okay. That takes us to the epidemic of addictions which are also mental health diseases."

KEMETIC MYTHOLOGY: THE BASIS FOR PSYCHOLOGY AND MENTAL HEALTH

The Kamitan Wisdom of Mind

In Kamitan Philosophy the mind is recognized to have varied levels of operation. Each level represents a plane of existence and vibration which manifests as a state or condition of consciousness. The table below shows the levels of mind and their Kamitan name and their function in the personality.

Kamitan Aspects of the psyche (psychology)	Kamitan Hieroglyphic term	Kamitan Name	Aspect of mind
		Nun	Undifferentiated Consciousness
		Amun	Hidden Witnessing Consciousness
		Ra	Universal Spirit
		Akhu	Individual spirit
		Asar	Eternal soul
		Aset	Wisdom and intuition
		Set	Ego
		Djehuti	Intellect
		Anpu	Mind (lower-purified)
Kamitan states of mind			
		Nehast	Resurrection, spiritual Enlightenment
		Såa	To Know
		Beq	Lucid, to be bright to see
		Neshsh.	Agitated, disturbed
		Wmet htp ab.	Dense Dull of heart-
		Såaa njset	To not Know, blindness, obtuseness weakness, evil of mind
		Kmn	Ignorant
		Riba	Madness, folly, insanity, delusion-
		Aun	Sleep Slumber
		Nehas	Wake up Awake

	[hieroglyphs]	***Mnab***	Firm of heart/steady minded
	[hieroglyphs]	***Ab.***	Imagination, let fancy run free in mind-
	[hieroglyphs]	***Mesqeh.***	Mental anguish, sorrow, pain-
	[hieroglyphs]	***Ass ab***	Light-minded man, mentally unstable

Table 9: Ailments of the Mind and their Remedies

Ailment of the Mind	Remedy: Practice the following
Anger	Forgiveness
Hatred	Understanding and Love forgiveness
Greed	Generosity, unselfishness
Lust	Purity, self-control, sex sublimation
Envy-Jealousy	Satisfaction with what God has given
Discontent	Contentment-not comparing yourself to others
Boredom	Right action
Pride	Humility

In Ancient Egypt, the mind was recognized as a primary factor in the cause of disease as well as its cure. Therefore, it was assigned a divinity to preside over it. The name of this divinity is *Djehuti.* He is representative of the Cosmic Mind of God. He enlightens human beings as to their spiritual nature through the wisdom which is transmitted through the hieroglyphic text that he brought to the world at the behest of Ra, the Supreme Being, and thereby heals human beings by making their consciousness, symbolized by the Divine Eye, 𓂀, "whole and sound again." This reconstitution process of the Eye is a metaphor of the spiritual evolution and resurrection (enlightenment) that every human being must pursue in life in order to discover true health and happiness on earth, and beyond. Ancient Egyptian mystical-religious philosophy therefore, is integral to the promotion of holistic health since it is from this source that we are able to derive the proper food for the mind, which leads to sanity, prosperity and physical health. So the Ancient Egyptian sages, priests and priestesses were the first to practice psychology and spiritual counseling as a means to promote good health.

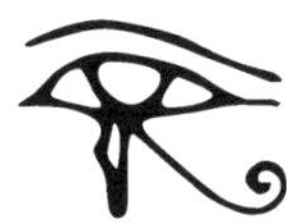

Figure 26: The Divine Eye of Heru

Psychological studies reveal a unique aspect of disease, psychosomatic illness. Psychosomatic disease relates to the phenomena of diseases that have physical symptoms but no physical causes that doctors can find. This points to the understanding that all disease is in reality has a mental source. In light of the previous teachings in reference to the mind-body connection, it is no surprise that the mind influences the condition of the body. In the following section we will explore the teaching of mental health from a spiritual perspective, relative to the practice of psychiatry (the branch of medicine that deals with the diagnosis, treatment, and prevention of mental and emotional disorders) and its spiritual ramifications. The Ancient Egyptian god Djehuti was known to the Greeks as ***Aesculapius***, the Greek god of medicine. He was also called Hermes or Thoth by the Greeks and Romans. He was the first practitioner of healing.

His art was not limited to healing the body, but also the mind, for it is only when there is health of mind, that it is possible to perceive the glory of life and the Divine essence.

The Ancient Egyptian Origins of the Western Medical Symbols

Djehuti, The God of Healing

Figure 27: Left: The Ancient Egyptian God Djehuti holding the Caduceus in his left hand and transmitting the life force with the ankh amulet in his right arm. (From the Temple of Asar (Osiris) in Abdu (Egypt, Africa)
Figure 28: Right: Modern caduceus (*staff with a serpent coiled around it*).

The Healing Power of Djehuti

The healing power of Djehuti consists of restoring the condition of the Eye, the symbol of healthy spiritual Consciousness, to its state before the impurities (ignorance about the Higher Self, anger, hatred, greed, lust, etc.) came in, that is, the Enlightened state. Thus Djehuti speaks:

> ***"I came seeking the Eye of Heru, that I might bring it back and count it. I found it (now it is) complete, counted and sound, so that it can flame up to the sky and blow above and below..."***

The name for the Eye of Heru may be pronounced as ***"Wedjat," "Udjat" or "Utchat"*** meaning: ***"the whole or restored one"*** and also ***"that which protects."***

Figure 29: Djehuti restoring to Heru the Udjat (Uatchit) Eye, 𓂀, which Set had blinded.

In the Asarian Resurrection myth saga, Heru's eye was damaged. Djehuti repaired the damage. In mystical terms, Djehuti, who symbolizes pure divine intellect, helps Heru to regain the divine vision and successfully meet the supreme challenge of life, overcoming Set, the lower self (anger, hatred, greed, spiritual ignorance, egoism, fear, etc,). He restored the Eye, which symbolizes divine consciousness. He accomplished this healing process through teachings, which bring wisdom that leads to right thinking, and right acting. These teachings lead to freedom from stress and mental imbalance. Thus, the ultimate and only true purpose of healing is to restore divine consciousness. This is to be considered "optimal health." This was the basis of the medical profession as Djehuti was the god of all doctors. The symbol of the eye of Heru (A), which was repaired by Djehuti, is still with us to this day in the form of the symbol of the pharmacist (H). It is used as an emblem denoting the drug store and medicaments for healing. It is an evolution from the alchemy that was practiced in medieval Europe, which was itself based on the medical science of Ancient Egypt.[137] The lineage of the symbol can be traced from the Eye of Heru symbol down to the pharmacist symbol of modern times.

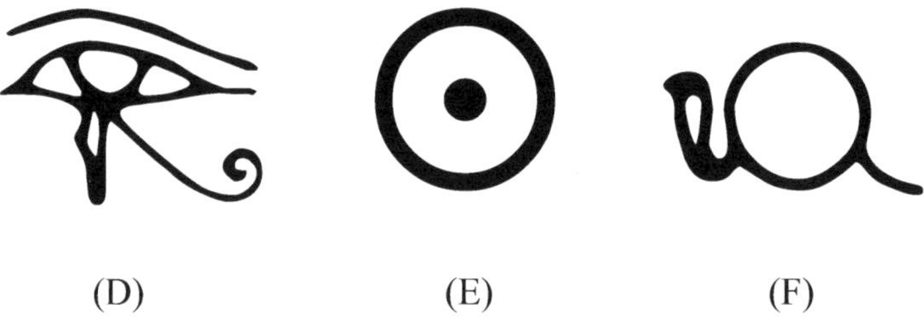

(D) (E) (F)

Figure 30: From left to right: D-The Eye of Heru Symbol. Heru was also known as the "Divine Hawk of Gold," a manifestation of the sun which is an embodied form of the Supreme Spirit.
E- The Ancient Egyptian symbol of the sundisk representing the golden sun, Ra, the Supreme Being.
F- The sundisk encircled by the solar serpent.

[137] The birthplace of alchemy was ancient Egypt, where, in Alexandria, it began to flourish in the Hellenistic period; simultaneously, a school of alchemy was developing in China. "Alchemy," Microsoft (R) Encarta. Copyright (c) 1994 Microsoft Corporation. Copyright (c) 1994 Funk & Wagnall's Corporation.

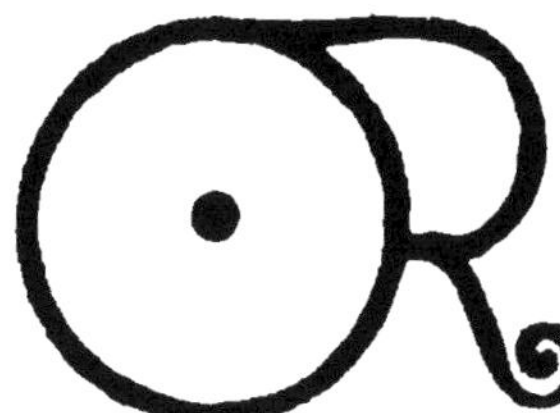

Figure 31: The Medieval Alchemical symbol of Gold.

Alchemy was the primitive form of chemistry practiced in Western Europe in the Middle Ages. Alchemy involved a search for the Philosopher's Stone, which is a mystic process for transmuting matter from state to state and worldly consciousness to divine consciousness. It was based on the Ancient Egyptian concept of the underlying unity of all matter and the unity of man with the universe. Similar teachings and alchemical practitioners existed in China and India during the middle ages as well. Alchemy was practiced in Western Europe, from the early Christian times until the 17th century. It then gave way to the modern "science" of chemistry.

Figure 32: The winged caduceus (G) with the Rx symbol (H), used by modern day doctors and pharmacists. In more recent times the symbol of the caduceus and the Rx have been increasingly replaced by the mortar and pestle (Fig. 33).

Figure 33: Mortar[138] and pestle[139] symbols used by modern pharmacies and drug stores.

AESCULAPIUS is the Greek god of medicine, **Asclepius** in Latin. **Aesculapius** is often depicted in art holding a ***staff with a serpent coiled around it.*** The serpent, which was sacred to him, symbolized renewal of youth, because it casts off its skin. It is also akin to the caduceus of Djehuti, which relates to the Serpent Power Energy.

In ancient Greek myth, Aesculapius was the son of the Greek divinities Apollo and Coronis. The centaur brought him up and taught him the art of healing. His daughter Hygeia personified health, and his

[138] A vessel in which substances are crushed or ground with a pestle.
[139] A club-shaped, hand-held tool for grinding or mashing substances in a mortar.

daughter Panacea, healing. Two of his sons appear in Homer's 'Iliad' as physicians in the Greek army. Their supposed descendants, called **Asclepiadae,** formed a large order of priest-physicians. The sacred secrets of medicine belonged only to them and were passed on from father to son.

The **Asclepiadae** practiced their art in magnificent temples of health, called **Asclepieia.** The temples were actually sanatoriums equipped with gymnasiums, baths, and even theaters. The patient was first put to sleep. His dream, interpreted by the priests, was supposed to furnish directions for treatment. All cures were recorded as miracles.

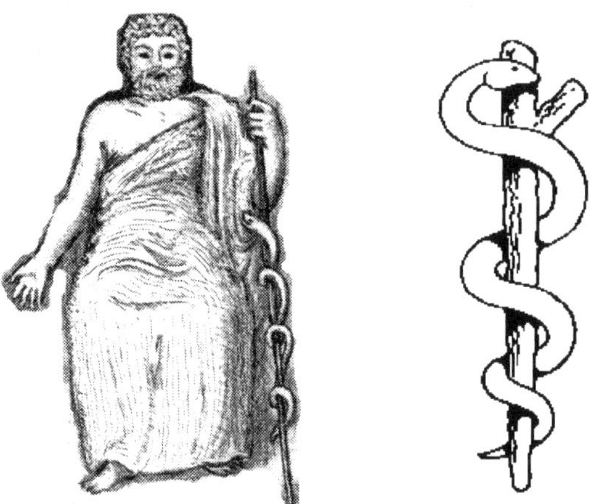

Plate 15: Aesculapius, the Greek god of medicine. Right- Caduceus of Aesculapius.

Sehu Djehuti: The Spiritual Preceptor for Mental Health

Djehuti is the god of learning, writing, mathematics and language. In Ancient Egyptian mythology, he is the scribe of the gods. He appears as the record keeper of the dead in the *Books of Coming Forth By Day.* He is the patron of learning and of the arts. He is the inventor of writing, and in the specific theology related to him, he is also seen as the Creator of the universe. Djehuti is depicted as a man with the head of a baboon or an ibis bird. He is also depicted sometimes holding a pen and ink. Other symbols of Djehuti are the lunar disk and crescent moon. The God Djehuti represents the principle of spiritual health and the maintenance of spiritual health is promoted when there is a viable spiritual discipline being practiced which leads one to spiritual enlightenment.

Djehuti is often depicted as an Ibis, a wading bird. 

The Kemetic term ***gem***, using an ibis picking into the mud, means “to find.” 

The ibis is a wading bird related to the stork and the heron. The choice of the ibis indicates a unique feature or quality which spiritual learning requires. This quality is related to the *wading* nature of the ibis. Wading birds have a special capacity to move through water and probe (gem) for specific items they desire with their long beaks. They find small insects and other edibles amidst the muddy waters and it is the cleansed and sharp intellect which can make sense of the world. Wading means *walking in or through a substance, as water, that offers resistance, impedes or makes movement difficult.* Djehuti represents intellect, the mind and its capacity to cut (wade) through the myriad of thoughts and concepts (water-ocean of consciousness) in order to get to the truth. The world is the ocean of consciousness and Djehuti is the aspect of the mind that can navigate through the world with healthy reasoning, and find vigor and intuition, making sense out of the cacophony of human life.

The illumination from the lunar disk is a reflection of the sun, so Djehuti's wisdom is a reflection of the Spirit just as human consciousness, which is limited, is a reflection of Cosmic Consciousness, which is unlimited and whole. The crescent moon symbol of Djehuti is a figure of the moon in its first quarter. It has concave[140] and convex[141] edges terminating in points. The crescent moon symbol signifies growing or increasing understanding, reason and spiritual wisdom. Therefore, Djehuti is the embodiment of knowledge. This is one of the reasons why he is said to have created writing. He is also the messenger of the Supreme Being, Ra, who brings the special words of power to Aset in the Asarian Resurrection Story in order for Aset to resurrect the young Heru, who was poisoned by Set. In this aspect Djehuti symbolizes the Spiritual Preceptor who brings the wisdom of the Divine Self to the aspirant so the aspirant can resurrect his or her spiritual aspiration each time it is attacked by the ego (Set).

Djehuti, Cosmic Mind, the moon, ☽, is a reflection of Ra, ☉ , the Sun - Spirit

The universe is understood to be like an ocean of subtle matter through which the Supreme Being, Ra, sails on his barque in order to sustain Creation. Djehuti is Ra's mind, the Cosmic Mind, with which Ra moves through the ocean of Creation. Thus, the universe is known as an ocean of consciousness or the Primeval Ocean, called Nu or Nun in Kemetic Mysticism. The Spirit (Ra) uses the Cosmic Mind (Djehuti) to create the objects and varied forms of Creation and maintain order in Creation. Therefore, matter (Creation) is in reality consciousness (Primeval Ocean) which has taken on forms (physical objects) in accordance with the will of the Cosmic Mind. The Cosmic Mind also brings forth learning and knowledge to Creation through the arts, sciences and language. Nothing is invented by human beings. Everything that is created by civilization comes from the Cosmic Mind, and not from any individual human being. To believe otherwise would be egoistic thought. The more a person is in tune with the Cosmic Mind, which actually means coming into harmony with the Cosmic Will, the more knowledge he or she obtains, and the more inner peace and fulfillment he or she experiences. The farther away a person gets from the Cosmic Mind through negative thoughts, actions, ignorance and delusion, the less able a person is to discover goodness, inner peace, knowledge, happiness and health in life.

140 Curved like the inner surface of a sphere.
141 Curved outward, as the exterior of a sphere.

Figure 34: Left-The Ancient Egyptian Goddess Hetheru
Figure 35: Right- Forms of the Ancient Egyptian God Djehuti as a baboon and as a man with the head of an Ibis with the crescent moon headdress.

In the myth of Hetheru and Djehuti of Ancient Egypt, Hetheru lost her mind and forgot her true (spiritual) identity. Djehuti devised a plan to approach Hetheru. Understanding that she was in a state of intense mental *dullness,* he knew that he could approach her directly by using his ordinary form and by giving her direct teachings as to the nature of the Self (Ra) and her true identity. After becoming embodied, Hetheru became caught up in the lust for sense pleasures, killing and meat eating. So he decided to transform himself into the form of a humble, harmless looking baboon instead of presenting himself in the form of a regal ibis headed divinity. Likewise, it would be very difficult for an ordinary person to behold and accept the real form of the Divine Self (Supreme Being). Therefore, the indirect means of spiritual preceptorship, religion, yoga, symbols, myth and parables are adopted until a spiritual aspirant is ready to have a direct experience. At that time the indirect means are placed aside in order to experience the Divine who transcends all forms, concepts, religions and symbols. So Djehuti presented Hetheru with some of the most profound teachings related to the nature of the Self in the form of parables, in order to gradually gain her confidence and stimulate her latent memories of her own true glory.

In the beginning, the Spiritual Preceptor must help the individual to somehow turn the anguish and pain experienced as a result of interaction with the world into a desire to rise above it. To this end, a series of techniques and disciplines have been developed over thousands of years. Some of these methods are myths, parables, mental disciplines, meditation and physical culture (Yoga exercises promote the development of the internal Life Force). The teacher needs to help the seeker to restructure and channel those energies which arise from disappointment and frustration into a healthy dispassion for the illusoriness of the world and its entanglements. The teacher shows the way to develop spiritual aspiration and self-effort directed at sustaining a viable personal spiritual program, known as *Sheti* in the Kemetic Smai Tawi philosophical system.

Djehuti is the quintessential image of the Guru in this story. The word "Guru" is an Indian Sanskrit term meaning "Spiritual Preceptor," a teacher of spiritual truths. A Spiritual Preceptor is a Sage who shows others the way to understand the higher reality beyond the ordinary phenomenal universe. He or she shows others how to discover their true identity and realize their oneness with the Divine. In essence, they are spiritual guides.

In Ancient Egyptian Myth, there are two great Spiritual Preceptors. Djehuti is one of them. He is the wonderful teacher of Hetheru. The other one is Aset. In the Shetaut Asar or The Story of Asar, Aset and Heru otherwise known as the Asarian Resurrection, Aset is the teacher of her son, Heru. She trains him in the arts, sciences and the mystical philosophy of Creation and the nature of the Divine Self. She enables Heru to receive the Divine Vision, which she obtained from Ra in the Story of Ra and Aset.

The Kemetic words related to spiritual instruction are ***Sehu*** "Spiritual Counselor" and ***Sebai*** meaning "Spiritual Preceptor." A Spiritual Preceptor is not only a person who has attained a high level of internal self-discovery and purity, but also a person who is well versed in the scriptural writings and has knowledge of parables and myths along with their mystical implications. He or she also knows the practices which lead a person to spiritual evolution (mystical disciplines).

If the teaching is given directly, it may be misunderstood or even repudiated altogether due to the state of mind of the individual. Hence, the student must be properly initiated into the teaching, and the proper relationship must be established between teacher and student.

The teacher offers humility and honesty with a beguiling wit, cheerfulness and an uplifting outlook. This is symbolized by the divine food Djehuti offered Hetheru. The teacher brings divine food in the form of wisdom teachings, which uplift the mind by relieving the burden of pain and sorrow, which weighs down the soul of a human being due to ignorance and negativity. The divine food is the taste of divine glory. It is a glimpse of the goal, which a disciple must aspire to experience in its fullness. However, this fullness is experienced in degrees as the teacher gives the spiritual teaching and as the student assimilates it.

Figure 36: The goddess Hetheru in the form of the lioness-holding the two serpents of the Kemetic Caduceus.

The student must learn to respect and trust the teacher. Also, the student must allow the teaching to penetrate deeply within the heart. It is only then that the teaching will have a transformative effect. Hetheru allowed Djehuti's words to penetrate her cold, anguished heart. Then she began to remember her past glory. This is the process of divine memory wherein she began to regain the remembrance of her true identity. The pain of seeing her current level of existence in comparison with her past glory brought her to tears. Also, she felt the pain of realizing that she was missing out on the boundless divine love of her true essence. This is the common emotional experience of a spiritual aspirant when understanding as to their true predicament begins to dawn. "What have I done to come down from the heights of divinity to the limited state of human life and mortal existence? How wretched am I? How degraded am I?" These are the kinds of questions asked by a spiritual aspirant before he or she begins to understand the meaning of the spiritual teachings. This form of thinking leads to a resolution to regain one's true glory and to rise up from the degradation of ignorance, "May I find a teacher who can guide me on the path to self-discovery and enlightenment at once!" Thus, Hetheru, came to respect Djehuti. She accepted his offering, listened to his teachings and later trusted him with her life. As one begins to reflect on the teaching, intuitional understanding opens up the opportunity to view the beauty and experience the infinite compassion of the Self. Then there are no more questions, only a keen desire to experience this elevated state more and more. An aspirant might say at this point, "I have glimpsed a wondrous bliss within. Let me fully discover it and abide in it."

The secret to mental health is in controlling the mind. And the secret to controlling the mind is being established in spiritual truth. Therefore, if one advances towards spiritual enlightenment one **will not** suffer from mental illness. Mystical Psychology leads the mind to experience greater peace, balance, contentment and inner fulfillment. This is why it is said that sages and saints are the most compassionate beings and that spiritual knowledge is the greatest gift of all. This is why the god Djehuti is known as the healer of the "Eye." The Eye is the symbol of inner spiritual vision. In the myth of Djehuti and Hetheru, the goddess Hetheru entered the world as the Eye and lost her way, and Djehuti healed her delusion and led her to spiritual enlightenment. In the myth of the Asarian Resurrection, Heru's spiritual Eye was damaged by Set and Djehuti healed it also. Therefore, Djehuti is the quintessential image of the spiritual preceptor who heals not just the body, but the mind and soul. Spiritual wisdom and spiritual instruction are the keys to alleviating and eradicating the greatest source of misery in life, spiritual ignorance. Spiritual ignorance is the greatest source of pain in life because it leads a person to a myriad forms of adversity, suffering and frustrations, not in just one lifetime, but in countless. In this regard, the promotion of physical and mental health is essential to transcending the lower states of consciousness. This is the purpose of the Mystical (Yogic) disciplines.

Emotions and their Effects of Physical Health

The mind is the source of the personality and therefore, the condition of the mind and its contents eventually infuse the body with either negative or positive energies. The following are specific emotions and attitudes, and their physical consequences. In order to correct the malady as it manifests in the physical world, one must correct not only one's actions, but the way of thinking that led to the problem must be corrected in the astral plane, the plane of the mind.

Ignorance- Ignorance is defined as the absence of the knowledge of the Higher Self. This is the root cause of all diseases. When the soul falls prey to the idea that it is an individual and not connected to the universe, it is said to have fallen into the delusion of ignorance. This delusion allows the soul to develop other maladies in the mental plane, which include:

Egoism- Egoism is defined as the exacerbation of the feeling of individuality, due to ignorance. Egoism is like a form of myopia of the heart. It causes constriction in consciousness and this constriction in turn promotes a short sighted and limited vision of life. Also, it promotes a limiting factor in one's intellectual capacity. This condition allows the soul to contract the primary disease of existence – human embodiment. After this, all other mental and physical ailments are possible. Egoism is like a rheumatic fever of the soul – characterized by restlessness, and discontent.

Desire- Desire is the illusory effort to satisfy the rheumatism by pursuing pleasures, relations and objects of the world of time and space. Since these can never truly and abidingly satisfy the ego, the desires never end and even become inflated, leading the soul to experience countless frustrations and disappointments (craving and greed when desires are fulfilled, or anger and hatred when they are not.).

Anger-Hatred- The prolonged experience of these lead to the development of nervous disorders, cancers, heart attacks, high blood pressure and breathing problems since they disrupt the flow of life force energy disturbing the peace of the body, and consequently the breathing rhythm as well. These conditions are agitating to the system, sources of extreme stress.

Fear-Anxiety-Worry- An un-enlightened person experiences fear in life due to the inability to understand the immortality of the deeper Self. One is dependent on situations of the world, and as these are always unpredictable, there is always a basis for fear. The prolonged experience of these leads to mental breakdowns (nervous breakdowns or other disorders), heart problems and low blood pressure because they are depressing to the system.

Greed- Greed is the accumulation of excess items not needed for life. Excess money, fame, worldly objects, etc., leads to excesses in other areas of life. One may experience excess emotions, excess recuperation time when becoming ill due to extra time needed to get rid of the mental and physical excess impurities taken in. One may go on for a long time discharging mucus from the body and or negative emotions.

Agitated & Dull Intellect- Ignorance, which began as benign tumor in the soul, has now, through the prolonged exposure to the negative emotions and thoughts (anger, hatred, greed, worry, anxiety, jealousy, passion-desire, etc.) and their intensification in the mind has developed into a negative way of being which leads the soul to all manner of degraded conditions, situations and adverse circumstances. Most people who consider themselves normal live in the agitated and dull states of mind, sometimes feeling good, sometimes feeling bad, sometimes sick and sometimes healthy, etc. In life there are more adversities than prosperities, more illness than health, more annoyances than sources of pleasure. The dull state is a mostly negative state wherein severe mental psychosis develop, and following this several physical ailments arise since the mind can no longer support the body in a proper and healthy way. The mind develops deep melancholy, depression, self-destructive behavior or the world seems to close in and life becomes miserable. The outlook is negative so the desires, thoughts, and actions are negative, promoting a continuous cycle of vice and adversity. This is like a cancer which destroys a person's ability to discover peace and contentment, and ultimately leads them to death since the opportunity to attain spiritual enlightenment is no longer possible in this lifetime.

Feelings, Emotions, Intuition and Health

"Feelings are good servants but poor masters."

-Ancient Egyptian Proverb

Emotions are expressions of the internal human condition. They are aspects of human feelings. Feelings are the internal experience of human beings as they make sense of their existence and their interaction with the world around them. Negative feelings arise when the soul is burdened by negative cognition. Negative cognition arises when the soul is ignorant of its own divinity and thereby acts out of selfishness. This deterioration in the mental condition of an individual is termed egoism. Egoism disturbs the internal arrangement of the personality, pushing it towards setian[142] (demoniac) qualities instead of heruian[143] (saintly) qualities.

When the internal arrangement of the personality is out of balance, the personality emotes negative expressions. These in turn shape the environment in ways that are distasteful to the ego itself that is doing the emitting. For example, when a desire is not fulfilled, the ego may curse what it considers to be the source of the obstruction preventing it from attaining what it believes is its object of desire. This emoting of hate as if causes the object to reflect hatred back and the personality is further tormented by this interaction. The person emitting hatred is incapable of experiencing true love and peace because of their own negative feeling and emission which cloud the intellectual capacity to resolve the issue of the true problem. The object of desire may be a person or an inanimate item, but the result is the same. The ego

[142]Relating to the Kamitan character "Set" from the Ausarian Resurrection Myth.
[143] Relating to the Kamitan character "Heru" from the Ausarian Resurrection Myth.

falls back on a coping mechanism based on ignorance wherein imagination and fantasy allow it to assign blame for the frustration it feels. Thus the frustration becomes projected upon the perceived source of the obstruction.

The ignorance by which this entire process proceeds is lack of knowledge of Self. The ignorant person acts out due to misunderstanding the true nature of their own being and the true nature of the external world. So perceiving itself as an individual in a universe of individual objects and random circumstances, the ego lives out of desire and fear, as well as hatred, constantly seeking to achieve situations or acquire objects that will fulfill it. Since this is impossible it experiences perpetual unrest.

The only peace that the mind experiences is when in dreamless sleep, for even worldly pleasures are a form of temporary tension relief. They ultimately lead to more frustration because the pleasure experienced from the world can never be fully and abidingly maintained, and so the desire can never be fully and abidingly fulfilled. Mental and emotional imbalances lead to imbalances in the life force energy and the hormones of the body. As a result, chemical reactions that occur within the body to keep it functioning optimally are disrupted, resulting in conditions such as headaches, ulcers and cancers. When the personality begins to discover higher and more fulfilling aspects of its nature, it finds peace and an intuitional capacity to lead itself to true happiness and health.

Three states of mind

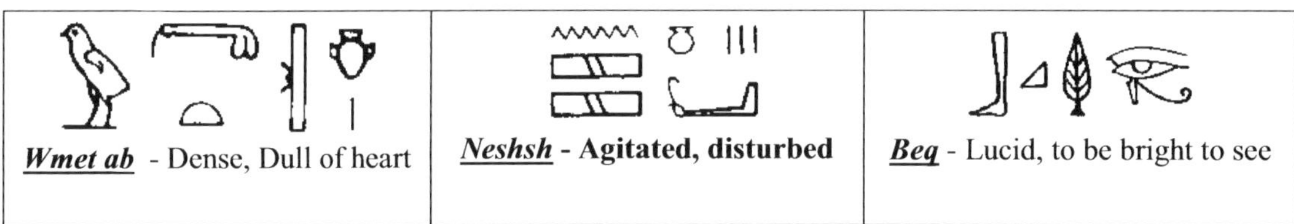

Wmet ab - Dense, Dull of heart	***Neshsh*** **- Agitated, disturbed**	***Beq*** - Lucid, to be bright to see

There are three important states of mind, the Dull, Agitated and Lucid. There are two basic states or poles of mental operation. These are Dullness and Lucidity. Most human beings lie somewhere in between these two opposite ends of the mental spectrum (varying degrees of disturbance or agitation). The Dull mind is beset with depression, anguish, hatred, and unrest, in varying degrees . The lesser agitated mind, the lucid mind, which operates on higher, universal principles and self-knowledge, or faith in the Divine, is free of or experiences less depression, worry, anxiety, etc. This mind is more prone to universal love instead of favoritism, conciliation instead of aggression, and understanding instead of just tolerance. This mind emotes forgiveness instead of lashing out and most importantly, due to its relaxed nature and trust in its own connection to the Divine, it has intuitional insight into its own spiritual, mental and physical condition.

The lucid mind knows when it is on the wrong path and how to get back on track when the path is temporarily missed. All human beings make mistakes in the realm of time and space, even sages. Unenlightened humans experience pain and or sorrow because of their "wrong" actions. However, advanced souls, sages, saints, etc., are freer from their pain and sorrow. Even these are understood to be Divinely inspired responses to the desires which fuel the ego's actions. So the Lucid-minded use these as remembrances of what is truly worth desiring. They accept these seemingly adverse situations and turn them into prosperities, using adversities as catalysts that turn them inwards, to push them towards a communion with Spirit. Lucid-minded people are therefore more in touch with their feelings and unlike the Dull-Agitated personalities, the feelings of the Lucid minded do not build up and control them, forcing them to express emotions that they will later regret. The Lucid-minded person gains the will and confidence to turn away from paths that are detrimental to spiritual, mental or physical health. Dull-minded persons continue to perform actions that are detrimental to spiritual, mental and or physical health. They stay on jobs that are causing them illness, or stay with marital partners that are unfaithful and or unrighteous, or acquiesce to family burdens that are unrighteous, or maintain activities that are injurious to health such as smoking and drugs, or accept religious burdens they know are un-spiritual, etc. Some people accept the dictates of their church even when they question certain actions or dogmas. But the acceptance is not complete and their conscience nags at them and yet they go one even if they feel they and their church, temple or synagogue are wrong. They may accept these things out of ignorance, a sense of family or cultural tradition, or a feeling of powerlessness to do otherwise. Dull-minded persons accept situations of abuse and mistreatment. They are tormented by the knowledge that they are doing something that goes against their conscience, but nevertheless continue performing the dull actions. They develop guilt and frustration, which they turn around and blame on the world or on others who they feel control their lives. All of this leads to undue stresses that are supported, not by the apparent perpetrator, but on the self-victimized ego. This way of life causes the personality to become unbalanced and diseased.

The answer to the burdens of the Dull-minded person is to seek a path that leads to truth. This is sometimes difficult to do, because it requires a change in the belief structure of the mind, a going against long held attitudes and values. The world opposes such changes in the form of family members, coworkers and others who still cling to the lifestyle of disease and frustration, and who expect the same out of the Dull person who is trying to make the change. So the person seeking transformation needs to find a support system outside his/her circle of Dull companions, in order for a higher vision of life may be glimpsed. Then the person needs to adopt the habits and practices of Lucidity that lead to healing and health. This is what the Kemetic Diet Program is all about, adopting a lifestyle that releases the inner light that is buried within the Dull personality, the light that can illuminate the ignorance and mental burdens of negative feelings, and thereby allow a person to take command of their own life and health. Such a person realizes when there is a spiritual, mental or physical problem and how to proceed to rectify the problem, be it a sudden pain in the side, a long time mental burden, a newly discovered cancerous tumor or an infection. Every person has the potential to gain these insights, and to recognize the words in this book as true and follow suit. The deeply Dull person, before they get far in this book, will label these words as the ranting of quacks and throw it out on their way to consult a traditional, orthodox, university trained M.D. who will not speak any mumbo jumbo about intuition or spirit and can prescribe some pill supposedly generated by "Hard Science" to treat their ailment. The Lucid minded person will recognize that while this book comes from a perspective of African spirituality, it applies to universal spirituality and all religions. The Dull person will try to dismiss it as a blasphemous text and put it out of their mind.

Yet, the examples are all around us, and in our own lives. Everyone has experiences where they followed a course of action based on an idea that came on the spur of the moment and if they had acted otherwise they would have been led to adversity. Examples are driving down the road and stopping even when the light has turned green and they have the right of way. Another car runs the light. If the first person had not stopped there would have been a serious accident. When asked why they stopped the simply said that "they just knew they needed to wait." Another example is a person who accomplished a days work on the computer and then all of a sudden had the idea to check to see if the information was backed up properly. It was not so they proceeded to back it up immediately and as soon as the backup was completed the computer crashed. If they had not backed up right then they would have lost all the work. These kinds of experiences abound in human life and they are evidence of a higher aspect of mind, the intuitional aspect.

The lucidity and intuition about life that we had when we were young has been subsumed in the depths of the ego due to the socializing force of culture. Yet even as adults we are amazed at some events such as our ability to know something before it happens, but we dismiss that as coincidence. The Lucid-minded person becomes sensitive to the internal voice that is connected to the Divine, and the Divine sees and knows all. So when a person moves towards the Divine in thought, word and action, the capacity to participate in the knowledge of the Higher Self becomes possible. This faculty is called intuition, and it is a healing power as well as an enlightening force that needs to be cultivated, just as any other aspect of the personality is cultivated. If a person wants to become a concert musician, he/she must practice and cultivate their art, and so too the intuitional capacity must be cultivated as well. This is done by study of the teachings and the practice of the disciplines enjoined by the teachings, which unburden the mind and expand the horizons of consciousness.

(Purification of the heart)

If this process of study and practice, termed *Shedi,* is adopted, the impurities of the mind are gradually removed, self-confidence is enhanced, and this new insight comes into effect. As stated before, it is a certain sensitivity, but unlike any other. There is an internal voice that is always there, but seldom acknowledged, in modern culture. The Dull person does not trust in this voice because it is often times urging a different action than that which the Dull person wishes to pursue, or it seen as imagination, and there is fear of losing the mind, and so on. The Lucid person recognizes this voice as that of the Higher Self, and not the imaginings or fantasies of the ego. Thus, the Lucid-minded person comes to rely on that internal voice for guidance and solace, and consequently they do not experience loneliness or devastation when the adversities in life occur. This internal guidance is a tremendous force for stopping negative activities such as smoking, drugs, meat eating, etc. It is an enlightening force that opens the door to a greater world beyond the physical and mental states, guiding the Lucid personality to the discovery of transcendental existence, the source of all life and where there is no burden, disease or death. Meditation is an integral part of the process of increasing self-awareness, self-confidence and spiritual strength, which allows a person to not only discover truth, but also to live it. The practice of purifying the personality and living by the precepts of Maat (righteousness and order) allows a person to be still enough to practice meditation. So purification and orderliness in life are essential first steps on the path to discovering intuition and supreme health.

THE CURE FOR THE GROSS IMPURITIES OF THE MIND

Unm ka un – medjat
"Feed the mind what is abiding"
Ancient Egyptian Proverb

How can one cure the mind that is fettered with gross and subtle impurities? Feelings, thoughts and emotions based on egoism (individuality) are considered to be gross impurities of the mind. These include anger, hatred, greed, worry, anxiety, jealousy, passion-desire, etc. In Kemetic Maat Philosophy, the scales of Maat delineate the precepts of righteous conduct for those personalities who must be guided by discipline. As previously discussed, there are seven aspects to the psycho-spiritual personality. Each of these is related to the psycho-spiritual consciousness centers of the Serpent Power. The Serpent Power is the Sekhem or Life Force, which sustains the personality. As a human being develops spiritually, each consciousness center opens and there is expansion. In order to achieve spiritual enlightenment, one must overcome the negative aspect of each center and cultivate the positive. In reality, the negativity at each center consists in the inability to open up and discover the expansion and freedom of the spiritual principle at each center. The three lower centers are related to worldly personalities, who are subject to the maladies listed above. Those who have overcome the lower nature experience the four upper centers. The way to overcome the lower nature is to practice the disciplines of mystical philosophy, which include performing good deeds and righteous action. This purifies the mind and allows one to promote purity of heart. The task of every spiritual aspirant is therefore to break the cycle of vice within themselves. This can be done by following the spiritual path of righteous action.

Figure 37: The Body-Mind-Soul-Spirit Connection

The first stage in the practice of the Path of Right Action is to control the organs of action. These three are the body (gross actions-physical body), the mouth (speech-subtle body) and finally the mind (thoughts-causal body). One must do righteous deeds, utter righteous speech and engender righteous thoughts. These three aspects of the personality must be brought into harmony with the teachings of physical, mental and spiritual purity. So this means that one must live by a higher principle of life, a higher truth, the truth of one's spiritual essence.

Table 10: The Cycle of Vice

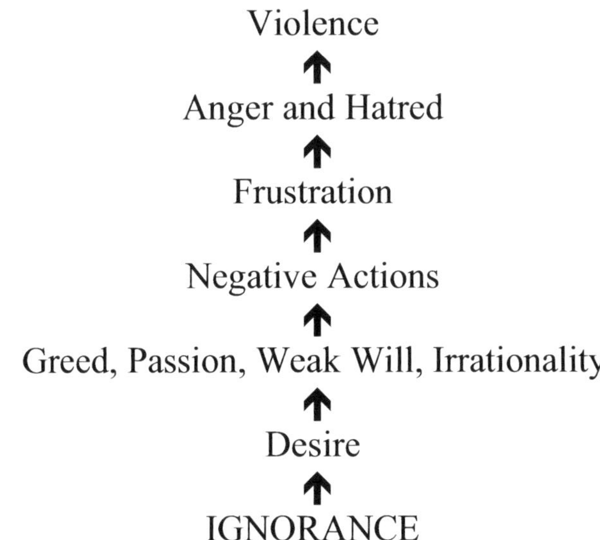

A human being needs to grow through the various psycho-spiritual principles as represented by each Serpent Power energy center in order to attain enlightenment. The principles are as follows. Center #1 relates to fear and survival. Center #2 relates to sexuality, and physical creativity. Center #3 relates to exercising power and control over others (egoism in the form of selfishness). Center #4 relates to universal love. Center #5 relates to self-control and inner expansion. Center #6 relates to transcendental awareness. Center #7 relates to union with the Cosmic Self.[144]

The goal of Serpent Power Smai Tawi practice is to unlock the hidden potential of the human being, which is being blocked by various psycho-spiritual forms of ignorance and negative feelings. The following diagram shows the main psycho-spiritual elements (obstacles to the full expression of consciousness) which are to be overcome at each center of psycho-spiritual consciousness.

[144] For more on the Energy Centers and the spiritual system involving their cultivation see the book *The Serpent Power* by Dr. Muata Ashby.

Table 11: Obstacles of the Psychospiritual Energy Centers

TRANSCENDENCE – ENLIGHTENMENT
(The Goal to Be Attained by Removing the Obstacles at each Center)

↑
7
Ego self - You think you are a mortal
human being instead of an Immortal Divinity.

↑
6
Lack of concentration. Sense of individuality. Lack of intellectual ability required to think properly and discover the true meaning of life. The intellect is clouded over by egoistic feelings,
desires and illusions about what reality is.

↑
5
Lack of self-control, Getting carried away with the whims of the mind and senses.

↑
4
Attachment, Egoistic Love

↑
3
Desire for worldly attainments, and control of others, Greed, Hatred,

↑
2
Gross Sexual Desire.

↑
1
Fear of death. Survival concerns. Where will next meal come from?

The following diagram shows the virtuous qualities of each center which are to be cultivated and developed in order to transcend that center on the upward movement towards total transcendence. Note that a horizontal line separates the centers 1-3 from 4-7, and that next to these the word Maat is written. This signifies that those people who are at the psycho-spiritual consciousness level between one and three are those people who have not reached the maturity for self-determination. They require rules and regulations imposed by society to guide them on the right path, which promotes self-development, sex-sublimation and self-control. Therefore, they must be taught the injunctions of Maat and they must be shown the wisdom of following its principles.

Table 12: Psycho-spiritual Principles of the Serpent Power-Maat Philosophy

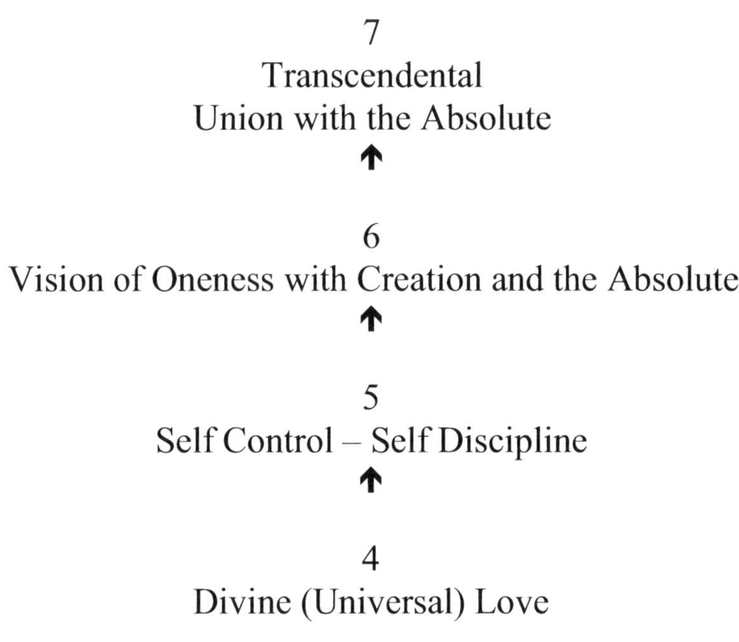

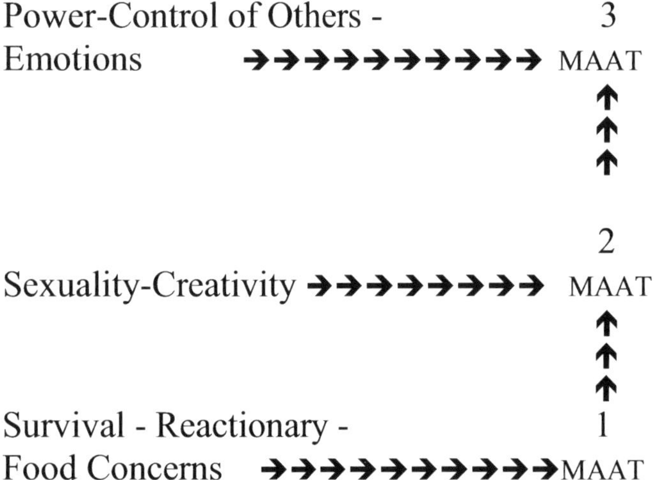

3
How to overcome: Surrender the ego to the Divine, to righteousness, to humility and service to humanity, the performance of good deeds without expecting rewards (selfless service).

2
How to overcome: Controlling sex desire. Understanding that all creation is essentially a manifestation of the Higher Self, and you are that Self. Your essence is all that exists so there is nothing to desire or covet. Rather, create wisdom, joy and contentment through dispassion and inner self discovery.

1
How to overcome: Faith and trust in the Divine. All needs in life are provided for by the Divine Self.

Those who have gained control over the first three psycho-spiritual consciousness centers will be able to discover a new, deeper essence of their own existence as they move beyond "animal" consciousness. Otherwise, they will remain in a horizontal movement through life, which will lead to pain, sorrow and disappointments, as well as the development of a karmic basis for reincarnation.

The Cure for the Subtle Impurities of the Mind

Once the gross impurities of the mind have been cleansed, that is, the unrighteousness of the lower three psycho-spiritual consciousness centers have been sublimated, it is necessary to cleanse the subtle impurities of the mind. For this task the Discipline of Wisdom was created. In brief, there are three stages or phases in the practice of Smai Tawi Wisdom. First the aspirant is to listen to the teachings and understand them. This stage alone is not easy if the heart is not already purified (cleansed from the gross impurities). Secondly, the task is to reflect on those teachings constantly and act in accordance with them in day to day life. Thirdly, the task now is to allow the mind to transcend the lower nature by meditating on the Higher Self.[145] This is accomplished by allowing the mind to freely flow towards the Divine continuously, an art that is learned in the practice of Smai Tawi Wisdom. The objective is to cultivate the four upper psycho-spiritual consciousness centers and their corresponding psychological principles, so as to transcend them and achieve Cosmic Consciousness and supreme health. When this discipline is perfected, the Ari or impressions from previous actions that would normally impel the individual to more egoism and ignorance, are cleansed.

Table 13:The Stages in the practice of Wisdom Yoga to Enlighten the Mind.

Spiritual Enlightenment
↑
Meditating upon and realizing the meaning of the teachings
↑
Study, Reflection and Practice of the teachings
↑
Listening to the teachings
↑
Ignorance

[145] For more details on the practice of Wisdom Yoga consult the book *The Wisdom of Isis* by Muata Ashby.

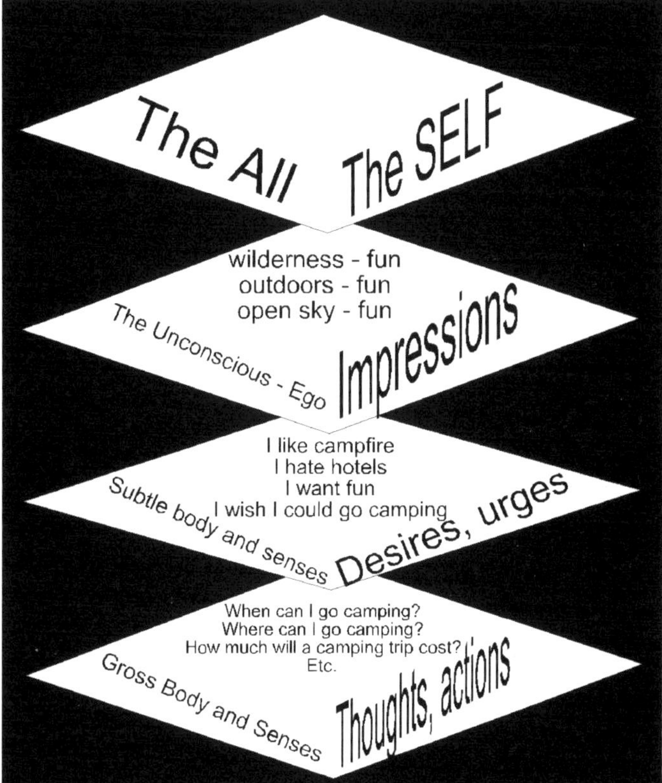

Figure 38: Structure of the mind.

The deeper implications of Serpent Power Yoga involve the control of thoughts and actions, understanding, and sublimation of desires and urges and the cleansing out of negative impressions in the energy centers which are blocking psycho-spiritual energy, the Serpent Power, which will allow you to discover the higher realms of existence.

Advanced Cleansing of the Mind

If the physical body is properly cleansed, and the mind is cleansed through the practice of virtue, the gross impurities will be purged in degrees. As this process occurs, the subtle energy channels and Life Force energy centers of the subtle body (mental body) will open up, and the Life Force, the Serpent Power energy, will be able to move freely through the personality. This movement of the Life Force will promote the higher cleansing of the mind and the subtle (Astral) body. It will allow the mind to become sensitive to subtle aspects of life that are not possible when the mind is caught up in the gross impurities of the lower emotions and the lower desires as well as the gross impurities of the physical body.

The Life Force energy operates to sustain the body and the basic mental functions when it is manifesting at the lower intensity. However, when the body and mind are cleansed, it is able to operate at a much higher level. In fact, it is able to elevate an individual's consciousness to the level of cosmic awareness, and ultimately to spiritual enlightenment.

When this form of higher spiritual cleansing begins to operate, the individual may experience subtle energies coursing through the body at different times. Sometimes it may accumulate in different areas. At other times it may feel like a sensation rising up along the spine or a pressure on the forehead. Still, at other times the individual may experience visions or a spontaneous sense of well being and bliss, and at other times it may be a sensation of showering light or fluid coming from the top of the head and encompassing the body in a subtle way. This is also referred to as the divine anointing.

All of these are manifestations of the Life Force that can occur when it is in motion and cleansing the mind and subtle personality. A practitioner only needs to observe these episodes and is advised to continue the normal day to day activities while moving along the path of self-discovery, allowing the energy to do its important work. In order to promote this cleansing through the Life Force, a special discipline of mystical spirituality has been developed. The practice of this discipline entails the cleansing of the body through the disciplines described in this volume and also cleansing the mind through the special disciplines of mystical psychology and meditation described further in the book, *The Serpent Power,* by Muata Ashby.

The reader should also keep in mind that if the practices laid out in this book, *The Kemetic Diet: Food For Body, Mind and Soul,* are followed, the awakening of the Life Force will occur in a natural and integrated way. The disciplines of the Life Force development Yoga are to be seen as a second step after establishing oneself in good mental and physical health and should not be attempted until then.[146]

Figure 39: Below- Diagram of the Psycho-Spiritual Energy Centers of Human consciousness also known as the Serpent Power, for concentration and meditation exercises.

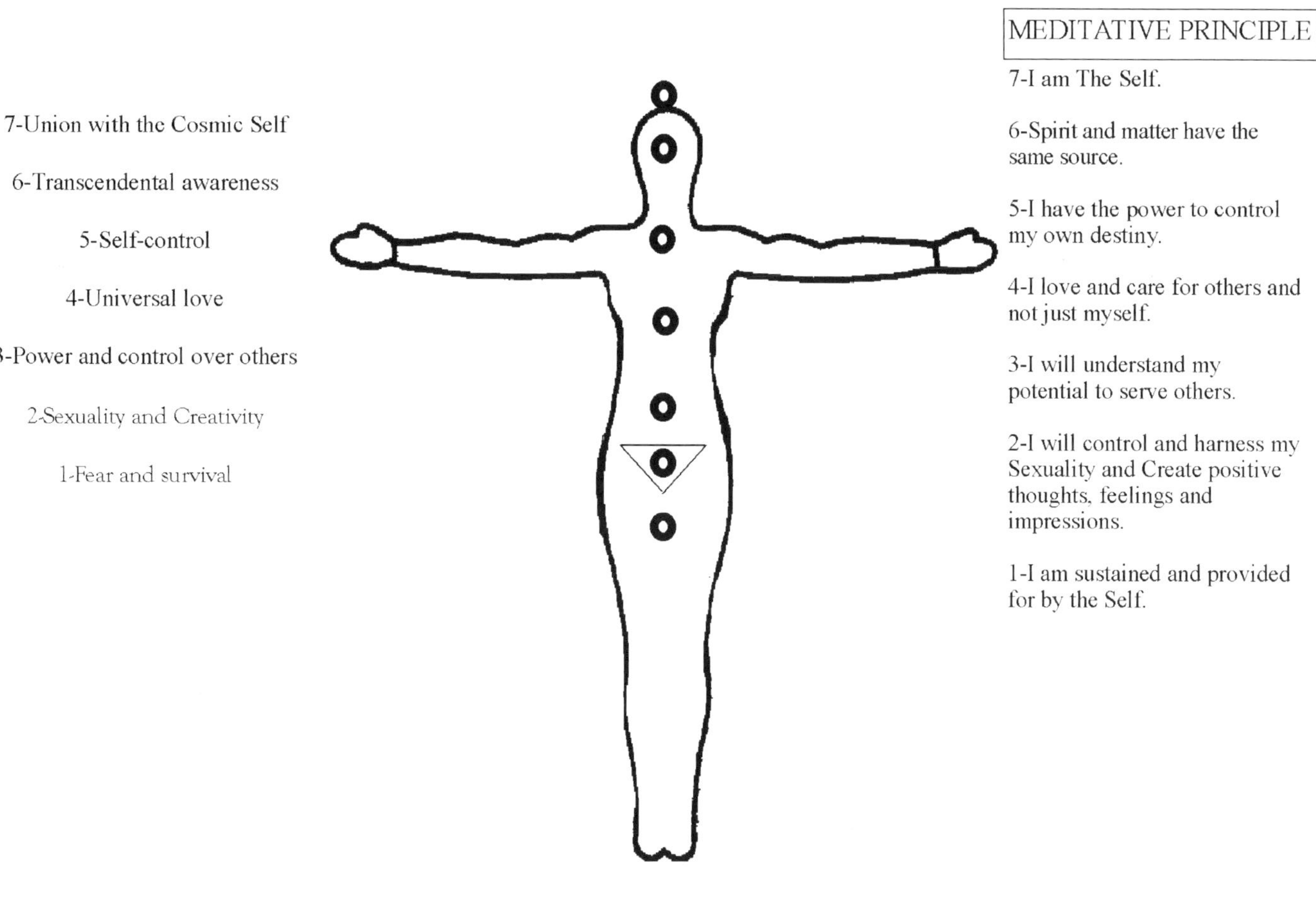
MEDITATIVE PRINCIPLE
7-Union with the Cosmic Self
6-Transcendental awareness
5-Self-control
4-Universal love
3-Power and control over others
2-Sexuality and Creativity
1-Fear and survival
7-I am The Self.
6-Spirit and matter have the same source.
5-I have the power to control my own destiny.
4-I love and care for others and not just myself.
3-I will understand my potential to serve others.
2-I will control and harness my Sexuality and Create positive thoughts, feelings and impressions.
1-I am sustained and provided for by the Self.

[146] For more on the Serpent Power wisdom see the book *The Serpent Power,* by Muata Ashby.

Positive Feeling and Positive Thinking

A related aspect of positive feeling is attitude. One's attitude has an effect on every aspect of life. One person can succumb to a particular circumstance while another can thrive while facing the same circumstance, all due to the attitude. One must maintain an indomitable attitude of being triumphant in the end no matter what the odds. If a person is truly religious, they should believe that the Supreme Being is with them always. So, how can there be any failure? This is real and powerful faith, which can indeed move mountains and restore health and maintain it. A positive attitude will make it easy to use the power of visualization.

The recent interest placed on the mind-body connection is something that mystics and practitioners of mystical spirituality and meditation have known for a very long time. As explained earlier, the human personality is a complex composed of soul, mind and body. The soul engenders the mind, and the mind engenders the body. If the soul desires to end the life, there is nothing that the mind or body can do to stop it. If the soul[147] is disturbed or distracted by the ignorance of life or the deep unconscious psychoses, the mind will suffer from insanity and consequently the body will suffer as well. If the mind were to be retrained to think positive thoughts, to be inspired by life, to understand its purpose and meaning, then it would work in harmony to allow the body to repair itself as needed.

> "The source of evil is in your body. Evil entices the body through temptation of its weakest virtue. There can be no divinity in the unclean temple where abomination rules."
>
> —Ancient Egyptian Proverb

Moral purity is an essential part of mental purity, and purity of the mind is the key to purity and health of the body. Therefore, anyone interested in optimal health should study the precepts of truth and righteousness of the spiritual tradition they follow and then begin to practice those teachings in day to day life. This will purify the heart and render it a proper vessel for Divine Consciousness.

> "Those who gave thee a body, furnished it with weakness; but The ALL who gave thee Soul, armed thee with resolution. Employ it, and thou art wise; be wise and thou art happy."
>
> —Ancient Egyptian Proverbs

"You are as you believe" is a powerful teaching in mystical religion. Your thoughts are based on your knowledge and your feeling. A person feels in accordance with what they believe, so if you believe in the wisdom that has been presented in this volume, you must allow yourself to freely feel it as well. That is, your feelings must match your beliefs. Understanding that your personality is united with the universe and that your soul provides it with Life Force energy to survive, you should begin adopting good feelings towards the world and towards yourself. This means that you must learn how to leave behind the negative thoughts and feelings of the past, which are in reality poisoning your own personality and wasting your life away. So just as there are herbs and medicaments for the body, there are also medicaments for the mind and the soul. These are listed below. They should be studied and practiced every day, and thereby all the levels of the personality (body, mind and soul) will discover health. The technique for their use and application in life is explained in the Ancient Egyptian Proverb preceding them.

> "To destroy an undesirable rate of mental vibration, concentrate on the opposite vibration to the one to be suppressed."
>
> —Ancient Egyptian Proverbs

---

[147] In the context of this teaching the soul is seen as the time and space manifestation of the Spirit. In this sense the soul can be disturbed and even suffer but the Spirit remains ever unaffected and free.

Positive Visualization

> "Strive to see with the inner eye, the heart. It sees the reality not subject to emotional or personal error; it sees the essence. Intuition then is the most important quality to develop."
>
> —Ancient Egyptian Proverbs

Using the mind, one can visualize the process of health, and bring thought into reality, thereby restoring health. The mind is so powerful that in a test of athletes, one group was allowed to practice on the field while others were only allowed to visualize themselves performing perfectly. The result when both groups played on the field was that the group which only practiced visualization performed better than the group which practiced physically.

If you were a carpenter who contracted a disease like cancer of the liver, for instance, you could visualize that you are tearing down the rotted beams in the house of your body and replacing them with new, specially treated beams (cells) that are immune to the termites and water damage (cancer). This technique can be applied to any occupation or one may see oneself as the doctor, curing oneself or one may visualize God or the Goddess coming to administer the healing treatment. If you are a clerk, you can visualize the healer or yourself taking out old files (diseased cells) and replacing them with new, updated ones (replacing diseased cells with vitality, and cleansed cells).

The most important element of visualization is that you must have hope and faith that a way is going to open up for you, and that whatever happens is God's will. The positive attitude is the first important key to restoring health and should never be abandoned. Even when the body dies as it must one day, there should be an intelligent hope in the heart that one will move on to the next best thing as per the Divine decree.

In a book and video series for PBS[148], the researcher, Bill Moyers, documented how alternative treatments such as visualization, meditation and manipulation of the subtle energies of the body are being used as healing techniques around the world. Spiritual and Yoga texts are replete with such techniques, and the technique of visualization is an art, which every spiritual aspirant needs to develop.

Positive Speech (Affirmation)

> "The fool who does not hear, can do nothing at all; looking at ignorance and seeing knowledge; looking at harmfulness and seeing usefulness; living on the things by which one dies; the food of evil speech."
>
> —Ancient Egyptian Proverb

Positive Affirmation is the next step in the process of implementing the positive attitude. Your words must be in line with your goals and desires. "If you can say it, you can do it" is the key teaching you need to follow. Do not believe and repeat the words of nay sayers and do not agree with or associate with pessimistic or depressed people. Do your research, and when you are sure you are following a righteous path, decide on what you want to believe in and affirm that belief with your speech. As you do, you will reinforce the positive thoughts and your words will act as positive vibrations that will reshape your mind and body.

[148] Public Broadcasting System-Television

> "To destroy an undesirable rate of mental vibration, concentrate on the opposite vibration to the one to be suppressed."
>
> "To change your mood or mental state, change your vibration."
>
> —Ancient Egyptian Proverbs

Positive affirmation and concentration of the mind on the opposite mood or thought is useful in counteracting negative states of mind. Since the mind is fluid, it takes the form of its impressions (aris or karmas). If the individual human consciousness identifies with a specific mood or thought, it will take on that feeling as its own and thus, partake in the repercussions of that feeling. Through practice, one can learn to train the mind to think in certain ways and develop new positive mental impressions or karmas. You must understand that all thoughts and states of mind are under your control. You can begin this practice by watching your thoughts closely. When you feel depressed, remind yourself that you, (that is, your true essence as the Higher Self, Neter, Asar, Aset, Heru or any deity you prefer), are the source of supreme joy (bliss). Repeat mentally, *"I" am Bliss* and see how your mind changes its state. Choose a sublime teaching to study or some words of power to chant, practice Yoga exercise, and listen to an uplifting audio or video recording. Do not allow the mind to develop a negative state. If you distract yourself by watching a movie or going to a party, your negativity will only be suppressed and it will come out at some future time. The wonder of working with the mind is the discovery that you can control it instead of it controlling you. You do not have to be a slave to the emotional swings or cravings of the mind. You have the power because you are innately the Universal Soul. Due to ignorance, your soul has allowed the mind to rule over it with desires and cravings. As you discover the immense power within the real you, you discover the true bliss of self-mastery.

> "What is the source of sadness, but feebleness of the mind? What gives it power but the want of reason? Rouse yourself to the combat, and it quits the field before you strike."
>
> "The house of God hates too much speaking. Pray then with a loving heart, whose petitions are all in secret. God will listen and do thy business, and will accept your offerings."
>
> —Ancient Egyptian Proverbs

Right Action and Right Thinking for Good Health

We previously elaborated on the concept of action, its consequences and relationship to reincarnation, as well as the mental impressions it creates which lodge deeply within the unconscious mind. In order to promote health, there must be right action, which implies right diet, right living and right thinking (positive thoughts, uplifting thoughts, etc.). It must be understood that even if one's present thoughts are righteous, there may still be some negative impressions lodged in the unconscious mind. Some of these impressions may have an effect on the present or future health of the individual, just as stored up Ukhedu (poisons, non-expelled excrement, rotten matter, drugs, etc.) in the cells of the body will have an effect even after the individual has resolved to lead a righteous life, and has embarked upon vegetarianism, correcting eating habits, giving up drugs and medicines, working for the benefit of society, etc. This individual may still become ill as this process is in reality a cleansing process. It is in effect a resolution of past actions and a moving beyond these.

Our ignorance causes us to look outside ourselves to someone else, a country, a group of people, a doctrine or a possession for happiness and pleasure, when we already have all the tools necessary for our own salvation and the power to provide for our own health and happiness. As human beings, people are used to making statements such as "I am hungry" or "I am sad." These statements, and the feelings which they evoke, constitute powerful vibrations which affect the mind. So by repeating them with conviction, one may truly believe that one is hungry, sad, angry, happy, etc. All matter, including your body, is only energy in a particular state of vibration. Therefore, through a purified and trained mind, you may control your vibrational state. Western psychology is only now discovering the power of affirmations to create new moods and feelings, and thus, new realities. The mind can either make itself feel "good" or "bad" according to its disposition. This in turn can affect the physical body, causing it to be healthy or ill.

One important effect that Ari can have on health is the manifestation of birth defects and abnormalities including mental illness. A person's karmic basis determines their next incarnation. Therefore, whether or not a person will be born into the home of righteous people, of practitioners of mystical spirituality, the home of drug addicts or people of poor hygiene, is determined by the actions of their previous lives. This ari (karma) cannot be easily overcome. The disciplines listed in this volume will serve to improve any such condition to some degree. However, there is a possibility that the individual may have to wait until the next incarnation in order to overcome those defects and be in a position to establish a level of health which will allow them to pursue a viable human existence. Then they will be able to resume their spiritual evolution. When there is an absence of such defects, the body has an excellent chance of overcoming all physical and mental ailments.

The impressions, which lead to anomalies in the physical body, are lodged in the unconscious level of the mind. Thus, in the process of healing it is important that the conscious mind should not be in disagreement with the unconscious. This means that a person should not reason "I have tried to live well but I am still getting sick." Rather they should resolve to endure the negative emanations of the mind and forge ahead towards an eventual ideal of complete recovery and health. Otherwise, they will defeat their own purpose, placing more negative thoughts into the mind, which will come back in the future as a force for more disease.

So a person seeking health should seek an understanding of the laws of Ari, the workings of Ukhedu and then resolve to follow the injunctions of righteous living which lead to health. At the same time they should affirm their goal of achieving optimal health, mentally, so as to infuse the unconscious with positive impressions that will bear fruit later on, as will power to follow the path of righteous living that leads to pristine health.

Positive Actions

"Knowledge without action is like hoarding precious metals, a vain and foolish thing.
Knowledge is like wealth, intended for use;
Those who violate the universal law of USE conflict with natural forces."

"Mastery of the passions allows divine thought and action."
—Ancient Egyptian Proverb

Positive affirmation and positive thoughts need to be followed up with positive actions. Positive actions are those actions that are in harmony with your positive thoughts and feelings. Seek out alternative health counseling, permanently change your diet and eating practices, and transform your life.

YOGA OF RIGHT ACTION AND RIGHTEOUS LIVING[149]

"No one reaches the Beneficent West (Enlightenment) unless their heart is righteous by doing MAAT."

"Speak MAAT; do MAAT."

—Ancient Egyptian Proverbs

Yoga of Action implies acting according to the teachings of mystical wisdom (Maat) throughout your normal day to day activities. It keeps the mind occupied with thoughts, which are uplifting to the mind. It is especially useful for calming the externalized-restless mind and redirecting thought patterns away from dwelling on mental complexes (worries), in order to allow the mind time to integrate its higher desire to overcome the difficulties through personality integration. Mental complexes will intensify rather than resolve if dwelled upon constantly. Many people have learned through experience that when there is a difficult problem, which will still be there the following day, it is better to "sleep on it" rather than dwell on it. When the clouds of egoism are no longer there, such as during deep sleep or in an advanced practitioner of yoga, the rays of the Self can shine through and illumine one's consciousness with *Hetep*.[150] Again it must be emphasized that this experience of peace is not an all or nothing experience. It occurs in degrees. You may still find yourself feeling entrapped and agitated, but now, in addition to these ego-based feelings, you have an increased sensitivity to the voice of wisdom within you. This is the voice which repeats a hekau, or prayers and reflects on the nature of your true essence when the ego wants to tie the mind up with worries and imaginations. You may hear this voice repeating: *"I" am fearless. "I" have all the resources within me to withstand and rise above any situation. Even this seemingly impossible situation is in line with my attaining enlightenment, and it too, like the clouds in the sky blocking the rays of the sun, will pass away.*

In the beginning stages of practicing Yoga when you are not very attuned to listening to your spiritual voice, you may not experience much peace. However, as you choose to listen to that voice more and more, and indulge in prayer, hekau and the other disciplines of Yoga more than you indulge yourself in egoistic practices, you will notice within yourself a river of peace, faith, security and devotion which will eventually overflow and wash away all ego based emotions from your personality. This is the victory of Heru over Set within your personality.

To the extent that you are able to control your temper, your inner war (between the Higher Self and the lower) will not affect others around you, however, there may be an already established tendency to lash out at people around you. One should do one's best to sublimate this tendency and to remain focused on the negative and positive forces battling within oneself and work to establish Maat within one's self. This can be a difficult task when one is used to looking outside himself or herself for the answers and means to solve life's problems and blaming others (i.e. spouse, children, church, childhood, parents, country, political and religious leaders) for the occurrence of those problems. Situations can only affect you if it is in line with your Ari for that to occur. Therefore, it is no accident or no one's fault or responsibility but your own, regardless of what situation (good or bad) you may find yourself in. You may not be able to see how your actions of this life could have resulted in your current circumstance, but remember, these situations are occurring as a result of actions not only in this lifetime, but previous ones. So your attitude towards dealing with all negative predicaments of life should be one of personal responsibility and forbearance. There is no need to feel bad or blame yourself or others. Blame and bad feelings are ego-based viruses, which infect the mind and further debilitate it. When you are typing and you make a mistake, you don't spend a lot of time blaming yourself and having regrets about having made an error.

[149] For more on the philosophy of right action see the book *The Wisdom of Maati.*
[150] Kemetic term meaning Supreme Peace (Spiritual Enlightenment).

You simply correct your error and carry on. The process with life should be similar. Pray for strength to endure and transcend the situation and put forth the effort to correct the error in your belief and thinking which predisposed you to have this situation manifest in your life. With patience and insight into the fact of your true underlying, boundless essence of your Higher Self, you can overcome all obstacles.

If you do not accept personal responsibility for your life, then you will never look to find that which may be in error in your thought processes and behavior, which predisposed you to your experiences, and there will be no chance for you to improve your situation. If you do not learn the spiritual lesson the situation is here to teach you, you are setting yourself up to have the experience repeat itself again. This is the nature of the karmic process upon which the world process is set up. These experiences are not meant to be painful or to make you bitter. Each of these experiences give you the opportunity to practice and secure spiritual qualities such as patience, equanimity, dispassion, detachment, universal love, freedom from resentment when persecuted or wronged and all the other precepts of Maat. In doing so, you learn to view every situation in your life as your path to enlightenment. In this way, performing your practical duties of life in a righteous manner becomes one and the same with your practice of spiritual discipline. Pain and suffering is a by-product of not living a life in harmony with Maat and with an awareness of your true essence.

The Yoga of Action also emphasizes the performance of selfless service, termed "Maat Ari" (Karma Yoga). When one performs selfless service, the ego loses importance and therefore, its needs and cravings become powerless illusions, which can no longer afflict the mind. The highest practice of Maat-Ari Smai Taui occurs in the state of enlightenment when there is no attachment to the fruits of actions. Work is performed in harmony with one's true nature without dependency on the results, be they good or bad from a practical standpoint. Right livelihood, the practice of making a living in such a way as to benefit oneself and all other beings is practicing Maat. Yoga of Action also implies a balanced movement and scheduling of time for spiritual discipline as well as other practical duties. Extremes are to be avoided because they also cause intensification of the mental complexes. The desired movement is relaxed and deliberate intensification of self-effort according to the capacity of the individual.

So a Positive Belief System leads to Positive Feeling, and this leads to Positive Thinking, and this leads to Positive Speaking (Affirmation), and this leads to Positive Action, and this all leads finally to Good Health. This is the ladder of Health of the Soul, Mind and Body. It works naturally and automatically, beginning with a positive belief system, not just of your own healing capacity, but also your relationship to the universe and the Divine. Once this fundamental factor is properly in place, the other factors come in of their own accord, without strain or stress. This is the power of the mind.

Table 14: Positive structure of the mind for good health.

SEMA (YOGA) OF WISDOM

The Yoga of wisdom is the discipline of learning how to think, feel and understand so as to lead oneself to prosperity, peace and spiritual enlightenment. From a state of ignorance, a spiritual aspirant purifies and sharpens the intellect so as to make it subtle enough to intuitively discover the nature of Self and Creation. Intuitional wisdom is the objective of the various practices of Yoga, but the study of wisdom teachings is the most important step in achieving intellectual knowledge which will be used to lead you to attain experiential (intuitional) knowledge. Study of the wisdom teachings is like mental food. It is this mental diet of sublime thoughts and affirmations, which will give fortitude and direction to your life.

Dispassion and Detachment

"Mastery of the passions allows divine thought and action."
—Ancient Egyptian Proverb

9. Detachment, absence of the feeling of mine-ness (sense of ownership) towards son, wife, house and the like and constant equanimity of mind in all happenings whether desirable or undesirable.

10. Unflinching devotion to Me (Higher Self) through the Yoga of inseparability, abiding in solitary places, not delighting in the company of the worldly-minded.

Gita: Chapter 13 Kshetra-Kshetrajna Vibhag Yogah--
The Division of Field and the Knower of the Field.
(Indian Yoga Text)

If any [man] cometh to me, and hateth not his father, and mother, and wife, and children, and brethren, and sisters, yea, and his own life also, he cannot be my disciple.
The Bible, Luke 14:26

What does the practices of dispassion and detachment really mean in practical life? When you develop a pleasurable feeling based on your interaction with an object, you develop a longing to experience that object more. You say: "May I get more of that." This desire leads to continuous mental unrest until the object is acquired, and frustration and anger when there is no possibility of your acquiring the object. When you begin to rely on objects (anything outside of yourself, i.e., land, money, cars, people, etc.) for your happiness, saying: "When I get that then I will be happy" or "When this happens then I will be happy," you are in reality cursing yourself or dooming yourself to unhappiness. This is because there is no situation or object in this changing world of time and space, which will make anyone truly happy. All things change and the human mind, once it acquires what it longed for, becomes happy---for a while, but then it grows tired of the situation and bored with the object; it then desires other objects and situations for its enjoyment. These desires of the mind are endless. This is the nature of the mind in an egoistic state and trying to satiate these desires is like trying to fill a bucket with holes in it.

When you live this way, you are in effect saying: "I don't have the inner resources to be happy; I need something outside of myself to make me happy." Your ignorance has led you to believe that happiness is to be found in objects, accomplishments or activities in the world. In reality, it is the Soul-Self, which sustains all life and is the source of all happiness, which you experience. In its purified form, this happiness is called bliss. Bliss is the experience of the state of enlightenment. The Neter (Self) sustains your free will, allows your mind to function and sustains the chemical processes of your body. Therefore, when you think that you are the one who sustains your daily activities, you are engaging in an egoistic illusion. It is your spirit, which gives life to your body, and it is the spirit, which gives you strength to pursue the activities of life. So the credit for your very existence should go to your innermost Self.

Therefore, your interest in objects is misplaced. You should be interested in this Self from which you arise and are sustained. It is the Self within you, which is infinite and boundless bliss. Objects have an enticing effect on the human mind because they all arise and are supported by the same blissful Self from which your very consciousness arises. This fact makes them enchanting to the human mind because the mind is always searching for what will make it happy. When you see an object, situation or person which makes you "happy," it is really the Self in that object which you are recognizing and not the object itself. However, your misguided notion that it is the object and not the Self, which brings joy, leads you to pursue the object, which is transitory and illusory. This leads to disappointment and frustration when the objects are not within your grasp or when the situations or persons you long for do not come to you.

Wisdom dictates that you should reverence the divine essence in objects, people and situations. Strive to recognize them as expressions of the Self as you are. Don't hold onto anything or anyone, rather love others with detachment, knowing that they are transient expressions of the Self.

All things die and are reborn, therefore, if you grieve over the loss of a loved one you are grieving over something which is based on erroneous understanding. No one dies in reality; they only change forms and move on in their quest for spiritual enlightenment through many incarnations, which are determined by their level of ignorance of their true Self, the Neter.

Therefore, do not become attached to anything outside of yourself and do not grieve over anything because there is no loss or gain in the Self. When you live your life according to this wisdom, you relieve the tension and pain of egoistic pursuits and open the doors of eternity.

GOOD ASSOCIATION: AN ESSENTIAL DISCIPLINE FOR HEALTH

Good Association Part 1

One of the most important ways of promoting awareness and constant reflection which will destroy the negative impressions (ari) in the deep unconscious mind is keeping the company of wise teachers or Sages. In Ancient Egypt, the Temple system served the purpose of instructing aspirants in the wisdom teachings. The initiates were then allowed back into the world on a regular basis in order to test their level of understanding and self-control by practicing the teachings when confronted with ordinary, worldly minded people. The Temple was a place where the initiate could go on a regular basis to receive instruction and counseling on the correct application of the teachings in day to day life. The idea is reflected in the Ancient Egyptian *Stele of Djehuti-Nefer*:

> *"Consume pure foods and pure thoughts with pure hands, adore celestial beings, and become associated with wise ones: sages, saints and prophets; make offerings to GOD..."*

The association with Sages and Saints (Good Association) is seen as a primary way to accelerate the spiritual development of the aspirant. Again, this is because it is the nature of the mind to imitate that which it focuses on. An important definition of the symbols associated with *Sma* or Sema is *to render clear or visible* . In ancient Egypt, the *gathering, assembly or reunion* was called *Smait* and *Smai* is a name for the Temple, the gathering place. In Egypt, the priest assumed the role of preceptor, *Sbai* , leading the initiate to understand the teachings of the hieroglyphs, to purification of the mind and body and eventually to intuitional realization through the practice of mental exercises and the application of the wisdom teachings. In ancient hieroglyphics, the scenes symbolize this where deities such as *Heru, Djehuti, Anpu, Hetheru, Aset*, etc., lead the initiate to meet Asar (his/her Higher Self). In India, this process is known as *"Satsanga"* where the aspirant receives teaching from the *Guru* (Spiritual Preceptor) on a continuous basis. In Buddhism the process is known as *Sanga*. In Christianity this idea was reflected in the relationship between Jesus and John the Baptist and later between Jesus and his disciples. Keeping the company of wise ones is an important and powerful tool for spiritual development because the nature of the unenlightened (ignorant) mind allows it to make subtle mistakes, which can lead the aspirant astray from the correct interpretation of the teachings. Thus, receiving the teaching is the real force which causes transformation through a baptismal ritual, and not the ritual itself.

Therefore, the teacher, guru, priest, etc., who is "close" to the Divine (enlightened) as it were, is seen as greater than the Divine because he or she can lead the aspirant towards the Divine (knowing who the Divine is and where the Divine is and how the Divine is to be discovered). Otherwise it would be a very difficult, long and arduous process for the aspirant to realize the truth. It would take millions of incarnations, wherein untold sufferings would occur in the process of gaining experiences, which would teach the proper way to discover the Self.

Your journey through this volume will impart one most important point about true spirituality, namely, that true spirituality is universal spirituality. This means that if you discover the truth about your own religion, you will have discovered the truth about all other religions therefore, true religion is a religion of the heart. You must always keep in mind that you are transcendental, immortal and eternal and as such, you are endowed with all the qualities necessary to achieve the highest level of spiritual realization regardless of your background or country of origin.

Another important point is to try to become the best possible disciple you can while still performing your every day duties of life. Once you honestly set in motion the mystical process of your own spiritual aspiration, you will one day encounter more advanced personalities from whom you can learn and progress further in your understanding. In every city, state and country, there exist more advanced personalities who can lead you further along your path of self-discovery. Have you known anyone who is able to control his or her emotions? Have you known anyone who has lived through a bad situation such as the loss of a loved one or a serious illness and has moved forward with composure, without losing enthusiasm for life? Have you met anyone who has been like a pillar for others, whom others go to in times of trouble or need? If you have the good fortune to know someone like this, get close to them and ask them to show you how they came to possess those advanced spiritual qualities. Ask their permission to spend time with them so that you may benefit from their knowledge and experience in living. You may find that some people are well developed in some areas but not in others. Learn what you can and emulate their virtuous characteristics. If you get to a point where you feel there is no more to learn from that person, continue seeking and you will discover the steps which lead upward on the ladder of spiritual aspiration.

There is no greater blessing than to meet Sages and or Saints who have attained Christ Consciousness, Nirvana, Buddhahood, Nehast (Heruhood), Salvation, Liberation, etc., themselves, while at the same time being well versed in the written teachings. They can best help you to understand the subtlety of the teachings and lead you to greater and greater awareness and comprehension which will lead to your own mystical realization in a shorter time than through any other method. They cannot transform you into a spiritual personality; you must do that yourself. However, they can direct you on the correct path and point out your mistakes if you are willing to listen. You need not specifically search for someone who is Enlightened in your own religion. You may continue to follow your own religion while still learning the subtlety of spiritual discipline and Yoga science as these apply to all religions equally. You should not become distracted by different religions or teachers, rather set your attention on the highest goal, Enlightenment, then all else will fall into place.

A disciple who does not practice the teachings of their spiritual preceptor with the notion that the preceptor will provide for his or her spiritual development is like a person who expects to become physically fit by merely going to a gymnasium without doing any exercise. The preceptor provides the mental food in the form of the wisdom teachings and then it is up to you to take this food, consume it, digest it, absorb it and allow it to become part of your being.

Since your innermost Self (God) is your Supreme Preceptor, all of the situations you find yourself involved with are divinely inspired to provide for your spiritual education. The same Divine Self is instructing you through the spiritual preceptor and it is this same Divine Self which aids your reflecting and understanding process.

Good Association Part 2

Good Association is a form of group therapy and counseling. It is similar to the process of psychotherapy of Western psychologists, helping the individual to see the error in understanding, which is causing the inability to cope with the world. The major difference between Good Association in Yoga, traditional Western forms of group therapy and individual counseling is that through the spiritual preceptor, Good Association assists and urges the individual to understand his or her transcendental true Self while traditional treatments seek to help the individual cope with life situations which produce stress and mental anguish. From a yogic point of view, ordinary human life is based on an erroneous view of existence, and psychological disciplines which do not include an understanding of the human soul, are also based on ignorance. Thus, treatments, which are based on ignorance, cannot provide effective and abiding results. From this point of view, modern psychiatry, psychology and modern medical science must be understood as disciplines which are only in their infancy because they have not yet acknowledged and discovered the hidden mysteries of the soul. Ordinary psychology is useful in taking extremely degraded individuals (psychotic) from the depths of abnormality and to some degree, helping them to become lucid enough to exist in the world. However, this level of existence and what modern psychology considers to be "normal" is not considered normal by yogic science. Mental abnormality exists to the degree of intensification of the ego and its accompanying complexes. The state of enlightenment or Self-knowledge is then the only state that can be called "the state of optimal mental health."

Good Association is a teacher-disciple relationship wherein yogic teachings are presented to promote spiritual, and thus mental and physical health. Through continuous association with sages or other spiritually advanced personalities, the aspirant is led to discover her/his true spiritual identity. When this process occurs, the general health of the individual is improved because mental complexes and stress diminish and in so doing, the body is able to maintain itself at a more optimal level.

Note: With few exceptions, television does not provide good association. You should strive to curb your viewing time in the beginning of your program and for the next three years. A casual time spent watching an educational television show may be useful in stimulating the mind, however, when television becomes a necessity to you and you spend much of your time "glued" to it for your "entertainment," television promotes dullness of the mind and intellectual weakness which lead to spiritual insensitivity.

Also, "hanging out" with those personalities who are Setian in nature (those who are continuously affected by **anger, hate, greed, lust, impulsiveness, selfishness, brutishness force, demoniac thoughts, thugs, thievery, violence, etc**.) is detrimental to the mental peace of an aspirant, especially to a neophyte (a beginner; novice). Those who are constantly moving around, constantly argumentative and constantly agitated are afflicted with intense identification with their bodies and senses and are unaware of their divine nature.

An important feature of the state of mind which is associated with those who are virtuous or vicious is that tranquility, repose, and peace are characteristic of the virtuous while frantic movement and struggle are associated with the vicious. These same characteristics of the virtues and vices are mentioned in the Ancient Egyptian (Maat), Indian (Dharma) and the Christian (Beatitudes, 10 Commandments) systems of moral development and the need for a state of peacefulness of mind is also emphasized as an imperative feature without which progress on the spiritual path cannot occur.

In general, a mental atmosphere of peacefulness and contentment is necessary for sublime thoughts and aspirations to emerge in the mind. Otherwise, through a life which is based on pursuing the satisfaction of the senses, there is constant desire and agitation of the mind and the individual will always be occupied with the petty thoughts and disturbances of day to day life. Therefore, the cultivation and maintenance of serenity and contentment should be a primary goal of a spiritual aspirant.

You can gradually wean yourself off of television and other negative associations by gradually engaging in them less and less until they are no longer needed. Though in the beginning you must put forth a conscious effort to abstain from these practices and to engage in spiritual work, the process becomes easier and easier until there is no more effort needed to sustain your withdrawal from these activities. This is because the positive spiritual experience provides such a sense of "Self" that you will loose your dependence on the objects of the world and instinctively refrain from associations, which will disrupt your growing sense of inner peace. In the mean time you must work with your mind to abstain from negative activities to the best of your ability. You must understand that you are not giving anything up. In fact, you will be gaining a closer relationship with yourself and true fulfillment of your inner desire.

Rest

Continued mental agitation and stress limits the possibility for engaging in reflection which promotes integration of feelings, thoughts and ideas. Rest is an integral part of the healing process and it is a pre-requisite for proper reflective abilities. In a practical sense, this is the purpose of sleep. From a yogic perspective, the technique of deep relaxation and the discipline of meditation can promote a state of restfulness far superior to that of the sleep state.

Silence

> *"The abomination of the sanctuary of God is: too much talking. Pray thou with a loving heart the petitions of which all are in secret. God will do thy business, hear that which thou sayest and will accept thine offerings."*
>
> —Ancient Egyptian Proverb

The practice of silence on a regular basis has the effect of allowing the individual to withdraw from interaction in the world, thereby calming the mind over time. Silence allows the individual to discover that many things do not need to be said. Inner peace awakens in those who can practice silence because the inner voice is given a chance to emerge from the mountainous thoughts and activities that externalization usually causes. Silence is seen as a mental austerity and it is considered among the practices of moral discipline and self-restraint. Silence should be practiced without making gestures to communicate with others, and at a prescribed time other than when one would normally be quiet. A specialized form of silence practice seeks to keep the body perfectly still for long periods of time (1-2 hours or more). This practice has the effect of developing strength of will as well as aiding the aspirant to remain quietly in meditative posture during the formal practice of meditation.

Being Alone

Practicing "alone time" need not be thought of as loneliness. Being alone can be an exercise in practicing being free from one's desires and attachments. These desires and attachments are the source of the mental complexes. By practicing aloneness, the mind is gradually able to conceive of life without the objects of attachment and is then able to discover its eternal companionship with the Self who is the mother of all mothers, the father of all fathers, the love of all loves, the best friend of all friends.

Recreation

Recreation is a seldom-discussed topic in philosophical treatises. It is usually seen as an "activity that is performed" in order to achieve some kind of regeneration of one's physical and psychological self. Also it is seen as a source of "fun" and excitement. The mind seeks to place itself in the most "pleasurable" environment or situations possible. From a deeper understanding of life and its purpose, the practice of many commonly accepted forms of recreation becomes inadequate because such activities have built into them, the elements of disappointment. Usually they are based on competition, which pits individuals or teams against each other in a format that is designed to produce and promote conflict. Since the happiness to be derived is based upon "winning" a game, one is bound for disappointment since that cannot occur each time that the activity is undertaken. If the times of disappointment are used for introspection, one will develop dispassion towards that which is illusory, painful and transient, and seek to find that which is real, constant and truly pleasurable. A whole new world opens for exploration and true recreation in the spiritual realm.

True recreation is fully conscious, detached and peaceful. Only then is it possible to "feel" and appreciate the nature of one's being, of creation itself. The highest degree of recreation is therefore experienced at the point of enlightenment, when Nehast (spiritual awakening) is realized. Here, every activity in life becomes "play." Life itself becomes a *"divine sport."* In Indian Vedanta philosophy this concept is called *"Leela."* There develops a continuous blissful feeling which does not pass from moment to moment as with those who move from activity to activity searching for a thrill to make them "feel alive," but existence becomes eternity, right in the very present moment. As modern physics shows, time is only a mental concept people put on intervals of eternity. The only reason why we believe time actually passes is because our minds are always concerned with the past or future events and rarely with the present moment. Raising one's spiritual awareness means becoming alive in the present, the here and now. This has been elaborated in the section on Meditation.

Recreation becomes a means to re-create one's consciousness at every moment instead of a means to forget oneself and to pass the time. It allows you to be able to deal more effectively with life's problems rather than serving to distract you for a few minutes, hours or days. Many enlightened personalities such as *Paramahansa Yogananda,* an Indian Sage who came to the West to spread the philosophy of yoga, would from time to time indulge in recreational activities. The difference is that he did not identify himself with the pleasure or illusoriness of the event. As a therapeutic practice, he advocated recreation as a means to gradually adjust the mind and body to greater and greater levels of spiritual discipline. In short, a spiritual discipline does not consist in "giving up" recreation or pleasure; it consists in understanding that the pleasure comes from within, the Self, and not from the object or activity.

SEMA (YOGA) OF DEVOTION TO THE DIVINE

Yoga of Devotion is the process of directing the mental energies (passion and love) to the Divine. It is a process whereby one uses one of the strongest emotions, love, to overpower mental afflictions and negative thoughts leading to union with the divine object of contemplation, one's Higher Self. In much the same manner that one rises above his or her problems and ailments when he or she falls “in love” with another person, so too when one directs feelings of love to the Higher Self, one is able to transcend problems and adversities in life. In addition, since human love is only a glimpse of cosmic love, imagine how much more powerful devotion to God can be in transcending the human condition. Devotion to God, also known as "Divine Love" is an effective way to produce mental health because it easily turns the mind towards the transcendental rather than towards the petty concerns of the ego. To practice Yoga of Devotion, throughout your day, feel that you are serving the Divine when you are serving others, since all people are essentially the Self. In this way your mind does not become distracted by their personalities. When snowflakes fall, you do not become so distracted with their individual shapes that you fail to identify them as snow. Likewise, as intuitional vision of your all-encompassing nature dawns in your heart, you will be able to look beyond all the different sizes, shapes, sexes and colors of people and recognize your Higher Self as the basis for their existence. All becomes loved for the sake of the Self.

> 43. Thou art Temu, who didst create beings endowed with reason; thou makest the color of the skin of one race to be different from that of another, but, however many may be the varieties of mankind, it is thou that makest them all to live.
>
> —Ancient Egyptian Hymn of Amun

> "Souls, Heru, son, are of the self-same nature, since they came from the same place where the Creator modeled them; nor male nor female are they. Sex is a thing of bodies not of Souls."
>
> —Ancient Egyptian Proverb from *The teachings of Aset to Heru*

> "O behold with thine eye God's plans. Devote thyself to adore God's name. It is God who giveth Souls to millions of forms, and God magnifyeth whosoever magnifieth God."
>
> —Ancient Egyptian Proverb from *Djehuti Hermes*

When the mind is continuously directed toward the majesty and glory of God, the Neter (Higher Self), the mind becomes imbued with that same glory and majesty. Thus devotion opens the way to the practice of the other disciplines of Yoga (Yoga of Action, Yoga of Wisdom, Meditation) and these in turn lead to the experience of deeper devotion.

Chanting and Words of Power in the Promotion of Healing

Sound has long been recognized as an instrument of healing because the vibrations can have an effect on physical matter, especially on the subtle matter of the mind. You may have noticed that certain music may make you feel happy, while other music makes you feel melancholy. Certain music brings up old memories (good and bad), while other music makes you feel vital and enthused. Thus, music can be used to engender a positive, stress free feeling in the mind. If the mind is positive, this will have the effect of allowing the relief of stress to promote the healing process by allowing the energy that would ordinarily go to stress and the promotion of harmful hormonal reaction, to be used for getting rid of impurities and repairing the damage which led to the disease.

In the practice of uttering words of power, (hekau, mantras, chanting, prayers) it must be understood that these are to be practiced in conjunction with sound healing techniques. In studying the writings of medical papyri from Ancient Egypt, it may be noticed that the number of papyri containing special utterances that were classified as medical, increased, while the application of practical medical techniques such as described here declined in the later eras, and with it, public health. This denotes, among other things, the level of corruption from outside forces, which degraded the practice of the medical arts in Ancient Egypt during the late period.

Music as a Healing Force

Pythagoras, a student of the Ancient Egyptian Mysteries, learned from his Ancient Egyptian Masters the teachings of mystical spirituality which included the art of music and how it affects the mind. He noted that certain music agitates the mind, and certain music does not. Music could be stimulating or pacifying if used properly. Therefore, there are certain forms of music that are conducive to peace, relaxation and harmony. This kind of music is suitable for promoting the healing and health maintenance process.

Figure 40: Musicians in Ancient Egypt

The Ancient Egyptian Sages instituted tight controls on theater and music because the indulgence in inappropriate entertainments was known to cause mental agitation and undesirable behaviors. The famous Greek Philosopher and student of the Ancient Egyptian Mysteries, Pythagoras, wrote that the Ancient Egyptians placed particular attention to the study of music. Even today, one can visit the temples of Ancient Egypt and note the prominently displayed musical instruments that were part of the temple rituals, and the birthing houses. Another famous Greek Philosopher and student of the Ancient Egyptian Mysteries, Plato, states that they thought it was *beneficial to the youths*. Plato further reports that *in the education of the youths they were particularly strict...they knew that children ought to be early accustomed to such gestures, looks and motions as are decent and proper; and not to be suffered either to hear or learn any verses and songs than those which are calculated to inspire them with virtue; and they consequently took care that every dance and ode*[151] *introduced at their feasts or sacrifices should be subject to certain regulations.*

Strabo confirms that *music was taught to youths along with reading and writing, however, it was understood that music meant for entertainment alone was harmful to the mind, making it agitated and difficult to control oneself, and thus was strictly controlled by the state and the priests and priestesses.* Like the sages of India, who instituted Nada Yoga, or the spiritual path of music, the Ancient Egyptians held that music was of Divine origin and as such was a sacred endeavor. *The Greek writer, Athenaeus,* informs us that *the Greeks and barbarians from other countries learned music from the Ancient Egyptians.* Music was so important in Ancient Egypt that professional musicians were contracted and kept on salaries at the temples. Music was given special consideration because it was recognized that it had the special power to carry the mind to either elevated (spiritual) states or (worldly) states.

When there is overindulgence in music for entertainment and escapism (tendency to desire to escape from daily routine or reality by indulging in fantasy, daydreaming, or entertainment), the mind is filled with worldly impressions, cravings, lust, and uncontrolled urges. In this state of mind, the capacity for right thinking and feeling are distorted or incapacitated. The advent of audio and visual recording technology and their combinations in movies and music videos is more powerful, because the visual element, coupled with music and the ability to repeat with intensity of volume, acts to intoxicate the mind with illusory and fantasy thoughts. The body is also affected in this process. The vibrations of the music and the feelings contained in it through the lyrics and sentiment of the performer evokes the production of certain bio-chemical processes in the mind and body. This capacity of music is evident in movies, musicals, concerts, audio recordings, etc., in their capacity to change a person's mood. Any and all messages given to the mind affect it, and therefore great care should be taken to fill the mind with the right kinds of messages in the form of ideas and feelings.

The Ancient Egyptians rated music highly, and Plato considered their music to be superior to the Greeks, both for melody and energy. But harmony and rhythm were always subordinate to the words, and the subject matter was paramount. There were two sorts of harmonies known to the Ancient Egyptians, which the Greeks designated as "Dorian" and "Phrygian."

The Dorian Mode is ***slow, meditative and devotional*** and it was used for processions, rituals and religious ceremonies. The second mode, Phrygian, is ***lively, exciting and devotional***. Thus, all music was dedicated to the Divine and not to frivolous entertainments. The singing of hymns was seen as an effective means to communicate with and propitiate the Divine. The Ancient Egyptian word for music means "to sing." Therefore, singing to the Divine was understood as the highest and only purpose of music. Unlike the case with ancient Greek music, the Ancient Egyptian musicians did not record notation, so the exact melodies used are not known. However, much is known about the theory of Ancient Egyptian music. There is evidence that the voice itself was the determiner of the melody. This, coupled with what is known about the modes, provides an approximation to work with in order to recreate, at least in part, the feeling of Ancient Egyptian music. Central to the music is the religion and the language. The Kemetic (Ancient Egyptian) language was called ***Medu Neter*** or Divine Speech or Speech is Divine. This means that the language was Divinely inspired and that when its words are used, they have special powers. This concept was known as ***Hekau*** by the Ancient Egyptians. In modern times it is known by the Hindus as ***Mantras***, Words of Power, or mystical chanting or divine singing. They have the power to invoke

---

[151] A lyric poem of some length, usually of a serious or meditative nature and having an elevated style and formal stanzaic structure. **2.a.** A choric song of classical Greece, often accompanied by a dance and performed at a public festival or as part of a drama. American Heritage Dictionary

positive vibrations and to transform the mind of those who utter them sufficiently, with understanding and feeling.

The author (Muata Ashby) has composed a number of musical selections, which are suitable for the promotion of relaxation and healing. This production made use of five musical instruments, of the many, which were used in Ancient Egypt: the voice, the hands (clapping), the Tar, hand drum, and the three stringed long lute, known as *Nefer.* To the Ancient Egyptians, the intent behind music was the overriding factor. All music, dancing and festivities should be dedicated to the Divine. On this teaching, the Ancient Egyptian Sages believed, depended the prosperity of the nation. In modern times we can see how the use of music and the performing arts has led to the degradation of society in the form of arts which are designed to engender passion and agitation in people's minds in an effort to stimulate sales, fortune and fame for those who produce it. This is, for the most part done without regard to the ill effects of music on the mind.

As of the date of this publication, the author (Muata Ashby) has prepared three musical collections that are suitable for aiding the healing process. The titles are *Merit's Inspiration, Nefer,* and *The Serpent Power Meditation and Music Level I.* These selections and their sequence were prepared with great care and feeling towards elevating the listener's mind. Based on the chants of Kemetic Religion and mysticism, and on traditional musical forms, they were designed to engender serenity, harmony and spiritual upliftment. See the rear section of this volume for more details.

Prayers For Health

Prayer is a special and potent way to charge your practice and the entire day with powerful spiritual vibrations. Prayers will be especially beneficial when the meaning is well understood. Pray in accordance with your faith, that you will be led to true understanding, peace and health.

You may consult the books *Initiation Into Egyptian Yoga* and *Egyptian Proverbs: TemT Tchaas* by Muata Ashby for other prayers and invocatory proverbs, which can be read as part of your prayer time. These serve the purpose of invoking the presence of the Divine Self to assist in directing you on your spiritual path. They bring auspiciousness to your life and uplift your mind for higher spiritual attainment.

All spiritually uplifting quotations from the Ancient Egyptian texts are to be considered as words of power. Therefore, you may choose from a variety of texts according to your inner-personal feeling. Try to let your mind flow freely as it gravitates toward particular teachings and let it flow to new ones as it matures and increases in intuitional understanding. Also, as you read the teachings and study the explanations, try to allow your heart to melt into the glory and majesty of which they speak. During your time of practice, inwardly let your feelings flow toward the Divine. This is very important. You must begin to understand that the teachings are talking about the Divine Self who is closer to you than anything on earth. Allow yourself to let your entire being flow in love and devotion toward the Divine. As you grow in knowledge and practice, you will discover the sweetness of divine love and cosmic union with the divine, which is beyond all human experiences.

In ancient Kamit the Swnus (doctors) prescribed healing treatments, herbs and cleansing modalities to heal the individual, but they also did something else that doctors in modern times have shied away from out of fear of appearing less "scientific." The Swnus also prescribed a prayer that was to be uttered by the person being healed. This form of healing technique has received attention in recent years with the writings of Larry Dossey M.D. through his books *Healing Words: The Power of Prayer and the Practice of Medicine* and *Prayer is good Medicine*. He presented surveys showing that "75 percent of patients believe their physicians should address spiritual issues as part of medical care, and 50 percent want their doctor to pray not just for them, but with them." This means that there is a need that is not being filled by the medical establishment, a spiritual need of the soul of its patients. Dr. Dossey also presented evidence that statistically proves that prayer has an effect on the healing process.

> "Statistically, God is good for you," says David B. Larson, M.D., of the National Institute for Healthcare Research in Rockville, Maryland, which studies the relationship between spirituality and health. Larson, a former senior researcher at the National Institute of Mental Health, says, "I was told by my [medical school] professors that religion is harmful. Then I looked at the research, and religion is actually highly beneficial. If you go to church or pray regularly, it's very beneficial in terms of preventing illness, mental and physical, and you cope with illness much more effectively. If you look at the research, in area after area, it's 80 percent beneficial. I was shocked."
> So was I. I stumbled blindly into the research on prayer during the 1980s, when someone sent me a scientific paper in which prayer was tested in a modern hospital in a large group of heart patients. It had never occurred to me that anyone would actually test prayer like a new medication -praying for half the patients and not for the other half, who were the "controls," and measuring the results. This study strongly suggested a therapeutic effect of distant, intercessory prayer. After I recovered from my surprise, I asked myself, If prayer works, shouldn't I be praying for my patients?[152]

So the practice of healing prayer which existed ancient Kamit has found its way into the halls of modern medicine. Dr. Dossey goes on to say that the effect does not operate exclusively in any particular religion.

> Following the publication of my book *Healing Words: The Power of Prayer and the Practice of Medicine, I* discovered that many of Rose's predictions were true. Fundamentalist groups from around the country reacted with outrage, condemning the scientific evidence as "occult" and "New Age" without stopping to consider whether or not the studies were valid. The primary reason they were offended seems to be that the prayer experiments show, as Rose states, that "people from many religious traditions do equally well on these tests." In other words, the experiments make clear that no specific religion has a monopoly on prayer. This is contrary to the belief of many fundamentalists that the Almighty is attuned mainly or exclusively to them; that those who are not "saved" can't really pray effectively; and that the only genuine prayer people outside their faith can offer is for mercy and forgiveness. To anyone holding such beliefs, the prayer experiments represent a colossal conflict between science and faith. When these two worlds collide, it is usually science that gets tossed out and dogma that is retained.[153]

These modern researches show that healing cannot be simply a matter of prescribing drugs or herbs for the body. It must take into account the needs of the mental-emotional and spiritual aspects of the personality as well. Therefore, the healer needs to be not just a scientist, but also a philosopher and a spiritualist. The scientist takes care of the body, the philosopher takes care of the mind and emotions, and the spiritualist takes care of the soul and leads a person to harmony and peace, and these are the springboards to health and enlightenment.

It is important to understand that while prayer and participation in religion do have an effect on healing, it is also true that ultimately the lifestyle will diminish or even cancel out any gains that are made through prayer and spiritual pursuits if the natural laws of healthy living are not followed. After building a large Christian ministry, the Reverend George H. Malkmus contracted cancer. He left the ministry in

---

[152] *Prayer is good* Medicine by Larry Dossey M.D.
[153] ibid

search of alternative therapies, since he did not want to die due to side effects of traditional western medical treatments for cancer like surgery, radiation and chemotherapy, as his mother did. He was shocked about his illness, thinking that as a minister, he and other ministers in the Christian church should have been exempt from such suffering due to their supposed piety and divine grace as Christian Ministers. For him, this also brought up the question of why should Christians suffer if they are supposed to be members of a religion that brings them closer to God? With this same idea he wondered how non-Christians could get healed without being part of this special religion (Christianity)?

> **"My Dilemma**
>
> Even more exciting than the healing I was experiencing in my own body was what I saw happening in the lives of others who were also at this nutritional institute. People were there from all over the world with all kinds of physical complaints. Many of these people were not professing Christians. Some of them were openly agnostics. Yet, when they applied the principles that were being taught ... truly miraculous healing took place and they got well.
> Now I was really faced with a dilemma. For nearly 20 years while in the Christian ministry, I watched Christians get sick and often die from a variety of illnesses in spite of many prayers and the efforts of the medical profession. Now I was faced with personally witnessing even non-Christians getting well without prayer, the medical profession or even acknowledging God in their lives. How was I to account for this?"[154]

Dr. Malkmus attended classes at a nutritional institute, and also he put the principles that were being taught there into practice. He healed himself without drugs and today preaches the gospel of vegetarianism and detoxification to Christians all over the world. Dr. Malkmus draws large crowds and focuses their attention on the Bible scripture that instructs all Christians to be vegetarians.

> *Then God said, "Behold, I have given you every plant yielding seed that is on the surface of all the earth, and every tree which has fruit yielding seed; it shall be food for you." (Christian Bible-Genesis 1:29)*

Most Christians as well as peoples of other world religions find the Genesis instruction too harsh and so for the most part they ignore it, and consequently his success among Christians appears to be largely with those facing health challenges. The question still remains however, how will people of any religion change if they are caught up in the morals of modern culture which promote excess and pleasure seeking? This question haunts many religions but especially the Christians because as Dr. Malkmus puts it, "Christians do not lead different lifestyles from the rest of the population." Therefore, statistics show that they suffer diseases in the same proportions as the rest of the population. Most Christians do not see anything wrong with meat eating, Burger King, McDonalds, Fried Chicken and Pizza fast food establishments, or in the illusions of Hollywood, or the contradiction of professing a culture of caring while promoting unlimited greed or promoting peace and forgiveness while at the same time being leaders of nations that are the most warlike and violent in history,[155] and so they develop the same ailments as the rest of the population. This includes mental-emotional illnesses as well. Dr. Malkmus continues:

> "During my nearly twenty years in the ministry, coming in contact with multitudes of Christians, I found an usually high percentage of Christians with

[154] Why Christians Get Sick by Dr. George H. Malkmus

[155] Western countries, led by Christians, have sponsored more violence and wars than all other groups combined.

emotional problems. In fact, there are many ministries that deal exclusively with Christians who have emotional problems.
Now emotional problems are definitely a form of sickness; however, it is a sickness that many do not want to recognize or acknowledge as a sickness. In fact, many do not want to acknowledge that they even have a problem. And sadly, when help is finally sought, the help often does not deal with the cause, but rather with the symptoms."[156]

Authentic spirituality serves two purposes in healing. First it gives the person hope that there is something greater than the suffering and that healing is possible. Then it gives the person spiritual strength to make the necessary changes in order to promote the healing process. Without the will to change their lifestyle, Christians and others will have a difficult time discovering true health. The lack of direction and stability through the practice of an effective religion prevents the capacity of the mind to discover true harmony and peace. Under these conditions health will be elusive and at best temporary.

So religion cannot be followed in name only, or in ritual only (prayer, chanting, singing, praising God, etc.). It must be an integral aspect of a life that is committed to the principles of universal religion (nonviolence, vegetarianism, mysticism, meditation and enlightenment). Otherwise, if the spiritual outlook of life is limited to ritual or exoteric and secular practices (Church, Temple or Mosque going) instead of mysticism and spiritual transcendence (discovering the Divine and becoming one with the Divine), the spiritual movement will always fall short and frustrate the individual, and inevitably lead to disease. Keep in mind here that religiosity is not necessarily authentic spirituality. Adolf Hitler was a member of the Catholic church, and yet look at the atrocities he comminted against humanity. The same can be said for the leaders of countries such as South Africa and the United States who allowed lynching and the murder of millions of Africans and Native Americans. Can they be considered as authentic and sincere practitioners of religion? While the efforts of Dr. Malkmus are commendable and should be supported, should other fundamental questions also asked about the religious traditions, practices and beliefs that have led people to practice religion in name only? Can anyone who does not follow the principles of their own religion, so that they can seek to satisfy their egoistic desires, be considered as religious or spiritual? And can there be any wonder as to the causes of their physical, mental and spiritual ailments in the presence of the cultural and theological deficiencies outlined above?

Prayer Before Dinners and Festivities

The Ancient Egyptian practice of saying grace before meals, was even carried out by ordinary householders. Prior to consuming food or engaging in festive occasions, such as parties, etc., the host of an ordinary household would invite the guests to view an image of a divinity, principally Asar, the god of the afterlife. They would bring out and display for all, the figure of a mummy, usually one and a half to three feet tall, standing erect or lying down. The purpose of this ritualistic act was to remind everyone about their own mortality, thereby showing the guests that life is fleeting, even as they are about to enjoy a sumptuous meal. In this manner, a person is reminded of the ultimate fate of life and a reflective state of mind is engendered rather than an arrogant, egoistic and deluded state. This practice also served to remind one of the purpose of life, to become one with the Supreme Self, in this case in the form of Asar, before the death of the body.

[156] Why Christians Get Sick by Dr. George H. Malkmus

Preparing For Death

Plate 16: Asar as figurine displayed at parties and dinners affairs

Taking into account the teachings related to ari (karma) and its effects in the life of a human being as well as the central teaching of Kemetic Mystical Philosophy (*Body to earth, Soul to heaven*), the true purpose of health must be defined as follows. From a philosophical point of view, human life is not the most desirable state of being. In reality, human beings are spirits who have forgotten their true identity. It is this true identity which is the desired state and it cannot be attained if there is a perpetual state of physical life. That is, a human being cannot grow fully if there is no physical death to allow their soul to move on (reincarnate) so as to learn new lessons of life until enlightenment is attained. This is the purpose of the death of the body. So, while the quality and quantity of life should be extended by reasonable and natural means, it must be kept in mind that everything that is born must die. Everything that begins must come to an end. The only way to escape this law of time and space is to transcend time and space altogether by discovering one's transcendental nature, the Spirit, which is beyond.

Death should not be shunned as most people in modern times do, as if they can escape its grasp. It should be viewed as a natural aspect of life.

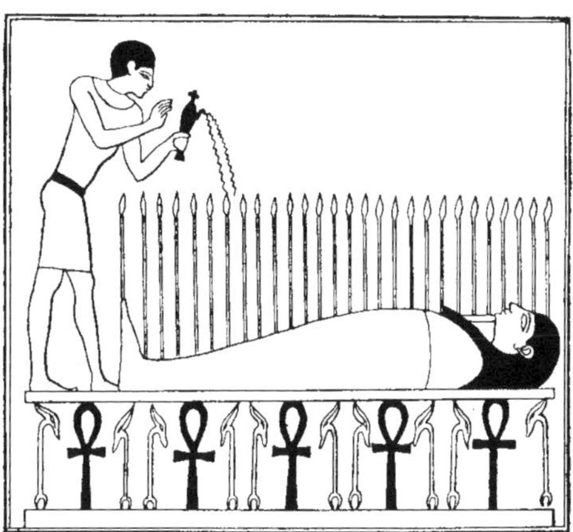

Figure 41: The God Asar as the Life Source in Vegetation

In Kemetic spirituality, the divinity Asar is often represented with a green hue. The picture above, which comes from the Temple of Aset (Isis) in Egypt, shows us the reason why. Wheat, representing all vegetation in Creation, is seen growing out of the dead body of Asar. In the Asarian Resurrection Myth, Asar was killed by his brother and resurrected by his sister and wife, Aset. While his spirit resurrected and became the lord of the "Beautiful West," his body became the sustaining essence which causes vegetation to grow. He, i.e. the spirit, is the 𓌀 𓋹 𓌀 , *Uas-Ankh-Uas,* or "flow of life force essence" which causes vegetation to grow and sustains human existence. Asar (Osiris) is green because he is the essence of life in the vegetables we eat. If we learn to eat the right "green" diets for our bodies, minds and souls, we are eating Asar himself, and thereby become divine beings ourselves. Isn't the saying "you are what you eat" well known now? This is the original teaching of divine food, which was later represented in Christianity as the eucharist. But you must know that everything you eat can be a eucharist leading you to health, vitality and spiritual enlightenment.

swadj – "May you become green" – "may you flourish and thrive"

In a mystical sense, Asar is the very sustenance of life. All food that is eaten is therefore Asar also. This idea is also expressed in the benediction of the Ancient Egyptian doctors, who, upon administering medicaments, would speak the special words of power *"may your mettu flourish."* The Kemetic term for flourish is "greening." So in order to become healthy, one is to become "green" like Asar. Thus, Asar is the sustenance of the *Duat* (Astral) as well as the *Ta* (earth) realms.

This theme is present in every aspect of Ancient Egyptian culture and others. In modern times, most people do not want to think about death, especially when they are "having a good time." This would have been considered a turning away from truth, a breach of one of the fundamental injunctions of Maat philosophy (Precept #24: *I have not stopped my ears listening to the words of right and wrong*). Thus, when the subject of death is broached, one should not turn away and act as if it does not exist or try to have a "good time and not think about it" attitude. Drugs, worldly entanglements, and other distractions may soften the blow of death in the short term, but some day the issue will have to be dealt with through the death of close family members and of one's very self. If you are not ready, the experience will be harrowing and painful. If you are ready, it can be "as smooth as silk." This is the prospect that initiates of the mystical sciences look forward to and discover.

Facing death and uncovering its mystery is the most important task for every spiritual aspirant. This is because the fear of death and the sorrow caused by disease, old age and death typify the pain, misery and frustrations of life. Therefore, conquering death means conquering life.

The goal of health practices is to allow the soul to have a useful body throughout its lifetime, a body that is not obstructed by disease and suffering. The body should be healthy even up to the time of death, for death is not determined by either health or illness of the body, but by the karmic necessity of the individual. It is one's own soul who makes the determination of when and how one will die. This is why death, sometimes seem senseless.

When all healing attempts have been made and despite those efforts, health deteriorates beyond any further action, it is time to help the dying person understand and accept what is happening, and even look forward to it. This process is made easier for those who have led a righteous life because their conscience can be clear, devoid of regrets, fears, discontent, and anger. While hope should be kept alive, the truth should be openly discussed and in this way, the higher purpose of health is also served, for death means that a new body will be acquired and the opportunity to apply the lessons of this life will once again be available to that person. When a society becomes so out of touch with the spiritual reality it fears death and dreads its coming, then it searches for ways to extend life, even after the soul has left the body. This misguided idea forces many to suffer unnecessarily, hanging on by machines which sustain the pain-racked body which is little more than a useless husk. This is very degrading to the soul, but yet it is in line with the karmic basis of those who perpetuate it and those who must suffer through it as patients.

Fasting Unto Death

In Western countries, the high degree of egoism (separation from the spiritual Self) has caused most people to suffer from the problem of clinging to life. This problem is seen as a powerful obstacle to spiritual enlightenment since the person is psychologically and emotionally tied to their physical existence, and therefore bound to worldliness and the negative aspects of life very intensely. This clinging process has led to the desire to hold on to life at any cost, even if that life is with a decrepit, useless shell of a body. The fear of death and the degree to which people have become out of touch with their own spiritual essence has led to this degraded condition. Even though many people consider themselves to be religious, in reality they are not progressing spiritually because they are not practicing authentic religious principles in life. In reality they are pursuing the world and its illusory pleasures, and this is all they know. Losing all they know is therefore a painful prospect, and so they try to hold on even when they know they will die. This state of affairs consumes valuable resources that would be better used to serve other purposes.

Coupled with this complex about death, there is another mental complex from which people suffer. It is the idea that youth is all-important and that old age is undesirable. This has translated into the culture of youth wherein older people are devalued and relegated to the fringes of society, and their wisdom is not accepted or even acknowledged by the younger generation. Yes, the same generation which will one day also become old! This is a ridiculous and misguided situation which has also led to a culture wherein all aspects of society are dedicated to the pursuit of youth and pleasure, especially sexual pleasure, the excess of which leads to many hormonal imbalances, sexual diseases and a depleted immune system. Good looks by any means including plastic surgery are the order of the day. When there can be no more surgeries, people become depressed and deluded, trying to hold on to their youth even when the body is incapable of doing the things it did previously. They have no greater prospect in life other than to continue pursuing the life they have known, albeit in a frustrating manner. When a person dies, everyone is shocked and dismayed, even when we all know we all must die some day. Where is the faith, the religion, the right thinking (living by truth), and the trust in the Divine? People are busy pursuing their own desires. They do not agree with or understand the divine purpose of death, and consequently life, otherwise they would accept it as an unavoidable and necessary part of life.

In ancient times and in other societies which survive even today, there was/is a recognition of the inevitability of death and the fact that it has a purpose. It is not to be feared or avoided; it is to be prepared for. Living the mystical spirituality lifestyle (promoting enlightenment of the mind and health of the body) is the best preparation. If a human being has led a good life, meaning that they have taken care of their body and used it for pursuing truth and performing righteous actions, then they will be prepared and even look forward to death as a doorway to greater aspect of life.

There is a practice of fasting unto death in which a person, realizing they have done all they needed to do in this life, and due to the deterioration of the body, that there is no longer a useful purpose for prolonging life, refrains from taking food until finally, they expire and move on. They recognize that they have used their time and that they must now go to the next experience, without burdening the living or making a fuss over their own departure. No feeding tubes, no miracle cures or respirators are to be expected. No legal maneuvers are to be used to prevent them from carrying out their wishes. This is the sign of mature human beings and a mature society.

CHAPTER 7: FOOD FOR THE SOUL

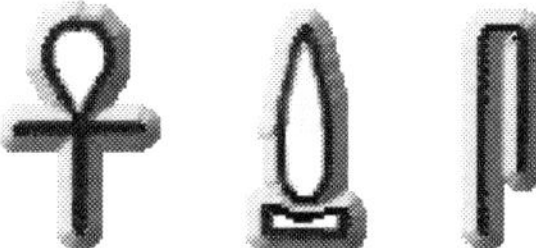

Table 15: The Ailments of the Soul and Their Remedies

Ailment of the Soul	Remedy: Practice the following
Impotence to change for the better	Meditation
Anguish-despair	Faith
Egoism	Altruistic, unselfishness
Heartache	Self-discovery, enlightenment

Cleansing of the Soul

When the disciplines of body and mind purification are practiced as described throughout this volume, the unconscious levels of the mind are gradually being cleansed of negative impressions from the past which have been obstructing the vision of the Higher Self. This allows the mind to fathom new horizons and to transcend its limitations, not just in the world of human affairs but also in the realm of the inner dimensions of the Soul. When a human being begins to awaken the virtuous qualities and to develop a sensitivity towards the glory of life and the sublime nature of the Spirit, the soul is becoming pure and the spiritual awakening of the personality is occurring. The latent gifts of the soul begin to emerge and the personality becomes powerful and dynamic and at the same time the spiritual strength and conviction also grows. This is the desired effect of the teachings and practices of Kemetic Health. They should be allowed to continue until the human being reaches the ultimate awareness of the divine nature, the coveted goal of spiritual enlightenment.

Introduction to Meditation

What is Meditation?

Meditation may be thought of or defined as the practice of mental exercises and disciplines to enable the aspirant to achieve control over the mind, specifically, to stop the vibrations of the mind due to unwanted thoughts, imaginations, etc. Just as the sun is revealed when the clouds disperse, so the light of the Self is revealed when the mind is free of thoughts, imaginations, ideas, delusions, gross emotions, sentimental attachments, etc. The Self, your true identity, is visible to the conscious mind.

The mind and nervous system are instruments of the Self, which it uses to have experiences in the realm of time and space, which it has created in much the same way as a person falls asleep and develops an entire dream world out of his or her own consciousness. It is at the unconscious and subconscious levels where the most intensive work of Yoga takes place, because it is here that the conscious identification of a person creates impressions in the mind and where desires based on those impressions develop. It is these desires that keep the aspirant involved in the realm of time and space or frees the aspirant from the world of time and space if they are sublimated into the spiritual desire for enlightenment. The desire to attain enlightenment is not viewed in the same manner as ego based desires; it is viewed as being aspiration which is a positive movement.

Externalized consciousness - distracted by egoism and worldly objects.

The light of the Self (consciousness) shines through the mind and this is what sustains life. The flow of consciousness in most people is from within moving outward. This causes them to be externalized and distracted and lose energy. Where the mind goes, energy flows. Have you ever noticed that you can "feel" someone looking at you? This is because there is a subtle energy being transmitted through their vision (which is an extension of the mind). Those who live in this externalized state of mind are not aware of the source of consciousness. Meditation, as well as the other disciplines of yoga, serve to reverse the flow of consciousness on itself so that the mind acts as a mirror which reveals the true Self.

Internalized consciousness of a Yoga practitioner.

Most people are unaware that there are deeper levels to their being just as they are unaware of the fact that physical reality is not "physical." Quantum physics experiments have proven that the physical world is not composed of matter, but of energy. This supports the findings of the ancient Sages who have taught for thousands of years that the reality, which is experienced by the human senses, is not an "Absolute" reality, but a conditional one. Therefore, you must strive to rise beyond your conditioned mind and senses in order to perceive reality as it truly is.

"Learn to distinguish the real from the unreal."

Human beings are not just composed of a mind, senses and a physical body. Beyond the physical and mental levels, there is a soul level. This is the realm of the Higher Self, which all of the teachings of mystical spirituality and the various practices of meditation are directed towards discovering. This "hidden" aspect of ourselves which is beyond the thoughts is known as Amun, Asar or Amenta in the Ancient Egyptian system of spirituality, as Brahman, in Indian Vedanta philosophy, as God in Christianity, etc.

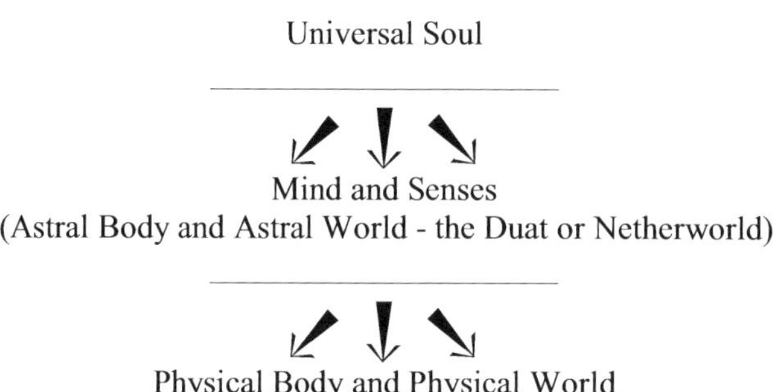

When you are active and not practicing or experiencing the wisdom of mystical spirituality, you are distracted from the real you. This distraction which comes from the desires, cravings and endless motion of thoughts in the mind is the *veil* which blocks your perception of your deeper essence, the Supreme Self. These distractions keep you involved with the mind, senses, and body that you have come to believe is the real you. When your body is motionless and you are thinking and feeling, you are mostly associated with your mind. At times when you are not thinking, such as in the dreamless sleep state, then you are associated with your Higher Self. However, this connection in the dreamless sleep state is veiled by ignorance because you are asleep and not aware of the experience. In order to discover this realm, you must consciously turn away from the phenomenal world which is distracting you from your inner reality. The practice of mystical spirituality accomplishes this task. Meditation, when backed up by the other disciplines of mystical spirituality, is the most powerful agent of self-discovery. The practice of meditation allows one to create a higher awareness, which affects all aspects of one's life, but most importantly, it gives the aspirant experiential knowledge of his/his true Self.

What is the Goal of Meditation?

Meditation may be thought of or defined as the practice of mental exercises and disciplines to enable the meditator to achieve control over the mind, specifically, to stop the vibrations of the mind due to unwanted thoughts, imaginations, etc.

Consciousness refers to the awareness of being alive and of having an identity. It is this characteristic which separates humans from the animal kingdom. Animals cannot become aware of their own existence and ponder the questions such as *Who am I?, Where am I going in life?, Where do I come from?,* etc. They cannot write books on history and create elaborate systems of social history based on ancestry, etc. Consciousness expresses itself in three modes. These are: Waking, Dream-Sleep and Dreamless-Deep-Sleep.

Ordinary human life is only partially conscious. When you are driving or walking, you sometimes lose track of the present moment. All of a sudden you arrive at your destination without having conscious awareness of the road which you have just traveled. Your mind went into an "automatic" mode of consciousness. This automatic mode of consciousness represents a temporary withdrawal from the waking world. This state is similar to a daydream (a dreamlike musing or fantasy). This form of existence is what most people consider as "normal" everyday waking consciousness. It is what people consider to be the extent of the human capacity to experience or be conscious.

The "normal" state of human consciousness cannot be considered as "whole" or complete because if it was there would be no experience of lapses or gaps in consciousness. In other words, every instant of consciousness would be accounted for. There would be no trance-like states wherein one loses track of time or awareness of one's own activities, even as they are being performed. In the times of trance or lapse, full awareness or consciousness is not present, otherwise it would be impossible to not be aware of the passage of time while engaged in various activities. Trance here should be differentiated from the religious or mystical form of trance like states induced through meditation. As used above, it refers to the condition of being so lost in solitary thought as to be unaware of one's surroundings. It may further be characterized as a stunned or bewildered condition, a fog, stupor, befuddlement, daze, muddled state of mind. Most everyone has experienced this condition at some point or another. What most people consider to be the "awake" state of mind in which life is lived is in reality only a fraction of the total potential consciousness, which a human being can experience.

Mental distraction, restlessness and extroversion characterize the state of automatic consciousness. The automatic state of mind exists due to emotions such as desire, anger and hatred which engender desires in the mind, which in turn cause more movement, distractions, delusions and lapses or "gaps" in human consciousness. In this condition, it does not matter how many desires are fulfilled. The mind will always be distracted and agitated and will never discover peace and contentment. If the mind were under control, meaning, if you were to remain fully aware and conscious of every feeling, thought and emotion in your mind at any given time, it would be impossible for you to be swayed or deluded by your thoughts into a state of relative unconsciousness or un-awareness. Therefore, it is said that those who do not have their minds under control are not fully awake and conscious human beings.

Meditation and mystical philosophy are disciplines, which are directed toward increasing awareness. Awareness or consciousness can only be increased when the mind is in a state of peace and harmony. Thus, the disciplines of Meditation (which are part of the mystical spirituality) are the primary means of controlling the mind and allowing the individual to mature psychologically and spiritually.

Psychological growth is promoted because when the mind is brought under control, the intellect becomes clear and psychological complexes such as anxiety and other delusions, which have an effect even in ordinary people, can be cleared up. Control of the mind and the promotion of internal harmony allow the meditator to integrate their personality and to resolve the hidden issues of the present, of childhood and of past lives.

When the mind has been brought under control, the expansion in consciousness leads to the discovery that one's own individual consciousness is not the total experience of consciousness. Through the correct practice of meditation, the individual's consciousness-awareness expands to the point wherein there is a discovery that one is more than just an individual. The state of "automatic consciousness" becomes reduced in favor of the experiences of increasing levels of continuous awareness. In other words, there is a decrease in daydreaming as well as the episodes of carrying out activities and forgetting oneself in them until they are finished (driving for example). Also, there is a reduced level of loss of awareness of self during the dreaming-sleep and dreamless-sleep states. Normally, most people at a lower level of consciousness-awareness become caught in a swoon or feinting effect which occurs at the time when one "falls" asleep or when there is no awareness of dreams while in the deep sleep state (dreamless-sleep). This swooning effect causes an ordinary person to lose consciousness of their own "waking state" identity and to assume the identity of their "dream subject" and thus, to feel that the dream subject as well as the dream world are realities in themselves.

This shift in identification from the waking personality to the dream personality to the absence of either personality in the dreamless-sleep state led ancient philosophers to discover that these states are not absolute realities. Philosophically, anything that is not continuous and abiding cannot be considered as real. Only what exists and does not change in all periods of time can be considered as "real." Nothing in the world of human experience qualifies as real according to this test. Nature, the human body, everything has a beginning and an end. Therefore, they are not absolutely real. They appear to be real because of the limited mind and senses along with the belief in the mind that they are real. In other words, people believe that matter and physical objects are real even though modern physics has proven that all matter is not "physical" or "stable." It changes constantly and its constituent parts are in reality composed of "empty spaces." Think about it. When you fall asleep, you "believe" that the dream world is "real" but upon waking up you believe it was not real. At the same time, when you fall asleep, you forget the waking world, your relatives and life history, and assume an entirely new history, relatives, situations and world systems. Therefore, philosophically, the ordinary states of consciousness, which a human being experiences, are limited and illusory. The waking, dream and dreamless-sleep states are only transient expressions of the deeper underlying consciousness. This underlying consciousness which witnesses the other three states is what Carl Jung referred to as the "Collective Unconscious." In Indian Philosophy this "fourth" state of consciousness-awareness is known as *Turia.* It is also referred to as "God Consciousness" or "Cosmic Consciousness." The corresponding terms in Kemetic philosophy are, *Nhast,* spiritual resurrection or *Maak-heru* –spiritual victory.

The theory of meditation is that when the mind and senses are controlled and transcended, the awareness of the transcendental state of consciousness becomes evident. From here, consciousness-awareness expands, allowing the meditator to discover the latent abilities of the unconscious mind. When this occurs, an immense feeling of joy emerges from within, the desire for happiness and fulfillment through external objects and situations dwindles and a peaceful, transcendental state of mind develops. Also, the inner resources are discovered which will allow the practitioner to meet the challenges of life (disappointments, disease, death, etc.) while maintaining a poised state of mind.

When the heights of meditative experience are reached, there is a more continuous form of awareness, which develops. It is not *lost* at the time of falling asleep. At this stage there is a discovery that just as the dream state is discovered to be "unreal" upon "waking up" in the morning, the waking state is also discovered to be a kind of dream which is transcended at the time of "falling asleep." There is a form of "continuous awareness" which develops in the mind, which spans all three states of consciousness, and becomes a "witness" to them instead of a subject bound by them.

Further, there is a discovery that there is a boundless source from which one has originated and to which one is inexorably linked. This discovery brings immense peace and joy wherein the worldly desires vanish in the mind and there is absolute contentment in the heart. This level of experience is what the Buddhists call *Mindfulness.* However, the history of mindfulness meditation goes back to the time of ancient India and Ancient Egypt. In India, the higher level of consciousness wherein automatic consciousness is eradicated and there is continuous awareness is called *Sakshin Buddhi.* From Vedanta and Yoga Philosophy, the teaching of the "witnessing consciousness" found even greater expression and practice in Buddhist philosophy and Buddhist meditation. Buddhi or higher intellect is the source of the word *Buddha,* meaning one who has attained wakefulness at the level of their higher intellect. The corresponding terms relating to "witnessing consciousness" in Kemetic philosophy is *Amun* -"witnessing consciousness" or "witnessing Self or Divinity" and *Shetaut Neter* – "Hidden innermost Divinity."

Informal Meditation: The Meditative Lifestyle

Meditation is not just an exercise that is to be practiced only at a certain time or at a certain place. In order for your meditative efforts to be successful, the philosophy of meditation must become an integral part of your life. This means that the meditative way of life, the Smai Tawi lifestyle, must become the focus of your life no matter what else is going on in your life. Most people who do not practice mystical spirituality cannot control the clamoring thoughts of the mind and because of this, do not experience inner peace or clarity of purpose in life; the teachings cannot help them. Others, beset by intensely negative thoughts, succumb to these and commit acts against their conscience, and suffer the consequences of a self-defeating way of life wherein painful situations and disappointments in life are increased, while happiness and contentment are decreased. The mind is weakened due to the mental energy being wasted in useless endeavors, which only serve to further entangle one in complex relationships and commitments. Another source of weakening one's will to act correctly to promote situations of advancement and happiness is caused by the susceptibility to negative emotions. Negative emotions such as anger, hatred, greed, gloom, sorrow, and depression as well as excessive positive emotions such as elation, serve to create mental agitation and desire which in turn cloud the intellectual capacity to make correct decisions in life.

When life seems unbearable due to the intensification of negative emotions and the obscuring of the intellectual capacity, some people commit suicide in an attempt to escape or end the painful onslaught of uncontrollable thoughts. Still others prefer to ignore the messages from the deeper Self which are beckoning them to move toward introspection. Situations of stress in life are motivators, the purpose of which is to turn you away from the outer world, because you have lost your balance. There is a place for material wealth and sensual experience (outer experiences of the senses), however, when the inner reality is ignored or when inner needs and inner development is impaired due to excess concentration on worldly goals and desires, then experiences of frustration and disappointment occur. If these situations are understood as messages from nature to pull back and find the inner balance, then personality integration and harmony can be discovered. However, if these times are faced with lack of inner strength, then they lead to suffering. Sometimes there are moments of clarity wherein the Higher Self is perceived in an intuitive flash, but people usually tend to discount the occurrence as a coincidence or other curious event while others, in bewilderment, believe they are going mad. Others prefer to ignore the issue of spirituality altogether and simply shun any thoughts about death or the afterlife. This is a reverse-spiritual movement that stunts spiritual evolution. Its root cause is fear of the unknown and fear of letting go. The practice of yogic meditation techniques can serve to counteract any and all negative developments in the mind if the correct techniques are used and the correct understanding is adopted.

There are four main components of meditation. These are: posture, breath-life force control, sound and visualization. In the beginning stages of practice, these components may be somewhat difficult to perform with consistency and coordination, but with continued effort, they become a pleasurable experience which will bring you closer to your awareness of your Self. It is difficult to control the mind in the beginning. Many aspirants lose heart because they have not obtained the results they had anticipated. They either quit prematurely or jump to different techniques without giving sufficient time for the exercises to work. They do not understand that although on occasion, profound changes will occur in a short time, for the most part it's a gradual process.

A meditative lifestyle should be developed along with one's formal meditation practices. This means acting in such a way that there is greater and greater detachment from objects and situations and greater independence and peace within. This can only occur when there is a keen understanding of one's deeper Self and the nature of the world of human experience, along with formal meditation practices and other activities which promote physical health (diet and exercise). Ordinarily, people "do" things in order to gain some objective or to derive some pleasure or reward. From a mystical perspective, they are "doers of action." They act out of the unconscious and subconscious desires arising in the mind at any given time and are thus, beset with a perpetual state of unrest and agitation. The meditative way of life means that your actions are always affirmations of your higher knowledge and awareness, and not based on the unconscious desires and emotions of the mind. Perfection in this discipline only comes with practice. When this art is perfected, the practitioner is referred to as a "non-doer." This is because even though they may be doing many things in their life, in reality they have discovered that the true rewards of life do not depend on the outcome of an activity, its fruit or reward.

Thus, true peace and inner fulfillment will never come through pursuit of actions when there is an expectation or desire for the fruits of those actions. The belief in objects or worldly activities as a source of happiness is therefore seen as a state of *ignorance* wherein the individual is caught up in the *illusions*, *fantasies* and *fanciful notions* of the mind. However, happiness and peace can arise spontaneously when there is an attitude of detachment and dispassion toward objects and situations in life. If actions are performed with the idea of discovering peace within based on the understanding of the philosophy outlined above, and for the sake of the betterment of society, then these actions will have the effect of purifying the heart of the individual. The desires and expectations will dwindle while the inner fulfillment and awareness of the present moment will increase. There will be greater and greater discovery of peace within, a discovery of what is truly stable and changeless within as opposed to the mind and outer world, which are constantly changing and unpredictable. Along with this there is greater effectiveness and perfection in one's actions.

Actions of any type will always lead to some result. However, this result is not as predictable as people have come to believe. In reality, the only thing a human being can control is the action itself, and not the fruits of the action. If there is concentration on the action without desire or expectation of the fruits of the action, then there can be peace and contentment even while the action is being performed. This is the way of the non-doer. Actions performed with expectations and desire are the way of the doer. The non-doer is free from the fruits because he or she is free from desires and expectations while the doer is dependent on the actions and is bound to the results, be they positive or negative. When desires and expectation in the mind are resolved, the mind becomes calm and peaceful. Under these conditions, the non-doer is free from elation or depression because his or her pleasure is coming from the present action in the present moment, promoting concentration of mind and expansion in consciousness. The actions are no longer based on memories of the past of pleasurable situations, which are impelling a movement to repeat those activities, or on expectations for future activities which will somehow bring happiness. The non-doer, not being bound to the memories or to the expectations is not bound by either the past or the future, and thereby discovers an eternal present. The doer is always caught up in the past or the present and thereby loses the opportunity to discover peace and true happiness. This is the condition of most people in the world. Before they realize it their entire life has gone by without their being aware of the passage of time. The art of true spiritual life leads one to detach from the world even while continuing to live in it and thereby to discover the hidden inner spiritual dimensions of the unconscious mind and what lies beyond. The doer is always bound to a form of experience which is determined by and bound to the world of time and space, because only in time and space can there manifest the memories of the past and the expectations for the future. The non-doer eventually discovers a transcendental experience of expanding consciousness in the present moment.

The philosophy of meditation may seem foreign to you at first but if you reflect upon it you will discover that it holds great truth as well as great potential to assist you in discovering abiding peace and harmony in your life. When you begin to practice and discover how wonderful it is to be in control of your mind instead of being prey to the positive or negative emotions and desires, you will discover an incomparable feeling, which goes beyond the ordinary concept of happiness. As with other human endeavors, in order to gain success you need to study the philosophy intensively with great concentration, and then practice it in your day to day life. Treat it as an experiment. The world and your life will not go away. Just ask yourself: What would happen if I were to become less attached and more in control of my mind? Follow the teachings and discover the inner resources you need to discover true happiness and to overcome the obstacles of life.

The practice of meditation requires regular and sustained practice. Failure is assured if there is no effort. Likewise, success is assured if there is sustained, regular effort. This is the key to accomplishing any goal in life and, enlightenment, is a goal like any other, albeit the highest goal. With respect to attaining the goal of enlightenment, all other goals are like dust blowing in the wind. The following instruction will serve as guidelines for meditation and is not intended to be a substitute for a competent instructor. There are many techniques of meditation. Here we will focus on basic techniques of "moving" meditations for initially calming the mind of the beginning practitioner. For more on the philosophy of Kemetic meditation and meditation instructions see the books *Meditation: The Ancient Egyptian Path to Enlightenment* and *The Glorious Light Meditation System of Ancient Egypt*–both by Muata Ashby

> **"I am steadfast, child of the steadfast One, conceived and born in the region of steadfastness. "**
>
> From the Egyptian
> Book of Coming Forth By Day

Formal Meditation Practice

Formal meditation practice means taking out a special time to turn away from the world, to sit in quiet contemplation and using special rituals such as burning incense, lighting a candle, uttering prayers, etc., in a special area chosen for this regular practice. First, locate an area of your home where you can perform spiritual practices such as Yoga exercises, prayers and meditations and not be disturbed. This area will be used only for Yoga practice. Gather the basic materials needed to create your own meditation area. An altar is a place of worship that contains certain artifacts that hold specific spiritual symbolism that lead to spiritual awareness. They do not need to have a specific religious affiliation. However, they should have spiritual significance. This will help to draw the mind away from worldly thoughts and lead it towards concentration on higher (spiritual) thoughts. The following items are to be considered as a basic listing of items. You are free to choose other items that resonate with your spiritual consciousness.

1- **Small table**

2- **Candle** - The candle holds deep mystical symbolism. It contains within itself all of the four elements of creation: fire, earth (wax in solid form), water (wax in liquefied form), and air. All are consumed in the burning process and all of them come together to produce light. This singular light represents the singular consciousness that shines throughout the entire universe. This light is the illumination that causes life to exist and it is the reason and source of the human mind. This light is life itself and life is God. Therefore, God is ever present in the candle, in the universe (nature) and in your heart and mind.

3- **Incense** - Incense invokes divine awareness through the sense of smell. When you perform spiritual practices and use a special incense consistently, every time that you smell the incense you will have divine thoughts and feelings even if you are not in the regular area of meditation. Therefore, select a fragrance that appeals to you and reflect within yourself that this is the fragrance of God in the same way as a flower emanates fragrance. Visualize that you are smelling divinity itself.

4- **Icon-** A picture, sculpture or other symbol of a Deity (as a symbol of the Supreme Being). This may be an Ancient Egyptian Deity such as Horus, Isis, etc., a Christian Icon such as Jesus or Mary, an Eastern icon such as Buddha (Buddhist), or Krishna, Rama or Saraswati of the Vedantic-Hindu tradition, etc. Choose an icon according to your spiritual inclination. This will help you to develop devotion toward the Divine and will hasten your progress in yoga. This is called worship of God with name and form. As you progress you will be instructed on how to worship the Divine in an abstract way without using any names or forms.

Rituals Associated With Meditation Practice

In the beginning the mind may be difficult to control. What is needed here is perseverance and the application of the techniques described here. Another important aid to meditation is ritualism. You should observe a set of rituals whenever you intend to practice meditation. These will gradually help to settle the mind even before you actually sit to practice the meditation. They are especially useful if you are a busy person or if you have many thoughts or worries on the mind. First take a bath. Water is the greatest cleanser of impurities. In ancient times the practitioners of Yoga would bathe before entering the temples and engaging in the mystery rituals. This practice has been kept alive in the Christian practice of baptism and the prayers using the Holy Water.

Once you have bathed, put on clothing that you have specifically reserved for the practice of meditation. This will have a strong effect on your mind and will bring meditative vibrations to you because the clothing will retain some of the subtle essence of the meditation experience each time you use them. The clothing should be loose and comfortable. It is recommended that you wear 100% Cotton or Silk because these are natural materials that will allow the skin to breath and feel comfortable. Keep the clothing clean and use the same style of clothing for your meditation practice.

When you are ready, go to your special room or corner that you have set aside for meditation. Take the phone off the hook or turn off the ringer and close the door behind you, leaving instructions not to be disturbed for the period of time you have chosen. When you sit for meditation, light a candle and some incense of your choice and then choose a comfortable position.

Posture for Meditation

Before you begin, practice some light physical exercises (yoga, tai chi, etc.) for several minutes. This will serve to free up any energy blockages and wake up the mind by stimulating the circulation of the vital forces within the body.

Now choose a comfortable posture. If you consistently practice meditation, you will gradually be able to stay in one position for longer periods of time. If you practice regularly, you will discover that your body will develop a daily rhythm that will be conducive to your meditation time.

Posture is one of the main components of the meditation practice. Maintain the back straight either sitting on the floor in the cross-legged posture (Lotus), or sitting in a chair with feet on the floor or lying on your back on the floor in the corpse-mummy pose (without falling asleep). This text prescribes a sitting position that is most comfortable for you which does not allow you to fall asleep. All the members of the body, the arms, legs, etc. should be motionless.

Tips for Formal Meditation Practice

Begin by meditating for 5 minutes each day, gradually building up the time. The key is consistency in time and place. Nature inspires us to establish a set routine to perform our activities; the sun rises in the east and sets in the west every day; the moon's cycle is every 28 days and the seasons change approximately at the same times of the year, every year. It is better to practice for 5 minutes each day than 20 minutes one day and 0 minutes the next. Do a formal sit down meditation whenever the feeling comes to you but try to do it at least once a day, preferably between 4-6 am or 6-8 pm. Do not eat for at least 2 hours before meditation. It is even more preferable to not eat 12 hours before. For example: eat nothing (except only water or tea) after 6 p.m. until after meditation at 6 a.m. the following morning. Do not meditate within 24 hours of having sexual intercourse. Meditate alone in a quiet area, in a dimly lit room (candlelight is adequate). Do light exercise (example: Kemetic Thef Neteru, Chi Kung or Hatha Yoga) before meditating, then say Hekau (affirmations, prayers, mantras, etc.) for a few minutes to set up positive vibrations in the mind. Burning your favorite incense is a good way to set the mood. Keep a ritualistic procedure about the meditation time. Do things in a slow, deliberate manner, concentrating on every motion and every thought you perform.

When ready, try to focus the mind on one object, symbol or idea such as the heart or Hetep (Supreme Peace). If the mind strays, bring it back gently. Patience, self-love and self-forgiveness are the keys here. Gradually, the mind will not drift towards thoughts or objects of the world. It will move towards subtler levels of consciousness until it reaches the source of the thoughts and there commune with that source, The Self. This is the desired positive movement of the practice of meditation because it is from The Self that all inspiration, creativity and altruistic feelings of love come. The Self is the source of peace and love and is who you really are.

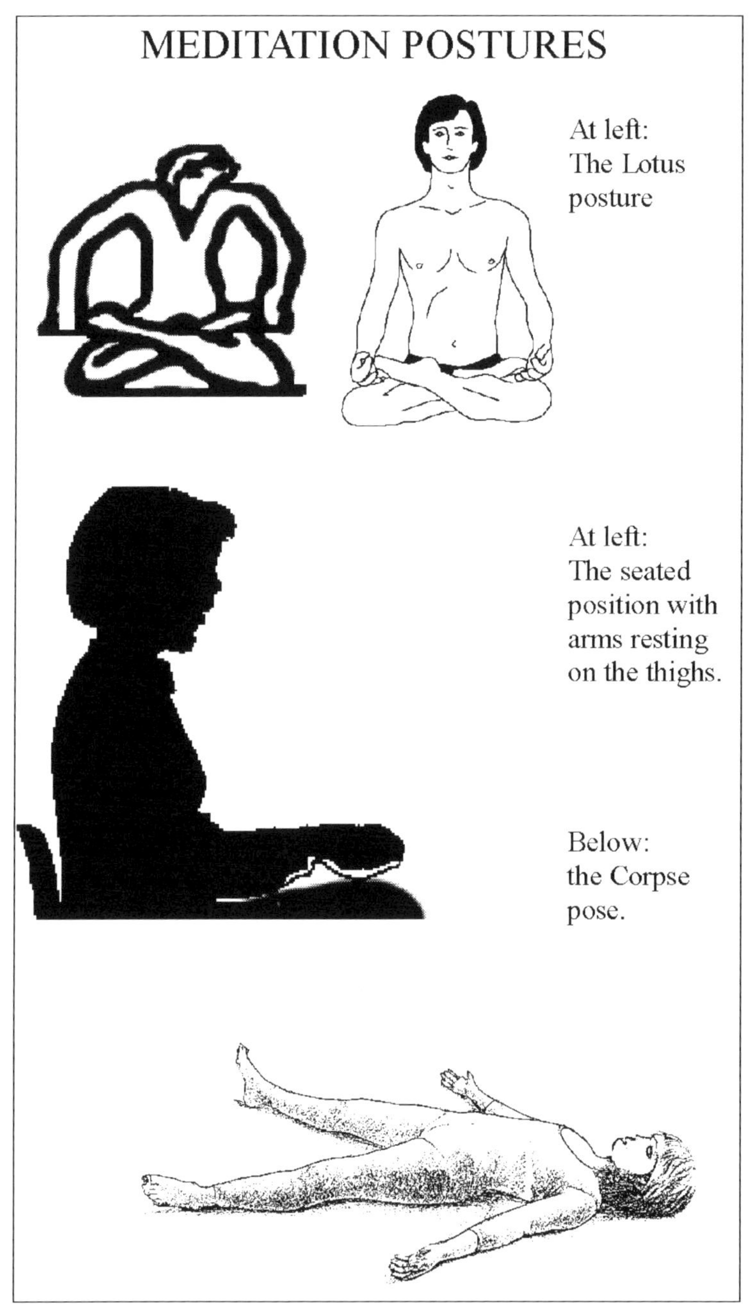
MEDITATION POSTURES
At left:
The Lotus
posture
At left:
The seated
position with
arms resting
on the thighs.
Below:
the Corpse
pose.

SIMPLE MEDITATION TECHNIQUE

Modern scientific research has proven that one of the most effective things anyone can do to promote mental and physical health is to sit quietly for 20 minutes twice each day. This is more effective than a change in diet, vitamins, food supplements, medicines, etc. It is not necessary to possess any special skill or training. All that is required is that one achieves a relaxed state of mind, unburdened by the duties of the day. You may sit from a few minutes up to an hour in the morning and in the late afternoon.

This simple practice, if followed each day, will promote above average physical health and spiritual evolution. One's mental and emotional health will be maintained in a healthy state as well. The most important thing to remember during this meditation time is to just relax and not try to stop the mind from pursuing a particular idea but also not trying to actively make the mind pursue a particular thought or idea. If a Hekau (Prayer) is recited, or if a special hieroglyph is meditated upon, the mind should not be forced to hold it. Rather, one should direct the mind and when one realizes that one has been carried away with a particular thought, bring the mind gently back to the original object of meditation, in this way, it will eventually settle where it feels most comfortable and at peace.

Sometimes one will know that one has been carried away into thoughts about what one needs to do, or who needs to be called, or is something burning in the kitchen?, etc. These thoughts are worldly thoughts. Simply bring the mind back to the original object of meditation or the hekau. With more practice, the awareness of the hekau or object of meditation (candle, mandala, etc.) will dissipate as you go deeper. This is the positive, meditative movement that is desired. The goal is to relax to such a degree that the mind drifts to deeper and deeper levels of consciousness, finally reaching the source of consciousness, the source of all thought; then the mind transcends even this level of consciousness and there, communes with the Absolute Reality, Neter. This is the state of "Cosmic Consciousness," the state of enlightenment. After a while, the mental process will remain at the Soul level all the time. This is the Enlightened Sage Level.

SLOWNESS MEDITATION METHOD

The Slowness Meditation Exercise is one of the easiest forms of practice to control the mind. As we discussed earlier, the ordinary human mind is in a constant state of motion. This motion originates from the desires which constantly compel the mind to think about ideas and how to acquire the objects it wants. These techniques are similar to the Chi Kung, Indian Yoga and Buddhist mindfulness visualizations which are designed to help you develop an awareness of the automatic consciousness so that you may gain control of your mindless tendencies. Since speed and constant movement are the main components of mindlessness or the automatic conscious state, the Slowness exercise is designed to gradually assist you in slowing yourself down at a physical, mental and finally the spiritual level. It makes use of three major components. These are 1-slowness, 2-silence, and 3- steadfastness.

Slowing the mind and body to allows concentration and meditation during any task at any time.

Silencing the body to hear the voice of NETER (GOD), the inner Self.

Steadfastness is keeping the idea ever present in the mind that you are a immortal and eternal being, made and given life by your Father-Mother CREATOR to experience the joy of living by remembering who you are, thereby becoming a God(dess) yourself.

"As You Believe So Shall You Become."

After a while, these ideas and practices will stay with you, even during your non-meditation time. You will become more conscious during work, play and other activities. Whenever possible, attempt a formal sit down meditation. The slowness exercise along with an integrated program of a vegetarian diet, reduced television or movie watching and reduced talking (eventually keeping silence for a minimum of 1 hour a day) will help calm down the restlessness which leads to the constant seeking of "fun" outside of one's self. Keeping the Highest Teaching or the Steadfast idea in one's mind at all times is also a form of meditation. You will gradually break down the illusion of what the world appears to be and gradually see it for what it is: your - Self.

Slowness- Stage One

Find a quiet room or area and with total silence proceed as follows:

The object is to train the mind to be one pointed and relaxed and to SLOW IT DOWN so as to be able to concentrate on one thing at a time.
The main activity on which one will concentrate is movement, but it MUST be slow... so slow as to be almost still.

While moving a particular limb or body part, concentrate on every movement. Every time you move a limb (i.e. arm, leg, etc.), THINK:

"Now I am moving my arm *."

*(you may move any body part, i.e. leg, arm, etc.)

Witness every movement and feel every time you take a step. Every time a limb moves concentrate on it. If something in the room catches your attention, look at it and think:

"Now I am looking at that."

You may walk in a circle, across the room, back and forth or stand in one spot and move a limb up and down. Use any movement you choose as long as it is quiet and "SLOW."

Practice this exercise for five minutes at a time gradually building up to as long a time as is comfortable. You may need to practice this stage for several days or weeks until you become aware of every movement with increasing serenity of mind. Practice daily, even if it's just five minutes a day.

Slowness-Stage Two

After some time of practicing Stage One, you will feel a new consciousness above your regular "automatic" "every day" consciousness. You will begin to feel you are living more in the moment, being more conscious of what is going on every second. This process is sometimes referred to as "Mindfulness" or "The Witness." This is the Amun consciousness that is the underlying essence of your soul. You will become more aware of your every action.

Witness: You will gradually feel you are a spectator, watching yourself perform as if in a grand theatrical show or movie.

Now carry on the slow movements as in Stage One and adjust the mental attitude as follows:

The object in Stage One was to help your Ba (soul-spirit) catch up with the mind and to slow the mind down. Now we will attempt to get ahead of the mind by controlling and directing the action.

Instead of noticing you are moving, now you will direct the movements by:

1- Starting from motionless state.
2- Decide what movement, direction and limb to move.

3- Then **BEFORE** you allow any movement, say mentally: "Now I'm going to move my arm up," "Now I'm going to touch the light switch," "Now I'm going to lift my right leg to step forward," etc.

Slowness- Stage Three

Here, the emphasis will be on motion as before but unlike the previous stages, the motion will be "mental."

Sit in a chair or on the floor in any comfortable pose or lay flat on your back. Regardless of the position you choose, the most important thing is keeping the back straight so that all energy centers can flow freely.

Remain completely motionless during this exercise. Now visualize yourself getting up, walking and moving as before, very slowly and deliberately. See the movement in your mind before it occurs and then send the command to your subtle body. See it moving about slowly according to your direction while you remain motionless in your meditative position. Do not allow any movement to escape your attention. Take notice of every single motion that is performed, no matter how slight.

Slowness-Stage Four

Remain motionless as in stage three. Visualize yourself traveling to far off lands, planets and universes. Imagine yourself communing with nature from the deepest recesses of the ocean to the farthest reaches of outer space - keeping motionless all throughout the exercise. Remain motionless for up to an hour and develop an awareness of yourself apart from the body. See yourself as being outside of the body and look on it as the "doer" of things in the world of time and space while "you" are the bystander who is watching the activities in the drama of the life of your body.
Meditate thus: "I am not that body, I am the spirit, immortal, eternal am I, the body dies but I live on for all eternity." "The body is not me!"

As you progress in this exercise, you will transcend the level of mental visualization. Your subtle astral body will actually leave your physical body and experience the disembodied state. At this Astral level of existence wherein the body is transcended, there is only awareness of the mind and senses.

Slowness-Stage Five

Now remain absolutely motionless. Do not move your physical or astral body. You will begin to see that even the astral body is not the real you. You will begin to experience an awareness of being and existing devoid of your astral body. See your thoughts as they move across the firmament of your mind coming out of eternity and going back to eternity from whence they arose. Do not attempt to hold onto them. Simply observe them. This is absolute motionlessness. The real you is the motionless witness to all of the thoughts of the mind and the actions of the body. This absolute witnessing consciousness is known as Amun or (Asar) and it is the support of all mental activity and all physical reality.

As you progress further, you will experience all pervasiveness, a oneness with all things. There will not be any place or thing wherein you are not. There will be an experience of pure consciousness. This pure consciousness is the soul and as you abide in your soul consciousness, your awareness expands until you discover that you are one with universal consciousness, God. This is the highest stage of experience wherein you strip yourself of all physical or mental actions. These actions are known as karma and when you do not identify with your pure, detached Self, you fall into identification with your thoughts and actions. This identification with your thoughts and actions which results from forgetfulness of your true Self is known as "ignorance." Therefore, true knowledge means detaching from the part of yourself that is involved in actions (thoughts, sense perceptions and physical movement) and discovering the silent, witnessing consciousness, and then consciously abiding in this knowledge regardless of the thoughts and actions you may find yourself performing in your daily life. This stage of spiritual practice is known as performing action while not performing action. This is Enlightenment. You are now steadfast or established in your essential nature, the Divine Self!

There are Ancient Egyptian hieroglyphs which portray the different parts of the human being such as the soul, the shadow, the Ka, etc. separating from the body of the initiate. This is an advanced portrayal of the concept of mystical self-discovery. The process of actually experiencing the different aspects of your being and realizing that you are not just a physical body and finite, mortal personality, is what opens the door to your discovering the true Self within you. In this manner, "out of body" experiences and experiences that transcend consciousness of even the astral body, lead to the discovery of existence without your mind and senses. When this level of experience is reached, you have attained true and absolute knowledge. In contrast, knowledge that was gained through the study of the teachings and the various other practices was indirect and incomplete. This is the highest goal of meditation, to assist you to go deeper within your own being and to help you discover that part of yourself, which you are not aware of.

Secrets of Longevity of Body Mind and Soul

What is the secret of longevity? We are constantly bombarded by the media, induced by the medical establishment's false claims that people are living longer, healthier lives. Yet, if we examine the statistics we will discover that this is actually the reverse. Prior to the advent of processed, chemicalized foods in the 20th century, humanity suffered from plagues, etc. In addition, many children died at birth and due to infectious diseases, and also many mothers died in childbirth, Today we have many machines that artificially prolong life. Two examples of such machines are artificial hearts, and kidney dialysis machines. Indeed the population of the world has increased not due to the improvement of life due to medical science, but to improved hygiene and first aid emergency assistance as well as artificial means that have allowed more people to survive the birthing process, better hygiene and artificial life support machines.

There are recorded cases of people, even in ancient times, who survived to be 100 years old and beyond. Currently less than 1% of the world's population reach that age, and the quality of life of those who grow old is dismal at best.

So how did the ancients do it? First of all they lived on whole foods and not denatured, chemicalized, processed foods. They also got plenty of sunshine and they breathed plenty of fresh air. Changing to a vegetable and fruit diet, a diet that is high in nutrition and low in calories, allows the body to live off of the necessary amount of food and not overwork the metabolism, which will cause the body to wear out sooner as it must work hard to process the excess calories from junk foods, candies, sodas, etc.

Also, it is important to reduce the stress of modern life. Thus it is necessary to work with the mind and develop a coping method that allows us to understand the world and our place in it without becoming frustrated and stressed. The disciplines of mind allow us to do this. Finally the spiritual outlook on life needs to be positive. Here the disciplines of spiritual evolution are necessary to bring the soul into harmony with the cosmic order. In this manner the personality is vibrating on all three levels (body, mind and soul) in synchronization and peace. This allows the personality to become elevated and wise, bringing meaning to the purpose of life. Therefore, the kind if diet advocated in this book is the way to pristine health and a fruitful old age.

HETEP!
(Peace)

The Holistic Guide to Food For the Body, Mind and Soul

THE KEMETIC DIET PROGRAM

By
Dr. Muata Abhaya Ashby

The following is a summary of the essential principles of the Kemetic Diet Health System, based on the Ancient Egyptian teachings of Health. These were extracted from the book *The Kemetic Diet, Food for Body, Mind and Soul* by Dr. Muata Ashby, which is a study of (Ancient African) practices and writings in the area of preventative health and healing, engendered by the first medical doctors in history…the *Sunus* or Kemetic (Ancient Egyptian) physicians.

Health For Body, Mind and Soul

The main principles of the Kemetic Diet encompass the understanding that the personality is a complex which includes, but is not limited to, the physical constitution. As such a human being requires more than just physical nourishment in order to survive and thrive as a healthy person. Therefore, a protocol has been enjoined to promote the purity of the body, mind and soul. There is a proper type of food for the body, a proper type of food for the mind and a proper type of food for the soul. If any of these foods are missing a human being will be malnourished and the personality will develop spiritual, mental or physical ailments.

Kemetic Principles of Disease and Health: *Ukhedu, Mettu* and *Swadj*

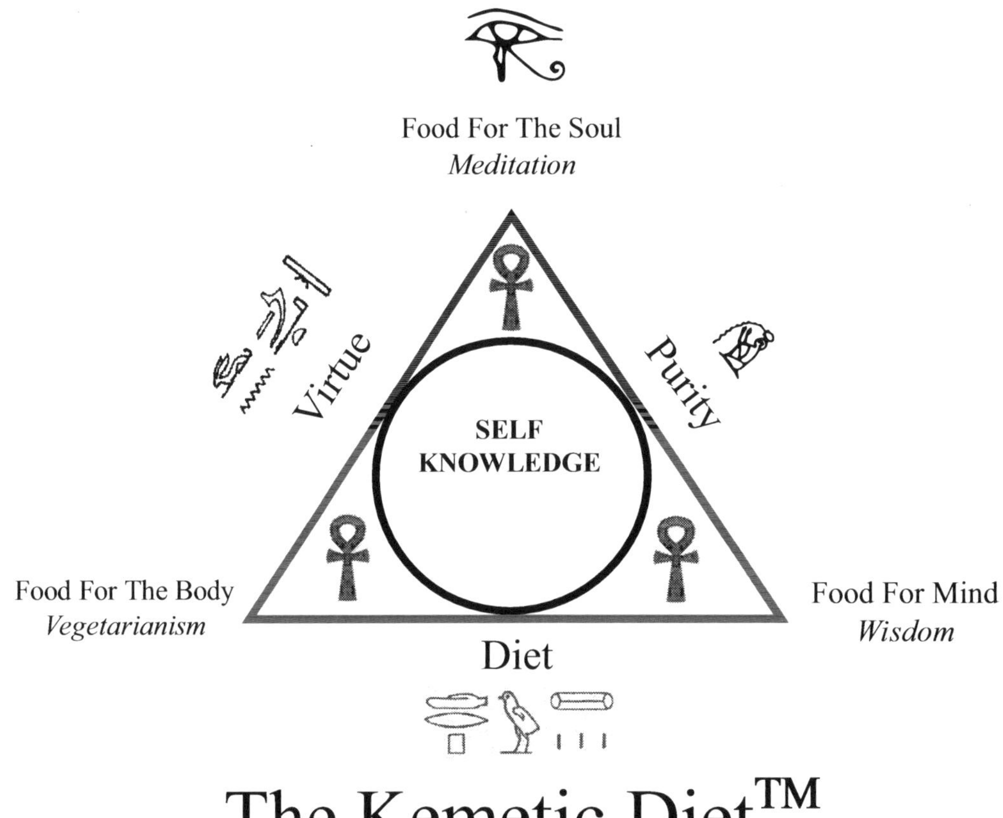

The Kemetic Diet™

The Kemetic Diet

The Ancient Egyptian concept of physical disease holds that it is due to indigestion. That is, some impurity has been digested that compromises the digestive system, which in turn deposits impurities into the *Mettu* or vascular systems. This has the effect of weakening the immune system. This process is called *Ukhedu*. The way to restore health is by *Swadj* or cleansing the mettu, to make it green again. This greening is accomplished by means of a vegetarian diet. However, there are obstructions for the mind and soul and a human being is not considered healthy until all the "bodies" (physical, mental and causal) are restored to their original state. The cleaning of the mind and soul requires a different kind of greening. All of this process leads to *Ankh, OOdja, Seneb* or Life, Vitality and Health.

Indigestion leads to malnutrition and malnutrition leads to the development of disease. Malnutrition, that is, ingesting foods and products that are poisonous or not getting sufficient nutrients for the proper functioning of the body, is the cause of Ukhedu (disease process). Ukhedu leads to mucus formation and this ukhedu, or the "disease process" as it was referred to by the doctors in ancient times, is commonly referred to by modern day wholistic health practitioners as "acidosis." So malnutrition and toxins in and around the body lead to acidosis, and acidosis leads to mucus formation. Mucus formation is a symptom of a disease that has developed to the extent wherein it cannot be contained in the body any longer. Therefore, a poor diet is referred to as a mucus-forming diet. Mucus formation is not a disease but the body's way of getting rid of excess impurities in order to restore health and not drown in the toxic environment. Drugs that suppress mucus are actually causing the body to hoard impurities. These will stay in the body longer, and have more opportunity to cause changes (mutations) in the body that will promote disease in the future.

Food For the Body:

- **Greening of the Body:** Vegetarianism-Veganism (Greening) is the aspect of maintaining physical health as it is the proper diet for the human body as opposed to meat eating (inc. fish and poultry) which is known to be injurious.

- Hygiene is the first important aspect of maintaining physical health since it prevents undue parasites and conditions that promote disease.

- Cleansing the physical body through fasting and diet are integral parts of the Kemetic diet system for those who have ingested items that may compromise the digestive system.

- Uplifting actions and pursuits (virtuous) are important aspects of health maintenance as they allow the body to receive exercise and to refrain from acts that would cause injury and disease. There are three forms of actions: thoughts, words and deeds. Uplifting actions include having a sublime goal in life. Life is more than just the pursuit of pleasures. It is a means to grow and discover abiding and transcendental peace and happiness. A primary means to achieve this is through selfless service to humanity.

Food For the Mind:

- **Lucidity of Mind:** Uplifting teachings cleanse the mind by removing ignorance which leads to unrighteous and harmful actions, and removes the ignorance of self which leads to stress and sorrow.

- Cleansing the mind is enjoined through listening to the teachings (wisdom-reason) of sages and saints and wise people so that the mind may have an altruistic outlook on life.

- Fasting is also to be practiced for the three forms of action (thoughts, words and deeds.).

Food For the Soul:

- **<u>Meditation and inner self-discovery:</u>** The mind that is calm through virtue and reason is capable of scaling the heights of inner self-discovery and higher consciousness. This allows a human being to discover higher forms of fulfillment and happiness in the spirit, which transcends time, space and death itself.

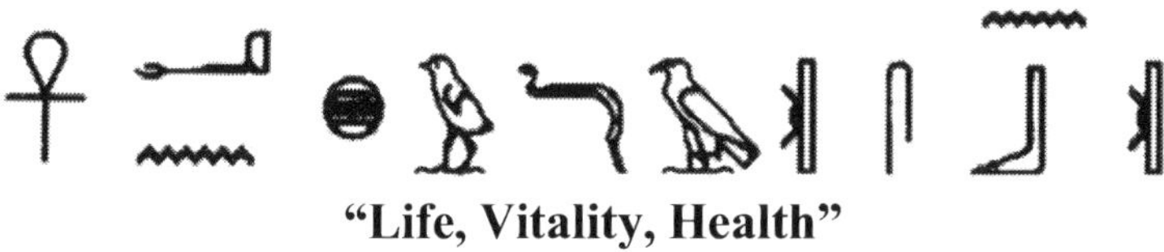

"Life, Vitality, Health"

Diagram Of Food For the Body

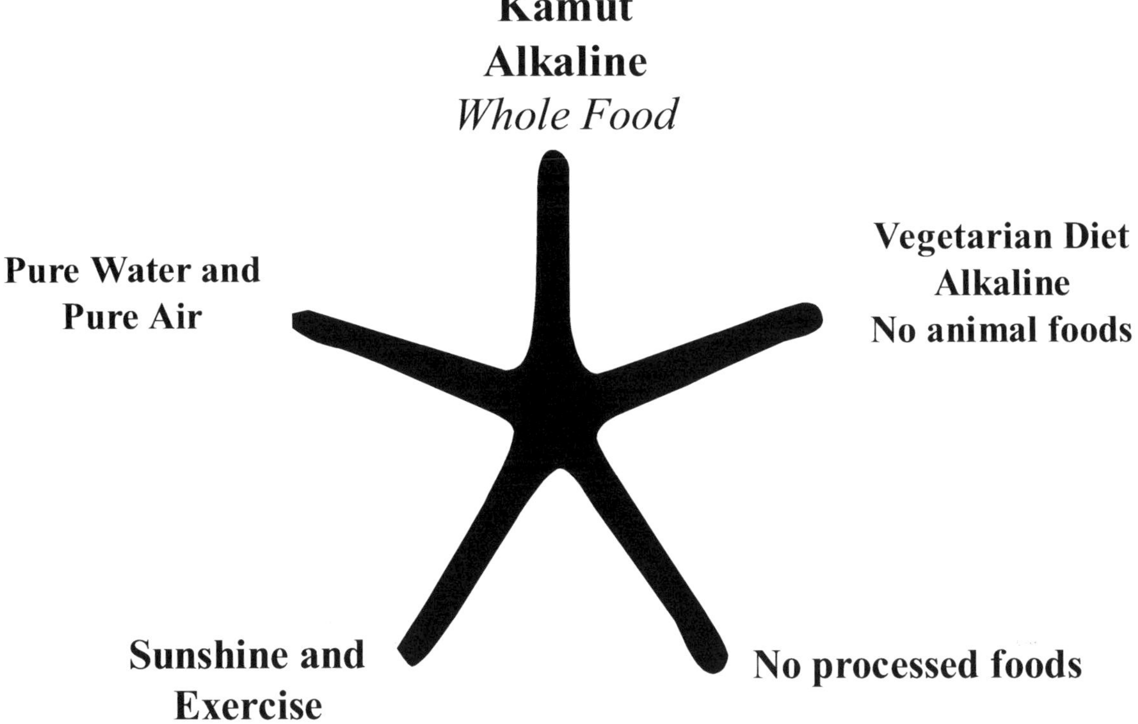

The "Foods For the Body" program has as its basis , the Ancient Egyptian whole food "Kamut," because of its highly nutritive qualities. Taken in juice form, it acts as an alkaline flush for the body to rid it of toxins as it delivers healthy chlorophyll, vitamins and minerals as well as amino acids for healthy cell reconstruction.

Next, it is important to have a plant based (green) diet to acquire the needed chlorophyll, fiber and other nutrients needed by the body. It is important to cut out processed food so as to avoid any more chemicals or denatured foods that will further damage the DNA and lead to degenerative diseases like cancer and heart failure. Pure water is used with the Kamut juice preparation as described earlier and any other preparations consumed, avoiding TDS (total dissolved solids-poisons) placed there during processing. Air is the other essential natural element needed for flushing the body's toxins and providing it with life force and oxygen to survive. Sunshine is also important for producing Vitamin D and inositol triphosphate, (INSP-3). Excersice allows the proper flow of body fluids to occur. This stimulates the systems and organs and aids the flushing of toxins from the body.

THE KEMETIC DIET AND MODERN RESEARCH

Green (Vegetable-Plant) Foods and Juices and Fruit Juices

Green leafy vegetables and Green (vegetable) juices form the foundation of the part of the Kemetic Diet system that relates to "Food for the Body." Many people moving towards a vegetarian diet experience varied changes in their physiology, as well as their sense of well being, depending on where they are coming from in their previous lives. People who have subsisted on a cooked food diet may experience an initial inability to maintain a high level of energy as they had when on the cooked food diet. This is because the body's ability to process the higher quality of fresh diet has been suppressed for so long that it no longer remembers how to handle fresh foods. Sometimes when people are confronted with the loss of energy they reason that it is because the fresh food diet, cannot provide them with the necessary nutritional elements they need, and they make the decision to go back to the cooked food diet and sometimes even further back to the meat based diet. What is actually necessary here is to move forward to a system that will allow the body to receive the nutritional elements. This can be accomplished through green juices. The body may not be able to properly break down the cellulose in the vegetable cells in order to thereby extract the nutritional elements in the vegetables. Juicing vegetables allows the cellulose to be broken down and the nutritional elements (including vitamins and minerals) are made readily available to the body's digestive system.

Many people emphasize fruit juices in their diets, but this can lead to excess sugar in the body that will lead to the formation of acids, thereby promoting disease. There should be a balance between green and fruit juicing and the kinds of fruits used in the juicing should be non-acid forming. for example, lemon juice, though apparently acidic metabolizes to an alkaline and promotes the cleansing of the body by flushing out the impurities. Other fruit juices (coconut, melons, cucumber, etc.) have alkaline properties and should be used accordingly (take at least 1-2 cups per day).

Red Blood Cell

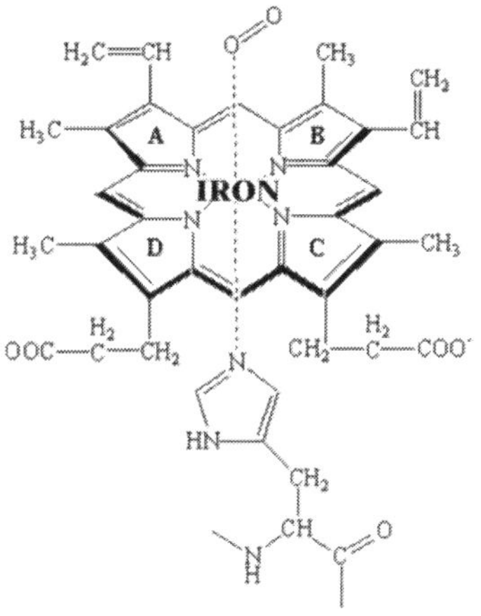

Chlorophyll Molecule

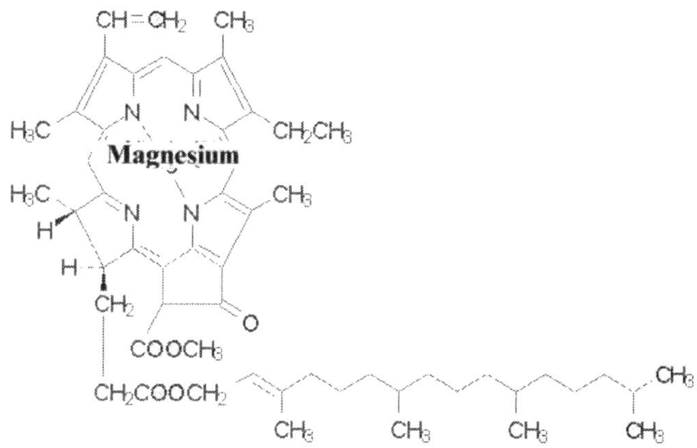

Green foods are essential to the human diet. The green color of plants (the leaves, stems, green fruit) is due to the pigment called chlorophyll which is located within their cells. Chlorophyll has the capacity to absorb light (from the sun) energy and transform it into chemical energy. The chemical energy in chlorophyll is used by human beings and animals to sustain themselves. In other words, human beings derive sustenance from the sun via plants. The molecules in plant chlorophyll and those of human hemoglobin are essentially the same, differing primarily in that chlorophyll carries an atom of Magnesium

(Mg), whereas the hemoglobin molecule carries an atom of Iron (Fe). Thus, the consumption of chlorophyll is a natural way to get the solar energy stored in the vegetables into the human body when they are eaten. The chlorophyll contained in green foods is like "green blood" and thus bolsters the red blood cell count in those who consume it. Some people have even avoided transfusions after consuming vegetable juices. Vegetable juices can also prevent anemia, a pathological deficiency in the oxygen-carrying component of the blood, measured in unit volume concentrations of hemoglobin, red blood cell volume, or red blood cell number.[157]

Due to the fact that fruit juices tend to be higher in sugar content than vegetables, juicing fruits tends to provide a higher concentration of sugars in a smaller serving. This infusion of such concentrated amounts of sugar can lead to acidosis in the body. Therefore, green juices should be emphasized more than fruit juices in general. Also, fruits tend to be acidic and though the body does require some of the elements provided by the fruits, including the acidity, one should take care to maintain the pH balance of the body. Fruits can be useful in preventing and recovering from Hypoglycemia - an abnormally low level of glucose in the blood. In this manner, one should eat fruits that are in season and not when there is an acid imbalance present, i.e. when there is gas in the gastrointestinal tract, mucus, sneezing, cold, etc. At these times, fasting in accordance with the dictates of the body should be allowed, followed by herbal drinks (teas, etc.), green drinks and green foods.

Whole Foods Concentrates and Vitamin Supplements Guidelines

- Taking vitamins and minerals alone cannot promote good health. for this, a "whole food" is necessary. A "whole food" or "superfood" is a food source that provides all of the vitamins, minerals and nutrients needed for the body's functions that the body does not produce itself.

- The preferable method of gaining higher nutrition (necessary vitamins and minerals) is through the consumption of real foods (vegetables), as opposed to synthesized foods (man made products or genetically altered products) or vitamin supplements (synthetic or natural). Food consumption may be of two kinds, solid or liquid.

- It is preferable to consume fresh whole foods as opposed to dried concentrates and vitamin supplements. This is because nutrients are not normally found in nature as dried concentrates (green {vegetable} drink powders that are mixed with water or juice or may be added to salads or other vegetable preparations or as vitamin supplements where elements are present in the form of isolated and synthetic nutrients. Vitamin and mineral substances in the form of isolated and synthetic nutrients do not occur as such in nature, but rather in conjunction with other elements of food. Therefore, vitamin and mineral supplements should be consumed with meals, and not alone. They serve a useful purpose in allowing the user to KNOW they are getting certain nutrients exactly.

- Concentrates make the essence of a food more potent, and can cause an imbalance in the body's systems that can lead to overdosing and imbalance. They can also cause an intense but natural and necessary detoxification event including increased production of mucus and loose stools.

- However, the problem of depleted soil due to over farming, environmental pollutants[158] and other problems have led to the necessity to rely on organic foods and vegetable juicing to concentrate the nutrients found in the depleted vegetables.

---

[157] American Heritage Dictionary

[158] Today, over 1,000,000,000 (one billion) pounds of insecticides are dusted or sprayed on the foods that people in the United States consume every year.

- If regular fresh vegetable juices are available (at least 1 pint {2 cups} every day), the use of vegetable concentrates and vitamin supplements may not be necessary at all.

- When high quality fresh juices are not available to take in the frequency and quantity described above, then whole food vegetable concentrates (juiced vegetables that have been dried and made into a powdered form which is to be mixed with water or juice for consumption) are definitely recommended.

- Kamut Juice is recommended by the Kemetic Diet System. It is a whole food product as opposed to a supplement. Some green powdered drinks offer large quantities of certain vitamins, minerals and chlorophyll, but not a whole range of those plus amino acids and other nutrient building blocks for the cells of the body. Some companies have put together whole food concentrates by combining many different plants because no one of these has all of the necessary ingredients to produce an overall preparation with all of the needed nutrients. This mixing of many different types of plant nutrients poses another question since foods are not found combined in this way in nature. Sometimes such preparations may contain as many as 20-30 different plants. The effect on the body of taking a product which combines so many plants (more than 4-7, even if organic) is of concern. There are certain plant foods that contain most of the needed nutrients and this is logically preferable since that single plant has collected all of those nutrients and has balanced them perfectly Kamut is such a plant, and it is especially highlighted here because not only is a whole food in the sense just described, but also, it is not crossbred or genetically altered or grafted as most, if not all, of the worlds foods are. This is because throughout history Kamut fell into disuse and seeds of the ancient form of the plant remained hidden until the mid 20th century. So it was not exposed to experimentation by modern farming or the evolution through the early industrial era with its intense pollution. Today North American it is cultivated at high elevation on land that up until a few decades ago was a lake in a volcanic region. These conditions rival the ancient soil on the banks of the Nile River, which were replenished by the fertile Nile silt every year as it came down from the mountains of Uganda and Ethiopia. Due to these special circumstances, there is no other food that can match the special qualities of Kamut.

Acidity, Alkalinity and Health

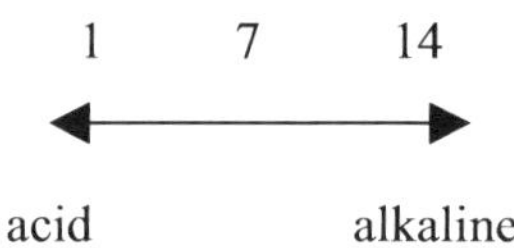

- If one's body pH level falls below the factor 7 (which can be tested with pH sensitive paper to which a small quantity of "fresh" saliva is applied[159], this signals that the body is becoming acidic and that disease process is developing.

Healthy range	Beginning Disease Range	Full Disease Rage
pH 6.6 – 7.4	pH 6.0 – 6.5	pH 4.5 – 5.9

[159] The procedure is to fast (no food or liquid) for 2 hours at least, and then spit out the saliva in one's mouth about 3-4 times before applying the pH paper to one's mouth to contact "fresh" saliva.

- When a disease condition arises one should:
    - cease consumption of acid forming foods and
    - stay on a strict diet of vegetable juices, vegetable juice concentrates and vegetables and
    - consume additional quantities of vitamin and mineral supplements including
        - vegetarian multivitamin
        - antioxidants
        - natural antibiotics (Garlic, Golden Seal, Echinacea, etc.)
        - living water
    - Supplements recommended by Dr. Ashby for use with the Kemetic Diet System are available through the Sema Institute (305) 378-6253 or semayoga@aol.com (see the back section of this book). (Also, see the listing of the supplement contents below.)

The Vegetable Drink Recommended for the Kemetic Diet Program: *Kamut Wheatgrass Juice*

"K A M U TT"

From Ancient Egypt comes an ancient grain to nourish the modern world! *Kamut Wheatgrass Juice* has been selected to fulfill the nutritional requirements of the Kemetic Diet Program. Kamut is a grain that was discovered in the Nile region of Egypt in the 1940's. Lost to history, this grain has been replanted and its health benefits surpass all other wheat. Some of the basic nutritional benefits of Kamut are listed below. It is also safe for those who have allergies to ordinary wheat.

In ancient times the grain was cultivated along the banks of the Nile River in Kamit (Egypt). The rich soil of Kamit, due to the replenishment of nutrients by the Nile and the lack of unrighteous farming practices, which are today being revealed as unhealthy (over-farming, genetic engineering, grafting, hybridizing, etc.), makes Kamut the purest grain on earth. The modern day farmers of this grain have vowed not to compromise this grain in modern times. It is prepared using all possible considerations so that the nutritional and enzymatic values are maintained at their highest possible levels from its harvesting to its bottling for use by the health seeker. Therefore, it is ideal as a staple part of the Kemetic Diet Program, just as it was used by the creators of the Kemetic Diet system in ancient times (over 5,000 years ago).

Other features of this grain include:[160]

[160] Kamut: Ancient Grain, New Cereal by Robert M. Quinn

- The complete nutritional analysis of Kamut brand grain substantiates that it is higher in energy than other wheat. **Compared to common wheat, it is higher in eight out of nine minerals, contains up to 65% more amino acids, and boasts more lipids and fatty acids. The most striking superiority of Kamut brand wheat is found in its protein level—up to 40% higher than the national average for wheat**. Because of its higher percentage of lipids, which produce more energy than carbohydrates, Kamut brand **can be described as a "high energy grain." Athletes, people with busy lives and anyone looking for quality nutrition will find Kamut brand products a valuable addition to their diet.** [161]

- For those suffering wheat sensitivities, Kamut brand products also play a unique role. Recent research by the International Food Allergy Association (IFAA) concluded "For most wheat sensitive people, Kamut grain can be an excellent substitute for common wheat." **Dr. Ellen Yoder, President of IFAA and a team of independent scientists and physicians reached this conclusion through their work with two different wheat sensitive populations—those who have immediate immune responses and those with delayed immune responses. In the delayed immune response group, a remarkable 70% showed greater sensitivity to common wheat than Kamut brand grain. In the immediate immune response group—the severely allergic—70%** had no, or minor, reaction to Kamut brand wheat. However, those with severe allergies should always seek the advice of a physician. Research is now underway in Austria to study gluten intolerance but is yet unfinished so no recommendations can be made for those suffering this affliction. For many wheat sensitive people, however, Kamut brand grain has become "the wheat you can eat." [162]

- May be used safely and effectively by most who have allergies to ordinary wheat.

- May be used safely and effectively by those who have diabetes.

Kamut Wheatgrass Juice:

There are five elements of *Kamut Wheatgrass Juice* which act as catalysts:[163]

Alkaline, Protein, Enzymes, Chlorophyll, Trace Minerals

- *Kamut Wheatgrass Juice* is an Alkaline forming food that does not artificially destroy the body's acids. Instead, it balances them.

- *Kamut Wheatgrass Juice* provides protein-completing factors, all of the eight essential amino acids, as well as a number of free form proteins that are reconfigured and used by the body to create lean connective tissue and enhance reproductive functions.

- *Kamut Wheatgrass Juice* contains enzymes identical to the most powerful and important enzymes manufactured by the body. The function of enzymes as catalysts is undeniable. Since every reaction in the body is triggered by enzymes, those which are taken in by the body as food supplant the need of the body to manufacture its own, therefore reducing a form of stress on the body. Some enzymes are responsible for enhancing the digestive function. Others are free radical scavengers that are similar to those manufactured by the body that have an anti-carcinogenic effect on the body.

[161] ibid
[162] ibid
[163] Green Kamut Corporation

- *Kamut Wheatgrass Juice* is a source of chlorophyll, the most health supporting green food phytochemical. The chlorophyll pigment in plants absorbs light energy, and in the process of photosynthesis whereby Carbon Dioxide (CO2) and water in the presence of the light energy produce organic matter (carbohydrate, sugars), oxygen is also produced and released into the atmosphere. Thus green plants are the planet's oxygen producers, the lifeblood of the planet kingdom. As discussed above, the molecular structure of chlorophyll is strikingly similar to that of Hemoglobin, the protein that makes human blood red. There are perhaps no two more vital elements working in tandem to benefit the human body. Chlorophyll is responsible for the release of oxygen. Hemoglobin captures the oxygen in the lungs and delivers it to the cells. Chlorophyll is known to have enormous benefits as a cleansing, detoxifying, and healing substance. The lists of infections, lesions, and inflammations "cured" by chlorophyll have been chronicled in medical journals for years:In her book "The Hippocrates Diet and Health Program, Dr. Ann Wigmore cites such an example: "In the early part of this century, chlorophyll was regarded as a top-notch weapon in the pharmacopeia[164]. Many physicians used it in the treatment of various complaints such as ulcers and skin disease, and as a pain reliever and breath freshener. One report by Dr. Benjamine Gurskin, then director of experimental pathology at Temple University, was published in the American Journal of Surgery. Dr. Gurskin discussed more than 1000 cases in which various disorders were treated with chlorophyll."

- *Kamut Wheatgrass Juice* contains the necessary trace materials, magnesium, potassium, and chromium without which the body would be prone to a proliferation of various immune, neurological and cardiac diseases. Magnesium activates enzymes that catalyze reactions between phosphate ions and energy to the muscle cells. It is also associated with regulation of body temperature, neuromuscular contraction and synthesis of protein. Potassium is the principle positively charged atom in intracellular fluid and is of primary importance in its maintenance. In conjunction with sodium and chloride, it aids in regulation of osmotic pressure (dissolved fluid absorption into the tissue) and acid-base balance. Chromium, a very hard metallic element, helps regulate metabolism and has recently become the superstar of the weight loss industry.

- *Kamut Wheatgrass Juice* is a potent source of anti-oxidants, alkaline, lightweight protein, chlorophyll, essential fatty acids, trace minerals, friendly bacteria, and key enzymes.

- *Kamut Wheatgrass Juice* causes a series of chemical reactions in the body that cleanse, detoxify, rebuild, and fortify at the cellular level. It helps boost the immune system, increase energy levels, combat fatigue, and most importantly-adds alkalinity to today's highly stressed, over-acidic body systems.

❖ TABLE A: NUTRITIONAL VALUES FOR COMMON WHEAT AND KAMUT BRAND WHEAT

	Common Wheat a.	Kamut Brand Wheat b.
PROXIMATE:		
water	11.5%	9.8%
food energy/100g (calories)	335	359
protein	12.3%	17.3%
total lipid (fat)	1.9%	2.6%
carbohydrate	72.7%	68.2%
crude fiber	2.1%	1.8%
ash	1.66%	1.82%
MINERALS: (mg/100g)		
calcium	30	31

164 A book containing an official list of medicinal drugs together with articles on their preparation and use.

iron	3.9	4.2
magnesium	117	153
phosphorus	396	411
potassium	400	446
sodium	2.0	3.8
zinc	3.2	4.3
copper	0.44	0.46
manganese	3.8	3.2
VITAMINS: (mg/100g)		
thiamin (B1)	0.42	0.45
riboflavin (B2)	0.11	0.12
niacin	5.31	5.54
pantothenic acid	0.91	0.23
vitamin B6	0.35	0.08
folacin	0.0405	0.0375
vitamin E	1.2	1.7
LIPIDS: (g/100g)		
saturated	0.303	0.550
16:0 (palmitic acid) monounsaturated	0.225	0.400
18:1 (oleic acid) polyunsaturated	0.733	1.580
18:2 (linoleic acid)	0.035	0.125
cholesterol 18:3 (linolenic acid)	0.0	0.0
AMINO ACIDS: (g/100g)		
tryptophan	0.194	0.117
threonine	0.403	0.540
isoleucine	0.630	0.600
leucine	0.964	1.23
lysine	0.361	0.440
methionine	0.222	0.250
cystine	0.348	0.58
phenylalanine	0.675	0.85.
tyrosine	0.404	0.430
valine	0.624	0.800
arginine	0.610	0.860
histidine	0.321	0.430
alanine	0.491	0.630
aspartic acid	0.700	0.980
glutamic acid	4.68	5.97
glycine	0.560	0.650
proline	1.50	1.44
serine	0.662	0.930

KAMUT Wheatgrass Juice®

100% Dried Juice of Organic Kamut® and Alfalfa Leaves

Kamut Wheat Nutritional Chemical Analysis

Nutrition Facts		**Vitamins**		**Minerals**		**Amino Acids**	
Kamitan name	Kamut						
		Vitamin A	<50 IU/100g	Calcium	11.1 mg/g	Alanine	18.4 mg/g
Chlorophyll	300 mg/100g	Beta Carotene	894 IU/g	Potassium	49.7 mg/g	Arginine	18.6 mg/g
Calories	3/g	Vitamin B1	0.61mg/100g	Magnesium	0.06 mg/g	Aspartic Acid	30.7 mg/g
Ash	14.70%	Vitamin B2	3.06mg/100g	Iron	0.21 mg/g	Glutamic Acid	33.5 mg/g
Moisture	7.10%	Vitamin B5	7.9 mg/100g	Silicon	0.29 mg/g	Glycine	15.2 mg/g
Protein	22%	Vitamin B6	11.7 mg/100g	Sodium	3.06 mg/g	Histidine	7.05 mg/g
Fat	2%	Vitamin C	84.5 mg/100g	Phosphorus	2.49 mg/g	Isoleucine	14.0 mg/g
Cholesterol	0%	Niacin	3.34 mg/100g	Boron	57 mg/g	Leucine	23.9 mg/g
Total Sugars	197mg/100g	Vitamin E	7.24 IU/100g	Manganese	0.13 mg/g	Lysine	18.8 mg/g
Carbs	400mg/100g	Vitamin K	1.08 mg/100g	Copper	0.16 mg/g	Methionine	41.2 mg/g
Iron	0.21mg/100g			Silver	0.20 mg/g	Phenylalanine	16.9 mg/g
Calcium	640mg/100g			Chromium	1.54 mg/g	Proline	19.2 mg/g
Sodium	3.06mg/100g			Zink	4.07 mg/100g	Serine	19.2 mg/g
		Enzymes				Threonine	14.8 mg/g
Shelf Life	2 years	SOD	1800/mg/g			Tyrosine	16.6 mg/g
Solubility	99%					Valine	16.4 mg/g
Total Dietary Fiber	< 5%					Total Protein	277 mg/g
Soluble Fiber	< 1%						

*Note: Kamut also contains small quantities of EFAs (Essential Fatty Acids) and Friendly Flora (Probiotics).

The Kemetic Diet Food Pyramid

The Food Pyramid, sponsored by the government as a "guideline" for healthy eating choices actually acts as a recommendation that most people and physicians follow. It has been adjusted in recent years from its original version in order to respond to the dire nutritional needs of the population. Some exponents have explained that it may be understood as follows: The items at the top (narrow section) should be consumed sparingly and those at the bottom (wide section) should be consumed in abundance. According to the pyramid scheme, this means that fats, oils, sweets should be consumed more sparingly than say meats. Mostly they are considering the fats and oils from items that are part of the regular diet of the general population. They give the following instruction.

> "You decide how to use the additional fat in your daily diet. You may want to have foods from the five major food groups that are higher in fat--such as whole milk instead of skim milk. Or you may want to use it in cooking or at the table in the form of spreads, dressings, or toppings."[165]

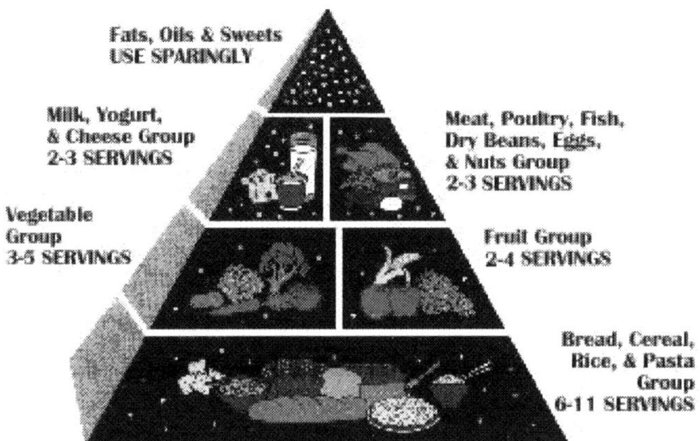

Food Pyramid of U.S. Department of Agriculture

The practitioner of the Kemetic Diet must understand clearly that based on the evidences presented in this book, the items listed above (milk and dairy, meat, poultry, fish, eggs, processed bread, processed cereal, processed rice, and pasta, fats and oils from animal products or processed and refined vegetable fats and oils) are not to be consumed in ANY QUANTITY. The Food Pyramid is designed to accommodate people who cannot resist the food items listed such as meats (including fish and poultry), cheeses, pastas, eggs, etc., and also to accommodate the lobbyists from the meat and dairy industry, as well as those in the food industry who, out of selfishness and greed, want to continue to provide those items to the consumer. This is not the way to promote health. This is similar to the tobacco industry's reckless disregard for human life in the pursuit of profits. This acquiescence of the U.S. Department of Agriculture Center for Nutrition Policy and Promotion which produced the "Food Pyramid" is reflected in the American Medical Association, which does not endorse Dr. Dean Ornish's PROVEN method to reverse heart disease by a regimen of the integral practice of the yogic disciplines, including vegetarian diet, because they feel people would not follow it since they would miss the foods (poisons) they like to eat, i.e. meats (including fish and poultry), cheeses, pastas, eggs, etc.

Living a life of health does not mean privation, but rather fulfillment and peace. Fulfillment and peace occur when people live life for the higher purpose instead of just for the pursuit of demeaning sensual pleasures such as those fleeting delights gained by foods that satisfy an abnormally excited taste.

---

[165] U.S. Department of Agriculture Center for Nutrition Policy and Promotion

As previously discussed, most grains have mucus-forming qualities. Some grains become detrimental to the body through processing and refining by the food companies. Some grains and beans have both acid inhibiting and acid forming qualities. Soybeans are acid inhibiting. Other grains and beans are considered to be acid forming. This list includes dried peas, dried beans, rye flour, oat flour, oat flakes. Cooking acts to release nutrients in some foods that would otherwise be difficult to digest (i.e. grains, beans), but also alters the chemistry of food, breaking down the nutrients and thereby rendering the food less nutritious. In view of the Kemetic Diet, the "Food Pyramid" should be adjusted to cut out (not just curtail) the detrimental foods and food preparation methods which ARE KNOWN TO CAUSE DISEASE AND CANCER entirely, and promote those foods and food preparation methods that sustain health and life (see below). For more on the specific grains recommended by the Kemetic Diet Program see the section in this book entitled ***"Calcium and Milk and Meats."*** (⊘ = cut out)

Breaking up the Acidic and Poisonous Food Pyramid

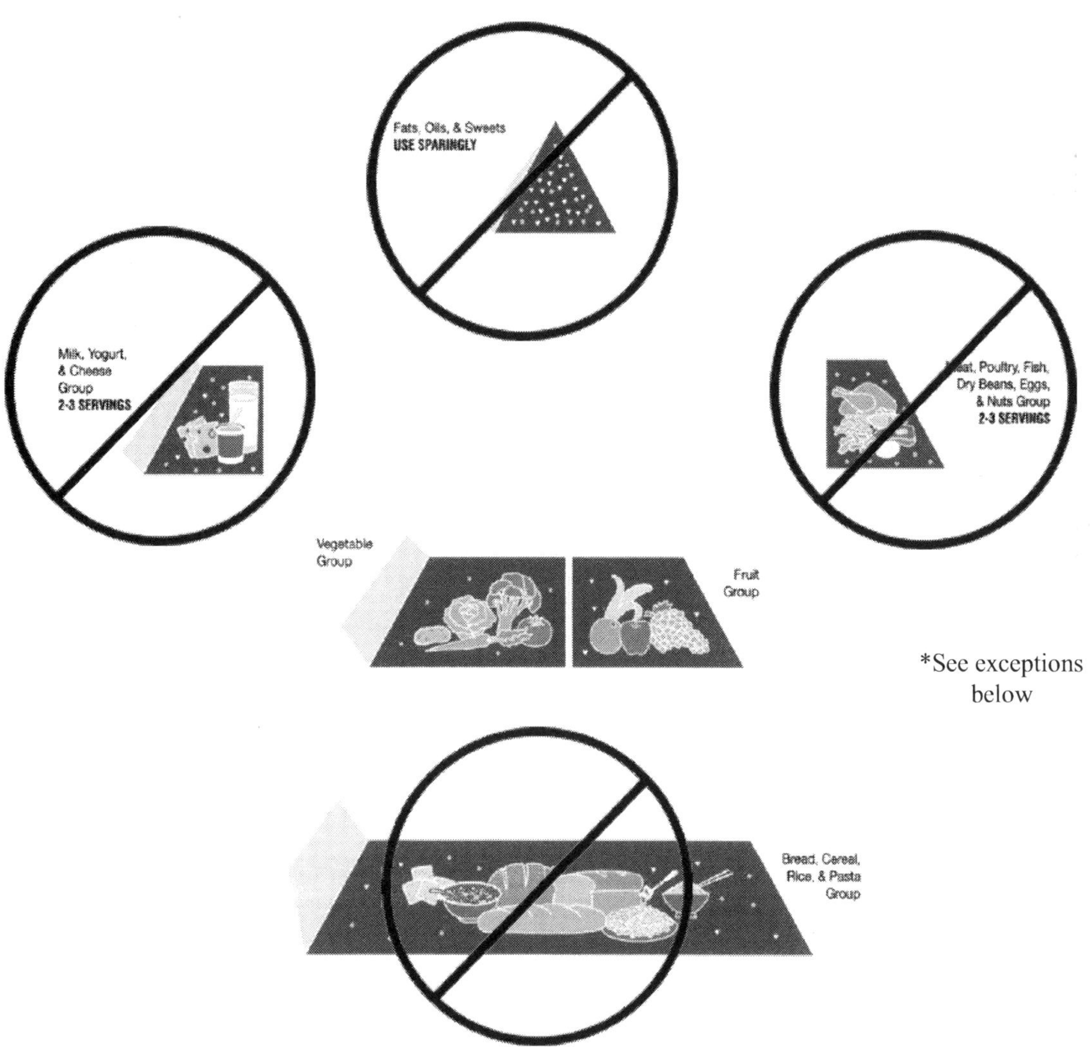

*Note: Organic Extra Virgin Expeller Pressed Olive oil (can be used for cooking) and Flax oil (cannot be used for cooking) are good oils that should be part of normal balanced vegetarian diet. Nuts such as almonds and beans such as garbanzos, lentils, etc- can be considered as positive and nutritious foods suitable for the Kemetic Diet Program. Unprocessed and unrefined organic cooked brown rice is also acceptable. Some breads such as organic sprouted Kamut and Spelt are acceptable in the transition diet.

The Kemetic Diet Food Pyramid

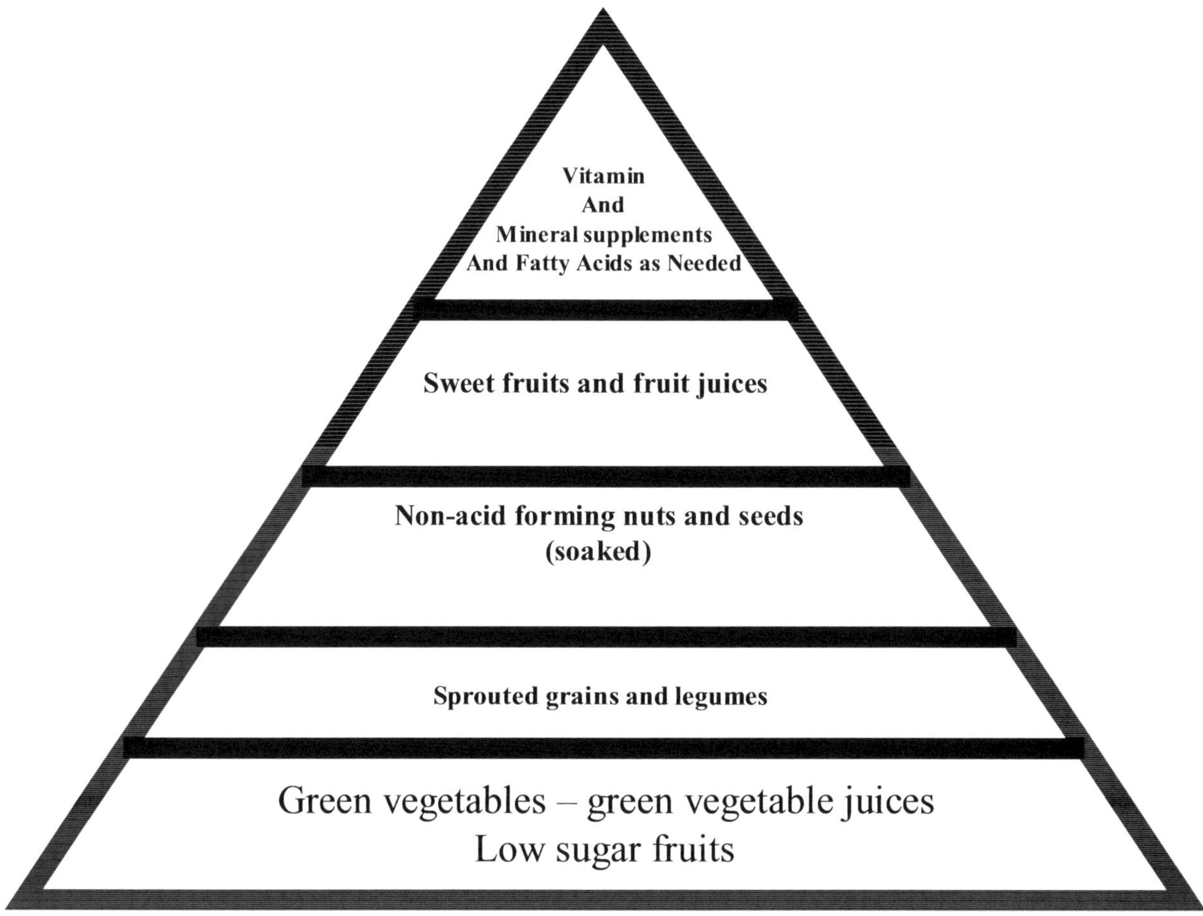

Living Water

Our planet consists of 70% water, but less than 1% of it is fit to drink, and it is estimated that in a few years to come there will be wide scale (planetary) drought conditions . In recent years many people have discovered the necessity of drinking clean and pure water. An entire industry has developed wherein water is more expensive than gasoline! Imagine that a most essential aspect of nature has been rendered so inaccessible to humanity due to pollution. For instance, the water in over half of the lakes in the United States of America is unfit for human consumption because they are contaminated with various poisons. The damming of rivers by municipalities has also depleted the supply. It is an extremely wasteful way of life that has led to a crisis. Regular tap water from city sources contain many chemicals which wholistic health practitioners cite as being toxic, to kill various bacteria, viruses and other microorganisms that regularly contaminate the municipal water supply. Companies have taken to searching out springs wherein clean water has not been affected by seepage of man made chemicals into the water table below ground.

The use of distilled water as a means to avoid the TDS (total dissolved solids) that survive standard filtration became popular a few years ago since there are over 60,000 known possible chemicals that can appear as TDS in water. However, in recent years natural health professionals have sounded the alarm that the process of distillation, being an artificial process not found in nature, kills the nutrients and filters out the minerals in the water, leaving only H^2O. Some companies distil the water and then add minerals back in for taste. This is not advisable since the new proportions may be out of balance. Mineral waters should be used cautiously because if a person is not in good health and their cells are not well hydrated, the minerals may crystallize or calcify in the vessels and in the brain leading to arteriosclerosis and or Alzheimer's disease. Those who use soft drinks are introducing a highly acid substance composed of 50% or more sugar which feeds Yeast and Candida bacteria. It would take 35 glasses of pH 10 water to neutralize one can of soda which has pH 2. Cooked foods produce free radicals and these damage the DNA leading to mutations like cancer. If the body is not well hydrated (it is de-hydrated) these will not flush out properly and will accumulate, causing great problems for the body including advanced degenerative diseases (cancer, heart disease, etc.). So those people who consume starches are also at greater risk for arteriosclerosis and or Alzheimer's disease because they are introducing elements that calcify easily in the body (arteries), and have low water content.

Living beings need more than the basic constituent chemical compounds of water. They need living water. Living water has naturally occurring vitamins and minerals in it as they were placed there by nature. So unprocessed or lightly processed purified natural spring water which has an alkaline pH is recommended. Distilled water can actually be detrimental since it will cause the body to release its stored nutrients in order to process the water as the body metabolizes it. If alkaline spring water is unavailable, distilled water can be "enlivened" by the addition of "live" foods such as the powered green grass/vegetable supplements, lime or lemon juice, etc. The pH level of natural living water is alkaline and this will promote an alkaline condition of the body when it is consumed. Do not forget that the body is over 75% fluid (living water). Many health experts agree that the best source of "living water" is the water from the young jelly coconut. Other sources include watery fruits such as melons.

In ancient Africa the river was seen as the "source of life." It was revered as a divinity and protected by law.

Living water should be used

- for mixing with the vegetable juice concentrates,
- for soaking nuts or dried fruits prior to consumption,
- for regular consumption during the day (herbal teas {not containing caffeine} may be added to the water in order to produce a good tasting drink that will refresh and alkalize the body).

Water also serves the purpose of hydrating the body, helping its cells to be oxygenated and removing toxic impurities. Therefore, it is important to consume living water to maintain and restore health.

Final note: The news is replete with reports of processed food recalls related to items that were once thought to be safe which were later discovered to be poisonous. The natural health enthusiast should look skeptically at ANYTHING that is processed or altered, including water, even if it is to make a "better" product that has more nutrients and higher pH. Beware of the word "enriched" on the labeling of anything you buy. This means that the product has been denatured and then "reconstituted." However, the reconstitution is unnatural and likely detrimental. There are many water brands on the market that claim to have produced water that is more easily assimilated by the body or that is of higher pH, etc. If it does not come out of a natural stream or underground river, they should be treated with caution, if consumed at all. Even the waters from those "natural" sources need to be checked first for pollutants or even excessive amounts of mineral deposits before they can be used. In short, being close to nature means coming to its way and not artificially trying to reproduce what nature has already perfected unless it is absolutely necessary. When the world's naturally healthy water supply runs out, then we can talk about heavy processing procedures to attempt to reproduce nature's miracle of water. Whichever water you use, make sure it is pH balanced. If you use distilled water which can be bought at a relatively cheap price as compared to other sources of healthy water, add a pH balancing nutrient (green juice powder, lemon juice, etc.) before consuming it.

Poor Ethics as Cause of Disease

The Ancient Egyptians recognized the Ukhedu as the main source of disease, but there were other subtler sources as well. One of these was ethical. It was noted that unrighteous behavior could lead to the deterioration of health. The modern medical establishment for the most part does not recognize the ethical basis, even though the mind-body connection is increasingly being accepted. The ethical aspect of life is integrally related to the mental state and the mental state, dictates the state of health because it controls the energies and hormones that direct the immune system. Therefore, feeling unrest due to unethical behavior will have a direct effect on the condition of the individual.

Ba ➔ Ka ➔ Khat

Another source of disease recognized by the Ancient Egyptians was the imbalance between the *Ba* (soul) and the *Ka* or mind. The Ba (soul) enlivens the Ka (mind-emotions-astral body) and the Ka enlivens the Khat (physical body). Since the soul has a higher program for human existence, and since human beings are often caught up in the ego desires of the mind, there is often an internal conflict within the personality. In this aspect the Ba can be thought of as Heru, the Higher Self and the Ka as Set, the lower self. The higher and lower self vie for control of the personality, and when there is harmony there can be health, vitality and greatness in the personality. When there is disharmony between these two aspects of the personality, there develops all manner of disease from misfortune and adversity to fatal physical ailments.

Fad Diets and Ego Diets

There have been many diets proposed by people in the medical establishments and others. Some examples were the Sugar Busting Diet, Fat Blocker Diet, Fen-Phen Diet, Macrobiotic Diet, Juice Only Diet, Cottage Cheese Diet, etc. Some were extremely detrimental and even led to deaths. Many were based on extremes in one food item, and extremes always lead to imbalances. Imbalances may provide seemingly positive results in the short-term, but detrimental results in the long-term. Most of these fad diets have come and gone over the years after being touted as the ultimate way, not necessarily to good health, but to what most people want even more, good looks. They are pursuing the diet to satisfy their egos, and not their health needs. Many people do not want to lose weight because of the health benefits. Rather, they want to lose weight so that they can look good to others, to be attractive and desirable. This has led to untold suffering. A recent craze was the Fen-Phen system of dieting using drugs that were later discovered to damage the heart and cause deaths. This led to a recall of the drugs and the system in the wake of multimillion dollar lawsuits that have gone on for years.

One of the most popular dieting programs currently is the "Atkins Diet," developed by Dr. Robert C. Atkins M.D.

> **July, 2002, Duke University Reasearch on the Atkins Diet**
> DURHAM, N.C. – "The high-protein, low-carbohydrate diet popularized by Dr. Robert Atkins Diet Revolution has been the subject of heated debate in medical circles for three decades. Now, preliminary research findings at Duke University Medical Center show that a low-carbohydrate diet such as the Atkins Diet can indeed lead to significant and sustained weight loss.

Like the Fen-Phen system, the Atkins Diet can produce weight loss, but the question is at what cost. The eminent developer of the proven and tested "Reversing Heart Disease" program, cardiologist Dr. Dean Ornish M.D., along with others in the orthodox medical, wholistic and alternative health fields, have been voicing their concerns over the Atkins system for some time. Dr. Ornish was so concerned that he labled the Atkins system as "mortgaging one's health." This means that one is putting one's future health at risk, in exchange for the short term gains (losing weight). The problems is that a high-protein, low-carbohydrate diet leads to mineral and vitamin deficiencies that will cause or predispose one to all kinds of diseases and conditions such as Heart Disease, including cardiomyopathy and heart failure, as well as osteoporosis.

> "Stress hormones such as adrenaline and steroids open calcium channels at the cellular level in the heart, causing the coronary arteries to constrict (spasm). (This is why calcium channel blocking drugs like Cardizem and Procardia are often prescribed.) Under conditions of intense chronic stress, even the muscle fibers inside the heart itself can begin to contract so vigorously that the normal architecture of these fibers is disrupted, damaging the heart muscle. This mechanism is known as "contraction band necrosis," "myofibrillar degeneration," or "coagulative myocytolysis," and it can lead to a condition called cardiomyopathy in which the heart doesn't pump blood very well. This, in turn, can cause heart failure."[166]

Just this year Dr. Atkins himself fell ill to this cardiac arrest.

> Statement on the Status of Dr. Robert C. Atkins' Health From Dr. Atkins and From the Chief Executive Officer/President of the Atkins Companies
>
> ***Thursday April 25, 2002 Press Release SOURCE: The Atkins Companies***
>
> NEW YORK, April 25 /PRNewswire/ -- On Thursday April 18, Dr. Robert C. Atkins, the well-known nutrition expert and best selling author, did, in fact, experience cardiac arrest during breakfast.

Most people get their protein from eating meats. As we have shown throughout this book, such a diet has innumerable problems. Some of the most important problems caused by such a diet are the lack of Omega-3 Fatty Acid and the problem of Calcium deficiency that develops due to the meat diet, in addition to taxing the body's systems that must deal with processing the overload of animal protein, and eliminating the waste products. These and other elements are essential to proper heart function. The following Texas Heart Institute research provides insight into the nature and prevention of cardiomyopathy.

---

[166] Dr. Dean Ornish's Program for Reversing Heart Disease" by Dr. Dean Ornish

"Cardiomyopathy[167]

"Cardiomyopathy" means "disease of the heart muscle." Cardiomyopathy damages the muscle tone of the heart and reduces its ability to pump blood to the rest of your body.

Although only about 50,000 Americans have cardiomyopathy, it is a leading cause of heart failure in the United States each year.

Can cardiomyopathy be prevented?

Although cardiomyopathy is one of the less frequent forms of heart disease, it's still important to be aware of the role heredity plays in the disease and to be familiar with its symptoms.

Check your family's medical history to learn if you are at risk. Even if nobody in your family has cardiomyopathy, you need to know the warning signs:

- unexplained shortness of breath,
- bloating,
- fainting, or
- chest pains.

Also, because drinking too much alcohol, eating foods without the proper vitamins, and exposure to toxins can all cause cardiomyopathy, you can lower your risk by adopting a heart-healthy lifestyle."

The last paragraph above is the key to this section. The article warns about alcohol, vitamin depleted foods, and toxins as causes of cardiomyopathy. What kinds of foods are depleated in their vitamin content? COOKED FOODS AND PROCESSED FOODS AND NON-ORGANIC FOODS! Also single item diets lacking variety. What are the sources of toxins? COOKED FOODS AND PROCESSED FOODS AND ENVIRONMENTAL POLUTION, STRESS AND SPIRITUAL FRUSTRATION.

It is important to understand that any diet program that requires the practitioner to go to extremes into one food item or chemical is bound to place the body in some kind of imbalance. Here again it is important to begin looking at oneself and the world in a mature fashion instead of looking for fanciful miraculous answers from science or programs that are not in harmony with nature. This takes hard work, changing from old habits and accepting the truth that the Standard American Diet, fast foods and processed foods are detrimental to health, no matter how good they may taste. Also, it must be understood that the lifestyle of stress and disregard for the laws of nature that characterize the modern culture of greed and selfishness underlies the mental imbalance that ultimately prevents a human being from having sufficient will power to make the necessary changes in their lives. This is why the Kemetic Diet program can be so powerful, because not only is it a diet for the body that will lead to physical health, but it also recognizes and addresses the deeper causes of illness in the mind and in the soul, which must be addressed in order to have truly optimal health.

[167] Texas Heart Institute

Climate Change as Cause of Disease

The peoples of ancient times noted that sudden changes in the climate could also lead to deterioration in health. In modern times, the change of climate would be attributed to a compromised immune system. Referring to the Nile Valley, the historians Herodotus and Plutarch said the following.

> "The river rises of itself, waters the fields, and then sinks back again: thereupon each man sows his field and waits for the harvest."
>
> -Herodotus

> "...they are the healthiest people in the world. I should put this down myself to the absence of changes in the climate, for change, and especially changes of weather, is the prime cause of disease."
>
> -Plutarch

What is it that allowed the first civilizations in our history to develop in the great river valleys of the world? What promoted the development of civilization in the Nile River Valley first in history? The river valley offers a unique opportunity for people to make use of the life giving benefits of water and to conduct farming along its banks, which from time to time flood into the valley and leave deposits. These deposits create extremely fertile soil, and therefore, good conditions for farming. The great river valleys of the world are known as the Nile River Valley (Africa), the Euphrates River Valley (Mesopotamia), The Indus River Valley (India), and the Yellow River Valley (China). However, in Ancient Egypt the situation was even more optimum than the rest. Noted by Herodotus, the regularity of the Nile flood allowed early farmers there to plan their crops and cultivate the land with greater ease than any other people in the world. This allowed them to use the longest and most reliable river in the world as a source of sustenance, so that they might engage in other pursuits such as civilization in the form of art, architecture, religion, philosophy, medical science, etc. The fertility of the Nile coupled with the stability of the climate went along way to promote the general health.

Breastfeeding

There are few things in this world that are more mysterious than life. Modern science still cannot explain life, that is, why life exists, how does it perpetuate and why does it reproduce. For all the answers about which science can theorize, the "how" of the reproduction process, there is no scientist that can penetrate the why of life. This glorious mystery, while unexplainable, is describable, and the means to promote health are known. The industrial and technological revolutions would have people believe that canned foods are better than fresh foods, and in the late 19th and for most of the 20th centuries these industries had convinced people in western countries that breastfeeding was one more unnecessary tradition. Now, in the late 20th century and as we commence the 21st, there is a growing realization that the lack of breastfeeding or shortened period of breastfeeding is a contributing source to compromised immune systems and children growing up with behavioral problems and other diseases.

It has been discovered that mothers transfer essential nutrients and antibodies through breast-milk, not to mention the impact of bonding and nurturing as well as the development of the child's emotions. There is no question of a correlation between lack of being nurtured as an infant and/or child, and the development of emotional and physical disabilities later on in life. The lack or reduction of breastfeeding has been found to promote more disease and mental disorders when compared to a group of the population who have been breastfed for longer periods as children. In non-western countries, the period of breastfeeding is 2 to 3 or more years after birth. By contrast, virtually all children in the United States are weaned by the 12th month, and many by the first, so that mothers can get back to their jobs or careers.

The Ancient Egyptian practice of breastfeeding provides further insight into the health of the people. It was general practice to breastfeed children to the age of three, and if needed, a wet nurse would be commissioned for the task. The following passage from the Wisdom Teachings of Any provides insight into the practice of breastfeeding in Ancient Egypt. Sage *Any* extols the virtue of taking care of one's parents, in this case the mother, who breastfed for three years.

> Double the food your mother gave you,
> *Support her as she supported you;*
> *She had a heavy load in you,*
> *But she did not abandon you.*
> *When you were born after your months,*
> *She was yet yoked (to you)*
> *Her breast in your mouth for three years.*

It is also noteworthy that the Ancient Egyptian doctors had a method of diagnosing breastmilk that was not suitable for breastfeeding. Breastmilk was tested before feeding the infant. If the milk smelled like fish it was deemed not suitable for breastfeeding. The pungent odor of the breastmilk would be caused by the ill health of the mother deemed and this health issue would have been also treated by the Sunu (doctor).

Dental Caries

It has been found by researchers that the later period in Ancient Egyptian history saw a higher incidence of dental problems as opposed to the earlier period. One reason that is commonly cited is the possibility that the Ancient Egyptian diet was full of sand due to the desert winds. However, no reports of increased winds have been noted in the later period versus the older. Therefore, this cause is suspect. Another explanation can be found in a cultural change. It is well known that Kemetic culture underwent a major change from the Middle Kingdom period to the New Kingdom. The Middle Kingdom period came to an end when the country was invaded by foreigners, who were called "Hyksos." These Hyksos were Asiatics who gained control of some parts of the country, sufficient to disrupt the society and expose it to new customs, foods, and new methods of food preparation. Thus, the previously healthiest people of the ancient world were affected by the stresses of military invasion as well as the stresses of social pressures, such as the desire to consume sweets, cooked foods, and add to these the unhygienic conditions engendered when there is any violence or adverse conditions imposed on a society. It has been found that when there is proper nutrition, the incidence of dental problems such as periodontal disease and cavities is reduced, and further, that the damage from these problems can be reversed without invasive surgeries or chemicals.

Fluoride, Dental Caries and Fluoride Toxicity

Since its introduction into the water supply of many western countries, Fluoride has been the object of much controversy. The argument has been that in order to protect public heath and promote better oral hygiene and dental heath, public officials needed to place fluoride into the public water supply. However, though fluoride is a naturally occurring compound in nature and in the human body, it has not been proven as an effective chemical for promoting dental health. Once again, just as the medical profession refuses to come out publicly and say that meat, milk and other foods are hazardous to health, the American Dental Association also refuses to publicly denounce the standard western diet and instead prefer to perform otherwise unnecessary surgeries and prescribe drugs to cope with the problems that have developed due to wrong eating habits and lifestyles.

Review of Fluoride Benefits and Risks,
Department of Health and Human Services, February 1991

Although fluoride compounds occur naturally both in the environment and in most constituents of the body, there is no conclusive evidence that fluorine or any of the fluoride compounds are essential for human homeostasis or growth … Investigators have failed to show a consistent correlation between anticaries activity and the specific amounts of fluoride incorporated into enamel.

Since the 1970s, caries scores have been declining in both fluoridated and non-fluoridated communities in Europe, the United States, and elsewhere. ... National decreases have not occurred in all countries, notably Brazil and France where the caries scores have not changed, and Japan, Nigeria, and Thailand where the scores have increased

Fluoride can be harmful in many ways. A specific disease related to fluoride is fluorosis.

©Copyright: Fluorosis Research And Rural Development Foundation:

Fluorosis is a crippling and painful disease caused by intake of fluoride. Fluoride can enter the body through drinking water, food, toothpaste, mouth rinses and other dental products; drugs, and fluoride dust and fumes from industries using fluoride containing salt and or hydrofluoric acid.

Fluorosis can affect young and old; men and women alike. Fluorosis occurs as · Dental Fluorosis · Skeletal Fluorosis and · Non-skeletal Fluorosis.

Fluorosis is a public health problem required to be managed by both Medical and Public Health Engineering Professionals (i.e. Water Supply Implementing Agencies).

Fluoride occurs naturally in nature and a well balanced diet will provide the body with the minute quantities of fluoride that it needs. However, toxicity can develop due to overdosing through drinking tap water or fluoride in tooth paste.

How much is too much?

In 1953, when Harold C. Hodge, chairman of the National Academy of Sciences toxicology committee, evaluated the dangers associated with excess fluoride, the best data available was Roholm's classic, ***Fluorine Intoxication***. Roholm had studied workers exposed to fluoride in dusts from aluminum ore. He reported that with an intake equal to 0.2 to 0.35 mg/kg/day, phase three skeletal fluorosis developed after about eleven years. In terms of milligrams per day, the equivalent is 10-20 mg/day for 10-20 years for persons weighing 100 to 229 pounds. As is generally true, toxicity depends on dosage per pound (or kilogram) of body weight. What wouldn't faze a 220 pound man might kill a newborn infant.

According to the Surgeon General, fluoride accumulates in a linear manner. Eighty to one hundred percent of ingested fluoride is absorbed from foods and beverages. ***The fractional retention or balance of fluoride at any age depends on the quantitative features of absorption and excretion. For healthy, young, or middle-aged adults, approximately 50 percent of absorbed fluoride is retained by uptake in calcified tissues, and 50 percent is excreted in the urine. For young children, as much as 80 percent can be retained owing to increased uptake by the developing skeleton and teeth. Such data are not available for persons in the later years of life ...*** Dietary Reference Intakes (1999) NAS/NRC

Additional time has been devoted here to alerting the reader to the hazard of fluoride because there is a danger of taking the simplest things such as tap water or tooth paste for granted as being safe with such arguments that "the government or public officials would not their own people. Time and time again the level of greed and the profit motive in western culture has proven to be more powerful than moral injunctions or legal regulation. Some people throw up their hands and surrender to what they see as an impossible situation, thinking they cannot escape the onslaught of the thousands of chemicals released into the environment, either legally or not, that affect everything in society. There is a way to find health but the seeker must be willing to give up their ignorance about the world and accept the hazards that their own lifestyle poses. In this way, when more and more people abstain from living in ways that are not in harmony with nature, they will gain collective strength to oppose the blind movements towards synthetic chemical solutions, and move towards organic methods to find peace with nature and health with the body. Examine the ingredients placed in your food or other products you use on your body or in your environment, and notice if there are any hazardous chemicals there, and then REFUSE TO EAT IT OR USE IT. Do not shrug it off and put it out of your mind saying "well everyone has to die some day." Everyone must die, but everyone need not live a life shortened by disease, filled with pain or suffering. Make the choice to stand up for your health and protect yourself and your family.

Note on Soy Products

As stated earlier, there are many meat substitutes that are made of vegetables and/or beans such as soy, that have textures and tastes similar to meat, and can be used to supplement the diet and provide protein as well as other nutritional elements. However, these products are processed and their nutritional value will not be as high as the fresh article. Also, taken to excess, processed soy products can cause the body to become acidic and the benefits of eating soy products as a source for protein and cancer fighting agents will be overshadowed by the detrimental effects. Therefore, the processed soy products in the diet should be limited and there should be an emphasis on sprouted soy and other less processed forms of soy products. The processed forms should be thought of and used primarily as transition foods when making the movement from a meat based diet to a vegetarian diet.

Soy milk is acceptable in controlled quantities and one should take care to use "unsweetened" or low sugar (using cane juice or other natural sweeteners-look on the contents label for no more than 2-4% sugars) soy milk. The sugar additives cause different reactions than would otherwise be present with soy alone. This will lead to excess acidity, gas and mucus, and a deterioration of the processes in the Mettu (vascular systems). Soy provides excellent nutritional value especially for the reproductive organs of both sexes as well as protein.

Pesticides

Another issue that has been substantiated by studies in American universities is the harmful effect of pesticides on young children. Many countries in Africa and the east as well as South America have attempted to counteract the problems such as malaria and malnutrition through the use of pesticides in the home, on the skin and on food crops. Now these actions are proving themselves to be extremely injurious to children especially[168], but to adults as well. It has been shown that people who receive proper nutrition

[168] In the book, The Food-Mood-Body Connection by Gary Null, Dr. Harold Buttram cites a Government Publication called "Identifying and Controlling Poisons of the Nervous System" which points out that one of the earliest signs of chemical toxicity is behavioral problems. This is a very significant correlation, and one that is also alarming, considering the epidemic proportions of so-called ADDH (Attention Deficit Disorder and Hyperactivity) and behavioral problems plaguing children in today's society.

have a lesser chance of contracting diseases because their immune systems are not compromised or weakened due to poisons in the environment, poor living conditions, ingesting the incorrect kinds of foods or ingesting incorrectly prepared foods.

Estrogen Replacement Therapy and Hormone Replacement Therapy

Both for men and women, the proper functioning of the endocrine system is an essential part of proper health. The Endocrine System is composed of all the endocrine, or ductless, glands in the body. These secrete chemical substances known as hormones directly into the bloodstream, and these act to control body functions. It has been referred to as a "liquid nervous system."[169] The most important endocrine glands are (1) The pituitary gland, (2) The thyroid gland, (3) The parathyroid glands, (4) The adrenal glands, (5) The islands of Langerhans in the pancreas, and (6) The sex glands, or gonads--in males, the testes, which secrete testosterone; in females, the ovaries, which secrete estrogens and progesterones.

Menopause is a condition that most women experience between the ages of 45 and 55. It is precipitated when the female reproductive capacity comes to an end. At this time many physiological and in some women, psychological changes occur, some of which *"have still not been completely elucidated."*[170] Many Western women complain of changes that include *Hot Flashes, Osteoporosis, Depression, Genital and Breast atrophy.* Also, many women report an increase in sex desire (associated with the relief of stress due to fear of conception), but also this is accompanied by a perception of loss of desirability and attractiveness. The medical establishment has associated these problems, with a loss in estrogen production.

> **ESTROGEN** Any of several steroid hormones produced chiefly by the ovaries and responsible for promoting estrus and the development and maintenance of female secondary sex characteristics.[171]

The Western medical establishment has devised a treatment called *Estrogen Replacement Therapy* and *Hormone Replacement Therapy.* The use of synthetic (produced in laboratories) hormones has yielded some positive results. However, the synthetic chemical hormones are not as easily digestible as the ones produced naturally by the body. Other natural hormones derived from horses, have been used, also with limited success. These pose a danger especially to women who are obese, or who smoke or suffer from high blood pressure. Thus it is clear that hormones from animals are unsuitable for human consumption. Further, Hormone Replacements Therapies using synthetic and other unnatural means have been linked to risks such as:

> Another important area to discuss is the risks of HRT. There is no evidence that HRT at post-menopausal doses increases hypertension or clotting abnormalities. Common possible side-effects include withdrawal bleeding with cyclic dosing, spotting during the first three to six months with combined continuous therapy, mastalgia, edema, abdominal bloating, and increase in the size of uterine leiomyomata. Rarely, symptoms of anxiety and depression can be worsened with initiation of HRT. Although there is no increase in

---

The orthodox medical and scientific communities and the pharmaceutical companies which are making recommendations for the treatment of these conditions, instead of addressing the issue of inciting environmental and nutritional causes of ADDH, such as food and environmental allergies, malnourishment, parasitic infestations, and this, chemical toxicity, seek to treat these children with harmful medications that have not been proven to be of benefit, and if anything, have been shown to be detrimental, in that they can trigger the exact or more severe behavioral problems which they are trying to inhibit.

[169] Random House Encyclopedia Copyright (C) 1983,1990 by Random House Inc.

[170] E.J. Mayeaux, Jr., M.D. Associate Professor of Family Medicine, Clinical Associate Professor of Obstetrics and Gynecology - Louisiana State University Medical Center Shreveport, Louisiana

[171] American Heritage Dictionary

asymptomatic gallstones, a 2.7-fold increase (3.4% to 9.8%) in cholecystectomy has been noted. Other risks include Breast Cancer and Endometrial Cancer.[172]

It was reported in the medical journal *The Lancet,* that Japanese women suffered from fewer symptoms of menopause than Western women. It is thought that this is due to the diet of the Japanese women, which includes *phytoestrogens,* estrogens from plants, such as soybeans, tofu, miso, flaxseeds, pomegranates, and dates.[173] Therefore, it is once again evident that natural sources rather than artificially produced remedies are more effective and safe for the promotion of healthy middle age in women as well as men.

Other studies reported by news agencies include:

CNN.com

Study: Estrogen increases ovarian cancer risk (20-Mar-01)
Women who use supplemental estrogen after menopause for10 years or more double their risk of dying from ovarian cancer, according to a study released Tuesday. This increased risk persists up to 29 years after a woman stops using the hormone therapy.

Hormone replacement therapy study halted (09-Jul-02)
In a move that may affect millions of women, U.S. government scientists Tuesday stopped a major study of hormone replacement therapy on the risks and benefits of combined estrogen and progestin in healthy menopausal women, citing an increased risk of invasive breast cancer.

FDA to reassess hormone replacement risks (14-Aug-02)
The Food and Drug Administration's Center for Drug Evaluation and Research has announced it will reassess the risks and benefits of Prempro, a hormone replacement therapy drug.

Stem Cell Research

There has been a great move in recent years to study Stem Cells. Before making a determination as to the Kemetic Diet view on this, we should first understand what Stem Cells are and why the scientific community is interested in them. The following update is representative of the two main groups involved in the Stem Research debate.

Overview:

A stem cell is a primitive type of cell that can be coaxed to develop into most of the 220 types of cells found in the human body (e.g. blood cells, heart cells, brain cells, etc). Some researchers regard them as offering the greatest potential for the alleviation of human suffering since the development of antibiotics. Over 100 million Americans suffer from diseases that may eventually be treated more effectively with stem cells or even cured. These include heart disease, diabetes, and certain types of cancer.

Stem cells can be extracted from very young human embryos -- typically from surplus frozen embryos left over from in-vitro fertilization procedures at fertility clinics. There are currently about 100,000 such embryos. However, a minority of pro-lifers object to the use of embryos. They feel that a few-days-old embryo is a human person. Extracting its stem cells kills the embryo -- an act that they consider murder. Stem cells can now be grown in the laboratory, so (in a pinch) much further research can be done using existing stem cells; no further harvesting needs to be made from embryos.

---

172 E.J. Mayeaux, Jr., M.D. Associate Professor of Family Medicine, Clinical Associate Professor of Obstetrics and Gynecology - Louisiana State University Medical Center Shreveport, Louisiana
173 *Prescription for Nutritional Healing,* James F. Balch M.D. and Phyllis A Balch, C.N.C.

Stem cells can also be extracted from adult tissue, without harm to the subject. Unfortunately, they are difficult to remove, are severely limited in quantity, and appear to be limited in usefulness.

Research using stem cells has been authorized in Britain, but was halted in the U.S. by President George W. Bush. Bush decided on 2001-AUG-9 to allow research to start again in government labs, but restricted research to use only existing lines of stem cells. Research continues in U.S. private labs and in both government and private labs in the UK, Japan, France, Australia, and other countries.[174]

NIH FACT SHEET ON HUMAN PLURIPOTENT STEM CELL RESEARCH GUIDELINES

Updated January 2001

The Promise of Stem Cell Research

Human pluripotent stem cells are a unique scientific and medical resource. In 1998, scientists at the University of Wisconsin and at Johns Hopkins University isolated and successfully cultured human pluripotent stem cells. The pluripotent stem cells were derived using non-Federal funds from early-stage embryos donated voluntarily by couples undergoing fertility treatment in an in vitro fertilization (IVF) clinic or from non-living fetuses obtained from terminated first trimester pregnancies. Informed consent was obtained from the donors in both cases. Women voluntarily donating fetal tissue for research did so only after making the decision to terminate the pregnancy.

Because pluripotent stem cells give rise to almost all of the cells types of the body, such as muscle, nerve, heart, and blood, they hold great promise for both research and health care. This advance in human biology continues to generate enthusiasm among scientists, patients suffering from a broad range of diseases, including cancer, heart disease and diabetes, and their families. For example, further research using human pluripotent stem cells may help:

- Generate cells and tissue for transplantation. Pluripotent stem cells have the potential to develop into specialized cells that could be used as replacement cells and tissues to treat many diseases and conditions, including Parkinson's disease, spinal cord injury, stroke, burns, heart disease, diabetes, osteoarthritis, and rheumatoid arthritis.
- Improve our understanding of the complex events that occur during normal human development and also help us understand what causes birth defects and cancer.
- Change the way we develop drugs and test them for safety. Rather than evaluating the safety of candidate drugs in an animal model, drugs might be initially tested on cells developed from pluripotent stem cells and only the safest candidate drugs would advance to animal and then human testing.

As stated above, stem cells are cells that can "become" other cells and thereby repair damage to tissue by replacing the damages cells. We must wonder why these stem cells exist to begin with and why they are found in great quantity in embryos but also in adults as well. In fact, the human body replaces every cell in the body every 1-2 years and how is this done? It is done by the body's own mechanism to

[174] **Copyright © 1998 to 2001 incl., by Ontario Consultants on Religious Tolerance Latest update: 2001-AUG-28 Author: B.A. Robinson**

regenerate. It has been discovered that blood cells also metamorphose into other kinds of cells as needed if the environment of the body is healthy.[175] It has also been found that the healthy cells of the body can also transform into fungi and other harmful cells (Cancer, etc.) if the inner environment of the body is toxic. So here we have another indication of the body's own ability to promote and maintain its own health and as it is often found, scientists are searching for a complicated scientific answer as opposed to a simple dietary one. The complicated nature of the scientific point of view is reflected in the following National Institute of Health update.

Natural Cell Metamorphosis vs. Cell Mutation

Our bodies have 100 trillion cells! The cells of the body are constantly metamorphosing themselves and reproducing themselves in a natural way. It has been shown that blood cells, for example, transform (metamorph) themselves into other kinds of cells that may be needed at a particular time in the body. Also, the body's cells exist in a constant state of "death and rebirth." Every minute millions and millions of cells are dying and new cells are reproduced to take their place, but with each reproduction, the quality is reduced until one day the copying process can no longer continue and the whole organism dies.

The body ages prematurely when 1)- it is toxic and 2)- it receives too many calories. These two factors cause the body's metabolic functions to speed up, which leads to deterioration, degenerative diseases and early death. If the quality of food provided to the body for building new cells is inadequate or deficient, the cells will take the nutrients from wherever they can find it. If they need calcium, they will take it from the bones and this will cause osteoporosis. The same is true for other minerals. If the body does not have the raw materials to create vitamin B-12, it will not be able to produce it on its own and supplementation will be necessary. However, with the proper diet the body can create the needed B-12.

Coming back to the cell copying process, if toxins such as nitrites, sugars, drugs or denatured foods are introduced to the body, the cells will deteriorate with each succeeding generation. This means not only that as a person gets older, they will develop more degenerative diseases, but that the genes they pass on to their offspring will be deficient, and consequently degenerative diseases will occur much sooner in the life of their children. This is what health professionals are now seeing in modern society. We often wonder why our grandparents smoked and ate all of the prohibited foods and lived into their nineties. Yet, our parent's generation developed cancers at a younger age, in their 50s and 60s, and our generation developed allergies and cancers earlier (at teens-50 years of age), and now the generation of our children are developing cancer and degenerative diseases from childhood. Recall the statistic at the beginning of this book: Cancer is the third leading cause of death in children less than 4 years of age, and the second leading cause of death in children 5 to 14 years of age! Why is this?

Dr. Francis Pottinger was a dentist and in the 1940s he performed experiments on cats in order to discover what the effect of processed foods would be on them. He took 800 cats and divided them into two groups. He fed one group unprocessed foods and he fed the other group processed foods. He discovered that the group that was fed the unprocessed foods had no change; they lived normally. However the first generation from the group that was fed the processed food diet (junk food) developed degenerative diseases (cancer, etc.) near the end of their life-span. The second generation of the group that was fed the junk food developed the same degenerative diseases but in the middle of their life span. The third generation of the group that was fed the junk food developed the same degenerative diseases but in the beginning of their life span. The third generation could not reproduce and so there was no fourth generation. They either could not conceive or the pregnancies were aborted prematurely.

[175] *Sick and Tired: Reclaim Your inner Terrain* by Robert O, Young, Ph. D. with Shelley Redford Young, L.M.T. (2001)

The Pottinger experiment holds serious implications for modern culture, which is so immersed in processed, and junk food diets. As of this writing western society is facing a problem of immense proportions. Right now in the United States 25% to 30% of young adults cannot conceive. This is the highest percentage that has ever been witnessed. This explains the explosion of fertility clinics in recent years and it is a sign of the effect of a heavily processed diet (Standard American Diet – SAD) which began in earnest around the year 1900. On the brighter side, Dr. Pottinger discovered that the trend to extinction could be reversed within three generations if the cats were once again fed a diet of unprocessed (not denatured) foods.

Summary Diagram: The Path to Disease

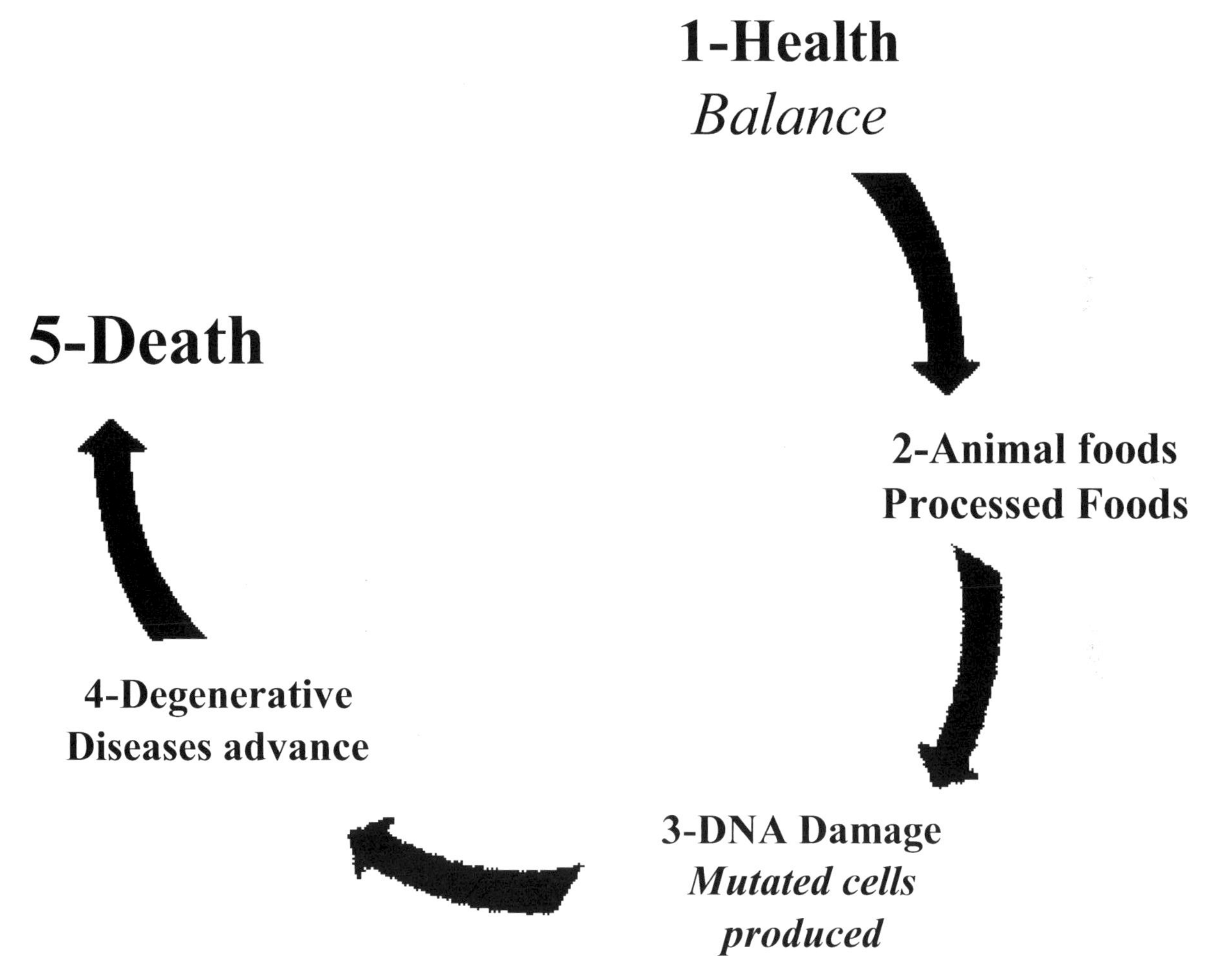

This brings us back to the understanding of the Kemetic Diet's principles of Health which holds that if the proper foods are taken in, the body will have sufficient raw materials to build healthy cells as needed. In addition, if the body is kept clean inside and out, there will not be a compromising (damaging) of the DNA that will tell the cells to transform into forms that cause disease, but rather, they will transform into forms that are in harmony with the physiology of the body. So it is a matter of protecting the DNA, and allowing it to do its job. It will direct the body's own already existing "stem cells" to metamorphose into the proper cells. Thus, authentic dietary and hygienic wholistic healing systems are successful because they work to prevent the DNA from being corrupted by toxins and poisons that would otherwise change the DNA and cause it to direct the stem cells to mutate into diseased cells. It is important that you realize the implication of what this means for your capacity to experience better health right now, as opposed to waiting for the orthodox medical and scientific fields to save you, assuming they can achieve these so-called "breakthroughs" in your lifetime. It means that you have the power and capacity to improve your health RIGHT NOW. It means that the greatest scientist ever has already made the greatest breakthrough, that scientist being the Divine Cosmic Intelligence who created your physical body with a capacity to heal and regenerate itself.

The predilection for "scientific" solutions has led humanity to waste valuable time, to experience untold suffering, and to inflict untold suffering on animals used in research, due firstly to not applying the common sense rules of health (as opposed to complicated theories), and secondly, by introducing foreign therapies, chemicals and drugs such as antibiotics which do not cure, but rather mask the symptoms and suppress the body's attempts to heal itself. As we learned in the overview (above), disregarding simple healing techniques such as nutritious diet and chemical free foods and reduction in stress, *"Some researchers regard them* (stem cells) *as offering the greatest potential for the alleviation of human suffering since the development of antibiotics."* The following report from the news media and the scientific medical establishment reflect a growing fear about the failure of antibiotics to cure disease as was once hoped.

> **YOUR HEALTH -- THE GROWING THREAT FROM DRUG-RESISTANT BACTERIA**
>
> June 16, 2000
> Web posted at: 5:52 p.m. EDT (2152 GMT)
>
> *From staff reports*
>
> **(CNN) -- Easily treatable infections may soon become immune to antibiotics, officials of the World Health Organization warned this week in their report "Overcoming Antimicrobial Resistance."**

It is the contention of natural health practitioners that the current emphasis on stem cells is just the latest in a long string of misguided applications of the scientific approach that will in a few years time end up in the same way as the antibiotics. This is because, even if stem cell research develops the capacity to regenerate new organs, as most people will return to their previous unhealthy habits (misbalanced lifestyle) which led to the development of the original disease condition in the first place, the "cure" will at most be short lived, just as if a person receiving a liver transplant after having cirrhosis of the liver secondary to alcoholism goes back to the negative habit of drinking alcohol, that person will end up at the doorway of death once again when the new liver becomes damaged.Rather than gaining health, independence and freedom, they will become more dependent on the orthodox medical and scientific fields, continually running to them to get more stem cells to cure this and that ailment, much in the same manner that a junkie must continually run to the drug dealer to get the next fix....for the right price of course! It must be realized that the scientific and medical communities also have a financial incentive to engage in these activities. It supports their current lifestyle. This statement is not to negate their talents and abilities, or even their intent and desire to want to help those in need, but to recognize their lack of development of the higher (spiritual) values of life, which has allowed them to become misguided in their endeavors, due the egoistic taints of pride or/and desiring prestige, or/and greed (desire to be wealthy), or/and desiring power to control others, or/and superiority, or/and vanity, etc., because they too, like their patients, do not practice a wholistic system of health for the body, mind and spirit. If their abilities were directed in a proper manner, a righteous manner, guided by the holistic principles of health for body, mind and spirit described here, that same energy, talent and ability could be used to truly heal the world.

It must be clearly understood that the body has the capacity to heal itself, that is, to manufacture healthy cells from cancerous cells, returning genetically mutated cells to normal again, IF the proper cleansing of toxins is enjoined AND the proper building blocks (nutrients) for healthy new cells are consumed. This means a complete lifestyle change away from habits that are detrimental and poisonous to those that are beneficial and life affirming.

The diseased person must first be cleansed (detoxified), and then the process of rebuilding new cells that are not cancerous or do not possess mutated DNA can begin. The main building blocks that the cells need are

- A clean environment (in and out of the body)
- Proper nutrition (vegetarian diet supplemented with vitamins, minerals and EFAs
- Peace of mind
- Spiritual expansion (self-discovery)

Summary Diagram: The Path to Recovery: From Disease to Health

5-Health
Balance

1-Disease
Imbalance

2 Cleansing + Whole Vegetable foods, Fresh Alkaline Foods

3-DNA Repair
New healthy Cell Production

4-Disease recovery

Why are Processed Foods so Poisonous?

Processed foods are dangerous. In an effort to cope with mass distribution to serve the growing population, manufacturers have devised ways to store consumables for longer periods than ever before. The following excerpts from the Encyclopedia provide insight into the procedures used in food processing and how the nutritive quality of the food is lost. Keep in mind that vitamins, enzymes and most organic proteins break down when exposed to temperatures greater than 100^0-118^0 Fahrenheit. Recall that a fever of 107^0 to 108^0 is usually fatal in a human being. However, microbes can survive this temperature, and thus, this is the reason why higher temperatures are used by the food industry. However, these high temperatures also kill, damage or destroy the nutritive elements of foods that support human life. The processing goal is also to eliminate the essential fatty acid, Omega 3 Fatty Acid, from the food, since this component of foods causes the food to become rancid and spoil. The modern food processing and preservation industry was born in 1809, when French chef and inventor Nicholas Appert, searching for a better way to provide food for Napoleon's army, devised a method for sterilizing food in tightly sealed glass bottles. In modern times, the principle antiseptic agents used in the preservation of food are heat and cold, in such processes as canning, pasteurization, and refrigeration. Irradiation is being investigated as a means of preserving food.[176] Prior to the advent of modern food processing people had to live closer to the land and take their food in a fresher state. Now they can get food that has been preserved with chemicals, denatured and stored for months or years, but the food is no longer food in the original sense of the term. Food processing is an artificial process that allows for an initial expansion of the population, but the quality of health of that population is dismal, and eventually the food will lead to its extinction. The denatured quality of the food forces people to eat a larger quantities in order to gain from the small quantity of nutrition that is left in the foods, and this leads to obesity, and/or higher metabolism and/or chronic health problems.

❖ Food additives are another cause of the denaturing of food. They are chemicals that are added to food in small amounts. Direct additives are placed in the food during processing to make it look and taste better, maintain freshness, and help in processing or preparation. As many as 3000 substances are approved by the Food and Drug Administration (FDA) for use as direct additives. An additional 10,000 substances are present in foods as indirect additives. These substances enter food incidentally during handling or from processing equipment or packaging.[177] One may ask, why is it necessary to add additives to food. Consider how tasty an apple or carrot that has been sitting on a shelf for months would be. Thus, additives are key to making the denatured, devitalized, unappetizing food look and taste "good" so that you would want to eat it. Additives and strong spices such as salt, pepper, garlic, etc., are used to mask the otherwise deplorable taste of denatured foods and trick the taste buds into accepting them. However, beyond the taste buds they meet with another challenge, the gastrointestinal tract (stomach and intestines). Often the gastrointestinal system cannot accept these items, thus it is not surprising that antacids, anti-gas and anti-diarrhea products top the list of products most purchased by consumers.

❖ Canning is used to preserve a wide variety of foods. Canning preserves food by heating it in airtight, vacuum-sealed containers. This process removes oxygen, destroys enzymes involved in food spoilage, and kills most microorganisms that may be present in the food. Up to half of the original content of water-soluble vitamins in a canned product can be lost in this way.[178]

❖ Irradiation is a process in which food is passed through a chamber where it is exposed to gamma rays or X rays. These high-energy rays are strong enough to break chemical bonds, destroy cell walls and cell membranes, and break down deoxyribonucleic acid (DNA), the substance that carries genetic information in all cells. Irradiation kills most bacteria, molds, and insects that may contaminate food. Irradiation also delays the ripening of fruits and sprouting of vegetables, permitting produce to be stored for longer periods of time. Because irradiation involves minimal heating, it has very little effect on the taste, texture, and nutritive value of food. The FDA first approved irradiation for use on wheat and wheat flour in 1963, and later approved its use on white potatoes, spices, pork, some fresh produce (onions, tomatoes, mushrooms, and strawberries), and poultry.[179]

❖ Pasteurization involves heating foods to a certain temperature for a specific time to kill harmful microorganisms. Milk, wine, beer, and fruit juices are all routinely pasteurized. Milk, for example, is usually heated to 145° F (63° C) for 30 minutes. Ultra-High Temperature (UHT) pasteurization, a relatively new technique, is used to sterilize foods for aseptic packaging. In UHT pasteurization, foods are

---

[176] "Food Processing and Preservation," *Microsoft® Encarta® Encyclopedia 2000.* © 1993-1999 Microsoft Corporation. All rights reserved.

[177] ibid

[178] ibid

[179] ibid

heated to 280° F (138° C) for 2 to 4 seconds, allowing the food to retain more nutrients and better flavor.[180] It is a little known fact that **Louis Pasteur** (1822-1895), world-renowned French chemist and biologist who was credited with founding the science of microbiology, proving the germ theory of disease, and inventing pasteurization, actually said that he had made a mistake. On his death-bed he said that he was wrong about the germ theory of disease.[181] In fact, his experiments revealed that disease and flies appear when he placed rotten foods and other materials to attract them. They were not attracted to healthy tissue. Again, why do people not develop strep throat, or tuberculosis (TB), which are supposedly "caused" by bacteria (*Streptococcus* and *Mycobacterium tuberculosis,* respectively) which are commonly found in the body and the environment? Why is it that only certain people develop these and other diseases and others do not?

❖ Genetic engineering refers to any deliberate alteration of an organism's DNA. Genetic engineering has been practiced for thousands of years, ever since humans began selectively breeding plants and animals to create more nutritious, better tasting foods. In the past two decades, genetic engineering has become increasingly powerful as scientific advances have enabled the direct alteration of genetic material. Genes have been cut and pasted from one species to another, yielding, for example, disease-resistant squash and rice, frost-resistant potatoes and strawberries, and tomatoes that ripen—and therefore spoil—more slowly.[182]

Author's note: Keep in mind that the nature of modern genetic engineering (available in the last 20 years) is different than what was available before. In the past, the possibilities for cross breeding plants and animals were still governed by nature. Now scientists can directly manipulate genes, circumventing the limitations of nature. This can lead to the creation of unknown organisms which may pose an unrestricted ecological threat to other organisms, such as microbes or viruses for which human beings have no defense, or foods that will irreparable damage human genes since they are not part of the natural food evolution process. For all the science and experiments, it is not known what effect the new organisms or other creations will have when relased into the environment. However, the profit motive has led many advocates of genetic engineering to play down the threat.

Antibiotics and Bacterial Resistance

It is ironic that prior to the advent of antibiotics and their so called potential to eradicate disease as miracle drugs in the 1950s, the medical profession was based on plants and herbs, and now we are moving back to the plants and herbs, that is back to nature. Now there is a steadily growing move away from synthetic chemicals and towards natural means to promote healing and maintain health. Many researchers and doctors in the medical establishment are fond of blaming veterinarians and others for "overusing" antibiotics and thereby allowing the bacteria to develop "immunities" to the drug. However, even if there was some value to this argument, how can there be any proper use of antibiotics in a society whose hygienic habits and food production and consumption practices necessitate the heavy use of the antibiotics and pesticides? That is, modern western society would not be able to survive and produce sufficient food (even denatured) to feed all the people and satisfy the craving for meat if it were not for the current level of pesticide and antibiotic use. So what is the overuse? A reduction in the use of

---

180 ibid

181 "Pasteur, Louis," *Microsoft® Encarta® Encyclopedia 2000.* © 1993-1999 Microsoft Corporation. All rights reserved.

182 ibid

pesticides and antibiotics could only be possible if there was a reduced need in the area of meat consumption. Meat consumption requires vast quantities of land that could be used for farming vegetables and fruits. Also, the diseases and health related problems caused by meat consumption would be reduced, if people eliminated meat from the diet. The animals would not require antibiotics and people would not develop diseases requiring antibiotics. The resources used to feed animals raised for human consumption would go towards feeding human beings instead of the animals, and since there would be less animals around because they are no longer being bred for this purpose, they would not need enormous stores of food. In addition, it must also be noted that the food that is fed to the animals is unnatural for them as well. It is not what they would be eating in their natural environment, under natural conditions. Where would cows or chickens or find large quantities of concentrated grains, and most likely grains that have been themselves genetically engineered to shorten the time span of their growth and maximize their production? Nowhere in nature. All animal husbandry practices (practices concerned with the care and breeding of domestic animals) in the food animal industry have developed around one concern: profit. Due to pressure and scrutiny as a result of various animal rights organizations, some of the more severe mistreatment practices have been discontinued, but many still exist, such as the castration and dehorning of young bulls without anesthesia, and the imposed mistreatment[183] and malnutrition of newborn baby cows for the veal industry.

As a result of the profit motive, the animal husbandry practices of the food animal industry have become focused on practices to shorten the interval of time it takes from the birth of the animal to the time to they can become slaughtered and sold to the public. Thus, they have created systems of food animal production to bring about these means by manipulating the animal's hormones, nutrition, breeding, environment and diet. Various methods are used such as hormone and light manipulation to bring the female animals to reproductive readiness at an earlier age, and hormones to induce ovulation or even multiple ovulations which are then used for embryo transfers to impregnate other females of that species (decreases the need for keeping a male animal around, plus the farmer can choose the genetic traits he wants; also, this is the technology that has been transferred to human reproductive medicine to deal with the issue of infertility in human females). In addition, growth hormones are given to the animals so that they can grow faster, and also they are fed diets that are very rich to so they can "fatten" sooner, so they can make it to market ASAP (as soon as possible). Interestingly, the meat industry has had pressure from the orthodox health systems to cut back on their "fattening" practices, because the amounts of fat in the animal tissue is a contributing factor in high blood fat levels (saturated fats, triglyceride and cholesterol) in people, and consequently in heart disease. As a result, they industry has come out with a "leaner" cuts of meat, for which they charge more since it requires that they exert more effort in the area of adhering to more natural techniques (such as feeding the animals more grasses) which slows down the usual process.

Naturally, the pressure that is put on the animal's body because of the above stated practices, as well as many more unnatural practices that are used, is immense, and consequently the animal's immune system becomes weakened. Now comes the need to supplement their diets with antibiotics, to spray pesticides on them to protect them from external parasites, and give them oral pesticides to rid them from internal parasites, to prevent them from succumbing to internal infections.

---

[183] Note: Veal calves are taken away from their mother right after their birth. They are not allowed to nurse from the mother, not even to get the, colostrum, the first important milk the mother produces which is rich in antibodies to protect the calf from various diseases. They are then kept in very small stalls and are tied so they cannot move. They are kept in a dark environment, away from sunlight, and fed a diet, which makes them anemic. The reason "veal" cutlets and other meats labeled "veal" are pale is due to the anemic condition of the animals as they are raised (purposely), and the reason the meat is tender is because the animals are tied and kept in confined stalls so they cannot move about and strengthen their muscle fibers, which would make the meat less tender. So in effect when someone buys veal which usually costs more than other cuts of meat and thinks they are getting a "better" food, in fact they are buying one of the most, if not the most unhealthy, un-nutritious, and unethical meat products.

All of these techniques and many more increase the "yield" of animals, or rather, the yield of meat available to the public. Then, through advertising, the industry induces and magnifies the desire in the susceptible public, either ignorant of what the proper diet of their bodies is supposed to be, or unable to control their desire due to lack of willpower, to eat meat...more and more, so they can continue to sell, more and more. So as stated previously, a reduction in the use of pesticides and antibiotics could only be possible if there was a reduced need in the area of meat consumption. Are you willing to make this change? Are you willing to give up old, familiar, comfortable, but spiritually, ethically and physically, bad habits, and an imbalanced lifestyle?

Yes, everyone does need to make a living now. But they needed to do so in ancient Kemet also; this situation was not different. However, making a living needn't be destructive for oneself, humanity, and the earth. Kemet had no shortage of doctors, lawyers, farmers, etc., but they also had true authentic leadership, spiritually and politically. They created jobs in other areas. How do you think the pyramids were built? Not by slaves as has been suggested. This "theory" had been scientifically and historically proven to be false. They were built by members of the society. How do you think the carvings and reliefs, the intricate details were created? By the members of the society. Thus, one need not worry about what will happen to all those people in the meat industry who will be out of work. Their energies can be used by the Divine Cosmic Intelligence to grow vegetables and fruits in wholistic ways. They can create a food industry that can feed healthy organic foods to the world, at a reasonable price. All this and so much more is possible in the realm of living a lifestyle based on the natural principles of health, of body, mind and spirit, not just on in individual level, but also on a community level, a national level, and at the world level.

There is one more factor that points to the illusoriness of vaccines and extremes in seeking hygiene.

> **THE FALSE COMFORT OF 'STERILE' LIVES[184]**
>
> Even as fewer people seek vaccinations -- in part because they believe that they are safe without them -- there has been a widespread increase in the use of antibacterial soaps and sprays at home, and parents and patients demand antibiotics at every sign of infection. These efforts at sterilizing our hands and countertops, and at killing every infection in our bodies can have just the opposite effect.
>
> Unless we soak our tables for many minutes and scrub our hands like surgeons, we can't kill all the bacteria on our skin, and what is left behind to survive and multiply are the stronger and more resistant germs. Our overuse of antibiotics has helped foster more numerous and stronger antibiotic-resistant microbes, to the point that we're running out of "last line" drugs to fight even the most resistant bacteria.

As the passage above suggests, in order to eradicate bacteria completely it would require extraordinary lengths and even then the idea of being free from microorganisms is faulty, because they not only live outside us, but also within us. There is a proper balance to be maintained, and keeping this balance in life allows us to live and maintain a condition wherein the microorganisms are, as it were, under control. Imagine what our ancestors did before the invention of antibacterial soaps? They lived without sterilizing their environment, or otherwise they would not have been able to think of anything else. Human life is possible due to a symbiotic relationship between bacteria and the chemical processes of the body. Without this balance life will not be possible. In fact, human beings are not individuals. Or rather, each individual is a walking, talking bundle of millions of individual living organisms. We are fooled because we only

[184] Free-riding microbes: stronger, more powerful, and our fault June 5, 2000 Web posted at: 3:38 p.m. EDT (1938 GMT) **by Jeffrey P. Kahn, Ph.D., M.P.H. Director, Center for Bioethics University of Minnesota**

see the largest one with two legs and two arms. So, balance, and not extremes between efforts towards health and living a fruitful life must be accomplished through the disciplines presented here, for outer physical and internal cleanliness.

Vaccines

Vaccines are another attempt by human beings to maintain a lifestyle that is incompatible with nature. Instead of complying with natural laws of living dictated by the body and the environment, people continue to search in vain for an artificial means to sustain the unrighteous desires of life. People do not need meat to survive; they desire it. People do not need antibiotics to survive; they want it because it allows them to live unbalanced lifestyles pursuing unnecessary desires through unnecessary means, and or in unhygienic conditions. People do not need cooked foods; they desire these because they want to satisfy the cravings of their palates to which they have become accustomed. Vaccines would not be necessary in a society where hygiene and proper nutrition are the foundation. Many people are fearful of vaccines as disease agents. This is because they are chemicals that do cause a real change in the chemistry and physiology of the body. While they may promote the development of antibodies to protect against a certain disease, many vaccines have the capacity to also promote the very same disease that they are supposedly trying to protect you from. It is a well-known fact that many people vaccinated for polio contracted the disease as a result of the vaccination. Other people have died from their use. Also, the long term effects of vaccines on individuals and the entire society are still unknown however, wholistic health practitioners feel that they have enough information to expect the worst, and most petition against vaccinating children (and adults). Even in the Veterinary Medical field, holistic and non-holistic Veterinary Medical practitioners are discussing the issue of vaccination. The discussion of this topic in the Veterinary Medical field has become more significant when it was found that in some animals, the vaccines were causing the development of malignant cancers where they were being injected. As a result veterinarians were advised to give the vaccines as far down on the legs as possible in some animals so if the cancer develops, the leg can be amputated! What a solution!

While the orthodox medical establishment attributes widespread vaccination campaigns for drastic reductions in illnesses that plagued the population in earlier decades, such as whooping cough, wholistic practitioners point out that these diseases were already on the decline prior to the introduction of the vaccines. Thus, the vaccines were falsely issued credit for the naturally occurring decline. All disease outbreaks go through a natural cycle. After the initial rise in the disease, the surviving population naturally develops immunity to the disease-triggering agent and or discovers and corrects conditions that predisposed to the disease, and the disease incidence declines in the population. Thus, wholistic practitioners feel that the trend for these conditions would have been a continued decline, without the introduction of vaccines, and thus, what the vaccine proponents are claiming as their victory is really a misinterpretation of the facts. To emphasize this point further, consider the following example. Suppose that you are running in a marathon race, and you are winning. Then, just with just a mile to go, with you still in the lead, I start to run along side you, to give you encouragement and support. Just as it would be highly questionable if I were to then make a statement of fact that the reason you won the race is because I intervened and ran along side you, it is erroneous for vaccine proponents to state that vaccines were responsible for the decline in these diseases, as a matter of fact. Rather, the most probable cause of the decrease in the incident of diseases was improved hygienic practices.

- History reveals that vaccines have not been helpful in eradicating disease. They have been introduced to society at a point when the plague or disease had already taken its toll on the population and was already waning. Thus it appeared that the vaccines had an effect.
- Actually, statistics show that 50% of those who take immunization shots actually "catch" the disease they were supposedly immunized against and actually take longer to heal from the disease when compared to those who were not immunized and "caught" the disease.
- CONCLUSION: vaccines and immunizations do not help but rather weaken the immune system and debilitate the body's ability to cope with disease.

Children are especially susceptible to the negative effects of vaccinations and immunizations. It is possible for a parent or legal guardian to file an AFFIDAVIT DECLARATION OF VACCINATION EXEMPTION with the state in which they reside in the USA. One can seek exception on grounds of Senate Bill #942, Section 1, Chapter 7, under the title "Exemption From Immunization" (one can file for a *MEDICAL EXEMPTION, RELIGIOUS EXEMPTION, PHILOSOPHICAL EXEMPTION).* For more information contact the Sema Institute.

Hygiene Inside the Body and the pH of the Body

We have spoken much about hygiene of the body. This gives most people the impression that outer cleanliness is the impetus. While outer cleanliness in undoubtedly important and enjoined by the ancient wisdom of the Kemetic diet system, the other aspect of hygiene –internal– is paramount. Internal purity allows the body to maintain health, and is promoted by proper nutrition (vegetarian-vegan, uncooked diet). The proper diet leads to maintaining an alkaline (basic) pH internal environment supporting the alkaline pH of normal blood. If the internal environment of the body becomes disbalanced by eating the wrong foods, ingesting drugs, negative thoughts, stress, poisons, etc., the body develops an acid environment. And just as acid corrodes and eats through materials, so too it eats through and corrodes the various systems of the body. This damage in all its forms is what orthodox medicine calls disease. Therefore, acidosis is a condition that one must prevent or correct in order to maintain or restore health. If this condition should develop, one must know how to bring the body back to balance. Understanding acidosis also facilitates one in understanding the genetic/inherited basis or predisposition to disease. For example, not everyone with acidosis develops diabetes. Some people may develop arthritis, or immune deficiency, or cancer, or high blood pressure, or high cholesterol, according to the organs and tissues in their body where they may have a congenital, hereditary[185], or acquired (due to trauma, toxins, previous illness, etc.) weakness or susceptibility to a certain condition. In other words, the weakest areas in a person's body will be affected by the acidity first.

---

[185] According to the Sema (Yoga-Kemetic Diet) concept of disease, conditions that are congenital (child is born with it) or hereditary (passed on genetically from parents to child) are tied to one's ari (karma) from previous life times. In terms of hereditary conditions, past arise from previous lifetimes lead one to be born to specific parents to pass on those genetic traits (which can be considered as tendencies or susceptibilities since there are usually elements of nutrition, environment, lifestyle, etc. which play roles in whether or not the condition will express itself as a "disease" process in a particular individual. This is elaborated on further in the upcoming section on Diabetes and sugar consumption.

> Acidosis, abnormal condition in which the acid-base balance of the blood is upset, with the blood becoming too acidic (pH below 7). May be caused by kidney malfunction, diabetes, or other diseases. Symptoms include weakness and malaise.[186]

It is important to note that whereas orthodox medicine describes acidosis as being caused by various diseases, wholistic health practitioners recognize it as the cause of metabolic "disease" conditions. Perhaps this is because traditional orthodox medicine does not pay attention to blood pH as a measure of health (denoting the level of toxicity in the body), screening for it the way they screen patients for high cholesterol or anemia, etc., as a part of a routine health exam.

The green diet, as well as the supplements given earlier, along with the disciplines for mind and soul, are the means to restore the body to the proper internal pH. When this is done, the body will be able to restore and maintain health once again. So acidosis is the primary problem. It is caused by malnutrition and a toxic lifestyle. Acidosis causes the body to react by producing an excess of mucus, which the body uses to move and excrete the toxins introduced through improper foods, drugs, etc., as well as those released by fungi and bacteria(s) that have proliferated within the body due to the imbalance of the body's chemistry.

Bacteria and fungi thrive in an acidic blood environment, so the answer to the problem of bacterias, viruses and fungi is not to produce vaccines, antibiotics and a host of pharmaceutical drugs, with all of the attendant side effects, with which to bombard them, but to restore the proper hygiene of the body that will eliminate or prevent the conditions under which they can survive and multiply. Focusing on microorganisms, as the cause of disease is the equivalent of saying that sewage causes flies. Sewage does not create flies, but rather attracts flies. And while the flies can further the spread diseases that may be present in the sewage, they are not the primary problem. Thus, no matter what is used to kill the flies, and how many flies are killed, flies will continually be present around the sewage for as long as it remains there, and disease will continue to be spread, until proper hygienic measures are taken to remove the sewage. While the flies can be cited as a complicating factor in the spread of disease, they cannot be considered as the cause of the disease. Likewise, the condition of acidosis creates an unhealthy internal environment within the body (which weakens the immune system) that attracts opportunistic fungi, bacterias and viruses which are ever abundantly present within us, on us and in our environment, and allows them to take hold. So what the orthodox medical doctors focus their attention and treatments on as the primary problem of a disease, that is, the fungi, bacterias and viruses (for example, viral pneumonia or bacterial pneumonia), is from the perspective of the wholistic practitioner, not the primary problem. Granted, once fungi, bacteria and viruses become involved they complicate matters, but their presence can be more easily and safely eliminated by addressing the primary problem, acidosis, just as the problem of the flies can be best handled by removing the sewage, rather than further complicating an already bad situation (the sewage) by applying toxic chemicals to kill the flies.

Antibiotics, antiviral agents, antifungal medications generally have side effects, upsetting the normal balance of the body. Eliminating the fungi, bacteria and viruses decreases the burden on the immune system and the body in general, and along with the forced rest one must take when ill, the self imposed fast from feeling too sick to eat or the doctor imposed fasts to allow for various blood and other testing procedures to be performed, the blood becomes cleansed to some degree, and depending on the degree of cleansing (alkalinization) relative the level of toxicity (acidosis) of the body, the body may be able to recover. Thus, traditional orthodox medicines "appear" to work. However, if habits are not changed, the problem is likely to recur.

[186] Random House Encyclopedia Copyright (C) 1983,1990 by Random House Inc.

Thus, year after year, people "catch" the "same" cold, again and again, and doctors, with all of their technology, are still unable to "prevent" or "cure" the common cold. With all of the billions of tax-payer and donation dollars the pharmaceutical and medical establishments have spent on research for all of the various cancers, AIDS, Diabetes, and other "diseases," they are yet to find cures. Rather, the statistics indicate that the incidence of these conditions (not to mention – side effects and complications due to the unnatural drug treatments they have devised) is higher now than when they began their research, and they are predicted to reach epidemic proportions in the next 10-20 years and totally overwhelm the current orthodox medical establishment and health care system. This is because they are researching the effect (presence of microorganisms) rather than the true cause (acidosis) of illness. As they are looking in the wrong place for the answers to their questions of disease and health, no matter how much "new" information their research reveals or how many breakthroughs they have, their results can never lead to true healing and health. And that money could be put to so much better use than to supporting their self-created, self-imposed and self-perpetuated paradigm: The Orthodox Medical Establishment. They have created their own difficulties and challenges by refusing to acknowledge the natural, simple and inexpensive route to health. They have chosen to pursue a model for health that can never produce a solution, and thus creating their problem, they now feverishly strive to pursue a solution, and in the pursuit, they look like heroes for undertaking such a daunting and challenging task. They have created their own language, often referred to as medical jargon, which the general public for the most part does not understand, and thus by obfuscation they seem to be so smart and trustworthy. Perhaps they can be left alone to eventually find out the futility in their pursuits, just the way a parent, after telling a child to not pursue a certain course of action based on the parent's experience, may just shrug their shoulders and let the child pursue the action if the child refuses to listen. But for most parents, they will follow this course IF AND ONLY IF the child's action will not seriously hurt the child or others. So, the wait and watch attitude cannot be undertaken in the case of the traditional orthodox establishment, as people are dying as a result of their erroneous assumptions, beliefs, practices and information and they have under their control the mouthpiece and finances of the government to impose their views on the general population through the media, schools, etc., and the power t orestrict or prevent the voicing of dissenting opinions or the work natural health practitioners. They have turned away from their sacred oath as doctors, "Above all do no harm," and taken on a new one, as voiced by a doctor on recent television medical show on The Discovery Health Channel, after he stapled the stomach of morbidly obese woman: " Well, we are doing more good than harm."

The monies that they are wasting on their futile researches, technologies and practices could be put to so much better use in these economically difficult times, especially with respect to health care. Most medical doctors are well meaning but misguided. However, one could make cases for murder or at least depraved indifference to human life for the many patients who have needlessly died at the hands of the orthodox health care system, which for the most part refuses to listen to wholistic health practitioners and take them seriously. At the very least they should be charged with "depraved indifference"! Why should they listen to wholistic health practitioners? What is in it for them? It would mean that the orthodox doctors would need to become trained in the areas of nutrition, meditation, stress management techniques, fasting, cleansing, and other wholistic health modalities to restore the body's alkaline pH, and they may not make as much money that they now do, but at least they will once again be able to say: "Above all, I have done no harm!"

True physical health can only come from a lifestyle which will promote spiritual fulfillment, mental lucidity and an alkaline blood pH, such as eating proper foods, cleansing, as well as reducing stress. The Stress Response creates acidity in the body, so the mental condition of the patient must also be addressed. As the ability to keep the mind calm is supported by spiritual insight, the process of returning the blood to an alkaline pH must include components which address issues of the body, mind and spirit of the individual. Under these conditions, the immune, endocrine, digestive, circulatory and other vital health maintenance systems of the body will function normally and healthily.[187]

Malnutrition toxins ➔ acidosis ➔ mucus formation ➔ disease

So malnutrition and toxins in and around the body lead to acidosis, and acidosis leads to mucus formation and the disease process of Ukhedu. Therefore, a poor diet is referred to as a mucus-forming diet. Mucus formation is not a disease but the body's way of getting rid of excess impurities in order to restore health and not drown in the toxic environment. As discussed previously, one manifestation of this process is the development of a "cold" which is really only a means to allow the body to rid itself of the excess toxins.

However if the body's cleansing mechanism is hampered, and it is not able to get rid of the excess mucus buildup, then the mucus will create a disruption in the structure and function of the tissues and organs where it becomes deposited, based on individual susceptibility, as discussed above. The result of this is what we call specific diseases. For example, a build up in the pancreas is called diabetes. A build up in the joints is called arthritis. A build up in the colon is called anything from constipation or diarrhea, to colon cancer, depending on the severity of the buildup. Drugs that suppress mucus are actually causing the body to hoard impurities; these will stay in the body longer and have more opportunity to cause changes (mutations) in the body that will promote usually more severe disease.

> *"There is no disease whose prime cause is better known, so that today ignorance is no longer an excuse that one cannot do more about prevention of cancer "... "But how long prevention will be avoided depends on how long the prophets of agnosticism will succeed in inhibiting the application of scientific knowledge in the field of cancer. In the meantime millions of men and women must die of cancer unnecessarily. "*

"The Prime Cause and Prevention of Cancer". Otto Warburg, two time Nobel Prize in Medicine winner, lecture at the meeting of Nobel Laureates, June 30, **1966** Director, Max Planck Institute for Cell Physiology, Berlin.

- Otto Warburg showed that cancer was related to the development of anaerobic conditions in the cells.[188]
- This deficiency in oxygen resulted in fermentation and a corresponding drop in pH (acidosis).[189]
- Carcinogens cause mutations in the normal cells (Cancer). This does not occur when the pH is between 7.4 and 6.6 which allows the breakdown of glucose into the A, C, G and T nucleotide radicals that permit healthy DNA synthesis.
- Malnutrition, leading to vitamin and mineral deficiencies that produce (toxic) acidic conditions in the cells are the cause of cell mutations (cancers). Therefore, the search for cancer causing genes is a waste of time, energy and money, not to mention the millions of people who contract disease and die needlessly every year. Further, the tonsils and appendix are natural parts of the body that should not be cut out. They become a problem only when the ipurities of the body are so severe that these structures are affected and compromised. So if they develop any problems, it is a sign

[187] Endocrine System, body system made up of all the endocrine, or ductless, glands that secrete chemical substances known as hormones directly into the bloodstream where they act to control body functions. Random House Encyclopedia Copyright (C) 1983,1990 by Random House Inc.
[188] *(Cause and prevention of Cancer;* Biochem, Zeits, 152: 514-520, 1924)
[189] (Low *pH Hyperthermia Cancer Therapy;* Cancer Chemotherapy Pharmacology 4; 137-145, 1980).

that the body is extremely toxic and not necessarily that surgery is needed, unless the problem has gone too far.

The Hygiene of the immediate environment is also extremely important. Human beings are not meant to live in cold and damp conditions where mold can form. Molds are any of various fungi that often cause disintegration of organic matter. Mold can lead to several health problems including respiratory distress and infections. Damp areas are usually closed in and curtailed ventilation can also be detrimental to the physical constitution.

Poor hygiene can promote infectious diseases, as Europe found out during the period of the plagues. Healing for Bronchitis and other infectious diseases in accordance with the Kemetic Diet Principles would be as follows. Bronchitis is an inflammation or obstruction of the bronchi which are the mettus (tubes) for leading air to the lungs. It can be chronic or acute. The acute is caused by infections (bacterial, viral, etc.). It can also occur after a "cold" or "flu". The chronic form can be due to continuing exposure to environmental pollutants, smoking, diet, climate changes, etc. If serious it can lead to heart disease and death. Therefore, the internal hygiene must be cleansed by ingesting whole green and nutritious foods and fluids. The external environment needs to be cleand also, eradicating chemical pollutants. The mental environment needs to be cleansed by promoting relaxation and positive thinking. And the spiritual environment needs to be supported also, through prayer and propitiation of the Divine.

Diabetes and the Overuse of Sugar

***Eliminating processed, refined, or concentrated sugars in the diet is an important aspect of health.**

> Diabetes Mellitus, a common metabolic disorder in which the body's inability to obtain and/or and use adequate amounts of the hormone insulin results in a disease process characterized by inability to handle carbohydrates. It may also affect many other body organs and functions. Susceptibility to diabetes mellitus is inherited, but the disease usually develops with obesity, pregnancy, menopause, infection, or severe emotional stress, and is slightly more common in females. A nonhereditary form is produced by cancer of the pancreas. Insulin is normally secreted by islets in the pancreas. In juvenile diabetes, the pancreas is diseased and too little insulin is produced, and severe symptoms result. In maturity, or adult-onset (after 40) diabetes mellitus, the effectiveness and/or speed of the release of insulin from the pancreas is often disturbed, producing minor, or in some cases, almost no symptoms. In diabetes mellitus, the body cannot handle the sugar end-products of carbohydrate metabolism and convert them to energy compounds. The excess sugar is excreted in the urine. Signs such as frequent urination, dry mouth, extreme thirst, weakness, weight loss, and blurred vision can result. Diagnosis depends on urine and blood tests as well as special glucose-tolerance tests. The disease cannot be cured but can be treated with carbohydrate-limited diet, exercise, and administration of drugs--either insulin injection or synthetic oral drugs--to lower blood-sugar levels.[190]

Firstly, it is important to understand that refined sugar is an addictive drug and a poison.

One of the main problems leading to acidosis in the body is the ingestion of sugar. When people think of sugar, they often think of refined sugar such as those added to candy, pastries and other synthetic products. However, there is a range of foods, that when eaten, produce excess sugar in the body. This eventually overloads the sugar handling mechanism of the body (insulin produced by the pancreas) and leads to its breakdown. Also it will lead to an internal environment of the body that is acidic, and thereby

[190] Random House Encyclopedia Copyright (C) 1983,1990 by Random House Inc.

perfect for microbes and fungi to multiply in excess of the norm, thereby producing toxic conditions and compromising the functions of the internal systems. Therefore, refined sugar should be strictly avoided, and certain foods obtained in nature should not be eaten to excess. These include sweet fruits. The green diet will automatically promote the proper conditions of the body since generally all vegetables fit for human consumption are pH base (alkaline). So, again, the vegetable based diet and sublime outlook on life and disciplines for inner self-discovery are the most compatible and harmonious diet (food for body, mind and soul) for human consumption.

One point deserves mention here. The concept that one is susceptible to "hereditary" problems follows the fact that one's coming into the world occurred through the ill preparation of the parents (ie. parents not living a wholistically balanced lifestyle in this and or previous lifetimes), and one's own negative Ari (one's own lack of living a holistically balanced lifestyle in a previous lifetime). As introduced earlier in this volume, if you acted in negative ways in past lives you will likely be drawn to parents who themselves are degraded (not living a balanced holistic lifestyle) your next incarnation. If the egg from the mother who leads a degraded lifestyle, and or the sperm of a father who leads a degraded lifestyle meet, there ensues the possibility of damaged DNA in one or both, causing or predisposing one to all manner of diseases from birth defects and mental illness to chronic illnesses. However, one's current actions, meaning one's adoption of a proper lifestyle now, will mitigate for past inadequacies and even repair some or all of the damage from the past. This is the message of yogic spirituality. You have the ability to improve your situation now, regardless of your past, and you can exercise that ability right now by first making up your mind to do so, and then by taking steps in that direction.

Refined sugar is an artificial and unnecessary additive which, like processed salt, is used to excite the palate and cause people to select foods not for their nutritional value, but for their ability to service an addiction. Additions to sugar are well documented. Simply test yourself by abstaining for several days (if you can hold out that long). Sugar is a scourge that has only recently become one, if not the most important source, of illness in modern times, so much so that this knowledge is reflected in up to date encyclopedias.

> **SUGAR**. A liking for sweet things seems natural to people everywhere. In ancient times people satisfied their desire for sweets with honey. Today sugar is the most widely used sweetener.
>
> Sugar is most often used to sweeten foods and beverages. In earlier times, sugar was used as a sedative, but today it is associated with a number of health problems. It is known, for example, that excessive consumption of sugar can contribute to obesity and promote tooth decay. In addition, sugar has been associated with hyperactivity in children and hypertension in adults. Nevertheless it remains a popular food and flavoring. "Sugar" is a general term for a category of carbohydrate compounds, but the granules or cubes of common table sugar are specifically sucrose. A group of related compounds belonging to the same group of carbohydrates and termed sugars by chemists are corn sugar (called glucose or dextrose), fruit sugar (called fructose or levulose), milk sugar (lactose), and malt sugar (maltose) (*see* Carbohydrates). In addition to these compounds there are the relatively indigestible sugars used in "sugarless" candies and gums manitol and sorbitol.[191]

One would necessarily want to ask the medical establishment why the use of sugar and other chemicals are allowed in foods if their goal is to promote health and well being. In ancient times honey was used, but remember that the honey produced by bees was not processed or refined and it was not abundantly available in most foods and in quantities that would saturate the body. In addition, the fruit trees that the bees used as their source to produce the honey were not trees that were sprayed with herbicides, pesticides and fungicides, etc., as we have today, except for a few sources that provide organic

[191]Excerpted from *Compton's Interactive Encyclopedia.* Copyright (c) 1994, 1995 Compton's NewMedia, Inc. All Rights Reserved

honey. With respect to honey also, while it can be used as to assist in the transition from table sugar, one should have the understanding that it should be stopped altogether. Honey is still technically an animal product of sorts, and also what most people are usually unaware of is that honey is a product of regurgitation (vomit) from bees. A better choice for a transition substitute is maple syrup, and even better is a natural herbal product called stevia.

You must take care to read the labels on the foods you want to eat and look for sugar in all of its processed forms: sugar, sucrose, dextrose, glucose, fructose, levulose, high fructose corn syrup, lactose, maltose, manitol and sorbitol, honey, maple syrup, etc. Stay away from any foods with processed sugars. You will obtain natural sugars by eating proper quantities of the foods recommended in this book. Consuming sugars that are extracted and concentrated will produce an imbalanced situation in the body because the other balancing compounds that one would ordinarily ingest along with the sugar when eating, let's say an apple, are not there. The microorganisms of the body that exist in a normal balance begin to multiply wildly in the presence of excess sugar, fermenting any other compounds that were taken in with the sugar, producing intestinal gas. The more they multiply, the more sugar they want, and herein lies the reason for part of the craving for sugar that one experiences; it is a stimulation by the bacteria to feed them...that is, to feed them more sugar. The more they multiply, the more they release chemical wastes into the mettus, and this of course is the beginning of toxin accumulation in the mettus, and ultimately diseases of all types.

Salt Requirements

Sodium is an essential mineral for human health. It is needed for maintaining proper mineral balance, and proper fluid balance in the cells as well as in the rest of the body. This bolsters the immune system and the effective functioning of the body's organs as well as proper muscle function and maintains the proper pH. When a person has an accident and the doctor calls for "fluids," the nurse does not bring distilled water, but rather a "saline solution." Saline solution is a special solution, containing salt, that is isotonic with blood and is used in medicine and surgery.

Many authorities state that the body requires small amounts, for example less that 500 miligrams of sodium per day[192] in order to remain healthy. Ingestion of large amounts of sodium, such as those found in canned foods or foods preserved with salt (salted fish, etc.), can lead to hypertension, and also it can exacerbate conditions like heart failure, premenstrual syndrome and kidney disease. Early experimentation led to the extreme belief that all salt should be cut out of the diet, and rightly so since the Standard Western Diet is already full of salt from the additives by manufacturers and canned goods. So people struggled to eat their bland tasting food. However, these very low requirements are usually put forth in reference to the arbitrary RDA minimum figures. Recent experiments have shown that those low numbers are not adequate.

> A recent four year study by the prestigious Albert Einstein College of medicine (done in association with the prestigious Cornell University Medical college) on 1,900 men with high blood pressure concluded that high blood pressure patients who ate less than 5 grams of salt a day had **more than four times as** many **heart attacks** as those who consumed over 10 grams a day. Although a *"tremendous"* increase in salt can lead to a *"small"* crease in blood pressure, low sodium causes the level of rennin hormone, secreted by the kidneys, in the blood to go up, and rennin is found in high levels of patients with high blood pressure.

---

[192] *Prescription for Nutritional Healing,* James F. Balch M.D. and Phyllis A Balch, C.N.C.

Thus, it is true that large amounts of salt in the diet can be detrimental but so too can all of the minerals and vitamins as well as the chemicals in food. Certainly, the extreme amounts found in canned foods should be avoided, but sodium need not and indeed should not be cut out from the diet entirely. Some will come from foods naturally. If more is needed there are viable alternatives that the health enthusiast can use as substitutes.

- ❖ Namashoyu (raw soy sauce – instead of regular soy sauce or Braggs Amino Acids) (organic)
- ❖ Kelp granules (organic)
- ❖ Sea salt (organic)

When the body is purified, a person can feel the authentic nutritional needs that it has, and they will automatically move towards and consume the kinds of foods that they need at any given time. So it is important to cleanse out the toxins, consume pure foods, and use supplementation if necessary, until the body may be able to function more normally. It is important to recognize that the body is designed to be a balanced system. If it is treated with extremes, it will move towards other extremes. Therefore, it is appropriate to seek balance. The Kamitan term for balance is Maat, which also means, truth, justice and order. So one must seek the truth of the balance that sustains life and therein will be discovered the path to harmony with nature. However, balance and moderation does not apply to synthetic and unnatural additives and chemicals. These must be avoided altogether. Processed salt is certainly one of the items to be avoided completely as extremely hazardous to health, as it contains a myriad of chemicals, is bleached, and the minerals are taken out. Rather, seek balance and harmony within the bounty of vegetables and herbs that nature provides. Nature's wisdom is far older than that of medical doctors who by comparison cannot be even compared as children. As the medical treatments put forth by medical doctors throughout their history reveal themselves to be dismal failures of medical science in their ability to handle *chronic degenerative disease* no other conclusion can be drawn other than to understand that the medical establishment does not know what it is doing, except perhaps in the area of trauma medicine and surgery.

Aids and other Diseases of the Immune System

There is no proof of the connection between HIV and AIDS.

There are many misconceptions related to the Auto-Immune Deficiency Syndrome (AIDS) and the Human Immunodeficiency Virus, as well as many other diseases of the immune system. First of all, despite the years of repetition in the news media or by scientist, as of this date **THERE IS NO SCIENTIFIC EXPERIMENT OR ANY KIND OF PROOF THAT SHOWS A LINK BETWEEN THE HIV VIRUS AND THE AIDS**. This is significant because it points to a failure of the scientific community to discover a cause and much less a cure for the problem (or disease-if there actually is one). It is often most comfortable for people in the general society to have an illusion as opposed to the reality, of situations going on in the world around them. They, therefore, seek no further information than that which they are presented with by the orthodox medical and research establishments and the general news media. They can relax in their idea of feeling that they know the cause of the disease, and that they or someone somewhere are working towards a solution, even if it is a false sense of security.

In fact there have been immune system diseases, cancers and other disorders in the world previously and what seems to have happened is that they are being ascribed to the HIV without any substantiation. What this does is that it lets politicians and business leaders "off the hook" as it were, since the blame for the diseases can be shifted from toxic waste, pollution, economic systems that maintain people in poverty, and unhygienic conditions, to some nondescript virus. The immune system diseases and their related problems existed in Africa and other parts of the world prior to the so-called discovery of the HIV. Since no causal connection between AIDS and HIV as been reported by anyone and a causative connection has been discovered between AIDS related diseases and non infectious factors, why is it that the media and drug companies as well as the medical establishment, including the WHO (World Health Organization), continue to promote the idea that there is a virus which causes AIDS.

It must be realized and understood that when HIV was discovered, it does not mean that was when HIV first appeared on the scene of human history. This marked only the development of the human capacity, via technology, to detect it. Due to the process of Ukhedu (acid/mucus buildup in the mettu) arising from living an imbalanced wholistic lifestyle (spiritually, mentally and physically), people's immune systems become overwhelmed and overactive. Because the tissues are so steeped in toxicity, the body goes into a life or death—self –preservation mode, revving up the immune system in an effort to rid itself of the toxicity. Under these conditions, it is reasonable to theorize that tissue damage results from the effect of the toxins as well as from the inability of the immune system to distinguish and remove the toxicity from the now severely diseased tissue.

The Divine Cosmic Intelligence within the body is always striving to keep it alive, and therefore, most of what the orthodox medical profession considers to be diseases or symptoms of diseases, from conditions such as hot flashes in menopause to cancer, are in fact mechanisms put in place by the body to keep it alive, to survive. While they can be used as warning signals or markers of toxicity in the body, they should not be treated as the enemy which must be destroyed, for example, the approach that is used with cancer. The body has many protective mechanisms built in. In a healthy body, at every moment it is working to destroy cancer and other denatured cells that are arising in the body due to various toxic chemicals and metabolic processes. However, when the toxicity is so severe and the damage too great that it cannot keep up with the destruction, it goes to its next level of defense, which may be to at least try to wall off the diseased cells. Hence it forms what orthodox medicine calls tumors. Many wholistic practitioners are reluctant to remove growths and tumors, because they say these are acting as toxic dumps for the body's wastes, and they feel that when these tumors are removed and the lifestyle remains the same, then the toxins are driven back into the body, and will disrupt other tissues and cause other more severe problems internally. That was why the body built this receptacle (tumor) in the first place, because it needed somewhere to isolate and deal with the toxic situation. So at each level of assault from toxic conditions, the body does its best, albeit under the compromised circumstances, so that may not appear to the outside world (orthodox medical doctors) that it is doing anything to keep the person alive. If this process is not understood, interrupting the body's mechanism, as orthodox medicine often does, rather than assisting it through wholistic means, can have severe consequences.

Consider the following example to try to understand this point a little better. Suppose that you visited a friend, and found her apartment in a mess...total chaos. You may leave with the impression that she is a very messy and dirty person, and that she is not even trying to clean things up. What you don't know is that your friend has a roommate who is the messy one, and your friend is actually an extremely neat person, and has actually been spending every moment of her free time running around trying to clean up the roomate's mess, but the situation is just overwhelming. So to someone just dropping by, things look very bad, but from your friend's point of view, even though things aren't optimal, they are better than the alternative that exists without her efforts. She's just trying to make the best out of a bad situation. She doesn't particularly like the choices she has, either living in a really dirty apartment where there is no floor space even to walk, or an apartment with boxes and papers stacked up everywhere around, but at least allowing space to walk on the floors, but opts for the latter since it at least allows her to be able to walk through the apartment. So, similarly, even the seemingly bizarre behavior by the immune system of creating a tumor is to keep the body alive, in hopes that the one who possesses the body will make a move engage in wholistic health practices to detoxify the body and bring it back into balance.

Consider another example. Increased blood cholesterol leading to blocked arteries is seen by the orthodox medical establishment as the problem or "disease" process, but by the body in a state of toxicity, as a protective mechanism to stay alive. From the body's perspective, if this plaque was not present on the blood vessels, the abnormally high acidity of the blood would burn through the blood vessels walls and cause internal hemorrhage, much in the same manner that sulfuric or any other strong acid poured onto the skin would severely damage it. Although the body knows that high cholesterol and plaque formation will eventually lead to death, it has chosen to take care of what it knows to be the most imminent danger first, preventing the formation of an aneurysm, which may then proceed to rupture and lead to internal hemorrhage. Thus, it is not surprising that one of the potential side effects of blood cholesterol lowering medications is hemorrhage. By pulling the cholesterol out of the bloodstream without resolving the issue of acidity, the protective mechanism to wall off the arteries from the acidity is prevented, and consequently the vessels are slowly eaten away by the acid, until they rupture.

Thus, just as orthodox medicine labels high blood cholesterol as a disease in and of itself, while wholistic medicine sees it as a hallmark of a deeper process of imbalance (imbalanced lifestyle - acidosis), the clinical signs that science labels as AIDS, holistic practitioners would regard as signs of toxicity in the body due to an imbalanced lifestyle – acidosis. So, the recommended approach for people with conditions that have been labeled as AIDS by the orthodox medical community, or those afflicted by any viruses, from the flu virus to the so-called and yet unidentifiable HIV, or any other autoimmune syndromes, and for that matter, for any so called "disease" states or conditions, would be the same: Implement the principles as outlined in this book for wholistic living.

Ordinary diseases are mislabeled as AIDS

So, the diseases that are considered as AIDS are actually a large list of disorders that are indistinguishable from diseases caused by any other unbalancing factors affecting the immune system. So what happens is that whenever the nondescript HIV antibodies are found in someone who develops one of the diseases, then the person is labeled as having AIDS, otherwise they are considered to have the particular disease.

THE LONG LIST OF AFRICAN AIDS DISEASES CAN NOT BE CLINICALLY DISTINGUISHED FROM THEIR CONVENTIONAL COUNTERPARTS

According to the WHO's Bangui definition of AIDS (Widy-Wirski et al., 1988; Fiala, 1998) and the "Anonymous AIDS Notification" forms of the South African Department of Health, **African AIDS is not a specific clinical disease, but a battery of previously known and thus totally unspecific diseases, for example:**

1. "weight loss over 10%,
2. chronic diarrhea for more than a month,
3. fever for more than a month,
4. persistent cough,
5. generalized pruritic dermatitis,
6. recurrent herpes zoster (shingles),
7. candidiasis oral and pharyngeal,
8. chronic or persistent herpes,
9. cryptococcal meningitis,
10. Kaposi's sarcoma"

Since these diseases include the most common diseases in Africa and in much of the rest of the world, it is impossible to distinguish clinically African AIDS diseases from previously known, and concurrently diagnosed, conventional African diseases. Thus African AIDS is clinically unspecific, unlike microbial diseases, but just like some nutritionally and chemically caused diseases (see above).[193]

It must be clearly understood that all scientists believe they have found is an "antibody" to the supposed virus. An antibody is an agent released by the body to combat foreign materials attacking the body. So it is an assumed discovery that there actually is a virus. Yet, these hard to detect antibodies are ascribed to the elusive virus in the face of contrary evidence which points to other factors such as environment, poverty, malnutrition, etc. Peter Duesberg P.h. D., a respected scientist, has been one of the leading voices dissenting from the general scientific and media propaganda. Peter H. Duesberg, Ph.D. is a professor of Molecular and Cell Biology at the University of California, Berkeley. He isolated the first cancer gene through his work on retroviruses in 1970, and mapped the genetic structure of these viruses. This, and his subsequent work in the same field, resulted in his election to the National Academy of Sciences in 1986. He is also the recipient of a seven-year Outstanding Investigator Grant from the National Institutes of Health.

[193] From the Peter Duesburg Aids web site (Aids and Africa) http://www.duesberg.com/africa2.html

In 1960 a veteran retrovirologist urged his peers to "raise questions whether the known facts about viruses suffice to account for it." The subject was cancer, the veteran was Peyton Rous, and the quote is from a paper in *Cancer Research.* Mindful of that example, in 1 987 1 asked a similar question in a paper likewise published in *Cancer Research:* whether the known facts about two human retroviruses suffice to account for leukemia and AIDS. Clearly, following Rous' example did not make me very popular with the multinational club of retrovirologists. My article was officially ignored and not "dignified" with a response because the AIDS virus establishment was "too busy ... saving lives" and testing for antibodies to HIV I was often shunned like an AIDS patient by my former fellow retrovirologists. My views were unwelcome for several reasons: after a frustrating, twenty-year-long search for a human cancer virus, the retrovirologists were craving for clinical relevance and hence happily adopted HIV-"the AIDS virus"-as the cause of AIDS. The discovery of HIV was announced in the U.S. at a press conference and the virus-AIDS hypothesis became instant national dogma. On this basis, the retrovirologists convinced their governments to spend billions of dollars to stop the predicted viral epidemic, already being labeled "the epidemic of the 20th century." The virus was also the immediate darling of the biotechnology companies. Due to its very low complexity, it can be readily cloned for diagnostic test kits and vaccines. In turn, the virus was a hit with the press because it mobilized in readers the instinctive fears of a contagious disease, and appealed to the public prejudice that all evil comes from without.

-Peter H. Duesberg, Ph.D.

There is no such thing as an "AIDS" virus.

The research of Duesburg and other scientists shows the invalidity of the virus claim, and since the mid 1980's when he began to contradict the party line about AIDS his research has been marginalized and for the most part ignored. The so called AIDS "epidemic" does not react like other epidemics but rather reacts like a poison in the environment, and when the poison is removed, the "AIDS" seems to reduce and disappear.

Likewise the American and European AIDS epidemics:

- rose steadily, not exponentially,
- were completely non-randomly biased 85% in favor of males,
- have followed first the over-use of recreational drugs, and then the extensive use of anti-AIDS-viral drugs (Duesberg & Rasnick, 1998),
- do not manifest in one or even just a few specific diseases typical of microbial epidemics,
- do not spread to the general non-drug using population.

AIDS manifests in a bewildering spectrum of 30 non-specific, heterogeneous diseases. This is consistent with the heterogeneity of the causative toxins. There is no evidence for AIDS-immunity in 18 years, but the American/European AIDS epidemics are now coming down slowly as fewer people use recreational drugs (Duesberg & Rasnick, 1998).

> For example, the American pellagra epidemic of the rural South in the early decades of the 20th century lasted for decades and no immunity emerged, until a vitamin B rich diet proved to be the cure. And it did not spread to the industrial North which had a diet rich in Vitamin B. Similarly the rather unspecific American epidemic of lung cancer-emphysema-heart disease-etc. rose steadily, not exponentially, in the 1950s and has lasted now for over 50 years without evidence for immunity. It did not spread randomly in the population but was restricted to smokers. And it is now slowly coming down as smoking slowly declines (Greenlee *et al.*, 2000). [194]

So the only thing that is clear from the research is that there is an epidemic of ignorance, hysteria and greed, since it is evident that the problems currently labeled as "AIDS" have other causes, and relatively simple solutions such as the institution of proper dietary and hygienic conditions, the removal of poverty, and the provision of education, opportunity and an ethical (spiritual) basis in life. However, a society that is bent on sustaining an unethical basis, miseducation and greed wherein the few control resources and wealth while the many suffer in poverty and miseducation will continue to deny the truth and even promote the ignorance. Consider how much false comfort it gives people to believe that we "know" what causes AIDS and that we are doing something about it through research that will lead to some antidote drug. Since the scientific model of the West can only hold such a view, it also promotes the revenues of drug companies who get moneys for research and then more moneys for selling the drugs.

In addition, the supposed antidotes (drugs and medicines to combat AIDS) are more deadly than the disease. The misrepresentation about Aids in Africa actually has led to a higher death rate from AIDS in the West than in Africa.

> Thus the AIDS risk of an American HIV-positive is about 15-times higher than that of an African! Since over 150,000 healthy (!) HIV-positive Americans are currently treated with DNA chain-terminating and other anti-HIV drugs (Duesberg & Rasnick, 1998), and since American HIV-positives have a 15-fold higher AIDS risk than African HIV-positives, President Mbeki must be warned about American advice on "treatments" of HIV-positives.
>
> (4) The discrepancies between African AIDS and infectious disease, and the discrepancies between the high AIDS risk of American compared to African HIV-positives can both be readily explained by the hypothesis that AIDS is caused by non-contagious risk factors and that HIV is a harmless passenger virus (Duesberg, 1996; Duesberg & Rasnick, 1998).
>
> According to this hypothesis the African AIDS diseases are generated by their conventional, widespread causes, malnutrition, parasitic infections and poor sanitation as originally proposed by leading AIDS researchers including Fauci, Seligmann et al. (Seligmann *et al.*, 1984).[195]

Many drug companies in the West have developed drugs that at first seem to help people who have contracted the AIDS syndrome (people can live with the "antibody" i.e. a positive test for HIV-without contracting AIDS). There are many people upset that Western drug companies are not selling or better yet, giving away their AIDS drugs to underdeveloped countries. This is actually an erroneous position based on the evidence outlined here. Such greed, as exhibited by the drug Western companies, is actually protecting the African people. These are deadly drugs that create conditions that are actually conducive for the "AIDS" syndromes to develop.

[194] From the Peter Duesburg Aids web site (Aids and Africa) http://www.duesberg.com/africa2.html
[195] From the Peter Duesburg Aids web site (Aids and Africa) http://www.duesberg.com/africa2.html

So what Africa needs is not drugs, vaccines, pesticides or processed foods, nor patronizing attitudes or complacency from missionaries and relief workers. These should be prohibited. What is needed is an import of natural health educators. People need to be free from colonialism, capitalism, dictatorships, wars, malnutrition and famine. The Western model of disease as being caused by viruses or microbes and not by chemicals in foods, recreational drugs (including alcohol), malnutrition, the partiality for processed foods, cooked foods, the mentality of indiscriminate pleasure-seeking, and the concept that democracy means people have the right to pursue political or business ideals regardless of their moral impact or that any form of sexual promiscuity, decadence or immorality is acceptable needs to be abandoned in favor of wholistic traditional African values, upliftment of ancient culture and ethics in business and government. The traditions and culture being referred to here are the traditions prior to the Islamic invasion, conquest and enslavement period, the European and American slave trade period and the colonial period which disrupted life, values, the economy and cultures of Africa.

There is also a psycho-spiritual (mental-emotional-spiritual) dimension to immune health that has to be evaluated with respect to immune dysfunction. From a spiritual level, the thymus gland which is found in the chest and is associated with immune function, is also associated with the heart energy center (chakra). The psycho-spiritual issues at this center relate to love, compassion, forgiveness, etc. Thus, psycho-spiritual implication of someone having an immune system that is attacking itself is that this person is experiencing an inability to love themselves, at a conscious level, or an unconscious level. For whatever reasons, in this or a past life, deep down they feel or felt unworthy, unaccepted, unloved, and this unresolved feeling expresses as their disbalanced lifestyle, which further contributes at a physical level to autoimmune system disorders. Once again this is why it is imperative that one engages in a process of psychological and spiritual cleansing as well in treating the physical body, because the cause starts first in the mind, and then orchestrates the means to become expressed physically. Therefore, one must also seek to the cure the mind. From the yogic mystical perspective, once the cure is effected in the mind, the body will follow suit. However, if the mental block is not resolved, then the body will continue to experience the effects of the mental imbalance, as this will express as a disbalanced lifestyle.

Finally, we can make the following statements about AIDS:

- ***There is no such thing as an "AIDS" virus.***
- ***There is no such thing as an "AIDS Epidemic."***
- ***The diseases referred to as AIDS can be eradicated with improved diet, hygiene and removal of toxins from the food and the environment.***
- ***The "AIDS problem" in Africa and elsewhere can be resolved through good nutrition, hygiene, positive cultural values and ethics.***

Important Supplements for the Kemetic Diet in Modern Times

The following supplements are the essential means to insure proper nutrition in modern times. Notice that the term "modern times" is being used here. This refers to the fact that in ancient times, the foods available to our ancestors were not denatured, processed, genetically modified or chemicalized. Also, the foods were not produced using farming techniques that render the crops low in vitamins, minerals and enzymes. In fact, the Nile flood left the soil so rich and high in quality that this contributed to extremely vital crops. This is of course not possible in modern Egypt due to the extensive system of dams used now to control and harness the Nile flood for producing electricity.

The following supplements are to be thought of as just that, supplements. The basis of the Kemetic diet is greenery, and the best way to achieve this is through fresh vegetables. In modern times it will be necessary to consume organic produce in order to approximate the original high quality of the Kemetic diet. However, after a life of eating cooked, denatured, processed foods, etc., the body may not be able to make full use of even the highest quality organic foods. Some people who go on a raw vegetable and fruit/nut diet sometimes complain of varied symptoms which may include, indigestion, gas, shallow breath, weakness, heart palpitations etc. These symptoms are not to be confused with the symptoms of the cleansing action caused by the infusion of higher quality foods.

> These symptoms are caused by deficiencies in the essential vitamins, minerals, amino acids and enzymes. Therefore, the first action is to make sure that the diet is balanced with sources of all the amino acids as described earlier in this volume. Even so, for reasons described above, supplements may still be needed for the first two or so years if transitioning to a raw diet. If these symptoms arise or to prevent them when one is starting a fresh foods diet, one may add the following supplements. Be sure you buy supplements suitable for vegetarians-vegans, and if the supplements are in capsule forms, be sure that the capsules are also vegetable based, and not the usual gelatin based (made from animal hoofs) capsules. Those following this advice have experienced an <u>immediate</u> (i.e. within hours) relief of symptoms, and also a quick buildup of vitality and a deep feeling of health. Multivitamin-Mineral supplement
> Calcium and Magnesium supplement
> Coenzyme Q10
> Flax
> Vitamin and mineral supplement
> Digestive enzymes
> Probiotics

It is important to understand the difference between therapeutic uses of supplements and the basic Kemetic Diet maintenance program. Varied supplements may be needed in the beginning as one is adopting a whole food lifestyle and moving away from a denatured-processed food lifestyle. Another reason may be if one is suffering from some vitamin or mineral deficiency due to imbalances in the chemistry of the body, as those times supplements may be used to bolster the body's systems. These are the times when the body needs "Therapy" in order to facilitate its return to balance. The use of supplements after the body has returned to a state of balance may cause an imbalance in the opposite direction, due to the body's having an overabundance of some elements. The goal of any natural health program is to lead a person to health by taking in nutrients from their natural sources and not supplemented sources since these are artificial and not for long-term use. You should consult with your health professional for your exact needs. The following is a general description of the methodology of the Kemetic Diet Program and is not intended to diagnose or treat medical problems or substitute for consultation with a competent health consultant.

Safety of Vitamins and Minerals

The body can absorb around 10 to 15% of the nutrients in an ordinary vitamin pill. So the rest is excreted, primarily in urine, and flushed down the toilet. So this means that for every $10.00 spent on supplements, one might be flushing $8.50 down the toilet. Therefore, the money would be better spent on food since the human body works better taking in a food item, breaking it down and taking the nutrients it needs from it. However, due to the problems with the depletion of the nutrients in the food, poor food choices, cooked foods, stressful lifestyles which further deplete the body's nutrient resources, etc., it is better to have expensive excretions than the medical, mental and spiritual costs of illness due to vitamin deficiencies.

As for the question of vitamin toxicity, the **United States Recommended Daily Allowances (USRDA)** are guidelines only. The RDA figures are suggested by the Food and Nutrition Board, a committee of the National Academy of Sciences-National Research Council, which meets every five years or so, to review and revise its recommendations. As the board defines them, the RDAs are "the levels of intake of essential nutrients considered, in the judgment of the Food and Nutrition Board, on the basis of available scientific knowledge, to be adequate to meet the known nutritional needs of practically all healthy persons."

The USRDA are based on standards to maintain marginal prevention of vitamin deficiency, the minimum level needed to maintain basic health. However, these figures do not relate to optimal health maintenance. Despite the cautions sounded by the agency and drug manufacturers, studies have shown that it is not harmful to consume two to three times the recommended levels of vitamins (including vitamin A[196] and vitamin D[197]). Many people regularly do consume two to three times the RDA of some of the vitamins through the foods they eat, especially if they take a multivitamin supplement along with their regular food intake.[198] Therefore, there is no basis for accepting the USRDA as a standard for optimal health. Thus, some wholistic nutritionists and medical doctors have taken to developing guidelines for *Optimal Daily Allowances* (ODA). The recommended vitamin dosages for optimal nutrition are as follows. These are suggested dosages and before using any supplements, one should consult with a health care provider. They should be adjusted for children in accordance with body weight.

> "**SONA Based Vitamin levels** - The vitamin levels in the **SONA** are based on the recently developed Suggested Optimal Nutrient Allowances (SONAs) as proposed to the US Senate. Through the effort of a 15 year study it is now possible to extrapolate suggested optimum daily nutrient allowances or SONA'S. The SONA'S are levels of nutrients found in a study of 13,500 male and female subjects living in six different regions of the United States conducted by senior investigators, Drs. Emanuel Cheraskin and W. M. Ringsdorf at the University of Alabama Medical School. The results of their $2 million dollar study are contained in 49,000 bound pages found in 153 volumes, whose results have been published in over 100 papers during the 1970's & 1980's. They correlated intakes of essential nutrients with signs and symptoms of disease. The healthiest individuals - those with the least clinical signs and symptoms, consumed supplements, and ate a diet richer in essential nutrients relative to calories than those with more signs and symptoms of disease. Based on the logical assumption that those who are free of symptoms are healthier than those showing clinical signs and symptoms of disease, the ideal daily intake of each essential nutrient was taken to

[196] Scientists in India used weekly vitamin-A supplements for school children and the result was a cut in deaths from disease by more than half. *The A Team* by Tim Beardsley, February 1991, Scientific American

[197] Comparative therapeutic Value and Toxicity of Various Types of Vitamin-D (c.Reynolds, M.D.). Also, studies by the Louisiana State University suggested that *doses of vitamin D in the millions of I.U.'s per day are safe.*

[198] Death by Diet by Robert R. Barefoot

be that level consumed by people who were free from symptoms and signs of disease. Cheraskin and Ringsdorf found optimum intakes of essential nutrients to increase with age. For more information please see the article: Establishing a Suggested Optimal Nutrient Allowance (SONA).

The **RDAs** - intakes of minerals and vitamins which prevent deficiency symptoms in healthy, average adults - are inadequate for optimum health, especially during stress, growth, pregnancy, lactation, strenuous and athletic activity, healing from disease and injury, and advancing age. At present, the RDA's represent the nutritional equivalent of the minimum wage. Just like the minimum wage, they offer little hope of significantly improving the quality of your life. For almost everyone, the SONA'S represent supplement levels of essential vitamins and minerals designed to maintain optimum health over a life-time."[199]

The Vegetarian Vitamin Supplement Recommended for the Kemetic Diet Program

The SONA Vegetarian Vitamin Supplement is created in the same way as the *Kamut Wheatgrass Juice*. It is not heated over 88^0 which would break down the nutrients and enzymes. It is a complement to the *Kamut Wheatgrass Juice* and the total Kemetic Diet Program.

Contents of the Vitamin-mineral Supplement for the Kemetic Diet

SONA

Vegetarian Multivitamin/Mineral/Enzyme Supplement

NUTRITIONAL ANALYSIS	
Energy	322 Kcal/100 g
Carbohydrates	54.8%
Fat	5.9%
Proteins (N x 6.25)	12.3%
Dietary Fibre	31.1%

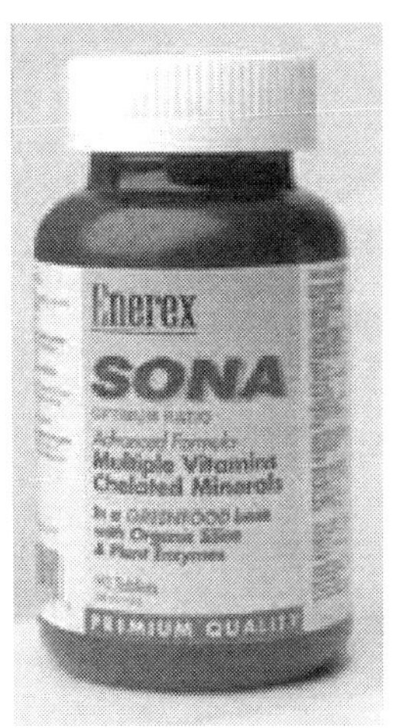

3 TABLETS CONTAIN	POTENCY
Organic Alfalfa Leaf Powder	450 mg
Organic Green Barley Juice Powder	225 mg
Spirulina Blue-Green Algae Powder	225 mg
Bamboo Gum (Providing 105 mg Organic Silica)	150 mg

[199] Enerex Botanicals

3 TABLETS CONTAIN

VITAMINS

	Potency	% EC RDA	% SONA°
Beta Carotene (15,000 IU)	9 mg		°°
Vitamin A (3000 IU)	880 mcg	110%	100%
Vitamin D (400 IU)	10 mcg	200%	100%
Vitamin E (100 IU)	74 mg	740%	100%
Vitamin C	400 mg	667%	100%
Thiamine (HCI)	9 mg	643%	100%
Riboflavin	3 mg	188%	100%
Niacin	30 mg	167%	100%
Pyridoxine (HCL)	10 mg	500%	100%
Folacin	800 mcg	200%	100%
Vitamin B12	3 mcg	300%	100%
Biotin	0.15 mg	100%	°°
Pantothenic Acid	21 mg	350%	°°
PABA (Para AminoBenzoic Acid)	21 mg		

AMINO ACID CHELATED MINERALS

	Potency	% EC RDA	% SONA°
Calcium+	300 mg	37%	°°
Iron+	18 mg	128%	°°
Magnesium+	300 mg	100%	100%
Zinc+	15 mg	100%	100%
Iodine	0.15 mg	100%	°°
Copper+	3 mg		°°
Manganese+	5 mg		°°
Chromium+	200 mcg		°°
Selenium+	200 mcg		°°
Vanadium+	75 mcg		°°
Molybdenum+	50 mcg		°°

+Hypoallergenic form, chelated with hydrolysed rice protein.

LIPOTROPIC FACTORS

Choline	21 mg	°°
Inositol	21 mg	°°

* European Recommended Daily Allowance
° Suggested Optimal Nutrient Allowances
°° SONAs Not Yet Established

ENZYMES

Protease	1,000 u**
Lipase	1,000 u**
Amylase	1,000 lu**
Cellulase	100 Cmcu**

** Based on AIE Standard

- The Vitamin/mineral/enzyme dietary supplement above in conjunction with the vegetarian lifestyle, regular fasting and vegetable juice program outlined in this book should be sufficient to take care of the nutritional needs of the average person. Adjustments should be made for children and also in accordance with the daily food intake.

Vitamin Supplements Prevent Deaths from Cancer

"It has been found, by several recent scientific studies, that eating 20 times the RDA of vitamin-A really does *inhibit cancer.* In 1993, in a medical trial in Linxian, China, Chinese scientists, along with scientists from the American National Cancer Institute, established that beta-carotene, a chemical cousin of vitamin-A, in combination with vitamin-E and selinium, reduces deaths from cancer. This supports the work done by medical researchers at the beginning of the century who found that a severe lack of vitamin-A caused stomach cancer in rats. The Chinese took the vitamins and mineral as a food supplement, but because of the American medical system, the National Cancer Institute scientists have rushed home *"to study drugs that might achieve the same effect".* In other words, *American scientists have found a nutritional and inexpensive way to treat cancer, but prefer instead to try to develop an expensive chemical for the drug companies.*"[200]

[200] Death by Diet by Robert R. Barefoot

- Thus it is evident that vitamin deficiency does not just lead to diseases, but more importantly, the presence of them can heal and prevent diseases – even cancer and AIDS.

Calcium and Magnesium

Calcium makes up 1.6 % of the human body weight, making it the most abundant metallic element.[201] Calcium is a mineral that is essential to the formation of bones and teeth, the functions of the blood, nerve conduction and also the proteins which structure the RNA and the DNA, the molecules which direct the vitality and formation of new cells. Calcium deficiency can cause heart palpitations, osteoporosis, tooth decay, muscle twitches, insomnia, arthritis, numbness, irritability, and many other problems. It's deficiency has also been implicated as a contributing factor in the development of colon cancer. Consult your herbal and vegetable manual or health food store for sources of calcium-rich foods, and include a calcium supplement in tablet form to your diet, unless you are on a well-balanced completely raw diet, including fresh vegetable juices and almond nut milk, and find that you do not need it. Calcium should be taken in conjunction with magnesium in a 1:1 to 2:1 ratio. Since these two normally interact in the body, if one is taken without the other, it will cause an imbalance. Vegetable juices are generally higher in Calcium and Magnesium content, and so you may choose to take a smaller quantity of supplements if you are juicing adequate amounts regularly. The following studies illustrate the importance of Calcium in the body's ability to carry out the normal physiological processes, and how deficiencies in Calcium, Vitamin D and Magnesium lead to an acidic condition in the body and promotes disease. The recommended daily minimum intake of Calcium and Magnesium to promote health is 1000 mg and 500 mg respectively. Calcium also has the effect of neutralizing acid and promoting an alkaline condition of the body. This is why calcium is used in antacids such as "Tums."

Calcium and Milk and Meats

- Increased milk consumption leads to HIGHER FRACTURE RISK due to osteoporosis.[202]
- Several cancers have been linked to dairy products.[203]
- There is a correlation between dairy products and diabetes.[204]
- Lactose intolerance affects 95% of Asian Americans, 74% of Native Americans, 70% of African Americans, 53% of Mexican Americans, and 15% of European Americans (Caucasians)[205] Cows milk proteins, sugars, and fats leads to chronic diseases, obesity, diabetes, and atherosclerosis plaques that cause heart disease.[206]

If maintaining adequate amounts of Calcium in the body for strong bones were as simple as drinking the levels of milk recommended by the Dairy Council or the current Food Guide Pyramid, Americans from the United States should have little to no problems with calcium deficiency, osteoporosis, etc. However, this is not the case. Rather the opposite is. Osteoporosis is rampant in this society. This is because the end product of dairy consumption renders the body acid, and acidity creates a condition whereby the body must try to restore the blood to its alkaline state. One way it achieves this is to break down bone and take the calcium and carbonate from the bone and move it into the bloodstream to buffer the acidity. This process is further exacerbated by the consumption of animal meat, which also creates acidity in the body that must be buffered by calcium from bones.

[201] The Calcium Factor by Robert R. Barefoot and Carl J. Reich M.D.
[202] Harvard Nurses' Health Study -See Physicians Committee for Responsible Medicine (202) 686-2210 PCRM@PCRM.Org
[203] Study by Daniel Cramer M.D. -See Physicians Committee for Responsible Medicine (202) 686-2210 PCRM@PCRM.Org
[204] Study by Scott FW, and Study by Karjalainen J, Martin JM, Knip M, et al -See Physicians Committee for Responsible Medicine (202) 686-2210 PCRM@PCRM.Org
[205] Study by Bertron P, Bernard ND, Mills M, Racial bias in Federal Nutrition Polict -See Physicians Committee for Responsible Medicine (202) 686-2210 PCRM@PCRM.Org
[206] -See Physicians Committee for Responsible Medicine (202) 686-2210 PCRM@PCRM.Org

In addition, animal meat is extremely low in calcium and very high in phosphorous. In animals such as dog, cats, iguanas, horses, birds, etc., feeding diets that are high in phosphorous and calcium deficient can lead to the metabolic disease syndrome called nutritional secondary hyperparathyroidism. It is seen when cats and dogs are feed all-meat diets, and when birds are fed diets consisting primarily of sunflower seeds and peanuts, as these diets are high in phosphorous and low in calcium. The mechanism of how this occurs is as follows. The low blood calcium level over a long period of time stimulates the release of the hormone called the parathyroid hormone, which will be found at a higher than normal level in the animal's blood. The main function of this hormone is to keep the blood levels of calcium in the normal range for proper functioning of the body. To do so, it breaks down bone. Thus, the bone becomes weakened, and susceptible to fractures. This condition can be termed osteoporosis, which refers to conditions in which there is a decrease in the overall bone mass as well as losses of both mineral and organic bone matrix (bone density).

The traditional human medical establishment, although they have named several factors which they believe contribute to osteoporosis, for the most part they still maintain that the exact cause is not known. It could be that they have not found a cause because they are working from the paradigm that eating meat and lots of grains are "normal and healthy," and are therefore looking for causes only within the framework of this paradigm. This would be like having documentation that poison ivy causes hives, yet telling people it is safe and healthy for them. Then, when they break out in hives, assuring them that you will not rest until you find the cause of their hives, no matter what it takes. Yet, because you have professed that it safe and healthy, you look at every possible cause, except the ivy. Since the answer to the puzzles rests in the ivy, you will never discover the cause of their hives, no matter how much money you throw at it or how many scientists you put to study the problem, until you are willing to face the fact that you may have made a mistake in your classification of the ivy as safe and healthy. This is the dilemma that the government, the food industry, the traditional medical establishment, meat and dairy farmers, the dairy and meat lobbyists and others who benefit from the meat and dairy industry must face. They have spent much time, effort and money creating and establishing the belief that meat and dairy products are safe and essential to the physical health of a person, and have excluded them from the scope of their researches to find answers to the many illness that plague society. Thus, it is not surprising that they have not been able to find the cures they have promised, even after the billions of dollars that have been poured into the research and medical sciences. There is a wonderful parable that expresses this point. Two young girls came upon their elderly grandmother on her hands and knees in her front yard searching for something. They asked if they could help. The grandmother explained that she had lost her knitting needle. They said that they would help her look for it, and asked her where exactly did she lose it. She told them she lost it inside house. They asked if she lost it in her house, why was she searching outside. She replied to them that it is very dark in her house and she could not see anything, so she was searching for it outside where there was light! Much like this elderly woman of our parable, traditional western medical science, with the exception of a few pioneers, continues to search for their "cures" where it is financially profitable for them to do so, but not where the true solutions can be found.

If in other animal species diets rich in phosphorous and low in calcium can bring on this condition of osteoporosis, could not the same mechanism exist for the human (animal) body? Animal meats are especially calcium deficient. This is why diets that promote meat eating or protein as the main source of nutrition or for the purpose of losing weight will produce short term seemingly positive results and long-term malnutrition. Many other food products such as grains, nuts and seeds have a higher calcium content, but still have relatively high calcium: phosphorous rations, and thus should be consumed in limited quantities. The optimum calcium: phosphorous ratio is balanced, about 2:1 to 1:2. Most meat, in addition to having low levels of calcium, have ratios ranging from 1:15 and higher, containing as much as fifteen times more phosphorous than calcium.[207] Most grains, though having slightly higher calcium content than most meats, are also low in calcium and high in phosphorous. Some notable exceptions in grains that are well balanced in calcium and phosphorous are Whole Grain Brown Rice, Amranth, and Whole Grain Buckwheat[208]. Most beans have a 1:2 to a 1:5 ratio, with Garbanzo beans and Soybeans being well balanced at approximately a 1:2 ratio. Most nuts have acceptable ratios, Almonds and Filberts (hazelnuts) being the most balanced, and Peanuts and Cashews being the worst.[209] Of the seeds, sesame seeds have a balanced ration of approximately 2:1 ratio, being higher in calcium than phosphorous. Sunflower seeds are high in phosphorous relative to calcium, having a ratio of about 1:8, and pumpkin seeds, which are recommended for prostate conditions due to their high zinc content, are relatively high in phosphorous at a ratio of 1:20, and thus should be used primarily as a supplement rather than a staple food.[210] (Note: Data for Flax seed was not reported). Interestingly, though not surprising after all we have learned about vegetable and fruits, most vegetables and fruits are relatively balanced in the their calcium: phosphorous ratios, and therefore can be eaten abundantly.

Why Calcium is So Important?

"Breathing Easy", by Lendon Smith, M.D., in the book Feed Your Kids Right, Dell Pub. Co. Inc., 1979.

*"Calcium is required all our lives for bones, teeth, muscle, nerve function, and for blood clotting. Muscle pains, cramps, twitches and even convulsions may suggest **calcium deficiency.** "*

The Recognition of the Importance of Calcium

***"Calcium must certainly be the major bioelement of the times.** Only a generation ago the calcium ion was known to physiologists and biochemists as a component of bone mineral and as a blood plasma constituent required in heart function and blood coagulation, but little more. But, in the 1970's a crescendo of calcium ion research developed. Today we know dozens if not hundreds of different cellular and extracellular processes that are regulated by the changes in cytosolic or extracellular calcium ions. Indeed, the calcium ion is emerging as a most important and ubiquitous intracellular messenger"* (Foreword, Albert Lehniger, Professor of Medical Science, John Hopkins University).

*"As we have seen, **calcium is central** to the ordered progression of replicating cells through their growth- division cycle. Neoplastic epithelia and mesenchymally derived cells can initiate DNA syntheses and proliferate normally in a low calcium medium, which does not support the proliferation of their normal counterparts. Besides needing calcium ions, normal cells must adequately spread out on a solid substrate before they are able to initiate DNA syntheses. Calcium is **specifically required** for spreading. Lowering the extracellular calcium and preventing spreading both block the initiation of DNA synthesis, without stopping on-going DNA synthesis. The elimination of extracellular calcium requirement for proliferation of viruses can be mimicked by exposing proliferatively inactive calcium-deprived normal cells to*

[207] The Book of Macrobiotics by Michio Kushi
[208] Note: Data for Spelt and Kamut grain {which were used in Ancient Africa and now being reintroduced to modern culture} were not reported.
[209] The Book of Macrobiotics by Michio Kushi
[210] ibid

calcium-independent-nucleotide protein Kinases located in the plasma membrane. Thus, addition of such subunits to the medium of normal cells cause them to behave like neoplastic cells by initiating DNA syntheses in calcium deficient medium. It is clear that the proliferative calcium independence in vitro is a universal property of neoplastic cells, the understanding of which may be ***the key to understanding cancer."*** (page 158, Volume 41)

Meat Eating and Consumption of Soft Drinks Depletes the Calcium in the body.

"The Green Leaves of Barley", Dr. Mary Ruth Swope,
1987,Swope Enterprises Inc., P.O. Box 62104, Phoenix, AZ
85082-2104. 1 (800) 447-9772
"There are many research studies which allude to the fact that high phosphorus and/or phosphoric acid (found in meat and soft drinks) pulls calcium out of the bony structures (bones, teeth and nails) in the process of digestion and assimilation. This has a disastrous effect on bone density, leaving them porous and spongy.When calcium is pulled from the bones, it is released through the kidneys, resulting in stone formation (kidney stones) before it is excreted

Calcium Is Necessary to Trigger Biochemical Functions in the Body

The Calcium Signal", **Scientific American,** November 1987, by Ernesto Carafoli and John T. Penniston:
'A common trigger precipitates biological events as diverse as the contraction of a muscle and the secretion of a hormone. The trigger is a minute flux of calcium ions. "
"To control cellular process effectively, calcium itself must be regulated. Knowledge of these intricacies (elaborate system of proteins that interact with the calcium ion regulating intracellular messages) may lead to greater clinical control over intracellular calcium,a possibility that has broad implications for the treatment of disease.

"Calcium in Synaptic Transmission", by Rodolfo R., Scientific American, October **1982.**

"The connection between the electrical activity of the cell and the release of the neurotransmitter is not direct; an ***essential intermediary is the*** *calcium ion. "*

Vitamin D production, Triggered By Exposure to the Sun Helps the Body Absorb and Use Calcium

"The Calcium Connection", Dr. Cedric Garland and Dr. Frank Garland, 1989, Foreside, Simon and Shuster Inc.
"Low cancer areas were far more frequent in the sun belt. (Thisstatement is contrary to the incorrect popular belief that sunshine causes cancer). *What was the significance of sunlight with regard to cancer rates? Sunlight reacts with cholesterol inside and on the surface of the skin to create vitamin-D. Vitamin D helps the body absorb calcium and plays a major role in the body's ability to use the calcium that is available. "*

Exposure to the sun is an essential practice in order to promote health. The widely disseminated notion that "exposure to the sun is bad for you" is contradicted by the facts. Overdosing on the sun is also a misunderstood phenomenon.

> "Assuming this to be true, and also assuming 12 hours of sunlight per day, the amount of vitamin-D produced in 30 minutes is 128,000 IU which calculates to " 3072000[211] IU per day". This means that they are advising that " 18,300 IU of vitamin-D are required by the human body per day" (which this author wholeheartedly supports), while saying, at the same time, that 1200 IU "may be toxic". Which is it, 18,000 or 1,200 ? The latter is ludicrous as the healthiest people in the world, the Hunzas in Pakistan, the Bamas in China, the Georgians in Russia, the Titi Cacas in Peru and the Okinawans in Japan, all of whom have virtually no diseases, all get about 7 hours of sunshine each day and therefore produce about 500,000 IU of vitamin-D each day (their skin is dark). Thus the logic of the Ph.D.'s who apparently cannot calculate, lies in the ruins of grade eight math."[212]

If the exposure to the sun is the causative factor in contracting skin cancer, then why is it that those peoples who live closer to the sun (close to the equator) are the groups that contract the least amount of skin cancer and those who live in northern or southern latitudes of the earth (away from the equator- and farther away from direct sunlight) contract the most skin cancer? All this means that, in our search for the causes of skin cancer we need to look at nutritional deficiencies rather than the deleterious effects of exposure to the sun, which is a natural aspect of the environment and has always been so. Why should we blame nature, which has existed long before our arrival? What are we doing that is deviating from the norms of Creation and leading us into disharmony and disease?

In addition to promoting a kind of photosynthesis process in the body in which Vitamin D is produced, which promotes mineral absorption (especially Calcium), the sun also stimulates the production of *inositol triphosphate,* INSP-3, which is an important mineral biochemical regulator.[213] Thus, exposure to the sunlight is an integral aspect of health and should be part of the daily program of a nutritious and healthy lifestyle.

Calcium and Cancer

"Calcium Takes Its Place As a Superstar of Nutrients"
Jane Brody, October 13, 1998, New York Times.

"Calcium is fast emerging as the nutrient of the decade, a substance with such diverse roles in the body that virtually no major organ system escapes its influence. A research team at the University of Southern California in Los Angeles reported in The American Journal of Clinical Nutrition that adding calcium to the diet lowered blood pressure. Dr, Susan Thy-Jacobs, a gynecologist at St. Lukes Roosevelt Hospital Center in New York believes that „a chronic deficiency or imbalance of calcium is largely responsible for the disruptive symptoms of PMS suffered by women ". Dr. Martin Lipkin of the Strang Cancer Research Laboratory at Rockefeller University in New York said that "Animal research indicated that increasing calcium levels to protect epithelial cells from cancer might also help prevent cancer in such organs as the breast, prostrate and pancreas ".

---

[211] Correction of original text math calculation by Ashby
[212] Death by Diet by Robert R. Barefoot
[213] ibid

Calcium and DNA and Cancer

"The Role of Calcium in Biological Systems", Volume 1, **1985,** CRC Press Inc.

As a prelude to the quotations in this book, the following comments, contained in the brackets, are made to help the reader better understand the quotations:

The Role of Calcium Biological Systems is a compilation of dozens of scientific publications by academically recognized scientists. This book deserves particular note because world-class scientists are *concluding* that there is a link between calcium deficiency and cancer. Also, the hundreds of scientific references contained in this book, as well as the other books quoted, could lead the reader to thousands of scientific publications on the importance of biochemical calcium. Although the first quote is self-explanatory, the second quote may be difficult for the reader to understand. Basically, it says that calcium deficiency in the body fluids outside and inside of the cell *stimulates the proliferation* of both virus and cell mutation (cancer) by regulating DNA synthesis. Furthermore it concludes that calcium deficiency is the universal property of *all* cancer cells, the knowledge of which may be *the key to understanding cancer.*

Living Longer With the Proper Amount of Calcium in the Diet

"How a Mineral Can Vitalize Your Health", by Dr. James K. Van Fleet, in the book Magic of Catalytic Health Vitalizers, .1980, Parker Publishing.

*"According to nutritional authorities, the American diet is more lacking in calcium than in any other essential food Dr. Henry C. Sherman, the noted biochemist, has stated in **effect that the prime period of human life could be extended by a moderate increase in calcium** in the diet. It would also be wise to get at least 400 units of vitamin-D daily to insure proper absorption of the calcium from the tract into the body where it can be utilized."*

***"When the body does not get enough** calcium, it will withdraw what little calcium it has from the bones to make sure there is enough in **the bloodstream,** then the body does its best to bolster the sagging architecture by building bony deposits and spurs to reduce movement and limit activity. "*

Calcium and Vegetarians

It is important to understand that since vegetarians do not eat meat, they will not suffer from the problem of the body leaching out calcium from the bones and from other sources within the body to process the meat protein as well as the acidosis caused by meat eating. If the diet is raw, then the need is even less because the foods will not cause acidosis that will require the need for calcium to neutralize the acidity. Therefore, the need for calcium by vegetarians will generally be less that that of non-vegetarians, and the need for calcium of those who consume a raw vegetable diet will generally also be less. The smaller quantities of calcium in ordinary vegetables will be absorbed more readily and will be retained more easily. Thus, the vegetarian and raw food diets are superior than a meat based diet in its most efficient use of calcium.

Coenzyme Q10

Coenzyme Q10 is an antioxidant. Some vitamins (C and E) also act as antioxidants. Antioxidants are natural agents that the body produces when it is working properly. When the body carries on its normal chemical processes, these give off stray atoms that combine with others in the body and cause chemical reactions that are not desirable; they oxidize or burn up the body, thus causing many diseases. These stray atoms are called "free radicals." In a normally functioning body, the antioxidants combine with the free radicals and process them in a beneficial manner. If the nutrient intake is of cooked foods, processed foods, imbalanced diet, stress, exposure to radiation and toxic chemicals, free radicals build up and deteriorate the systems of the body. Supplementing the diet with antioxidants has been found to be beneficial in the treatment of cancer, drug abuse, asthma, brain anomalies including Alzheimer's, aging, MS, periodontal disease, immune system problems, allergies, repair the stomach lining, and other problems.

Coenzyme Q10 is one of the most powerful "Coenzyme Qs." Other coenzymes are Vitamin C, Vitamin E, Vitamin A, L-Cysteine, L-Glutathione, Selenium, Superoxide Dismutase and Gamma-Linoleic.

Olive oil and Flax oil

Bk-uadjit - fresh olive oil

Bk-ndjum - Sweet olive oil

Olive oil is one of the oldest known oils in human history. It was cultivated in the Mediterranean and traded widely throughout the entire region and exported to far off lands in ancient times. It was one of the commodities that the Ancient Egyptians traded with the Greeks. The program recommendation is "Extra virgin cold pressed organic olive oil." It is an excellent and natural source of EFAs or "Essential Fatty Acids and is therefore recommended for the Kemetic Diet. It is also desirable because of its taste, and can be added directly to foods prior to consumption, mixed with dressings for salads and other sauces. In addition, although the Kemetic Diet does not advocated cooking, and especially not frying, this oil can be used for cooking. As with all oils, it should be stored in the refrigerator. Olive oil may be used as part of a natural and balanced vegetarian diet. Flax may also be used if there is a concern for EFA deficiencies or during illness.

Flax is a plant that has blue flowers, and seeds that yield linseed oil. It also has slender stems from which a textile fiber is obtained for clothing. Flax formed an integral part of the Ancient Egyptian diet and in this manner the Ancient Egyptian people received much benefit from receiving the *essential fatty acids* (EFA) which have in modern times been referred to as Omega fatty acids. There are several kinds of fats, however only two kinds are essential fats needed for human health: *omega 3 (n-3 or w3) and omega 6 (n-6 or w6).* Both of these are unsaturated fats. The EFAs are converted into several elements by the body, if they are provided to the body in sufficient quantity and in the right ratio. Also, the quality in which they have been prepared is important. Once again, the preparation must be through a cold-press process if it is provided in a liquid form, and it must not be heated beyond room temperature. Also, it must be kept refrigerated. All the other fats, such as, omega 7, omega 9 (monounsaturated) and saturated fat are considered as non-essential because the body can produce them on its own from sugars and starches.

Every cell in the body needs EFA. They are necessary for rebuilding and producing new cells. They are not manufactured by the body, and therefore must be taken in through the diet. Thus, a deficiency in

EFA will lead to many disorders in the body, and conversely, supplementation with EFA have many beneficial effect of alleviating disease conditions such as arthritis, pain, high cholesterol and triglyceride levels, hardening of the arteries, memory loss, impaired learning, eczema, and heart disease, to name a few. Flax seed is available at health food stores in its seed form which can be pulverized in a coffee grinder, and then sprinkled onto the food, or as a cold pressed oil, found in the refrigerated section, which must be used in an uncooked form. It too can be added to the food just before one eats it, or used in dressings. Flax can also be found in a gel cap form, however, the gel caps are often non-vegetarian.

It is notable that the people of modern day Okinawa are some of the healthiest and long-lived in the world even though they receive their omega fatty acids mostly from eating fish. The Okinawans also believe in a healthy wholistic lifestyle which includes exercise, spirituality and other aspects which make it very similar to the Kemetic Diet system. Another source of oil for the Ancient Egyptian Diet was the fruit from the Horseradish tree. (Available at health food stores)

The Critical Need for Essential Fatty Acids

Medical Research has found a positive correlation between Omega-3 fatty acid deficiency and over 50 disease conditions, including the top three causes of death in the USA, heart disease, cancer and stroke.[214] Other conditions which were correlated with Omega-3 deficiency include Diabetes, Immune disorders, Alzheimers, Psoriasis, Multiple Sclerosis, High Blood Pressure, dry skin, PMS, etc.

Omega-3 fatty acid is an Essential Fatty Acid (EFA). There a many “essential” nutrients that the human body needs. “Essential” means that the body either does not make these nutrients at all or does not make them in sufficient quantities which the body needs for health, and so they must be ingested in foods or supplements. The two Omega fatty acids that are of primary interest are Omega-3 fatty acid and Omega-6 fatty acid. EFA’s are found in every cell in the body, and are involved in several metabolic processes in the body, thus, it is understandable how a deficiency in these vital nutrients can lead to a break down and mal-functioning of so many parts of the body resulting in over 50 degenerative conditions. In the *European Journal of Cancer (2000) 36: 335-40,* French researchers reported that the results of a study of women with breast cancer showed that women with high levels of alpha-linolenic acid (Omega-3 fatty acids) in their breast tissue had a 60% lower risk for breast cancer than women with lower levels.

Omega-3 fatty acids have received much more notoriety than Omega-6’s because modern food practices have rendered the diet of the average person rich in Omega-6 fatty acids and deficient in Omega-3 fatty acids, so much so, that the historical ratio of Omega-3 to Omega-6 in the human diet which used to be 1:1 is now around 1:10 to1:25. This means that most people in society are suffering from Omega-3 deficiency[215]. They are taking in 10 to 25 times the amount of Omega-6’s as Omega-3, and some health experts feel that there is an overall deficiency of the EFA’s, both Omega-3’s and 6’s. Thus, the emphasis in addressing the Omega fatty acids if most often in terms of recommending Omega-3 fatty acids, as opposed to Omega-6’s, and Omega-3 is sometimes given the title of being the “good” guy and Omega-6 the “bad” guy. However, this is far from the truth. What is important to the body is having the proper ratio, as the effects of these two groups of fatty acids offer a counter balancing within the systems of the body.

For example, one of the reasons that Omega-3 fatty acids are known to be beneficial for heart disease is because of its effect of preventing blood clots. While this effect is beneficial in preventing heart attacks and strokes, if one were to only consume Omega-3 fatty acids, this could lead to hemorrhage. But nature

---

[214] Jade Buetler, R.C.P., R.R.T., CEO of NatrueMed Research Inc., *The Critical need or Omega-3 Supplementation.*
[215] ibid

is inherently wise, and installed a counterbalancing mechanism, Omega-6 fatty acids. The effect of the Omega-6 fatty acids is the opposite, that of promoting blood clotting, thus, when one gets a cut, the Omega-6's assist in the ability of the blood to clot. Similarly with the immune system and the inflammatory response, the Omega-3's have an anti-inflammatory effect, which is beneficial in preventing conditions such as arthritis and immune mediated inflammatory conditions such as lupus, rheumatoid arthritis, etc., whereas Omega-6's promote the inflammatory response, which is of benefit in the healing process. Autoimmune disorders, which are also prevalent in modern culture, are also related to Omega-3 deficiency.

So it is not a matter of good or bad fatty acids, but a matter of having the correct quality and balance of Omega-3 and Omega-6's in the body, so that the body can effectively modulate its responses according to the situation. When the balance of the Omega-3 and Omega-6 fatty acids is disrupted, various conditions erupt in the body according to the nature of the imbalance. Years ago it was widely reported that Eskimos consume large quantities of fat but do not suffer from high rates of heart disease, as would be expected. What was not publicized by the media with respect to the Eskimos eating the high fat blubber but having lower rates of heart disease was that the studied Eskimos had a higher incidence of hemorrhagic stroke, presumably from ingesting more Omega-3 than Omega-6's. In modern society outside of the Eskimos, however, with ratios of 1:10 to 1:25 Omega-3: Omega-6 fatty acids, there is the opposite effect in place. The effect of the excess of Omega-6's (relative to Omega-3's) in the body promotes the clotting of blood. This is exacerbated by the stress of modern day life which evokes the body's stress or fight or flight response, which also increases the "stickiness" of the blood and promotes clot formations which can lead to conditions such as heart disease and stroke, the number one and number three leading causes of deaths in modern day western society.

Traditional western medicine's attempt to counter the increased propensity for blood clot formation in westerners, instead of recommending bringing the Omega-3:Omega-6 ratios back into balance and changing one's diet to a low fat, whole foods vegetarian, vegan or raw food diet, and one's lifestyle to decrease stress, came in the form of a recommendation that seemed to indicate that just about everyone in western society should take aspirin daily. This recommendation was based on a study, funded in part by one of the companies that make aspirin, which revealed that taking aspirin can reduce the incidence of heart attacks. Aspirin works by interfering with blood clot formation, so the mechanism by which aspirin decreases the incidence of heart attacks is by keeping the blood from clotting so it can flow freely through the arteries. This is especially important if the person has atherosclerosis, whereby the vessels are partially occluded by plaque buildup along the walls. Then it becomes imperative to keep the blood as clot free as possible, because it would take only a small clot to become stuck in the narrowed vessels and cause a heart attack, if the clot blocks one of the heart arteries, or a stroke, if the clots blocks one the arteries in the brain. Thus, stroke is also referred as "brain attack" by the medical establishment. However, while taking aspirin did decrease the incidence of heart attacks in the subjects tested, what was not revealed to the mass media about the subjects of this study was also equally important. Since aspirin prevents the blood from clotting normally, it also increased the incidence of hemorrhagic strokes (bleeding into the brain), gastrointestinal bleeding from ulcers, and sudden cardiac death in the test subjects.

One major reason that the incidence of sudden cardiac death was not helped by taking aspirin is that aspirin does not affect the basic factors which contribute to heart attacks such as the build up of cholesterol plaques and other deposits in the arteries, which are for the most part diet related, or/and spasms in the arteries, most likely due to stressful stimuli and the release of the stress hormones. Also, this idea of taking aspirin leads many people to develop the erroneous assumption that as long as they take aspirin regularly, they are doing something beneficial for their heart, so they do not have to change their diet or lifestyle. Nature has already created several built in mechanisms by which one's blood can be free of blood clots, yet maintain its ability to clot when needed, such as through the regulation of the

Omega-3 and Omega-6 fatty acids in the body, when they are present in high quality and in their proper ratios.

Table 16: Diseases Associated with Omega3 Deficiency:

• Acne	• Cancer	• Kidney Disease	• Psoriasis
• AIDS	• Cystic Fibrosis	• Learning Disorders	• Reyes Syndrome
• Allergies	• Dementia	• Leukemia	• Schizophrenia
• Alzheimer's	• Diabetes	• Lupus	• Stroke
• Angina	• Eczema	• Malnutrition	• Vision Disorders
• Atherosclerosis	• Heart Disease	• Menopause	
• Arthritis	• High Blood Pressure	• Mental Illness	
• Autoimmunity	• Hyperactivity	• Metastasis	
• Behavioral Disorders	• Infection	• Multiple Sclerosis	
• Breast Cancer	• Immune Deficiencies	• Neurological Disease	
• Breast Cysts	• Inflammatory Conditions	• Obesity	
• Breast Pain	• Intestinal Disorders	• Post Viral Fatigue	

Reference: Medline Medical Database 1999: Review of 1757 peer-reviewed articles

The Deficiency of Omega-3 fatty acids in the Western Food Industry: Out of Balance

Omega-3 fatty acids are found in trace quantities in greens, walnuts, sea-vegetables, some seeds, and more abundantly in flax seeds, and deep-water ocean fish. Thus, there are few sources of naturally occurring Omega-3 fatty acids. Consider that in the west, the food industry has moved away from promoting whole foods such as vegetables, fruits, whole grains and beans, legumes, in favor of eating meats, processed and refined foods. Omega-6 fatty acids, on the other hand, are more abundantly found in whole foods, especially in seeds, and in the industrialization era, the capacity to expel oil from seeds to produce vegetable oils, such as derived form peanut, sunflower, safflower, corn, soy, etc., has contributed greatly to the shift in the Omega fatty acid balance. These oils provide very concentrated sources of Omega-6 fatty acids. Further adding to the imbalance, whatever little amounts of Omega-3 fatty acids may be found in foods are generally removed in the processing and refining of foods to extend their shelf-life, since Omega-3 fatty acids become rancid easily.[216] Other factors making maters worse are that the process by which these vegetable oils are produced using high temperatures cause up to 20-50% of their fatty acids to be converted to the "trans" form, which is associated with increased cancer rates.[217] The formation of "trans" fatty acids is compounded in the process of hydrogenation, the process which is applied to vegetable oils to make them solid and create products such as shortening, margarine, etc. Most processed refined foods contain hydrogenated or partially hydrogenated oils, and should therefore be avoided. Thus, even though there is an abundance of Omega-6 fatty acids in the western diet, the quality is generally poor, and dangerous, consisting of "trans" fatty acids rather than the high quality "cis" forms present in whole foods. This is why some health and nutrition experts feel that there is a general deficiency of Omega fatty acids (both Omega-3's and Omega-6's) in the western diet.

OMEGA FATTY ACIDS: WHY FLAX IS BETTER THAN FISH OILS

Many health sources, when recommending the omega-3 fatty acid supplement, list flax seed oil and flax seed oil combinations, and also fish oils as sources for the EFAs, but rarely do they guide the reader to make a choice. Fish oils are derived from fish, and therefore are not vegetarian. They promote and perpetuate the needless killing of animals, unnecessarily. In his book, *Conscious Eating*, Dr. Gabriel

[216] This is why flax oils must be stored in dark containers and refrigerated, or the ground up flax seeds is best used right away.
[217] Dr. Gabriel Cousens, M.D, *Conscious Eating*

Cousens, M.D., says that "there are no nutrients found in fish that cannot be found in safer and more healthy vegetarian sources," and this holds true for the Omega-3 fatty acids. Flax seeds have been found to have the highest content of Omega-3 fatty acids of all foods, surpassing even fish. Flax seeds contain 18-24% Omega-3 as compared to 0-2% of fish.[218] The media, fish industry and conventional medical establishment popularized fish oils after researches found that Eskimos eating high levels of fat (blubber) had low levels of heart disease. They related this to the high levels of Omega-3 fatty acids in the food (blubber, fish) of the Eskimos.

However, in his article, *The Critical need or Omega-3 Supplementation*, Jade Buetler, R.C.P., R.R.T., says "fish oils must undergo complex refining to reduce odor, peroxides, free fatty acids and potential toxins[219] due to contaminants such as DDT and methyl mercury. Despite these measures standards of quality for fish oils have proven extremely inconsistent. Many companies have been penalized for manufacturing fish oils in excess of toxicity guidelines." Cardiologist and researcher, Dr. Dean Ornish, makes the point his book *Dr. Dean Ornish's Program for Reversing Heart Disease*, that fish oils contain saturated fats and increases blood cholesterol levels. This is because it is an animal product, and unlike vegetable products, animal products contain cholesterol. Thus, Dr. Ornish does not recommend fish or fish oils for his "reversal" diet for heart disease, as high cholesterol is one of the key factors contributing to heart disease, the number one killer in the USA. Rather, he recommends vegetarian sources of Omega-3 fatty acids. Dr. Ornish also states that fish oils may cause insulin resistance and increased blood glucose levels in diabetics, and voices concern about the potential contamination of fish with toxins such as pesticides, chlorinated hydrocarbons, and heavy metals.

NOTE on the ancient Kamitan views on fish eating:

> In ancient Egypt peasant food was regarded as fish (fresh water or salt water). In some periods those who ate fish were considered as unclean. (Ancient Healing p 46) Recall that the method used by the ancient Egyptian doctors to test breastmilk was to reject it if it smelled like fish. (A History of the Egyptian People, Budge – pp 202)
>
> Plutarch: "No Egyptians would eat the flesh of sheep, except the Lycopolites."

Organic Flax seed, on the other hand, is readily available, and flax seed contains a very restorative ratio of Omega-3: Omega-6 fatty acids of approximately 3:1. Thus, flax seed and flax seed oils can be consumed in a pure state. Most flax seed oils are cold (expeller) pressed, which means that they are processed at temperatures below the normal standards for other types of oils. The temperatures at which they are pressed varies with the individual companies. The recommended ones are the companies that press them at temperatures under 100 degrees Fahrenheit, which maintains the highest quality of the oil. Flax oil is best kept refrigerated, having an unrefrigerated shelf life of approximately 3 weeks, and up to 4-6 months refrigerated. It must also be protected from light so as not to become rancid.

An added benefit flax seed over fish oils is that flax contains fiber, unlike fish. It is particularly high in a fiber called lignin, which, according to Dr. Cousens, "our bodies convert to lignans, which help to build up the immune system and have specific anticancer, antifungal and antiviral properties."

Flax seed – Back to Balance

---

[218] Dr. Gabriel Cousens, M.D, *Conscious Eating*

[219] See section on *Fish and Seafood*

In any endeavor, the key to regaining balance is two-fold. Stop engaging the actions that are moving you further away from balance, and engage in actions that will bring you back to balance. So, first and foremost, stop over ingestion of Omega-6 fatty acids, especially trans fatty acids by not eating foods containing refined vegetable oils, hydrogenated or partially hydrogenated oils and margarine. Secondly, eat whole foods containing the healthy forms of Omega fatty acids. Barlean's and Omega Nutrition [220] researchers recommend approximately 1 to 3 teaspoons[221] of flax seed oil daily to meet the recommended Essential Fatty Acid supplementation[222]. Of course they recommend that one should consult a health care professional in regard to the personal use of any health-related products, especially if one has any existing medical condition or unusual symptomology. Other researchers and clinicians recommend 2-5 tablespoons per day, however, Dr. Cousens feels that this is more of a therapeutic dose. Flax seed oil can be taken directly, however, some people find the taste to be a bit too strong. It can also be mixed with dressings, and used in smoothies or other dishes. The companies that sell the flax oils usually have many recipes available, in addition to vegan and raw foods cookbooks. An alternative is to soak the seeds to a smoothie and blend in a blender, make dehydrated raw flax cracker, or to grind the dry seeds in a coffee grinder and sprinkle on salads, foods or beverages. It is best to grind the seeds immediately before eating it, to minimize loss of the nutritive elements. There are also cold-milled ground flax products available. When one returns to balance and stops eating foods that are cooked or overly cooked, processed, refined or otherwise manipulated to be made a nutritional hazard in favor of organic, whole vegan foods, then it is possible to eliminate the need to take flax as a daily nutritional supplement. Rather, it can be incorporated into one's diet as a whole food[223].

The *Omega 3 (n-3 or w3) and Omega 6 (n-6 or w6)* Supplement is Recommended for the Kemetic Diet Program

Probiotics

Probiotics are friendly bacteria that normally live within the human gastrointestinal tract and are helpful to digestion. They are non-pathogenic (not capable of causing disease). They also combat unfriendly bacteria and fungus and thus prevent disease. There are hundreds of strains of bacteria. The two most common types of probiotics are *Bifidobacterium* and *Lactobacillus acidophilus.* Probiotics fulfill other important tasks like aiding in the detoxification process.

> "...when bifidobacteria (a probiotic) are in a good state of health, they will detoxify pollutants and carcinogens (cancer-causing substances), as well as manufacture the various B vitamins...When in a poor state of health, however, they just cannot do these jobs as well or at all."[224]

The use of antibiotics, cooked food, dairy products, etc. depletes their number and promote indigestion and diseases including candidiasis and yeast infections and other diseases caused by pathogenic bacteria:

---

[220] Barlean's and Omega Nutrition are two of the producers of the highest quality of flax seed oil available.
[221] 3 teaspoons = 1 tablespoon
[222] 1 teaspoons of flax seed oil = approximately 3 teaspoons of whole flax seeds
[223] Flax tips: Flax oil can be used as an oil substitute for the more hazardous oils in dressings. Flax can also be added to raw and cooked veggie burger recipes as a binder: Ground flax seed in a coffee grinder, and put in a food processor or blender with enough water to process/blend it. It will become quite thick. This mixture must then be quickly added to raw or cooked veggie burger recipes as a substitute for egg and other processed egg substitutes to bind the burgers together. Soak or wash the blender/food processor right away before the flax dries.
[224] Naturopathic physician Leon Chaitow of the University of Westminster, England.

- ❖ Salmonella
- ❖ E. coli
- ❖ Staphylococcus
- ❖ Listeria

The probiotic bacterias, besides promoting proper digestion, also acts as a defense against the pathogenic bacteria and produce B vitamins including niacin, folic acid-vitamin B12 and biotin. They can work to reduce cholesterol levels by contributing to cholesterol metabolism and utilization.[225] Since friendly bacteria continually die off, they need to be constantly replenished.[226] Unprocessed (raw) vegetables have a natural amount of friendly flora that are consumed, say when eating a salad. This naturally replaces the friendly flora that die off or are lost during the natural process of waste elimination. Therefore, it is wise to take probiotic supplements when using antibiotics and / or after their use or when the body has undergone some disease, especially those related to the gastrointestinal tract. The probiotic supplement used should contain stable, human strain bacteria. Specifically, the use of probiotics should be considered in the following situations:

- ❖ After treatment with antibiotics – use for 14 days
- ❖ If one travels frequently (domestic and international);
- ❖ If one has a history of cancer, high cholesterol, or heart disease;
- ❖ If one is under emotional and/or physical stress;
- ❖ If one frequently experiences constipation or diarrhea;
- ❖ If one is lactose intolerant, using dairy products;
- ❖ If one is inactive;
- ❖ If one has an unhealthy diet;
- ❖ If one is exposed to Pathogens in the food, water, or air
- ❖ Change in diet

The Limitations of the Scientific Method: Another Reason for the Failure of Medical Science

The scientific method is an attempt to remove ambiguity from the body of human knowledge and the means by which knowledge is added to the storehouse of human learning. The problem with this method of gathering knowledge is that it necessarily receives information only from empirical evidence. However, as the great scientist Einstein and the modern day quantum physicists have proven, Creation is not absolute or empirical. Creation is composed of variables wherein some aspects operate in different ways under different circumstances. This is why the concept of cause and effect is also flawed. Ignorance of the mystical law of cause and effect known as the law of *Ari* in Kamitan philosophy and Karma in Indian philosophy, leads scientists to seek for causes or reasons for what they see in nature, somewhere within the confines of the time and space of the event in question. In reference to Yoga and mystical religion, as concerns people and their actions, mostly, what is occurring today could be a result of what happened in a previous lifetime (philosophy of reincarnation-already proven in parapsychology experiments).[227] As concerns nature, what occurs today is sustained by the Transcendental Essence, i.e. Supreme Being. Further, the observers, the scientists themselves, and the very perception of these experiments are factors in the experiments and are therefore, factors in the results. This is where the problem of skewing of the results and interpretations of results based on conscious or unconscious prejudices or misconceptions comes in, that is, the problem of "falsifying observations to accord with some preconceived worldview."

---

[225] Protecting your health with Probiotics by George Weber, Ph. D.

[226] ibid

[227] for evidences see the book *The Conscious Universe: The Scientific truth of Psychic Phenomena* By Dean Radin, Ph. D.

As the modern discipline of Quantum Physics has shown, the physical world itself is not what it appears. It is not solid and distinct but rather interrelated energies in varied forms of expression. Physics experiments have shown that matter is not solid as it appears but that it is rather, energy in different forms of manifestation. So the instruments used to discern reality, the logical conditioned mind, and the limited senses, are inadequate for discriminating between what is real and what is unreal. The fallacy of believing in the absolute authority of science is evident in the inability of science to discover anything that is absolute. Something absolute is unchangeable in the beginning, middle and end. Every decade medical science makes "new breakthroughs." This means that they are discovering something "new" which supersedes their previous knowledge. This necessarily means that the previous knowledge was conditional and imperfect and therefore, illusory. Thus, science has its value, but it is not to be considered a reliable source for truth or as a substitute for the disciplines of self-knowledge. So, only a mind that has been trained in transcendental thinking and intuitional realization can discover "truth." Yoga and mystical religion are spiritual sciences that promote the cultivation of the higher faculties of the mind. The mystics of Yoga the world over have for thousands of years proclaimed that the mystical reality which is to be discovered through the disciplines of Yoga and Mystical religion is the same Absolute essence which has always sustained Creation and all existence, including human consciousness. It is the same essence that was discovered by Imhotep and other Sages of Kamit, the Upanishadic Sages of India, Buddha, Jesus, etc., and it is the same absolute reality that can be discovered by anyone today or in the future, who applies the teachings of Yoga and Mystical religion.

So, the idea of the objective observer or that only experimental results which can bring forth repeatable results or parameters that show "consistency with the totality of other aspects of the scientific framework" are valid is sometimes contradictory with respect to nature and logic. Nature is not a machine and even if it were to be treated as such it is not a machine for which the parts are all known and understood. There is an aspect of nature that transcends empirical observation; it must be intuited. This aspect of nature is ignored by the scientific method, by its own bindings, and therefore, the ability to use science as a tool to discover truth, is limited. Since the world is variable (relative), then it follows that any "scientific" data obtained from experiments will also be relative and variable. It is useful within the framework of science, but not beyond that framework. In other words, it cannot be used to ascertain anything about realities outside of its framework. This is why philosophy is an important tool of science. It allows the intuitive faculty of the mind to be cultivated and directed towards discovering the aspects of nature that no physical testing equipment can penetrate.

The world cannot be fully discerned through the intellect because the intellect is also limited. It cannot comprehend the totality of Creation. However, by intuitional (knowing that transcends the thought process) reasoning through transcendence of the relativity of nature, it is possible to discover that absolute reality which is common, and therefore uniform in its *"consistency with the totality"* of human and spiritual experience. The problem is that this aspect of existence can only be approached through a scientific application of philosophical principles and disciplines that can provide results only in the mind of an individual. The Western scientific community shuns this approach, likening it to primitive and unscientific speculations. By ignoring the "why" of things, as the definition of the scientific method above suggests, the scientific method is cutting itself off from the source of knowledge, and looking only at its effect, the "what," and then accepting this as a basis to discern reality. It is like experimenting on the sunrays, neglecting to notice the sun, but extrapolating from the limited experiments and making assertions about what the sun is. In like manner, science looks at nature and notices the relativity, but does not allow itself to explore the mystical-spiritual dimensions of cause. Rather, it seeks to ascribe factors within the realm of the flawed relative field of Creation itself, as the reason behind existence. In fact, for all the knowledge that Western Culture has amassed, in reality there is perhaps no more important knowledge than that which has been recently derived from Quantum Physics, because these clearly point to a transcendental essence of Creation.[228 / 229/230]

Western Culture's adherence to the "Scientific Method" has turned it away from the science of self-development (myth, religion and yoga mysticism) since it (spiritual evolution) cannot be proven

[228] Memphite Theology, Muata Ashby
[229] The Tao of Physics, Fritjof Capra
[230] Dancing Wu Li Masters by Gary Zukov

empirically according to its current criteria as different people are at different stages of evolution and the process may require many lifetimes to complete. Here again, even the parameters set by Western Culture as the procedure of the "Scientific Method" are not being followed. The statement that there is no science beyond the existential aspect of Creation is in effect a violation of the "scientific" rule of objectivity to *"observe things as they are, without falsifying observations to accord with some preconceived world view."* The predilection to discount the transcendent as "un-provable" is a worldview which typifies Western Culture. Thus, the objectivity in the scientific method has at least two built in flaws. First, is the insistence on determining scientific fact based on evidence that can be observable to the physical senses with or without assistance from technology, and therefore can only exist in time and space. Secondly, the necessity for human standards in determining *"conclusions"* based on the data, for it has been shown that the same data can lend itself to different interpretations based on conflicting views, even within the scientific community. A true scientific method should require an objective standard which cannot be violated by the whims of the observers or scientists. Its conclusions must be accepted and not refuted by opinions or desires to uphold particular worldviews. However, again, all of the best standards will be useless if the scientists are biased.

A further connotation, prevalent in Western Culture arising from adherence to the "scientific method" is that what is transcendent is imagined, superstition and unfounded illusion, and only what the "Scientific Method" deems as provable is correct and acceptable. Hence, since myth and mysticism are in the realm of the transcendent, then by this type of Western logic it follows that they are also un-provable and unreal. This is a very powerful argument that further develops into the most dangerous concept, that Western Culture is the determiner of what is truth and that the art, culture, science and religion, etc., of other cultures, past or present, are inferior due to their primitive and "unscientific" manner of approaching nature.

In a scientific investigation, opinions have no place beyond the stating of the hypothesis. Also, the constraints of social propriety do not apply. It is perfectly scientific to state a theory that the Ancient Egyptians were not black Africans, but rather Asiatics, or that Indian Vedic culture and not Kamitan culture gave rise to civilization. There is nothing wrong in making those statements. However, if the person stating these ideas wants to put them forth as "facts" or "reality" or consider these ideas as "proven," then a more rigorous process of supporting those ideas must be undertaken. The evidence must be accurate, available to all investigators, and it should be primary and not second-hand conjectures. Therefore, the opinions of other scholars, no matter how reputable they may be, must be based on primary evidence, and that evidence cannot be substituted by the scholars conclusions or opinions about it. Therefore, scholarly dictums[231] are worthless if the scholar cannot or does not support them with evidence. Other terms, often used synonymously in scientific discussions are "postulate" or "axiom."

> An **axiom** is a self-evident or universally recognized truth; a maxim.
>
> A **dictum** is an authoritative, often formal, pronouncement.
>
> A **postulate** is a *statement or proposition that is to be assumed to be true without proof and that forms a framework for the derivation of theorems.*[232]

Many times scientists or others relying on them treat corollaries as proofs.

> A **corollary** is *a proposition that follows with little or no proof required from one already proven, A deduction or an inference.*[233]

So corollaries, postulates, etc., are also useless in a presentation of scientific findings. They should not even be discussed because they have no merit. Sometimes merit is placed on dictums or corollaries due to the reputation of a scientist, or for political, social or economic reasons but these have no place in a scientific discussion. Thus, if a scientist is not dispassionate, an unconscious or conscious alternative

[231] American Heritage Dictionary
[232] American Heritage Dictionary
[233] American Heritage Dictionary

agenda will be put forth. Further, if no evidence is produced to support a contention, then a scientist might be in danger of appearing biased, promoting a political or social point of view or expressing personal beliefs and sentiments about a particular issue. Over time, they themselves begin to believe in those opinions. This is the power and danger of the human mind. A prime example of this is the belief in drugs. Some drugs have been helpful but usually only when the body has been mistreated so much that it needs drastic measures in order to survive. Almost weekly now we hear of drugs that were once touted as safe and helpful are being removed from the market as unsafe or dangerous.

New Diseases and the Economics of Drug Therapy

Every year there are more and more new diseased being "discovered" or being "recognized" as needing to be treated. The primary means of this treatment is through drugs. Profits are increased when some condition is discovered to which drug therapy can be applied. Therefore, drug companies are constantly searching for drugs that can be used to treat diseases and conversely diseased that can be treated by drugs. Many times drugs have been developed by accident and there is no purpose for them. The drug companies may not want to lose the time and money put into its development so they search to see if the drug is useful in the treatment of any disease. We have already seen how the very theory of drug therapy is flawed. However, the search for new diseases or finding new conditions that can be considered as new treatable diseases has reached new and ridiculous heights. This is not to say that new conditions have not arisen in humanity due to modern society's unparalleled deterioration of the environment and development of unprecedented levels of stress and toxins in the body. However, the naming of new diseases is now beyond the rational and still the predilection is to seek out drugs instead of simple and natural practices to deal with such problems as "Acid Reflux Disease" – by stopping the ingestion of acid forming foods. Another condition recently named is "Social Anxiety Disorder" – another term for acute stress. Instead of looking to lifestyle problems and societal pressures there is a predilection to seek out new drugs to deal with the problem. Instead of looking to discover why there is a problem with nutritional deficiency in foods the move is to Genetically Modify the food.

> In fact, the mainstream health industry has been rushing in the opposite direction. Less time. Less individuality. More and more drugs. Every year, more conditions are "diagnosed" as requiring medication. I recently saw a scientific paper claiming that the disease of "imagined ugliness" should be treated with anti-depressants. The direction is toward more pills, more "quick fixes," and more profit for the pharmaceutical industry.[234]

The same problem exists when dealing with mental disorders:

> In the early 21st century, the money is also in genetic research, based upon the idea that mental illness can be found and treated in the genes. We're told that disorders such as schizophrenia and depression seem to be passed down from generation to generation, therefore it's in your genes. A lot of research talent and money is going into trying to find vaccines so that anyone with a genetic expression of a mental disease will be able to be vaccinated against it. Dr. Ty Colbert, a clinical physiologist and active member of the National Association for Rights, Protection and Advocacy, reminds us that "while there are some true genetic disorders, like Huntington's disease, with which they are making a lot of progress, there has actually been no progress made with any mental illness. No pathophysiological evidence whatsoever exists for mental illness; it's all a series of theories."[235]

[234] The Food-Mood-Body Connection by Gary Null

[235] The Food-Mood-Body Connection by Gary Null

The Politics of Disease

Drug therapy is the primary concern of drug companies and they have a strong influence over the medical establishment and the government through lobbying the American Medical Association and the Congress. But this situation is not particular to the United States. It is endemic in western governments and it is spreading to the governments of other countries as the western companies cause western governments to forcibly curtail natural health practices in developing countries by in effect extortion. To obtain loans and aid developing countries (especially in Africa) are required to purchase western products and curtail their production of domestic products. This coercion entered into by the developing governments, forces an untenable situation in which the developing economy is wrecked and the western economies flourish since they have a new and ever increasing supply of consumers to purchase the products. The governments of the developing countries enforce these rules by intimidation, often times using the same funds obtained through the aid in order to create armies and purchase weapons to subjugate their own populations. These dictatorial and tyrannical governments are supported by the western countries and this has led to civil wars in the developing countries and increasing hatred of western governments and western peoples. This where natural health professionals, especially those interested in following the Kemetic Diet Program, come in. It is part of their responsibility to promote the knowledge and adoption of the correct health wisdom and practices nationally and internationally.

Conclusion: Summary of The Philosophy of Healing in the Kemetic Diet

You may by now realize that there are three aspects of health and therefore three causes of disease. The human being is composed of a composite consisting of the body, mind and soul. Therefore each aspect must be treated in order to promote healing and health. So there are physical factors to consider, mental factors to consider and spiritual factors to consider. If any of these are in disharmony, disease arises. The human being is a complex of these three main aspects. Thus, health cannot be gained only by a special pill or uttering words of power or prayer or expecting miracles without taking care of every aspect of your personality, that is, doing your part and letting the Divine do its part to promote your health and well being and prosperity. Perhaps the capacity itself of making lifestyle changes that lead to health instead of death, the main pathway to health, should be considered as the real miracle, since most people find it so hard to change their ways from how the culture has conditioned them. The will to change arises when the mental and spiritual capacities are expanded. Therefore, the mind and soul need to be taken into consideration when promoting real healing and not just relief from the symptoms of illness.

For the body one should adopt a healthy lifestyle (detailed in this book). Look at the sections on natural antibiotics for the acute problem of infection. But realize that infections occur when the immune system is compromised due to poor eating habits, malnutrition, stress and spiritual frustration. The body is overwhelmed with the opportunistic bacteria that normally live in the body but not in the higher quantities that lead to a diseased condition. Yeast[236] and Candida[237] are examples of such organisms. When the body is out of balance such as when too much sugar is consumed, these microorganisms multiply in greater numbers and overwhelm the systems of the body causing disease. This condition arises due to imbalance. The same occurs with the mind. It becomes overwhelmed with the "bacteria" of negative thoughts, desires and longings. Thoughts, desires and longings are always there, but in healthy

[236] **yeast** (yēst) *n.* **1.a.** Any of various unicellular fungi of the genus *Saccharomyces,* especially *S. cerevisiae,* reproducing by budding and from ascospores and capable of fermenting carbohydrates. **b.** Any of various similar fungi. **2.** Froth consisting of yeast cells together with the carbon dioxide they produce in the process of fermentation, present in or added to fruit juices

[237] ***Candida Albicans:*** Parasitic yeast like fungus that lives in a natural balance in the body: intestines, genital tract, mouth, esophagus, and throat. When out of balance it leads to Candidiasis- aliments of various organs and systems of the body.

individuals, not in an overwhelming quantity (that obstructs reason) or lower quality (that leads to mental imbalance – anger, hatred, greed, lust, jealousy, envy, etc.) unless there is an imbalance in the way we think and feel. We think and feel in ways we choose or choose to allow ourselves to be affected in life either due to ignorance or based on wisdom. Ignorance leads to mental illness and wisdom leads to sanity and enlightenment.

For the mind there must be relief of stress. Relaxation comes when the mind discovers peace through wisdom. Therefore, study the teachings and utter Medu Neter (divine speech) that will cleanse the mind. The prescribed Hekau (words of power) to promote health – enjoined by the Swnus (ancient African-Egyptian doctors was "Hetep di si Neter iri mettu wadj." (look up in the book for the full meaning). Also, repetition of the teachings is a form of Medu Neter.

For the soul there needs to be self-knowledge and self-discovery, which transcends words, thoughts and concepts. This comes of its own accord as the aspirant moves on the path, as the body and mind are purified and meditation leads the personality to transcend its conditioning.

Kamitan tradition holds that in order to receive something there must be an offering. So if you pursue health you must make an offering (Hetep) at your altar. The offering in exchange for health is purity of body, purity of mind and purity of soul. Seek to cleanse your physical, mental and spiritual self and all disease will be healed in accordance with the Divine dispensation and your own effort.

Peace and Blessings and May All Life, Health and Vitality be on to you!

Kemetic Vegetables, Fruits and Herbs Used in Ancient Times

Vegetables used by the Ancient Egyptians included:

Barley
Celery
Chickpeas – excellent source of vitamins and minerals and proteins
Cucumber
Dates
Edible roots of turnip and carrot class
Egg-plant
Emmer wheat
Figs
Flax (source of Omega 3 and 6 Fatty Acids)
Fruit of the moringa or horseradish tree – for oil
Garlic
Grapes
Leeks
Lentils
Lettuce
Melons
Olive oil (source of Omega 3 and 6 Fatty Acids)
Onions
Pea
Radishes
Raisins
Seeds of cumin
Spinach
Tamarind

Herbs included

Aniseed
Carob
Chervil
Cinnamon
Coriander
Cumin
Dill
Fennel
Fenugreek
Flowers
Hemp
Marjoram
Parsley
Thyme

Animal products:

Peasant food was regarded as fish (fresh water or salt water). In some periods those who ate fish were considered as unclean. *Recall that the method used by the ancient Egyptian doctors to test breastmilk was to reject it if it smelled like fish.

Cows were sacred and therefore were not eaten.

Plutarch: "No Egyptians would eat the flesh of sheep, except the Lycopolites." Goat, gazelle, ox, geese, etc. were eaten by well to do families in certain periods. Milk and cheese were also consumed in different periods. However, recall that these foods were prohibited for the Initiates.

*The following listing can be thought of as an expansion on the Kemetic listing above, for modern times. The local vegetables and herbs, which grow in the area where one lives, should form the staple of the diet. Therefore, foods similar in quality to those included in these lists should be sought and consumed.

Alkaline Vegetables for the Kemetic Diet

All of the following vegetables are suitable for use with the Kemetic Diet and will provide the required nutrients while promoting the pH balance of the body in order to prevent disease. So most preparations with these vegetables that are fresh and uncooked or processed will be in keeping with the Kemetic Diet system. Therefore, the combination of these vegetables (consuming some each day and alternating) can be the staple of the daily diet.

Alfalfa grass ☥
Artichokes
Asparagus
Barley grass ☥
Brussels sprouts
Cabbage lettuce, fresh
Cauliflower
Cayenne pepper
Celery
Chives
Comfrey
Cucumber, fresh ☥
Dandelion ☥
Dog grass
Endive, fresh
French cut beans (green beans)
Garlic
Green cabbage, December harvest
Green cabbage, March harvest
Kamut grass ☥
Lamb's lettuce
Leeks (bulbs)
Lettuce (green – leafy)
Onion
Peas, fresh
Peas, ripe
Red cabbage
Rhubarb stalks
Savoy cabbage
Shave grass
Sorrel
Soy sprouts ☥
Spinach (other than March)
Spinach, March harvest
Sprouted chia seeds ☥
Sprouted radish seeds ☥
Straw grass
Watercress
Wheat Grass ☥ (*Kamut* as opposed to regular wheat)
White cabbage
Zucchini

☥ These vegetables provide the greatest nutrient and alkaline qualities and should be the foundation of every green diet.[238]

[238] *Sick and Tired: Reclaim Your inner Terrain* by Robert O, Young, Ph. D. with Shelley Redford Young, L.M.T. (2001)

Alkaline Fruits for the Kemetic Diet

Apricot
Avocado (protein) ☥
Banana, ripe
Banana, unripe ☥
Black currant
Blueberry
Cantaloupe
Cherry, sour ☥
Cherry, sweet
Coconut, fresh ☥
Cranberry
Currant
Date
Fig Juice powder
Fresh lemon ☥
Gooseberry, ripe
Grape, ripe
Grapefruit ☥
Italian plum
Limes ☥
Mandarin orange
Mango
Orange
Papaya
Peach
Pear
Pineapple
Raspberry
Red currant
Rose hips
Strawberry
Tangerine
Tomato ☥
Watermelon ☥
Yellow plum

☥ These fruits provide the greatest nutrient and alkaline qualities and should be the foundation of every green diet.[239]

[239] *Sick and Tired: Reclaim Your inner Terrain* by Robert O, Young, Ph. D. with Shelley Redford Young, L.M.T. (2001)

NOTES

Use this section to take notes on the important concepts you have learned.

NOTES

Use this section to take notes on the important concepts you have learned.

Your Plan of Action

Use this section to begin developing a plan of action, which you will implement for yourself. List the ideas you would like to begin to follow up on right away beginning now. Beside each action write what day and time you will take that action on. On the third column write in your initials when you accomplish that goal.

Today's Date	Actions I want to take based on what I have learned and know is good for my health	How I will implement those actions	Today I have accomplished this goal

Daily Kemetic Diet Basic Maintenance Plan (Summary)

- Food for Mind and Soul-Relaxation period – after taking care of the morning routine, sit quietly for 20 minutes, focusing on your breath (proper breathing) to draw in life force energy and center yourself for the day ahead.

- Breakfast (Breaking the Fast):
    - Say the following chant four times just before having breakfast: *"Hetep Di Si Neter Iry Mettu Wadj"* which means "Offerings given to cause the Divine to make the channels of the body healthy (green).
    - Water from a young jelly coconut or 1 teaspoon of Kamut Wheatgrass Juice* with six ounces of purified spring or distilled water, alkaline water if possible.

- Mid-morning:
    - Repeat *"Hetep Di Si Neter Iry Mettu Wadj"* four times
    - Watery Fruit – melon, cucumber, grapes, etc., or freshly juiced carrot/green vegetable juice or Herbal Tea (cool or very warm, but not Cold or Hot)
    - 1 capsule of Sona Vitamin

- Lunch: (noon time-not necessarily at 12 P.M., but rather when feeling hungry-between 12-2 P.M.)
    - Repeat *"Hetep Di Si Neter Iry Mettu Wadj"* four times
    - Before lunch, have another 1 teaspoon (1½ if had coconut water for breakfast) of Kamut Wheatgrass Juice* with six ounces of water.
    - Then 30 minutes later, a Large salad:
        - Large All Raw Vegetable Salad
            - Can add Raw Hummus or Nut Pates, etc. –Check with food combining chart
        - Or Raw Fruit / Fruit salad
    - 1 capsule of Sona Vitamin with lunch

- Mid-Afternoon:
    - Repeat: *"Hetep Di Si Neter Iry Mettu Wadj"* four times
    - Nut Milk or Nut snack (nuts soaked for 12 hours; soaked almonds best)

- Dinner:
    - Repeat: *"Hetep Di Si Neter Iry Mettu Wadj"* four times
    - 30 minutes before supper: 1 teaspoon (1½ if had coconut water for breakfast) Kamut Wheatgrass Juice* with six ounces of water.
    - Large Vegetable salad
    - 1 capsule of Sona Vitamin
    - For those Transitioning to the Kemetic Diet System or those on the Kemetic Diet who are not eating a completely raw diet, AFTER salad is eaten, you may have small portion of cooked vegan foods, in accordance with the guidelines of the transition diet, lightly steamed vegetables being preferred.

- Evening:

    - Food For the Body
        - Repeat: *"Hetep Di Si Neter Iry Mettu Wadj"* four times
        - Light Fruit, Fruit salad, dried fruit (soaked) or fresh fruit juice.
        - Herbal tea (cool or very warm, but not Cold or Hot)

    - Food for the Mind- spend a minimum of 20 minutes reading uplifting literature that expands your understanding about the world and yourself.
    - Food for the Soul- Meditation- Prior to going to bed sit quietly for minimum 20 minutes meditation period.

Daily Kemetic Diet Basic Maintenance Plan (Detailed)

- Food for Mind and Soul-Relaxation period – after taking care of the morning routine, sit quietly for 20 minutes, focusing on your breath (proper breathing) to draw in life force energy and center yourself for the day ahead.

- Breakfast (Breaking the Fast):
  - Say the following chant four times just before having breakfast*: "Hetep Di Si Neter Iry Mettu Wadj"* which means "Offerings given to cause the Divine to make the channels of the body healthy (green).
  - Water from a young jelly coconut or 1 teaspoon of Kamut Wheatgrass Juice* with six ounces of purified spring or distilled water, alkaline water if possible.

- Mid-morning:
  - Repeat *"Hetep Di Si Neter Iry Mettu Wadj"* four times
  - Watery Fruit – melon, cucumber, grapes, etc. or freshly juiced carrot/green vegetable juice or Herbal Tea (cool or very warm, but not Cold or Hot)
  - 1 capsule of Sona Vitamin

- Lunch: (noon time-not necessarily at 12 P.M., but rather when feeling hungry-between 12-2 P.M.)
  - Repeat *"Hetep Di Si Neter Iry Mettu Wadj"* four times
  - Before lunch, have another 1 teaspoon (1½ if had coconut water for breakfast) of Kamut Wheatgrass Juice* with six ounces of water.
  - Then 30 minutes later, a Large salad:
    - All Raw Vegetable Salad
      - Should have a variety of vegetables
      - Should include fruits which are traditionally eaten with salad such as cucumbers, red or green bell peppers, tomatoes, etc
      - Use leaf lettuce, Romaine, and not head (iceberg) lettuce for greater nutrition
      - Raw hummus or other raw vegetable, nut or seaweed preparations which are compatible may be added
    - Or Raw Fruit / Fruit salad
  - 1 capsule of Sona Vitamin with lunch

- Mid-Afternoon:
  - Repeat: *"Hetep Di Si Neter Iry Mettu Wadj"* four times
  - Nut Milk or Nut snack (nuts soaked for 12 hours; soaked almonds best)

- Dinner:
  - Repeat: *"Hetep Di Si Neter Iry Mettu Wadj"* four times
  - 30 minutes before supper: 1 teaspoon (1½ if had coconut water for breakfast) Kamut Wheatgrass Juice* with six ounces of water.
  - Large Vegetable salad
    - Should have a variety of vegetables-some preferably different from lunch menu and
    - Should include fruits that are traditionally eaten with salad such as cucumbers, red or green bell peppers, tomatoes, etc.
    - Raw hummus or other raw vegetable/ nut/ seaweed preparations may be added

  - 1 capsule of Sona Vitamin
  - For those Transitioning to the Kemetic Diet System or those on the Kemetic Diet who are not eating a completely raw diet, AFTER salad is eaten, you may have cooked food according to the following guidelines:

    - Vegan foods, in accordance with the guidelines of the transition diet (no more than half serving).

- Lightly steamed vegetables being preferred.
- May include other transition foods here such as brown rice, beans (No Pasta, No Cooked Breads)
- vegetable soup

- Evening:

  - Food For the Body
    - Repeat: *"Hetep Di Si Neter Iry Mettu Wadj"* four times
    - Light Fruit, Fruit salad, dried fruit (soaked) or fresh fruit juice.
    - Herbal tea (cool or very warm, but not Cold or Hot)

  - Food for the Mind- spend a minimum of 20 minutes reading uplifting literature that expands your understanding about the world and yourself. Or you may listen to lectures on philosophy and the means to work through and transcend obstacles of ignorance, negative emotions and adversity in life.
  - Food for the Soul- Meditation- Prior to going to bed sit quietly for minimum 20 minutes meditation period. For the first 10 minutes reflect on the teaching you have read or heard. For the next 10 minutes focus on your breath (proper breathing) using the chant if you have one allow your mind to relax and go deeper into yourself.

In addition to the above, the following is part of the Kemetic Diet System

- Flax seed supplementation: Flax seed oil – Children 1/3 to 1 teaspoon / 33 lbs., Adults – 1 teaspoon to 1 tablespoon / 100 lbs. Not recommended for cooking. Can take straight or mixed with salad dressing. Ground Flax seeds- Milled Flax seed-1 teaspoon to 2 tablespoons daily

- Sunlight: Spend 10-20 minutes in direct sunlight – to stimulate vitamin D production and life-force rejuvenation. If possible take two 10-minute sunbaths during the day. This can be easily accomplished if you take your lunch in the outdoors. (allow the sun to touch your skin directly).

- Exercise: Minimum spend ½ to 1 hour practicing Kamitan Tjef Sema Paut Neteru Yoga Exercises (Egyptian Yoga Tjef Neteru Book and/or videos available), or other gentle yoga styles or other exercises like Tai Chi which work with the physical and energy bodies– morning or early evening practice.

*Note on Kamut Wheatgrass: Beginners should start with:

- For first 2 - 4 weeks: A total intake of 1/8 teaspoon of Kamut daily, for breakfast
- For next 2 - 4 weeks: 1/8 teaspoon twice a day (1/4 teaspoon daily) for breakfast and dinner
- For next 4-8 weeks: ¼ teaspoon three times a day,
- For next 8 weeks: ½ teaspoon three times a day,
- Then begin Kemetic Diet Program of 1 teaspoon of Kamut three times a day.

This regimen may be extended over a longer period of time if one is experiencing moderate to severe cleansing reactions at the level where one is. Should this occur, one should return to the lower level where one did not experience such cleansing reactions, and continue at this level for another 2-4 months before trying to go to the next level.

- Additional liquids may be taken throughout the day according to the demands of your body. You may use coconut water from young jelly coconuts, purified alkaline water or herbal teas (not very cold or too hot).

Nutritional Supplements For Use With the Kemetic Diet Program

(Available through Sema Institute / C.M. Books and Health)

These supplements are recommended for the following situations:

1. When starting the Kemetic diet program, those who have been on a well-balanced raw food diet for over 2 years may take supplements at their discretion. If stopping taking vitamins, it is best to wean yourself off slowly, so that you may determine any negative effects and be able to correct them without severely unbalancing the body. So, for example, if you are taking 3 vitamins daily, cut down to 2 for 6 months or so, and if no ill effects are perceived, then to 1 for another 6 months or so, then you may try stopping completely. However, be aware that some vitamin and mineral deficiencies may not show up for years. It is best to have yourself tested to be sure there are no deficiencies.
2. Those who have been practicing vegetarianism with cooked and or uncooked food and who are in reasonably good health may take the supplements (containing digestive enzymes) until one completely transitions to a compete well-balanced raw food diet and is on this diet for 2 years (follow the guidelines above -see # 1).
3. Those who have been eating meat should turn to vegetarianism completely, and may use probiotic supplementation for 1-6 months, and vitamin supplementation (containing digestive enzymes) . As you transition from non-vegetarian to vegan, and from vegan to raw, follow the guidelines above (see #'s 1 and 2)

Daily Kemetic Diet Plan for Illness Condition

- The plan for illness is the same as the Basic Plan except
  - there is to be no cooked food at all.
  - there is to be no nut food at all.
  - fruit intake is minimal. (no sweet fruits at all – consume only alkaline watery fruits. – no dried fruits.
  - Freshly juiced green leafy vegetables with carrot juice daily.
  - Fasting: practice fasting in accordance with the intuition of the body or the outline in this book- if you are not hungry do not eat solid foods but continue with green vegetable juices.

- Food for Mind and Soul-Relaxation period – after taking care of the morning routine, sit quietly for 20 minutes, focusing on your breath (proper breathing) to draw in life force energy and center yourself for the day ahead.

- Breakfast (Breaking the Fast):
  - Say the following chant four times just before having breakfast: *"Hetep Di Si Neter Iry Mettu Wadj"* which means "Offerings given to cause the Divine to make the channels of the body healthy (green).
  - Water from a young jelly coconut or 1 teaspoon of Kamut Wheatgrass Juice* with six ounces of purified spring or distilled water, alkaline water if possible.

- Mid-morning:
  - Repeat *"Hetep Di Si Neter Iry Mettu Wadj"* four times
  - Watery Fruit – melon, cucumber, etc. or freshly juiced carrot/green vegetable juice or Herbal Tea (not Hot)
  - 1 capsule of Sona Vitamin

- Lunch: (noon time-not necessarily at 12 P.M., but rather when feeling hungry-between 12-2 P.M.)
  - Repeat *"Hetep Di Si Neter Iry Mettu Wadj"* four times
  - Before lunch, have another 1 teaspoon (1½ if had coconut water for breakfast) of Kamut Wheatgrass Juice* with six ounces of water.
  - Then 30 minutes later, a Large salad:
    - All Raw Vegetable Salad with or without raw Hummus
    - Or Raw Fruit / Fruit salad
  - 1 capsule of Sona Vitamin with lunch

- Mid-Afternoon:
  - Repeat: *"Hetep Di Si Neter Iry Mettu Wadj"* four times

- Dinner:
  - Repeat: *"Hetep Di Si Neter Iry Mettu Wadj"* four times
  - 30 minutes before supper: 1 teaspoon (1½ if had coconut water for breakfast) Kamut Wheatgrass Juice* with six ounces of water.
  - Large Vegetable salad
  - 1 capsule of Sona Vitamin

- Evening:

  - Food For the Body
    - Repeat: *"Hetep Di Si Neter Iry Mettu Wadj"* four times
    - Light Fruit, Fruit salad, fresh fruit juice.
    - Herbal tea (not Hot)

- Food for the Mind- spend a minimum of 20 minutes reading uplifting literature that expands your understanding about the world and yourself. Or listen to lectures on philosophy and the means to work through and transcend obstacles of ignorance, negative emotions and adversity in life.
- Food for the Soul- Meditation- Prior to going to bed sit quietly for minimum 20 minutes meditation period. For the first 10 minutes reflect on the teaching you have read or heard. For the next 10 minutes focus on your breath (proper breathing) using the chant if you have one allow your mind to relax and go deeper into yourself.

How to Adopt the Kemetic Diet Program

The chart below is divided according to the different levels of advancement from a meat eating and processed food diet to a 100% raw and organic diet. It is a general guideline, designed in succeeding stages of advancement so that the user may gauge his/her own current level and thereby choose the next higher level at which to adopt the program. It is recommended that the program be adopted in stages and that the user should not skip stages as this may induce a cleansing reaction (detoxification) that is more severe than would be expected by progressively adopting a better diet gradually. The length of time in each stage may be adjusted according to the condition of an individual. The poorer your diet is in each stage, and the more backtracking you do (eating items or quantities of items from a previous level that you were supposed to have given up), take the upper limits (longer times) to make the transition.

A	B	C	D
If your current diet consists in	For the next 6 months to 1 year Adopt Kemetic Diet maintenance Plan	For the next 1-2 years	After 1-2 years on well-balanced 100% raw diet
❖ over 50% cooked food, ❖ meats and processed foods ❖ refined sugar ❖ white flour ❖ non-organic food] ❖ fried foods	❖ 50% cooked food, and processed foods/ 50% Raw-Live foods – fresh vegetables and fruits ❖ Cooked foods are to follow guidelines in this book for transition diet foods ❖ no meats ❖ use maple syrup, dates, or stevia herb instead of refined sugar ❖ use whole wheat flour (Kamut flour) instead of white flour ❖ No Fried Foods	❖ 80% Raw foods – fresh vegetables and fruits /20% cooked ❖ Cooked foods are to follow guidelines in this book for transition diet foods ❖ Other items as in B ❖ Green vegetable juices ❖ use organic instead of non-organic food preferably ❖ No Pasta ❖ No cooked breads ❖ No Potatoes or Cassava (Yucca)	❖ 100% raw foods – fresh vegetables and fruits ❖ Green vegetable juices ❖ use organic instead of non-organic food preferably
Instruction: begin the Kemetic Diet program by adopting stage B	Instruction: advance the Kemetic Diet program by adopting stage C	Instruction: advance the Kemetic Diet program by adopting stage D	Instruction: maintain this program for the rest of your life ☺
	Food Supplements Vitamins (with Digestive enzymes) Probiotic Flax oil or meal Kamut Juice Practice intuitional fasting for the body as dictated by the wisdom of the body (if not hungry do not eat).	Food Supplements Vitamins (with Digestive enzymes) Flax oil or meal or Olive Oil Kamut Juice Practice fasting as needed (daily, 1 day per week and - at equinoxes and solstices, for 3 days)	Food Supplements Vitamins (with Digestive enzymes) Flax oil or meal Flax oil or meal or Olive Oil Kamut Juice Practice fasting as needed (daily, 1 day per week and - at equinoxes and solstices, for 3 days)

NOTE: if you are in the midst of dealing with a severe life threatening illness you should seek the counseling of a qualified health counselor to adopt the most advanced program immediately.

YOUR 30 DAY HEALING DIET AND FASTING PLAN FOR BODY, MIND AND SOUL

Use this section for the next 30 days to record your daily diet and natural health practices. Record what you have eaten in the way of good food for the body, mind and soul each day. Remember, you must do something for each aspect of your personality each day in order to be healthy. Take care to follow the instructions given in this volume when deciding on what type of food you want to consume. Do at least one of the activities listed in the first box for your body, mind and soul health each day.

Instructions: In the first 20 days of the program you will not eat meat or dairy products. Consume only vegetables and fruits as outlined in PART II of this volume. Use the guidelines for the transition diet and proper eating habits guidelines. On the 21st day eat only fruits. Begin your fast on the 22nd day. On the 22nd and the 24th day drink only freshly squeezed juices. On the 23rd day drink only lemon or lime and water or coconut water. On the 25th day eat some solid fruits again. On the 26th and 27th day eat only raw vegetables and fruits. On the 28th day resume eating fruits, vegetables (preferably raw, or lightly steamed), nuts, and meat and dairy substitutes if needed. After the 30th day resolve to maintain this way of life for your body, mind and soul health. Gradually try to wean yourself off of the more dense (cooked) foods in favor of raw/live foods. Adopt a regular fasting program as described in PART III, from then on. Check with your personal health care professional before, during and after practicing any diet or fasting program. NOTE: FOR THOSE WHO HAVE RECENTLY CONVERTED TO A VEGETARIAN DIET DO NOT TAKE FRUITS OR FRUIT JUICES DURING THE FASTING DAYS IN YOUR FIRST YEAR OF THE KEMETIC DIET.

DAY	Today's Date	Food For the Body What physical food (vegetables and fruits) did I eat today? How have I used my body in a righteous manner to serve others today? How have I cared (exercise, bathing, herbs, massages, reflexology, etc.) for the body today?	Food For the Mind What uplifting teachings have I heard, or what uplifting books have I read today? What have I done today that is good for my own well being, my family, the community, and the world?	Food for the Soul What food have I eaten for my soul today? Practice meditation, chanting and prayer twice daily (minimum 15 minutes in the morning before breakfast and in the evening before bed time.)
1				
2				
3				
4				
5				

DAY	Today's Date	Food For the Body What physical food (vegetables and fruits) did I eat today? How have I used my body in a righteous manner to serve others today? How have I cared (exercise, bathing, herbs, massages, reflexology, etc.) for the body today?	Food For the Mind What uplifting teachings have I heard, or what uplifting books have I read today? What have I done today that is good for my own well being, my family, the community, and the world?	Food for the Soul What food have I eaten for my soul today? Practice meditation, chanting and prayer twice daily (minimum 15 minutes in the morning before breakfast and in the evening before bed time.)
6				
7				
8				
9				
10				
11				
12				
13				
14				

DAY	Today's Date	Food For the Body What physical food (vegetables and fruits) did I eat today? How have I used my body in a righteous manner to serve others today? How have I cared (exercise, bathing, herbs, massages, reflexology, etc.) for the body today?	Food For the Mind What uplifting teachings have I heard, or what uplifting books have I read today? What have I done today that is good for my own well being, my family, the community, and the world?	Food for the Soul What food have I eaten for my soul today? Practice meditation, chanting and prayer twice daily (minimum 15 minutes in the morning before breakfast and in the evening before bed time.)
15				
16				
17				
18				
19				
20				
21		Fruits only (vegetarians only) Steamed veggies for non-vegetarians and new vegetarians		
22		Juices only (vegetarians use fruit juices. Non-vegetarians or new vegetarians use vegetable juices)		

DAY	Today's Date	Food For the Body What physical food (vegetables and fruits) did I eat today? How have I used my body in a righteous manner to serve others today? How have I cared (exercise, bathing, herbs, massages, reflexology, etc.) for the body today?	Food For the Mind What uplifting teachings have I heard, or what uplifting books have I read today? What have I done today that is good for my own well being, my family, the community, and the world?	Food for the Soul What food have I eaten for my soul today? Practice meditation, chanting and prayer twice daily (minimum 15 minutes in the morning before breakfast and in the evening before bed time.)
23		Lemon and water only. Rest and relax all day. Practice breathing exercises and light physical exercise.	Read uplifting spiritual texts, listen and visualize peace, good will, understanding, and well being.	Practice silence, reflection, and meditation.
24		Juices only (vegetarians use fruit juices. Non-vegetarians or new vegetarians use vegetable juices)		
25		Fruits only (vegetarians only) Steamed veggies for non-vegetarians and new vegetarians		
26				
27				
28				
29				
30				

For a detailed exposition of the Kemetic Diet System please consult the book:
The Kemetic Diet: Food For Body, Mind and Soul by Dr. Muata Ashby

Available Video courses:

Lecture Series: The Kemetic Diet in six lessons (A six hour series on the Kemetic Diet system) by Dr. Muata Ashby

Lecture Series: Mysticism of The Kemetic Diet & Christianity and the Kemetic Diet, by Dr. Karen "Dja" Ashby

Kemetic Diet Personalized Counseling Program

Founder of the Sema Institute:
Sebai Dr. Muata Ashby

Need Assistance In Starting or Practicing the Kemetic Diet Program?

If you are new to the healthy lifestyle, self-healing culture, nutrition or alternative health or advancing in your practice of natural health and nutrition practices you may need some counseling as you implement the principles of conscious living and detoxification to your life and pursue the path of self-healing, self-empowerment and self-mastery. In order to be a successful human being in the world, attain personal fulfillment and spiritual insight one must have three kinds of health: health of the body, mind and soul. Health and healing are fast becoming the most important issues for all people of the world. The staff at The Sema Institute now offers counseling on all levels of the Kemetic Diet System (for the Body (diet, nutrition, exercise, lifestyle change), for the Mind (mental health), and for the Soul (spiritual disciplines). You may communicate via mail or telephone and receive expert counseling and instruction on the ancient African methods of nutrition and other natural life changes that can restore health and prevent disease. Return the Application for Personalized Kemetic Diet Counseling at the back of this sheet or call 305-378-6253 for more information or go to the web site www.Egyptianyoga.com.

Sema Institute of Yoga, P.O. Box 570459 Miami, Fl. 33257

(305) 378-6253

Web: **www.KemeticDiet.com_** or www.Egyptianyoga.comm Email: Semayoga@aol.com

RESOURCES TO COMPLEMENT THE KEMETIC DIET

Organic Food Sources

Local Health and Whole Food Stores

Many local supermarkets carru organic produce, usually next to the inorganic produce, or in its own separate area. You can also speak to the produce manager and request that they carry specific organic products you may desire. Many local supermarkets also now have health food sections.

Living-Food Retreats

Ann Wigmore Institute
P.O. Box 429
Rincon, Puerto Rico 00677-0429
Phone:787-868-6307
Fax-.787-868-2430

Aris La Tham
C/O Sunfire Food
Ligunea Post Office
Kingston, Jamaica
876-377-3983
Sunfirefood@hotmail.com

Juicing and Juice Machines

The Champion Juicer

Distributor.-
The Raw Gourmet
P.O. Box 4133
Carlsbad, CA 92018

Phone:760-967-6664
1-888-316-4611
email: rawgourmetc&aol.com

The Green Power Juicer

Distributor.
The Sema Institute of Yoga,
P.O. Box 570459,
Miami, Fl 33157
305-378-6253

Books for Vegetarian and Raw Recipes to Complement the Kemetic Diet

Cookless Recipes by Aris La Tham

Eat Right, Live Longer by Jennifer Raymond

Food For Life by Neal D. Barnard, M.D.

Fresh Vegetable and Fruit Juices: What's Missing in Your Body? By N.W. Walker D.Sc.

Raw Kids by Cheryl Stoycoff

Sunfire Cuisine- The Tropical Art of Raw Food by Aris La Tham

The Garden of Eden Raw Fruit & Vegetable Recipes by Phyllis Avery

The Raw Gourmet by Nomi Shannon

Books and Information for Alternative Healing Approaches

Physicians Committee for Responsible Medicine
(202) 686-2210 PCRM@PCRM.Org

Prescription for Nutritional Healing, by James F. Balch M.D. and Phyllis A Balch, C.N.C.

Sick and Tired: Reclaim Your Inner Terrain by Robert O, Young, Ph. D. with Shelley Redford Young, L.M.T. (2001)

Women's Bodies, Women's Wisdom by Christine Northrup MD

INDEX

A

B

E

F

G

Q

R

S

T

U

V

W

X

Y

Audio Lecture Series on Health For Body, Mind and Soul by Dr. Muata Ashby

For a detailed exposition of the Kemetic Diet System please consult the book:
The Kemetic Diet: Food For Body, Mind and Soul by Dr. Muata Ashby

Available Video courses:

Lecture Course: The Kemetic Diet in six lessons (A six hour series on the Kemetic Diet system) by Dr. Muata Ashby

Kemetic Diet Class 1
Kemetic Diet Class 2
Kemetic Diet Class 3
Kemetic Diet Class 4
Kemetic Diet Class 5
Kemetic Diet Class 6

Lecture Series: Mysticism of The Kemetic Diet & Christianity and the Kemetic Diet, by Dr. Karen "Dja" Ashby

Audio Cassettes $9.99 U.S.

207 CLASS 5 Initiation: Health, Vegetarianism and Yoga - 90 min
3005-3008 Yoga and Mental Health Seminar (4 tapes)
9002 Class 1: The principles of Health Part 1
9003 Class 2: The Kemetic Concept of Health-Doctors in Ancient Egypt and the source of disease-how wrong foods and wrong eating habits cause all diseases.

9004 Class 3: The Kemetic Concept of Health-Fasting for body mind and soul

May the blessings of Life, Vitality and Health be yours!

OTHER BOOKS FROM C. M. BOOKS

P.O.Box 570459
Miami, Florida, 33257
(305) 378-6253 Fax: (305) 378-6253

THE YOGA AND MYSTICAL SPIRITUALITY BOOK SERIES

This book is part of a series on the study and practice of Ancient Egyptian Yoga and Mystical Spirituality based on the writings of Dr. Muata Abhaya Ashby. They are also part of the Egyptian Yoga Course provided by the Sema Institute of Yoga. Below you will find a listing of the other books in this series. For more information send for the Egyptian Yoga Book-Audio-Video Catalog or the Egyptian Yoga Course Catalog.

Now you can study the teachings of Egyptian and Indian Yoga wisdom and Spirituality with the Egyptian Yoga Mystical Spirituality Series. The Egyptian Yoga Series takes you through the Initiation process and lead you to understand the mysteries of the soul and the Divine and to attain the highest goal of life: ENLIGHTENMENT. The Egyptian Yoga Series, takes you on an in depth study of Ancient Egyptian mythology and their inner mystical meaning. Each Book is prepared for the serious student of the mystical sciences and provides a study of the teachings along with exercises, assignments and projects to make the teachings understood and effective in real life. The Series is part of the Egyptian Yoga course but may be purchased even if you are not taking the course. The series is ideal for study groups.

Prices subject to change.

1. **EGYPTIAN YOGA: THE PHILOSOPHY OF ENLIGHTENMENT An original, fully illustrated work, including hieroglyphs, detailing the meaning of the Egyptian mysteries, tantric yoga, psycho-spiritual and physical exercises. Egyptian Yoga is a guide to the practice of the highest spiritual philosophy which leads to absolute freedom from human misery and to immortality. It is well known by scholars that Egyptian philosophy is the basis of Western and Middle Eastern religious philosophies such as *Christianity, Islam, Judaism,* the *Kabala*, and Greek philosophy, but what about Indian philosophy, Yoga and Taoism? What were the original teachings? How can they be practiced today? What is the source of pain and suffering in the world and what is the solution? Discover the deepest mysteries of the mind and universe within and outside of your self. 8.5" X 11" ISBN: 1-884564-01-1 Soft $19.95**

2. EGYPTIAN YOGA II: The Supreme Wisdom of Enlightenment by Dr. Muata Ashby ISBN 1-884564-39-9 $23.95 U.S. In this long awaited sequel to *Egyptian Yoga: The Philosophy of Enlightenment* you will take a fascinating and enlightening journey back in time and discover the teachings which constituted the epitome of Ancient Egyptian spiritual wisdom. What are the disciplines which lead to the fulfillment of all desires? Delve into the three states of consciousness (waking, dream and deep sleep) and the fourth state which transcends them all, Neberdjer, "The Absolute." These teachings of the city of Waset (Thebes) were the crowning

achievement of the Sages of Ancient Egypt. They establish the standard mystical keys for understanding the profound mystical symbolism of the Triad of human consciousness.

3. **THE KAMITAN DIET GUIDE TO HEALTH, DIET AND FASTING Health issues have always been important to human beings since the beginning of time. The earliest records of history show that the art of healing was held in high esteem since the time of Ancient Egypt. In the early 20th century, medical doctors had almost attained the status of sainthood by the promotion of the idea that they alone were "scientists" while other healing modalities and traditional healers who did not follow the "scientific method' were nothing but superstitious, ignorant charlatans who at best would take the money of their clients and at worst kill them with the unscientific "snake oils" and "irrational theories". In the late 20th century, the failure of the modern medical establishment's ability to lead the general public to good health, promoted the move by many in society towards "alternative medicine". Alternative medicine disciplines are those healing modalities which do not adhere to the philosophy of allopathic medicine. Allopathic medicine is what medical doctors practice by an large. It is the theory that disease is caused by agencies outside the body such as bacteria, viruses or physical means which affect the body. These can therefore be treated by medicines and therapies The natural healing method began in the absence of extensive technologies with the idea that all the answers for health may be found in nature or rather, the deviation from nature. Therefore, the health of the body can be restored by correcting the aberration and thereby restoring balance. This is the area that will be covered in this volume. Allopathic techniques have their place in the art of healing. However, we should not forget that the body is a grand achievement of the spirit and built into it is the capacity to maintain itself and heal itself. Ashby, Muata ISBN: 1-884564-49-6 $24.95**

4. **INITIATION INTO EGYPTIAN YOGA Shedy: Spiritual discipline or program, to go deeply into the mysteries, to study the mystery teachings and literature profoundly, to penetrate the mysteries. You will learn about the mysteries of initiation into the teachings and practice of Yoga and how to become an Initiate of the mystical sciences. This insightful manual is the first in a series which introduces you to the goals of daily spiritual and yoga practices: Meditation, Diet, Words of Power and the ancient wisdom teachings. 8.5" X 11" ISBN 1-884564-02-X Soft Cover $24.95 U.S.**

5. ***THE AFRICAN ORIGINS OF CIVILIZATION, MYSTICAL RELIGION AND YOGA PHILOSOPHY* HARD COVER EDITION ISBN: 1-884564-50-X $80.00 U.S. 81/2" X 11" Part 1, Part 2, Part 3 in one volume 683 Pages Hard Cover First Edition Three volumes in one. Over the past several years I have been asked to put together in one volume the most important evidences showing the correlations and common teachings between Kamitan (Ancient Egyptian) culture and religion and that of India. The questions of the history of Ancient Egypt, and the latest archeological evidences showing civilization and culture in Ancient Egypt and its spread to other countries, has intrigued many scholars as well as mystics over the years. Also, the possibility that Ancient Egyptian Priests and Priestesses migrated to Greece, India and other countries to carry on the traditions of the Ancient Egyptian Mysteries, has been speculated over the years as well. In chapter 1 of the book *Egyptian Yoga The Philosophy of Enlightenment,* 1995, I first introduced the deepest comparison between Ancient Egypt and India that had been brought forth up to that time. Now, in the year 2001 this new book, *THE AFRICAN ORIGINS OF CIVILIZATION, MYSTICAL RELIGION AND YOGA PHILOSOPHY,* more fully explores the motifs, symbols and philosophical correlations between Ancient Egyptian and Indian mysticism and clearly shows not only that Ancient Egypt and India were connected culturally but also spiritually. How does this knowledge help the spiritual aspirant? This discovery has great importance for the Yogis and mystics**

who follow the philosophy of Ancient Egypt and the mysticism of India. It means that India has a longer history and heritage than was previously understood. It shows that the mysteries of Ancient Egypt were essentially a yoga tradition which did not die but rather developed into the modern day systems of Yoga technology of India. It further shows that African culture developed Yoga Mysticism earlier than any other civilization in history. All of this expands our understanding of the unity of culture and the deep legacy of Yoga, which stretches into the distant past, beyond the Indus Valley civilization, the earliest known high culture in India as well as the Vedic tradition of Aryan culture. Therefore, Yoga culture and mysticism is the oldest known tradition of spiritual development and Indian mysticism is an extension of the Ancient Egyptian mysticism. By understanding the legacy which Ancient Egypt gave to India the mysticism of India is better understood and by comprehending the heritage of Indian Yoga, which is rooted in Ancient Egypt the Mysticism of Ancient Egypt is also better understood. This expanded understanding allows us to prove the underlying kinship of humanity, through the common symbols, motifs and philosophies which are not disparate and confusing teachings but in reality expressions of the same study of truth through metaphysics and mystical realization of Self. (HARD COVER)

6. AFRICAN ORIGINS BOOK 1 PART 1 African Origins of African Civilization, Religion, Yoga Mysticism and Ethics Philosophy-<u>Soft Cover</u> $24.95 ISBN: 1-884564-55-0

7. AFRICAN ORIGINS BOOK 2 PART 2 African Origins of Western Civilization, Religion and Philosophy(Soft) -<u>Soft Cover</u> $24.95 ISBN: 1-884564-56-9

8. EGYPT AND INDIA (AFRICAN ORIGINS BOOK 3 PART 3) African Origins of Eastern Civilization, Religion, Yoga Mysticism and Philosophy-<u>Soft Cover</u> $29.95 (Soft) ISBN: 1-884564-57-7

9. **THE MYSTERIES OF ASET: The Path of Wisdom, Immortality and Enlightenment Through the study of ancient myth and the illumination of initiatic understanding the idea of God is expanded from the mythological comprehension to the metaphysical. Then this metaphysical understanding is related to you, the student, so as to begin understanding your true divine nature. ISBN 1-884564-24-0 $24.99**

10. **EGYPTIAN PROVERBS: TEMT TCHAAS *Temt Tchaas* means: collection of ——Ancient Egyptian Proverbs How to live according to MAAT Philosophy. Beginning Meditation. All proverbs are indexed for easy searches. For the first time in one volume, ——Ancient Egyptian Proverbs, wisdom teachings and meditations, fully illustrated with hieroglyphic text and symbols. EGYPTIAN PROVERBS is a unique collection of knowledge and wisdom which you can put into practice today and transform your life. 5.5"x 8.5" $14.95 U.S ISBN: 1-884564-00-3**

11. **THE PATH OF DIVINE LOVE The Process of Mystical Transformation and The Path of Divine Love This Volume will focus on the ancient wisdom teachings and how to use them in a scientific process for self-transformation. Also, this volume will detail the process of transformation from ordinary consciousness to cosmic consciousness through the integrated practice of the teachings and the path of Devotional Love toward the Divine. 5.5"x 8.5" ISBN 1-884564-11-9 $22.99**

12. **INTRODUCTION TO MAAT PHILOSOPHY: Spiritual Enlightenment Through the Path of Virtue Known as Karma Yoga in India, the teachings of MAAT for living virtuously**

and with orderly wisdom are explained and the student is to begin practicing the precepts of Maat in daily life so as to promote the process of purification of the heart in preparation for the judgment of the soul. This judgment will be understood not as an event that will occur at the time of death but as an event that occurs continuously, at every moment in the life of the individual. The student will learn how to become allied with the forces of the Higher Self and to thereby begin cleansing the mind (heart) of impurities so as to attain a higher vision of reality. ISBN 1-884564-20-8 $22.99

13. **MEDITATION The Ancient Egyptian Path to Enlightenment Many people do not know about the rich history of meditation practice in Ancient Egypt. This volume outlines the theory of meditation and presents the Ancient Egyptian Hieroglyphic text which give instruction as to the nature of the mind and its three modes of expression. It also presents the texts which give instruction on the practice of meditation for spiritual Enlightenment and unity with the Divine. This volume allows the reader to begin practicing meditation by explaining, in easy to understand terms, the simplest form of meditation and working up to the most advanced form which was practiced in ancient times and which is still practiced by yogis around the world in modern times. ISBN 1-884564-27-7 $24.99**

14. **THE GLORIOUS LIGHT MEDITATION TECHNIQUE OF ANCIENT EGYPT ISBN: 1-884564-15-1$14.95 (PB) New for the year 2000. This volume is based on the earliest known instruction in history given for the practice of formal meditation. Discovered by Dr. Muata Ashby, it is inscribed on the walls of the Tomb of Seti I in Thebes Egypt. This volume details the philosophy and practice of this unique system of meditation originated in Ancient Egypt and the earliest practice of meditation known in the world which occurred in the most advanced African Culture.**

15. **THE SERPENT POWER: The Ancient Egyptian Mystical Wisdom of the Inner Life Force. This Volume specifically deals with the latent life Force energy of the universe and in the human body, its control and sublimation. How to develop the Life Force energy of the subtle body. This Volume will introduce the esoteric wisdom of the science of how virtuous living acts in a subtle and mysterious way to cleanse the latent psychic energy conduits and vortices of the spiritual body. ISBN 1-884564-19-4 $22.95**

16. **EGYPTIAN YOGA MEDITATION IN MOTION Thef Neteru: *The Movement of The Gods and Goddesses* Discover the physical postures and exercises practiced thousands of years ago in Ancient Egypt which are today known as Yoga exercises. This work is based on the pictures and teachings from the Creation story of Ra, The Asarian Resurrection Myth and the carvings and reliefs from various Temples in Ancient Egypt 8.5" X 11" ISBN 1-884564-10-0 Soft Cover $18.99 Exercise video $21.99**

17. **EGYPTIAN TANTRA YOGA: The Art of Sex Sublimation and Universal Consciousness This Volume will expand on the male and female principles within the human body and in the universe and further detail the sublimation of sexual energy into spiritual energy. The student will study the deities Min and Hetheru, Asar and Aset, Geb and Nut and discover the mystical implications for a practical spiritual discipline. This Volume will also focus on the Tantric aspects of Ancient Egyptian and Indian mysticism, the purpose of sex and the mystical teachings of sexual sublimation which lead to self-knowledge and Enlightenment. 5.5"x 8.5" ISBN 1-884564-03-8 $24.95**

18. **ASARIAN RELIGION: RESURRECTING ASAR The path of Mystical Awakening and the Keys to Immortality NEW REVISED AND EXPANDED EDITION! The Ancient Sages**

created stories based on human and superhuman beings whose struggles, aspirations, needs and desires ultimately lead them to discover their true Self. The myth of Aset, Asar and Heru is no exception in this area. While there is no one source where the entire story may be found, pieces of it are inscribed in various ancient Temples walls, tombs, steles and papyri. For the first time available, the complete myth of Asar, Aset and Heru has been compiled from original Ancient Egyptian, Greek and Coptic Texts. This epic myth has been richly illustrated with reliefs from the Temple of Heru at Edfu, the Temple of Aset at Philae, the Temple of Asar at Abydos, the Temple of Hetheru at Denderah and various papyri, inscriptions and reliefs. Discover the myth which inspired the teachings of the *Shetaut Neter* (Egyptian Mystery System - Egyptian Yoga) and the Egyptian Book of Coming Forth By Day. Also, discover the three levels of Ancient Egyptian Religion, how to understand the mysteries of the Duat or Astral World and how to discover the abode of the Supreme in the Amenta, *The Other World* The ancient religion of Asar, Aset and Heru, if properly understood, contains all of the elements necessary to lead the sincere aspirant to attain immortality through inner self-discovery. This volume presents the entire myth and explores the main mystical themes and rituals associated with the myth for understating human existence, creation and the way to achieve spiritual emancipation - *Resurrection.* The Asarian myth is so powerful that it influenced and is still having an effect on the major world religions. Discover the origins and mystical meaning of the Christian Trinity, the Eucharist ritual and the ancient origin of the birthday of Jesus Christ. Soft Cover ISBN: 1-884564-27-5 $24.95

19. **THE EGYPTIAN BOOK OF THE DEAD MYSTICISM OF THE PERT EM HERU $26.95 ISBN# 1-884564-28-3 Size: 8½" X 11" I Know myself, I know myself, I am One With God!–From the Pert Em Heru "The Ru Pert em Heru" or "Ancient Egyptian Book of The Dead," or "Book of Coming Forth By Day" as it is more popularly known, has fascinated the world since the successful translation of Ancient Egyptian hieroglyphic scripture over 150 years ago. The astonishing writings in it reveal that the Ancient Egyptians believed in life after death and in an ultimate destiny to discover the Divine. The elegance and aesthetic beauty of the hieroglyphic text itself has inspired many see it as an art form in and of itself. But is there more to it than that? Did the Ancient Egyptian wisdom contain more than just aphorisms and hopes of eternal life beyond death? In this volume Dr. Muata Ashby, the author of over 25 books on Ancient Egyptian Yoga Philosophy has produced a new translation of the original texts which uncovers a mystical teaching underlying the sayings and rituals instituted by the Ancient Egyptian Sages and Saints. "Once the philosophy of Ancient Egypt is understood as a mystical tradition instead of as a religion or primitive mythology, it reveals its secrets which if practiced today will lead anyone to discover the glory of spiritual self-discovery. The Pert em Heru is in every way comparable to the Indian Upanishads or the Tibetan Book of the Dead." Muata Abhaya Ashby**

20. **ANUNIAN THEOLOGY THE MYSTERIES OF RA The Philosophy of Anu and The Mystical Teachings of The Ancient Egyptian Creation Myth Discover the mystical teachings contained in the Creation Myth and the gods and goddesses who brought creation and human beings into existence. The Creation Myth holds the key to understanding the universe and for attaining spiritual Enlightenment. ISBN: 1-884564-38-0 40 pages $14.95**

21. **MYSTERIES OF MIND AND MEMPHITE THEOLOGY Mysticism of Ptah, Egyptian Physics and Yoga Metaphysics and the Hidden properties of Matter This Volume will go deeper into the philosophy of God as creation and will explore the concepts of modern science and how they correlate with ancient teachings. This Volume will lay the ground**

work for the understanding of the philosophy of universal consciousness and the initiatic/yogic insight into who or what is God? ISBN 1-884564-07-0 $21.95

22. **THE GODDESS AND THE EGYPTIAN MYSTERIESTHE PATH OF THE GODDESS THE GODDESS PATH The Secret Forms of the Goddess and the Rituals of Resurrection The Supreme Being may be worshipped as father or as mother. *Ushet Rekhat* or *Mother Worship*, is the spiritual process of worshipping the Divine in the form of the Divine Goddess. It celebrates the most important forms of the Goddess including *Nathor, Maat, Aset, Arat, Amentet and Hetheru* and explores their mystical meaning as well as the rising of *Sirius*, the star of Aset (Aset) and the new birth of Hor (Heru). The end of the year is a time of reckoning, reflection and engendering a new or renewed positive movement toward attaining spiritual Enlightenment. The Mother Worship devotional meditation ritual, performed on five days during the month of December and on New Year's Eve, is based on the Ushet Rekhit. During the ceremony, the cosmic forces, symbolized by Sirius - and the constellation of Orion ---, are harnessed through the understanding and devotional attitude of the participant. This propitiation draws the light of wisdom and health to all those who share in the ritual, leading to prosperity and wisdom. $14.95 ISBN 1-884564-18-6**

23. ***THE MYSTICAL JOURNEY FROM JESUS TO CHRIST* $24.95 ISBN# 1-884564-05-4 size: 8½" X 11" Discover the ancient Egyptian origins of Christianity before the Catholic Church and learn the mystical teachings given by Jesus to assist all humanity in becoming Christlike. Discover the secret meaning of the Gospels that were discovered in Egypt. Also discover how and why so many Christian churches came into being. Discover that the Bible still holds the keys to mystical realization even though its original writings were changed by the church. Discover how to practice the original teachings of Christianity which leads to the Kingdom of Heaven.**

24. **THE STORY OF ASAR, ASET AND HERU: An Ancient Egyptian Legend (For Children) Now for the first time, the most ancient myth of Ancient Egypt comes alive for children. Inspired by the books *The Asarian Resurrection: The Ancient Egyptian Bible* and *The Mystical Teachings of The Asarian Resurrection, The Story of Asar, Aset and Heru* is an easy to understand and thrilling tale which inspired the children of Ancient Egypt to aspire to greatness and righteousness. If you and your child have enjoyed stories like *The Lion King* and *Star Wars you will love The Story of Asar, Aset and Heru.* Also, if you know the story of Jesus and Krishna you will discover than Ancient Egypt had a similar myth and that this myth carries important spiritual teachings for living a fruitful and fulfilling life. This book may be used along with *The Parents Guide To The Asarian Resurrection Myth: How to Teach Yourself and Your Child the Principles of Universal Mystical Religion.* The guide provides some background to the Asarian Resurrection myth and it also gives insight into the mystical teachings contained in it which you may introduce to your child. It is designed for parents who wish to grow spiritually with their children and it serves as an introduction for those who would like to study the Asarian Resurrection Myth in depth and to practice its teachings. 41 pages 8.5" X 11" ISBN: 1-884564-31-3 $12.95**

25. **THE PARENTS GUIDE TO THE AUSARIAN RESURRECTION MYTH: How to Teach Yourself and Your Child the Principles of Universal Mystical Religion. This insightful manual brings for the timeless wisdom of the ancient through the Ancient Egyptian myth of Asar, Aset and Heru and the mystical teachings contained in it for parents who want to guide their children to understand and practice the teachings of mystical spirituality. This manual may be used with the children's storybook *The Story of Asar, Aset and Heru* by Dr. Muata Abhaya Ashby. 5.5"x 8.5" ISBN: 1-884564-30-5 $14.95**

26. **HEALING THE CRIMINAL HEART BOOK 1 Introduction to Maat Philosophy, Yoga and Spiritual Redemption Through the Path of Virtue Who is a criminal? Is there such a thing as a criminal heart? What is the source of evil and sinfulness and is there any way to rise above it? Is there redemption for those who have committed sins, even the worst crimes? Ancient Egyptian mystical psychology holds important answers to these questions. Over ten thousand years ago mystical psychologists, the Sages of Ancient Egypt, studied and charted the human mind and spirit and laid out a path which will lead to spiritual redemption, prosperity and Enlightenment. This introductory volume brings forth the teachings of the Asarian Resurrection, the most important myth of Ancient Egypt, with relation to the faults of human existence: anger, hatred, greed, lust, animosity, discontent, ignorance, egoism jealousy, bitterness, and a myriad of psycho-spiritual ailments which keep a human being in a state of negativity and adversity. 5.5"x 8.5" ISBN: 1-884564-17-8 $15.95**

27. **THEATER & DRAMA OF THE ANCIENT EGYPTIAN MYSTERIES: Featuring the Ancient Egyptian stage play-"The Enlightenment of Hetheru' Based on an Ancient Egyptian Drama, The original Theater -Mysticism of the Temple of Hetheru $14.95 By Dr. Muata Ashby**

28. **GUIDE TO PRINT ON DEMAND: SELF-PUBLISH FOR PROFIT, SPIRITUAL FULFILLMENT AND SERVICE TO HUMANITY Everyone asks us how we produced so many books in such a short time. Here are the secrets to writing and producing books that uplift humanity and how to get them printed for a fraction of the regular cost. Anyone can become an author even if they have limited funds. All that is necessary is the willingness to learn how the printing and book business work and the desire to follow the special instructions given here for preparing your manuscript format. Then you take your work directly to the non-traditional companies who can produce your books for less than the traditional book printer can. ISBN: 1-884564-40-2 $16.95 U. S.**

29. **Egyptian Mysteries: Vol. 1, Shetaut Neter ISBN: 1-884564-41-0 $19.99 What are the Mysteries? For thousands of years the spiritual tradition of Ancient Egypt, S*hetaut Neter,* "The Egyptian Mysteries," "The Secret Teachings," have fascinated, tantalized and amazed the world. At one time exalted and recognized as the highest culture of the world, by Africans, Europeans, Asiatics, Hindus, Buddhists and other cultures of the ancient world, in time it was shunned by the emerging orthodox world religions. Its temples desecrated, its philosophy maligned, its tradition spurned, its philosophy dormant in the mystical *Medu Neter*, the mysterious hieroglyphic texts which hold the secret symbolic meaning that has scarcely been discerned up to now. What are the secrets of *Nehast* {spiritual awakening and emancipation, resurrection}. More than just a literal translation, this volume is for awakening to the secret code *Shetitu* of the teaching which was not deciphered by Egyptologists, nor could be understood by ordinary spiritualists. This book is a reinstatement of the original science made available for our times, to the reincarnated followers of Ancient Egyptian culture and the prospect of spiritual freedom to break the bonds of *Khemn,* "ignorance," and slavery to evil forces: *Såaa* .**

30. **EGYPTIAN MYSTERIES VOL 2: Dictionary of Gods and Goddesses ISBN: 1-884564-23-2 $19.99 This book is about the mystery of neteru, the gods and goddesses of Ancient Egypt (Kamit, Kemet). Neteru means "Gods and Goddesses." But the Neterian teaching of Neteru represents more than the usual limited modern day concept of "divinities" or "spirits." The**

Neteru of Kamit are also metaphors, cosmic principles and vehicles for the enlightening teachings of Shetaut Neter (Ancient Egyptian-African Religion). Actually they are the elements for one of the most advanced systems of spirituality ever conceived in human history. Understanding the concept of neteru provides a firm basis for spiritual evolution and the pathway for viable culture, peace on earth and a healthy human society. Why is it important to have gods and goddesses in our lives? In order for spiritual evolution to be possible, once a human being has accepted that there is existence after death and there is a transcendental being who exists beyond time and space knowledge, human beings need a connection to that which transcends the ordinary experience of human life in time and space and a means to understand the transcendental reality beyond the mundane reality.

31. EGYPTIAN MYSTERIES VOL. 3 The Priests and Priestesses of Ancient Egypt ISBN: 1-884564-53-4 $22.95 This volume details the path of Neterian priesthood, the joys, challenges and rewards of advanced Neterian life, the teachings that allowed the priests and priestesses to manage the most long lived civilization in human history and how that path can be adopted today; for those who want to tread the path of the Clergy of Shetaut Neter.

32. THE KING OF EGYPT: The Struggle of Good and Evil for Control of the World and The Human Soul ISBN 1-8840564-44-5 $18.95 Have you seen movies like The Lion King, Hamlet, The Odyssey, or The Little Buddha? These have been some of the most popular movies in modern times. The Sema Institute of Yoga is dedicated to researching and presenting the wisdom and culture of ancient Africa. The Script is designed to be produced as a motion picture but may be addapted for the theater as well. 160 pages bound or unbound (specify with your order) $19.95 copyright 1998 By Dr. Muata Ashby

33. FROM EGYPT TO GREECE: The Kamitan Origins of Greek Culture and Religion ISBN: 1-884564-47-X $22.95 U.S. FROM EGYPT TO GREECE This insightful manual is a quick reference to Ancient Egyptian mythology and philosophy and its correlation to what later became known as Greek and Rome mythology and philosophy. It outlines the basic tenets of the mythologies and shoes the ancient origins of Greek culture in Ancient Egypt. This volume also acts as a resource for Colleges students who would like to set up fraternities and sororities based on the original Ancient Egyptian principles of Sheti and Maat philosophy. ISBN: 1-884564-47-X $22.95 U.S.

34. THE FORTY TWO PRECEPTS OF MAAT, THE PHILOSOPHY OF RIGHTEOUS ACTION AND THE ANCIENT **EGYPTIAN WISDOM TEXTS ADVANCED STUDIES** This manual is designed for use with the 1998 Maat Philosophy Class conducted by Dr. Muata Ashby. This is a detailed study of Maat Philosophy. It contains a compilation of the 42 laws or precepts of Maat and the corresponding principles which they represent along with the teachings of the ancient Egyptian Sages relating to each. Maat philosophy was the basis of Ancient Egyptian society and government as well as the heart of Ancient Egyptian myth and spirituality. Maat is at once a goddess, a cosmic force and a living social doctrine, which promotes social harmony and thereby paves the way for spiritual evolution in all levels of society. ISBN: 1-884564-48-8 **$1895 U.S.**

MUSIC BASED ON THE PRT M HRU AND OTHER KEMETIC TEXTS

Divinity

Music of Ancient Egypt

Muata Ashby

Available on Compact Disc $14.99

Sung with original Ancient Egyptian language and musical instruments

WHAT IS KEMETIC (Ancient Egyptian Spiritual) MUSIC?

From the Ancient Sounds the *Music of Ancient Egypt* Collection is an exploration of Ancient Egyptian musical forms and mystical teachings using Ancient Egyptian musical instrument reproductions to discover the mysteries of Kemetic (Ancient Egyptian) devotional musical feeling. Music that fuses Ancient Egyptian feeling with modern rhythms of the world including West African, Middle Eastern, Soul, Jazz, and East Indian styles. Using authentic the Ancient Egyptian words derived from inscriptions and hymns.

MERIT'S INSPIRATION
NEW Egyptian Yoga Music CD
by Sehu Maa
Ancient Egyptian Music CD
Instrumental Music played on reproductions of Ancient Egyptian Instruments– Ideal for meditation and reflection on the Divine and for the practice of spiritual programs and Yoga exercise sessions.
©1999 By Muata Ashby
CD $14.99 –UPC# 761527100429

ANORATIONS TO RA AND HETHERU
NEW Egyptian Yoga Music CD
By Sehu Maa (Muata Ashby)
Based on the Words of Power of Ra and Hetheru
played on reproductions of Ancient Egyptian Instruments **Ancient Egyptian Instruments used: Voice, Clapping, Nefer Lute, Tar Drum, Sistrums, Cymbals** – The Chants, Devotions, Rhythms and Festive Songs Of the Neteru – Ideal for meditation, and devotional singing and dancing.
©1999 By Muata Ashby
CD $14.99 –
UPC# 761527100221

SONGS TO ASAR ASET AND HERU (HERU)
NEW
Egyptian Yoga Music CD
By Sehu Maa
played on reproductions of Ancient Egyptian Instruments– The Chants, Devotions, Rhythms and Festive Songs Of the Neteru - Ideal for meditation, and devotional singing and dancing.
Based on the Words of Power of Asar (Asar), Aset (Aset) and Heru (Heru (Heru)**)** Om Asar Aset Heru is the third in a series of musical explorations of the Kemetic (Ancient Egyptian) tradition of music. Its ideas are based on the Ancient Egyptian Religion of Asar, Aset and Heru (Heru) and it is designed for listening, meditation and worship. ©1999 By Muata Ashby
CD $14.99 –UPC# 761527100122

HAARI OM: ANCIENT EGYPT MEETS INDIA IN MUSIC
NEW Music CD
By Sehu Maa

The Chants, Devotions, Rhythms and Festive Songs Of the Ancient Egypt and India, harmonized and played on reproductions of ancient instruments along with modern instruments and beats. Ideal for meditation, and devotional singing and dancing.
Haari Om is the fourth in a series of musical explorations of the Kemetic (Ancient Egyptian) and Indian traditions of music, chanting and devotional spiritual practice. Its ideas are based on the Ancient Egyptian Yoga spirituality and Indian Yoga spirituality.
©1999 By Muata Ashby
CD $14.99 –
UPC# 761527100528

RA AKHU: THE GLORIOUS LIGHT
NEW
Egyptian Yoga Music CD
By Sehu Maa
The fifth collection of original music compositions based on the Teachings and Words of The Trinity, the God Asar and the Goddess Nebethet, the Divinity Aten, the God Heru, and the Special Meditation Hekau or Words of Power of Ra from the Ancient Egyptian Tomb of Seti I and more...
played on reproductions of Ancient Egyptian Instruments and modern instruments - **Ancient Egyptian Instruments used: Voice, Clapping, Nefer Lute, Tar Drum, Sistrums, Cymbals**
– The Chants, Devotions, Rhythms and Festive Songs Of the Neteru – Ideal for meditation, and devotional singing and dancing.
©1999 By Muata Ashby
CD $14.99 –
UPC# 761527100825

GLORIES OF THE DIVINE MOTHER
Based on the hieroglyphic text of the worship of Goddess Net.
The Glories of The Great Mother
©2000 Muata Ashby
CD $14.99 UPC# 761527101129

ORDER FORM

Telephone orders: Call Toll Free: 1(305) 378-6253AMEX, Optima, Discover, Visa or MasterCard ready.Fax orders: 1(305) 378-6253

Please send the following books. I understand that I may return any books for a full refund-for any reason, no questions asked.

ITEMS	Cost
Sub-total	

Shipping-Book Rate: Air Mail: $6.50per book and $.50 for each additional

Shipping ______________

Name:______________________________________

Address:____________________________________

City:____________ State:_______ Zip:_________

Sales tax: Please add 6.5% for books shipped to Florida addresses

_____Payment:_____________________
_____Check_______________________

_____Credit card: _____ Visa, _____ MasterCard, _____ Optima, _____ AMEX, _____ Discover

Card number:______________________________

Name on card:_____________________________

Exp. date:______/_______

Copyright 1995-2005 r. R. Muata Abhaya Ashby
Sema Institute of Yoga
P.O.Box 570459, Miami Fl. 3327

www.Egyptianyoga.com

EGYPTIAN YOGA
The Philosophy of Enlightenment
Muata Ashby
Edited by Karen Clarke-Ashby